POLITICS IN ISRAEL

THE SECOND REPUBLIC

SECOND EDITION

ASHER ARIAN

The Graduate Center,
City University of New York
Israel Democracy Institute
University of Haifa

CQ PRESS A DIVISION OF CONGRESSIONAL QUARTERLY INC.
WASHINGTON, D.C.

CQ Press
1255 22nd Street, N.W., Suite 400
Washington, D.C. 20037

(202) 729-1900; toll-free, 1-866-4CQ-PRESS (1-866-427-7737)

www.cqpress.com

∞ The paper used in this publication exceeds the requirements
of the American National Standard for Information
Sciences—Permanence in Paper for Printed Library Materials,
ANSI Z39.48-1992.

Printed and bound in the United States of America

08 07 06 05 04   5 4 3 2 1

LIBRARY OF CONGRESS CATALOGING-IN-PUBLICATION DATA

Arian, Alan.
    Politics in Israel : the second republic / Asher Arian.
        p.   cm.
    Includes bibliographical references and index.
    ISBN 1-56802-932-2 (pbk. : alk. paper)
    1. Israel—Politics and government.   2. Political parties—Israel.   3. Political
culture—Israel. I. Title.

    JQ1830.A58A75 2005
    320.95694—dc22
                                                    2004020929

It is a delight to dedicate this book to children
Leor (Dukie), Aviv, Shelly

spouses
Carol, Yael, Michal, Guy

and grandchildren
Mor, Tal, Keren, Ofer, Mika

CONTENTS

LIST OF TABLES AND FIGURES

TABLES

FIGURES

PREFACE

Politics in Israel seems to be in a constant state of flux—deals are brokered and broken, careers soar and sour, statements are refined and retracted—but a surprising consistency survives beneath these fluctuations. Strands of the familiar run through the years: the instability of coalitions, the reemergence of groups thought to have lost political salience, the resilience of political actors once believed extinct, the flexibility of platforms and promises, and the permanence of the temporary.

Politics in Israel provides readers with a comprehensive overview of the key institutions, actors, and events that shape Israeli politics. This edition emphasizes the changes that have remade Israeli politics in recent years and includes an updated discussion of political institutions to reflect the mid-period of the Knesset (parliament) elected in 2003. It also offers a broad perspective of the ongoing development of the Israeli political system.

Demography continues to be an essential element of Israeli politics. Israel's bid to become competitive in the global high-tech industry has largely depended on the human resources and brainpower provided by the influx of one million immigrants from the former Soviet Union over the past decade. These immigrants have also, however, contributed to an unprecedented degree of turnover in Israeli elections, as they have frequently supported the opposition candidate in successive elections. The number and proportion of Arabs in Israel have also been increasing. Their rising education levels and growing expectations have changed the nature of their demands and the behavior of leaders from their community.

Since the last edition of this book, an important structural change took place in Israeli politics: repeal of the direct election of the prime minister. Adoption of a system of direct election had put Israel on a course of instability from 1996 to 2001. Binyamin Netanyahu and Ehud Barak, as directly elected prime ministers, tried to run the government as if their personal mandates somehow eliminated the need to work with a majority coalition in the Knesset. The resulting political chaos was more intense than the coalition crises that the direct election of the prime minister was supposed to reform.

The results of the 1967 Six-Day War continue to rend the country, with a substantial minority determined to hold on to the territories captured in that war and a sizable group convinced that only their return will make nonbelligerent arrangements with the Arabs possible. The largest portion of the population falls between these two extremes, and appealing to this group has become the secret of success in Israeli electoral politics, as Ariel Sharon demonstrated in 2001. Sharon promptly repealed the direct election of the prime minister, and in 2003 set out to withdraw unilaterally from the Gaza Strip even though he did not have the support of the majority of Likud party voters. The art of achieving goals even without a clear majority is at the nexus of ideological and electoral politics. Most Israelis acknowledge the importance of ideology, but respond to pragmatic, legitimate leaders. Sharon knows this, as did Prime Ministers David Ben-Gurion, Menachem Begin, and Yitzhak Rabin before him.

Readers will find that the organization of this book remains largely the same as that of the previous edition. The introduction, which provides a snapshot of current Israeli politics and historical context, delineates the key themes and questions that shape the discussion in the rest of the book: How can the rule of law be accommodated when there is such intense competition for political legitimacy? How might religious and nationalist passions be contained in order to establish a consensual and tolerant society? What does "Israel" mean to a population consisting of citizens from various religious and ethnic backgrounds? How can Israel achieve participatory democracy in an age of technological innovations and a society characterized by individualism? What protections should be put in place to act as checks and balances for the branches of government and to safeguard individual liberty? These and related issues are addressed in the book's chapters on demographics, political economy, parties and other political actors, party organization, elections, institutions of government at the national and local levels, the media, and political culture. Newcomers to the politics of Israel will find what they need to become conversant in the study of this complex and compelling state. I hope others will find new reasons to continue to be interested and engaged in the topic.

Acknowledgments

My work on this edition of *Politics in Israel* was facilitated by the collegial atmosphere and intellectual stimulation I have encountered at the Israel

Democracy Institute in Jerusalem, and I offer my thanks to the fellows, officers, and staff of that institution. Shlomit Barnea, Sandra Fine, Anat Roth, Nir Atmor, Yoav Artzieli, Shir Barlev, Yagil Levy, and Ofer Kenig provided assistance and advice for this edition, and I thank them.

I wish to remember with fondness Ed Artinian, the founder of Chatham House Press, whose support and encouragement resulted in the initial publication of *Politics in Israel* and its various revisions before his untimely passing. I would also like to thank my reviewers, whose comments helped me tailor this new edition: Donna Robinson Divine, Smith College; Zvi Gitelman, University of Michigan; and Itai Sened, Washington University in St. Louis.

Finally, I am pleased to acknowledge the assistance of the staff of CQ Press—Charisse Kiino and Sally Ryman for their help in publishing this edition and Elise Frasier for her encouragement and wise counsel. I want to thank Katharine Miller as well for her fine editorial instincts. I am grateful to all of them for their help.

1 INTRODUCTION

A POLITICAL SYSTEM must be understood in terms of the people who live under it, their values and ideals, the resources at their disposal, the challenges that face the system, and the institutions developed to meet these challenges. Israel is a fascinating example of a complex system that has developed in a relatively short time (since the 1880s) into a dynamic country that has undertaken colossal commitments in the military, economic, and social fields. There seems to be never a dull moment, with Israel capturing an inordinately large share of the world's attention.

Israel has undergone tremendous changes over the decades. Recent developments have included the onset of accommodation with its Arab neighbors; the continuation of the struggle of the Palestinians over land and political rights; a major constitutional change to direct election of the prime minister, which lasted five years before it was repealed; the introduction of competitive features into the highly centralized economic system; and the continued ingathering of Jews from around the world—especially a very large wave of immigration by Jews from the former Soviet Union.

The Six-Day War of 1967 divides Israel's political history into two distinct periods: (1) the period of independence and state consolidation between 1948 and 1967; and (2) the period after 1967, which has been consumed by the dilemmas attendant on the struggle to extricate the country from the fruits of that victory, including the seeking of accommodation with the Palestinians. The Labor Party dominated the entire first period and some of the second, while the Likud has largely led the second period, with occasional moments of competition between the two groups.

1

A peace treaty has been in effect with Egypt since 1979, but it was with the signing of the mutual recognition agreements between Israel and the Palestine Liberation Organization (PLO) in Washington in 1993 (also called the Oslo Accords) that peace was recognized as a policy option in the war-torn Middle East. A peace treaty was signed with Jordan in 1994, and negotiations were begun with the Palestinians, Syrians, and Lebanese to end the long period of confrontation. Those negotiations with the Syrians and Lebanese were not successful; the vision of coexistence with the Palestinians faded with the beginning of the intifada in 2000. Years of suicide bombing, violence, and political stalemate have ensued.

The promise of peace was challenged by the specter of disunity and terror. A Jew assassinated the prime minister of Israel in November 1995, and Arab suicide bombers terrorized the population, killing more than a thousand Israelis in such attacks in the period between 2000 and 2004.

The political system abandoned the smoke-filled rooms of the party bosses and emerged into the open air of the public arena by instituting the selection of party heads and Knesset lists by the members of the major parties in primary elections; the aborted experiment of the direct election of the prime minister between 1996 and 2001 was another expression of this impulse. But the oligarchic party system was not successful in grafting on the new patterns of democratization, and by 2004, the system was in shambles. Likud had a strong leader in Ariel Sharon but he was often at odds with his party's convention. Labor was not able to rebound from its recent defeats or to generate a confident leadership group for the twenty-first century. The fractiousness of the Knesset during the period of the direct election of the prime minister (1996–2003) left in its wake a series of mid-size parties committed to sharply defined sectors of the population.

With the decrease in power of the political bosses, the political parties had yet to find the appropriate mechanisms to fulfill their classic functions of aggregating interests and articulating demands. The parties were largely eclipsed by an emerging politics of fleeting popularity based on television talk shows and opinion surveys. The legitimacy of the Knesset (parliament) was at a very low level, leaving it unable to provide meaningful parliamentary checks to balance the power of the prime minister. And, at the very moment of declining influence of parties and parliament, and the significant strengthening of the executive, the Supreme Court of Israel became more activist than ever before.

The economy's growth during the 1990s was stymied by world conditions and by the upswing of terror at home and abroad. Its transformation from centralization and state monopoly to more openness and market-orientation had been spurred by the partial lifting of the Arab boycott and by significant international investment, but that progress was stalled by the worldwide collapse of the hi-tech bubble and the eruption of the intifada (Arab uprising). The demographic revolution that occurred with the arrival of a million immigrants from the former Soviet Union was partially offset by a very high birthrate among Israeli Arabs.

The booming economy occasioned an ever-widening gap between the rich and the poor in Israel, with many—half of them Arabs—below the poverty line. In addition, the relaxation of government control of various sectors of the economy often led to the emergence of a few dominant actors in these sectors rather than to a pattern of pluralistic competition.

The large-scale immigration from the Soviet Union, as well as the much smaller one from Ethiopia, brought to the country many individuals whose classification as Jews was in doubt, according to the Orthodox rabbinate charged to decide on such matters. The demographic transformation of the country, along with the fear of increased terror, resulted in the partial replacement of workers from the territories of the Palestinian Authority, who had been squeezed out of the labor market by new immigrants, at least in some occupations and for a certain period of time, and also by foreign laborers who had been brought to the country in very large numbers.

Well into Israel's sixth decade, its strong sense of isolation resurfaced. Faced with vocal international pressure and censure, with anti-Semitism growing around the world, the Israel of the 2000s was much like the Israel of the 1950s—defiant, besieged, determined. The brief eclipse of these feelings in the years following the signing of the Oslo Accords in 1993 was receding. However, the collective ethos that had characterized the country during its formative years was now replaced by individualism. While this individualism had existed in the past, it was often denied; now it was celebrated. Choice among options in such areas as university education, travel, communications, and entertainment were more plentiful than before, and growing. Health care was now provided as a national service, and that development created an attendant weakening of the major labor union, the Histadrut, whose membership base had once been ensured because it was the major health care provider. Even the esteemed Israel Defense Forces (IDF) was in danger of losing its status as the key mechanism of social integration in the country, as it reconsidered its future needs and policies of recruitment in an age of changing military threat and warfare technology. And there had been a parallel growth of both secularism and religion in the country, decreasing the spirit of coexistence and pluralism, and increasing the anxieties and fears of a "war of cultures"—or worse—among the Jews of Israel. Shinui, a major winner in the 2003 elections, presented itself as an anticlerical party.

Since independence in 1948, Israel had changed enormously. From a population of 780,000, it had increased by 2003 to 6.6 million. There were 130,000 students in 1948, compared with 2 million in 2003, as well as 700 university students before the war of independence (one-third were killed in that war) compared with 120,000 in 2003. Exports amounted to $35 million in 1950 and to $25.6 billion in 2003. In 1948 less than 6 percent of the Jews of the world lived in Israel; 39 percent did so in 2003. The percentage of the population with thirteen years or more of formal education jumped from 9 percent in 1960 to 39 percent in 2003 (42 percent for Jews, 22 percent for others). One-half of one percent of the population lived in housing with three or more persons per room in 1993, compared with 21 percent in 1960; 54 percent of the population lived in housing with one or fewer persons per room in 2002, compared with 7 percent in 1960. Israel's gross national product rose from $2.5 billion in 1960 to $122.6 billion in 2003. The number of tourists arriving jumped from 110,000 in 1960 to 2.4 million in 2000 (before the onset of the intifada). The number of private cars in Israel increased in that same period from 24,000 to almost 1.5 million in 2002, while the number of telephone subscribers went from 68,000 to 3 million (92 percent of households), with another 2.5 million cell phones, and the number of air passengers grew from 223,000 to 9.6 million in 2000.

Despite all these dramatic changes, Israel's political system has retained its democratic form, and that is a remarkable achievement on its own. Israel is unique just as any other country is unique. And yet because of its record, it is tempting to declare Israel "truly unique." Merely by virtue of its membership in the exclusive club of democratic nations (in which parties compete for power in free elections), Israel is in a special category. In the 1970s and 1980s, when this club shrank until only a couple of dozen countries in the world met the criteria, Israeli democracy persisted—and this in a period in which the defense burden on Israel was unparalleled in other countries, democratic or not. Other countries had large immigrant populations, but proportionate to its size none had absorbed so many immigrants in so short a time as had Israel. When the ranks of the world's democracies again swelled with the collapse of the Soviet Union, Israel was one of the older established democracies in the world.

Political scientists who compare political systems find difficulty in fitting Israel into their schema. Discussing political parties, Giovanni Sartori found the extended dominance of Mapai exceptional, while Arend Lijphart, in his study of relations between major ethnic, religious, and language groups, left Israel outside his framework because of its uniqueness. In respect to the relations between the military and civilian sectors, or its success in curbing runaway inflation without causing large-scale unemployment or political and social upheaval, Israel is often regarded as special; and discussions of political modernization point to Israel as falling outside many general patterns.[1] The system of separately electing the parliament and the prime minister was certainly unique.

But we should resist the temptation of establishing a "truly unique" category for Israel. We should recognize special conditions and achievements but strive at the same time to recognize the similarities and patterns that are familiar to students of other societies. For in other senses Israel's political and social experiences are similar to those of other countries.[2] The scarcity of local resources meant continual searching for foreign sources of import capital, and importing this capital gave the central authorities great sway not only over the economy of the country but over its politics as well. The large number of immigrants facilitated the development of machine politics, but the children of these immigrants provided the votes for the successful challenge to the dominant party. Politics in Israel tended to be party politics, and party politics tends to be hierarchical. Because no single party held a majority in the system, smaller parties (usually religious ones in Israel) held the balance of power in coalition formation.

As Israel moves well into its second century of development—independence came in 1948 but modern Jewish settlement in Eretz Israel (the land of Israel) began in the early 1880s—it faces problems and issues that are neither new nor unique but will have a strong impact on the system. Through its response to these issues, the politics of Israel will be played out.

Legitimacy

Almost six decades after independence, the issue of legitimacy still poses a potential threat to the country. Political legitimacy is the basis on which the exercise of political authority is established; a system is legitimate when its decisions are generally and widely accepted as just and proper by major groups in the system.

The pre-state period in Eretz Israel witnessed the development of a regime that had authority without sovereignty. That is, the population on the whole voluntarily undertook to obey the rules and laws set down by the leadership, including taxation and conscription. This was in addition to the rules set down by the mandatory power that held sovereignty. For our purposes, however, what is important is that the overwhelming majority of the population perceived the organized decision-making bodies of the Yishuv (the pre-state Jewish community) to be legitimate.

The pre-state period saw both secular and religious challenges to the legitimacy of the Yishuv's decisions. The Revisionists split from the organized Yishuv over issues of policy toward the British mandatory power, arguing that Yishuv institutions and their decisions were not binding on them; in a word, that they were illegitimate. David Ben-Gurion never forgave the Revisionists and their Herut successors for this withdrawal, and he attempted to deny them standing when he placed them in the company of the communists, the other ostracized group of mainstream Israeli politics in the years following statehood, by declaring that all parties were candidates for his coalition government except the communists and Herut.

In the Yishuv period and even in the state period, some (especially the haredi ultra-Orthodox Neturai Karta group) have adopted an anti-Zionist position that denies legitimacy to the laws of the state and the rules by which decisions are to be made. The basis of their opposition is theological, and thus it represents a potentially dangerous challenge to the State of Israel. There are, likewise, elements in the ultranationalist fringes of the Zionist right whose rejection of government decisions regarding the peace process led to the assassination of the prime minister in 1995; the basis of this political opposition is also theological, and it represents no less of a challenge. Most of the Jewish terrorist groups active in the 1980s and 1990s were religious, and they justified their behavior on religious grounds, but whatever the basis of the opposition, when religious authorities (or others) declare that their divinely revealed law is superior to and in contradiction of man-made law, severe crisis is inevitable. The existence of competing bodies of law to which significant segments of society owe their allegiance is a prescription for disaster. This fate has been avoided in Israel thus far because most religious groups accept the legitimacy of the laws of the state (see chapter 10), but the potential for crisis exists, especially if highly emotional issues emerge to divide the public.

The rules by which decisions are made must be perceived as legitimate; so too must the decisions themselves. One may disagree with a decision yet concede that the decision-making process is legitimate and that those who participate in it have the legitimate right to make it. It is important to distinguish clearly between *legitimacy* and *legality,* for the question is not only whether the decision makers have the legal right to make the decision but whether the decision is generally accepted. If the debate over the future of the post-1967 territories is between returning them and annexing them, it is likely that major groups in the country (military, press, politicians) hold that either or both options are legitimate. A crisis for the political system arises when people are asked to support or act on decisions they perceive to be illegitimate.

Legitimacy in Israel is by no means assured simply because the government has been duly elected and constituted. Sensitive issues have the potential for polarizing the body politic. The future of the territories taken in the Six-Day War is such an issue. But even then, the matter must be broken down further: there was little real opposition in 1995–1996 to the transfer to Palestinian control of the Gaza Strip and of cities on the West Bank of the Jordan (Bethlehem and Nablus, for instance); there was some opposition to the transfer of Hebron. However, there is likely to be strong opposition to a treaty that turns over the Golan Heights to Syria, and fierce opposition to any agreement that is perceived as giving up sovereignty over parts of Jerusalem.

The population is divided between those who felt strongly about retaining sovereignty over these territories and those who felt that annexing them would change the basic nature of the state and would therefore be detrimental. This kind of basic issue holds great danger for a democratic society because a mere majority for either position will not assuage the intense feelings of the other group. In the light of the polarization of public opinion, Prime Minister Menachem Begin showed masterful political skill in calling on the Knesset to determine whether the Israeli settlements were to be removed from Sinai as part of the peace treaty with Egypt in 1979. By involving the entire political system in the decision, and not just his governing coalition, he won an overwhelming vote for his position, which was supported more by the Alignment opposition than by his own Likud. The coalition of these two groups was more than enough to overcome the fervent opposition of those who wanted to stop the withdrawal from the Sinai.

Identity

Whether or not an individual has a clear conception of the nation-state and his or her place in it is an important question asked by political scientists.[3] The state is the most pervasive object of identification in modern political life, surpassing in importance the family, clan, village, movement, and political party. The Zionist idea was catalyzed into the Zionist movement at the end of the nineteenth century as nationalist ideas and movements were sweeping Europe; Israel was born in a period that saw the emergence of many new states. But Israel calls itself a "Jewish state"—this notion has been expressed in legislative declarations and is fervently supported by most Israeli Jews. When asked, "Are we in Israel an inseparable part of the Jewish people or a separate people?" 85 percent chose the first option.

An overwhelming and growing majority of Jews in Israel identify themselves as both Jews and Israelis. More than two-thirds in 1965 and almost three-quarters in 1974 responded that being Jewish played an important part in their lives. When asked about the centrality of being Israeli, 90 percent of the same samples reported in both 1965 and 1974 that "Israeli-ness" plays an important part in their lives.[4]

In a 2004 survey, respondents were given four identities to rank: Jewish, Israeli, their degree of religious practice (observant or secular), and their ethnic classification (Ashkenazi or Sephardi). As figure 1.1 shows, 83 percent chose as their prime identities either "Jewish" or "Israeli"— almost 40 percent of the respondents chose one of these categories as

Figure 1.1   Identities among Jews, 2004 (in percentages)

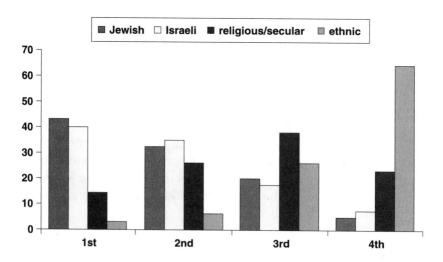

Source: Asher Arian, Shlomit Barnea, Pazit Ben-Nun, *The 2004 Israeli Democracy Index: Auditing Israeli Democracy* (Jerusalem: Guttman Center at The Israel Democracy Institute, 2004). Jewish respondents only: http://www.idi.org.il/.

their first choice and the other as their second choice. Ethnic and religious observance identities were left far behind, and these results were very similar to those observed in 1996.

There was a clear difference in ranking when the responses were broken down by political orientation based on a right-left self-placement scale (see figure 1.2).

Presented with a 7-point scale and asked to place themselves on it, 26 percent of respondents placed themselves in the three places on the left of the scale, 27 percent in the middle place, and 47 percent in the three places on the right of the scale. Of the left identifiers, 56 percent ranked "Israeli" first, compared with 26 percent that ranked "Jewish" first. The opposite pattern occurred on the right, where 55 percent ranked "Jewish" first and 30 percent ranked "Israeli" first. The center group chose "Israeli" at a 47-percent rate and "Jewish" at a 37-percent rate. None of the ideological groupings has a monopoly on either of these two identities; very few Israelis chose the more particularistic ethnic or religious observance categories in first or second places.

For most Jews in Israel, then, there is no discrepancy between being Israeli and being Jewish. Israel is "Jewish" in the sense that its language is Hebrew, its school curriculum is heavily laced with biblical and Jewish

Figure 1.2 Identities among Jews, by Left-Right Self-Indentification, 2004 (in percentages)

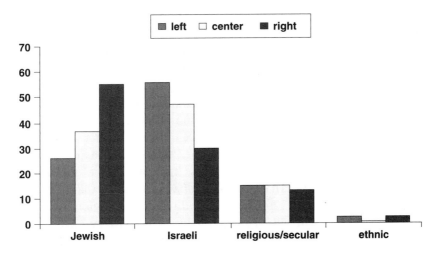

Source: Asher Arian, Shlomit Barnea, Pazit Ben-Nun, *The 2004 Israeli Democracy Index: Auditing Israeli Democracy* (Jerusalem: Guttman Center at The Israel Democracy Institute, 2004). Jewish respondents only: http://www.idi.org.il/.

history, and its holy days are Jewish in origin and are set in accord with the Hebrew calendar (although important events, such as summer vacation, payday, and even the date when winter uniforms are distributed in the army, are determined by the Gregorian calendar).

Enormous efforts are expended in the educational system to promote both Jewish and Israeli identities. Politicians have developed a status quo agreement that supposedly freezes the religious identification issue as it was in the pre-state era—in effect, it is the basis for all further negotiations while claiming nothing has changed. Since the Second World War, the Jewish world has almost unanimously accepted Zionism and the security of Israel as the top priority on its agenda. It is not surprising, then, that few Israelis feel cross-pressured regarding these topics. To be sure, there have been expressions of support for one end of the continuum or the other. The Canaanite movement of the 1950s held that the geographical expression of its identity as originating from the land of Canaan was more meaningful to its identity than the Jewish identity that included two thousand years of Diaspora; this latter identity was adopted by the Zionist movement. At the other extreme are individuals who reject the national expression of Judaism—the State of Israel—and whose sole identification is with the Jewish religion. For some of them, such as the Neturai Karta group, citizenship in a Jewish state is a secular detail of no religious significance since the state was not wrought by divine decree; for others, it is outright blasphemy to support such a state, and hence it follows that obstructing it becomes laudable.

While the identity issue seems resolved for most Israeli Jews, the system is faced with three other crucial issues: the meaning of a Jewish state; the role of the State of Israel for Jews who do not live in Israel; and the relationship to the state of non-Jews living in Israel. What does it mean to have a Jewish state? Is Israel a country of Jews or a country with Jewish content? How is this Jewish content to be institutionalized in the life of the state and who is to decide? What expression is Judaism to have in the life of the state? More specifically, can both freedom of religion and freedom from religion be ensured? And what of pluralism of Jewish expression?

Israel has dealt with these problems in two ways: by promising to retain the status quo in synagogue-state affairs (meaning that arrangements in effect during the pre-state period regarding religion and religious practice would be extended into the state period), and by affording monopoly status to Orthodox Judaism—to the virtual exclusion of other forms, such as the Conservative and Reform movements—on matters in which the state provides a role for religion (as in personal law issues such as marriage and divorce). The implications of this latter practice are to circumscribe certain personal liberties, such as prohibiting marriage in cases in which the Orthodox rabbis have deemed it forbidden; to limit access of organizations and individuals to funding provided by the government for religious affairs; and to legalize, approve, and institutionalize limits on the role of women in communal religious life.

This state of affairs is a constant problem in a population that is not particularly observant. It is estimated that about a quarter of Israeli Jews are observant in an Orthodox sense or even beyond that, including 6 to 10 percent haredi, or ultra-Orthodox; that about 40 percent are determinedly secular; and that the rest are somewhere between those poles. While many are tolerant and even sympathetic to a religious way of life, many are not, and a sizable minority would resist imposition of a religious lifestyle.

The irony of the situation is that as Israel becomes more secular, the perception persists that the power of the Orthodox religious parties is growing. In 2003 they won 22 seats of the 120-member Knesset compared to 27 seats in 1999; Shinui, a party that ran on a campaign of decreasing the power of the haredim, won 15 seats. The Orthodox parties can tolerate the seculars and try to educate them; they abhor the Conservative and Reform denominations, feeling that they have usurped the titles, prayers, and ceremonies of Judaism. Orthodoxy becomes more influential in Israel as the power of the other denominations of Judaism increases in other Jewish communities around the world.

The second crucial issue unresolved is the role of the State of Israel for Jews who do not live in Israel. Conceiving itself as a Jewish state has been translated in practice to a policy that makes every Jew a citizen of Israel virtually for the asking. The Law of Return is the concrete expression of the prophetic vision of the "in gathering of the exiles." The statistical fact is that almost 40 percent of the world's Jews live in Israel, but the boundaries of Israel's political system are hard to set because the spiritual and material influence of Jews who are not Israelis is often felt. Many Israelis see their national undertaking as providing a refuge for the world's Jews; and many Jews in the world show pride, concern, and anxiety (or other emotions) toward Israel in a manner unusual for citizens of foreign countries. Regardless of the distribution of opinion regarding Israel among the Jews in other countries, the question of which identity predominates is always near the surface—sometimes it is asked by Jews themselves and sometimes by those who wish to question the loyalty of Jewish citizens to their home country. It is not a new question: if Jews were persecuted in the Middle Ages for having a distinct religion, in modern times this dilemma is compounded by the existence of the State of Israel and the difficulties this raises regarding both religious and national loyalties.

The third issue is the difficult dilemma faced by non-Jewish citizens of Israel, most of whom experience fundamental conflicts of identity. Let us begin by noting that the Arab population in Israel (within the boundaries preceding the 1967 war) is referred to as the "minorities"—what a wonderful example of a Hebrew expression laden with ideological meaning! The Arabs are a minority (almost 20 percent) in the formal sense, but this does not accurately reflect the demography of Eretz Israel or the Middle East, nor does it take into account Arab sensibilities. Being expected to support a Jewish state in a period of intense Arab nationalism, and when other forces are calling for the establishment of a Palestinian state, is a difficult position to be in. Israeli Arabs are not called upon to serve in the army (as the Druze and Bedouin are), and this exclusion can be seen as a measure of semi-citizenship because army service is so important in determining the pecking order of Israeli political and bureaucratic life.

The way this non-Jewish group identifies itself is both a crucial challenge to the system and a heavy burden on the members of the group. Israeli Arabs are confronted with multiple identities: their religion (most are Muslim), Palestinian, and Israeli. Most Israeli Arabs have demonstrated prudence in handling their dilemma, despite the killing by Israeli police of thirteen Israeli Arabs who were demonstrating in 2000, and the intifada that began a few weeks earlier. Their ambiguous position, however, places enormous strain on them; for the system, it represents a tremendous source of potential crisis.

During the mass immigration from the former Soviet Union, many people who were related to Jews but who were not themselves Jews arrived in Israel and were granted citizenship through the Law of Return. These citizens and their Israeli-born children confront unsettling issues when they need religious services such as marriage, divorce, or burial and find they are denied them by the Orthodox Jewish establishment.

Integration

Over a hundred years ago, modern Jewish settlement in Eretz Israel began. The first hundred years were dominated by Eastern European immigrants and their children. Positions of power, institutions, the culture, the economy, and the educational system were in their hands. But a great historical asymmetry occurred. The Zionist movement—based on secular, nationalist European ideas—was not particularly successful among secular European Jews: while most were ready to subscribe to its ideology, fewer were actually willing to live in Israel. In a sense, the Zionist movement generated a leadership but failed to attract its natural followers.

After independence, large-scale immigration of Jews from Arab countries began. The people who arrived in this period tended to be more traditional than their European counterparts who came to Israel or their cousins from Arab lands who did not. They also proved to be much more loyal to the Zionist cause as a group. A minority of the world's Ashkenazi (European) Jews live in Israel, compared with two-thirds of the Sephardim (generally from Asian and African countries). The progress of the Sephardi immigrants in terms of education and occupation was swift; undergoing extremely rapid development, they also faced negative aspects of modernity such as the breakdown of the patriarchal family and soaring crime rates.

In the early 1980s, as the Israeli-born sons and daughters of Sephardi immigrants became a vocal and numerous factor in Israeli elections, the issue of their integration into the system emerged in a boisterous and sometimes violent manner. On the whole, extreme positions have not been taken, although there have been occasional outbursts of violent group behavior. Undoubtedly, the Sephardim have lately achieved higher levels of influence and power than they had in the past; they have made substantial gains in the political arena and have advanced socially and economically as well, but not nearly as much as the Ashkenazim. The majority position of the Sephardim among the Jews of Israel did not last long, since most of the immigrants in the wave from the former Soviet Union were Ashkenazim. The issue of the integration of the Sephardim into Israel's political and social life will remain a touchy one for years to come.

It is clear that the demographic and sociological changes that the Israeli population is experiencing will profoundly affect the political system. A century of Ashkenazi dominance was followed by a brief period with a Sephardi majority before the immigration from the former Soviet Union changed the balance again. What is likely to emerge in the not-too-distant future is a native-born leadership that is more Israeli than Ashkenazi or Sephardi. The children of Israel wandered in the desert forty years before they entered the land of Israel, before a new generation emerged to take on the burdens of nationhood. The elections of Binyamin Netanyahu in 1996 and Ehud Barak in 1999 marked the emergence of a young, Israeli-born leadership; Netanyahu was born in 1949, a year after the state was founded.

A problem of integration in another sense is posed by Arabs living in the territories Israel acquired in the 1967 war. Many of those Arabs now live under the Palestine Authority, but in terms of security and foreign policies they are still under Israel's control. The vast majority of them have known only occupation by the Israel Defense Forces or semi-autonomy under the Palestinian Authority. The issue of their future remains the most pressing issue on Israel's political agenda, and the Israeli political system will be tested as the Palestinians and Israelis attempt to work out a permanent status agreement. Should the Palestinians have their own state? Could a sovereign state (or would it) commit to permanent demilitarization? And if it should do so, how meaningful would that commitment be? What is to be done with the Jewish settlers and settlements in the territories? Should Jews not have the right to live anywhere in Eretz Israel? The dilemmas are stark; the answers will be complex.

Political Culture

As change occurs in Israel's relations with its neighbors and in its position in the world, the character of the issues that dominate its domestic politics is likely to shift. The topics of security and foreign policy will likely remain central in public awareness, but the nature of the debate and the domestic implications are likely to change. In the past, security and the welfare state were dealt with as consensual issues. Maintaining strong defenses will continue to be the overriding concern of all Israeli governments, and many policies will still be cast in the name of defense. The welfare state has been shrunk as the leadership fashions an economy that is less protective of its weakest citizens and more competitive, but there is still a need to provide citizens with minimum standards so that the youth will be fit for army life and the economy will be competitive in the international marketplace.

However, these issues have become more divisive and the debate will likely spill over into the political system more openly than in the past. What type of army is best suited to the changing conditions—a broad-based conscription army as in the past, or a much smaller, professional volunteer army with high levels of technological capability? What are the implications of these choices for the defense of the country, and what is the likelihood that an officer class will emerge that sees itself not only as different from but better than the elected leaders? How much welfare can the imperatives of international economic competition allow? Are the rewards of national economic success to be shared, or should the successful be allowed to enjoy the fruits of their effort, while many others live at a much lower economic level?

If the country succeeds in resolving the issues of the territories and of the Palestinians, will it then be able to come to grips with the real questions of Zionism, such as the definition of a Jewish democratic state? What is the meaning of a Jewish state: a state full of Jews, or a state filled with Jewish content? And who is to define Jewish content? For that matter, who is to define who is a Jew? In a postwar period, one could imagine public concentration on issues such as these, and perhaps even a Labor-Likud coalition of secular Zionist parties defining the relations with the Jewish religious parties and with the Arab parties.

Certain characteristics are likely to persist. Politics in Israel has always been party politics, and party politics has been elite politics. The party system has undergone a shift from dominance to competitiveness. The Knesset as an institution has become the weakest of the three branches of Israel's government, mostly because the political parties have lost their cohesiveness and focus.

Responsiveness to the public has grown over the years, yet Israel's political system retains features of centralization and hierarchy. The prime minister has enormous power, with few checks or balances on his ability to control the Knesset majority and the major ministries. The Israeli political system is hierarchical in the sense that a party, a politician, and a citizen all tend to know their place in the power structure and rarely overreach themselves. The opposition accepts its relatively powerless role, just as a junior coalition power accepts its relatively subordinate role in the calculus of power. All eyes tend to focus on the leader, waiting for the cue. Individuals and groups fit into this structure, and political parties tend to be collections of factions, or nuclei, around leaders, jockeying for position in the pyramid of power. The hierarchical nature of the structure is facilitated because subordinate groups and individuals are likely to be dependent on decisions regarding appropriations and appointments that are made at higher levels of the hierarchy.

All this fits in nicely with Israel's bureaucratic public life. The centralized economy encourages dependency, with the government controlling about half of the economy's activity and directly influencing much of the country's economic life. These proportions register enormous economic influence and hint at enormous political power. Add to that the facts that almost two-thirds of those employed work in services and that three-quarters of the employed are salaried, and the impact of the control of the centralized economy is clear.

The future of the political party, the centralized economy, and the role of ideology are likely to persist in Israeli politics. All of these features will shift in content and style, but they will still be central. The style of Israeli politics will remain ideological: the use of symbols, rhetoric, and coded phrases has always been evident in the Israeli political experience and is not likely to diminish soon. What is also true is that Israeli politicians can be very pragmatic and can review long-expressed ideological formulations if their understanding of political reality so demands. The population on the whole tends to be less ideological but shows a high degree of deference to the ideological expressions of politicians, just as it does to the decisions of the leadership.

Israel's political culture demonstrates a fascinating mix of ideology and pragmatism.[5] The socialist ethic that ruled for decades has withered, although some signs of it can still be found. The element of nationalism, on the other hand, has retained its intensity, if not strengthened. The materialism of many Israelis is obvious to the observer, and it seems to have become the norm; despite very high levels of taxation, the ethos developed is one of seeking creature comforts in the present tense. This materialism does not blunt, and indeed perhaps enhances, high levels of identification with the system by most Jews, as well as a willingness to sacrifice for its preservation and maintenance.

The most enduring feature of the system is likely to be the politician. Israeli politicians tend to be dependent on the party and its institutions for their influence and livelihood. But all of them, except two or three at the apex of the pyramid, share a generally low level of prestige. In the late 1970s, "Knesset member" was ranked 64th out of 90 preferred occupations by a national sample.[6] A taste of the orientation of the public is gleaned from the story of the Haifa-area resident arrested for attacking his neighbor with a knife: in explaining his behavior, he claimed that his neighbor had called him a politician.[7]

The politician and the political system have three distinct spheres of activity—electoral politics, coalition politics, and bureaucratic politics—each with its own rhythm and rules. The politician divides his time among the three, but the nature of his investment and his expectation of profit are different in each sphere. Electoral politics may be the most important formally because it is the selection of the prime minister and the allocation of Knesset seats as determined by voters on election day that establishes the division of political power. Electoral politics is limited to the campaign period, although the press and public (and perhaps politicians as well) think of political life as an unending campaign.

Coalition politics can come up at any time, and it usually involves only a handful of actors. Since the coalition is necessary to rule, however, the payoff of the coalition game is high. Coalition politics determines who will control important government ministries, Knesset committees, policies, and budgets. Creating crisis in the coalition is an effective way of pressuring for more, but there is also a danger that power already achieved will be lost if the coalition crumbles.

Bureaucratic politics is likely to be the major investment of the politician, who must retain or enhance his position within his organization if he is to continue his career. He may well assume that others covet his position: if he is the representative of a group, he may assume that others in the group would like to see him rotate out of office; within his party, other groups may feel deprived as they are denied representation because of his group's success in achieving positions of influence; certainly, outside his party, members of other parties have set their goal to replace him and his party. He must keep the politics of his constituency organization, his party, and the country clearly in mind as he meets, speaks, maneuvers, and negotiates to retain power for himself, his group, and his party. This group infighting is the kind of politics that is most hidden from the public eye but the one that probably takes up most of the energies of the politician.

The world of Israeli politics often seems confusing to the uninitiated. One reason is that names of parties and alignments change, although the basic uniformities are strong, and concentrating on major issues and patterns shows that the system often follows a few basic rules. For readers familiar only with Anglo-American politics, a word of advice: try not to transfer your understanding of politics and its terminology to the Israeli system without adjustment. Terms such as *left-right, checks and balances,* and even *democracy* are widely used in Israeli politics, but it would be misleading to interpret them in the same way they are used in other systems. The Israeli system is much more easily understood by someone who knows political systems in continental Europe, as the forms and usages are more directly traceable there. Even then, however, Israel poses special problems, for its history is unique, and its politics must be understood in that light.[8]

The dilemmas faced by Israeli democracy are similar to those that other advanced democracies confront in the twenty-first century. The details will depend on each country's unique historical developments, but the complexity and confounding nature of the perplexities are familiar. These themes will recur in the following chapters:

- Can the rule of law be maintained when many have intense and conflicting views of the appropriate sources of legitimacy in the system?

- Can pluralism and tolerance be fostered when religious and nationalist passions well up?

- How is it possible to forge into a single nation citizens of various ethnic backgrounds and different religions?

- What is the meaning of participatory democracy when technological innovations atomize society and individualism is rampant?

- How are the branches of government to be balanced so that abuses of power will be checked and individual liberty maintained?

- How can public needs by met by a profit-driven media?

- What is the responsibility of the state to weaker elements in the society during a period of globalization and open borders and markets?

- What is the meaning of parliamentary democracy when political parties are in serious decline?

- How can a sense of responsiveness and accountability be promoted within a political system that is perceived by a cynical electorate to be peopled by manipulative politicians?

2   PEOPLE OF ISRAEL

A KEY ELEMENT in the development of any country, and certainly in Israel, is its population—its size, quality, and morale. It is fitting to focus on the people of Israel for many reasons, not the least of which is the fact that the Zionist movement's overt goal was to change the place of residence of the world's Jews from the Diaspora to Zion. In that sense the Zionist movement has been very successful. In 1882, there were 24,000 Jews in Eretz Israel, or 0.3 percent of the world's Jews. By 2003, Israel's 5.1 million Jews constituted 39 percent of the 13 million world Jewish population (see table 2.1).[1]

The size of Israel's population at the end of 2003 was 6.6 million, including Jews living in the territories taken in the Six-Day War of 1967 but not including non-Jews living there.

Some 77 percent were Jews, 16 percent Muslim, 1.5 percent Arab Christians, 1.5 percent Druze, and less than one half of one percent non-Arab Christians.[2] Another 3 percent were listed by the *Statistical Abstract of Israel* as "Religion unclassified." This category first appeared in 1996 to account for the growing number of immigrants from the former Soviet Union who were Israelis but not Jews; of the more than one million immigrants from the former Soviet Union, estimates of the proportion of non-Jews among them range from 10 to 30 percent.

One of Zionism's major achievements has been its absorption of immigrants; in fact, Israel has absorbed more people, per base population, than any other country in the world. Mass immigration of Jews to Israel has been actively encouraged, with exceptions during certain periods and

Table 2.1   Population of Jews in Israel and the World, 1882–2003

Year	Size of population (in thousands)	Number of Jews in Israel (in thousands)	Percentage of Jews in Israel	Number of Jews in world (in millions)	Percentage of world's Jews in Israel
1882	600	24	4.0	7.7	0.3
1922	752	84	11.2	8.0	1.1
1939	1,545	464	30.0	16.6	2.8
1948	806	650	80.6	11.5	5.7
1954	1,718	1,526	88.8	11.9	12.8
1967	2,777	2,384	85.8	13.6	17.5
1986	4,331	3,561	82.2	13.0	27.4
1996	5,619	4,550	81.0	13.0	35.0
2003	6,631	5,094	76.8	13.0	39.0
Including non-Jews in the territories:					
1967	3,744	2,384	63.7		
1986	5,712	3,561	62.3		
1996	7,489	4,550	60.8		
2003	9,800	5,094	52.0		

Sources: Dov Friedlander and Calvin Goldscheider, *The Population of Israel* (New York: Columbia University Press, 1979); Dan Horowitz and Moshe Lissak, *The Origins of the Israeli Polity: Palestine under the Mandate* (Chicago: University of Chicago Press, 1978); and various volumes of *Statistical Abstract* and the *American Jewish Yearbook*.

Note: Population figures up to 1939 are for Eretz Israel; the 1948 through 2003 numbers in the upper set relate to the pre-1967 borders and include Jewish residents of the territories but not non-Jews living there.

regarding certain groups. Between 1948 and 1951, Israel admitted 666,000 Jewish immigrants, mostly from Mediterranean countries and survivors of the Holocaust from Europe, who joined a base population of only 600,000. Since 1989, more than one million immigrants have arrived in Israel, mostly from the former Soviet Union, ironically making that country, which opposed Israeli policy for many years, the largest supplier of Jews to Israel.

Zionism has been successful in reversing the two-thousand-year Diaspora characterized by the dispersion of many sizable Jewish communities throughout the world (particularly in Europe, the lands of the Middle East, and North Africa). By the beginning of the twenty-first century only two sizable Jewish communities remained—the United States and Israel. Compared to Israel's 39 percent of world Jews in 2003, the 5.2 million Jews in the United States made up 40 percent of the Jewish people. The next largest communities of Jews elsewhere in the world are much smaller: only France and Russia have Jewish populations larger than a half million, and an additional four (Argentina, Canada, the Ukraine, and the United Kingdom) have Jewish communities between a quarter million and a half million people.

Mass immigration of Jews to Israel continues to enjoy wide support on an abstract level from Jews in Israel and abroad, but the fact is that most Jews of the world do not live in Israel. Any understanding of Israeli politics must rely heavily on an appreciation of who came and who did not, when they came, why some left, and how those who stayed became part of the system. We must take into account the relations between the Jews of Israel and the Jews of the world during the 125 years of Zionist activity, the impact of the growth of the number of Jews in Israel on the Arab population of the country, and the demographic changes occurring in the country as a result of differing rates of emigration, immigration, and fertility among the various groups.

The bottom line of the immigration balance sheet is determined by a large number of forces, including developments taking place abroad, the attitudes of the ruling power, and the psychological predispositions of the immigrating population. These in turn affect the likelihood of successful absorption and the effect of immigration on the political institutions of the country. The following points should be kept in mind:

1. There is no easy explanation for immigration. It is convenient to think of "pull" factors making a country attractive and "push" factors making the country from which one emigrates unattractive; often these forces work in tandem. Usually there is no experience in a normal adult's life parallel to the dependency encountered after immigration to a foreign country. If the "pull" factors outweigh the "push" factors, absorption is likely to be easier. If one is imbued with ideological passion or religious vision, making *aliya* ("coming up") to Israel will be managed even more successfully. Also, the social context is important: individuals coming alone are likely to have a much harder time than if they belonged to a group, be it family, village, or political group. It is no accident that immigrant groups develop after every substantial immigration, for they answer a very basic need of community, roots, and ties to the familiar—things that are usually initially denied the immigrant.

2. While Zionism has provided a ready ideology for immigration to Eretz Israel, most Jews with other options have chosen not to come. That was especially true of the mass migration from Russia and Poland to the United States at the beginning of the twentieth century, and it is equally true of those Jews allowed to leave the

Soviet Union at the end of the century. Note, however, that Jews of North African and Middle Eastern extraction came to Israel in higher percentages when they left their countries, although many better educated and urban Jews preferred to emigrate to France and the United States and not to Israel.

3. Much immigration is caused by external factors. Large numbers of Polish Jews arrived in Eretz Israel in the mid-1920s because of the double pressures of a general boycott declared on Jewish industry and commerce in their country of origin and a simultaneous legislation of quotas formulated in the Johnson-Lodge Immigration Act of 1924 in the United States, which limited access to that desirable country of destination. A record high number of 66,000 immigrants arrived in 1935, about a quarter of them from Germany, as conditions in pre–World War II Europe deteriorated. In 1957 a substantial number of immigrants from Morocco arrived, reflecting anxieties felt by Moroccan Jews as nationalism in North African countries began to emerge. Mass immigration from the Soviet Union toward the end of the century could be undertaken only when Soviet authorities granted exit visas; the huge influx following the dissolution of the Soviet Union is even more understandable in light of the U.S. immigration restrictions, which barred access to the country of first choice for many Soviet émigrés.

4. Every immigration has its emigration. Some immigrants—especially if they are physically and financially able—are likely to return to their country of origin or to move on to another destination. In the massive immigration of many nationalities to the United States between 1908 and 1924, every one hundred immigrants were balanced by thirty-four emigrants. Of those who arrived during the second *aliya* (1904–1914), Ben-Gurion estimated that only one in ten remained (the true figure is probably closer to three in ten).[3] Over time, about 10 to 15 percent of Israelis have left Israel. For historians, sociologists, and demographers, this is a natural and well-known phenomenon. To the Zionist it is saddening, since one who believes in the ideological correctness of his or her cause sees immigration to Zion as a key element in its platform.[4]

5. Earlier waves of immigrants are advantaged compared with those who come later. This tends to be true both for groups and their leadership. As a new group is introduced at the bottom of the absorption ladder, the group with longer tenure is "pushed up."

The new group generally finds it harder to acclimate to the new country than those who preceded it, in part because the old-timers are likely to be very jealous of their privileges and suspicious of the demands of new groups, especially regarding jobs, housing, and political power. The groups that perceive themselves as deprived thereby are likely to call for a reallocation of resources to alleviate their deprivation rather than expenditure of large sums on absorbing new immigrants.

Periods of Immigration

The years between 1882 and 2004 can be divided into five periods. Each witnessed an expansion of the Jewish population in Israel, and each had an effect on the politics of the country.

1882–1924

The formative period saw the smallest immigration numerically, but it was the most significant politically. The very limited and select immigration of rather homogeneous populations set the scene for the initial emergence of the political leadership that was to dominate Israel's years of creation.[5]

Before 1880, fewer than 25,000 Jews lived in Eretz Israel. They were concentrated in the four holy cities of Jerusalem, Hebron, Tiberias, and Safed and spent their time largely in study and prayer. Sustained by monies collected from Jewish communities outside Eretz Israel, they prayed for the redemption of the land and the coming of the Messiah. Their reception of secular settlers who came to fulfill their prayers without divine help was notably cool.

The settlers of the first *aliya* (1882–1903), numbering between 20,000 and 30,000, came in reaction to the growing anti-Semitism in Russia. Whereas most of their fellow Jewish immigrants went to the United States, this handful (compared with the 2.5 million Jews who left Eastern Europe between 1880 and 1924) responded to the nationalist awakening among Jews and immigrated to Eretz Israel. Many of them had received ideological instruction in the first organized nationalist Jewish groups known as *Hovevei Zion* but were dramatically lacking in funds and agricultural skills. Established Jewish settlers were especially hostile, seeing the newcomers not only as religious offenders but as competitors for the limited charity sent from abroad. Relatively educated, from urban backgrounds, and totally unprepared for the barren wastelands they encountered in Eretz Israel, these brave beginners were rescued from ignominious failure by "import capital," money sent from abroad—a feature of Israeli life that would persist. The efforts of Baron Edmond de Rothschild, a noted Jewish philanthropist, rescued the settlers but installed Rothschild agents as overseers; soon the settlers became accustomed to turning to Paris for help and even sent their children to France to school. Many of them did not return.

The second *aliya* (1904–1914) came out of the ferment of the unsuccessful Russian revolution of 1905, with its attendant ideas of social equality and freedom. Of the 35,000 who came during this period, almost all were from Russia, a few thousand from Rumania, and 2,000 from Yemen. About 10,000 were pioneers in the sense of abandoning the easy life and comforts of home in order to participate in the Zionist revolution. Reports of malaria and other tribulations received from members of the first *aliya* did not daunt them, but many proved unable to meet the challenge and left. This was the most important of the original *aliyot* both because three top leaders of the formative period in Israel's history—David Ben-Gurion, Yitzhak Ben-Zvi, and Yosef Shprinzak, Israel's first prime minister, second president, and first chairman of the Knesset, respectively—arrived then and because the political organizations they founded would have the greatest impact on the future of the country.

Largely young, single, dedicated socialists, the members of the second *aliya* proved more innovative than their counterparts in the first. Of course, they had a firmer base on which to work, thanks to their predecessors' efforts. The newcomers were successful in developing new kinds of agricultural settlements and industry, and in promoting Jewish cultural activities. During this period political parties emerged, and the Histadrut (the federation of labor unions) was later created by them. These developments occurred naturally in response to challenges and problems faced in everyday living and not as a result of an ideological blueprint.

The interests of members of the first and second *aliyot* soon clashed. The young pioneers wanted to work at physical labor but found themselves shut out of the businesses of their natural employers, the members of the first *aliya*, because indigenous Arab labor was cheaper, more plentiful, and more experienced. Both sides offered national-interest arguments, the landowners claiming that they were building a viable economy, the job-seekers pointing out that Jewish labor was essential to a viable economy and that in its absence sizable immigration would not be possible. The battle over the "conquest of labor" was begun, and the laborers were successful in winning to their side the World Zionist

Organization.[6] They set the tone for Jewish settlement and would ultimately emerge as national leaders. They also won the undying enmity of the plantation and orchard owners—an antagonism passed on from generation to generation in Israeli politics.

The success of the labor leaders was not in their ability to organize the workers or to increase immigration substantially. In fact, most of the laborers were not organized in either of the two labor parties of the day, nor did they work predominantly in agricultural occupations. But they set a course and developed a commonality of cause and internal cohesion, which are preconditions of any politically successful organization.

The years of the First World War saw a cessation of immigration and the ultimate liberation of Palestine from the Ottoman Empire by the British and Allied armies. In 1917 the British secretary of state for foreign affairs, Arthur James Balfour, sent Lord Rothschild his famous declaration announcing the support of the British government for Zionist aspirations in Palestine. And in the 1922 League of Nations Mandate for Palestine, article 6 stated that "the Administration of Palestine, while ensuring that the rights and position of other sections of the population are not prejudiced, shall facilitate Jewish immigration under suitable conditions."

Immigration to Eretz Israel picked up again at the beginning of the 1920s with the end of the First World War and during the convulsions that swept over Russia in its revolution and attendant civil war. Most of the 35,000 members of the third *aliya* (1919–1923) came from Russia—15,000 of them identifying themselves as pioneers. This influx of Jews brought the population to 85,000 in 1922, the same as it had been in 1914, counterbalancing those who had left.[7]

The third *aliya* consisted mostly of young, single males from Poland and Russia who had been prepared for their immigration by participation in agricultural training programs organized by Zionist organizations in Europe. They entered a more structured environment than had the members of the first and second *aliyot,* and strong ideological motivation was prevalent among them. Their experiences in Europe had taught them the importance of political organization and control, and their nationalism brought them to Eretz Israel rather than to America or other destinations. They accepted the authority of leaders already living in Israel (who were only a few years older than they) but pressured for their own goals. Many of them were members of groups, which afforded internal cohesion to their efforts and magnified their influence in the system. They and their predecessors of the second *aliya* formed the generation of Israel's founding fathers.

We have seen how immigration was shaped by international developments as well as by the motivation of the immigrants. A third factor was the policy of the ruling authorities to immigration. The Turks opposed immigration, but because of the system of capitulations under which Europeans enjoyed extraterritorial privileges throughout the Turkish Empire and because of the ineffectiveness of the officers of the Ottoman administration in policing immigration, about 80,000 Jews arrived in Eretz Israel between 1880 and 1914.[8] The British were conscious of Arab sensitivities to the growing Jewish population and were more aggressive in attempting to establish a policy of immigration during their Mandate.

The formula developed by the British was "economic absorptive capacity," and the immigration ordinance of 1920 tried to implement the formula by allowing in Jews of independent means, those with religious occupations, and dependents of residents. Beyond that, only "subsidized immigrants" (those whose maintenance was guaranteed by the World Zionist Organization for one year, later to be redefined as those who had a definite prospect of employment) were admitted, and then only up to the quota set by the authorities. The subsidized immigrant category was specified in the labor schedule that the Jewish Agency's department of immigration prepared; when approved by the British High Commissioner, labor schedule certificates were issued to the World Zionist Executive, which distributed them according to a party key, with each party receiving certificates in rough proportion to its political strength in the country.

1925–1948

The immigrants of the period from 1925 to 1948 were the generation of the Mandate, the struggle against the British, the struggle against the Nazis, the struggle for immigration, and, ultimately, independence.

Quotas were being set in the United States to restrict the inflow of immigrants in the 1920s, and so when conditions in Poland provided a "push" for many Jews to leave that country, and as the economic depression in Europe worsened, the fourth *aliya* (1924–1930) arrived. Eighty-two thousand Jews arrived in this period—35,000 in 1925 alone.[9] If the third *aliya* was Russian and ideological, the fourth was Polish and middle-class. Unlike the penniless socialists of the earlier *aliyot*, many of the Poles had some independent means, and their capitalism flourished. But in 1927 there was a severe economic crisis, and the economic foundations of the Yishuv, concentrated in agriculture, could not absorb large numbers of urban-oriented migrants. Unemployment was very high, and starting in late 1926, Jewish emigration gained momentum: some 23,000 of the 80,000 immigrants of the fourth *aliya* are estimated to have left the country. In 1927 emigration exceeded immigration.

The fifth *aliya* (1932–1938) was a reaction to the spread of anti-Jewish activities in Central and Eastern Europe, especially the rise of Hitler in 1933. This was a huge immigration by local standards, numbering some 200,000. In 1935 alone a record 66,000 Jews arrived. The Jewish population of the country more than doubled in five years. Although the fifth *aliya* is often called the "German *aliya*," in fact only a quarter of its members were German and Austrian Jews. The largest group numerically was from Poland, which did, after all, have the largest concentration of Jews in the world at that time; the biggest decline was from the USSR, where restrictions on emigration were being enforced. These Central European Jews brought with them capital for investment and, along with their middle-class backgrounds, urban lifestyles and organizational skills.

In the aftermath of the mass immigration of the 1920s and 1930s, the local Arab population reacted violently with demonstrations, strikes, and attacks. By 1939 the Jews, who had made up 4 percent of the population in 1882, had grown to 30 percent through immigration (see table 2.1). Economic difficulties fed Arab resentment, and the British reaction was to severely limit the immigration of Jews. In 1933 and 1934 the Jewish Agency requested 60,000 labor certificates, but the British allocated fewer than 18,000. In 1936, 10,695 were requested but only 1,800 were approved. Still, the problem could not be easily overcome, for in seventeen years the Arab population had increased by 50 percent, the Jewish population by 500 percent.

The British introduced political criteria, as opposed to economic criteria, in setting the quota of Jewish immigrants and determined that 12,000 Jews per year would be the "political high level," or upper limit. This figure was more or less achieved for the years between 1936 and 1938, the figure jumping to 30,000 in 1939. Most of the immigrants came from Germany and Austria. As the clouds of war gathered, international immigration slowed to a trickle, but for the first time, Eretz Israel became the major migration destination of world Jewry.

The British White Paper of 1939 limited Jewish immigration to 75,000 for the next five-year period, making the Jews a third of the population and then terminating immigration. By the date the White Paper had immigration ending, however, only about 50,000 Jews had arrived. Illegal immigration had existed throughout the Mandate, and since 1934 illegal immigrants had been deducted (if their number could be determined) from the quota of Jews permitted to enter Eretz Israel. After

World War II, tens of thousands attempted to enter illegally, and many were successful. But after mid-1946, most of these Jewish survivors of European persecution were intercepted, and 56,000 of them were imprisoned on Cyprus. Between 1945 and mid-1948, about 75,000 Jews came, most of them illegally.

The organizational efforts required to sustain illegal immigration, prepare the Yishuv for armed conflict with the Arabs or the British by manufacturing or procuring weapons, and raise and train an effective fighting force—all this alongside the legal activities of absorbing immigrants, strengthening the economy, and developing a social infrastructure—were enormous. The busyness of the period swept up groups and individuals, generating national enthusiasm and levels of self-sacrifice whose loss were sometimes bemoaned by later generations who wished to return to "basic values." But on the verge of the symbolic victory of national independence there occurred the greatest modern tragedy to befall the Jewish people—the Holocaust. David Ben-Gurion's political wisdom in navigating these difficult straits raised him to a peak of popularity and general acceptance both in Israel and abroad. It was during this period of the multiplicity of tasks confronting the Yishuv that lieutenants were recognized for their organizational and leadership abilities, and careers in the public sector were begun.

The 1948 Declaration of Independence proclaimed that "the State of Israel is open to Jewish immigration and the ingathering of Exiles." The first order enacted by the provisional government abolished the British restrictions on immigration and defined as legal those residents who had been "illegals" under British rule. Two years later, in 1950, after hundreds of thousands of Jews had come to the country, the Knesset passed the Law of Return, which granted to every Jew in the world the right to immigrate to Israel.

When this Law of Return was drafted in the shadow of the Holocaust, the definition of who is a Jew seemed self-evident. Whomever the Nazis had identified as a Jew and sent to the death camps was to be offered refuge in the newly established state. Over the years, however, this debate grew more heated: should Israel adhere to the definition of *halacha* (Jewish religious law), which identifies a Jew as one born of a Jewish mother or one who has converted, or should one's paternal legacy count, or perhaps one's own self-identification? The only new legislation that resulted from this debate was the 1970 amendment defining a Jew as one born to a Jewish mother or one who had converted to Judaism, but this did not settle the issue because the legitimacy of conversions by non-Orthodox rabbis (rabbis of the Reform and Conservative Jewish movements, for example) were challenged.

The anomaly of admitting non-Jews to the country as Israeli citizens did not occur to the lawmakers in the formative years. The 1952 Law of Citizenship granted citizenship to every Jew, his or her spouse, children, and grandchildren. In effect, this meant that a single Jewish grandparent was sufficient to ensure the right to citizenship upon immigration to Israel. The granting of Israeli citizenship thus bore no relation to the determination of the Orthodox rabbinate regarding the question of whether the person was or was not a Jew. Stories abound of immigrants tracing their rights to Israeli citizenship to a grandparent who had no connection to Judaism other than by an accident of birth. Imagine a young Bolshevik whose progeny, decades later, came to Israel. Or those of a Jewish woman in Kurdistan who married a Muslim man and bore him nine sons; eventually, she was allowed to enter Israel along with her family of 170 people—children, grandchildren, and their spouses. Were Americans to contemplate immigrating to Israel at the beginning of the twenty-first century under existing rules, perhaps as many as 50 million people would be eligible under the Law of Return.

1948–1954

In 1948 the remnants of the European Jewish society immigrated, but soon after the founding of the state, communities of Jews born in Asia and Africa made up the bulk of the new immigrants. The large number of these immigrants doubled the Jewish population of the country within these years and heightened the already difficult economic conditions faced by the new country. Between 1948 and 1951, 700,000 immigrants were added to the 650,000 Jews already in Israel. Despite the enormous demographic change, the political leadership successfully adapted and remained in power. The Arabs again protested, this time through force of arms, with neighboring Arab states attacking the new state in an attempt to abort its birth. Many local Arabs left, thinking that this was a temporary exodus until the fighting halted, and they became the crux of the Palestinian refugee problem that is still festering in the region. The reaction of the refugees is familiar: many German Jews in the 1930s believed that they had left "temporarily" until the Hitler nightmare passed, just as many Iranian Jews fifty years later set up temporary homes in Israel, France, or the United States, convinced that the Khomeini revolution would be short-lived.

After the establishment of the Israeli state, waves of immigration came at a fast and furious pace. First came the European immigrants imprisoned on Cyprus and in camps in Europe. Soon after, Jews from Bulgaria, Yugoslavia, Yemen, Aden, and Algeria arrived. In early 1949 there came Jews from Turkey and Libya and the entire community of 35,000 Jews in Yemen. Toward the end of 1949 the doors of Poland and Rumania were opened, and the Jews streamed out, followed the next year by Iraqis and many more Rumanians. The government was hard-pressed to absorb, feed, and house the new immigrants. A war was being fought, and resources were scarce. Rationing of foodstuffs was introduced, and demands were made by leaders of the United Jewish Appeal in the United States to slow down immigration for six months in order to balance the budget. Ben-Gurion rejected all such pleas, arguing that "economic conditions should be adjusted to immigration volume rather than the reverse."[10] The highest monthly immigration rate was recorded during the first seven months of 1951, when some 20,000 immigrants a month arrived in the country, mostly from Rumania and Iraq. This monthly rate was almost as large as the entire first *aliya*.

1954–1989

In 1951 the Jewish Agency announced "rules of selection," hoping to reduce the number of sponsored immigrants who were chronically ill, nonproductive laborers, or unwilling to settle in agricultural areas. The major realistic sources of potential immigration in the mid-1950s were Turkey and Iran, where about 130,000 Jews still lived, and North Africa, with half a million. Western countries did not seem a likely source, and the 3 million Jews in Eastern Europe and the Soviet Union were prevented from leaving. Before the restrictions were set, only about 30,000 had come to Israel from North African countries, with many of the middle and upper classes making their way to France instead. It is not clear whether the restrictions prevented larger immigration; what is clear is that after the Israeli economy started to pick up again, after the German reparations began, and especially after the victory of the Sinai campaign of 1956, immigration from North Africa, especially Morocco, began to increase. After reaching a low annual figure of 18,000 immigrants between 1952 and 1954, the figure rose to 70,000 in 1957, with Jews arriving mostly from Morocco, Poland, and Egypt.

The controversy over the issue of quotas for North African immigrants reached a peak in the mid-1950s, and Prime Minister Moshe Sharett raised the quotas from 2,000 per month to 3,000. The reasoning behind the government decision was that the economy could absorb no more; the similarity between this and the original 1922 British position is striking. When Ben-Gurion returned to office as prime minister in 1955, the policy was nevertheless unchanged. The Herut movement consistently opposed all immigration restrictions during these years, while others regarded them as unfortunate but necessary. Herut's ideological stance was not put to the test for most of its period in office (1977–1992), for Israel's major problem was generally a lack of immigration and a growing *yerida* (emigration, or "going down"). It was challenged with the beginning of the mass immigration from the former Soviet Union in 1989.

Immigration between 1961 and 1965 reached 230,000, coming mainly from Morocco and Rumania, with some from Argentina as well. By the Six-Day War in 1967, the sources of potential immigration had changed: the Eastern European and North African reservoirs were largely dried up, leaving Western countries and the Soviet Union. Of the 250,000 Jews given exit visas from the Soviet Union in the 1970s, however, only 160,000 came to Israel.[11]

The task of dealing with immigration was complicated by the emergence of two competing bureaucracies: the Jewish Agency and the government Ministry of Immigrant Absorption. The fact that politicians and bureaucrats dealing with the complex issue of immigration were often from different factions or parties made the competition for resources and control of immigration more intense.

1989 to the Present

The end of the Soviet Union saw a resurgence of Jewish immigration to Israel, at a time when the options for population change from outside sources seemed very bleak. And it came from two very different sources—the vast majority were immigrants from the former Soviet Union, most of whom were Jews only because it was so recorded in their identity cards, and a smaller fraction were immigrants from Ethiopia, most of whom had retained traditions for centuries.

Between 1989 and 2004, many more Jews—more than one million—came to Israel than had been in the country at the time of independence in 1948. Not only did they come in great numbers, but most of them came in the first years of this period. In 1990, 185,200 Jews arrived from the former Soviet Union, and in 1991, an additional 147,800.

The great bulk of Ethiopians came as a result of the airlift named Operation Solomon in 1991, an operation that involved 14,200 immigrants.

Total immigration decreased in each of the first four years of the twenty-first century, from 61,000 in 2000 to 21,000 in 2003. The Ethiopian immigration remained steady in this period, at less than 3,000 each year.

The government was completely unprepared for the task of absorbing such large numbers of immigrants, despite the pressure it had tried to exert over the years to force the Soviets to "let my people go." In the past, most immigrant absorption activities had been hands-on projects by government ministries, the Jewish Agency, and philanthropic organizations; this time, the decision was made to provide grants and then to let the immigrants fend for themselves. The Likud government declared a policy of "self-absorption," which basically meant giving cash to the immigrants and hoping for the best. Perhaps because there was no other choice, perhaps because it was the era of similar small-government ideologies in Thatcher's Britain and Reagan's United States, perhaps because the Likud was in power, the government wanted the market to deal with the problems and potentials of such a large influx of people.

The ambition and ingenuity of many of the immigrants, along with an upturn of the economy after the 1993 peace accords, prevented disaster. After very difficult beginnings, many of the Soviet immigrants found employment and housing, but the Ethiopians were much less successful. Eventually deemed unable to cope, they were absorbed by government bureaucrats in a manner familiar to many who had immigrated earlier, with all the attendant resentments.[12]

A majority of the 609,900 immigrants from the former Soviet Union between 1989 and 1995 were Ashkenazim, who were well-educated, secular, and steeped in western and Russian culture. They came because the Soviet Union was crumbling, the political and economic future was very uncertain, and they were concerned about anti-Semitism. Most of them discovered Zionism and Judaism in Israel, not in the Soviet Union.[13] Many had brothers, sisters, and cousins who went to the United States and other western countries during the same period, and many of these immigrants would have joined them there if they could. Instead, the familiar combination of a desire to leave their home country and the unavailability of alternative destinations brought them to Israel. Israeli authorities tried to convince other governments, especially the United States, to limit the number of immigrants from these countries so that Israel would get more of them.

They came from various parties of the Soviet Union: about 30 percent each from Russia and the Ukraine; 21 percent from the central Russian republics of Kafkaz, Azerbaijan, and Georgia; 9 percent from Belorussia; 6 percent from Moldavia; and 3 percent from the Baltic republics of

Estonia, Latvia, and Lithuania.[14] Almost 80 percent of the immigrants were Ashkenazim; Sephardi Jews were concentrated in the central republics. They came to a country with many familiar (if inferior, in their opinion) features and many residents who traced their ancestry to those same lands. They recognized the bureaucratic system with which they had to deal, many learned the language quickly, and most adapted to the new environment through a combination of personal, group and communal efforts.

The major feature of this Soviet immigrant group was their high level of education. Sixty percent were professionals—compared to 28 percent for the Jewish population already in the country. In the 1989–1995 period, 68,000 engineers arrived, comprising 11.2 percent of the group. Doctors and dentists made up another 5 percent—almost 10,000 doctors arrived in the 1990–1991 period alone—and another 5 percent were teachers. More than 40 percent had thirteen or more years of education, compared to 24.2 percent in the general population.

By contrast, the Ethiopian immigrants, who had been literally picked out of their underdeveloped African homeland overnight, came to a country that was very different from the one they had left and one that had very few former immigrants like them. Tracing their Judaism back to King Solomon and Bat Sheba, they brought traditions that had developed separately from the rest of the Jewish world, and they lacked the development of the Talmud and the rabbinical oral tradition that the Ashkenazi and Sephardi Jews shared. Accordingly, in addition to their economic and cultural "backwardness," many were seen as lacking in a religious sense as well. While their immigrant group features hundreds of Ethiopians in universities and in the army, and a few dozen officers, their social and economic integration faces serious challenges. The rate at which Ethiopian students pass the high school matriculation examinations is less than half the national average; and the number of juvenile delinquents among the Ethiopian population is double that of the other groups.[15]

An unsolved issue in the case of the Ethiopians is that of the Fala Shmura, part of one of the oldest known Jewish communities, tracing its origin to the Queen of Sheba in the times of King Solomon. The Fala Shmura, estimated to be about 18,000 in number, say their ancestors were forced to convert from Judaism to Christianity, but they insist they are Jews. The religious authorities—and hence the Israeli government—oppose their recognition as Jews on the ground that the only legally valid conversions are those performed by Orthodox rabbis. Since Jews are eligible for automatic Israeli citizenship, the ingathering of the Fala Shmura becomes embroiled in the politics and the financing of immigration.

Immigrants from the United States form a very small but important group in Israeli politics and society.[16] Of the 21,767 immigrants to Israel in 2003, less than 10 percent came from the United States, although Americans made up nearly half of world Jewry.[17] However, American immigrants have been very visible in the settlers' movement in the territories on the one hand and in civil rights and peace movements on the other. U.S.-born immigrants in Israel make up about 2 percent of the population. Over the years, these immigrants have tended to be younger and more educated than the general American Jewish population, a telltale sign of a pull, not push, immigration. Half of the American immigrants in 2003 came as singles.

Some Americans came before the Six-Day War, but the two largest groups came afterward, with 30,000 immigrants arriving between 1967 and 1973, and some 50,000 after 1973. Of the post-1973 group, about two-thirds were Orthodox, many of whom chose to settle in Judea and Samaria; the town of Efrat, for example, is comprised of some 10 percent Americans. Although more than a third of those who came to Israel as immigrants from the United States eventually gave up and left the country, the rate of leaving for the Americans who were Orthodox was about half that.

Emigration

In Israel, where every new immigrant is viewed as an important contribution toward the goal of the ingathering of the Jews, those who leave the country, by contrast, are not highly regarded. As a general estimate, about 10 to 15 percent of Israelis have left the country over time. A Central Bureau of Statistics report estimated that a total of 270,000 Israelis had emigrated between 1990 and 2001, including 68,000 (mostly not registered as Jews) from the former Soviet Union.[18]

It is very hard to give an exact number of emigrants because as a rule democratic countries do not collect data on the "returns." The determination of who is an emigrant itself presents difficulties because Israelis living abroad, when asked, often insist that they are planning to return. Also, while it might be possible to guess that persons born in Israel but now living in another country are emigrants, it is harder to identify the status of a person who lived in Israel for many years but who neither was born in Israel nor presently lives there. In addition, it is likely that a considerable number of people born in Israel and living abroad are Arabs and not Jews.

The early 1950s witnessed the highest rate of outflow in Israeli history. The ratio of emigrants to immigrants was higher (although the absolute number was lower) in the 1950s than in the late 1970s, a period in which problems of emigration concerned the public. Many of those who left in the 1950s spent a few months or a couple of years in Israel after the Holocaust and then left for other countries. For those who had never been ideologically committed to Zionism, Israel offered a temporary safe haven in a very long nightmare. For others, living conditions in Israel were simply too hard.

In the 1970s, Prime Minister Yitzhak Rabin denounced this emigration, calling Israeli emigrants "the fallen among the weaklings," and the government admitted that this large demographic loss was a matter of serious national concern. The government attempted to encourage the return of citizens living abroad, but with only mixed success.[19] The program included offering customs rebates and housing benefits similar to those granted new immigrants to those who returned to Israel after being abroad for a number of years. Those who came back increased from 8,000 in 1991 to 14,000 in 1995, and those returning to Israel were of higher educational level than those staying in the United States. This return migration was reinforced during that period by the booming economy in Israel and the peace process.[20] In 2004, many of these benefits were discontinued, a reflection of the difficult economic times and the individualistic ideology that pervaded Israel's political economy.

The stigma attached to emigration has decreased considerably over the years. One of the results of Israel's becoming a more open and competitive society is a growing acceptance of the fact that where one lives is a private decision as well as a public one. It is evidently no longer socially unacceptable to express a desire to leave the country, depending on conditions; the range of positive response fluctuates depending on how the respondents relate to the issues facing the country. In surveys conducted in 1995 and in 1996, the proportion saying they wished to remain in the country was 83–84 percent, but in each of the years between 1999 and 2002 the range of positive response was only 58–64 percent, reflecting the economic slowdown, disappointment with the Oslo peace plan, and the intifada.[21]

The other side of this growing acceptability of emigration is a declining sense that *aliya* is essential to the country's future. In the 1970s, 85–90 percent agreed with the statement that *aliya* is essential to the country's future; in 1986 and 1990 surveys, the number was 82 percent;

in 1992, it was 71 percent; and in the 1994 and 1995 surveys, it had fallen to 64–67 percent.[22]

The pattern of responses to the question of why people consider leaving is also revealing. Most think that it is because of economic reasons, but security concerns are also in play. In a 1986 survey, 73 percent responded that people might express doubts about staying in Israel for economic reasons; in 2003 economics was still the majority answer, but it was offered by only 52 percent of the sample. In 1986, 14 percent said that security concerns were the major reason; in 2003, that answer was given by 35 percent of the respondents.[23]

Jews are known as a wandering people. The Zionist vision was that in a national homeland, certain "negative" features of the Diaspora would be expunged from the Jew, including his wanderlust. This has obviously not happened. Not only have most of the Jews not returned to Zion, but many continue in their mobile patterns. This was so even in the time of the second commonwealth (two thousand years ago), when the Jews made up 10 percent of the Roman Empire.[24] We also know that today, at every educational and income level, American Jews travel more than non-Jews do. Every indication points to the fact that the wandering will continue in the future.

Sephardim-Ashkenazim

Demographic developments within the Jewish community are very important in understanding the politics of the State of Israel. Because its citizens come from a variety of backgrounds, it is no wonder that communal and institutional differences became a major factor in structuring the political landscape of the country.

In Israeli politics one of the dominant criteria is ethnicity—not the Jewish and non-Jewish distinction, but intra-Jewish ethnicity. The subject is a complex one, but the major distinction among Jews is between *Ashkenazim*, who came to Israel from Europe and America, and *Sephardim*, who immigrated from countries in Asia and Africa. While these terms are commonly used in contemporary Israeli politics, they obscure as much as they reveal because they are borrowed from other spheres. They have their origins in the medieval period of the various communities' sojourning in the Diaspora following different expulsions throughout history.[25] More appropriately, three divisions should be recognized: an Oriental (Eastern, also referred to as *Mizrachi*) community of Jews who never left Asia and Africa; the Sephardim, whose language

(Ladino) and ethnic culture originated in Spain before the expulsion of 1492; and the Ashkenazim (referring to Germany), whose hybrid language was Yiddish. Sometimes language is suggested as a basis for distinction, but today both Ladino and Yiddish are vanishing languages, and in any case they did not penetrate everywhere.[26] Hebrew, not the other languages, is widely spoken in Israel, and Jews around the world are likely to be more exposed to Hebrew than to Yiddish or to Ladino, so the earlier language distinction is failing.

The ethnic terms themselves are related to different ritual practices and usage adopted by scattered Jewish communities. The Ashkenazi-Sephardi terms are very problematic and imprecise. Thus, for example, many Jewish communities of southern Europe were Sephardim, while communities in the eastern Mediterranean, India, Yemen, and Ethiopia could not appropriately be put in either category. Especially in the latter half of the twentieth century, flourishing Sephardi communities were established in the Americas and especially in France. On the other hand, Ashkenazim lived in Egypt and China. Regardless of the misleading inaccuracies incorporated in the terms, this Sephardi-Ashkenazi nomenclature became part of the political reality of Israel and has emerged as a major theme in Israeli politics.

Of the 13 million Jews in the world, the majority are Ashkenazim, but only about a quarter of them live in Israel, compared with about two-thirds of the Sephardim. Israel's Jewish population is roughly half Sephardi and half Ashkenazi, although as the children of "mixed marriages" are coming of age, these distinctions become difficult to maintain.

Keeping in mind that we are compressing too much into the popular dichotomy of Sephardim (or Mizrachim) and Ashkenazim, we shall also rely on the usage of the government's Central Bureau of Statistics, which reports place of birth and father's place of birth (see tables 2.2 and 2.3). There are very high correlations between the European- or American-born and the Ashkenazim, and between the Asian- or African-born and the Sephardim, and hence we shall use the terms interchangeably. We should remember, though, that differences between Iraqi and Moroccan Jews (both called Sephardim here) are as great as or greater than differences between Russian and German Jews (both Ashkenazim). The more recent interaction of these Jews with their host country varied their common heritage as Sephardim or Ashkenazim just as a more distant history varied the common heritage shared by all Jews as they were developing the rituals, traditions, and language shared only by Ashkenazim or Sephardim.

Table 2.2 Place of Birth of Jews in Israel, 1948–2003

	1948	1961	1972	1983	1990	2003
Total (in thousands)	716.7	1,932.4	2,686.7	3,350.0	3,946.7	5367.2
Percentage in population:						
Israeli-born; father Israeli-born	35.4[a]	5.5	8.4	15.9	22.3	29.8
Israeli-born; father Asian or African-born		14.9	22.6	25.4	24.3	19.1
Israeli-born; father European or American-born		17.4	16.3	16.1	15.3	14.2
Asian- or African-born	9.8	27.4	24.8	18.6	15.0	10.1
European- or American-born	54.8	34.8	27.9	23.9	23.1	26.8

Sources: Statistical Abstract, 2003, 2–76.

a. Total of all Israeli-born, not broken down by father's origin in 1948.

The proportions of the groups in the population have changed over time (see table 2.2). Assuming that a large portion of those born in Israel of Israeli-born fathers were of Asian-African origin, it is likely that Jews of Sephardi background outnumbered the Jews of Ashkenazi background in the population during the 1980s. But the influx of immigrants from the former Soviet Union, most of whom were of Ashkenazi origin, probably reversed that situation. The proportion that has changed most dramatically is the percentage of the population that is Israeli-born of fathers also Israeli-born, which grew steadily from 5.5 percent in 1961 to 29.8 percent in 2003. In 1972, 47.3 percent of Jews were Israeli-born; that figure had increased to 63.1 percent by 2003. Even though immigration will continue to be important, the future will be molded by the Israeli-born.

As ever larger percentages of Israeli Jews were native-born, the ethnic cleavage became more distant. As indicators, consider that a majority of Israeli Jewish voters and 90 percent of Jewish children in elementary schools during the 1990s were native-born. They were exposed to a culture that downplayed—even if it did not successfully alleviate the disparities of—these ethnic distinctions. The rate at which a member of one group married a member of the other group was a high and constant 20 percent. The number of children from these "mixed marriages" grew, and the meaning of the ethnic distinctions blurred. In response to a question about whether the respondent is Ashkenazi or Sephardi, about a third of the sample now responds "neither" in survey after survey.

Beyond the labeling is the question of social and political meaning. Although fading, the labels are still of enormous importance. The major political parties vie to recruit politicians who can be presented as authentic

Table 2.3 Voting Potential of the Jewish Population in Israel

	Percentage in population			Percentage under 18			Knesset seats[a]		
	1967	1986	2003	1969	1986	2003	1969	1988	2003
Israeli-born; father Israeli-born	6.5	19.5	29.4	62.3	74.7	62.4	4	8	19
Israeli-born; father Asian- or African-born	18.7	25.7	19.2	81.6	47.6	18.8	5	22	27
Israeli-born; father European- or American-born	16.4	16.2	14.2	49.1	37.1	19.4	13	16	20
Asian- or African-born	27.8	17.2	10.2	11.5	2.4	3.8	38	27	17
European- or American-born	30.6	21.4	25.7	3.6	5.8	23.9	46	33	23
Total numbers and percentages	2,344,877	3,561,400	5,324,300	31.6%	34.1%	28.5%	106	106	106

Sources: Statistical Abstract, 1969, 42–43; Statistical Abstract, 1987, 73–75; Statistical Abstract, 2003, 2–74.

a. Assuming 80-percent participation; 12,000 votes per seat in 1969; 17,600 votes per seat in 1988; and 25,000 in 2003.

leaders of these groups, and the lists of both Labor and the Likud feature impressive and almost equal numbers of Sephardi politicians. And yet, in spite of significant headway achieved by Sephardim in and through politics, equality in terms of actual power has not been achieved.

Population growth is the key to potential political shifts, especially in a democracy. The fertility rate (the number of births divided by the population of females of child-bearing age) for the total population was 86.2 in 2003; for Jews, 74.7; for Christians, 71.6; and for Muslims, 150.1. The rate for Jewish women born in Europe was 52.2, and for those from the former Soviet Union was 45.3. For Asian-Africans it was 55.9; for those born in America, 85.0 was the highest. The fertility rate for women born in Israel whose mothers had also been born in Israel was 74.7.[27] The electoral potential of the various groups has changed over time (see table 2.3). European- or American-born voters and their Israeli-born children constituted a majority of the electorate in 1969; the Ashkenazim could elect fifty-nine Knesset members and the Sephardim could vote in forty-three members. By 1988, the European- and American-born and the Asian- and African-born voters and their Israeli-born voting children each had the potential of electing forty-nine Knesset members. The Sephardim had higher growth rates than the Ashkenazim and their family size was larger; the Ashkenazim tended to be older and to have fewer children. In 2003 the potential was forty-three seats for the Ashkenazim and forty-four for the Sephardim. The potential for second-generation Israeli Jews grew from four seats in 1969, to eight seats in 1988, to nineteen seats in 2003.

Non-Jews, Arabs, and Palestinians

Israeli Arabs

The Jewish state of Israel has a sizable population of non-Jews. Table 2.1, where the complement of the percentage of Jews in Israel is made up of non-Jews, clearly indicates that the picture is not static. Before the establishment of the state, non-Jews were a large minority: 96 percent in 1882 and 70 percent in 1939. With statehood in 1948, their relative weight fell (to 19.4 percent) because the pre–1967 war boundaries excluded most of them. By 1954, after the Jewish population had more than doubled as a result of immigration, the concentration of Jews was at its highest, almost 90 percent. After that, the relative weight of non-Jewish Israelis grew steadily in spite of continued Jewish immigration because the non-Jewish rate of reproduction was higher than that of

Jews. By 2003, non-Jews made up 23.2 percent of the population within the State of Israel not including the territories taken in the Six Days' War.

There were over one million Muslims in Israel at the beginning of 2004; comprising 16 percent of the population, they were the largest non-Jewish group by far. In addition, there were 120,000 Christians and 110,000 Druze.[28] However, Muslim children made up approximately one quarter of those under fifteen in the country. The annual rate of growth of the Muslim population in Israel in recent years (3.4 percent) is 2.4 times that of the Jewish population (1.4 percent). This growth rate is among the highest in the world, and even higher than that of the neighboring Arab countries.[29]

If the Arabs of the territories are added to these calculations, Jews make up a much smaller majority of the Eretz Israel population—52 percent in 2003 (see table 2.1). Projecting these figures into the near future is the basis of the demographic time bomb that concerns many in Israel. According to this projection, Jews will be a minority in Eretz Israel in the not-too-distant future, and this prospect upsets many for whom a Jewish state is a cherished goal. This point of view equates the numerical balance with the nature of the state, while others prefer to look to the policies of the state when discussing a "Jewish state." The demographic dilemma is real; the policy implications of the dilemma are less clear, and they have been at the core of the deadlock that has characterized Israeli politics for decades. Some conclude that the territories should be relinquished in order to alleviate the impending imbalance, while others think that the solution to the dilemma is to transfer the Arabs out of Israel, in a form of ethnic cleansing. The debate regarding the future structure of Israel's population involves assumptions regarding politics, demography, immigration, emigration, fertility, and morality. There is no doubt that the demographic factor will continue to be dominant in the political discourse and social realities that develop in the future.

It is imperative to make a very sharp distinction between Arabs who are citizens of Israel and those who live under the jurisdiction of the Palestinian Authority. The Arab citizens of Israel are those who remained after the 1948 war; they are full citizens of the country. There is debate among historians and other observers about the responsibility of each side in causing the movement of Arabs.

Israeli Arabs are full citizens in the sense that they organize politically, vote, and may be elected to the Knesset. Psychologically, however, their position is much more complex. They live in a Jewish country whose symbols, flag, and national anthem are all Zionist. They are not called to serve in the army—one of the important rites of passage for Israeli youth and a key to advancement in the adult world, where, as nonveterans, they are precluded from some of the benefits of Israel's welfare state. They comprise some 20 percent of the population but account for half of those below the poverty line. Their towns and communities receive different and unequal treatment by the authorities than that given to comparable Jewish municipalities. Their schools are even more crowded than the Jewish ones.[30]

But it is important to realize that Israeli Arabs have been, on the whole, law-abiding citizens. They are conflicted; they are cross-pressured.[31] Most identify with their Arab background, with their Palestinian roots and their refugee cousins, but many also identify themselves as Israelis. As a community they have conflicting identities; moreover, both Jews and non-Israeli Palestinians are unclear about where their loyalties lie.[32]

Relations between Israel and its Arab citizens faced a very serious challenge with the killing of thirteen Arabs by the Israeli police during demonstrations in October 2000, days after the onset of the al-Aqsa Intifada in the territories. The official report regarding the confrontation concluded that the government and the police had failed in their handling of the crisis and that Arab leaders, including Knesset members, had incited violence. But there has been no marked improvement in the relations between the two groups. The foundations of the citizenship of the Arab minority seemed to be shrinking, and the influence of Arab citizens on Israel's internal and external policies seemed to be at an all-time low.[33]

Palestinians

The Jewish-Arab conflict is more than a century old; it began when Zionists started to settle in Palestine. The origins of the Israeli-Palestinian conflict are much more recent: One prominent turning point in that struggle was November 29, 1947, the day that the United Nations decided on the partition of mandatory Palestine between the two peoples living in the territory—the Jews and the Arabs. The leadership of the Yishuv, representing the Jewish community, accepted this decision, but the Higher Arab Committee rejected it.

On May 14, 1948, the day the British Mandate ended, Israel's independence was proclaimed. The Arabs did not accept this development, and the armies of Egypt, Jordan, Lebanon, Syria, and Iraq attempted to prevent the establishment of Israel by force. The conflict that had simmered for years between two indigenous groups in a colonial territory escalated to the more visible status of armed conflict among nation-states.

The war ended with an Israeli victory that left the new country with a territory about 50 percent larger than that approved by the United Nations. Under the partition plan, Israel was to have been some 5,200 square miles in area; after the war, it annexed an additional 2,500 square miles, making the postwar country about the size of the state of New Jersey. The territory west of the Jordan River held by the Kingdom of Jordan ("the West Bank") was annexed by Jordan in 1950; the Gaza Strip was controlled by Egypt, although never annexed by it.[34] According to the original United Nations scheme, Jerusalem was to be an international city; as the cease-fire went into effect, the city was divided: the army of Jordan controlled the Old City and the eastern sections, the Israeli army the western neighborhoods.

The Palestine refugee problem originated during this 1948–1949 war. About 700,000 Arabs who lived in mandatory Palestine left, some voluntarily, some at the insistence of the Arab armies who promised they would be allowed to return after the hostilities, and some at the hand of the Israelis during the war.[35] Some 60 percent of them found their way to Jordan, about 20 percent to the Gaza Strip, and another 20 percent to Syria and Lebanon. The solution of the refugee problem will be one of the more difficult issues to be tackled by Israel and the Palestinians in working on the permanent status arrangement.

The Six Days' War of 1967 was a major turning point in the conflict. Israel won an amazing victory, unified Jerusalem, added another million Arabs to those already under its rule, and conquered lands claimed by Egypt, Jordan, and Syria. During this war, many of the refugees from the war of independence in 1948–1949 again came under Israeli jurisdiction.[36] In the 1979 peace treaty with Egypt, Israel agreed to return the largely uninhabited Sinai Peninsula.

Despite the impression sometimes given by discussions of its strategic importance and military might, Israel is not a big country. The total area of the state and the territories under its control is comparatively small. After the Sinai was returned, Israel comprised about 10,500 square miles—about the size of the state of Maryland, yet smaller than Armenia, Albania, or Belgium.

Israeli authorities have historically conceived of the conflict in the region as being between nation-states. Once Israel was established, the question was if, when, and on what terms, Arab states would recognize Israel. Arabs living in Israel were granted citizenship but they were treated with circumspection; in fact, they lived under military government for the first twenty years of statehood. Israelis have historically rejected the notion of a Palestinian state; some, such as Golda Meir in the 1970s and Binyamin Netanyahu in the 1990s, have argued that there was no such thing as a Palestinian nation and hence no Palestinian state was possible. Others added that the Arabs already had twenty-plus states and that an additional one was not needed for the relatively small Palestinian population—Jordan could become the Palestinian state.

Between the 1967 war and the 1993 Oslo Accords, the policy of Israeli governments was to avoid changing the legal status of the territories, except for Jerusalem and the Golan Heights, while supporting Jewish settlements in the territories (with varying degrees of enthusiasm). The entire city of Jerusalem and much of the countryside around it were annexed by Israel soon after the 1967 war, and Israeli law was applied to the Golan Heights (which belonged to Syria) in 1982. Applying Israeli law was less than annexation but left little doubt regarding the intentions of the ruling power. The prospect of returning territories in order to make peace was consistently the platform of the Labor Party, and it became the policy of the government of Israel after 1993.[37] The Likud did not accept this principle, and the dilemma of the Netanyahu government was to remain loyal to the traditional hard-line Likud platform while conforming to international agreements based on the land-for-peace principle that had been entered into by previous Israeli governments.

A sense of "creeping annexation" was prevalent among Palestinians because of the persistent policy of all Israeli governments to expropriate land for Jewish settlements. This expropriated land, added to that taken over by the Israeli authorities after the retreat of the Jordanian army in 1967, and the properties purchased by Israelis from Arab owners, brought the total holding by Israel to about a third of the land on the West Bank. This development was deemed most dangerous by Palestinian nationalists.[38]

The Labor government headed by Levi Eshkol proceeded with settlement soon after the 1967 war, especially along the Jordan River and around Jerusalem. The beginning of Jewish settlement in territories with a large Arab population also began under Labor, in 1974, when Yitzhak Rabin and Shimon Peres, both of Labor, were prime minister and defense minister, respectively. Capitulating to the symbolic pressures of potential Jewish settlers living in temporary camps on lands central to the biblical past of Israel, and to the political pressure of the rightist parties demanding government sanction and support for this policy of settlement, the Labor leadership initiated the policy that eventually led to large-scale settlement in the territories.[39]

The big leap in settlement activity came during the Likud years between 1977 and 1992. In 1976, there were a little more than 3,000 Jewish settlers on the West Bank (Judea and Samaria). By 1988, the number had increased more than twenty-fold, to about 70,000 Jews living there. In May 1977 there were 34 settlements in the West Bank; by 1984, the number had climbed to 114. In 1985 only one additional settlement was added. During the periods of the National Unity Governments, the pace of settlement represented a compromise between the desires of the Likud to go faster and the wishes of Labor to proceed more cautiously, although neither of the big parties opposed continued settling. The 1984 National Unity Government agreement limited new settlements to five or six new settlements annually, and the agreement that established the 1988 National Unity Government set eight settlements a year as its target, assuming that funds were available.

The 1990–1992 Likud government made settlement a high priority. The Shamir government refused to halt settlement in 1992 in order to receive $10 billion in loan guarantees from the United States to absorb immigrants from the former Soviet Union. This rift with the first Bush administration (along with the Likud's other problems) led to the 1992–1996 Labor government, which froze new settlements. By 2004, there were about a quarter million Jews living in the disputed territories, providing every new government with a promise or a problem, depending on its ideology. Not all of the settlers were ideologues. Residing in the territories became a popular alternative for young Israeli-born Jews seeking reasonably-priced housing in the suburbs of Jerusalem and Tel Aviv.

The Palestine Liberation Organization (the PLO), generally considered to represent the Palestinians, was established in 1964. It pursued a very checkered political and diplomatic career in trying to achieve the visibility and the legitimacy needed to reach its ultimate goal of achieving national independence for the Palestinians. The PLO was often associated in the public mind of the West with terror and terrorism, accusations to which it sometimes admitted. The inhabitants of the territories achieved high levels of national solidarity, even though they were cut off from the PLO leadership. Although Israel prided itself on its democratic forms, the Arabs in the territories were deprived of political and civil rights, and they experienced the frustrations, inconveniences, and even humiliations of living under military occupation.

The Palestinians' refusal to accept the status of Israeli occupation erupted in the intifada, an uprising of the Arabs in the territories, which began in December 1987. A year later, when the U.S. government agreed to enter into discussions with the PLO, the role of the PLO and its legitimacy were at a high point. Gradually, the portion of Israelis who were prepared to enter into negotiations with the PLO grew, although both major parties, the Likud and Labor, rejected the notion.[40] Some Israelis feared that Arab recalcitrance went beyond solving the issues raised by the Six-Day War, and that ultimately the Palestinians wanted to dismantle the State of Israel. Therefore, tough policies—even distasteful ones—were a matter of continued survival. Others felt that a solution could be reached only by political, and not by military, means. Caution, strength, and vigilance were needed, they felt, but so was a solution that would allow all sides to live in peace.

In Washington in September 1993, a handshake between Prime Minister Yitzhak Rabin and PLO Chairman Yasir Arafat marked the signing of the Oslo Accords (formally known as the Declaration of Principles on Interim Self-Government Arrangements) between Israel and the PLO. The agreement included provisions for Palestinian self-rule in Gaza and Jericho, and the transfer of specific government functions on the West Bank to the Palestinians. Two years later, in September 1995, the Oslo 2 Agreement was signed.[41] It created three zones on the West Bank: (1) Area A, to be controlled solely by the Palestinians, included the cities of Bethlehem, Jenin, Nablus, Qalqilya, Ramallah, and Tulkarem, and parts of Hebron; (2) Area B, including many towns and villages, in which activities of the Palestinian Authority would be coordinated and confirmed with Israel; and (3) Area C, consisting mainly of unpopulated areas of strategic importance to Israel, and Jewish settlements, to remain under sole Israeli control. Oslo 2 included, among other things, a timetable for the redeployment of the IDF, elections to the Palestinian national council, and the beginning of negotiations regarding the permanent status between the negotiating sides.

The appropriate degree of interaction between the two societies has always been a hot political issue. Closure of the territories was often imposed after terrorist incidents as a form of defense, but it also had the effect of punishing the many Palestinians who worked in Israel—they could not get to their jobs, and the territories could not provide alternative employment. But this policy of temporarily isolating the territories raised the possibility of two separate entities, a development that might make an independent Palestinian state more likely. In parallel, Palestinians began to work out for themselves what their society should be like.[42]

The onset of the al-Aqsa Intifada in 2000 coincided with the pressure brought to bear on the Palestinians by U.S. President Bill Clinton just before he was to leave office. Clinton and Prime Minister Ehud Barak pressed Arafat and the Palestinians at Camp David and at Taba to agree to a comprehensive plan that would require considerable concessions from both sides, but that pressure failed and the Palestinians balked.[43] The failure of this attempt to reconcile the opposing parties was followed by years of suicide bombings and Israeli operations that left both sides drained.

As the impasse continued, the popularity of the notion of separation grew among Jews. The right was skeptical, thinking that accepting such a division might imply a weakening of Israel's commitment to the territories, while the left feared that separation might institutionalize inequality and lower the chance for peace, but the large middle of Israeli public opinion saw separation as a protection against suicide bombings and continued terror attacks.[44] Labor's Amram Mitzna ran on a platform of unilateral separation in 2003 and was defeated in a landslide by Prime Minister Ariel Sharon. By 2004, however, unilateral separation, which was supported by a majority of the population, had become Sharon's own policy preference as well, although it was rejected in a referendum among Likud members. The building of an actual security barrier around Jewish settlements on the West Bank was related to this policy. The controversy it generated was where to put it, not whether to build it. Should it be placed on the 1967 borders, or should it protect settlements far inside the territories established since 1967?

3 POLITICAL ECONOMY

THE FORM OF ECONOMY in Israel is a mixture of government activity and state planning, along with free enterprise. Since the mid-1980s there has been a marked shift away from government intervention and toward market economics and an atmosphere friendlier toward initiative, and especially investment.[1] Increasingly, the rhetoric of the country's economic ideology, regardless of the party in power, favors competition and market forces while shrinking the welfare state; in practice, there is still a high degree of concentration of economic might at the centers of power, and a growing gap between rich and poor.

The relative poverty of the country in resources and the tremendous expenses of defense and immigration absorption have coincided with a highly centralized, overstretched economy. But defense also has provided an arena for technological innovation and creativity, and the mass immigration from the Soviet Union in the 1990s introduced an enormously talented pool of engineers, doctors, and computer specialists. Israel's economy benefits from the infusion of funds from abroad, but it is very competitive in many fields, and the standard of living of its population has reached European standards. The gap between rich and poor has grown, while increasingly shifting the provision of minimum standards for its population to the institutionalized network of organizations and bureaucracies of the overextended civil society.

The economy provides an excellent example of many of the major features of Israeli public life.[2] The economy is very centralized and is characterized by a high level of government influence. It provides the Jewish people living outside Israel with a tangible link with the country and its development. The economy has increasingly encouraged enterprise and initiative, and yet it is still dominated by a small number of principal actors, most of them well connected to government leaders. Repayment of past debt is a major burden for the economy, and the economy has been dependent on loans and grants from foreign countries, especially the United States.

Costs of the defense effort make up the single largest expenditure and influence the structure of the entire governmental budget. Subsidizing basic consumer goods and public transportation once characterized the policies of both Labor and the Likud, but this practice has declined in recent years, compared to the past. Unemployment reached a very high 11 percent in 2003, while inflation was kept in check; this was a reversal of the pattern established in the 1990s, when relatively low unemployment accompanied high (and in the 1980s, even raging) inflation.

Decisions that appease growing consumer demand while simultaneously continuing expensive government projects have led to the mortgaging of future generations to the standards of today. Trade imbalances are huge, and they are met by indulging in loans in foreign and local currencies. The economy usually skews in favor of the salaried class immediately before elections. Attempts to reform the economy are difficult both because the vested interests protect existing structures and because such moves are politically unpopular, but since 1985 the shift away from patterns of the past has been constant.

Prime Movers

Israel's political economy can be understood only in terms of the historical developments that produced the system. Imagine an economy with few if any raw materials; with great needs for funds to finance political and social projects; with connections to individuals, institutions, and governments abroad interested in aiding it; and with an administrative elite intensely loyal to the overriding goals of the economy yet flexible and ambitious enough to attempt an enterprise that was theoretically not promising. Add to this the need for secrecy, and the result may be something resembling the Israeli economy. These generalizations have held for the entire period of modern Jewish settlement in Eretz Israel, although the details have changed. The need for secrecy, for example, was originally intended to prevent the British mandatory power from discovering clandestine efforts at absorbing illegal immigrants. Secrecy was often justified because of a project's connection with security needs or, later, to allow Israel to deal with firms or countries that did not want these dealings to become public knowledge. Today, the habit remains long after the need has vanished.

Three prime movers—the World Zionist Organization (WZO), the Histadrut, and the Israeli government—were responsible for fashioning the Israeli economy and for developing it. At different points in the development of the economy of Eretz Israel since the 1920s, economic power has been distributed differently among the three. In the pre-state era, the WZO and the Histadrut reigned; following the establishment of the state, the Histadrut and the government wielded enormous influence; in the 1980s, the role of the Histadrut changed drastically, leaving economic power even more centralized in the hands of the Israeli government.

National Institutions

The most important economic force in the pre-state period was the WZO. After World War I, development of the economy was spurred by immigrants coming with capital of their own, but mostly it came about because of the activities of the WZO and the moneys it collected abroad and expended in Eretz Israel. The WZO, founded by Theodor Herzl in 1897, now meets once every four years based on elections held by Jews all over the world. Since statehood, the results of the Knesset elections determine the relative size of the Zionist parties that represent Israel in the Zionist Congress. Since 1959, Israel has selected 38 percent of the delegates; the United States, 29 percent; and all other countries together, 33 percent.

The structure of the WZO is pyramidal; above the broad base of the Zionist Congress is the 518-member Assembly, and above that an executive committee with 192 members, and a smaller directorate. Israeli parties are dominant, and the payoffs and politics of the WZO are often a direct extension of party politics in Israel. In addition, representatives of the right-of-center Maccabi, WIZO (the women's auxiliary of the Zionist organization), Bnei Brith (a Jewish communal organization), the Sephardic Federation, and the Orthodox, Conservative, and Reform movements in Jewry are members. Power tends to be shared, although important functions are kept for the major party if possible.

When the League of Nations established a Mandate for Palestine in 1922, it provided that "an appropriate Jewish agency" be set up to cooperate with Britain, the mandatory power. The aim of the resulting "Jewish

Agency" was to assist and encourage Jews throughout the world to help in the development and settlement of Eretz Israel. Its Executive was the chief decision-making body in Eretz Israel and became the "state in the making."

Because of its close working contacts with the mandatory power, the political importance of the Agency far exceeded that of local institutions such as Knesset Israel, the Electors' Council (Asefat Nivharim), and the National Committee (Vaad Leumi), and by 1930, as the outlook for the future of European Jewry darkened, it became even more important. By 1935 Mapai had won control of the Agency Executive, and Ben-Gurion had become its chairman. Such control was important symbolically because the fight over control of the Zionist movement between Jews living in Eretz Israel and those living abroad had gone on for a long time. Even more important were the political implications, for the ascent of Mapai shifted control of the moneys collected from abroad to Eretz Israel and from nonsocialist parties to socialist ones.

Upon achieving independence, it was natural for the chairman of the Agency Executive (Ben-Gurion) to become prime minister, and the head of the political department (Sharett) to become foreign minister. Relations between the State of Israel and the WZO and the Jewish Agency were formalized in 1952. This in effect froze the situation that then existed and recognized the WZO's and the Jewish Agency's continued activity in the fields of settlement, immigration, and education. After independence, the Agency was very active in the economy, owning Raasco (which mainly provided construction and had set up forty settlements), and Bank Leumi, then the country's largest bank. In addition, the Agency had partial ownership and control of Mekorot and Tahal, which developed water projects; Amidar, which provided and managed moderately priced housing developments; El Al, Israel's national airline; Zim, Israel's major shipping line; and the Israel Museum in Jerusalem. This partial list, along with a series of affiliated corporations, indicates the wide scope of the Agency's activities and its role in the economy.

Two other important organizations of the WZO in the pre-state period still exist, although their functions have largely been eclipsed by the state. The first is the United Jewish Appeal (Keren Hayesod/Magbit), which is the money-raising arm of the Zionist movement. Founded in 1920, it operates in forty-five countries around the world (though not in the United States). Since it is often less problematic for Jews throughout the world to contribute to a Jewish philanthropic organization rather than directly to the State of Israel, the organization serves important functions, although its efforts are closely coordinated by the finance minister and the government. The ideology of the appeals is that Jews around the world have a responsibility to support Israel and therefore should contribute to it through a worldwide organization. As Israel prospered and the Jewish diasporas were challenged by assimilation or by oppression, a debate emerged about what share of the moneys raised by the UJA should be transferred to Israel and what share should be used for the needs of Jewish communities outside Israel.

The second important organization is the Keren Kayemet (Jewish National Fund), which was charged with purchasing and reclaiming the land. When the state was formed, many of its functions passed naturally to state authorities. The caretaker of nationalized land is the Israel Lands Administration, which controls more than 90 percent of pre-1967 Israel. Thus the Lands Administration is a very valuable asset, and politicians fight over it when negotiating for ministries. Accordingly, the Administration has been located at various times in a number of different ministries; when the Ministry of National Infrastructure was set up in 1996, headed by Ariel Sharon, the Lands Administration was one of the key building blocks.

In 1971 the Jewish Agency was reorganized, becoming a partnership between the Zionist movement, controlled by the dominant Israeli political parties, and the leaders of Diaspora Jews, generally identified as "non-Zionists." Differing agendas clearly drove the two groups of leaders, but, in reality, Israeli parties continued to control the Agency's governance, structure, policies, budget priorities, and senior staff appointments. In 1995 Avraham Burg was elected chairman of the Jewish Agency and World Zionist Organization. At the age of forty, he was the youngest person ever to serve in that position and he also happened to be a Labor leader, a dove, and an Orthodox Jew in favor of religious pluralism. When Burg returned to parliamentary politics, Sallai Meridor of the Likud, aged forty-four, was selected head of the Jewish Agency and the WZO.

Funded mainly by Diaspora donations, the WZO and the Jewish Agency bring immigrants to Israel and help them start their new life in the country, as well as providing Jewish and Zionist education in the Diaspora. But the organizations have suffered from an aura of stagnation and occasional petty corruption. Fifty years ago, most money raised by the UJA in Jewish communities worldwide went to Israel. Concerned that the intermarriage rate among American Jews might be as high as 50 percent, that three-fourths of U.S. Jews have never visited Israel, and that many Jews in Israel are alienated from Judaism, it was proposed that half the $500 million raised be spent in Israel and the other half in the Jewish communities in which the money was raised; WZO leaders from the Diaspora demanded to keep an even larger portion at home. This debate occurred as some of the main American federations announced that they would reduce their allocations to the Jewish Agency from 39 percent to 37.5 percent of funds raised by the UJA. A court decision in 2000 further threatened the organizations by ruling that developing settlements only for Jewish citizens denied equal rights to other citizens.[3]

The WZO and the Jewish Agency are faced with a disputed agenda, a shrinking staff (cut in half from its 3200 employees level in 1990), and friction with ministries in Israel which have overlapping mandates, since the organizations are active in encouraging *aliya,* in youth and educational work, in settlement, and in welfare work, all functions also filled by government ministries. Compromises are worked out, such as the division of labor regarding immigrant absorption—with the Jewish Agency dealing with potential immigrants outside of Israel, and the government's Ministry of Immigrant Absorption handling immigrants in Israel—but personal, bureaucratic, and political interests keep getting in the way.

The WZO and the Jewish Agency provide alternative sources of income for social projects in Israel, thus freeing the government's budget for other purposes. Also, the continued existence of these organizations allows for activity and involvement by many non-Israeli Jews. As for settlements in the territories, different policy preferences have been expressed by senior bureaucrats of opposing parties. The result is conflicting bureaucratic initiatives with personal and organizational interests at stake. The WZO and the Jewish Agency have been downsized considerably, but they still have important symbolic value and continue to be active in the economy. Controlling them provides patronage and activity, and although the size of the workforce and the range of activities have been reduced over the years, they still remain attractive political plums in Israeli politics.

The Histadrut

The clearest organizational expression of political and economic power in the pre-state period was the Histadrut. Formed in 1920 by socialist parties to further the economic, social, and cultural interests of the Jewish worker in Eretz Israel, it became an important power base for socialist parties.[4] Apart from representing workers in the negotiation of contracts with employers, it also incorporated the important collectivist enterprises of the country, including the collective kibbutz and the cooperative moshav. In addition, the Histadrut was a major employer in its own right, supplying social welfare and economic services such as education, health, housing, construction, manufacturing, culture, banking, insurance, and sport.

The Histadrut's cooperation with the WZO, and later with the state, allowed a pooling of resources. Bank Hapoalim, for instance, was set up by the Histadrut with the help of the WZO. Through the first four decades of statehood, the government's Ministry of Finance allowed the Histadrut's pension funds to be invested in Hevrat Ovdim, the Histadrut's holding company, giving it a sure source of capital. With the dramatic changes of the 1980s and 1990s—featuring the government's takeover of Bank Hapoalim, the collapse of Hevrat Ovdim, and government regulation of pension plan investments—those days were over.

The structure of the Histadrut changed little between its founding in 1920 and its streamlining (some called it gutting) in 1994, although over the years, many activities that formed the backbone of the Histadrut were transferred to or transformed by the state. The Histadrut holds elections among its members every four years, using a list system, in which most of the political parties of Israel compete. Until 1994, the Labor list (Mapai, or the Alignment, or whatever name was being used at the time), always won an absolute majority in Histadrut elections and thus completely controlled this important source of power and patronage.

In the May 1994 elections, Labor was challenged by one of its own, Chaim Ramon, who was the minister of health in the Rabin government at the time. He split with Labor because it refused to support his proposed national health scheme. This topic was especially sensitive, since one of the Histadrut's remaining bastions of power was Kupat Holim, its system of health clinics and hospitals. Ramon's list won 46.2 percent of the vote, running against the Histadrut secretary-general, Chaim Haberfeld, who headed the lackluster Labor list and won only 32.5 percent. Although Ramon thus won control of the Histadrut convention, Labor retained control of the labor councils, leading to low-intensity conflict between the two groups. If conceived of as two factions from the same camp, they did very well, but upstart Ramon's success was a cruel rebuke to the Histadrut's establishment and to those who had opposed Ramon in the Labor Party.[5]

In 1993, 42 percent of salaried workers in the economy had been members of the Histadrut,[6] placing Israel in a category of countries with similar rates such as Germany, Italy, and Canada, well ahead of the United States, Japan, or France, but far behind the Scandinavian countries.[7] In 1994 the Histadrut had 1.8 million members, but at the conclusion of its membership drive in October 1995, there were only 650,423 members,[8] 84 percent of them salaried and about 9 percent pensioners.

The reason for this severe drop in membership was that one no longer needed to be a Histadrut member to have access to the health insurance of the Histadrut's Kupat Holim. The National Health Insurance law that went into effect in 1995 (see chapter 11) declared that applicants for insurance could not be turned down by a health plan, and that acceptance could not be made conditional on membership in another organization. In the past, many workers had suffered their membership in the Histadrut because of the health insurance coverage, but even if we assume that the previous numbers were accurate and not bloated, membership had been falling at a rate of about 2 percent per year even before the law was enacted.

Ramon served as head of the Histadrut for eighteen months and then returned to the government after the Rabin assassination. He was followed as head of the Histadrut by Amir Peretz, with whom Ramon had run in their successful elections. Before the 1999 elections, Peretz broke with Labor over economic policies and established "Am Ehad" (One Nation), but he rejoined Labor in 2004. The Histadrut redefined itself as a defender of the interests of workers and retired persons, facing off against the government in strikes and work stoppages over the government's plans for privatization and the shrinking of the public sector.

The Histadrut's economic activities were historically significant because it was willing to pioneer in sectors that would not have attracted a capitalist investor. Since the ideological goals of the leadership were developing the economic base of the homeland and creating a class of Jewish workers in Eretz Israel, its economic behavior was often prone to risk-taking.[9] Its historic role in the economy involved administration, economic enterprises, its cooperative organizations, and the cooperative economy.

The administration involved bureaucrats and functionaries of the central administration, the executive committee, workers councils, trade unions, Kupat Holim (the sick fund), pension plans, social welfare funds, *Davar* (the Histadrut's newspaper), and the *Jerusalem Post* (the English-language newspaper, which until 1989 was jointly owned with the Jewish Agency). The most important of these was Kupat Holim, which employed almost 30,000 in the 1980s, and was a major consumer of medical supplies and other commodities.

The Histadrut played a major role in the country's economic enterprises. In 1986, 27 percent of the country's industrial production was generated by Histadrut corporations, which included Koor, Shikun Ovdim, Hasneh, and Bank Hapoalim—leaders in industry, building, insurance, and banking, respectively. Each of these enterprises had an important impact on the economy. Koor, for example, had more than 100 industrial firms, some 100 commercial firms, and 50 administrative and financial firms, including pension funds whose moneys financed many other projects. The country's largest industrial exporter, employing 30,000 workers in 1986, Koor was listed in *Fortune* magazine's list of the 500 largest companies in the world.[10]

In the mid-1980s, many of these enterprises felt the impact of the slack management practices that had characterized their operations. Historically their role in the economy had been very significant, but facing enormous deficits and a reduced labor force, they had to curtail their bloated bureaucracies and their patronage—a serious departure from past practices. In order to raise the capital to see them through the crisis, some of these enterprises sought government loans or guarantees; in the past, with the Finance Ministry controlled by the Labor Party, this type of appeal was natural. But under the Likud administrations of the 1980s, the government was less forthcoming; it made governmental support conditional on administrative reform of the enterprises. For example, in 1980 Finance Minister Yigael Horowitz reversed the policy that had allowed Hevrat Ovdim to take unlinked loans from the pension funds run by the Histadrut. When Shimon Peres of the Labor Party served as prime minister in the mid-1980s, and when he became finance minister in 1988, he, too, supported the curtailing of policies that in the past had been extremely beneficial to the Histadrut.

Ideological issues also came to the fore: there were suggestions that the needed capital be raised by turning to private investors. This would indicate much more than economic trouble for the working-class Histadrut; it would also signify an important deviation from the socialist principle of class or national ownership of the means of production. The policies followed in the 1990s by the Likud's Binyamin Netanyahu as prime minister and, more recently, as finance minister have confronted the Histadrut with continuing challenges.

Histadrut organizations set up to facilitate cooperative marketing for members include Hamashbir Hamerkazi department stores, supermarkets, and Tnuva, which is still the largest food concern, providing 70 percent of the country's dairy products. Other aspects of its cooperative economy, encompassing the kibbutz, the moshav, and other cooperative ventures, are still intact, but diminished. However, only about half the workers are members of the cooperatives, and that raised difficult ideological problems because of the norm against exploiting hired labor. Egged and Dan, for example, transportation cooperatives that accounted for 80 percent of the country's passenger movement, were periodically plagued by tensions between drivers who were cooperative members and drivers who were salaried employees. Another example is the eleven regional enterprises set up by the major kibbutz movement; of the 6,000 workers, 1,200 were kibbutz members. The perceived exploitation by these enterprises of the surrounding (largely Sephardi) population in development towns became symbolic in the ethnically charged elections of the 1980s.[11]

The kibbutz and moshav are prime examples of Israeli inventiveness and adaptation. Kibbutzim continue to be active in agriculture, but increasingly their income is from industry, service provision, and the professional activities of their members. During the pre-state and early state periods, these agricultural settlements—especially the kibbutz—were the focus of political and ideological power as well as economic success. This role of moral leadership has been eclipsed, and the decline of the kibbutz in the public mind is both cause and effect of the decline of Labor. But its economic achievements stand.

The overhead organization of the settlement movements is the Agricultural Center, which represents 401 moshavim and 267 kibbutzim. These cooperative enterprises are dominant in most fields of agricultural endeavor, and in some fields (such as milk or flowers) they control almost all production. Cooperatives provide most of Israel's produce and some 80 percent of its agricultural exports, involving about two-thirds of those working in agriculture.

When the Histadrut and the government were controlled by the same party—as was the case between 1948 and 1977—the potential political and economic power was awesome. Even with the ascent of the Likud, the Histadrut continued to play a major role in the economy, but the rules changed, and so has the Histadrut.[12] Gone are the organizational base, the patronage, and the power enjoyed by the Labor Party for seventy-five years. The reformers of the mid-1990s believed that the behavior of Labor regarding the old Histadrut was like that of a "suicidal whale," in Ramon's unforgettable phrase, while the New Histadrut (they actually changed its name) would allow for the reemergence of the labor movement as a vibrant leader of Israel in the future. The new leadership decided to focus on the trade-union aspect of the Histadrut.

The New Histadrut moved its headquarters to Jerusalem from Tel Aviv, sold many of its property holdings, reorganized the regional and local workers' councils, and retired or did away with the jobs of many of its activists. The Histadrut newspaper, *Davar*, was sold to the paper's employees, as were other publishing and cultural enterprises. After several false starts and partial Histadrut participation, *Davar* published its last issue in 1996. The role of the Histadrut in supporting competitive sports, and especially its *Hapoel* teams, was severely restricted.

The economic base of the New Histadrut was far different from the old Histadrut in terms of both scope and influence. The National Health Insurance Law of 1995 redefined the role of the Histadrut as an actor in health delivery; Kupat Holim was confined to providing facilities, with the collection of dues and the funding of expenses regulated and conducted by the National Insurance Institute and the Ministry of Health. Most important, the law abolished the requirement of Histadrut membership for those insured by the Histadrut's Kupat Holim.

Government legislation regulating pension plans effectively took control of a major source of capital out of the control of the Histadrut in exchange for covering the commitments of plans which were not actuarially sound because of growing life expectancy, lowered investment rates, and poor management.[13] The Histadrut's share of Koor was sold to a California-based company; Bank Hapoalim, Israel's largest commercial bank, which had been taken over by the government after the shares-manipulation scandal of 1983, was sold to private investors.[14]

The Government of Israel

The government is by far the largest actor in the Israeli economy, and its role is growing. The public sector can be divided into three categories: units that provide governmental services, business enterprises of the state, and state-owned corporations.

The first category, units that provide governmental services, is the most extensive of the three. Activities are undertaken by governmental ministries or special units set up by the Knesset and financed by the public treasury. The category includes defense; ministries concerned with promoting certain aspects of the economy (energy, agriculture, atomic energy, transportation, industry and commerce, tourism, communication) or activities important to the economy (subsidizing credit and supporting public transportation); ministries concerned with the social welfare (education, health, labor, immigrant absorption, religious affairs, building, and housing) and activities related to public welfare (aid to the broadcasting authority, subsidizing basic food articles, and agricultural production); services of a general or administrative nature (the president, the Knesset, the prime minister's office, the ministries of Finance, Interior, Police, Justice, Foreign Affairs, the state controller, financing political parties); and municipal and local government arrangements for firefighting, water, and sewage.[15]

The second category of public-sector activity includes the business enterprises of the state, such as railroads, lands administration, the port of Jaffa, the government printer, and the arms industry. These enterprises sell services and goods, financing their operations largely by these sales. Another area of government activity is the statutory authority, established by law, which overlaps with activities already mentioned. They include the commissions for production and marketing in the various agricultural areas (vegetables, tobacco, milk products), Magen David Adom (the Israeli Red Cross), Yad Vashem (the Holocaust memorial organization), the national social security institute, local authorities, the Bank of Israel, the council for higher education, the employment service, the ports authority, the airports authority, religious councils, the broadcasting authority, and the national sport lottery. This list does not have to be exhaustive to underscore the point that the government is very active in many facets of the Israeli society.

Government corporations, the third category, operate in areas such as natural resources, development, and tourism. The Government Corporations Law identifies a government company as one with at least 50-percent government ownership or 50-percent participation in its direction. Using this definition, there were 101 such corporations in 2002, down from 189 in 1987. In 2002, 55,248 people, or about 2.5 percent of the workforce, were employed by government corporations, down from 72,655 in 1992.[16] The reduction in these numbers occurred because the government sold its share in some corporations. The actual scope of government activity becomes clearer if we add the subsidiaries of these government companies and joint ventures between government and private owners and the more than 120 corporations set up by municipalities.

Government corporations allow the government more flexibility of action in the marketplace than is usually the case with units under strict public scrutiny and financed by the treasury. But these corporations may become empires unto themselves, either not responsive to public demands or too dependent on the politicians who set up the corporations. In Israel each corporation is responsible to a minister, but the diversity and complexity of the corporations demand unusual talents to direct them effectively.

The picture of the Israeli economy painted here so far heavily emphasizes the structures created by public institutions both before and after
the founding of the state. But, while the public sector is undoubtedly
very influential, the private sector must not be ignored. Despite all its
centralization and the heavy influence of the government on its economy, Israel has encouraged private investment and economic activity,
and many of these undertakings have proved beneficial to the investor
and the economy alike. Corporations such as Clal and Hevra Leisrael
were set up under very favorable terms in order to attract investment by
Jews abroad.

As in most market economies, and maybe a decade behind others, the
key word now is *privatization.*[17] In Israel, however, in addition to the
usual questions regarding privatization, the defense issue looms large.
What activities should be recognized as monopolies? Does it make sense
to replace concentration of government economic control with concentration in the hands of a few individuals? What are the motivations of
the buyers? Are there crucial or sensitive spheres whose transfer to
private hands could endanger national security?

The motivation of most investors seems to have been profit, rather than
control of Israeli politics or economic life. Here are some recent examples:

1. In the largest privatization deal in Israel's history, a group headed
   by Ted Arison and the Dunkner family (owners of the Dead Sea
   Works) purchased 43 percent of Bank Hapoalim from the government for $1.36 billion in 1997.[18]

2. In 1999 the government gave Intel an unprecedented $600 million
   grant covering 35 percent of the investment in a plant in Kiryat Gat
   to manufacture electronic chips. The plant was a major success,
   exporting in 2003 product worth $1.5 billion and employing 3,700
   workers. (Nevertheless, the unemployment rate in Kiryat Gat was
   still 14.7 percent.)

3. El Al, the national airline, is in the process of being privatized, with
   completion scheduled for the end of 2004. An obstacle in the path
   of privatization is the fact that El Al does not now fly on the Sabbath
   or Jewish holidays; investors are uncertain about the effects of
   leaving that situation unchanged or the possible commercial ramifications of changing this policy.

4. Zim, the national shipping company was sold in 2000 to Hevra
   Leisrael, a holding company owned by the Ofer brothers, under
   very favorable terms.[19]

5. Bezeq, the national telephone company, still in the hands of the Israeli government, is in the process of being privatized; agreements regarding the transfer have been worked out with management and the employees.

6. In 2004 Finance Minister Netanyahu began privatizing Bank Leumi by giving every taxpayer a share of the bank.

The debate regarding privatization continues. A moderate view sees it as beneficial only when privatization spurs competition, or when changed market conditions demand efficiency and better management. Regarding many national assets, the government continues to hold a "golden share," through which it retains some measure of control and protects the national interest in companies such as El Al and the Israel Electric Company. Prime Minister Sharon and Finance Minister Netanyahu, however, made privatization a high priority in their economic reform plan of 2003. The government persisted in its policy to continue privatization, aiming to sell some $2 billion worth in 2003–2005, a very ambitious goal considering that income from privatization in 2002 was less that $100 million.[20]

Dramatic changes have taken place in the daily life of Israelis because of marked improvement in telephone, postal, and train services. Long operating within government ministries, these functions were transferred in the mid-1980s to the status of government corporations, which allowed management greater flexibility in terms of planning and increased the workers' motivation. One incentive to the workers who provided these services was more flexibility in the wage structure—like all salaried employees, they were involved in the popular Israeli sport of comparing salaries and wanted to be "linked" to the wages of other groups. The government favored the change to remove entrenched anomalies in these service areas; the workers were counting on higher wages. The results were very impressive.

Bezeq, the telecommunications corporation, was privatized in the 1990s, when 25 percent of Bezeq's shares were offered on the open market, with 10 percent of the offering going to the concern's workers, and the new corporation created a revolution in its sphere of activity. An indication of this revolution was cutting the waiting time for installation of a telephone line: whereas in 1984 a quarter-million households were waiting to have telephones installed, and half of them had already been waiting for three years, the waiting time virtually disappeared by 2003. Likewise, passenger trains have become an independent government corporation; the number of riders tripled between 1998 and 2003.

Performance and Government Activity

Israel's economic achievements are impressive. Between 1950 and 1976, the gross national product (GNP) increased by nearly 9 percent a year in constant prices and by 4.7 percent a year on a per capita basis. After that, growth stagnated (as it did in the rest of the world), with GNP increasing by 2 percent in constant prices in 1975 and by only 1 percent in the late 1970s. When calculated on a per capita basis, this gave Israel a standard of living higher than that of Italy. On an absolute basis, Israel's GNP was higher than that of Egypt's, although Egypt had a population more than ten times the size of Israel's, and this fact is even more impressive given that the Israeli economy's GNP was about 40 percent that of Egypt's economy after independence in 1948.

Israel attained the highest gross domestic product (GDP) growth rate among Western (OECD) economies in 1991 (6.2 percent) and 1992 (6.7 percent), but the trend slowed with the economic crisis of 1997 and soured in 2000 with the outbreak of the intifada. Israel experienced negative growth rates in 2001 and 2002 and a 1.2 growth rate in 2003.[21] After encountering double- and even triple-digit inflation in the 1980s, Israel's unemployment rate soared at the beginning of the twenty-first century. Inflation and growth were low, but so was economic activity.

Still, the country's per capita GDP placed Israel 22nd among 200 countries in the world. A small country with a population of 6.5 million, Israel's international position in some areas of industrial and agricultural production capacity and exports is remarkable. Free Trade Agreements with Europe's EU and EFTA and the United States facilitate Israel's exports and its participation in international business enterprises, affecting its anticipated growth during the twenty-first century (see table 3.1). Despite a number of bad economic years at the beginning of the decade, Israel's per capita GDP in 2002 was greater than those of European countries such as Spain and Greece.

The government has played a very active role in the Israeli economy. Its control of the budget, the rate of exchange, the money supply (nominally controlled by the Bank of Israel), and the granting of licenses, loans, and grants makes it the single most important actor in the Israeli economy, affecting as much as 90 percent of the economy's performance. The government is the country's biggest employer and its largest customer. It controls important economic resources: land, money, raw materials, water, and the right to grant or deny the use of these and related potential sources of income. The government determines subsidies,

Table 3.1 Economic Indicators in Selected Countries

Country	GDP, 2002 (in $millions)	GDP per capita, 2002	Annual growth in GDP, 2002/2001	Average annual rate of inflation, 1999–2002	Unemployment rate, 2002 (as % of workforce)	Total debt as % of GDP, 2002	Human Development Index (HDI)
United States	9,186.0	36.1	2.9	1.8	5.8	60.8	0.937
Japan	5,606.5	31.3	−0.7	−1.25	5.4	147.3	0.932
Germany	2,707.9	24.1	0.2	0.74	8.6	62.8	0.932
Great Britain	1,354.9	26.5	1.5	2.5	5.1	52.0	0.930
Spain	737.2	16.1	1.8	3.6	11.3	65.6	0.918
Greece	150.0	12.1	3.6	3.4	10.0	104.7	0.892
Israel	116.3	17.6	−1.5	3.6	10.3	102.9	0.905

Sources: For GDP and annual growth in GDP: *Israel Statistical Abstract 2003*, table 28.6. For GDP per capita: Organization for Economic Co-operation and Development, *OECD Economic Outlook—2003*, vol. 2003/2, no. 74 (December 2003). For average annual rate of inflation: Bank of Israel, *Inflation Report 2003*. For unemployment rate: *Israel Statistical Abstract 2003*, table 28.5. For total debt as % of GDP: The General Auditor, The Management Unit for the Government Debt, *Annual Report 2002*, 39. For HDI: United Nations, *Human Development Report, 2003*.

wages, and taxes and, in effect, determines the standard of living for the bulk of the population.

Most imported foodstuffs are imported by the government or by government license, while food production is regulated by public commissions on which the government has major representation. Many raw materials are imported by government monopolies. Wage guidelines are set for salaried workers in consultation with the government; cost-of-living increases, so important in a country that has experienced triple-digit inflation, are also determined after government consultation. Prices can be fixed by the appropriate ministry on goods deemed vital or on goods that enjoy the status of monopolistic commodities. Capital formation, investment programs, and the licensing of banks are other areas of government influence and activity.

The key ingredient in the government's influence over the economy is that for all practical purposes it has monopolized the capital market. This was the case both when the major banks were controlled by the prime movers of the economy and again after the government controlled the banks as a result of the bank shares scandal. In 2003 the two largest banks (Hapoalim and Leumi) controlled two-thirds of the capital market, and the two bank groups (including banks affiliated with them) 80 percent. The three largest banks (including Discount) controlled 80 percent of the capital market, and the three bank groups 90 percent.[22]

Israelis save at a very high rate, mostly through retirement funds partially financed by employers, through investment plans, and through the stock market. Most of this activity is supervised by the Finance Ministry by way of issuing licenses to banks or to financial institutions, under the control of the banks, that conduct such investments. Although this supervision is ostensibly meant to protect the public, in effect it allows the ministry tremendous leverage on the economy; in this manner the ministry can control the investment activity of the banks and financial institutions. In practice, most of these moneys are channeled into projects in tune with the priorities and goals of the government budget. For example, the finance minister, with the approval of the Finance Committee of the Knesset, can approve bond issues with tax reductions that obviously have a great influence on how the public invests its money. Other bonds are issued for institutional investments, thus creating a mechanism to absorb the very large amounts of money in pension funds. Poorly administered funds, on the other hand, are prone to turn to the government for aid, thus creating an incentive for the Finance Ministry planners to control the pension funds and their policies. To truly privatize and encourage competition, the bureaucrats and politicians must relinquish their control of this source of power.

One legacy of Israel's unique history is the expectation that any problem worthy of solving would be financed by the government or one of its agencies. Also, most projects could be presented in a way that would appeal to leaders anxious to implement Israel's priorities of security, economic development, social justice, and full employment. Loans would have to be guaranteed to attract industry; settlements would have to be built to enhance security; communication and transportation could be important in time of emergency; scientific and technological excellence must be pursued; housing must be provided; health services and hospitals must be improved; and so on. Few activities were outside the scope of government.

There were political consequences to these economic activities. Regardless of the motivations of the leaders who initiated the projects, they led to a tremendous concentration of power and resources in the hands of a very small number of politicians and civil servants. And when new immigrants widely perceived that their promotions and even their jobs depended on retaining the present bosses in power (as was the case through the 1950s and perhaps later as well), these perceptions could be translated into electoral victories and power perpetuation.

The key to Israel's political economy is dependence and influence rather than outright control and direction. Given the government's power to control prices and provide licenses, its near monopolization of the capital market, and its subsidizing of foodstuffs, transportation, land, and housing (in certain areas), most actors in the Israeli economy are influenced by and many are dependent on government policies. This dependency makes the economy highly sensitive to changes in personnel and policy, and it makes the positions of leadership of the Finance Ministry potentially powerful. But this dependency lowers the likelihood of change in the system because radical change breaks the dependency relations that are so important to both sides. It is easy, for instance, to raise wages before elections; it is extremely difficult to cut them back afterward.

The ministries that deal with economic matters are aided by the Knesset's penchant for delegating to the appropriate minister many of the details of legislation. This transfer of legislative activity to the executive branch allows the Knesset to act in principle while the ministries deal with details, but in reality it means that enormous economic and political power is concentrated in the economic ministries. What is even more notable from a political point of view is that economic decision making in Israel ultimately leads to the government and within the government to the Finance Ministry, especially to the minister and the director of the budget. Enormous power rests in these positions in the Israeli system, the Finance Ministry usually having an "agent" participating in key deliberations throughout the public sector *before* budgetary decisions are made. Having the information beforehand prevents the ministry from being surprised by an enterprising governmental unit and gives it an effective veto on all plans and projects.

The use of the term *veto* is important because it would be incorrect to foster the impression that the Finance Ministry, its minister, or the budget director can easily bring about a revolution in the economic arrangements of Israel. The Israeli economy is simply too complex, and the interests and organizations at work are too many to be easily bent to the will or policy of determined men. For example, in 1980 Yigael Horowitz talked gloomily of the Israeli economy not being able to continue at its rate of government activity and expenditure, but he was forced to resign when the political calculations of the government brought in very different conclusions. However, when the top political leadership is united in attempting to achieve a goal, the chances of achieving it are greatly enhanced. This was most obvious in 1985, when Labor Prime Minister Shimon Peres cooperated with the Likud's Finance Minister Yitzhak Modai in controlling an inflation rate that exceeded 400 percent yearly. Peres used the influence he had with the Histadrut, headed by Labor's Israel Kaisar. The Likud and Labor, both members of the National Unity Government, cooperated in holding back rampant inflation by agreeing to hold down prices, wages, and taxes, without causing undue inflation or social unrest.[23] Avi Ben-Bassat concludes that the stabilization program introduced in that period paved the way for later growth but also erased the ideological differences between the two big parties.[24] Netanyahu's term as finance minister in the 2003 Sharon government will also be remembered as a period of cooperation and firmness (some termed it callousness) in forming and pursuing economic reforms.

Except for very unusual circumstances, the political-economic leadership has more power to prevent developments it sees as negative or unnecessary than to make drastic changes in the regular order of things. Most change that can be effected is incremental in nature. The system is simply too enmeshed, the interests too variegated, and the force of habit too great to allow for sweeping change. Furthermore, comprehensive change demands much more political and bureaucratic clout than most political-economic leaders have had or have wanted to expend. The rule of thumb gleaned from Israeli political history is that finance ministers have usually been left to do their own thing, the prime minister being either too inexpert or too preoccupied with other issues to involve himself in the economy. Other ministers become spokespeople for ministries they are charged to lead and fiercely resist cuts in their budgets or perceived infringement on their turf. The high degree of concentration of Israel's economy should not be misunderstood to mean that structural changes can be brought about overnight. Almost all enterprises in the Israeli system see in the Finance Ministry the source of support or funds for expansion in good times or salvation and enmity in bad ones. And these, of course, are political and not exclusively economic issues.

An extremely important source of power for the finance minister and his advisers is their ability to determine the appointment of key figures in the economy. Many industries and economic units are directly tied in with government, and others are dependent on it. If the politicians who head the Finance Ministry desire to do so, they can influence the composition of boards of directors in the public sector by placing people loyal to them or by placing party activists in key positions throughout the economy. This practice stems from their power—or their perceived power. Indeed, their influence is not always needed; often appointments will be made in anticipation that they will find favor in the eyes of government leaders. This is the sure test of power because anticipatory behavior is a sign of a very large measure of influence and control.

The structure and statutory arrangements of the economy provide the government in general and the finance minister in particular with large measures of responsibility regarding the national economy, as well as tempting possibilities to utilize their power to further economic and political ends. But the finance minister is not omnipotent; his major resource lies in his ability to direct, develop, suppress, or reduce the activities of the public and private sectors. But as the economy has developed, complete dependence on the government has been reduced; in the 1950s employment and housing were almost completely dependent on government activity, but this is no longer the case. At the same time, powerful groups and institutions within the economy have emerged—largely thanks to government policy. Large unions within the Histadrut, important financial institutions, and major investors have the potential for opposing government policy in an effective manner.

It is little wonder that the finance minister is considered to be one of the most powerful figures in Israeli politics. In the twenty-nine years of Alignment rule, Finance was one of the few ministries never to be held by anyone but a Mapai member. Even the Defense Ministry was given to Rafi after 1967 (first to Moshe Dayan and then to Shimon Peres), but the powerful leaders who served as finance ministers (Eliezer Kaplan, Levi Eshkol, Pinhas Sapir) were all Mapai leaders, as were two weaker personalities but important Mapai functionaries (Zeev Sharf and Yehoshua Rabinowitz) who also held the post. It was natural for the Likud in 1977 to give its top post to Prime Minister Begin and the role of finance minister to Simha Ehrlich, the leader of the Liberals, the other major party of the Likud along with Herut. Ehrlich was followed by Yigael Horowitz of a smaller Likud party, then by Yoram Aridor and later by Yigael Cohen-Orgad, both dedicated Herut members. In the National Unity Government of 1984, the finance minister was Yitzhak Modai of the Liberal Party, followed by Moshe Nissim, also of that party. With the advent of the 1988 National Unity Government, Shimon Peres became finance minister. Avraham Shochat, an ally of Rabin in the Labor Party, was finance minister between 1992 and 1996, followed by the Likud's Dan Meridor in 1996.

Meridor clashed with Prime Minister Netanyahu and was replaced by Yaacov Neeman, a well-known lawyer but not a Knesset member. As Israel entered a period of political instability and constant shifting of governments and prime ministers, the Finance Ministry tended to be held by only a handful of people. After Neeman resigned about a year after taking office, he was replaced by Netanyahu (who was also prime minister at the time) and then by Meir Shitreet of the Likud. In the period of Barak's prime ministry after the 1999 elections, Shochat returned, to be followed by Silvan Shalom when Sharon replaced Barak in 2001. When Netanyahu agreed to return to head the Finance Ministry after the 2003 elections, Sharon gave him both increased authority and political backing.

For certain financial decision-making cases, such as the setting of salaries for Knesset members, ministers, and judges, or the amount to be paid to political parties for financing their activities or the activities of government corporations or special allocations, the approval of the Knesset Finance Committee is also needed. This committee reflects the composition of the governing coalition and usually presents no problem (see chapter 9), but the cooperation of the committee chair is essential, making the chair one of the most powerful people in Israeli politics. Close cooperation between the finance minister and the chair of the Finance Committee can mean an enormous concentration of power.

An idea of the direct involvement of the government in economic matters can be gleaned by the development of the economy by sectors. While it is not easy to measure precisely, the relative size of the government sector in the economy is growing. It was once customary to speak of three sectors of the Israeli economy: the private sector, the government sector, and the Histadrut sector. During the first fifteen years of statehood, the public sector and the Histadrut sector (excluding the Jewish Agency) accounted for about 20 percent each of the net domestic product, with the government sector share in net product growing since 1953.[25] In 1969, based on employment figures, the public sector employed 33.6 percent of salaried workers, the Histadrut sector 18.1 percent, and the private sector 48.3 percent.[26] Using economic figures of the early 1980s (not employment statistics), the estimate was that the private sector accounted for about 40 percent of economic activity in the country, the Histadrut 20 percent, and the government 40 percent. Since the retreat of the New Histadrut from economic activity, the shares of both the private and government sectors have risen.

Political leaders at times undertake economic risks because they fear that not doing so will expose them to even larger political dangers. Two examples are the bank shares crash of 1983 and the issue of the kibbutz debt, and they are related.

The banks ensured persistent upward demand for their shares by regulating the price through schemes such as having bank subsidiaries post demand for their shares. While illegal, the process was undertaken with the full knowledge of the government, the Knesset, and the Bank of Israel. This regulation resulted in an average appreciation of the value of the banks' shares at a rate of 30 to 40 percent per annum in real terms; after a few years of such activity, the shares of the banks were grossly overvalued in terms of their economic value. In October 1983 the prices of bank shares collapsed abruptly. The government came to the rescue of threatened shareholders and covered much of their loss. The government set a floor on the price of the bank shares and agreed to purchase all the outstanding shares at a predetermined dollar amount over a period of six years. The guaranteed prices were above market price, so the government held the shares. However, the government obtained almost no voting rights, even though the shares constituted almost 100 percent of the banks' equity. Later legislation procured the voting shares for the government as of 1993, so the banking industry was nationalized, not by intention but because political considerations overrode economic ones.[27] Although the heads of the major banks were tried and convicted of fraud for manipulating the price of their shares, the political leadership was never put on trial.

In the same period, eager to expand their farms and factories, and tempted by unlinked, long-term bank loans at a time when triple-digit inflation took the pain out of repayment, many kibbutzim (as well as many others) borrowed at the old values, planning to pay back at the new ones. Shimon Peres, as prime minister of the National Unity Government, desired to introduce a measure of discipline into the economy in 1985 by reducing inflation to double-digit figures and raising interest rates. At that moment, the banks demanded their money back, and the kibbutzim could no longer afford to pay. The kibbutz movement faced a debt of $10 billion.

In 1989 the government and the kibbutzim worked out an arrangement that canceled some of the debt, deferred payment on other parts, and forced some kibbutzim to liquidate their obligations by selling land to real-estate developers. In early 1992, the Likud government responded to skyrocketing urban housing prices and an insatiable hunger for land to build on, along with the pressure of the huge immigration from the former Soviet Union, by ordering the Israel Lands Administration, official caretaker of state land, to free some farmland for residential building. A handful of kibbutzim and moshavim in the Tel Aviv and Jerusalem areas were paid handsomely by real-estate developers for land they had been leasing.

The largest part of kibbutz debt was held by Bank Hapoalim, formerly owned by the Histadrut, and the second largest part by Bank Leumi, formerly owned by the Jewish Agency. The government was in the process of selling Bank Hapoalim and wanted to put Bank Leumi on the market soon afterward, but the unresolved question of what the kibbutzim owed the banks created a major obstacle delaying finalization of the Hapoalim sale. Unless a buyer knew the value of the assets on the bank's books, it was impossible for a final price to be set. In the Finance Ministry and the Central Bank, reconsideration of the idea of selling the banks was under way, reflecting the close relationships between the government bureaucracy and former bureaucrats who held the top private banking jobs. The banks had substantial holdings in their investment companies, and control of Bank Hapoalim provided major stakes in Koor and Clal holding companies.

The role of the government in the economy of Israel is unprecedented among democratic regimes; the involvement of political actors in the economy is enormous, and has increased over the years. Direct government activity is very high: the national budget's share of the gross national product (GNP) rose from 32.5 percent in 1950 to 95 percent in 1980; in 2003 it was 55 percent. This would be unimaginable if there were not sources of income outside the country. A time-series study of the relations between government consumption and GNP (without the Histadrut or the national institutions) revealed that the ratio was between 0.33 and 0.36 until the 1960s, when it contracted to about a quarter; it rose above 40 percent after 1967.[28]

Defense expenditures fell from 25.5 percent of the GDP in 1982 to 12.2 percent in 1990 and 7.7 percent in 2001. Defense expenditure as a percentage of total government expenditure was 18.5 percent in 2002 (see table 3.2), but because of the intifada, these percentages rose after 2002. While defense took a smaller slice of the total, in Israel that slice was larger than in other countries.[29] The ratio of defense budget to the GDP was about three times higher in Israel than in other Western countries.

The government budget supposedly reflects the priorities of the government.[30] In Israel this is so only indirectly, because much of the budget is based on moneys generated and spent abroad, and because activities supported by the government need not be directly financed by it (Jewish Agency activities, for example). Calculating the budget as a percentage of the GNP may be a misleading figure because transfer payments are not included in the gross national product. Thus, for example, when the National Insurance Institute supports a retired person or gives a family allowance, these payments are not incorporated in the GNP, although they play an important role in the nation's economic and social policy. Similarly, subsidies paid by the government are not calculated as part of the GNP. Transfer payments ranged between 4.4 and 8.7 percent of the GNP annually between 1980 and 2003.

Import Capital

Israel's achievements would not have been possible without the importation of capital. Just as other countries have imported foodstuffs, raw materials, or automobiles, Israel has, in addition, imported money. The

Table 3.2 Defense Expenditures in Selected Countries

	Defense expenditure as % of GDP, 1990	Defense expenditure as % of GDP, 2001	Defense expenditure as % of government expenditure, 2001
United States	5.3	3.1	15.7
Japan	0.9	1.0	6.1
Germany	2.8	1.5	4.7
Great Britain	3.9	2.5	6.9
Spain	1.8	1.2	6.1
Greece	4.7	4.6	16.4
Israel	12.2	7.7	18.5

Source: United Nations, Human Development Report, 2003, table 17, p. 295.

most consistent sources of this money have been the Jews of the world, who have regularly contributed to Israel through donations, loans (Israel Bonds), or investment. Between 1948 and 1978, collections (not including loans or investments in Israel) reached a level of more than $5 to $7 billion, nearly two-thirds of it from the United States.[31] Between 1951 and 2003 Israel Bonds raised $25 billion.

What has become even more important than the support of the Jews of the world is the support given Israel by other governments, especially Germany and the United States. Reparations paid by the West German government to the government of Israel in the 1950s aided Israel in overcoming one of its earliest and most difficult economic periods. Food was rationed as hundreds of thousands of new immigrants continued to pour into the country. By 1978 over $4 billion had been received from the Bonn government, of which $836 million was reparation payments to the Israeli government for Nazi actions in World War II (these payments ended in the 1960s). In addition, personal restitution payments to Israeli citizens for acts against them during the Nazi rule continued; in 2002 restitution payments amounted to $760 million.[32] An agreement was reached in 1998 with Swiss banks that held moneys of Jews during the Holocaust, whereby the banks would reimburse descendants $1.25 billion.

The bulk of Israel's import capital in recent years has come from the government of the United States. Since the early 1980s, Israel has been receiving about $3 billion a year from the U.S. government, approximately 60 percent in military aid and 40 percent in economic support. Most of this aid has been given as grants; only a small portion have been loans that had to be returned. (Israel, however, still had very large payments to make on past debts.) These figures represent a dramatic rise in the level of American aid, as is illustrated by the fact that in 1970 U.S. aid to Israel totaled $71 million, of which $30 million was military aid, and only $1 million of the total was in grants.

Foreign aid allows policymakers to avoid decisions regarding the country's priorities; since expenses need not be reduced, programs that otherwise would not be funded can be continued. While the aid has continued to flow, Israel has learned that not all its demands would be met: the government was forced to discontinue development of the Lavi jet-fighter in 1987 when it became clear that the United States would not continue to underwrite the project. In 2003 the government deficit (income minus expenditures) stood at $6 billion, the lowest level since 1991—but at 5.7 percent of gross domestic product, it was still high by comparative standards.

Israel's total foreign debt at the end of 2002 reached $67.6 billion, or 110 percent of the GNP, with about 40 percent of that sum in government liabilities payable in foreign currency, a result of the long-term independence and development bonds sold mostly to Jews abroad; an additional amount was owed by the government but payable in local currency. The developing trends in this regard are striking and unmistakable: a sharp rise in the public foreign debt and a lowering of the role of debts to Jews (bonds) in the equation. In 1955 the total national debt payable in foreign currency was $491 million, with the government owing $398 million of it; $198 million, or almost 50 percent of that government debt, was owed to bondholders. By 1980, bondholders made up a little over a quarter of the total foreign debt of the government payable in foreign currency. This, even while the size of the debt to bondholders increased 14.5 times in the twenty-five years between 1955 and 1980, while the total foreign debt of the government increased by double that rate, 28 times.

Israel's yearly debt, however, is greater than the support it receives from the United States. In 1982 Israel was pledged to repay $3.2 billion—about 14 percent of the GNP was expended on servicing the yearly debt! In that year about $1 billion was spent returning principal and servicing the interest on the first large loans given by the United States in 1973. In the 2004 government budget, 34.5 percent was earmarked as interest.

In the 1990s, the U.S. government guaranteed $10 billion in bank loans for Israel to aid in immigrant absorption, and in 2003 another agreement was reached, under which the United States would guarantee up to $9 billion in bank loans for the 2003–2005 period.

As U.S. support jumped after 1973 and then stabilized, the proportion of Israel's needs supplied by the contributions of world Jewry shrank in comparison to the billions supplied by the American treasury. American Jews donated more than half a billion dollars a year to the United Jewish Appeal, which must finance local activities as well as programs in Israel. The amount generated by the sale of Israel Bonds in the United States in the same period was more than half a billion dollars a year.[33]

Moreover, as Israel proved itself militarily strong, many Jewish communities began to rethink the tradition of putting Israel's needs before more localized ones. Slowly a shift in priorities developed, and the share of contributions sent to Israel tended to decrease. This development coincided with the passing of the older generation of American Jewish community leaders whose formative years had coincided with the Holocaust and the formation of the State of Israel. For the younger generation of leaders, Israel was a fact of life, and other needs of the Jewish community had also to be attended to. Some Jews outside Israel also became critical of Israel in an unprecedented manner. The war in Lebanon, the Who is a Jew? issue, the handling of the Arab uprising, and the future of the territories divided many of these Jewish communities (just as they divided Israeli Jews). This dissension further decelerated the traditional rate of contributions to Israel—Jews continued to contribute, but their proportionate share in Israel's import capital was lower.

The relationship between economics and politics is especially interesting from this perspective. The government's ability to influence much of the economy of Israel gives power wielders within the state a potent tool. Yet this enhanced power to influence the policies of the Israeli government does not seem to extend to the Jewish fund-raisers abroad nor to the major government supporter of the Israeli economy, the United States. We must seek the explanation to this difference in the ideology of supporting Zionism on the one hand and the practicalities of trying to influence a sovereign power on the other.

Dependence on someone else's money would not seem to be the best recipe for independence of action, but the Jews of the world, while often politely listened to, have long been excluded from policy decisions in Israel. This customary exclusion followed Ben-Gurion's thinking that one who wants to influence Israeli policy should live in Israel. Inevitably, strains have resulted from the attempted division of labor, whereby Jews outside Israel collect the money but leaders within Israel decide how to spend it.

In the 1920s the WZO tried to influence social and economic development within Eretz Israel from its headquarters abroad; this brought about a series of conflicts with the pioneers, especially socialists. When Mapai became the dominant force in the World Zionist Organization's Executive in 1933, it acted to consolidate its control over the inflow of moneys. Since then, tensions between donors and receivers have been mitigated by consultation and by passing out honorific titles without allowing economic power to be translated into political power by outsiders over Israeli politics.

The dependence of Israel on U.S. funds has traditionally been cited by Arab states as proof of American complicity in Israeli policies. It is clear to them that economic power can be translated into political influence, and American protestations notwithstanding, the U.S. government has not seriously attempted to alter Israel's foreign policy course. The Americans have indeed used their economic weapon, usually in Israel's favor. They have generally been careful to avoid putting pressure on Israel by cutting off aid, although more subtle devices such as withholding a shipment of purchased material, failing to approve suggested increases in aid, or threatening not to guarantee loans given by others, have been used. How a big power influences a smaller power is a complex and fascinating topic; what seems clear is that the options open to the big power are not unlimited. Short of cutting off aid completely, history has shown that translating economic aid into political obedience is a difficult task. But there are intermediary steps, such as impeding the flow of money. One of the arrangements that advantages the United Jewish Appeal in the United States, for example, is that it is recognized there as a charitable organization and hence, according to U.S. tax law, contributions to it can be deducted from one's income tax. It is sometimes financially rewarding for Americans to donate to the UJA (or other charities) and thus put themselves in a lower tax bracket. Should these rules change, a different atmosphere, psychological and economic, might be revealed.

The most economically beneficial way to import capital is through export based on foreign investment. In the 1990s, Israel provided many foreign investors with an attractive option: the likelihood of a quiet and stable political environment, a well-trained workforce, and the strong probability of profit. The first was achieved by the partial lifting of the Arab boycott as a result of the Oslo Accords with the PLO; the second by the successful spinoff of technologies developed in military and defense-related industries, along with the educated professionals who recently immigrated from the former Soviet Union; and the third through government subventions for investors. Its talented labor force, its strategic location between North America, Europe, and the Far East, and its free-trade pacts with both the United States and Europe endow Israel with a potential as spectacular as that of Hong Kong or Singapore.[34]

In 1995 a total of $2.3 billion was invested in Israel—a twenty-fold increase from 1992, and a signal from the investment world that the mutual recognition agreement between Israel and the PLO would bear economic benefit. Most opportunities were seen in high-tech industries, where salary levels were relatively low by international standards and quality was good. Venture capital in Israeli industry soared to $480 million in 1995 from $55 million in 1991.[35] Major high-tech companies such as Intel, IBM, Digital Equipment, Motorola and National Semiconductor all created major research and development centers in Israel. The Intel Corporation, one of the world's major producers of integrated circuitry and chips for microprocessors, for example, accepted a Ministry of Industry and Trade offer of a $600-million grant that was conditional on its making Israel the site of a $1 billion expansion project. Unfortunately, much of this growth was curtailed when the intifada broke out in the 2000s.

While import capital—loans, grants, contributions—has always been important in the Israeli economic equation, much of the burden has fallen on Israelis themselves, who are very highly taxed. Like any other government, Israel has tried to finance its activities by absorbing capital from the Israeli public. By 1978 about 45 percent of the total government income came from domestic sources, with 55 percent collected abroad. Financing Israel's massive public consumption has required such heavy taxation that, in some years, the Israeli citizen has borne the highest tax burden, relative to income, in the world. During its first decade, taxes equaled one-eighth of the GNP; in the 1960s, the proportion reached one-quarter; then it wavered between one-third and one-half in the 1970s, and peaked at 52 percent in 1986; since then it has fallen again. At no time, however, has taxation covered more than two-thirds of the government budget.

Employment and Distribution

Israel's economy is dependent on foreign capital, its defense budget is large, and it is a country of immigrants—all these features promote dependency relations. Lacking land, capital, and a profession (or the opportunity to work in their profession), many who came to Israel found themselves dependent on the various bureaucracies for all their needs. The kind of labor market that developed accelerated the economic concentration delineated earlier in the chapter.

Attempting to resolve the problems of economic scarcity, unemployment, security, and integration of the new immigrant groups led to governmental policies that structured the labor market. The logic behind labor absorption in the economy was political as well as economic, favoring services, especially in the public sector. The government, by virtue of its economic concentration and primary role in setting wages and price policies, had a major role in determining public welfare. Much of the workforce was salaried, and many worked in public sector enterprises, making them financially dependent and within relatively easy grasp of the tax authorities. A very large majority of salaried people were directly affected by the wage policy of the government.

In 2002 there were 90,510 government employees, excluding teachers and employees of government corporations.[36] About a third of the nation's 2.3 million employed people worked in jobs for which the government was either the direct or the indirect employer, including the armed forces, teachers, employees of municipalities and local authorities, the Jewish Agency, workers in government corporations, Kupat Holim, and civil servants. This figure does not include workers in industries still under the control of the Histadrut, whose salaries are influenced by a national wage agreement that does not require the approval of the Finance Ministry, or employees of banks that were taken over by the government after it rescued them from the bank-shares collapse and had not yet been privatized.

A second important feature of the labor market is that most of the work is concentrated in the services sector. Of the 2 million employed persons in 2002, 75 percent worked in such service occupations as commerce, hotels, communication, finance, and business; 23 percent worked in industry including mining, manufacturing, electricity, water, and construction; and 1 percent in agriculture. About a third of the total, or half of those working in services, were employed in public and community services. These figures support the notion prevalent in Israel that working in industry does not provide the status or economic rewards of working in services, but it also means that a great many jobs are dependent on government and public budgets, not on the productive capacity of the economy. When broken down by nationality and sex, the magnitude of the trends changes a bit: non-Jews are more active relatively in agriculture and industry, while Jews—and especially women—are more concentrated in services.

It was difficult to construct a modern industrial society with a population whose largely middle-class backgrounds gave them inadequate preparation for such a task. Most important in solving this difficulty from a political point of view was the willingness of the leadership to provide employment by creating jobs, even if some of them were redundant or unnecessary. One of the direct results of such high levels of government control and influence was that social and political goals (and not only economic ones) could sometimes guide decision makers in their deliberations. For example, industries might be located in developing areas in order to disperse the population or to provide employment for people sent to inhabit these areas, even if the location itself made little economic sense. Some of the workforce is involved in compulsory army service, including reserve duty of a month or so for many men until middle age. Israeli leaders, regardless of party, have tended to rank full employment very high on their list of policy goals. The 11-percent rate of unemployment in 2004 was high and politically sensitive. In addition to Israelis, some 100,000 Palestinians who had worked in the local economy were largely barred from their workplaces in Israel with the onset of the intifada in 2000; in their place, foreign workers were used. By 2004 it was estimated that 250,000 legal foreign workers were in the country, along with an additional 100,000 illegals.

The mechanism of setting wages underscores the central role of the government.[37] The process begins with negotiations between officials of the Finance Ministry, the Histadrut's trade union division, and the coordinating committee of the employers; the result of the negotiations is a national wage agreement. The government's role is usually one of arbitrator, because the workers want more but employers want to pay less. The government is not only a major employer but is also elected by the largely salaried electorate and, no less important, is responsible for the national economy. After the guidelines have been set, attempts are made to reach specific agreements in the various economic sectors and later in individual plants. This long and extended process means that labor issues are almost always in the news, and many contracts are signed long after previous ones have expired.

The Histadrut and the government are influenced by political and economic considerations; both are major employers, and the leadership of both must stand for reelection. When both the Histadrut and the government were headed by Labor, cooperation was the rule, although arguments, even heated ones, did occur. But their solution was generally achieved through intraparty committees or discussions. When the Likud headed the government and Labor controlled the Histadrut, an attempt was made by the government to limit the role of the Histadrut to economic matters and thus diminish the Histadrut's role in decisions with political importance.[38]

The point of major interest here is that the wage policy of the country, not just of civil servants, is monitored by the center. Industrial enterprises are bound by general guidelines determined in wage negotiations, municipal workers are bound by the dependency of the municipalities on national budgets, and so on. The Civil Service Commission was relieved of its role in these wage negotiations in the mid-1980s, and power over this sensitive area was transferred to the controller of salaries, who is more closely under the control of the finance minister. According to the 1985 law, a unit that receives funding from the national budget may pay salaries, fix pensions, or provide other benefits only in accordance with the general guidelines of the Finance Ministry's controller of salaries.

The finance ministers of Israel have used their power in this centralized wage structure for political benefit. The relative growth rate of nondefense spending has been largest and the increase in real wages greatest in election years. Data through 1973 show the growth of average annual per capita consumption in the year preceding elections compared to generally low levels in previous years.[39] Changes in real general income grow slowly, reaching a crescendo during election years. One analysis showed that in the first year after an election, the average wage change was 0.9 percent, followed by 1.8 percent in the second year after the election, and 4.2 percent in the third; the peak was reached in the fourth year, when the average wage change was 6.5 percent.[40] Extra-economic factors are clearly at work here. Using this kind of analysis, it is less surprising that Labor held power through eight elections and that the Likud could use its economic clout after 1981 to perpetuate its power. In a sense, it is more surprising that the Alignment lost political power at the polls in 1977 than that it had held it for so long.

The economy has generally not been a major political issue in elections because the government strives to make people feel as good as possible about the economy before elections. The most startling example of economic interference was Yoram Aridor's policy of decreasing excise taxes on goods such as color television sets before the 1981 elections. Coming on the heels of Finance Minister Yigael Horowitz's resignation and his predictions of catastrophe for the Israeli economy, Aridor's policy caused a subjective change in mood that probably did as much as anything else to turn around the Likud's poor performance in the polls and get it moving in the "right direction"—the party's slogan for election day.

The turnover of 1977 can be partially understood as a result of the Alignment's policy in the mid-1970s of cutting government nonmilitary spending and services and increasing taxes, especially among the higher-income portion of the population. It was precisely that latter group that defected most heavily from the Alignment (although not only because of the tax increase) and gave its votes to the Democratic Movement for Change (DMC), in this way accelerating the ascent of the Likud. The Bank of Israel reported that real available income per capita dropped by 8 percent between 1973 and 1976. For the lower classes this was but another reason to vote Likud and not Alignment, but for members of the upper classes who wanted to vote for neither the Likud nor the Alignment, the available alternative was the DMC. To be sure, the economic downturn was related to the Yom Kippur War, and the upswing for the Likud had begun earlier and had been associated with demographic changes within the population, but the inability of the Alignment to fashion an economic policy consistent with vote-getting was another sign of its deterioration and another reason for the turnover.[41]

Although the ethos of Israel was once egalitarian, now inequality and poverty are great by comparative standards, and growing. Using the Gini coefficient (for which perfect equality is 0.0) as a measure, the inequality index reported in table 3.3 puts Israel behind all countries except Germany and the United States in terms of economic inequality in the year 2002. Inequality had been lower in the past, but its increase has been steady over the years: in 1982 Israel's index was 0.222, in 1985 it was 0.327, and by 2002 it had risen to 0.369.[42] Not only did the country's index increase, but the percentage of the population below the poverty line grew to 21.1 percent. (Although less than 20 percent of the population, Arabs make up half of those in poverty.)

In 1987 the income available for the highest decile to spend after meeting basic expenses was 7.6 times as large as the available income for the lowest decile. National Insurance Institute figures showed that in 1988 the two highest deciles earned 49.7 percent of the gross national income, while the lowest two deciles earned only 2.2 percent; when welfare payments were added in, the share of the lower two deciles was 6.3 percent.[43] In 2001 the income of the highest decile was 12.1 times higher than the lowest decile; after taxes and transfer payments, the gap was 7.4 times higher. Government policy still works to close the gap, but less effectively than in the past.[44]

The income data presented by continent of birth in table 3.4 make it clear that Ashkenazim have been favored. Israeli-born Jews had a gross income of 112.1 in 1995, when 100 is set as the base rate for those born

Table 3.3   Inequality and Poverty in Selected Western Countries, 2002

	GINI index of inequality	Percentage of population under poverty line
Sweden	25.0	5.9
Netherlands	32.6	8.7
France	32.7	8.6
Great Britain	36.0	NA
Israel	**36.9**	**21.1**
Germany	38.2	12.3
United States	40.8	18.8

Source: Human Development Reports 2003, 282. For Israel, National Insurance Institute, *The Dimensions of Poverty and Inequality in Income Distribution 2002* (Jerusalem: The Research and Planning Section, 2003).

Note: NA = not available.

Table 3.4 Gross Income per Urban Household, by Continent of Birth

| | | | | Base: Born in Europe or America = 100.0 | | | | |
	1965	1970	1975	1980	1985	1990	1995	2000
Jews, total	90.1	90.0	94.2	91.5	92.2	92.5	105.4	115.5
Israeli-born Jews	108.6	103.3	102.5	93.8	95.4	90.8	112.1	126.2
Asian- or African-born Jews	71.7	73.9	82.2	80.1	80.7	88.2	98.4	107.6
European- or American-born Jews	100.0	100.0	100.0	100.0	100.0	100.0	100.0	100.0
Non-Jews	—	61.1	86.9	64.9	62.1	59.0	69.3	67.3

Source: Israel Statistical Abstracts, 1981, 293–295; *1995,* 331. The data for 2000 were received through personal communication from the Central Bureau of Statistics. The numbers do not appear in the *Abstract* because that series was discontinued after 1995.

in Europe and America. By 2000, Asian- and African-born Jews did better than the European-born, many of whom at that point were new immigrants from the former Soviet Union. It was the non-Jews who were consistently below all Jewish groups in income. Analyses by period of immigration and level of education, not displayed here, show that the longer one is in the country and the more education one has, the better the gross income, but that continent of birth and ethnic group still matter.

Inequality in the society is steadily growing and is at a higher level than the egalitarian expectations of the founders of Israel. Per capita income, for example, has grown over the years, but income differentials between the veteran Ashkenazi and the newcomer Sephardi groups have also widened, fostering a sense of relative deprivation among the less advantaged Sephardim. This increasing gap has occurred because Ashkenazim have tended to save more and to invest more, thus increasing the original disadvantage of the Sephardim in relative terms. The gap also has been fostered by differing levels of education, by differences in knowing how to work the system by networking in the labor market (especially among employees), and because the Ashkenazim have tended to dwell in the country's major cities as opposed to the outlying regions.

Before the al-Aqsa Intifada, Palestinians enjoyed a high standard of living compared with Arabs in other countries or with the two million Palestinians in Jordan or among the other two million scattered around the world. Still, it was much lower than that enjoyed by Israeli Arabs, not to mention Israeli Jews. Between 1969 and 1987, the number of noncitizen Arabs (from the territories) in the labor force tripled, from about 2.5 percent to about 8 percent. Following the outbreak of the intifada in 2000, however, the Palestinian workers virtually disappeared from the labor market and were replaced by foreign workers.

The introduction of other workers contributed to an improvement in the position of the Sephardi workers, but in relative terms the Ashkenazi groups gained even more. Among the self-employed, Sephardim have done well—their average income was higher than that of the Ashkenazi group. Nonetheless, the Sephardim tended to fill lower-prestige occupations and hence this "alternative route of social mobility" was partial at best.[45]

4   THE POLITICAL ELITE

POLITICS IN ISRAEL is party politics, and party politics is elite politics. The Italian political sociologist Gaetano Mosca, writing at the end of the nineteenth century, accurately described the situation in Israel a century later:

> In all societies . . . two classes of people appear—a class that rules and a class that is ruled. The first class, always the less numerous, performs all political functions, monopolizes power and enjoys the advantages that power brings, whereas the second, the more numerous class, is directed and controlled by the first.[1]

The character of society and the direction it takes can be understood in terms of the composition, structure, and conflicts of the ruling group.

Implicit in the unequal distribution of political power in a democracy is the realization that voting and elections are not the only avenue of expressing political preferences and getting them adopted. Instinctively we know that some individuals have more influence than others. In organizations the hierarchy of ranks clearly identifies those who have a higher likelihood of having their decisions implemented in general: a teacher has more power than a student; in the army an officer is more powerful; in a plant the manager determines what the worker will do; and in the home usually the parents decide what is to be done. In democratic situations, equality is the rule. Each of us has considerable power because our vote is equal to everyone else's and—no less important—everyone else's vote is equal to ours.

But in reality, a ruling elite emerges. Even if we are able to change elites by voting in the opposition party at the next election, even if we are able to limit them by the constitution (written or unwritten) the country has developed, effective political power is never in the hands of the people. Moreover, an elite is not usually a collection of isolated individuals but is likely to be homogeneous, unified, and self-conscious. Individuals in the elite know one another well, have similar backgrounds, and share values, loyalties, and interests, although they may have differences of opinion on political issues and their personal ambitions may lead them to clash with one another.

It is important to appreciate that the preceding generalization regarding the unequal distribution of political power is a universal phenomenon. Only an extremely small proportion of the citizens of any country has any real chance of directly influencing national policy. Most people most of the time do not have the resources, access, or interest to involve themselves in policy decision making. In matters of curbing inflation (because the issue is so complex) as in matters of peace and war (because the issue is so sensitive), small groups of decision makers make decisions that affect all of us. This is true in all countries and at all times.

Participation and the Elite

Patterns of political stratification tend to be pyramidal in shape throughout the world;[2] it may well be that the Israeli political pyramid is higher than that found in some other democratic countries and its slope more sharp, but the general contours are the same. Most of the population does but one political act and that is to vote. This public is crucial to the politician, but as individuals the voters have very limited influence. Voters have one important collective political resource: numbers. In Israel the ranks of *nonparticipants* are very thin; voting participation is high, although it has been in decline. Among Jews, it used to be that those who failed to vote did so almost universally for technical reasons; there are growing signs that some of the nonvoting in recent elections reflects dissatisfaction with politics and politicians. There is more purposive abstention among non-Jewish Israelis, but even among this group a very large majority participates (see chapter 8).

The *attentive public* is composed of those who have the skills and resources to become activists, who follow politics intently, but who take no active part other than voting. Data on very high levels of news consumption in Israel, as expressed by reading newspapers, listening to and watching news on radio and television, suggest that the size of the attentive public may be greater than in other countries (see chapter 12).

Activists may be party members, middle-level bureaucrats, or educators. They may be classified as those who take some active interest in politics by talking occasionally with a politician or writing a letter to a newspaper, but usually their action is limited to the issues to which they react.

The *influentials* are turned to by leaders and decision makers for advice. Their opinions and interests must be taken into account because their potential sanctions are feared. This stratum may include party officials, media personalities and journalists, university professors, army officers, labor union officials, high-level bureaucrats, industrialists, financiers, religious leaders, and officers of Jewish groups abroad. This group is even more limited in numbers but is likely to react to a broader spectrum of issues of public policy.

The second highest stratum consists of the *proximate decision makers,* those individuals directly involved in policymaking, usually ministers and senior administrative officeholders. At the apex of the pyramid is the group of *top leaders,* which in Israel may consist of the prime minister and perhaps another two or three individuals. The symbiosis between the two highest strata is extremely important, for while proximate decision makers provide support, legitimacy, and organization for top leaders, top leaders in their turn provide ideological direction, backing, and considerable status and power to the proximate decision makers. People in the second stratum are anxious to sustain the top leadership because their own careers may depend on the continued success of the leadership and their own ambitions may be based on succeeding to the top leadership when the time comes.

At the apex of the pyramid, the top leaders have the final say if issues reach them. In Israel many issues of foreign and security policy are regularly brought for decision to the top leadership, while matters of internal and economic policy are not. In foreign affairs the top leadership tends to be the decision makers; in internal matters it tends to act as a final court of appeal if lower levels of decision makers cannot reach agreement among themselves.

The entire political system of Israel is stratified in terms of power, and so are the Knesset and the various political parties. The single member of the Knesset has relatively little power unless he is joined by many others, and this generally implies coalition support for his positions, and support by the prime minister if possible. In turn, the government can almost always block unfavorable motions in the Knesset, and since it also has control of the government ministries, it controls the administration as well as the legislation of policy. Moreover, individual Knesset members are almost always dependent on their political party for reelection, whether their party features primaries or not, and so they are likely to gauge their behavior accordingly.

Crises of Succession

An indigenous Jewish political elite emerged in Eretz Israel only after the establishment of the British Mandate in the 1920s. Before then, political activity was circumscribed; Zionist politics, on the whole, was conducted in Europe. Theodor Herzl spent little time in Eretz Israel, Vladimir Jabotinsky had his headquarters in Europe, and many leaders spent a good deal of their time abroad eliciting support and attending meetings.

With the second and third *aliyot*, the political organizations and the leaders of the country for the next generation and a half emerged. Many were imbued with the ideals of socialism and collectivism that had become fashionable in the Russia they left after the unsuccessful Russian revolution of 1905. They were composed of two major groups: those born in the period between 1885 and 1890, and those born at the turn of the century. These groups represented two distinct generational units in Israeli politics. The first group immigrated as part of the second *aliya* between 1905 and 1912 and was instrumental in setting up the major political organizations of their day: the Ahdut Haavoda Party in 1919 and the Histadrut in 1920. These organizations were to dominate much of the political and economic activity of the Jewish community in mandated Palestine. The leader of this group, David Ben-Gurion, became Israel's first prime minister, holding the post, with brief interruptions, until 1963. The younger group arrived in the third *aliya* (1919–1923) and was greatly influenced by the Russian Revolution of 1917.[3]

Both groups came from Poland and Russia, both were highly motivated ideologically and politically, and both constituted a small fraction of the Jews who immigrated. These groups set up the important organizations in a political void. They were young, energetic, and self-sacrificing, and their successful efforts meant that they would be the leaders of the State of Israel when it was founded in 1948.

An implicit symbiosis developed between these two socialist groups. The older ones were the statesmen, making the grand decisions and setting policy, while the younger group controlled the party machine, was faithful to the leadership, depended on it, and worked for it. The younger group thus ensured the perpetuation of the power of the older group because in the last analysis the leadership was also dependent on the party machine. When the acknowledged leadership began fading from the scene in the 1970s, a crisis of succession loomed. The informal hierarchical relations that had been such an important part of the division of labor within the generational units of the party could not be easily transferred. The long years of shared experience and the generational solidarity that this produced prevented the flow of young, new leadership into the ranks.

A fascinating case in point is the political career of Moshe Dayan. After Dayan left the army as chief of staff in 1957, Ben-Gurion wanted to make him a government minister. The major objections came, as one might expect in a hierarchical system in which political apprenticeship is very long, from the second stratum of the ruling elite. Golda Meir and Zalman Aranne pointed out that Dayan should be trained as a politician in more humble surroundings than the government. By trying to bypass the third *aliya* group of Mapai leaders, Ben-Gurion infuriated the party machine.

Ben-Gurion had no choice but to relinquish power to the third *aliya* group, but upon leaving office he became a bitter critic of this group and ultimately split with the Mapai Party he had founded. In 1965 Rafi was established by Ben-Gurion along with some of the bright "young Turks" he had fostered in the defense establishment, such as Dayan and Shimon Peres. The new party appealed to many young Israeli-born supporters who resented the perceived fact that the older party machine prevented adaptability to changing problems and blocked access to positions of power. Many, however, were torn between two long-standing allegiances: between the former leader of the party, Ben-Gurion, and the traditional leaders of the party machine.

The party machine was revitalized quickly by Pinhas Sapir, then minister of the treasury, before the 1965 elections. Sapir was younger than many in the leadership of the machine group, and as minister of finance he was able to hold the machine together by setting policies that favored groups and individuals supportive of the party and its clients. As long as the structure of the party machine was hierarchically autonomous, career aspirations had centered on the apex of the power pyramid. Now the key positions of the party machine became less attractive than key posts in the national government; ambitious politicians now strove to be members of the Knesset or government ministers. The symmetrical relationship of the machine with the top leadership was broken. Machine leaders were suddenly dependent on the top leadership for career advancement, and they could no longer trade off its support and activity for influence on ministers and policy. They were also less effective as brokers between the leadership and the followers. With the ascension of the third *aliya* group to power, the party organization suffered, and this effect was eventually to be felt in the voting results.

The leadership attempted two methods of solving the crisis of succession.[4] One was to ally themselves with other parties, thereby gaining depth of leadership. Before the 1965 elections they formed a joint list with Ahdut Haavoda, whose leaders had split from Mapai in 1944. Preceding the Six-Day War of 1967, Mapai exhibited a lack of leadership in foreign and security policies—areas in which Ben-Gurion had predominated, but he was no longer leader of the party. After some hesitation, Dayan was made defense minister and Rafi was included in the National Unity Government. In 1968 the Mapai leadership consolidated this process by forming, along with Rafi and Ahdut Haavoda, the Israel Labor party.

The second method of solving the crisis of succession was by introducing new elements into the party leadership. Before the 1973 elections (and war), Sapir and his party decided to appoint army heroes to positions of importance in the government, thus introducing an additional "social force." Gaetano Mosca writes that "as civilization grows, the number of the moral and material influences which are capable of becoming social forces increases. For example, property in money, as the fruit of industries and commerce, comes into being alongside of real property."[5] The social force in this case was that it became natural for those who had been endowed with success in the military field to play an active role in politics. Their backgrounds did not prepare them for party politics, however, let alone for the intricacies of running a party machine.

Following Mosca's analysis, the social forces in a society indicate the reservoir of potential talent to be tapped for the ruling elite. The young pioneers who set up the dominant political organizations in the 1920s were at the peak of their careers in the 1940s when their children came of age and began seeking their own way. Most of these children did not find politics an attractive career because the best jobs were filled by relatively young people (who could not be expected to retire soon). Moreover, a clear "social force" had emerged: defense. The army, the security establishment, the procuring of arms for the Jewish community, and service with the British armed forces in the Second World War—all these activities attracted the bright young men and women of the 1940s. By the 1960s two processes overlapped: the aging and retirement of the traditional political leadership and the retirement in their mid-forties of a generation of defense and army leaders due to the early retirement policy of the Israel Defense Forces (IDF). The apex of the political pyramid was vacated just as the apex of the military pyramid was being rejuvenated. It was only natural for experienced army officers who had succeeded in a field that was clearly a "social force" to assume positions of responsibility and authority in politics.

This horizontal movement from the apex of one elite pyramid to the apex of another is called in Hebrew "parachuting." Instead of climbing to the top of the political hierarchy the way a foot soldier would, a general is parachuted in, bypassing the customary apprenticeship of years at the lower levels of the national party hierarchy. It is not surprising that the objections to bypassing traditional channels of advancement came from those who had been serving as second-stratum leaders waiting their turn to assume the role of top leaders.

The problem was that parties were crisis-prone because there was no accepted way to replace a leader who had become entrenched in office. In the case of a Ben-Gurion or a Begin, this entrenchment afforded the respective party years of sure leadership. When the succession crisis started, however, it was very intense. Both Labor and the Likud experienced an influx of political leaders with army backgrounds who vied for the top spot. In Herut, Ezer Weizman and Ariel Sharon—both of whom had completed impressive army careers before entering politics—tried unsuccessfully to unseat Begin or at least to share power with him. Both figured prominently in the Likud's creation and victory in 1977, but Begin's role as top leader remained unchanged. Ultimately Weizman served as the country's president and Sharon became prime minister in 2001.

Ex-generals joined both Labor and Likud: Ehud Barak was foreign minister in the Peres government formed after the Rabin assassination in 1995; Yitzhak Mordechai became defense minister in the 1996 Netanyahu government; Shaul Mofaz went directly from the position of IDF chief of staff to become Sharon's defense minister in 2002.

The period of direct election of the prime minister (1996–2001) accelerated the processes that stunted the emergence of elite group solidarity—a more individualistic orientation at the expense of collective instincts of the group. Netanyahu's father had been active in politics with Jabotinsky but was shunted aside when Begin took over Herut in the 1940s. To watch Binyamin Netanyahu's insensitive treatment of his colleagues as he rushed to form his government after the 1996 election, one could not help but have the sense that he was wreaking vengeance on the sons of the Herut leaders who had treated his father so harshly fifty years before. Barak's relations with political colleagues were also notoriously callous.

The parachuting of military leaders was obvious between 1973 and 1977, when a fascinating process of differentiation began to develop among the ruling elite of the Labor Party. Cabinet members who had primary responsibility for security and foreign affairs (Yitzhak Rabin, Shimon Peres, Yigael Allon, Israel Galili, Aharon Yariv earlier) tended to be from a military background *and not* historically associated with Mapai, while some who dealt with internal matters were also those whose political careers *had been* dependent on the Mapai party machine (Yehoshua Rabinowitz, Avraham Ofer, Aharon Yadlin, and Moshe Baram). A sense of common purpose never developed between the two elite groups. When he was prime minister in the 1970s, Rabin failed to bridge conflicting interests, styles, and backgrounds. The party's lack of accepted leadership was the backdrop against which the details of a political drama were played out: the competition between Rabin and Peres for the right to head the list (Rabin won), Rabin's resignation from first on the list because of his wife's personal foreign currency problems, and Peres's ascension to first place a month before the election in 1977. It is little wonder that the military heroes were not successful in running their party. They were the victims, not the causes, of the crisis of leadership succession and the attendant passing of dominance from the Labor Party.

The emergence of the Democratic Movement for Change (DMC) in 1977 also reflected the crisis of succession. The DMC provided an alternative channel of upward mobility for leaders (political, military, economic, and university) who disdained the opportunity of competing for positions in the disreputable governing parties. The setting up of a new party reflected the disarray of the party system in 1977; both party leadership and electoral support was in flux. A bold move might create a party that would have a pivotal position in coalition calculations. While the DMC could not claim to be pivotal—the Likud and the religious parties could rule without them—their achievement in winning fifteen seats was impressive in Israeli political terms.

Leaders change for many reasons; the only one that affects all of them is aging. When the political elite of the second and third *aliyot* faded from power, no successor generation was primed to take its place. Living in the shadow of giants can be a daunting experience for young, ambitious politicians. Rabin and Peres emerged as the successors, but they lacked the qualities that make an elite work: a shared vision of the future and the willingness to work within the group to achieve political goals.

As the Rabin-Peres generation faded in the 1990s, Labor again faced the dilemma of leadership succession. There were many candidates but no group emerged that could cooperate and rule cooperatively. In the 1990s, a loose alliance of eight politicians—including Chaim Ramon, successful challenger of Labor in the Histadrut elections; Avraham Burg, the head of the Jewish Agency; Yossi Beilin, architect of the Oslo Accords with the PLO; Yael Dayan (Moshe's daughter); and Amir Peretz, head of the Histadrut after Ramon resigned in the wake of the Rabin assassination—was moving quickly up the ranks and showing the potential of being such a future elite. They had all been active in politics for many years, they were "yuppies," reform-oriented Labor activists, all very ambitious, and they shared a dovish viewpoint and a strong drive to power, but their ties to the group were always an open question. For example, Ramon's run for the Histadrut was not supported by most of the others; Burg's run for the Jewish Agency, on the other hand, was supported by the others after he was denied a cabinet position by Rabin.

The inability of this group to take over the party lay both in their personalities and in the obstacles to success in the path they had chosen. By the year 2004, some of them were still potential leaders of Labor, while others had split from the party. Ramon and Burg had competed unsuccessfully for head of the party; Beilin and Dayan had become leaders of Yahad, a social-democratic party established with Meretz; and Peretz had set up his own Histadrut-based party called Am Ehad (One Nation).

Former army leaders abounded in the party—among them Ehud Barak, Binyamin (Fouad) Ben-Eliezer, Matan Vilnai, Efraim Sneh, and Amram Mitzna—but none fared much better than the group of politicians. Barak won the party's nomination in 1999 and then beat Netanyahu convincingly, only to have his rule crumble after unsuccessful negotiations with the Palestinians. In 2001, after only a year and a half in office, he faced the Likud's Ariel Sharon in a special election and lost in a landslide. Ben-Eliezer served as defense minister in the Sharon government of 2001, but he failed to beat former Haifa mayor Mitzna in the primary for head of list. In the 2003 elections, the Labor list headed by Mitzna turned in Labor's weakest performance in history.

The Labor Party constitution required that a primary be held for party head within a year of an electoral defeat; Barak became head of the party after the 1996 defeat and Mitzna was selected after the 2001 loss. When they in turn resigned as head of the party after their own defeats, the party convention turned each time to Shimon Peres to head the party. Eighty years of age, Peres had been active in the party for sixty years when he was reelected in 2004. This pattern underscored the failure of a ruling elite to take over the party; instead, a number of ambitious individuals competed with one another.

In the Likud, Begin's reign between 1977 and 1983 represented continuity with the Labor leadership in the sense that he was the last of the older generation still active in politics. His undisputed leadership of the Herut and the Likud between the 1940s and the 1980s was facilitated by the loyalty of his colleagues from the pre-state period, when all had fought in the underground together. The Liberal Party chose ministers to the Likud government, but none of them challenged the supreme leadership role of Herut's Begin. When Begin relinquished power in 1983 and was followed by Yitzhak Shamir, it was unclear if his would be an interim premiership or if Shamir could win control of the Likud and the Herut movement. In fact, Shamir controlled the party and the country for ten years, many of them in coalition with Labor in National Unity Governments.

The Likud crisis of succession burst out after the 1992 victory of Labor's Rabin over Shamir. The subsequent decision by the defeated Shamir not to compete for the party leadership left the field open to the next generation—Benny Begin, David Levy, Dan Meridor, Binyamin Netanyahu, Uzi Landau, Ehud Olmart—and the older Ariel Sharon. This next generation of political leadership included the "princes" of the movement, since the fathers of Begin, Meridor, Netanyahu, Landau, and Olmart had been prominent in the movement in the past. Netanyahu won control of the party—but not the admiration of his colleagues—in the Likud primary. The makings of a cohesive elite were available in the Likud because so many of the contenders were sons of the "fighting family," but Netanyahu's individualistic style thwarted this possibility. This once-young, now middle-aged successor generation, with decades of service already behind them, inevitably had an advantage compared to other ambitious party activists, and they became Likud ministers in Sharon's government.

The ranks of the next generation were thinned after the Netanyahu defeat in 1999, when Benny Begin left politics after a disastrous showing as head of a right-wing party and Meridor bolted Likud to join the Center Party. Those who remained were mostly loyal to Sharon, waiting for their moment, even if they favored a different candidate to head the Likud. They were joined by a second tier of activists that included Tzipi Livni (who, as the daughter of a prominent leader of the Irgun in the pre-state period and a Likud Knesset member, might be dubbed a "princess"), Tzachi Hanegbi (son of Geula Cohen, a prominent Likud and right-wing stalwart), Limor Livnat, and Silvan Shalom (who was connected by marriage to the country's foremost telecommunications and newspaper family).

Religious parties were successful in passing political leadership to the second generation. The National Religious Party's (NRP) leadership struggles were mild compared to those of Labor and Likud, but, paradoxically, at the same time political power was slipping from its grasp. Outmaneuvering the veteran political activist and head of the NRP machine, Yitzhak Rafael, Zevulun Hammer's Youth Faction gained the status of party leader in 1977, along with the older group led by Yosef Burg (Avraham's father). By careful coalition-building and adroit use of parliamentary procedure, Hammer's Youth Faction was able to prevent Rafael's inclusion on the party list and to have Rabbi Chaim Druckman, identified with the Gush Emunim settlers movement, placed second on the list. When Burg finally retired, Hammer was in place as leader.

But the picture clouded. One of the young leaders, Aharon Abu-Hatzeira, split from the NRP and set up Tami before the 1981 elections. Then Rabbi Druckman split from the NRP after the election and set up his own Knesset delegation. The ethnic issue raised by Tami and the nationalist issue raised by Gush Emunim plagued the NRP's ability to win votes. Thus, although the NRP (1) held impressive bases of power in the religious education system and the interior and religious affairs ministries, (2) had a platform of intense nationalism that tended to be in tune with the nation's mood, and (3) had determined their political succession, they were weak in an electoral sense, winning only four seats in 1984, compared to six seats in 1981 and twelve in 1977. Hammer prevailed over Avner Shaki, who represented Sephardi hardliners, but these two "young" leaders grew older competing with one another. Upon joining the government in 1996, Hammer remained the recognized leader until his death in 1998. In 2002, Effi Eitam, a former general and a strong supporter of the nationalist point of view, led the NRP.

Haredi leaders are appointed by the respective councils of rabbinical sages. Meir Porush's father, Menachem, had been elected on the ultra-Orthodox Agudat Israel list for ten elections. In 1996, at the age of forty, son Meir was head of the party. Arye Deri emerged as a shrewd national politician as head of Shas when he was still in his twenties. After Deri was convicted of misuse of public funds and served time in jail, Shas was led by Eli Yishai, an unknown but loyal activist approved by Deri and the rabbis. After their disastrous 2003 showing, dropping from seventeen to eleven seats, Deri's group was very critical of Yishai's leadership and the internal competition within the party intensified.

Knesset Members

Knesset members are an easily identified positional elite, a category often studied by political scientists. Israel held Knesset elections sixteen times between 1949 and 2003. On each of those occasions, 120 members were elected to the Knesset. In all, a total of 737 individuals have served as Knesset members through the 2003 elections.

About a third of each elected group is new (see figure 4.1); about two-thirds of Knesset members have served more than one term. The average number of terms served through 1992 was 2.74, or about eleven years; the median was two terms, or about eight years. In the first elections, all members were necessarily new; in the July 1961 elections, held less than two years after the November 1959 elections, and decided upon months earlier, only nine new members entered. Outside those two unusual years, the number of new Knesset members has ranged between thirty (in 1955) and fifty-five (in 1999); in 2003, forty new Knesset members were elected.

Figure 4.1   Incumbency in the Knesset, 1949–2003

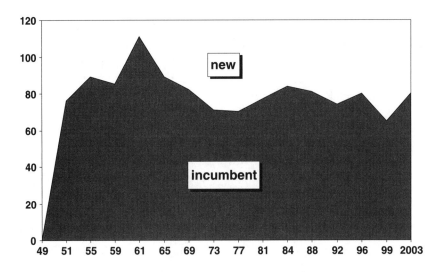

About 10 percent of the total number of those elected to the Knesset have served nonconsecutive terms. This was generally because after one term in office these candidates achieved places in the list below the cut-off point decreed for their parties in the next election; in a later election, they were more successful and were reelected. In 1999 four of the fifty-five "new" members had previously been in the Knesset; in 2003 the number was three out of forty.

The average age of Knesset members has varied a good deal. In the first twenty years of Israel's history, the average age of Jewish members of the Knesset tended to grow older and older, from 49.4 in 1949 to 54.3 in 1965; but this trend has moderated. In 1988 the average age was 52. The explanation for the aging trend is that many of the original members continued their parliamentary careers for a number of years, blocking entrance to the Knesset by younger members. As these older members faded, a more normal distribution was generated. Inbal Gamliel, 28, was the youngest member elected in 2003.

Even this pattern varied from party to party depending on size. A small party with a tight-knit leadership that perpetuated itself over the years (such as Menachem Porush of the ultra-Orthodox Agudat Israel, who was elected ten times) tended to have a higher average age from Knesset to Knesset. Larger parties such as Labor and Likud could retain their leadership and introduce new blood at the same time. Consistent winners were Shimon Peres of Labor, elected thirteen times (also elected on the Rafi and Mapai lists), and the Herut's (the major faction of the Likud) Menachem Begin, elected ten times. The aging of the Knesset is likely to be cyclical, especially if members pursue the parliament as a way of life and if the election results are relatively stable.

Age-based parties have never won representation in the elections, however, although both pensioners' parties and a youth party have stood for election. The major parties are aware of the importance of appealing to these large age groups, but the general rule is that parliamentarians in Israel begin at middle age and hold on if they can.

The different rates of longevity reflect political developments in the country. The first two decades were decades of consolidation, and the political elite perpetuated their rule in hierarchical parties little affected by the demographic changes occurring in the country. Even in the 1973 election, which was held soon after the traumatic Yom Kippur War and generated high levels of turnover, the Labor Party was able to retain power, despite doing less well than in the past.

The 1977 election saw the largest political upheaval in Israeli political history, with the dominant Labor Party losing its place of primacy to the Likud. These elections were influenced by the emergence of a reform-oriented party, the Democratic Movement for Change, which successfully siphoned off a considerable fraction of Labor's leadership and voters, partly because of scandals uncovered within the Labor Party.

After the 1977 elections, Israeli politics returned to a more stable basis, but turnover in Knesset membership became a familiar feature. The 1992 and 1996 elections reflected other political swings, although the electoral shifts were smaller than in 1977. With the direct election of the prime minister and the success of sectarian parties, and swelled by the introduction of hundreds of thousands of new voters who had immigrated from the former Soviet Union, the fates of the parties and their Knesset members became less secure, and fifty-five of the winners—almost half the house membership!—were not incumbents. In 2003, aided by the fact that Shinui's success added many new faces, a third of the new Knesset had not been seated in the outgoing Knesset.

The path to incumbency in Israel is simple.[6] The first rule is to be high on the party list; the second is to have your party win seats greater in number than your place on the list. If you are first, one seat will do; if you are tenth, ten would be the minimum number of seats needed by your party to ensure your incumbency. Add to the general uncertainty of elections the fact that big parties have often held primary elections for places on their lists, and the picture of job insecurity is more complete.

Since election results are obviously not known in advance, the likelihood of being elected or reelected diminishes as one approaches the last place on the list that the party has usually won. Between 1973 and 1996, all Likud and Labor candidates above the thirty-ninth position on their respective lists were elected, with the following exceptions: for Labor in 1977 and the Likud in 1992 and 1996, thirty-two members were elected; the magic number for Labor in 1996 was thirty-four. But there has also been a cap on success: since 1973, neither party has elected more than fifty-one members, so those placed in the range of the forties in either party had every right to be anxious. Since then, matters have been worse: in 1999 for the Likud and in 2003 for Labor-Meimad, only nineteen Knesset members were elected.

Candidates competing in the 1996 Likud primary were exposed to a previously unknown danger occasioned by the newly implemented law for the direct election of the prime minister. The law called for a second round of voting if no candidate got more than half the votes, which put enormous pressure on the candidates of the two big parties to prevent others from their side of the political spectrum from running for prime minister. In 1996 the pressure was on Netanyahu because other viable candidates from the right had announced their candidacy, and there was a reasonable chance that Peres would win the needed 50 percent of the vote on the first round. Just as the Likud was holding its primary for places on its list, Netanyahu cut deals with David Levy's Gesher Party and with Rafael ("Raful") Eitan's Tzomet Party to present a joint Likud-Gesher-Tzomet Knesset list in order to win the support of these politicians. Netanyahu assured Gesher and Tzomet seven seats each of the first forty places on the new joint list—at the expense of Likud candidates. While the agreement was duly approved by the Likud center, the appropriate decision-making body, the effect of it was disastrous for ambitious Likud politicians. In the end, only the first thirty-two places on the Likud-Gesher-Tzomet list were elected to the Knesset, yielding only six each for Gesher and Tzomet and twenty places (instead of the forty they had expected) for Likud aspirants.

Being high on the list obviously increases the probability of being elected and reelected. Even if one is not elected, the chance of becoming a Knesset member remains, since the next candidate on the list fills the place if a vacancy should occur. Some who entered the Knesset in this manner have had a chance to build an important political future. For example, Ovadia Eli was tapped by prime minister-elect Netanyahu in 1996 to be speaker of the Knesset, despite the "slight" detail that Eli had not been elected to the Knesset. The plan was to delay his election as speaker until the Knesset had passed a law—known in Hebrew as the Norwegian law—mandating the resignation of ministers from the Knesset and their replacement by the next person on their list. A revolt in the Likud Knesset delegation prevented this development. Another example occurred when the Knesset elected Chaim Herzog in 1988 to be the president of the state; when he resigned from the Knesset he was replaced by the next candidate on the Labor list who had not been elected, Chaim Ramon. Ramon, a young, ambitious politician, became the head of the Labor delegation in the Knesset, achieved a high place on the 1992 Labor list, was appointed minister of health in Rabin's government, and led a successful coup against his party in the Histadrut—all this even though he had almost not been seated in the Knesset four years earlier.

The sexual composition of the Knesset shows no tendency toward equality.[7] Women have never been numerous; the seventeen women elected in 1999 represented an increase over previous elections. In 2003 a new high of eighteen women, or 15 percent, were elected—eight represented Likud; four, Labor; three, Shinui; and one each, the NRP, Am Ehad, and Meretz. The representation of the National Religious Party increased from zero to one woman in 2003, just as it had in 1977. Women are obviously very far from achieving equality with men, although the 2003 government included three female cabinet members—an all-time high.

In the 1973 elections Marsha Friedman was elected to the Knesset on Shulamit Aloni's Citizens Rights Movement list; at that time, Friedman was leader of the Women's Liberation movement. In 1977, 1981, and 1992, a women's list ran but failed to achieve representation. The woman who achieved greatest power in the system was Golda Meir, who was prime minister at the end of her colorful and eventful career. An important Labor Party leader who happened to be a woman, she could not be accurately characterized as "representing" women in her many roles.

The political system of Israel was developed by new immigrants from Eastern Europe during the first decades of the twentieth century, and it was only natural for these politicians to continue dominating the political system during their lifetimes.[8] As the percentage of East European-born in the population diminished and the percentage of native-born increased, the numbers of native-born Israelis in the Knesset increased. But in an important sense this statistic is misleading, because the overwhelming tendency was for the second generation of Israeli Knesset members to be the sons of the East European-born first generation. The frequency distribution in the country of birth category may have changed, but the focus of political power and membership in the Knesset remained firmly in the hands of Europeans and their children, leaving the Sephardim grossly underrepresented.

In any new endeavor, those who are the founders—and especially if they are young—are likely to persist and dominate the endeavor for many years. This was the case with the Histadrut, many of whose leaders were in their twenties when it was founded in 1920.[9] The dominance of East Europeans is demonstrated dramatically in an analysis of the place of birth of the thirty-seven signers of Israel's Declaration of Independence. They were members of the National Committee and later the Provisional State Council that served up to the first general election of 1949. Of these "founding fathers," twenty-nine came from Eastern Europe and six from the rest of Europe; one was born in Israel, and one in Yemen. There was significant carryover from this body to the First

Knesset, elected in 1949. Of the forty members of the expanded Provisional State Council, twenty-seven were elected to the First Knesset; twenty years later, ten of them were still members of the Knesset.[10]

The numbers of European-born Knesset members have decreased and those of the Israeli-born have continually increased over the years. More than 85 percent of the Knesset were European-born as a result of the first three elections; their proportion was 79 percent following the next two elections, and 68 percent in the Sixth Knesset, elected in 1965. After the seventh election, the percentage of European-born members had fallen to 63 percent, then to 56 percent after the eighth, and 38 percent after the ninth.[11]

Israeli-born Knesset membership was increasing. The Israeli-born rose steadily from 11 percent in the First Knesset to half by 1977; in 2003 almost three-quarters of the Knesset members were born in Israel.

Knesset members of Asian and African birth have also increased steadily, and they now replicate more accurately their relative strength in the population. From 3 percent in the First Knesset to 8 percent in the Fifth (1961), they grew to 12 percent in both the Eighth and Ninth (1973 and 1977), to 25 percent in the Tenth (1981), to 20 percent in the Eleventh (1984) and Thirteenth (1992) Knessets. The gradual increase of representation of the Sephardi Jewish community in the Knesset is evident.

Both Labor and Likud, as well as many of the smaller parties, placed Sephardi candidates in prominent places on their lists. In a major revision compared with past lists, Labor in 1988 fielded eleven candidates born in Asia or Africa among the first forty on its list; the corresponding number for the Likud was six. Twenty of Labor's first forty in that year, and twenty-nine of the Likud's first forty, were born in Israel. Rabin and Netanyahu were born in Israel, but both Peres and Shamir were born in Poland. In 1999 there were forty-five Sephardim and sixty-four Ashkenazim among the Jews in the Knesset. Not only were the numbers increasing, but also the Sephardi candidates' place on the lists was improving. Prominent Sephardi leaders included Shlomo Ben-Ami, Dalia Itzik, David Levy, Yitzhak Mordechai, Silvan Shalom, and Meir Sheetrit. The composition of the Knesset delegations was coming more in line with the demographic changes taking place in the society.

The bias in favor of persons of European origin can be seen even more strongly in the composition of the governments in Israel. From independence until April 1974, fifty-eight of the seventy ministers were born in Europe, North America, and South Africa, compared with only four born in Asia and Africa. In the Likud government of 1977 as well, the vast majority of ministers were of European extraction. Of the nineteen ministers in 1981, three (Aharon Abu-Hatzeira, David Levy, and Moshe Nissim) were Sephardim, while in the less important category of deputy minister, three of the nine were Sephardim. In 2003, with Shas not included in the government, the number of Sephardi ministers decreased. Prominent Sephardi leaders in 2004 included President Moshe Katzav, Chief of Staff of the Israel Defense Forces Shaul Mofaz, Foreign Minister Silvan Shalom, and Legal Adviser of the Government Meni Mazoz.

Apologists for the system excuse this inequality on the grounds that Sephardi Jews have not had the experience with democratic institutions and therefore have not been adequately prepared to take their proper role in the running of the country—their day will come. Protesters argue that Sephardim have been consistently discriminated against in many spheres of life and that the political sphere is the most obvious area of this discrimination. Both sides point to the emergence of Sephardi political leaders in the politics of local government to prove their point. Apologists point to examples of successful politicians there as proof that they are learning the rules and will ultimately emerge on the national level. Protesters respond that these leaders are already capable of much more important roles but are confined to busywork at the local level in order to harness their energies and co-opt them into the major-party frameworks.

In 2003 ten Knesset members were Arab or Druze, compared with seven elected in 1984, five in 1988, and eight in 1992. Arabs and Druze made up about 16 percent of the population, about 12 percent of the electorate, and about 8 percent of the Knesset in 2003. Arab and Druze representatives were found not only in Arab parties; in 2003 two Druze were elected on the Likud list. Labor placed non-Jews in places 20 and 21, confident that they would be elected, but then won only nineteen seats. The Arab vote fails to realize its electoral potential because Arab votes do not go uniformly to Arab lists and because of the high rate of abstentions. As with other groups in a proportional representation system, voting potential does not automatically transform itself into parliamentary seats. In the early years of the state, a majority of Arabs voted for Zionist or Zionist-related parties; since the 1990s most Arab and Druze votes go to Arab lists; about 30 percent of the Arabs and Druze vote for Zionist parties.

Politics as a Vocation

The emergence of a popular leader enhances the chances of any party. But in addition to the top leader, a party must be endowed with strata of leaders and activists who will carry out the day-to-day tasks of running the party and the organizations in its control. Max Weber made the important distinction between those who see politics as a vocation and those who see it as an avocation—those who live off politics rather than for politics.[12]

Weber suggested that a system dominated by those who live off politics will tend to be conservative and static. A system dominated by those who live for politics has a better chance of generating innovative political leadership that will present new ideas and directions largely because they are free of the party and its vested interests. This analysis applies well to Israel. After an initial period of ideological and organizational creativity, the political elite became conservative and its institutions static. In the popular idiom, the politician became more concerned with retaining his seat than convincing others of his position.

The best way to understand this distinction is to contrast the *apparatchik* with the *cincinnatus,* as Zbigniew Brzezinski and Samuel Huntington did in their book *Political Power: USA/USSR.*[13] The apparatchik is the bureaucrat-politician commonly found in the former Soviet system. He has devoted his life to the party and has progressed from one bureaucratic post to another and from one agency to another. His socialization, his livelihood, and his career are all dependent on hierarchical relationships, on slowly climbing the bureaucratic ladder and on doing the job well but in the framework of the organization, its demands, and its ideology. The cincinnatus, on the other hand, dominates the American political system. He is the "distinguished citizen who lays aside other responsibilities to devote himself temporarily to the public service." He is likely to be more independent in thought and action than his Soviet counterpart because he is less dependent on the party and its affiliated organizations for power, status, or livelihood. In fact, an American businessman, banker, or lawyer who agrees to go into politics or accept an administrative appointment with the government usually takes a very substantial cut in salary. But he is likely to be on the job only a few years, lacking experience in government bureaucracy when he enters service and leaving with his experience when he exits.

The Israeli system has been dominated by the apparatchik. This was especially true during the 1948–1977 period, when the Alignment parties dominated the government. Then, of Israel's seventy-seven ministers, fifty-two had spent most of their professional lives in bureaucracies (including military and religious bureaucracies), and it is reasonable to suppose that their promotion stemmed from their success in learning to survive in that kind of organizational setting. The numbers for the Likud governments between 1977 and 1981 showed a more nearly even split between the two types of politicians. But the concentration of the apparatchik was especially great among those six ministers of the Likud period (Menachem Begin, Moshe Dayan, Chaim Landau, Yosef Burg, Zevulun Hammer, and Ezer Weizman) who had also served during the Alignment period.[14]

Politics in Israel is not only a way of life for many politicians, it is also a way of earning a living. This point sheds important light on the mechanisms of control of the party over its political activists. With the gradual growth of activity on the part of the Jewish community in the pre-state period, the number of offices expanded, as did the number of individuals for whom politics was the primary, if not exclusive, endeavor. The parties were able to attract talent not only because of their ideological appeal but also because public service was rewarded by a salary. Of the eighty-two political leaders of the pre-state period studied, 42.5 percent earned their living from party-related activities.[15] When these findings are broken down by political party, a significant pattern emerges: leaders of the parties of the labor movement were much more likely to be on the party payroll than were leaders of the center and right parties. Of the pre-state leaders, two-thirds of the left party leaders and one-third of the nonleft party leaders were salaried by party-sponsored organizations.

Yet another 20 percent of the labor movement leaders were members of kibbutzim. They could be assigned party work in order to fill ideological goals and political-economic interests of the kibbutz movement without any financial sacrifice or risk on their part. Their needs were provided for by the kibbutz, and they were free to devote themselves to public service. This was one of the important explanations for the over-representation of kibbutz members and kibbutz interests in Israeli politics.

The material dependence of politicians on political organizations did not cease with the establishment of the state. This dependence—with all that it implies regarding conformity, timidity, and loss of enterprise—continued to be the pattern in the large parties, especially those of the labor movement. The structure of these parties and their vast administrative networks, most clearly seen in the myriad activities of the

Table 4.1 Occupations of Knesset Members, by Major Parties, 1949–1977

Party	Politician N(%)	Other N(%)	Total N
Mapai (including Rafi)	99 (63)	58 (37)	157
Ahdut Haavoda	15 (94)	1 (6)	16
Mapam	25 (78)	7 (22)	32
NRP	20 (58)	14 (41)	34
Agudat Israel	4 (57)	3 (43)	7
Poalei Agudat Israel	2 (50)	2 (50)	4
Herut	16 (36)	28 (64)	44
Progressives/Independent Liberals	7 (50)	7 (50)	14
General Zionists/Liberals	7 (18)	33 (82)	40
Communists	6 (75)	2 (25)	8
Others	4 (22)	14 (78)	18
Total	205 (55)	169 (45)	374

Source: Emanuel Guttman and Jacob Landau, "The Israeli Political Elite," in *The Israeli Political System*, ed. Moshe Lissak and Emanuel Gutmann [in Hebrew] (Tel Aviv: Am Oved, 1977), 227.

Histadrut, provided a training ground for ambitious members who sought to fill the ranks of the party leadership. When the occupations of the 374 Knesset members who served from 1949 through 1977 are analyzed (see table 4.1), it is seen that the distribution of Knesset members by source of livelihood was similar to the pre-state period, and that the parties of the left were much more likely to be represented by apparatchiki than were the parties of the right and center.[16] Activity in the movement and the party was seen as an expression of a commitment to a way of life—as public servants they identified with the party and put themselves at its disposal. This was a great source of strength for the parties of the labor movement, which could easily be reinforced, especially during the forty-odd years when they were in control of the national institutions as well as the Histadrut. These psychological and economic dependencies accelerated oligarchical tendencies in these parties and assured support for the established leadership.

The Center (*merkaz*) of Mapai, the legally constituted decision-making body, was dominated by people in the party's employ, most of whom had no independent means of support.[17] As we go up the power pyramid, the higher the stratum, the higher the concentration of individuals dependent on the party.[18] This dependence on the party could be translated into political obedience if necessary. When engaged in battles with other parties or in gathering votes, the internal cohesiveness and esprit de corps were high. When faced with internal dilemmas, party bosses could usually count on the loyalty of party activists.

The Alignment parties were most likely to generate the apparatchik pattern, as was evident in the 1977 elections, for example. Twenty of the Alignment's thirty-two Knesset members worked for the party as its representatives in the outgoing government, in the Knesset, or in party-related enterprises and local government. The forty-three-member Likud delegation was much more varied in terms of the occupational structure of its members: only six Likud members were primarily involved in political life. It is not surprising that the Likud had a much less intense organizational life, since it had been in opposition throughout most of its existence and never had control of the bureaucracies that the Alignment led. The DMC was the least apparatchiki of all: of its fifteen members, only one reported that he was a party worker. Looking at this dimension only (momentarily ignoring the differences of ideology and personality that existed), it is not surprising that the DMC did not remain intact throughout the session of the Ninth Knesset. The DMC leaders could "afford" to break up their organization, both because the organization was very young and had few vested interests and because the leadership had prestigious careers other than politics to which they could return.

The 1996 Netanyahu government, limited by law to eighteen members including the prime minister, was completely made up of individuals who had active public lives in their respective parties, had served in the Knesset before, or had developed their careers in the military; only one was not an elected Knesset member. One of the first acts of Barak as prime minister in 1999 was to rescind the law limiting the number of ministers, but the basic patterns of recruitment, in his and in later governments, did not change.

Former leaders of Israel's defense establishment, including army commanders, have been prominent in the life of the Knesset and the government. In 1999 two former chiefs of staff, Amnon Lipkin-Shahak and Ehud Barak were elected to the Knesset. In 2003 another former chief of staff, Shaul Mofaz, served as defense minister; he would have also been elected to the Knesset, but he had not been out of the army long enough to be allowed to compete in the elections.

Prime Ministers and Presidents

Two roles in Israeli politics stand out as being at the head of the pyramid of power and prestige: that of prime minister and that of president. They are fundamentally different in nature. The prime minister's position is of supreme political importance, and the various issues of political struggle usually end up on his desk or close to it. The prime minister is selected by the Knesset to be head of the executive branch and the cabinet, and as such, head of the coalition that rules the Knesset. As the leader of his party he also wields great political power, which enhances his authority as prime minister. The president's role, on the other hand, is largely honorific and symbolic, although he is formally head of state and is entrusted with appointing the person who would attempt to win a majority of the Knesset in support of his proposed government coalition.

Short biographies of the people who have occupied these positions illustrate the structure of the Israeli political elite. Between 1948 and 2004, ten men and one woman have served as prime minister. Seven were born in Eastern Europe, and four (Rabin, Netanyahu, Barak, and Sharon) in Israel to parents with East European backgrounds. Most became prime minister at relatively advanced ages, after long careers in party-related political work. Eight of them—Sharett, Rabin, and Shamir are the exceptions—were also the heads of their political parties, and all of them could be considered professional politicians (or apparatchiki) in that none of them had a profession or means of support outside the bureaucratic structures of the party and the state.

The symbolic presidency, as we would expect, leaves more room for exceptions and deviation from the stated generalizations. Three of the eight presidents (Chaim Weizman, Ben-Zvi, and Katzir) were intellectuals and academics. Navon and Katzav were the only Sephardim among the nineteen holders of the two top positions, and it is no accident that both served as president rather than as prime minister; both were active party politicians, one in Labor and one in Likud.

Prime Ministers

David Ben-Gurion, first prime minister of Israel, was born in Poland in 1886. In 1906 he came to Eretz Israel as part of the second *aliya* and as a leader of Poalei Zion. In 1908 he returned to Russia to join the army, and in 1912 he began studying law in Constantinople. With the outbreak of World War I he again came to Eretz Israel, only to be expelled by the Turks to Egypt. In 1919 he was one of the initiators of the establishment of Ahdut Haavoda; in the following year he was active in setting up the Histadrut and the first assembly of the Jewish settlers in Eretz Israel, called Knesset Israel. Between 1921 and 1935 he served as the general secretary of the Histadrut. In 1930, when Mapai was founded, he was considered its leader. Between 1935 and 1948 he was the chairman of the Jewish Agency Executive. In 1948 he announced the establishment of the State of Israel and became its first prime minister and defense minister, serving in these capacities from 1948 to 1953 and from 1955 to 1963. By 1965 he had left Mapai and founded Rafi to compete with his former party. After most of Rafi returned to Mapai in 1968 to form the Labor Party, Ben-Gurion set up the State List before the 1969 elections. Ben-Gurion retired from political life in 1970 and died in 1973.

Moshe Sharett, second prime minister of Israel, was born in the Ukraine in 1894 and immigrated to Eretz Israel with his parents when he was twelve. He studied law in Constantinople and served in the Turkish army in World War I. After the war he joined Ahdut Haavoda. In 1920 he went to London to study and became active in the World Zionist Organization. Between 1925 and 1931 he was editor of *Davar*, the Histadrut newspaper. In 1933 he was appointed head of the political department of the Jewish Agency in place of Chaim Arlozoroff (who had been murdered). Sharett retained this post until independence; in effect, he was the foreign minister of the state-in-the-making. When Ben-Gurion resigned in 1953, Sharett was chosen to succeed him. He lacked the political and bureaucratic skills of Ben-Gurion, and in policy matters he tended to be more moderate and less activist than his predecessor. He set up Israel's diplomatic service and retained the post of foreign minister while he was prime minister. In 1955 Ben-Gurion became defense minister in place of Pinhas Lavon in Sharett's government, and before the 1955 elections, he replaced Sharett as prime minister as well. In 1956, four months before the Sinai Campaign, Sharett resigned from the government, objecting to Ben-Gurion's activist policies. He remained active in public affairs until his death in 1965.

Levi Eshkol, Israel's third prime minister, was born in 1895 in Russia. In 1914 he immigrated to Eretz Israel, where he toiled as a worker and was one of the founders of Degania B, the kibbutz of which he was a member until his death. In the 1920s he was sent to procure arms in Europe, and at the end of the 1930s he was a member of the national command of the Haganah (the Yishuv defense force). In 1937 he initiated the establishment of Mekorot, the Histadrut's water company. Eshkol was secretary of the Tel Aviv workers' council in the Histadrut; in the 1940s he managed the Haganah's treasury. He was appointed by Ben-Gurion as the first director general of the Defense Ministry. From 1949 he was a member of the Jewish Agency Executive and head of its settlement department. In the early 1950s he was treasurer of the Jewish Agency, and minister of agriculture and development. By the 1950s he was a major figure within Mapai; between 1952 and 1963 he was minister of finance. In 1961 he formed the government that was headed by Ben-Gurion; later Eshkol was Ben-Gurion's chief opponent in the Lavon Affair (see chapter 5). When Ben-Gurion resigned in 1963, Eshkol took over the posts of prime minister and defense minister. His conciliatory nature (along with political considerations) led to an alignment between Mapai and Ahdut Haavoda before the 1965 elections, the formation of the National Unity Government before the Six-Day War in 1967, and the merger of Mapai, Ahdut Haavoda, and Rafi to form the Labor Party in 1968. He died in 1969.

Golda Meir, Israel's fourth prime minister, was born in Russia in 1898. When she was eight, her family moved to Milwaukee, Wisconsin, and in 1921 she immigrated to Eretz Israel as part of the third *aliya.* She was a member of kibbutz Merhavia until 1924. In 1925 she joined Ahdut Haavoda; in 1928 she was elected secretary of the women's workers' council; and in 1933 she became secretary of the Histadrut's executive committee. When many Mapai leaders were detained by the British on the "Black Sabbath" in June 1946, she ran the political section of the Jewish Agency. Before independence, Sharett ran the political section in the United States and at the United Nations, and Meir ran the department in Jerusalem. In 1947 and 1948 she held secret talks with Jordan's King Abdullah. After independence, she served as head of Israel's first mission to the Soviet Union, then as minister of labor and national insurance (social security) between 1949 and 1956. Upon Sharett's resignation in 1956 she became foreign minister and held the position until 1965, opposing Ben-Gurion in the Lavon Affair. In 1966 she was appointed secretary of Mapai. She resigned from most of her positions in 1968, only to be called back to active political life in 1969 at age seventy-one, after Eshkol's death. She served as prime minister until 1974; during this period the Labor-Mapam Alignment won its biggest plurality (fifty-six seats in 1969), and the Yom Kippur War of 1973 shocked the country. In the aftermath of the war and amid criticism of her and her government, she resigned in 1974. She died in 1978.

Yitzhak Rabin, Israel's fifth prime minister, served two terms, 1974–1977 and 1992–1995. He was born in Jerusalem in 1922, to parents who had come from Eastern Europe and were active in the Histadrut and Mapai. He was a leading officer of the Palmach during the war of independence; by 1953 he was made a general, and between 1956 and 1959 he served as commander of the northern front. In 1964 he was appointed chief of staff and led the army during the Six-Day War. In 1968 he was appointed Israel's ambassador to Washington. He ran on the Alignment list in the 1973 Knesset elections, and in 1974 was appointed minister of labor in Golda Meir's last government. When Meir resigned a month later, Rabin was earmarked for the prime ministry by the Mapai king-maker, Finance Minister Pinhas Sapir; Rabin was chosen because of his past connections with the labor movement and his famous military record, and because he was not involved in the military mistakes of the Yom Kippur War. Rabin won the job over Shimon Peres after a close vote in the Labor Party center—the first such contested election for the post in Labor Party history. Rabin was the first native-born prime minister and the first to lack a strong political background. For three months he led a minority government without the participation of the NRP in the coalition; by October 1974, the NRP had reentered the coalition. In 1977 he again beat Peres for the leadership of the party, this time in the party convention. But in April 1977 foreign currency infractions by his wife were discovered, and Rabin removed himself from first place on the Labor list and was placed in the twentieth spot. After the 1984 and 1988 elections, he became minister of defense. Again chosen as head of the Labor list before the 1992 elections, Rabin was elected prime minister. The decision to recognize the PLO led to his being awarded, along with Peres and Arafat, the Nobel Peace Prize in 1994. In November 1995, Rabin was assassinated after a peace rally in Tel Aviv.

Menachem Begin, sixth prime minister of Israel, was born in Poland in 1913. Until he was thirteen, he was a member of Mapam's youth group (Hashomer Hatzair); when he was sixteen, he joined Beitar, the Revisionist youth group. In the 1930s he studied law and was active in the Revisionist movement. In 1939 Jabotinsky appointed him head of Beitar in Poland, the chief concentration of power of the movement. In 1940 Begin was arrested by the Soviets and sentenced to eight years' imprisonment for Zionist activities; he was sent to Siberia but then released because he was a Polish citizen. After his release, he joined the Polish army and at the same time was appointed head of Beitar in Eretz Israel. He arrived in Eretz Israel in 1942 and became head of the Irgun in 1943; he led that organization until independence in 1948. A £10,000 bounty was offered by the British for his capture, but he evaded arrest. After the Irgun was disbanded and the Israel Defense Force established, Begin was the natural candidate for leading Herut. He became the leader of the opposition, objecting strenuously to reparations from Germany and arms sales with Germany. In 1965 he ran at the head of the Gahal list, a joint list of Herut and the Liberal Party that was further expanded in 1973 and named the Likud. Between 1967 and 1970 Begin served as minister without portfolio in the National Unity Government. After eight unsuccessful attempts, Begin's Likud won a plurality of the votes in 1977 and 1981. Begin was the first Israeli prime minister to sign a treaty of peace with an Arab state, the 1979 treaty with Egypt; he was awarded the Nobel Peace Prize, together with Anwar Sadat, in 1978. Begin resigned in 1983, evidently shaken by the results of the 1982 Israeli incursion into Lebanon and by the death of his wife. He died in seclusion in 1992.

Yitzhak Shamir, the seventh prime minister, was selected by the Herut faction of the Likud to succeed Prime Minister Begin in 1983 and served intermittently until 1992. Born in Poland in 1915, Shamir came to Eretz Israel in 1935 and joined the underground movement fighting the British in defiance of the official Jewish policy of self-restraint. He joined the radical Lehi (Lohamei Herut Israel—the Israel Freedom Fighters—also known as the Stern Gang), and was widely considered to have played an active role in planning the assassinations of senior British officials. After statehood, he worked for Mossad, Israel's intelligence agency, and later became a Herut member of the Knesset. He served as chairman of the Knesset after the Likud's ascension to power in 1977 and as foreign minister after Moshe Dayan resigned that post in 1980. In 1979 he opposed the peace treaty with Egypt, but since he was chairman of the Knesset at the time, he abstained rather than vote against it. In 1984, he became foreign minister in the National Unity Government headed by Shimon Peres and then rotated with Peres in 1986 and became prime minister again. After the 1988 elections, Shamir was successful in establishing another National Unity Government, which he headed. In 1992 he headed the Likud list in the election but lost to Labor's Yitzhak Rabin.

Shimon Peres, the eighth prime minister, served in the 1984–1986 and 1995–1996 periods. Born in Poland in 1923, he immigrated to Israel in 1934. When he was twenty, he was elected head of the youth group associated with Mapai. In 1947 he became active in the Haganah, procuring arms. During the war of independence he served in the Defense Ministry and after the war was the ministry's representative in the United States. Between 1953 and 1959 Peres served as director general of the Defense Ministry. He was elected to the Knesset on Mapai's list in 1959 and served as deputy defense minister until 1965. He was one of the architects of Israel's nuclear energy program and of the cooperative efforts with France in military and political spheres. In 1965 he left Mapai and followed Ben-Gurion to form Rafi; he served as secretary general of Rafi but broke with Ben-Gurion when Rafi decided to form the Labor Party in 1968 along with Mapai and Ahdut Haavoda. Between 1969 and 1977 Peres served at various times as minister of immigration absorption, transportation, communication, information, and defense. In 1974, 1977, and 1992, he competed unsuccessfully against Yitzhak Rabin for the Labor Party's support for the role of prime minister. In 1977, after Rabin removed himself from the top spot, Peres headed the Labor list in the election; between 1977 and 1984, he led the opposition to the Likud governments. He headed the National Unity Government from 1984 to 1986, at which time he rotated with Shamir—Peres became foreign minister and Shamir prime minister. In 1988, despite heavy opposition from his Labor Party, Peres led the party into the National Unity Government and became finance minister in Shamir's government. Before the 1992 elections he was defeated by Rabin in an election held among the party's membership for first position in the Labor Party. After Rabin won the election, Peres served as foreign minister, bringing to fruition the Oslo Accords with the PLO. Peres, Rabin, and Arafat shared the Nobel Peace Prize in 1994. In 1995, after the assassination of Rabin, Peres assumed the prime ministry, only to be defeated by Netanyahu in the 1996 elections. In 2003 Peres was selected temporary leader after the election failures of Barak, Ben-Eliezer, and Mitzna.

Binyamin Netanyahu, Israel's ninth and youngest prime minister, was the first to be directly elected. He was also the first prime minister to have been born in Israel after the establishment of the state. Born in Tel Aviv in 1949, he spent a number of years in the United States while growing up. He served as Israel's ambassador to the United Nations, and as deputy minister of foreign affairs, in which capacity he played a role in the 1991 Madrid Peace conference. Netanyahu won the leadership of the Likud in 1993 in an election among the party's members and was elected in the first direct election of the prime minister in 1996. Losing that office to Ehud Barak in 1999, he became finance minister in Sharon's government in 2003.

Ehud Barak, Israel's tenth prime minister, was chief of staff of the Israel Defense Forces. He was born in Israel in 1942 and served much of his army career in a highly regarded commando unit. When he left army service in 1995, he joined the Labor Party and Rabin's government as interior minister. After Rabin's assassination, Barak was appointed foreign minister in the Peres government. He was elected head of the Labor Party in 1997 and defeated Netanyahu in a landslide victory in 1999. His efforts to affect Israel's foreign and security policies included a unilateral withdrawal from Lebanon and aborted peace talks with the Syrians and the Palestinians. The unsuccessful peace talks at Camp David and Taba in 2000, in conjunction with U.S. President Bill Clinton, presaged the call for early elections in 2001. Ariel Sharon defeated Barak handily, and Barak retired from politics.

Ariel Sharon, Israel's eleventh prime minister, was born in Israel in 1928. He became a leader of the Liberal Party after retiring from the army in 1973 and was instrumental in forming the Likud with the Herut movement. In the 1973 Yom Kippur War he returned to military service. He resigned from the Likud Party in 1976 and ran as head of the Shlomzion list in 1977. After returning to the Likud, he was appointed defense minister in 1981 but was relieved of that position in 1983 in compliance with a finding by the Kahan commission of inquiry regarding the events in the Palestinian refugee camps of Sabra and Shatilla in Beirut. After Netanyahu's defeat in the 1999 election, Sharon assumed leadership of the Likud and went on to defeat Barak in 2001 and the Labor Party in 2003.

Presidents

Chaim Weizman, Israel's first president, was born in 1874 in Russia. He studied in Germany and Switzerland and received his doctorate in chemistry in 1899. In 1898 he participated in the second Zionist Congress, and before the fifth Congress in 1903 he was among the founders of the Democratic Party. In 1904 he accepted a position at Manchester University in England. In 1907 he visited Eretz Israel for the first time but decided not to settle there. In 1910 he became a British citizen. He emerged as a Zionist leader after World War I as a result of his connections with the British establishment. During the war he had aided the war cause through his scientific work, and in 1917 his diplomatic efforts brought about the Balfour Declaration, promising the establishment of a Jewish national home in Eretz Israel. Weizman was then head of the Zionist Federation in England; with the Balfour Declaration he achieved political stature throughout the Zionist movement. In 1919 he signed an agreement with King Feisal regarding cooperation between Arabs and Zionists. In 1921 he was elected president of the WZO and continued sporadically in that position, occasionally losing to the socialists, who often opposed him. In 1937 he settled in Rehovot in Eretz Israel. His pro-British policies were rejected by the Zionist Congress in 1946. In 1947 he settled in New York and was active in recruiting the support of President Truman to the Zionist cause. He was elected president of Israel in 1948; he continued in this post until he died in 1952.

Yitzhak Ben-Zvi, second president of Israel, was born in the Ukraine in 1884. In 1904 he came to Eretz Israel for a few months; in 1905 he began studying in Kiev. During the 1905 pogroms he was active in the Jewish self-defense movement. In 1907 he again came to Eretz Israel, this time as part of the second *aliya*. He was active in socialist organizations. In 1910 he began studying law in Constantinople but was interrupted by the First World War. He was arrested and expelled along with Ben-Gurion. He was a founding member of Ahdut Haavoda and a member of the secretariat of the Histadrut's executive committee. When the National Committee of the Yishuv was formed, he was elected to its directorate; in 1931 he was elected chairman of the committee's executive, and in 1945 he became its president. The National Committee dealt mostly with local matters, leaving the important international matters to the Jewish Agency and the Histadrut. After independence, he was elected to the Knesset but was never appointed a minister. He was elected president in 1952 and then reelected twice before his death in 1963. He was widely regarded as a historian and intellectual, dealing mainly with various Jewish ethnic groups.

Zalman Shazar, Israel's third president, was born in Russia in 1889. In 1912 he immigrated to Eretz Israel as part of the second *aliya*. He studied in Europe until the First World War and worked as a historian. In 1920 he returned to Eretz Israel as a member of a study mission and finally settled there in 1924. He became a member of the secretariat of the Histadrut's executive committee and a member of *Davar's* editorial staff. He was given various missions for Ahdut Haavoda and later Mapai. He was a founding member of the Knesset and was appointed minister of education and culture in 1949. In 1951 he resigned from the government to head Israel's mission in Moscow, but the latter appointment did not materialize. In 1963, at the age of seventy-four, he was elected president; he continued in this post until his death in 1973.

Efraim Katzir, Israel's fourth president, was born in the Ukraine in 1916. When he was six, he immigrated to Eretz Israel with his parents. He completed his studies in Eretz Israel by earning his doctorate from the Hebrew University in 1941. In 1948, at President Weizman's invitation, Katzir joined the Weizman Institute for Science in Rehovot and headed its biophysics department. His career was academic and not political. He was elected president in 1973 and served until 1978.

Yitzhak Navon, Israel's fifth president, was born in Jerusalem in 1921 of a Sephardi family that had lived in Eretz Israel for generations. He studied Hebrew literature and Islamic culture at the Hebrew University and taught at a local high school. Between 1946 and 1948 he was head of the Arab section of the Haganah. From 1952 to 1963 he served as an aide to Ben-Gurion, and in 1965 he was a founder, along with Ben-Gurion, of Rafi. He was elected to the Knesset on the Rafi list in 1965 and again later on the Alignment list. In the Eighth Knesset, he served as chairman of the foreign affairs and security committee. In 1978 he was elected president; he served until 1983. In 1984 and 1988 he became minister of education and culture in the National Unity Governments.

Chaim Herzog, Israel's sixth president, was born in 1920 in Ireland, where his father was the chief rabbi. He immigrated to Eretz Israel in 1935 and studied law as well as attending the yeshiva in Hebron. After serving in the British army in the Second World War, he served as head of intelligence in the Israeli army, as military attaché in Washington, and as Israeli ambassador to the United Nations. He was a member of Rafi and then of the Labor Party, and was elected to the Knesset. He was elected president in 1983 and reelected in 1988, and he served until 1993.

Ezer Weizman, the seventh president, was born in Tel Aviv in 1924. He served in the British Royal Air Force in World War II and was a commander of the Israeli air force between 1958 and 1966, formulating the air strategy that was successfully implemented in the Six-Day War. He retired from the IDF in 1969, after serving as deputy chief of staff, and joined the National Unity Government as minister of transport representing Gahal. After the Likud's ascension to power, he was appointed minister of defense, and in that capacity he took part in the Camp David talks with Egypt. He resigned from the government in 1980, displeased with the pace of the peace process. He formed a list named Yaad in 1984 and was reelected to the Knesset; before the 1988 elections Yaad negotiated for secure places on the Labor list. After both elections, Weizman served in the National Unity Governments between 1984 and 1990. He resigned from the Knesset in 1992 and was elected president in 1993 and then reelected in 1998. In 2000, after learning of a movement afoot in the Knesset to remove him from office, he became the first president to resign from office.

Moshe Katzav, the eighth president, was born in Iran in 1945. Katzav, a longtime Herut and Likud activist, was the first president to be elected without the support of the Labor Party. He emerged as an activist in Kiryat Malachi, a development town with a large immigrant population, then served as a Knesset member and as a government minister since 1984. In 2000 he competed for the presidency against Shimon Peres and received sixty-three votes in the second round of the secret Knesset balloting.

A Sephardi for President

While political power has stayed firmly in the hands of East Europeans and their descendants, more Sephardim and others have achieved positions of prestige and influence over the years. Symbolically, the most important office in Israel is the presidency of the state. The president's role is nonpolitical, with important moral, symbolic, ceremonial, and educational functions. The president symbolizes the sovereignty of the state, receiving the credentials of ambassadors. He also has the power to grant pardons, which he usually does only after consultation with other authorities. While the president wields some power because he has the task of appointing the person who will attempt to form the government, the task itself is largely nonpolitical. Nevertheless, the decision of who will be president is a very political one.

The president is elected by the Knesset, by secret ballot, for a period of five years and may serve no more than two consecutive terms in office. The election is by majority vote after the candidates have been nominated by at least ten Knesset members, with the agreement of the candidates. On the first two ballots an absolute majority of the Knesset (at least sixty-one votes) is needed for election; after that, a plurality is sufficient. The president may be removed from office if three-fourths of the Knesset members so vote.

In 1973, after the death of Zalman Shazar at the age of eighty-four, a popular candidate for the presidency was Yitzhak Navon. The son of an old Sephardi family in Jerusalem, he had pursued a long career in public affairs, serving with Sharett and Ben-Gurion. The party machine, and especially Golda Meir, opposed Navon's candidacy for political rather than ethnic reasons—Navon had been disloyal to Mapai by aiding Ben-Gurion, Dayan, Peres, and others in forming Rafi in 1965. Many thought that her opposition was an act of anti-Sephardi discrimination, when in fact it penetrated to the real heart of the matter—political loyalty. Meir added another (nonethnic) dimension to the issue when she declared that she would find it inappropriate to have Ben-Gurion's aide ask her in his new capacity as president to form a government. When Efraim Katzir was ultimately elected to the post, it was a blow to many Sephardim who had been keen on Navon's election, but the Labor Party machine won the day and chose a distinguished scientist as president.

When Katzir's term ended in 1978 and he declared himself unwilling to seek reelection, Prime Minister Begin announced that it was his intention to elect a Sephardi as president and that Yitzhak Navon of the Labor Party would be an appropriate candidate. What followed was a valuable lesson in how politics seeps into many areas of Israeli life: the election of the president, increased sensitivity to the ethnic issue, the desire to grant Sephardim representation at the highest symbolic levels of the state, and the inability of the Likud at that time to elect its own candidate to the presidency. After the elections in 1977, which had brought them to power after thirty years of opposition, the major factions of the Likud could not agree on a candidate. In addition, and in a more general sense, the case points up the dilemma known as the Arrow Paradox of Voting.

The paradox, named after the economist Kenneth Arrow, occurs in a democratic setting when the voters (in a country or in a committee) have more than two alternatives and order their preferences in such a manner that no majority outcome is possible. The election of Navon in 1978 is a demonstration of the dilemma presented by the paradox. When Begin announced his support of Navon, he had not fully taken into account the reaction of the Liberal Party, which was anxious to elect Elimelech Rimalt, a longtime Liberal leader. Navon, supported by the Alignment and the DMC, was strongly opposed by the Liberals. Since Begin was adamant about the importance of electing a Sephardi as president, he proposed the candidacy of Yitzhak Shaveh, an obscure physicist, for the post. Begin's Herut supported the prime minister's candidate, as did La'am. The Alignment wanted Navon but preferred Rimalt to Shaveh. The following situation developed: Shaveh had the support of forty-one Knesset members from Herut, La'am, and the NRP; Rimalt won the support of forty-seven Liberal and Alignment Knesset members; and Navon was supported by fifty-two members of the Alignment, DMC, and smaller parties. Equally important, the preferences of the groups differed, as shown in the following rankings:

(1) Alignment and others	(2) Liberals and others	(3) Herut and others
Navon	Rimalt	Shaveh
Rimalt	Shaveh	Navon
Shaveh	Navon	Rimalt

At a crucial moment Navon announced his unwillingness to continue as a candidate. It was clear that in the situation as it had developed,

Rimalt would be the winner. As Shaveh would not be elected, he too withdrew his candidacy, and then Navon returned to the fray as an alternative to Rimalt. Begin's group preferred the Sephardi candidate—even though he was an Alignment politician—to the candidate of the Liberals. Despite the fact that Herut and the Liberals were the major factions in the victorious Likud, Herut joined the Alignment and the DMC in voting for Navon for president. Navon received eighty-six votes and was elected in April 1978.[19]

Moshe Katzav, the second Sephardi elected president, ran against Shimon Peres in 2000. Peres, a political perennial, and Ashkenazi, seemed assured of victory. But party, ethnic, and religious factors surfaced in the secret ballot and combined to give the victory to Katzav. Each elected president until then had been the candidate of the Labor Party. Peres was no longer leader of his party and it is likely that he did not win the votes of all the Knesset members from his own Labor Party. The religious parties, and especially Shas, were anxious to have an observant or at least a traditional Jew as president; Katzav fit that description, while Peres certainly did not. And then there was the ethnic factor, often overlapping with the party and religious ones: Peres was born in Poland, Katzav in Iran. In all, Peres's legendary ability to pry defeat from the jaws of victory was again tested and, sure enough, again he lost.

5 POLITICAL PARTIES

THE BASIC DIVISION of the Israeli party system is between Likud and Labor. In 2003 Likud won 38 seats in the 120-person Knesset, while Labor (along with the moderate Orthodox Jewish party Meimad) received only half that number, 19 seats. If we conceive of these two parties as the major building blocks of the system, the political spectrum becomes focused (see figure 5.1). Clustering around them are other parties of the left and the right, respectively; each of these other parties may once have been part of one of the bigger parties or may align with one of them in the future. In addition to these two clusters, there are a group of Jewish religious parties, the Arab parties, and some scattered smaller parties.

In Israel's proportional representation system of elections, many lists and parties compete. The record was set in 1999 when thirty-five different lists formally competed, although two announced their withdrawal a week before the election; in 2003, "only" twenty-seven lists competed. A minimum threshold is needed to win representation—before 1992 it was 1 percent of the valid votes cast; since 1992 it has been 1.5 percent, although there is always pressure to raise it even higher.

It is important to distinguish between parties and lists. A *party* is a registered entity that seeks power within the established rules of elections. A *list* is a roster of candidates prepared by a party or a group of parties to run in elections (see chapter 6).

In 1984 Labor and Mapam jointly set up a single list called the Labor-Mapam Alignment, and the Likud list was made up of two autonomous

Figure 5.1   Knesset Results for Labor and Likud, 1965–2003

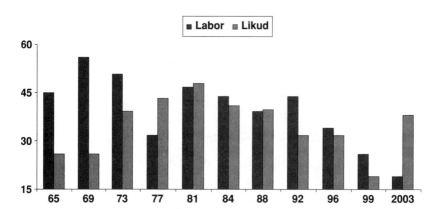

parties, Herut and the Liberals. In 1988 Labor and Mapam ran separate lists, and Herut and the Liberals merged into a single party called the Likud. By 1992, Mapam had joined with two other parties, the Citizens Rights Movement, and Shinui, to form a single list known as Meretz. In 1996 the Labor list was made up of one party, while the Likud list, formally called Likud-Gesher-Tzomet, combined the candidates of three parties: the Likud, David Levy's Gesher, and Raful Eitan's Tzomet.

Likud's list in 2003 was made up of one party, Labor's of two, as Labor and the moderate Orthodox party Meimad agreed to field a joint list. Some die-hards in the Shinui movement had refused to join Meretz and had persisted as Shinui, and they were the big surprise in 2003, winning fifteen seats. In 2004 Meretz in turn merged with some who had left Labor and formed Yahad, the Israel Social-Democratic Party.

For a politician facing the challenge of forming a coalition in the Knesset, or in setting public policy, the size of the groups participating in the discussions and the interests they represent are crucial. The initial question for a politician is how many votes can I control in the Knesset? How big is my party? In other words, how far are we from a Knesset majority and how much do I need others to help me form that majority? The next question is how big is the next largest party—meaning also what chance does my opponent have to form a coalition if I failed to do so? The point of departure is the size of the two large parties, Labor and Likud.

Another way of approaching Israeli politics is to consider the party system in terms of the distribution of power among the two largest

Figure 5.2   The Two Largest Parties' Shares in the Knesset, 1949–2003

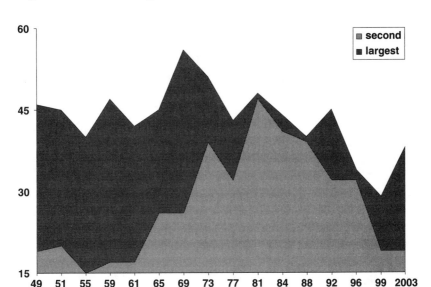

parties, as represented in figure 5.2. This diagram is based on much the same election results as figure 5.1, but it focuses on electoral size without distinguishing between political parties. Figure 5.2 clearly indicates three major periods in Israeli politics: one of dominance by Labor until 1977, a second of competitiveness between 1981 and 1996, and a third of flux and dealignment since 1999. Note that in 1999 the combined size of the two largest parties was the lowest ever—between them they controlled slightly more than a third of the Knesset. Sectarian politics and fractionalization coincided with the introduction of the direct election of the prime minister in 1996, making that election, rather than the Knesset vote, the focus of party competition. After the repeal of the direct election procedure, the Knesset elections again became crucial in the 2003 elections.

Two major policy breakthroughs (the Likud's 1978 peace with Egypt and Labor's 1993 accord with the PLO) came in the years following elections in which the gap between the two parties increased. In each case, the party in government that made the breakthroughs had been the big winner in the elections previous to the change in policy. But they were winners only in a relative sense; they were able to shift policy not because they were relatively strong, but rather because the second party was relatively weak.

Labor's uninterrupted reign ended in 1977, after which the Likud and Labor competed closely for power. The Likud emerged as the largest party in 1977, grew more in 1981, and then began a downward trend. Labor peaked in 1969; its reemergence in 1992 was only relative to the poor showing of Likud that year. In the period of dominance, the system was one-sided; the period of competition saw a heightening of the concentration of the vote at first and then a reemergence of the smaller parties.

By 1981 the race between the Likud and the Alignment was very close; between them they won nearly 1.5 million of the almost 2 million votes cast, but only 10,405 votes separated them. The Likud continued its steady growth, adding more than 100,000 votes to its 1977 total, while the Alignment bounced back from its 1977 trauma, growing by 50 percent. Within the Jewish population, the Likud was a bigger winner, since Arabs had accounted for more than 40,000 of the Alignment total. Comparing the results of the elections between 1984 and 1996 to the Alignment's more glorious past, however, leads to the inevitable conclusion that despite its good showing in 1981, it remained a party in decline. The number of people who actually voted increased between 1969 and 1988 by almost 900,000, but the difference between the Labor vote of 1988 (685,363) and the Alignment (Labor and Mapam) vote of 1969 (632,035) was only slightly more than 50,000 votes. In 1988, Mapam ran alone and won 56,345 votes. The Likud, on the other hand, added more than 370,000 votes in that period, growing from 338,948 in 1969 to 709,305 in 1988.

The 1992 election brought Labor back to power and allowed Rabin to reach an accord of mutual recognition with the PLO in Oslo; it was made possible more by the decline in the Likud vote than by a renewed Labor Party. Labor won forty-four seats, the same number that it had in 1984.

In the 1996 election Labor won 818,570 votes to the Likud-Gesher-Tzomet's 767,178 votes, but the drop to thirty-four seats and thirty-two seats respectively was a harsh blow to both of the major parties. Likud had also won thirty-two seats in 1992, but in 1996 Gesher and Tzomet were its partners in a joint list—Levy's Gesher had been part of the Likud until 1995, but Eitan's Tzomet had independently won eight seats in the 1992 elections. In 1999 both Labor and Likud focused on the direct election of the prime minister, ignoring the Knesset race, and the ultra-Orthodox Shas and Russian immigrant parties flourished. Following the crumbling of the peace plans of Labor's Barak, the Likud rebounded in 2003, but Labor did not.

Table 5.1   The Two Largest Parties' Shares in the Knesset, 1949–2003

	Biggest winner	Second-biggest winner	Total Seats	Competitiveness ratio[a]
1949	Mapai: 46	Mapam: 19	65	0.41
1951	Mapai: 45	Liberal: 20	65	0.44
1955	Mapai: 40	Herut: 15	55	0.38
1959	Mapai: 47	Herut: 17	64	0.36
1961	Mapai: 42	Herut: 17 Liberal: 17	59	0.40
1965	Alignment[b]: 45	Gahal[c]: 26	71	0.58
1969	Alignment[d]: 56	Gahal[c]: 26	82	0.46
1973	Alignment[d]: 51	Likud[e]: 39	90	0.76
1977	Likud[e]: 43	Alignment[d]: 32	75	0.74
1981	Likud[e]: 48	Alignment[d]: 47	95	0.98
1984	Alignment[d]: 44	Likud[e]: 41	85	0.93
1988	Likud: 40	Labor: 39	79	0.98
1992	Labor: 44	Likud: 32	72	0.73
1996	Labor: 34	Likud[f]: 32	66	0.94
1999	One Israel: 26	Likud: 19	45	0.73
2003	Likud: 38	Labor-Meimad: 19	57	0.50
PM 1996	Netanyahu 50.5%	Peres: 49.5%	100%	0.98
PM 1999	Barak: 56.1%	Netanyahu: 43.9%	100%	0.78
PM 2001	Sharon: 62.4%	Barak: 37.6%	100%	0.60

a. Competitiveness ratio = second biggest winner/biggest winner.

b. Mapai and Ahdut Haavoda.

c. Herut and Liberals.

d. Labor and Mapam.

e. Herut, Liberals, and others.

f. Likud-Gesher-Tzomet.

The trend toward consolidation of large parties began in 1965 with the emergence of the Mapai-Ahdut Haavoda Alignment and the Herut-Liberal Gahal, and it peaked in 1981, when ninety-five seats were divided between Likud and the Labor-Mapam Alignment (see figure 5.1 and table 5.1). It is not an unrelated fact that growth of the two parties' share of the vote coincided with the emergence of amalgamated parties, that is, lists set up by a combination of parties.[1] In 1965, in reaction to the split in Mapai caused by the setting up of Rafi by Ben-Gurion, Dayan, Peres, Navon, and others, old-time Mapai leaders formed an electoral coalition with Ahdut Haavoda in order to avoid political defeat. By 1968 Rafi, Mapai, and Ahdut Haavoda had formed the Labor Party, and in 1969 Labor joined Mapam in the Alignment. Meanwhile, the right Herut and center Liberals were founding an electoral bloc for the 1965 elections, expanded in 1973 under pressure from Ariel Sharon, with the acquiescence of Begin, to form the Likud.

This consolidation of the parties afforded party activists many advantages. Their quota of parliamentary seats was fixed through negotiation with the other partners in the amalgam, reducing the organizational and personal tensions usually associated with elections. The relative strength of a partner in one of these arrangements was fixed; if the list did well, the absolute number of representatives in the Knesset increased. This arrangement also afforded ideological benefits to the politician, who could be extreme (or moderate) in the councils of his (or her) own party and yet explain that in order to reap the benefits of the larger amalgamation, his (or her) position must be flexible in negotiation.

The appearance of breakaway third parties tempered the trend of two-party vote concentration: in 1965 Rafi won ten seats, in 1977 the Democratic Movement for Change (DMC) won fifteen, and in 2003 Shinui won fifteen seats. Most of these votes were at the expense of the Alignment; without the appearance of these breakaway parties the trend toward consolidation would be even clearer. A related trend was the growth of the Likud, whose advent in 1977 was aided mightily by the emergence of the DMC—because the DMC took many votes away from the Alignment, lowering the Alignment to the second largest party.

At independence, Mapai (Labor's precursor) was perceived as legitimate, Herut (Likud's antecedent) as illegitimate. The weakening dominance of Mapai and Labor, the achievement of legitimacy and equal political status by Herut and Likud, and the eclipse of Labor's legitimacy by the Likud sum up the political history of Israel since statehood. The key questions of Israel's future are likely to involve legitimacy: Will secular and religious Jewish parties develop a shared notion of the legitimacy of Israel's Jewish and democratic nature? Will Israeli Arabs accept the legitimacy of the state? Will Arab parties ever be regarded as legitimate by Israeli Jews? Dealing with these issues will likely introduce new parties. Will a new political alignment emerge in the future? If the country becomes less entangled with issues of the territories and the Palestinians, will it be then be free to come to grips with the real questions of Zionism, including the meaning of a Jewish democratic state? If the political issues regarding the neighboring Arabs recede, will a secular coalition of Labor and the Likud emerge and come to grips with post-territorial issues by competing with Jewish religious parties and/or with Arab parties?

A Dominant Party System

At first glance, the Israeli political party system seems to fit the multi-party pattern. In 2003, twenty-seven lists ran for election, and thirteen gained at least the 1.5 percent of the vote then needed for representation. But simply counting the number of parties in a political system does not reveal enough about the functioning of the system. For much of the pre-state era and for the first twenty-nine years of independence, political power was centered in one party. Since the subject of politics is power and not merely formal, legal, or constitutional issues, the *competitiveness of the system* and the *rotation of power* between parties must also be considered.

On closer reflection, the multiparty model with its implicit assumption of government instability is inadequate. At least until 1977, the Israeli case is an important example of a dominant-party political system, which is characterized by one party winning a plurality of the votes over a long period of time. But more important is the following consideration:

> A party is dominant when it is identified with an epoch; when its doctrines, ideas, methods, its style, so to speak, coincide with those of the epoch. . . . Domination is a question of influence rather than of strength: it is also linked with belief. A dominant party is that which public opinion *believes* to be dominant. . . . Even the enemies of the dominant party, even citizens who refuse to give it their vote, acknowledge its superior status and its influence; they deplore it but admit it.[2]

In Israel we have an example of a democratic system in which competition was allowed and free elections took place, and yet the ruling party was not rotated out of power. Italy, India, and Japan in the decades following World War II, and state-level politics in certain regions of the United States at times, have also been known continually to elect members of one party (e.g., the Democrats in the South and the Republicans in the Midwest), even though competitive politics was allowed.[3]

One attempt to come to grips with the dilemma of competition without party rotation in a democratic system was proposed as "an alternative way to democracy," [4] an analysis relevant to Israeli politics into the 1970s. The argument was essentially that a nonrotating system could be democratic if the internal organization of the ruling party was open to competition among its constituent elements. Moreover, the party could be responsive to shifts in public opinion in the country by revising its formula for coalition formation. Having a plurality, not a majority, of the seats in the Knesset meant that the government was always formed by a coalition of parties. This meant that power was diluted, at least to some extent (see chapter 9).

In the years immediately following independence, Mapai was presented with an opportunity shared by few parties in democratic polities—that of presiding over the creation of a constitutional and political order. As a consequence, it was closely identified with the new state, and it was the party of those segments of Israeli society most involved with those heroic years. It was able to translate this identification into an organizational network that complemented and amplified the advantages conveyed by its image. Furthermore, most of this network consisted of channels maintained largely at the expense of the state, with the result that party and government tended to merge in the popular mind. The role of governmental personalities in this image-building process was most important, and until 1977 almost all were from or associated with labor and left parties.

The strategy of the dominant party vis-à-vis other parties in the system thus has two principal goals: (1) to keep the party near the center, where the action is, and (2) to mobilize and demobilize segments of the population selectively in relation to the needs and absorptive capacity of the party. In the development of this strategy the party benefits from its symbiotic relationship with the society in that its dominance ensures it a major role in the definition of where the center is. Moreover, its orientation toward power encourages it to move with long-term shifts in public opinion regardless of its ideology. Party strategists labor under obvious and not-so-obvious handicaps in moving the party in new directions; there is nothing inevitable about their success, just as nothing is inevitable about the continued dominance of the party. Wrong interpretations of public opinion, inadequate attention to the demands of major groups, misjudgments concerning the importance of marginal groups, poor organizational work—all can lead to disaster.

As long as the dominant party performs intelligently, the opposition can do little that is effective. As Maurice Duverger has written: "The dominant party wears itself out in office, it loses its vigor, its arteries harden. It would thus be possible to show . . . that every domination bears within itself the seeds of its own destruction." [5] Even bad decisions by the dominant party are not disastrous unless the opposition is in a position to take advantage of them, which is seldom the case. And it is not in such a position because the dominant party has systematically excluded it and its leadership from positions of control and from the symbols of legitimacy.

As a result, the dominant-party system is remarkably stable. Disorder and even violence may be recurring features of the system, but they are surface disturbances that lead to little change. The opposition cannot replace the dominant coalition, and its frustration leads only to superficial instability. Although governments may not last long, the same parties and usually the same politicians continue to dominate the ruling coalition. The faithful are rewarded; the opposition is shut off from power.

As in other dominant-party systems, in Israel the role of centralized hierarchical structures (especially bureaucracies) in the society is very important. The democratic internal processes that often exist in two-party systems are absent here. The apparatus of mobilization typical of single-party systems is likewise negligible as a base of power, though it exists. Society tends to be held together by hierarchies that serve as the principal links between government and citizen. Indeed, these lines of communication, extended and humanized by networks of personal ties, are the true instruments of control in society, and they are either co-opted or controlled by the dominant party.

Mapai and Labor were identified with an epoch and its values, and they provided the leadership and ideology of the first thirty years of independence. With the passing of Labor from its position of dominance in 1977, however, it was clear that the Labor leadership had failed to remain attuned to changes within the society. All the problems are discussed at length elsewhere, but listing them here is instructive: no new generation of leadership had been groomed for when the old guard would pass from the scene; the passing of the old guard coincided with a blow to Israel's military, political, and psychological prowess in the Yom Kippur War of 1973; the party's organization had grown lax, and nasty evidence of corruption had surfaced; the steady change in the demographic structure of the country was not responded to in a convincing way. In sum, not only had the opposition become convinced of the dominance of Labor, but Labor leaders themselves had fallen into the reassuring trap of believing in perpetual dominance. This was the start of their undoing.

What follows a dominant-party era? The question is not easily answered. Some Labor supporters assumed that in 1981 Labor would return to dominance after its temporary setback in 1977; this was not to be. Another possibility was rotation between the two large parties. Labor's partial return to power in 1984 showed that many of the symbiotic relationships that characterized the first generation of Israeli politics had withered. It took the party until 1992 to put in place a candidate

(Rabin), organizational work, and structural change adequate to regain the support of the some of the working-class and Sephardi voters it had once claimed to represent. But in 1996, those gains were diminished and Peres was unable to retain control.

A third possibility was that the Likud would emerge as Israel's new dominant party, and thus the dominant-party system would continue but with a new dominant party. But just as the loss of dominance is not an abrupt matter, so too the establishment of dominance is a process rather than a moment. If the Likud was to emerge as a dominant political party in Israel, it had to overcome the lack of organizational contact with the citizenry on an extended basis. Likud parties had never had the organizational strength possessed by Labor and left parties, a factor that facilitated Labor's dominance.

The Likud of the late 1970s possessed three characteristics that could have been used as levers to dominance, but they were not capitalized on: (1) a major national turning point—the peace process with Egypt; (2) the broad support of growing sections of the population—the young and the Sephardim; and (3) the absence of serious ideological opposition on the part of the Labor-Mapam Alignment. These three were necessary, but obviously not sufficient, conditions for the emergence of a new era of political dominance.

By 2003, the Likud had been on a thirty-five-year quest for dominance. When it was in a position to capitalize on its 1977 electoral victory and on the 1978 peace treaty with Egypt signed by Begin, dominance eluded it. Tensions erupted between Begin and Defense Minister Sharon after the Lebanon War of 1982; Yitzhak Shamir, Begin's replacement, was less attentive to internal party dynamics and to the measures needed to build a competitive party machine. Democratization became fashionable and in the 1990s both the Likud and Labor introduced primaries into the process of selecting candidates for the Knesset. The leadership thus had less control of the selection process, while greater transparency and oversight in public financing made it more difficult to use the resources of the state for party-related goals—a feat Labor had mastered with memorable results.

The Likud had been very successful in stigmatizing Labor and the left since the 1977 turnabout. Identifying the left with the establishment is a common feature of Israeli politics, even when the left is far from power. Economic and social problems are popularly explained as stemming from the policies of the left and from the corruption and party-power hunger of its leaders. The second intifada begun in 2000 led to a widely heard claim that all security troubles stemmed from the Labor/Rabin/Peres–led

Oslo Accords and that Barak had been prepared to make an even more fundamental mistake at Camp David and Taba when he seemed on the verge of agreeing to return almost all the territories and accepting the establishment of a Palestinian state. The claim was given added weight when it was pointed out that he was even willing to divide Jerusalem and to relinquish claims to sovereignty over the Temple Mount.

Over the years, the Likud was also able to encroach on Labor's traditional bastions of power, such as local government, the Ministry of Finance, the Ministry of Education, and the National Broadcasting Authority. The election of Likud's candidate, Moshe Katzav, as President of Israel in 2000 is one of the best illustrations of these processes. Katzav, a middle-range Likud leader, defeated Shimon Peres, Nobel Prize winner, longtime Labor Party leader, and former prime minister, in a secret Knesset ballot. Perhaps most significant, however, was the decimation of the Histadrut, the national labor federation—a major political, social, and economic institution in Israeli society since the 1920s, and the most important vestige of Labor dominance. This was a long-term process, but the deathblow came in 1994, when the National Health Insurance scheme reduced the Histadrut to a strictly labor union function.

Typically, a dominant party will bring about its own demise, rather than falling victim to its opposition, and this was certainly true of the Labor Party. Ironically, it was the actions of the Labor leadership itself that had undermined the strength of the Histadrut—especially the decision to reform the health system in a way that weakened the Histadrut's health clinics (Kupat Holim). Decisions to nationalize other realms that had been bastions of party strength, such as education and the labor exchanges, also eroded Labor's power. Finally, charges of corruption eroded the moral standing of the Labor leadership and led to calls for good government.

The Likud had the wherewithal to achieve the status of dominant party—it was identified with the era, its leaders set the public agenda, and even its detractors recognized its uncontested position of rule. What the Likud lacked and what Labor had had in the pre-state period and early years of independence was the party organization to perpetuate its rule and sustain the loyalty of its activists. What Likud lacked was the functional equivalent of the labor union, the Histadrut, which had been dominated by the parties of the left.

The Likud has never attempted to establish institutions that would extend its power and increase the loyalty of its activists. The major source of party strength, besides the patronage afforded by being in power, is local government, and the Likud has achieved great success in this area. Local government is an important party resource, since building contractors and businessmen are anxious to be close to the party in power, and activists are able to procure jobs for themselves and their supporters. The centralized nature of Israeli public policy reinforces network ties and mutual dependence. While this resource is important to many involved in politics, it is not deeply rooted enough to ensure the perpetuation of the party in power. Besides, other parties such as Shas and some Arab parties have developed other mechanisms to closely tie voters to parties, successfully establishing organizations that provide social services, while the two major parties, Likud and Labor, have consistently avoided these activities in recent years.

Moreover, the Likud has been tied up in a morass of multiple inconsistencies with regard to ideology, policies, and constituencies. The party had to compromise its Greater Israel ideology to pursue peace and win the goodwill of the American administration, leaving the party split over the issues of returning territories for peace and the establishment of a Palestinian state. At the same time, the Likud's adherence to right-wing policies stemming from its ideology, as well as its affiliation with the religious camp, prevented it from significantly enlarging its electoral base. The Likud's social-economic program of liberal and neoliberal reforms has led to the alienation of many in the lower class who are its natural constituency.

Left-of-Center Parties

One key group in understanding Israel's political system is the left-of-center party group known in the past as the Alignment. This was the name of the list set up in the elections between 1969 and 1984, including candidates from the Labor Party and Mapam. Mapam decided to run alone in 1988, but the term *Alignment* (*Maarach* in Hebrew) is still used occasionally to refer to Labor and its affiliates. It refers to those parties that formed and ruled Israeli political life during the formative pre-state period and the first generation of statehood. After winning eight elections since independence, in more recent years the Alignment has only managed to control the prime ministry during the 1984–1986, 1992–1996, and 1999–2001 periods.

The Alignment is the appropriate group with which to begin because the history of parties on Israel's left and their leadership is closely tied to the history of the pre-state years, the period of independence, and the first three decades of statehood. Its organizations—the Histadrut, Kupat Holim, kibbutz, and moshav—were mainstays of the country until the 1990s.

The Pre-state Period

The political organization Ahdut Haavoda was established in 1919, bringing together various organizational undertakings begun under Turkish rule. After the defeat of the Turks by the British in World War I, these undertakings gained momentum. In 1920, the Histadrut was set up, providing a structure to further the social, economic, and cultural interests of the workers. The socialist leaders of Ahdut Haavoda were an integrated group of militants who were imbued with shared goals; aware of traditional Jewish culture, values, and scholarship; and open to the revolutionary movements and ideas sweeping Europe. Their ideological world was a confluence of the urges for social justice, class awareness, and Zionist aspirations; their leadership instinct told them that their goals of national independence and social justice could be achieved only if the requisite political and organizational work was adequately done. Their varying brands of Marxist analysis all led to the conclusion that economic foundations had to be laid for the Zionist enterprise and that the Jews in Eretz Israel had to undergo a radical social transformation in order to realize the Zionist goal of a new Jewish nation.[6]

The 1920s saw the expansion of the Histadrut and its activities, although it was increasingly threatened by a largely bourgeois immigration, which failed to join its ranks, and later by the severe economic crises of 1927 during which major enterprises, including the Histadrut's Sollel Boneh, went bankrupt. By 1930, faced with new issues, Ahdut Haavoda merged with a former rival party in the Histadrut to form Mapai, led by David Ben-Gurion, who was at the time secretary-general of the Histadrut. By 1935 Ben-Gurion had become chairman of the WZO Executive and thus the leader of all Jews in Eretz Israel. As Ben-Gurion and the leadership became ever more preoccupied with national concerns, their socialism waned and became more pragmatic in nature.

As the old Ahdut Haavoda moved to the right with the formation of Mapai, an active left-wing opposition emerged both within and outside the party. The left favored a less centralized and less powerful Histadrut and called for the strengthening of local units, especially the kibbutzim. This left-wing opposition was led by Hashomer Hatzair, the ideological center of the Kibbutz Haarzi, although it refrained from declaring itself a party until the mid-1940s. The group endorsed a vision of Jews and Arabs living together in a condition of binationalism, pursuing the class struggle for the mutual benefit of all. It was strengthened in the 1930s with the arrival of immigrants trained in its vigorous youth movement abroad.[7]

The left-wing opposition within Mapai took up the cause of the kibbutzim, which resisted the enhancement of the authority of the Histadrut. Kibbutz Hameuhad, a left-wing kibbutz movement, was influential in urban matters as well, its faction winning a majority in the local labor council of Tel Aviv. The leftist opposition was active in 1935, preventing the ratification of an agreement reached between Ben-Gurion and Zeev Jabotinsky regarding cooperation between the Histadrut and the trade union movement set up by the rightist Revisionist Party. Ben-Gurion had negotiated the agreement without consulting the second stratum of leadership, and most of those leaders opposed the agreement. They were not prepared to compromise with a rival organization that stemmed from a party that had aroused extreme negative feelings in the Yishuv.[8]

The left opposition in Mapai fully emerged in the 1941 Mapai Conference, calling itself Siah B. It opposed the change in Zionist policy that called for the creation of a Jewish state, as well as plans for the partition of Palestine. Instead these leaders called for socialist control of all positions of power in the country and further settlement and development. The Biltmore Program, named after the New York hotel in which the American Zionist Organization endorsed the goal of Jewish statehood in 1942, became official Zionist policy in November of that year. Siah B, more favorably inclined toward the Soviet Union and Marxism, demanded recognition within Mapai as a separate faction with the right to veto majority decisions.

At the party conference in 1942, all internal factional activity was banned. But when the opposition faction persisted in its opposition, Ben-Gurion staged a showdown at a meeting of the Histadrut executive in 1944. Siah B left Mapai, renaming itself Ahdut Haavoda to indicate that Mapai had abandoned the ideals of the old party and that they were being carried on by the new one.

In 1948 Hashomer Hatzair and Ahdut Haavoda formed Mapam. Each component group had a kibbutz movement—Haarzi and Hameuhad, respectively—which dominated it, but these movements were not combined or integrated. This enlarged left intended to remind Mapai of its socialist origins even if it could not win power on its own. In 1954 Ahdut Haavoda left the merged party (and retained that name) because Hashomer Hatzair had persisted in its pro-Soviet policy, which was unacceptable to many in Ahdut Haavoda. Moreover, the Ahdut Haavoda leadership, especially the high concentration of the group that had served as officers of the Palmach, demanded a more activist foreign and defense policy than was acceptable to the Shomer Hatzair faction of Mapam.

Socialism was a major theme of conflict running through the history of the Alignment parties. Some of them opted for orthodox Marxist-Leninism; others preferred a Marxist-Zionist brand or a humanistic social-democratic orientation with emphasis placed on nationalistic Zionism. Differing international conditions reflected the lineup of parties at any given time. For example, immediately after the Russian Revolution of 1917, some parties urged following the path of class struggle. After the defeat of Nazi Germany in 1945, some followed the Soviet model, while others opted for a brand of Western European social democracy. On issues specific to the country, extreme leftist parties often take a binational position, whereas others take a much tougher line regarding the Arabs. Differences developed within the Alignment over the eventual resolution of the status of territories taken in the Six-Day War of 1967—some were prepared to return most or all of them, others none.

The State Period

In the years immediately following independence, Mapai epitomized the dominant party. The largest vote-getter, the key ingredient of any government coalition, the standard-bearer of the society's goals, and the articulator of its aspirations, Mapai also had the tremendous political advantages of a united and integrated leadership; a broad-based, well-functioning, and flexible political organization; no serious political opposition; and control over the major economic and human resources flowing into the country. But Mapai failures, especially internal disputes over political leadership and ineffective party organization, were as important in explaining its eventual decline as was the gradual strengthening of the Herut movement and the Likud.

The starting point for seeking the seeds of decline is the notorious Lavon Affair.[9] When Ben-Gurion decided to retire (temporarily) from political life in 1953, Foreign Minister Moshe Sharett was appointed prime minister, Pinhas Lavon became defense minister, Moshe Dayan chief of staff, and Shimon Peres director general of the Defense Ministry. The latter two appointments foreshadowed the emergence of the "young Turks" in Mapai; along with Ben-Gurion, they would oppose the old guard.

In autumn 1954 undocumented reports circulated that Israeli intelligence had ordered a cell of Egyptian Jews to engage in bombing and arson against American installations in Cairo in order to harm relations that were at that time improving between Egypt and the United States.[10] The thirteen members of the group were detained, and two of them were hanged by the Egyptian authorities. An Israeli retaliatory raid into Gaza killed forty Egyptian soldiers but could not wipe out nagging questions about the degree of training and readiness of the spy unit and the political wisdom of the plan. More critically, Minister of Defense Lavon claimed that he had not given the order for these acts and that his signature on the order had been forged. Isolated, he was compelled to resign.

The issue was revived in 1960 when Lavon received evidence that, in his opinion, cleared him. Ben-Gurion, however, declined to exonerate him, reasoning that since Lavon had not been convicted, he could not be exonerated. Dissatisfied with this treatment, Lavon infuriated Mapai by bringing the matter before the Knesset Committee for Foreign and Security Affairs, and the story leaked to the press. Since Lavon was also reported to have called into question the integrity of Dayan and Peres, the developing split along generational lines within the party was brought into sharper focus.

The findings of a committee headed by Justice Chaim Cohen were not conclusive. Next, efforts made by Levi Eshkol brought about an admission by Sharett, acceptable to Lavon, that had the evidence placed before the Cohen committee been available in the mid-1950s, it would have brought a different decision concerning Lavon's role in the affair. A ministerial committee appointed to study the matter concluded that Lavon was free of responsibility. Nevertheless, Ben-Gurion insisted that as Lavon had evidence that imputed guilt to others, only a court of law could undertake the exoneration.

Ben-Gurion resigned as prime minister on January 31, 1961, bringing about the resignation of the government based on the rules pertaining at that time. New elections were held in August 1961, with Ben-Gurion heading Mapai's list for the last time. The party closed ranks for the elections, and only four seats were lost, compared with the 1959 vote. But the party would never be the same again. Ben-Gurion had been defeated by his former disciples on an issue that he considered one of principle. Moreover, unlike the situation when Ben-Gurion had resigned ten years earlier, his colleagues now realized that they could assert themselves and run things without him.

Conditions were ripe for Ben-Gurion's split from the main corps of second stratum leaders in Mapai—a development that forecast tensions in the party for years to come. Ben-Gurion and the younger generation of party leaders he had promoted opposed the alignment with Ahdut Haavoda; the old guard favored it, regarding the Ahdut Haavoda leadership as a counterbalance to the appeal of the "young Turks" and an alternative source of future leadership if the young, ambitious pretenders should actually split from Mapai. More important, by neutralizing the younger generation, the leaders of the third *aliya* would be able to prolong their rule. At the 1965 party convention, the alignment with Ahdut Haavoda was approved by a vote of about 60 percent to 40 percent. At the same convention, the delegates rejected Ben-Gurion's demand that the next government headed by the party must reverse the decision to approve the recommendation of the ministerial committee exonerating Lavon. Rafi emerged when Ben-Gurion then simply announced the formation of a separate list. Six weeks later, the party expelled those members who had set up the new list; soon after, a reluctant Moshe Dayan joined the Rafi ranks. The Lavon Affair thus split Mapai, fostered the aspirations of the "young Turks," and gave the leaders of the third *aliya* their chance to rule.

The decade between 1963 and 1973 was one of third *aliya* leadership. Eshkol, the genial conciliator and finance minister under Ben-Gurion, served as prime minister from 1963 to 1968. He was also defense minister until 1967 when, before the outset of the Six Days' War, a National Unity Government was formed that included Rafi and Herut, with Moshe Dayan as minister of defense and Menachem Begin as minister without portfolio. Begin, head of the Gahal faction (Herut and Liberals) in the Knesset, was instrumental in the formation of the National Unity Government—he even suggested that his old nemesis, Ben-Gurion, be recalled to power to head the new government. As the prolonged crisis that preceded the war simmered, the old-time leaders of Mapai, led by Eshkol, finally acquiesced. Eshkol's government was expanded to include Dayan and Begin.

The three years of the National Unity Government (1967–1970), including the period of the Knesset elections of 1969, were most important in changing the perceived illegitimacy of Begin and Herut in the system. Eshkol agreed even before the war to a proposal (which Ben-Gurion had rejected) to have the body of Zeev Jabotinsky, the Revisionist leader and Begin's mentor, reinterred in Israel by formal decision of the government. After the war, even Ben-Gurion relented in his intense animosity toward Begin and Herut, and the two leaders maintained correct, if not warm, relations until Ben-Gurion's death in 1973.

The National Unity Government symbolically presaged future developments. In 1968 Dayan and most of Rafi returned to Labor, and, along with Ahdut Haavoda and Mapai, formed the Israel Labor Party. Begin and Herut remained in the unity government until the summer of 1970; they withdrew when the government decided to consider the proposals of U.S. Secretary of State William Rogers for a settlement of the Israel-Arab conflict. Begin's participation in Eshkol's government did more than anything else to legitimize the former head of the outcast Irgun as a respectable, and ultimately alternative, leader.[11]

Golda Meir was the second member of the third *aliyah* to serve in the role of prime minister (1968–1974). Selected by Mapai on Eshkol's death, she served through the Yom Kippur War and the 1973 elections. Soon after, she resigned, leaving an Israel weakened by war, in increasing political isolation and burdened with an enormously inflated defense budget, and a Labor Party that would have difficulty overcoming the shocks of the experience.

When the Labor Party was formed in 1968, its constituent parties comprised its institutions on the basis of the following formula: 57.3 percent for Mapai, 21.35 percent each for Ahdut Haavoda and Rafi (see figure 5.3). The remnants of these three parties were partially intact six years later when the issue of succession arose. The candidate who had the support of the old-time leaders was Pinhas Sapir, an effective finance minister and party kingpin. Even in 1974, fifty-four years after the Histadrut was established, it was clear that if they had an agreed-upon candidate, the older generation could dictate the choice of prime minister to the party institutions; although formal power had passed to younger hands, the old guard had the influence and the votes to determine the outcome. Yigael Allon and Shimon Peres were unacceptable to the majority Mapai group because they came from Ahdut Haavoda and Rafi, respectively. That they were now all in the same party and that these candidates were admittedly loyal leaders of the new party did not shorten the memories of an old guard trained in the tradition that the first rule of politics in Israel is loyalty to your faction. Yitzhak Rabin, chief of staff during the Six Days' War and ambassador to Washington until a short time before the Yom Kippur War, became the choice of the convention; his political background was less clear than those of the others, and he had no obvious factional affiliation that could be used to veto his candidacy.

Rabin served as prime minister between 1974 and 1977, with Shimon Peres as defense minister. Before the 1977 elections, Peres contested for the top spot with Rabin and was defeated. Shortly before the elections, however, word was released of an illegal foreign currency account held by Rabin's wife. Rabin thereupon left the prime ministry and abandoned

Figure 5.3   Splits and Mergers in the Israeli Labor Movement

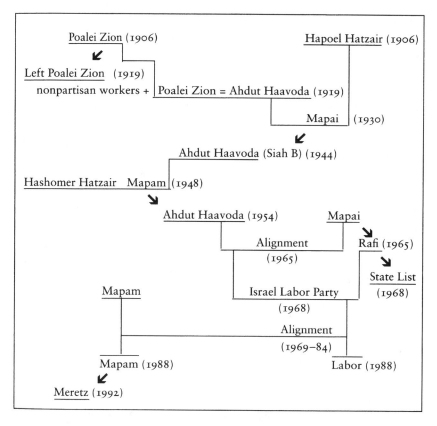

Source: Myron Aronoff, *Power and Ritual in the Israeli Labor Party* (Assen: Van Gorcum, 1977).
Note: Solid connecting lines indicate mergers; arrows indicate splits.

his plans to be number one in the Alignment's list for the elections. Peres was named in his place, and it was his misfortune to lead the party into opposition. Although the ideological differences between Rabin and Peres were minimal, competition between them continued. After the 1984 election, Peres became prime minister as part of the agreement that set up the National Unity Government.

That agreement called for rotation in office between Prime Minister Peres and Foreign Minister Shamir after two years. Despite tensions and crises, the agreement held, and Peres exchanged ministries with Shamir in 1986, assuming the office of foreign minister. Although Peres earned high grades as prime minister for curtailing the runaway economy, for withdrawing the Israel Defense Forces from Lebanon, and for effectively winning control of party institutions, many in the party and in the public preferred Rabin.

As a result of the inconclusive 1988 elections, in which Labor won thirty-nine Knesset seats to the Likud's forty, another National Unity Government was established. But this time, rotation was not part of the agreement because Likud support among other potential coalition partners was greater than it had been in 1984. Under Prime Minister Shamir, Rabin was made defense minister, Peres finance minister.[12]

Before the 1992 elections, Rabin again challenged Peres in Labor's convention and barely won the 40 percent needed for victory on the first round of voting. Had he fallen short, Peres would most likely have won in the second round, because other candidates who ran in the first round had supported Peres in the past against Rabin. However, Rabin led the party to electoral victory in 1992 and then appointed Peres foreign minister, while he himself served as both prime minister and defense minister.

Despite their decades-long terrible interpersonal relations, the two Labor leaders worked more closely together than ever in this period. Prompted by the collapse of the Soviet Union, prodding from the United States, and recognition of the high cost in life, moral rectitude, and property extracted from Israel by the intifada, Rabin and Peres drastically changed Israel's foreign policy. Israel and the PLO agreed in Oslo in 1993 on mutual recognition and on a cessation of terrorist activities. In ceremonies viewed with favor by much of the world, Rabin and Peres were celebrated as peacemakers, and the two of them, along with PLO Chairman Yasir Arafat, won the Nobel Peace Prize.

The history of conflict and cooperation between the two men ended on November 4, 1995, with the assassination of Rabin in Tel Aviv. This cruel act threw the country into a period of extended mourning, culminating in an unusually quiet election campaign in May 1996. Unfortunately for Labor, Peres again failed to lead the party to victory.

Whereas the Labor Party platform of 1992 had opposed a Palestinian state and called for the continued control and presence of Israel on the Golan Heights, by 1996 these two planks were erased, giving the party leader maximum latitude in negotiations after the election. In the past, platforms had been framed as instruments of constraint for leaders in power or as documents reflecting compromise over competing positions. This new situation of discretionary latitude was especially appropriate for a party with a single dominant leader, Peres, positioning himself to continue making peace. Peres's loss to Netanyahu, however, changed those plans.

In 1999 Ehud Barak campaigned on tough security and foreign policy platforms, but after beating Netanyahu convincingly, Barak proceeded to negotiate with the Syrians and then with the Palestinians. In both cases Barak's positions were much more conciliatory than anything that Labor had proposed before—Barak agreed to return almost all the territories taken in 1967—but in neither case was the deal consummated.[13] Quite naturally, however, many thereafter identified those positions as starting points for future negotiations.

Details of the Barak plan with Syria included the demilitarization of the Golan Heights, with neither Syria nor Israel having armies near the boundary; Mt. Hermon returned to Syria, but with Israel having an early-warning system there; Golan settlers remaining for a limited period of time; the Golan Heights under Syrian sovereignty; the international boundary at the waterline of the Sea of Galilee. The details were rejected by most Israelis[14] and by the Syrians.

In January 2001 Barak's government, with the active encouragement and participation of U.S. President Bill Clinton, negotiated with the Palestinian Authority regarding details of a final agreement between the two sides. Elements of the negotiations included establishment of a Palestinian state on 95 percent of the West Bank and Gaza, with Israel retaining clusters of settlements; transferring the Arab neighborhoods in Jerusalem to Palestinian control, with the Temple Mount held by the Palestinians and the Western Wall retained by Israel; a limited number of Palestinian refugees allowed to return to Israel; territories in Israel exchanged for territories controlled by the Authority; and Israel giving up control of the Jordan Valley in a number of years. This plan was proposed in the last days of Clinton's presidency and as Barak's parliamentary coalition was crumbling. There was no evidence of majority support in Israel for the plan, and it was rejected by the Palestinians.

After Barak's peace plans disintegrated and Sharon trounced him in the special election for prime minister in 2001, support waned for a moderate Labor position on security matters. The intifada raged on, and in 2000–2003 about 1,000 Jews and 3,000 Arabs were killed, making it one of the bloodiest periods in the 120-year conflict. Amram Mitzna led the Labor Party in 2003, calling for unilateral withdrawal from the territories. Labor fared as poorly in the elections as it ever had, yet a year later Prime Minister Sharon proposed a slim version of Mitzna's plan. After Mitzna's defeat and resignation as head of the Labor Party, Peres was again chosen to head the party, and he promised to support Sharon's unilateral separation from the Palestinians even if Labor did not join the coalition.

Out of power and out of vote-attracting leaders, Labor seemed to be out of steam. Even on social and economic matters, with the gap between rich and poor as pronounced as it had ever been in Israel and higher than in most advanced industrial democracies, Labor was no longer able to fire the public imagination with its social programs and economic proposals. Its association with the moderate Orthodox Jewish Meimad assured that most traditionalist religious groups would avoid cooperating with the party.

Mapam was the junior partner of the Alignment between 1969 and 1984. In this period, it lost some of its distinguishing features as the country's premier Marxist socialist party. While it retained its own party institutions, it appeared subservient to Labor's policies and interests, and some voices within Mapam occasionally called for breaking up the Alignment. When the Labor Party agreed to form a coalition with the Likud in 1984, Mapam left the Alignment.

Mapam remained in opposition during the period of the National Unity Government between 1984 and 1988. In 1992, Mapam joined with the Citizens Rights Movement and the original Shinui, to form Meretz, which did very well, winning twelve seats, and making it an important player in the Rabin government by supporting Rabin's peace initiatives and fostering civil rights and social welfare legislation. In the 2003 elections, Meretz took a hit, along with the other moderate parties, winning only six seats. The fortunes of the left-of-center were as low as they ever had been. In 2004 Meretz and former Labor leaders such as Yael Dayan and Yossi Beilin formed a social-democratic party named Yahad (Together).

The entire political spectrum is sprinkled with former Labor activists. A fascinating feature of the party structure is the shift to the right by people originally in the Labor camp. Rafi split in 1968 over the decision of returning to the Labor camp. Some remained in the State List, headed by Yigael Horowitz and Zalman Shuval; they later were leaders in such parties as La'am and Ometz, but were ultimately incorporated into the Likud. A second group with a similar history was the Greater Israel Movement, headed by Mapai leaders such as Zvi Shiloah, Eliezer Livne, Moshe Shamir, and Avraham Yaffe. Some of these former Mapai activists founded Tehiya after rejecting the Camp David agreements with Egypt in 1979.

In 1996 this phenomenon was seen with the founding of the Third Way. Many of the founders found the parting with Labor painful, since they were leading members of the defense establishment, personal friends and devoted followers of Prime Minister Rabin who split with him because they were disappointed with his government's course. The platform of the Third Way was almost indistinguishable from the security-oriented Labor Party platform of 1992, especially regarding the Golan Heights, an area populated mostly by Labor followers, which they considered vital for the country's security. Its plan for a territorial compromise in Judea and Samaria was essentially a modified version of the Allon plan, which in effect had been Labor's platform for over a quarter of a century, calling for the Jordan River to be Israel's security border.

Likud Parties

The Likud itself was an amalgamation of a number of other parties. Like Labor, the Likud found itself attracting a wide variety of like-minded political leaders. Some groups that split with the party later formed joint lists with it, and then rejoined the party, such as David Levy's Gesher.

The Herut movement, set up by former Irgun leader Menachem Begin in 1948, was the most important element in forming the Likud in a political and ideological sense. The Liberal Party was the political continuation of the General Zionists of the pre-state and early state years, and represented a bourgeois point of view. A third party of the pre-1988 Likud list was La'am, a remnant of the Rafi faction of Mapai that refused to return to the Labor Party camp in 1968 when the united party was formed. After Ben-Gurion's death, La'am aligned itself with the Likud. In the 1988 elections, its representatives ran on the Likud list but were not part of the newly united party.

As with the Alignment parties, the period of amalgamation began in 1965. Gahal, a bloc of the Herut movement and the Liberal Party, competed in 1965 with the Mapai-Ahdut Haavoda Alignment and in 1969 with the Labor-Mapam Alignment. In 1973 the Likud was formed, joining the Free Center and La'am to Gahal.

The parties of the right have remained in power for most of the period following the 1977 Likud victory despite the high degree of competitiveness that characterized the end of Labor's dominance of Israeli politics. In the ten elections between 1969 and 2003, the right bloc consolidated its domination while the left lost support. The 2003 election continued the trends of the previous three decades, extending the decline of the left and further consolidating the right's control over the parliament, the policy agenda, and the nation's priorities. The strength of the two large parties, Labor and Likud, had declined significantly throughout the 1990s, but in 2003 the right-wing Likud doubled its Knesset representation to thirty-eight seats, while the left-wing Labor saw a further decrease. After the 2003 election Likud reigned as the single party clearly at the top of the heap. Ariel Sharon in 2003, like Menachem Begin twenty-five years before him, had triumphed over the left (with the help of Shinui, a breakaway center party—the role played by the DMC in 1977); he held uncontested power and was positioned to make historical decisions regarding the future of the territories.

Herut

The Herut movement is the direct ideological descendant of the Revisionists, a party founded in 1925 by Vladimir (Zeev) Jabotinsky.[15] That party's name reflected the belief that the policies of the Zionist Organization had to undergo immediate revision if the goals shared by all Zionists were to be achieved. Opposing the paths of conciliation and gradualism advocated by the socialists, the Revisionists demanded militancy in achieving their nationalistic goals. Jabotinsky offered a myth of martial strength to compete with the myths of the conquest of the land offered by the socialists and *tora veavoda* (religious law and toil) offered by religious Zionists. Not by the patient accumulation of another cow and another *dunam* (1,000 square meters), but by blood and iron would the country be won. Beitar, the Revisionist movement's youth movement, contains the initial of Joseph Trumpeldor in its acronym; Trumpeldor's heroism and labor ideology made him a hero in both Revisionist and labor camps.[16]

Jabotinsky, a fiery speaker and original thinker, had been active in Zionist circles for years before resigning from the Zionist Executive in 1923 and conceiving the idea of forming a political party and youth movement. At first, the Revisionists worked within the frameworks of the General Zionists and the WZO, but Jabotinsky's ideas were seen as too militant and were unacceptable to the leadership. In the 1931 elections to the local Electors' Council, the Revisionists won 23 percent of the delegates, second only to Mapai's 42 percent. In the 1931 elections to the Zionist Congress outside of Eretz Israel they did even better, winning 21 percent compared to Mapai's 29 percent. But by 1933, with the advent of Hitler and the murder of Chaim Arlozoroff (discussed later), Mapai surged to 44 percent and the Revisionists slipped to 14 percent. By 1935 the Revisionists had given up hope of taking over the WZO and formed their own New Zionist Organization. It was precisely during this period that Ben-Gurion and Mapai consolidated power in the WZO, with Ben-Gurion becoming chairman of the Zionist Executive. Jabotinsky's refusal to cooperate with the organized Yishuv headed by Mapai would earn him Ben-Gurion's undying political enmity.

Because participation in the organized Yishuv was voluntary, there was no possibility of coercing dissident groups. Operating outside the organized Yishuv and stigmatized by the establishment, which effectively denied them legitimacy, the Revisionists were branded irresponsible opportunists, unworthy of support and likely to pose a danger to the Zionist cause. Three incidents left a heavy layer of ill will: Arlozoroff's murder, the "season," and the sinking of the *Altelena*.

In June 1933, Arlozoroff, a prominent leader of Hapoel Hatzair and a gifted thinker and writer, was gunned down at the age of thirty-four at the seashore near Tel Aviv. The leadership of Mapai was convinced that the Revisionists were behind the murder, although the young immigrant Revisionist arrested and convicted of the murder was later released for lack of evidence.[17] While Histadrut leaders remained certain that Arlozoroff's murder was a Revisionist plot, the Revisionists were equally sure that the trial was the product of a conspiracy between Mapai and the British police. Years later it was revealed that two Arabs had confessed to the murder but had been silenced by British authorities so as not to force the police to admit that they had falsely charged the Revisionist. In 1982 an official commission of inquiry was established to look into the matter; more important than its inconclusive results was its impact in underscoring the fact that memories and passions had not faltered much.

The "season," which occurred at the end of 1944 and beginning of 1945, amounted to cooperation by Jewish authorities with the British mandatory power in rounding up members of the Irgun and Lehi.[18] The Irgun Zva Leumi was the major nucleus of Herut; it was formed in 1937 after Jabotinsky negotiated a return to the Haganah command structure of dissidents who had formed Haganah B in 1931. These dissidents numbered 100 at the time of formation and 3,000 at the 1937 reunification. They were more militant than the Yishuv leadership and feared what they considered the pacifist policies of Histadrut leaders.

In 1940, after the Second World War had broken out, the Irgun was faced with the issue of cooperation with the British in fighting the war. Whereas the Yishuv adopted Ben-Gurion's formulation of fighting the war as if there were no White Paper (severely limiting Jewish immigration) and fighting the White Paper as if there were no war, Jabotinsky called for a truce with Britain, giving priority to waging war against Hitler. Abraham Stern rejected this path, and immediately after Jabotinsky's death in 1940, Stern took the majority of Irgun members with him in establishing Lehi (Lochamei Herut Israel). Stern's plan was to trade Europe's Jews for Lehi's support in defeating Britain and aiding the Germans to capture Palestine.

The Haganah, the military force of the organized Yishuv, had long operated an intelligence unit to follow the activities of other underground organizations, but rounding up and turning in fellow Jews to the hated British was an unusual act. The leadership's willingness to participate in this activity followed the assassination in Cairo of Lord Moyne, the British minister of state in the Middle East, by two Lehi agents. This high point of the campaign of terror against the British led Yishuv authorities to agree to cooperate with the British security forces in detaining Irgun and Lehi "freedom fighters," but this was often done in a clandestine manner in order to ease the troubled conscience of Jews turning in other Jews—and this at the height of the European nightmare. The "season" successfully dampened the activities of the nonestablishment underground, but it did not extinguish its fire. Its leader, Menachem Begin, successfully avoided capture, and young new enthusiasts volunteered, filling the ranks thinned by arrest.

Some six weeks after independence, less than a month after the establishment of the Israel Defense Force and a few days into the truce worked out by the United Nations, a third trauma poisoned relations between the nationalist right and the socialist left.[19] The *Altelena* was a ship procured by the Irgun to carry some 800 volunteers, 5,000 rifles, and 250 machine guns and ammunition. Although Irgunists claimed that the government knew about the shipment and that negotiations were under way for its distribution, Ben-Gurion did not disabuse his cabinet of the impression that the shipment was against the law and meant to arm the Irgun's men, thus defying the authority of the government. The ship was scuttled by army fire, resulting in the loss of the much-needed ammunition. After the public agitation died down, Ben-Gurion appeared to be the victor; he had upheld the rule of law and had crushed possible defiance of the primary rule of the modern state— that it is to have a monopoly on the use of violence. The Irgun disbanded, and many of its members reorganized as the Herut Party. The traditions, leadership, and values of the Irgun and Lehi were transferred to Herut, but the new organization clearly accepted the supremacy of governmental decisions.

The leaders' perceptions of one another and of the groups they led lingered for decades, creating fissures so deep that only time could heal them. This explains why Herut's achievement of legitimacy and eventual power was so long in coming: Ben-Gurion and Mapai understood that to deny legitimacy to another enhanced their own. The causes of the antagonisms have faded, but the mutual recriminations and passionate expressions of political views have been passed on to the next generation.

Menachem Begin was thirty years old when he became commander of the Irgun in 1943; five years later, he set up the Herut movement, in which was to be found many features of the Revisionists, the Irgun, and Lehi. Most obvious was the role of the leader. Begin was still "commander"; his former staff became his aides. He tended to surround himself with his "fighting family" (former members of the Irgun and Lehi), retaining the fiery rhetoric and tough posture that had characterized his underground life. His first years in Herut were as stormy as the Irgun days. Immediately after the sinking of the *Altelena* and a roundup of Irgun and Revisionist Party members, Begin declared that the State of Israel had become a totalitarian police state. During the debate over German reparations in 1952, he said that there should be no negotiations with Germany under any conditions; mobs influenced by Begin's stance attacked the Knesset, and the future of Israel's parliamentary life seemed imperiled. A less intense furor took place seven years later when the issue of the sale of Israeli arms to Germany came up.

Ben-Gurion declined to call Begin by name, referring to him in Knesset debates as the man seated next to Dr. Bader, but he labeled Begin a *fascist*—a particularly weighty word in Israel right after the Second World War. Political passion was never higher, nor was Ben-Gurion's popularity. The combination of the two forced Begin to bide his time, confining himself to mostly parliamentary efforts, attempting to provide the Israeli Knesset with a dynamic opposition; this he effectively achieved, especially on matters dealing with Israeli and Jewish honor and defense.

Begin removed himself as head of Herut after the party lost almost half its Knesset seats in the 1951 elections, but he soon returned to head the party with added gusto. In 1965, after the newly formed Gahal did less well than anticipated in the elections against the newly formed Mapai-Ahdut Haavoda Alignment headed by the lackluster Levi Eshkol, a challenge was mounted against Begin's leadership of Herut by a group led by Shmuel Tamir, an Irgun veteran and a prominent criminal lawyer. After a bitter fight, Tamir lost and was suspended for a year by a party court. Perhaps taking his cue from the "young Turks" in Mapai, Tamir split with Herut to form the Free Center.

Because of the party's relatively poor showing in the 1969 elections, Ezer Weizman then tried to wrest control from Begin, but he too was defeated by Begin's superior control of the party's institutions. Weizman went into political limbo, to return as architect of the Likud's electoral victory of 1977 and as minister of defense in Begin's cabinet. After Weizman resigned in 1980, arguing that the government was not pursuing the peace treaty with Egypt energetically enough, and even voting against the government on a no-confidence vote sponsored by Labor, he was expelled from Herut.[20] In 1984 he returned to head a list called Yahad, which won three seats; by 1988 Weizman and his group were full members of the Labor Party, and Weizman was seventh on the Labor list and running its election campaign. He promised to make Peres prime minister just as he had done for Begin eleven years earlier, but this time he was less successful. He became minister of science and development in the 1988 National Unity Government, and then was elected president of the country by the Knesset in 1993.

Begin retired from politics in 1983, soon after the abortive Lebanon war of 1982 and the death of his wife. Some speculated that the post-Begin period would introduce instability to Herut and the Likud, but in fact Shamir's "temporary" ascension to leadership turned out to be long-lived. Proving to be an accomplished political tactician, and despite tensions with younger leaders such as David Levy and Ariel Sharon, Shamir maintained power. This was especially impressive because it was the first time since 1940 that Herut had been led by anyone but Begin. Moreover, as leader of Herut and as prime minister, Shamir became the caretaker of Begin's Camp David agreement with Egypt and the United States, even though he had abstained on the Knesset vote and the man he appointed as foreign minister in 1988, Moshe Arens, had voted against it.

Shamir outlived the end of the National Unity Government and the "dirty trick" move by Shimon Peres to replace him as prime minister in 1990. Shamir led the country to the Madrid Peace Conference in 1991, but it was never clear how committed he was to his peace policies, since he continued the mass expansion of settlements in the territories and the payments to religious parties for their continued support of his government. He headed the Likud's list in the 1992 elections, opposed by Labor's Rabin, and saw the Likud fall from forty Knesset seats to thirty-two. He thereupon resigned as head of the party but retained his Knesset seat. In 1993, in an unprecedented vote among Likud members and not only among the activists or convention members, Binyamin Netanyahu was selected head of the Likud.

As Herut's electoral fortunes improved, the visibility of its leadership cadre increased. There were old guard leaders, especially Shamir, and those who rose to prominence when the Likud came to power in 1977, such as Arens. Then there were the sons of former leaders, such as Benny Begin and Dan Meridor; Sharon, the former general; and politicians with special representational qualities, especially Sephardim (David Levy, Moshe Katzav) and the young (Ron Milo, Netanyahu, and Ehud Olmart). In the 1994 municipal elections, Milo was elected mayor of Tel Aviv, and Olmart defeated Teddy Kolleck in the race for mayor of Jerusalem.

A serious rift occurred between Netanyahu and Levy, who had opposed him and lost, and over a purported videocassette of Netanyahu's extramarital behavior. Netanyahu accused Levy of being behind the exposure; in fact, no videocassette existed. The rift came to a head over the details of the upcoming Likud primaries: Levy wanted a large proportion of the 1996 Knesset list to be reserved for the party's districts, an arrangement that would enhance his power. Levy left the Likud and formed a new party called Gesher (Bridge), together with one ally, David Magen; both, however, continued to be members of the Likud's Knesset faction. This strange development came about because the law regulating political party financing from the public treasury required that at least a third of those Knesset members elected on a list would have to resign from the faction in order to have it recognized as a new faction. Since Levy was far from that number and the money would be lost to both the Likud and to the breakaway faction if they resigned from the Likud, Levy and Magen remained members of the Likud Knesset faction.

Levy announced that he would run for prime minister. Gesher was duly registered as a party and a list was selected. Finally, however, Ariel Sharon succeeded in convincing Levy to return to the Likud fold in order to avoid a first-round election for prime minister that would feature a united left headed by Peres against a divided right. Should Peres win the needed majority in such a contest, there would be no need for a runoff between Peres and Netanyahu. Levy acceded, in return for placing seven of Gesher's candidates among the Likud's top forty places, thus promising for his new party much better results than they were likely to have achieved by facing the electorate on their own. Raful Eitan's Tzomet

(Intersection) won the same terms that Gesher had been given, allowing for the emergence of Likud-Gesher-Tzomet in 1996.

Netanyahu's razor-edge victory over Peres was accompanied by a fragmented Knesset that was difficult to control, and then Netanyahu alienated many of his government colleagues and his coalition partners by his inconsistent policies and his personal style. A bevy of former Herut associates broke with him, including Benny Begin, Dan Meridor, Yitzhak Mordechai, and Roni Milo. Begin was to form a more extreme party on the right, while the other three were active in forming the Center Party before the 1999 elections. After the Likud's rule was swept away by Barak's victory over the isolated Netanyahu and after Netanyahu resigned as the head of the party, Sharon was selected as a temporary replacement to revitalize the party organization. Sharon retained the chair, however, winning both the 2001 and 2003 elections handily.

The 1979 peace treaty with Egypt had prompted the emergence of new political organizations to the right of Herut. The Tehiya (Rebirth) Party emerged when Herut movement leaders Geula Cohen and Moshe Shamir left the party in opposition to the treaty, negotiated by Begin, which mandated Israeli withdrawal from the Sinai. Tehiya was led by Yuval Neeman, a nuclear physicist and former president of Tel Aviv University. In 1984 Tehiya was joined by Tzomet, whose head, Raful Eitan, was a former chief of staff of the Israel Defense Forces. In that year, Tehiya was the third largest party, winning five Knesset seats. In 1988 Tehiya and Tzomet ran separately and won three and two seats, respectively, but in 1992 Tzomet, as a major benefactor of the Likud's loss of voters, took eight seats, while Tehiya failed to win the minimum number of votes to win representation. In 1996 Tzomet folded itself into the Likud.

Another ultranationalist party is Moledet (Homeland), formerly led by General Rehavam ("Ghandi") Zeevi (who was assassinated in 2001). Calling for the transfer of the Arabs from the territories to Arab countries, Moledet won two seats in its first attempt in 1988, three seats in 1992, and two seats in 1996. The idea of transfer was championed in the political discourse of Israeli politics by Rabbi Meir Kahane, but his list, Kach, was not allowed to run in the 1988 elections. The Central Elections Committee ruled, in a decision later upheld by the Supreme Court of Israel, that Kahane's party had disqualified itself from running in the elections by advocating an anti-Arab racist platform. Some of the votes that might have gone to Kach were undoubtedly won by Moledet, others by the Likud and religious parties.[21] Rabbi Kahane was assassinated in New York in 1990.

Herut's ideological plank on foreign policy was revised over the years in response to changing conditions. At first it championed Israel's claim over all of the territory of Palestine held during the period of the British Mandate and refused to recognize the 1949 borders as legitimate, arguing that this would prevent Israel from taking advantage of circumstances if war were forced upon it. When the Herut movement formed Gahal with the Liberals, no changes were needed; each party retained its own platform. Herut supported the idea of *shlamut haaretz* (an undivided Eretz Israel), and after the Six-Day War its platform stressed the importance of continued Jewish settlement in Judea, Samaria, Gaza, Sinai, and the Golan. Immediately after the 1967 war, however, Begin, along with the rest of the National Unity cabinet, agreed to return Sinai to the Egyptians as part of a peace treaty. The Arabs refused; a decade and a bloody war later, Sadat and Begin agreed to the same thing.

The Likud forcefully opposed the 1993 peace accords with the PLO, and its boisterous rallies during this period were part of the verbal violence that foreshadowed the assassination of Prime Minister Yitzhak Rabin in 1995. But when forced to write a plank for its 1996 platform, the party's tone changed: as prime minister, Netanyahu would abide by Israel's treaties, although his government would be more careful in ensuring that the other side was carrying them out fully; the PLO would have to be dealt with, but President Arafat would be shunned because of his terrorist past. Most of the Likud leadership went along with this moderation of tone and content; Benny Begin was a notable exception, opposing contact with the PLO under any circumstances. In 2002, against the wishes of Prime Minister Sharon, the Likud convention passed a resolution opposing the establishment of a Palestinian state, but Sharon, sensing that Likud voters were more moderate than his party's governing institutions, seemed prepared to ignore the decision.

A nationalist party, Herut's social and economic planks favored free enterprise, but not in a dogmatic sense; if government activity or intervention was needed to achieve national goals, this was ideologically permissible. The socialists and Mapai were anathema to Herut for historical, organizational, and ideological reasons. The Histadrut was perceived as a tool of the socialists to exploit the workers, and strikes were seen as a poison in the nation's system. After the General Zionists did so well in 1951, jumping to twenty seats from seven seats in 1949, Herut attempted to appeal to General Zionist voters by adopting a more liberal-bourgeois economic and social platform in 1955. While not a religious party, neither was Herut anticlerical, as the socialists were purported to be. The party's platform declared, as did the original statement of the New Zionist Organization set up by Jabotinsky in 1935, that the movement would "implant the eternal values of Israel's heritage in the life of the nation."

Liberals

The Liberal Party was the successor to the General Zionists, who represented the core of the World Zionist Organization; their goal was to remain politically united for the common purpose of achieving Zionist programs. In the 1920s the General Zionists split into two factions. Faction A was led by Chaim Weizman, then president of the WZO, and had a prolabor policy supportive of a conciliatory approach to the mandatory powers. Faction B, which was more bourgeois and middle-class, supported private enterprise in Eretz Israel and had a more activist policy against the British.

Faction A, bolstered by the German immigration of the 1930s, came to be called the Progressives; Faction B retained the name General Zionists. By 1961 the two factions merged and formed the Liberal Party, but the merger was short-lived. The two factions again split in 1965, this time over the issue of electoral cooperation with Herut.

The Progressives retained their gradualist ideology and favored cooperation with Labor, a position they regularly achieved over the years by participating in Labor governments (and even joining the Alignment in 1982). But the majority of the Liberal Party opted for the formation of the Gahal list, and the party split. The Liberals (former General Zionists) retained the name Liberal; the Progressives called themselves Independent Liberals, which seemed to refer less to their independence of thought or action and more to their independence from the General Zionists and Herut.

Clearly, parties such as these were at a disadvantage compared with the ambitious and well-organized parties of the left and the religious groups whose members were in networks that extended beyond the political dimension of life to encompass social, cultural, and often economic aspects as well. As their name proclaimed, the General Zionists were interested in the generalized goals of the movement and less so in the specifics of the project. They supported free enterprise and tended to disdain grassroots organizational work, believing that their enlightened ideas would carry the day.

The General Zionists and the Liberals tended to resemble middle-of-the-road European parties advocating limited government, a constitution, and free enterprise. They believed that if individuals were allowed to pursue their own goals, it would be to the advantage of the nation as a whole. Their prominent role in the WZO afforded them close ties and functional advantages with important organizations such as Hadassah, Maccabi, and WIZO; but the General Zionists never developed patterns of party control over these organizations as did the parties of the left and the religious parties over organizations within which they were dominant. The General Zionists did not identify with the class politics of the left stressed by Mapai; they perceived the importance of the economic and agricultural enterprises undertaken by the socialist parties of the Histadrut in national terms and not in sectoral or political party terms.

The Liberals in the Likud were always relegated to second place. Because no leader of national stature ever emerged from the party, its decision to accept Begin's leadership made political sense. The relations between Herut and the Liberals in the Likud were governed by rules set up over the years to divide power and jobs, by the practices that developed, and by compromise. The Liberal leader Simha Ehrlich was "kicked upstairs" from the job of minister of finance to the deputy premiership when the economic policies he introduced after the 1977 elections not only liberalized the economy but brought about an inflation rate of more than 130 percent a year; as he was the leader of the second major partner in the Likud, firing him outright would have been out of the question. Ehrlich's opposition to the appointment of Ariel Sharon as minister of defense, after Ezer Weizman resigned, prevented the appointment before the 1981 elections. Once the elections were out of the way, however, Begin could disregard Ehrlich's implicit threat of the Liberals rocking the Likud boat and appointed Sharon. The Likud council had decided that Begin would have the right to appoint ministers to his government, and so Ehrlich's and the Liberals' veto power were overcome formally. This was one more indication of the weak political role of the Liberal Party. In 1984 Herut leaders tried to reduce drastically Liberal representation in the Likud list; after a tense period of negotiation, they agreed to a moderate reduction of Liberal strength.

Before the 1988 elections, the Liberals formally merged with Herut, forming a party called the Likud; their leader, Yitzhak Modai, was third on the Likud list, and Moshe Nissim was in seventh place. Both of them had been ministers of finance in the 1984–1988 National Unity Government. While both were also ministers after the 1988 National Unity Government was formed, it was clear that the Liberals had lost their clout. Modai was made minister of economics, a largely planning function with no political punch, and Nissim was appointed minister without portfolio. Modai ran on a separate list in 1992 and failed to win representation. Before the 1996 elections Nissim resigned; two other Liberal leaders, Zalman Shuval and Gideon Pat, failed to win high places in the Likud primaries.

The Independent Liberals were once considered to be at the center of Israeli politics. After achieving a handful of votes for years, their fortunes were cruelly dashed when the Democratic Movement for Change (discussed later in this chapter) reduced their power to one Knesset seat in 1977; by 1981 even that had disappeared. Still, their economic and settlement organizations, especially Haoved Hatzioni, allowed them at least a formal existence. In 1984 they opted not to run independently and accepted a place on the Alignment's list. They accepted the third place in the centrist Shinui (Change) list for the 1988 elections; unfortunately for the Independent Liberals, Shinui won only two seats. By 1992, they were no longer partners in preelection negotiations.

Religious Parties

On the whole, religious groups came to terms with Zionism late, if at all. Although religious motifs, groups, and leaders were affiliated with Zionism from its inception, the most vociferous opposition to Zionism among Jews came from religious circles. It is therefore not without irony that these religious parties are growing, and are certainly the most stable organizationally, of the groups competing in Israeli politics.

All of the competing parties in Israeli politics are Orthodox Jewish parties. The uninitiated should be warned that we are discussing the distinctions among Orthodox, ultra-Orthodox, and ultra-ultra-Orthodox Judaism. Reform and Conservative Judaism are simply not in the picture, although both of these groups make efforts, especially through the courts, to win approved status.

Three topics are useful to differentiate among these Orthodox religious parties: (1) their willingness to cooperate in the Zionist enterprise;[22] (2) the representation of Sephardim in these parties, which were largely formed and run by Ashkenazim; and (3) the degree of militancy regarding the territories that each displays.

The original religious parties in Israel were the Mizrachi, Hapoel Hamizrachi, Agudat Israel (Aguda), and Poalei Agudat Israel (Poalei Aguda). The National Religious Party (NRP), made up of two major former parties, the Mizrachi and Hapoel Hamizrachi, was most willing to cooperate in the Zionist enterprise, as its name attests. Its cooperation with the secular Zionist parties in building the Jewish state has been complete, with its sons (and some daughters) serving in the armed forces, and the party itself joining in the "historical partnership" with Mapai and Labor in the formative years and then in the government coalition with the Likud. The members of NRP blend their religious fervor and Zionist zeal into a potent mix.

At a lower level of cooperation are the haredi parties of Aguda, Poalei Aguda, Shas, and Degel Hatorah (the Torah Flag). The word *haredi* connotes awe-inspired, fearful of God's majesty, in the same way that the Christian Quakers and the Shakers use the term. The haredim maintain separate organizational and social structures, although they agree to limited political participation. Their shared conviction is that Israel will be restored by a divine act and not by acts of man. Accordingly, their religious beliefs do not drive their political positions, making them endlessly flexible and often cooperative coalition partners, whichever larger party is in control.[23] They do not consider themselves Zionists and do not participate in Zionist institutions such as the WZO. Instead, they see their role in influencing the Israeli government as similar to their role of influencing the local government in Boston or Brooklyn, where some of them also have large numbers of adherents. To ensure their support, Israeli governments (led by either Labor or Likud) have allowed them unusual privileges, such as exempting their sons from army service while studying in yeshivas (daughters are completely exempt) and allowing them to maintain an "independent" school system partly funded by public moneys yet not controlled by the Ministry of Education.

Although the Aguda has participated in government coalitions, its participation has been restricted since 1952. Until 1977, Aguda leaders often cooperated with Alignment policies but refrained from assuming cabinet positions, and this pattern continued after the ascension of the Likud in 1977, with the Aguda formally agreeing to support the Begin government but not accepting a cabinet appointment. Aguda leaders were, however, awarded chairmanships of important Knesset committees. In the 1996 Netanyahu government, as in the 1988 National Unity Government, the Aguda was given responsibility for a ministry (Housing in 1996, Labor in 1988), but since it declined having a minister participate in cabinet meetings, the portfolio was formally held by the prime minister, and an Aguda deputy minister was appointed to handle the day-by-day operations of the ministry. It also held the crucial position of chair of the Knesset Finance Committee.

Religious separatists, including the Eda Haharidit and other extreme elements (some of whom are in the Aguda), pursue a policy of noncontact with Zionists, seeing in them a threat to religious purity. Neturai Karta, a small group of a few hundred families in Jerusalem and Bnei Brak (a religious suburb of Tel Aviv), refuses to recognize the legitimacy of the State of Israel to this day and accuses those who do so of blasphemous behavior. There have even been reports that members have conspired with elements in the Arab world to rid themselves and their Jerusalem of the Zionist oppressors.

Three religious lists won representation in 2003—Shas with eleven seats, United Torah Jewry (made up of Agudat Israel and Degel Hatorah) with six seats, and the National Religious Party with five seats; these twenty-two members represented 18 percent of Knesset seats. In 1999 these three parties had won twenty-seven seats—an unprecedented achievement. In 1996 the number was twenty-three, and before that, the highest number won by religious parties had been eighteen seats, which they had gained in four different elections (see table 8.1, pp. 234–235). The religious parties have adopted various forms of electoral cooperation in the past. In 1949 they all ran together as the United Religious Front, and in 1955 and 1973 Agudat Israel and Poalei Agudat Israel ran together on a joint list as the Torah Religious Front.

The 2003 display of strength by the religious parties continued the pattern begun in 1988, when non-Zionist religious parties won more seats than did the Zionist religious parties. Until 1988, the Zionist religious parties had bettered the non-Zionist religious parties by a ratio of 2 to 1; in 1988 the NRP—the only Zionist religious party to win representation in that year—won only five seats, while the three non-Zionist religious parties won thirteen. In 1996 the division was nine for the NRP and fourteen for the others (ten for Shas, and four for United Torah Jewry).

If there was ever an example of a political group whose power is greater than its strength in the country, the religious parties provide it. The third largest winners in Knesset elections after Labor and the Likud, religious parties have usually served as coalition partners with the biggest winner. To the big winner this makes good sense: it is better to pay the smaller price demanded by the third biggest winner than the higher price that the second biggest winner could demand. With the exception of a number of months in 1958–1959, a number of weeks in 1974, and a number of years in the 1990s, the largest of the Zionist religious parties, the NRP, has always been a coalition partner, whether that coalition was formed by Labor or by the Likud. In the 1984 and 1988 National Unity Governments, and in the 1996 Netanyahu government, most of the religious parties participated. Shas had spectacular years of coalition achievement prior to 2003, when the very secular Shinui refused to serve in a coalition with Shas and Sharon accepted that condition, thereby weakening Shas's ability to provide patronage and services.

The splits and divisions within the religious group indicate the issues it faces. One cleavage is ethnic, the other nationalist. In 1981 Tami, lead by Aharon Abu-Hatzeira, scion of an important Moroccan rabbinical family, split from the NRP over the issue of ethnic representation, winning three seats in 1981 and one seat in 1984.[24] By 1988, Abu-Hatzeira had been co-opted into the twelfth place on the Likud's list. The nationalist split was related to Gush Emunim, the organization supporting settlement in the territories. In 1981 and 1984, the NRP lost strength to nationalist lists such as Tehiya and Morasha. Morasha was set up by Rabbi Chaim Druckman, a former NRP Knesset member, and Hanan Porat, a former Tehiya Knesset member, both Gush Emunim leaders. When they failed to set up a joint list with the NRP in 1984, they ran with Poalei Agudat Israel and won two seats. By 1988, Porat had returned to the NRP; in 1996 he was sixth on the NRP list.

The passion for pioneering that had characterized the left in the first half of the twentieth century shifted to Gush Emunim after the Six Days' War. Gush Emunim sprang from the ranks of the NRP, its members bringing to the project of settlement and redeeming the land of Israel the same kind of youthful excitement, dedication, and self-sacrifice that early generations had identified with the kibbutz movements.[25] One clear indication of this passion is the size of the youth groups in the country. Labor-related youth groups were the largest by far in the pre-independence period and in the first decades of statehood. In 1996 the NRP's Bnei Akiva was the largest youth group, according to a survey by the Ministry of Education. Bnei Akiva registered 28 percent of youth group members, the Labor related group had 23 percent of the total, and the non-affiliated scouts accounted for 16 percent.

The eclipse of the labor movement even in this field is especially ironic since the kibbutz movements have continued to settle—both Labor-led and Likud-led governments supported settlement in many ways—but the public mind seemed to identify settlement with Gush Emunim. One reason was that Gush Emunim broke with past practice and settled in Arab-populated areas of the territories taken in the 1967 war. Another reason was that the Labor parties had settled so long ago and so successfully that their continued settlement was simply not news. A third reason was that the Labor-led governments tended not to publicize their efforts in this field because it could be antagonistic to its peace policies. Likud-led governments were not bashful about their efforts, but they had neither the personnel nor the organization to undertake tasks such as Labor did, so identifying themselves with Gush Emunim pioneers was a reasonable solution for them. The NRP benefited from this development; the Youth Faction and others strongly supported this behavior; still others, such as the religious kibbutz federation, were more cautious. Also, the shift of policy in the NRP to support of an activist settlement and foreign policy coincided with the structure of opinion and changing demography of the country. Gush Emunim, with the implicit and often explicit support of the NRP, could capitalize on the religious claim to the land of Israel, and the national and security importance of the territories, while using forms of settlement developed mostly by others in earlier times.

Another factor that weakened the NRP came from Meimad (Dimension). This group broke off in 1988 to present a more moderate platform regarding the territories than that of the NRP. Meimad won 15,000 votes in 1988, enough to drain off support from the NRP, but not enough to win representation in the Knesset. Meimad still existed in the 1990s but did not field a list.

In 2003, seventeen of the twenty-two seats of the religious group went to the haredi non-Zionist Shas and United Torah Jewry (Agudat Israel and Degel Hatorah). To understand the politics of these ultra-Orthodox parties, one must know something of the mindset of deeply religious people whose first loyalty is to their theology (not to the laws of any nation-state), who try to live religious lives in a secular country that is strongly nationalist. The ultimate authority for their political decisions (as well as religious decisions, of course) is the Council of Torah Sages. Some political parties have one council that is made up of party leaders, who make the important ideological and practical decisions for the party. In these ultra-Orthodox parties, however, the senior rabbis decide what is to be done, and a secondary group of politicians (many of whom are also rabbis) carry it out.

Ethnic tensions and personal rivalries are two other dimensions affecting the developments in these haredi parties. To understand the complicated story of these three parties, it is important to know that Agudat Israel is the oldest one among them. Traditionally led by Ashkenazi rabbis, the Aguda was surprised in 1984 when a group of Sephardi rabbis (headed by Rabbi Ovadia Yosef, former Sephardi chief rabbi) broke off from the Aguda and set up a list called Shas (Guardians of the Torah). Shas split off after the Aguda rabbis refused to place enough Sephardi candidates on the 1984 Aguda list.

In 1988 additional actors became involved: Chabad (an ultra-Orthodox group led by Rabbi Menachem Schneerson from Brooklyn, the Lubavitcher Rebbe) made its first appearance in Israeli electoral politics. Chabad had long been active in religious, educational, and social welfare work but had never before been active politically. Chabad's purpose was to bolster the Aguda's share of the vote by providing the Aguda with Chabad's experienced organizational cadres; the Lubavitcher Rebbe would then gain influence in the Israeli political system through the Aguda's Knesset delegation. But rivalry between Chabad and other groups, notably the one headed by Rabbi Eliezer Shach, an old and venerable rabbi from Bnei Brak and an old-time Aguda leader, split the ranks. The relations between Rabbi Shach and the Lubavitcher Rebbe (and their followers) had been tense for many years on theological as well as other grounds. For example, the followers of the Lubavitcher Rebbe were convinced that their rabbi (who had never set foot in Israel) was the messiah and should be recognized as such; Rabbi Shach and his entourage characterized this position as blasphemy. The competition between them was for political turf and, as this example shows, for otherworldly stakes as well.[26]

Rabbi Shach's relations with the Aguda became more tenuous over the years, and, in parallel fashion, his relations with Rabbi Ovadia Yosef and with the Shas Party improved. Before the 1988 elections, Rabbi Shach and his court set up the Degel Hatorah Party to appeal to his Ashkenazi supporters, but he continued as a spiritual leader for the mostly Sephardi Shas. Shas, while predominantly Sephardi, was not exclusively so. For example, Uri Zohar, a very popular comedian in his secular days, before he became an ultra-Orthodox rabbi, was an appealing Ashkenazi spokesman for Shas.

The competition between these parties was fierce, involving cajoling, threats, and charges of election fraud. In one of the highlights of the 1988 election campaign on television, for example, Shas presented the proceedings of a rabbinical court that absolved the oaths of potential voters who had promised to vote for the Aguda. The intense competition and the fervent organizational efforts paid off: Shas won six seats, the Aguda five, and Degel Hatorah two. After that election, the Knesset passed a law making it illegal in Israel to try to influence voters by promising to provide a blessing or by threatening to withhold a blessing or to curse someone for voting (or for not voting) for a specific party, just as it is a crime in Israel to buy votes with money or favors. In 1996, despite this legislation, the fierce competition for votes continued, and the use of amulets and promises of blessings for "correct" voting were reportedly widespread.

The religious parties in Israel today are the clearest cases of total inter-penetration of religious, social, cultural, political, and often economic life. Their members tend to live in religious districts, send their children to religious schools and youth groups, read religious party newspapers and journals, pray together, and vote together.[27] Their organizations provide housing, schools, and even food to the members. In the pre-state period, this interpenetration existed among socialist groups as well, and there are still strong remnants of it, especially in kibbutzim. One of the last sizable communities in which political affiliation is still so inter-twined with social life, however, is the religious neighborhoods. The religious parties' educational activities are much more clearly identified organizationally and in terms of social and political values with their parties than is the case in parallel secular situations; less so in the state-religious school system controlled by the NRP, more so in the "independent" school systems of the haredim, which receive public money without being supervised by the state. Religious youth groups are more successful in recruiting and conveying a clear social, cultural, and political message; the unifying effects of national sovereignty have only partially penetrated their value structure. Whereas statism (see chapter 11) has tended to blur differences among parties in the secular camp, especially in schools and youth groups, members of the religious parties have retained a central core of religious belief that differentiates them from the general population. This particularistic orientation is reinforced by the social, educational, and political structures that exist in their environment.

The existence of separate communities is reflected in the dress of the adherents. In modern Israel it is likely that a man whose head is covered (unless he is in the sun) is religious and supports a religious party. But the differentiation is likely to be even finer: a knitted *kipah* (skullcap) has become a symbol of the NRP and especially of its youth movement; a nonknitted *kipah,* by extension, is likely to indicate support for the reli-gious point of view but probably not for the NRP. Black wide-brimmed fedoras and suits generally identify non-Zionist Orthodox supporters—popularly known as "black hats" in Israel—while the more traditional garb (common to nobles in Poland in the Middle Ages) of long-flowing robes and fur hats identifies the dress of the Aguda and their supporters and separatists. Different subgroups also have different-colored socks, gowns, and other identifiable garments. This survey provides a rough measure only, presented here to point out how complete is the penetra-tion of the community into the lives of the adherents, even including the clothes they wear.

As one would expect, the competition among the religious parties is intense. Each group grades the others in terms of categories important to it. The Aguda argues that the NRP is not religious enough, finding fault with the NRP's record of compromise and cooperation with secular governments and policies. The NRP emphasizes its record of contribution to the Zionist cause and education, arguing that a separatist Aguda can have no impact on the larger society and its values. The rabbis of the Council of Torah Sages, the spiritual and ideological guides of the Aguda, Shas, and Degel Hatorah, took to task the chief rabbis of Israel, formerly associated with the NRP, for their interpretations and scholarly exegesis of the Halacha. This competition is made possible because both sides accept the same basic texts, the Bible and the rabbinical teachings, as holy and binding. All ideologies face the issue of interpreting dogma (witness Marxism), and all use the argument of ideological orthodoxy to bolster their interpretations.

Challenge from the Center

The Israeli political party system is firmly rooted in its historical origins. The public and the leaders of the Likud and Labor perceive themselves as representing the left and the right, respectively, even if the difference in policy is not always clear. Their ideas, vocabulary, organization, and imagery come from the first half of the twentieth century and not the second half. Their political world is one with a strong and leading socialist party and a beleaguered but persistent right. That the power roles have changed is beside the point; the rhetoric persists.

And so it came to pass that the three serious challenges to the established parties since independence came from within the left establishment and attempted to fill the void perceived to exist between the dominant Labor party and the revisionist right. The first challenge emerged in 1965 with Rafi, the second in 1977 with the Democratic Movement for Change (DMC),[28] and the third with Shinui in 2003. Rafi and the DMC appeared only once; Shinui in a different form had run in the past, but it had never had such a prominent leader as it did in this incarnation with Tomi Lapid.

In their single appearances, Rafi and the DMC were more successful than many long-established parties had been. Rafi won ten seats, the DMC fifteen; Shinui in 2003 also won fifteen seats. Each party consciously attempted to fill the political and ideological middle ground between what they saw as a decaying Labor Party and an irresponsible and out-of-touch Likud. Each projected the image of a centrist party.

Both Labor and Likud having become amalgamations of smaller, more ideologically oriented parties, often with muted or scrambled ideologies, the insertion of a center party into the formulation allowed the larger parties to present themselves as left or right. The center parties perceived themselves as parties of the future, rejecting both Labor and Likud, which they considered parties of the past. Rafi and the DMC took their major leadership and electoral strength from the Alignment camp, returning most of these resources to Labor after each aborted experience ended.

But there the similarities end. Rafi split from Mapai, and with the exception of Ben-Gurion and the renegade La'am group, returned to it. As time passed, former Rafi leaders played a more and more important role in the Labor Party and in the country. Shimon Peres was to become prime minister; and both Moshe Dayan and Peres were to serve as defense ministers—roles previously reserved for the Mapai leadership. Yitzhak Navon and Chaim Herzog were to serve as president of the country. Ben-Gurion's bright "young Turks," impatient in their youth with their likely rates of ascent up the ladder of political power in Mapai, achieved positions of importance in Labor despite their disloyalty to Mapai. This was all the more likely to happen because of the lack of alternative leadership in Mapai itself.

If the Rafi challenge came from the heart of the party system, the DMC challenge came from its periphery. The existing parties could ultimately ignore the challengers because the threat could not be sustained over time. Their leadership was ad hoc, without the bonds of mutual respect and understanding necessary for sustained political action. Rafi returned to the fold; the DMC disintegrated. Neither was characterized by effective organization at the grassroots. Neither was especially effective among the lower class, the workers, or the Sephardim (groups that often overlap). The appeal for good government and for "throwing the rascals out" worked in certain middle-class and professional groups, but it could not compete in 1965 with the organization of Mapai, nor in 1977 with the shift to the Likud among many Sephardi voters.

The twelve years between the Rafi and DMC challenges to the prominent parties saw two important wars. In both, Israel was victorious militarily, but in the second the country suffered terrible political and psychological blows that shook national self-confidence. The Rafi campaign was a direct challenge to the leadership of Mapai, and it hurried the process of party amalgamation by bringing about the Mapai alignment with Ahdut Haavoda and, in reaction, the Herut bloc with the Liberal Party. Rafi featured a young generation of political leaders straining to assume major roles of power sponsored by a charismatic political patron (Ben-Gurion) who felt wronged by the party he had set up. The generational effect was central to its appeal for efficiency and modernity, and in the face of a ruling power that spawned bureaucracy and was perceived to equate the good of the party with the good of the nation.

The DMC also had a reformist air about it, but the conditions that led to its creation were dramatic and troubling. The 1973 election took place weeks after the Yom Kippur War, and the lists submitted before the war were still in effect. The 1977 elections, then, were the first elections at which the terrible frustrations of the war and its aftermath could be expressed. The protest groups that had grown in strength and volubility after the war had largely disappeared (except for the original Shinui). The Labor Party had also witnessed cases of corruption by key officials and even the suicide of a minister, Avraham Ofer, who evidently feared that he was being investigated. The unrest within the Labor Party was at its height, and many leaders felt that the organization was too brittle to change in any meaningful way.

The differences notwithstanding, the common plank in the Rafi and DMC platforms was electoral reform. The Israeli penchant for seeing cultural and political problems in procedural terms—change the method and you change the system—was again expressing itself. Neither Rafi nor the DMC was successful in bringing about this change, although the electoral achievements of both were impressive.

The DMC leadership disintegrated along with the movement during the tenure of the Ninth Knesset, between 1977 and 1981. Never an integrated leadership group to begin with, it attempted to set up a party with democratic structures, and this presaged its downfall. The three major components of the DMC were the Democratic Movement, led by Yigael Yadin, former chief of staff of the IDF and a renowned archeologist; Shinui, headed by Amnon Rubinstein, who had been dean of the law school at Tel Aviv University and was a prominent newspaper and television personality; and part of the Free Center, led out of Herut by Shmuel Tamir. Preparations for the organization of the movement were rushed, partially because Prime Minister Rabin surprised the country by having elections in May rather than in the fall. The DMC decided on an open primary for determining its Knesset list, and for the first time in Israeli political history, some 30,000 citizens participated in setting up a Knesset list. Allegations of noncollegial behavior, heard even before the results were counted, stemmed from practices of recruiting members and arranging deals to vote for (or not vote for) certain candidates. But the enthusiasm of the volunteers and the vocal public support pushed these concerns to the background as the excitement of a new, reformist party prepared for election day. The DMC determined that of the conditions for its participation in the government, most of them procedural and constitutional, the most important were an immediate revision of the electoral law and a call for new elections.

After the elections, however, it turned out that Begin could form a coalition without the DMC, and he did so, relying on the coalition-wise NRP and Aguda parties. Realizing that they did not hold the balance of power, many DMC leaders pressed for participation in the coalition anyway, feeling that their constituents expected action and not loyal opposition. The call to join the Likud-NRP-Aguda coalition split the party, and Shinui withdrew. Some DMC leaders attempted to curb the excesses of Likud policy, especially regarding further settlement in the territories during the negotiations with the Egyptians and the Americans after Camp David, but on the whole their role was marginal. By the end of the term, Yadin returned to the Hebrew University and his archeology, Tamir tried unsuccessfully (despite Begin's acceptance but lukewarm support) to return to Herut, and Minister of Welfare Israel Katz joined Dayan's largely unsuccessful (two seats) Telem list in the 1981 elections. Thus ended one of the most promising, yet disappointing, chapters in Israeli politics for those who wanted to see new blood and new ideas reinvigorate the business-as-usual atmosphere of intrigue and personality groupings.

Shinui persisted and won two seats both in the 1981 and 1988 elections and three in 1984, a quiet echo of the clarion call for change heard in 1977. In 1992 and 1996 the original Shinui was the smallest partner in the newly formed, left-wing Meretz. However, when the majority of Shinui decided to merge with Meretz in the early 1990s, a tiny splinter group led by Avraham Poraz balked. Poraz retained the name and the formal organization of Shinui and continued to run. In 1999 his group won six seats, and in 2003 the party hit it big, expanding to two and a half its size by winning fifteen seats.

With both Rafi and the DMC, we can detect a reluctance on the part of the electorate to support the challenging party. We can see this by comparing the parties' results in Knesset and Histadrut elections. The two parties ran in both elections, and in both cases they did relatively better in the first of the two elections. In 1965 the Histadrut elections were held before the Knesset elections; Rafi won 12 percent of the votes of the Histadrut members and 7.9 percent of the votes to the Knesset. This was surprising, since a new, young party should have been especially attractive to the emerging professional middle class, many of whose members were likely not to be Histadrut members. Making some liberal estimates, we may conclude that Rafi barely held its own between the Histadrut elections and the Knesset elections. About two-thirds of Israelis are members of the Histadrut, and Rafi's 80,000 votes in the Histadrut elections are almost two-thirds of the 118,500 votes it won in the Knesset elections. In other words, Rafi was unable to pick up a disproportionate share of the non-Histadrut voters or, alternatively, was unable to keep the loyalty of those who voted for it in the Histadrut elections till the time of the Knesset elections. Mapai's political machine worked overtime in 1965 to try to overcome the appeal of Ben-Gurion and his Rafi list, and, judging from these figures, the machine was at least partially successful.

The DMC case in 1977 reiterates some of these points. In the Knesset election, the DMC won more than 200,000 votes, or 12 percent of the total. In the Histadrut elections six weeks later, it received only 8.1 percent, or about 75,000 votes. That is less than 40 percent of the votes it had won at the Knesset election. We can again use the alternative explanations proposed in the case of Rafi—that the DMC was unsuccessful in picking up an unusually large share of Histadrut members; or that the Alignment was successful in returning voters to its fold by the second vote. Both explanations are partially true. Parties of the center that emerged from the Alignment were not able to attract masses of Histadrut members' votes. But the homing mechanism that had worked in favor of the Alignment when faced with this kind of challenge seemed to malfunction after the Histadrut was weakened by the passage of the National Health Insurance Act (see discussion in chapter 10). When many ex-Labor voters voted for Shinui in 2003, it was less than clear that they would ever vote again for the Labor Party.

The party of Shinui led by Poraz, which had not joined Meretz, enjoyed an astonishing victory in 2003, winning fifteen Knesset seats by running on a centrist, middle-class, antiharedi platform. Tomi Lapid, a prominent journalist and television personality, joined the Shinui leadership as head and became minister of justice in the coalition formed by Sharon after the elections. Shinui was successful in preventing Shas from joining the coalition, thereby depriving Shas of the government jobs and easy access to funds that the party had enjoyed for years.

Arab Parties

Three Arab lists won representation in the 2003 elections, totaling eight Knesset seats. They won about 6 percent of the Knesset even though Arabs make up about 12 percent of the electorate. Some Arab voters choose Zionist parties, and many do not vote, but the Arab vote has increasingly gone to these Arab parties, and less to Zionist ones. In 1996, 77 percent of Arabs participated in the elections and about 70 percent of them voted for Arab parties. Arab parties have never been included in government coalitions, and no Arab has ever served as a cabinet minister. While Arab parties helped block the formation of a right-wing government after the 1992 elections, thus allowing Labor to pursue the peace accord with the PLO, they were not officially members of the government. Arabs have served as deputy ministers, but these Knesset members were from Zionist parties.

In the early years of statehood, Arab voters were afforded symbolic representation by having delegates in the Knesset in lists sponsored by Mapai, the dominant party, and most Arab voters supported Zionist parties.

Arab leaders of a nationalist bent found an outlet for their activities in Maki, the Israel Communist Party, which was dominated by Jews.[29] Rakah, the New Communist List, which split from Maki in 1965, was more clearly anti-Zionist and non-Jewish, calling for recognition of Israeli Arabs as a national minority. In 1977 Rakah merged with the Jewish Black Panthers headed by Charlie Biton, to form Hadash (the Hebrew acronym for the Democratic Front for Peace and Equality). Biton left the party in 1990, but Hadash retained its place as one of the largest parties among Arab voters, winning three seats in the 2003 elections.

Balad (Sons of the Country Movement) provided a clear voice of Arab nationalist expression. Led by the fiery Azmi Bishara, it split from Hadash in 1999. In 2003 it won three seats.

By 1984, the Progressive List for Peace emerged, a nationalist Arab group that drew most of its votes from Arabs. The legality of the party was challenged before the 1984 and 1988 elections on the grounds that the party opposed the existence of the State of Israel, but the Supreme Court denied the petitions.

A more moderate Arab position was advanced by the United Arab list, headed by Abd Daroushe. This party's platform is more moderate than Hadash's, calling for influence and not only protest. Daroushe had been a member of Knesset on the Labor list but resigned from Labor soon after the onset of the intifada (Arab uprising) in 1987. In 2003 the United

Arab list won two seats, down from the five seats it had won in 1999 when the United Arab list led by Daroushe agreed to participate in a joint electoral list with Islamic groups.

Other Parties

The parties that once made up what are now Likud and Labor, plus the religious parties, explain most of the action of Israeli politics. Sometimes the support of small independent parties became crucial to the system because of their contribution to the stability of the government, but this will be less likely to happen in the future since the minimum vote share needed for representation has risen to 2 percent, meaning that the smallest delegation elected in the future will have at least three members. Until 1992, the minimum was 1 percent, and between 1992 and 2003 it was 1.5 percent.

Successful ethnic lists are rare. While all parties want Sephardim and Ashkenazim on their lists for their electoral potential, ethnic groups in Israel have rarely been successful in winning Knesset seats on their own. There was a Sephardi list in 1949 that won Knesset representation *before* the massive influx of Sephardi voters in the early 1950s, and Abu-Hatzeira's Tami, which won three seats in 1981 and then joined the Begin coalition. The Progressives/Independent Liberal Party had large measures of support in the 1950s from German immigrants and was largely dominated by them, unlike almost all the other parties (even the Arab-based communist Rakah Party), which were dominated by East European Jewish political elites.

In 1996 two exceptions to this rule expressed the group consciousness of Jews of North African and Soviet Union backgrounds, in Shas and Israel b'Aliyah, respectively. Shas had been growing in its ultra-Orthodox environment as a Sephardi version; it reached ten seats in 1996, making it the third largest delegation in the Knesset. There was a Russian immigrant list in 1992 that did very poorly, but in 1996 Natan Sharansky's Israel b'Aliyah list won seven seats.

Many of the successful small parties were headed by leaders who had once belonged to bigger parties but who broke off and ran in elections on their own. Shulamit Aloni was elected to the Knesset on the Alignment list in 1969 but antagonized the party leadership by her outspoken stands in party and Knesset debates. It was clear that she would be relegated to a low position on the 1973 list, making her reelection very doubtful. Before the 1973 election (and war), she presented a list along with a women's group and a group advocating electoral reform; her Citizen Rights Movement (CRM) list won three Knesset seats with support from voters who wanted to punish the Alignment for its mishandling of the opening phases of the war but who were not willing to vote for the Likud. In 1974 her three seats became crucial in Rabin's attempt to form a government without the National Religious Party, and the CRM was in the government until the NRP joined it, at which time the CRM withdrew. In 1988 the CRM, still headed by Aloni, won five seats, and it became one of the mainstays of Meretz in 1992 and 1996.

Aharon Abu-Hatzeira's Tami Party found itself in a similar position in 1981. The list was set up after the leader withdrew from the NRP a short time before the deadline for submitting lists to the Central Elections Committee. Abu-Hatzeira was annoyed at the lack of support he had received from the NRP leadership during his trial on charges of accepting bribes and because of the lack of representation in the NRP of Sephardi Jews. (In the 1981 trial he was acquitted because of insufficient proof; in a different trial involving misuse of public funds, he was found guilty and sentenced to serve a three-month prison term.) The three votes Tami won were instrumental for Menachem Begin in setting up his sixty-one-vote coalition. In 1988 Abu-Hatzeira's Tami ran as part of the Likud list.

Moshe Dayan headed Telem in 1981. In 1984 there were four examples: Ezer Weizman's Yahad; a list headed by a former Likud finance minister, Yigael Horowitz; one headed by former Labor Party secretary-general, Lyova Eliav; and another headed by Likud minister and former Dayan running mate, Mordechai Ben-Porat. It is not clear from the 1984 experience if running alone was good electoral strategy then, as the first two won representation while the second two did not. By 1988, three of these leaders were elected on major lists, Weizman and Eliav with Labor, and Horowitz with the Likud. By 1992, this practice of running alone decreased, at least in part because the minimum percentage needed for representation had increased to 1.5 percent.

Barring a role in coalition politics, small parties lend local color (and at times comic relief) to Knesset deliberations, but their political role is insignificant. Individual party members may play an important educational or moral role, and the work of these individual members may be important on Knesset committees, but since we are talking about political arrangements in which votes count, the small party is almost always at a disadvantage. Examples of colorful Knesset members whose presence enhanced the visibility of the Knesset were Uri Avneri, editor of *Haolam*

Haze and head of a list by the same name; Meir Pail, who represented the New Left and Shelli; and self-proclaimed representatives of lower-class Sephardim, such as Charlie Biton of Rakah. Rabbi Meir Kahane's rabid anti-Arab positions added a tense dimension to Israeli parliamentary life until his party was disallowed before the 1988 elections.

While Israel's electoral system no longer encourages very small parties, its political and cultural traditions do not prevent them from having a role in governing. They are given a platform for their ideas in the Knesset—if they know how to use it—and there is no constitutional barrier to a small party's using this platform as a springboard to grow into a major party. While this has not yet happened, it could.

6 PARTY ORGANIZATION

THE PARTY IS the focus for politicians ambitious to run the country or at least to be on the fringes of power. It is the forum where ideological issues are raised, if not ultimately and formally decided. It is where the rules are drawn under which a candidate may have a good chance of being elected to the Knesset, and Knesset membership is generally considered the natural reservoir of those with increased probabilities of attaining significant levels of power. Most crucially, the political party is the prime agent in selecting the person who will be the candidate for prime minister.

A political party is a group organized for the purpose of achieving power and holding office within a political system. This distinguishes it from a pressure group, which is intent on influencing policy on a certain issue. Israeli politics can be thought of on three levels: *electoral politics*, *coalition politics*, and *bureaucratic politics*; all three levels are associated with the political party. The electoral list was historically composed by the party, and lately the major parties have held primaries in which party members vote to form the list. Voters perceive elections as a contest among parties and the leaders of parties. Coalition decisions stem from the strength the parties have won at the polls and the decisions of party leaders. The efforts of the politician to achieve advantage in his or her organization by increasing influence and concentrating resources is a basic characteristic of bureaucratic politics, and a major locus of this behavior is the political party.

Political parties fill many functions: They set the political agenda; they select candidates and choose leaders; they contribute to the process of political socialization of the electorate by transmitting political values and information to voters; they aggregate interests, form and sustain government coalitions, and play a role in social integration.[1] They may also serve as a unifying force in the divisive Israeli political system, for while the electoral campaign is usually intense and marked by stinging attacks, the democratic contest among parties has generally been conducted within the rules, although the system was sorely tested by the assassination of Yitzhak Rabin in 1995. This controlled competition tends to bridle antagonism and stresses shared goals and ideals as much as it highlights differences among the parties.

Forms of Party Organization

As power shifts in a society, so organization of the political party changes. In a society run by the nobility and clergy, politics is confined to the shifting coalitions in the king's court. When elections determine the division of power, it becomes politically advantageous to organize the electorate better than your opponents do. When the important resources are controlled by the state, it is advantageous to coalesce with opponents to assure a steady flow of money.

Concepts such as the *mass party*, the *cadre party*, the *devotee party*, the *catch-all party*, and the *cartel party* provide analytical tools to make sense of the Israeli political scene. There is no ideal form of party organization, nor are forms of organization static. Forms used by successful parties are often mimicked by other parties. Party organization adapts to meet existing conditions. Organization reflects interests, needs, and motivations, but it also generates all of these—and in so doing, party organization itself changes.

At any given moment many organizational forms of political parties may coexist, but a smaller number will be dominant. Different organizational structures correspond to specific historical periods. The cadre party flourished in a time of limited suffrage when the leadership was made up of notables and the appeal was to the middle and upper classes. The mass party was introduced by the socialists between 1890 and 1900; shortly thereafter, the fascists and communists introduced the devotee party. The catch-all party was a post–World War II development, and the cartel party appeared after 1970.

The mass party was the most successful form in Israeli history, spawning the parties that reigned between the 1930s and the 1970s. Adopted by parties of the left, both secular and religious, characteristic forms of mass parties spread out among other parties that attempted to imitate the success of the winners. The basic organizational unit of the mass party is the branch, and the working class is the major focus of organizational efforts. Organization must be conceived in a broad sense, for not only the attainment of office is at stake, but also the necessity of transforming society and the minds and lives of the workers organized in the parties.

The mass party generally has a socialist orientation, one in which centralization and discipline are strong. Properly motivated individuals do not need explicit instructions about how to act in their jobs or their public lives. The good of the party incorporates notions of the good of the state and individual good as well. Leadership tends to be oligarchical; elites of mass parties are developed by the parties themselves. This is perhaps one of the few instances in history in which political power can be obtained through organizational skill alone, rather than in conjunction with military, commercial, or ecclesiastical skill or office.

Membership in a mass party is very important, for the party not only needs sources of financial support but also must promote class consciousness among the membership. A very large number of members is desired, and a high degree of enthusiasm is expected of the membership. Doctrine is important in a mass party to keep enthusiasm high, to stir class consciousness, and to suggest that the political and social payoffs for the party's strivings are attainable in the near future.

The proliferation of party-related bureaucracies in Israel followed neatly from the conception of the organization of a mass party and from the special conditions that existed in the country in its early years. Not only was there a scarcity of social services, but the country lacked the basic economic infrastructure of roads, docks, and energy that are a prerequisite for economic growth and development. In the case of the Yishuv, the situation was basically unique because the political elite preceded the bulk of the population in arriving in the country and making plans for its future. Political organizations, then, provided some services and much ideological instruction, as they did in many European parties; in addition, the socialist parties of the Yishuv were key agents of socialization as new waves of immigrants arrived in the country. The immigrants were dependent on these parties, which absorbed them not only as party members benefiting by their party's activities but also as immigrants grateful to the absorbing authorities.

The development of parties of social integration stemmed from ideological and organizational needs. Peter Medding described the reality well when he wrote,

> ... the activities in the party branch embraced much of the member's social life and were his major source of information and guidance in political and social affairs. His employment, friendships, cultural interests and leisure hours were all deeply influenced by his party membership focused on the local branch. Attempts were also made to encourage the member to live in politically homogeneous Histadrut housing developments. In addition, he read the Histadrut newspaper, *Davar*, which because of Mapai's control of that body, was in reality a Mapai paper, and subscribed also to one of the party journals, such as *Hapoel Hatzair*. A Mapai member could, if he so desired, lead his life in a completely party circumscribed environment, hardly coming into major political contact with outsiders, and barely subject to competing political influences or conflicting sources of information.[2]

It was inevitable that the large scale of membership-oriented activity should lead to drives for an expanded budget, larger membership, and ever-increasing bureaucracies. Larger bureaucracies also meant more political control, because more people were dependent on party activities for a livelihood, and these people could easily be mobilized when demonstrations or elections took place. Larger bureaucracies also meant more jobs in the cities for an immigrant population that was on the whole of urban origin and was not anxious to fulfill the ideological imperative of agricultural settlement. And so the clerks, bureaucrats, and apparatus members involved in the delivery of health services, culture, economic activities, and education grew in number as the parties grew in power and control. As the bureaucracies expanded, more programs were sought, and the role of the bureaucracies and their leaders in the party strengthened.

The devotee party structure is also evident in certain communist, fascist, and religious party organizations in Israel. There is a clear justification in grouping these forms of party organizations together, for, despite their ideological differences, there is a basic similarity in the kinds of followers these parties attract: individuals capable of fanatical devotion to the party, to the cause the party supports, and to the dictates of the party. There must be a basic acceptance of the notion that, whatever the behavior, the party is working for the good of the class or the cause; blind adherence to the leadership is expected. While communists may be considered on the extreme left of the social and economic continua and fascists on the extreme right—with religious fundamentalists on a different continuum altogether—there is a sense in which all the adherents of these parties are very much alike. In figurative terms, if the continuum were bent and the extremes joined to form a circle, it would be clear that in psychological terms the values and attitudes of communists and fascists (and fundamentalists) tend to be authoritarian, antiliberal and close-minded, unwilling and unable to put up with the frustrations and compromises necessary in a democratic form of government.

Perhaps the greatest similarity is in the extreme authoritarian structure of leadership within these party forms. Whether by the Council of Rabbinical Sages of Orthodox fundamentalist parties, or by the communist politburo, or by the fascist supreme leader, decisions are made at the top and obedience is expected from the members. Sanctions may be positive or negative, and they may include promises of blessings, jobs, or contracts, or threats of curses, expulsion, or worse, depending on the organization and its ideology. What is similar is that leadership is developed by the party, and fundamental obstacles to alternation in leadership are built into organizational structures; stable, if not always inspiring, leadership tends to emerge. Stability lasts as long as the leader lasts. After that, the crisis of succession is often severe.

Characteristic elements of the devotee party were evident in the Israel Communist Party and Mapam—especially the democratic centralism in the former and the ideological collectivism in the latter—in that party members were required to accept the decisions of the party's decision-making bodies as ideologically binding. Debates and division of opinion are appropriate only until the party's authoritative bodies have ruled; after that, the membership must acquiesce in the decisions adopted.

Elements of devotee organization were also evident in the Revisionist movement and its successors. Jabotinsky was given absolute power by a referendum of the membership in 1933, while the leaders Ahimeir and Yevin openly advocated a totalitarian party led by a dictator.[3] The underground military organizations of the Irgun and Lehi continued this tradition, which also answered the needs of a secretive fighting unit. The values of discipline and obedience were exalted, and the use of ceremony and pomp was familiar to those who followed developments on the continent of Europe during the 1930s. Begin was called the "commander" by members of the "fighting family" who followed him from the Irgun to Herut. When he arrived at a Tel Aviv outdoor election rally in the early 1950s, flanked by uniformed motorcycle guards, the imagery for many was indelibly imprinted.

The major organizational difference between the various forms outlined here has to do with the basic units adopted by each party. For the communists it is the cell—a secretive, small group of party members organized at the place of work. This location of organization was an important innovation of Lenin, emphasizing the Marxist analysis of the importance of economic factors in the life of the individual and the state. The cell can fill functions of encouragement, disruption, intelligence, or dissemination of ideas, all according to the needs of the moment. The branch of the mass party is connected with an individual's place of residence, thus making party activity an after-work enterprise; the branch therefore concentrates on providing individual services as well as cultural, educational, and instructional activities because members lack a common workplace. The branches of mass-membership Israeli parties, especially in the heyday of party activity, filled all these functions and were augmented by the Histadrut with a complementary organization of the workers at the place of employment, where the political and occupational work of the parties could be pursued. The militia was the form developed by fascist parties as the unit of organization. Recruiting mainly from middle and lower-middle classes (as opposed to the working-class appeal of the socialists and communists), the fascists used the militia with its overtones of army discipline and patriotic symbolism to increase levels of allegiance of members.

The emergence of catch-all parties occurred in the 1960s and 1970s, when various parties' leaders discovered a capacity to appeal to the electorate at large and the mass parties weakened as the mass media developed, as the children of the immigrant generation came of age, and as social services were transferred from party-related organizations to the state.[4] Voters were beginning to behave more like consumers than active participants, and this new model of party was sometimes incorrectly identified as part of a process of Americanization of Israeli politics. Elections were seen to revolve around the choice of leaders rather than the choice of policies or platforms, especially in the 1980s, while the formation of those policies became the prerogative of the party leadership rather than of the party membership. Popular control and accountability were weakened as the public seemed to judge politicians prospectively rather than retrospectively, in terms of promises rather than record, in terms of what they would do in the future rather than in terms of what they had done in the past.[5] The persistence of National Unity Governments in the 1980s also contributed to this pattern. Parties were not over, nor were they in decline, but they were changing.

Israel's abortive affair with the direct election of the prime minister and the simultaneous election of the Knesset using proportional representation was an expression of a cadre party mentality superimposed on a mass party structure. When it was adopted in the early 1990s, the mass party in Israel had already crumbled and many were anxious to replace the old system. But the inherent contradictions in the new system threatened the parties to the core, and so the remnants of the mass parties coalesced in 2003 to repeal the change.

The cadre party model presupposes that the elected notables can identify and pursue the national interest, while the model of the mass party was one of competing visions of appropriate social policy. Where the cadre party relied on the quality of supporters, the mass party relied on the quantity of supporters. The mass party became a victim of its own success as the state began to provide on a universal basis the welfare and educational services that had been the responsibility of the party. The improvement of social conditions increased social and electoral mobility. The catch-all party recruited members on the basis of policy agreement rather than social identity. Parties began making universal appeals directly to voters rather than communicating principally to and through their core supporters, further weakening the ties between particular parties and particular segments of society. The party began to act as a broker between the electorate and organized interests, rather than in its traditional role of organizing and then representing interests.

The capacity of a party to perform the brokerage function depends not only on its ability to appeal to the electorate, but also on its ability to manipulate the state.[6] A party that can use the state in the interests of its clients can also use it in its own interests. In their role of law-makers it was "natural" for party leaders to turn to the state to provide and regulate financial support for political parties, and to acquire easy access to the electronic media, controlled by the state, to pursue their goals. The introduction of party financing in 1969 and the generous amount of free television and radio time provided during election campaigns in the Israeli case, fit this model perfectly. In a sense, the state is invaded by the parties; the state rules are determined by the parties in concert, providing resources to existing parties to ensure their own survival and aiding them in resisting challenges from newly mobilized alternatives. The state becomes an institutionalized structure of support for sustaining insiders while excluding outsiders. The parties become absorbed by the state rather than acting as brokers between the state and other groups. No longer trustees (cadre party), delegates (mass party), or even entrepreneurs (catch-all party), party leaders become functionaries of semi-state agencies. In this sense a cartel emerges, in which all the existing parties share in resources and in which all survive.

Likud and Labor were good examples of cartel parties that relied on government support to persist. They still had branches and placed a premium on membership, but these were holdovers from mass party forms, occasionally important resources in intraparty fights, but no longer vital for the survival of the party organization. This explains how leaders of such parties could even consider "open primaries" in which any citizen, whether a member of the party or not, could participate in choosing the party's candidates for office. The NRP also retained the forms and functions of a mass party while enjoying the party-funding legislation passed by the other cartel parties. The haredi parties were closest to cadre parties, with their established rabbinical leadership, and the total unimportance of membership and party branches. They flourished by providing their supporters with access to government money and ideological clarity.

Membership

The historical development of political party organization in Israel featured a tendency toward mass-membership parties with oligarchical tendencies. The tone was set by the parties of the left, both secular and religious, and the other parties followed. We might have expected that a bourgeois party with centrist ideological inclinations, such as the Liberal Party (General Zionists), would have organized differently, but at least at the formal level, many characteristics that occurred in the more successful parties of the left were copied by the Liberals. There is obviously a propensity in political life to mimic success, and this may explain why, at least on paper, most parties in Israel seem to resemble one another.

Today the organizational structures of most Israeli parties are similar, although there have been historical differences of emphasis depending on the type of party. Take membership, for example. While formally all Israeli parties wanted members, this aspect was more important in parties whose ideologies demanded political and educational work in the electorate, whose program called for party activities that demanded budgets and bureaucratic organizations and for outlays of funds otherwise unattainable. Obviously, these characteristics better corresponded to socialist parties than to the General Zionists, especially during the period before the state was founded, for then much of the activity was based on party-related organizations, especially the Histadrut (to which the General Zionists did not belong).

In the pre-state period, membership was significant for a number of reasons. First, it was necessary to raise money, and a steady stream of funds flowing in from the payment of dues was an organizational innovation of extreme importance in the history of political parties. But it was predicated on the assumption that parties did something, that they provided services. All Zionist parties engaged in fund-raising activities abroad, and none of them relied exclusively on membership in Eretz Israel to fund their activities. But the General Zionists and Revisionists had two advantages: (1) the level of their activity in Eretz Israel was much lower than that of the other parties, and (2) the extent of their success at fund-raising was higher abroad than it was in the Yishuv. For the socialist mass-membership parties, dues from members in Eretz Israel were relatively more important.

Second, parties provided important services that were available only to members. The polity of the Yishuv was a voluntary structure, and few services were available on a universalistic basis because no central authority existed. The party (often through the Histadrut) could provide housing, employment, and health, cultural, and educational services. Being a member of the "right" party could enhance the probability of receiving these services.

Third, membership was important because it was believed that in the political struggle each additional member raised the likelihood of success. Membership was not conceived of as a passive role entered into only to receive material benefit but as an indication of agreement with the party's ideology and the efforts of the party's leadership. The party played an important role in educating the public through the education of its members.

Fourth, the assumed relationship between voting and membership was always at the back of the minds of party leaders. Growth in membership indicated growth in the potential number of votes at the next election. Besides granting the leadership important psychological support, added members seemed to indicate that the party's program was growing in acceptability.

Fifth, the party machine, its bureaucracy, was very interested in members as a sign of its success. Short of elections, no clearer indication of organizational prosperity was available than membership. Another incentive for the bureaucrats was that with each jump in membership, additional programs—hence additional funds and additional jobs—must be added.

An important distinction to be made is between direct and indirect membership. A direct member applies to the party and is accepted on an individual basis. In most Israeli parties during the period when strong ideological divisions seemed to separate the parties, an applicant had to be recommended by a party member in good standing, in addition to accepting the party's platform and paying periodic dues. A much more practical arrangement in terms of the party organization is indirect membership, in which one becomes a party member by virtue of membership in another organization, most often a trade union. Not only is the member offered a social support system within the party, but he is represented in party affairs by the same leaders who represent him in union affairs. In reality, as we can imagine, the worker is not overly aware of his party membership because he joins automatically when joining the union.

The conveniences for the organizational bureaucrats are clear. They can count on a steady income from the dues of the union membership that are deducted from the worker's salary and forwarded directly to the party by the union. No more uncertainty regarding membership funds; no more fear that party positions will alienate members and bring about large-scale resignations. Another aspect of this same "benefit" from the point of view of the party bureaucrats is that they can now deal with trade union bureaucrats on political matters and no longer have to deal with the members themselves. The two sets of bureaucrats are likely to have similar backgrounds, goals, and lifestyles; hence they will probably get along quite well with each other.

A key dispute regarding the National Health Insurance Law was the relationship between party membership and other activity. The practice had been that the Histadrut's sick fund was available only to Histadrut members, and since the Histadrut was comprised of political parties, a portion of the dues went to those parties. The reformers wanted a clear separation between health insurance provision and political party activity, while the Histadrut leaders wanted to retain the connection. After a bitter fight (see chapter 10), the reformers won; the Histadrut today does not have the regular and automatic income for its constituent political parties from those insured. Provision has been made for a voluntary deduction for political activities, but that is much closer to direct membership than to the indirect membership of yesterday.

A good example of indirect membership comes from the National Religious Party (NRP). When the Mizrachi and Hapoel Hamizrachi merged in 1956 to form the NRP, the merging organizations were not disbanded. Hapoel Hamizrachi handled issues of labor, agricultural settlement, the protection of workers' rights, and the development of labor and pioneering values. Its members had access to Histadrut sick-fund facilities on the basis of an agreement drawn up in the 1920s: Hapoel Hamizrachi members (but not all members of the NRP) were provided services by the Histadrut, while their organization transferred a percentage of their dues to the Histadrut sick fund. These individuals were not members of the Histadrut, although they paid the same dues as did Histadrut members, but they were members of Hapoel Hamizrachi, and by virtue of indirect membership, NRP members as well. This complex arrangement allowed Hapoel Hamizrachi to continue providing these services to its members without renegotiating the agreement, and also to merge with another party to form a new one and yet retain its original organizational identity.

This arrangement was continued even after the advent of the National Health Insurance Law and the reorganization of the Histadrut after its 1994 elections. The decision by the Histadrut to renew its historical alliance with the NRP and Agudat Israel workers' organizations meant that affiliated workers would join the Histadrut and that more than half of the organization tax paid from their salaries would be refunded to the religious parties.

Indirect membership still exists in Israel today, but at a much lower level than in the past. This is a sign of the times, and of the relative weakness of the parties. The introduction of the party primary came about in part because leaders wanted to increase party membership (and the dues generated), and because older alternative forms of membership had withered away. In a party with a weakened bureaucracy, calls for democratization were more likely to be heeded.

Membership rates fell with the lessening ability of the parties to provide material benefits. The percentage of respondents in surveys reporting that they were party members fell from a high of 18 percent in 1969 to a low of 8 percent in the 1984 and 1988 polls, and then rose again to 9 percent in 1996 (see figure 6.1). The downward trend was gradual but consistent; the upward swing was punctuated by the spike in 1996, corresponding with the democratic interlude of primary elections in most parties. In 1999 and 2003 that upward trend faltered.

In parties with primary elections, membership drives take on added importance beyond the increased dues they generate. It becomes imperative for a candidate to recruit people whose votes he thinks he can count on in the primary election. These drives inevitably raise charges of corrupt practices, with reports of activists recruiting members by questionable means.

Figure 6.1   Party Membership, 1969–2003 (in percentages)

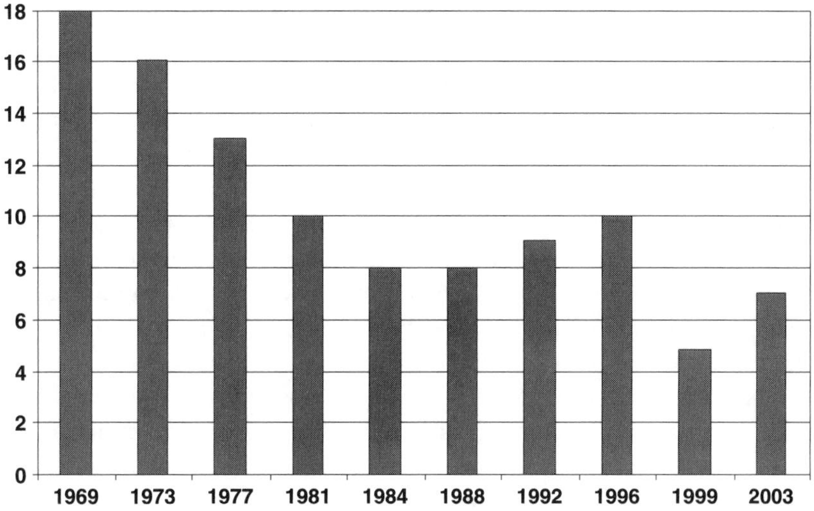

Source: Israel National Election Surveys.

Political parties still control the path to power in Israel. In the past, members were at the bottom of a top-down structure, but today they control one key step on that path in parties with primary elections. Groups and individuals sign up to further their own candidates or issues, or they are courted in the hope that they will support a candidate. Membership in more than one party is illegal, and in 1996, some 30,000 cases of joining two parties were discovered by the office of the Registrar of Political Parties. Individuals were notified that they had to relinquish their membership in all but one party to be eligible to participate in any party's primary election.[7]

There are important organizational implications of different kinds and degrees of connection with a party—voters, members, and those actually participating in party affairs—and the meanings of high and low ratios involving these categories. The leadership of a party must keep in mind these different types of participants, and the timing of appeals to each group must be different. Ideally these three groups should overlap at the highest possible numerical level, but most people do not become members, let alone activists. A party with high numbers of voters, members, and activists would indicate great appeal and a high likelihood of stability in future elections. A party that registered a high number of voters but a low number of members could celebrate for that one election, but would have to suspect that its performance over time might be unsteady. It would not be unusual for a party in this position to begin a campaign for new members immediately after the election. If the number of members was nearly equal to the number of voters, the party would have a firm nucleus of voter support but might have exhausted its potential because it was not successful in recruiting voters who were not members.

These implications can be explored using the experience of 1996, the year in which many parties held primary elections. Table 6.1 contains the numbers of voters, members, and those who voted in the primaries for selected parties in 1996, and the ratios between the pairs of numbers. The three religious parties, Shas, Agudat Israel, and the NRP, exist in a different organizational culture. The highest ratio of voters to members was for the haredi parties Shas and Aguda, mostly because membership in the party alone is meaningless in these ultra-Orthodox, non-Zionist parties—the former Sephardi, the latter Ashkenazi. Their ranks are fed by congregations of faithful worshippers and students of the Torah, which band together with other communities to form the myriad of sects and courtyards allegiant to diverse rabbinical authorities. Matters of policy and appointments to official positions are controlled by the respective Councils of Torah Sages and are not issues of participatory democracy. Political membership, meetings, and primaries are out of place and unnecessary for these parties.

Shas and Aguda are as close to total parties as one can find in twenty-first century Israel: their organizations nurture their followers in activities along much of the social, economic, and cultural spectrum. Both parties are committed to the well-being of their membership, providing schools outside the national education system but largely funded from the public treasury, and both are active in procuring government funding to construct housing in communities earmarked for their membership, and in providing other goods and services. Although there are no manifestations of democratic process, the allegiance of the faithful is very impressive, and in 1999 Shas was able to attract many regular Likud voters who supported Netanyahu for prime minister and Shas for the Knesset.

If Shas and Aguda are classic cadre parties, the National Religious Party is perhaps the clearest extant example of the type of mass party organization that characterized the first generation of Israeli politics. Its 1996 voters-to-members ratio is the lowest of the parties presented in table 6-1. The NRP has a vibrant membership based in the synagogues

Table 6.1 Members, Primaries Voters, and Voters

	In selected parties, 1996						Labor and Likud, 2003		
	Labor	Likud	NRP	Meretz	Shas	Aguda[a]	Primary for Labor Knesset List	Primary for Labor Leader	Primary for Likud Leader
Members	261,169	178,582	107,772	34,111[b]	141	101	110,988	305,000	305,000
Primaries voters	194,788	91,907	—	18,968	—	—	58,783	66,256	140,918
Voters	818,741	767,401	240,271	226,275	259,796	98,657	455,183	455,183	925,279
Approximate ratios									
Voters/members	3:1	4:1	2:1	7:1	1,842:1	976:1	4:1	4:1	3:1
Members/primaries	1.3:1	2:1	—	2:1	—	—	2:1	4.6:1	3:1
Voters/primaries	4:1	8:1	—	15:1	—	—	6.6:1	7:1	7.7:1

a. Part of United Torah Jewry.

b. Members of the three constituent parties, and members of Meretz.

affiliated with its movement; it is closely involved in religious state-supported educational institutions ranging from preschool through universities; it is identified with special training-and-Torah-learning units in the army; it prides itself on the organizational and economic commitment by the party's leaders and most of its members to the settlements in the territories; and it has a very active youth group. The NRP has preserved a form of total party activity originally developed and perfected by the parties of the secular socialist left, but which have increasingly vanished in Israeli society.

Labor, the mother of mass-membership parties in Israel, retained some signs of its organizational past in 1996. One such indicator was its 3-to-1 voters-to-members ratio, which indicated that many of its 818,741 voters were organizationally involved in the party. The Likud, less than a mass-membership party but more than a cadre one, had a lower voters-to-members ratio. Its appeal had to be beyond organizational attachments; the Likud evidently overcame its organizational weakness by presenting an attractive candidate in Netanyahu.

A party would want to have many voters and just about as many members. While its ratio may be steady, however, this indicator may be misleading if the vote for the party diminishes—this is the dilemma faced by both Likud and Labor. The total vote has become more fragmented, as parties with a higher voters-to-members ratio are increasing their strength among voters at a much faster rate than are the mass-membership parties. The result is a fractionalized party system, with a nearly equal division between the two candidates for prime minister in 1996. For both Likud and Labor in 1996, the primaries were crucial moments, since they determined the relative popularity of the leaders of the two big parties, which in turn would likely impact the winner's choice of ministers in the government formed after the election. The primaries may have been good for the activists, but they failed to generate the popular support needed to win the elections convincingly.

The 1996–2001 period of the direct election of the prime minister left the parties in disarray. Party identification weakened and organizational loyalty frayed, as the candidates for the prime ministry worked assiduously to attract votes for themselves, but the party was largely overlooked. In 2003 Labor's voters and its members were about half of the number in 1996, and the size of its primaries electorate was a quarter of its previous size (see table 6.1). In contrast, Likud's membership had doubled, and the number of its primaries voters and general elections voters had increased.

Of the secular parties, Meretz had the highest voters-to-members ratio. It fielded a relatively small group of leaders and militants in 1996 but was able to attract others at a high rate—for each member of Meretz, seven voters chose the party in the elections. Meretz was a conglomerate of three parties: Mapam had 15,517 members; the Citizens Rights Movement, 5,132 members; and Shinui, 1,311. Prior to the 1996 elections, primaries were held in each of the constituent parties, followed by a ranking by all Meretz members (including an additional 12,151 members of Meretz not associated with any of the three constituent parties) of those candidates selected in the primaries according to a key reflecting the relative sizes of the three parties. The three constituent parties merged into one party before the 1999 elections.

Party Institutions

The major feature of internal party structures, in addition to the primaries for the parties that hold them, is indirect representation, which has been called "an admirable means of banishing democracy while pretending to apply it."[8] Its major characteristic is simple: members cast their ballots only once, for the broadest-based institution of the party; this broadest-based institution elects the next-highest-level institution; the members of the third tier are then elected by those on the second; and so on. This arrangement facilitates control of the party by a group or groups of activists while professing concern for the demands and wishes of the broader membership. Indirect democracy can be thought of as a many-layered pyramid, with each layer reduced or distilled to form the layer above it until the topmost layer is finally reached. Each layer is called upon to select only the layer directly above it, but all higher layers can commit the party as a whole, unless specifically prevented from doing so by the constitution.

Anyone with experience in administration will recognize the pattern and will applaud its logic and appreciate its potential efficiency. If something is to be done, endless debate and mass decision making can be disruptive and time-consuming. On the other hand, this special version of democracy prevents the sustained control of the organization by the rank-and-file and lends itself to control and manipulation by groups of activists.

The typical structure of an Israeli party is a multitiered one, including a broad-based convention and a narrower-based central committee that elects an executive committee, which in turn selects a secretariat. While

the number of tiers and their respective sizes may vary, the general principle applies. As a rule, the more tiers between the mass membership
and the leadership, the more unlikely is direct democratic control, or, in
other words, the more indirect the form of representation.

There is a great temptation in this setting to perpetuate the power of
supporters and friends and to shut out the opposition—the very essence
of oligarchic organization. As Duverger notes: "Party congresses are just
like a meeting of employees facing their employers: obviously the former
will tend to keep in office the latter, whose creatures they are."

The major parties in Israel are all constructed on the basis of indirect
representation. The Likud central committee, with its 2,913 members
selected in 2002, also served as the party's temporary convention because
of political difficulties in selecting that group. These difficulties were partly
bypassed by the leadership by retaining in place the Likud secretariat,
numbering 499 members, that had been selected in 1994. Obviously,
power is distilled to a very high degree in this situation. The selection of
the central committee becomes crucial in controlling the party; usually
great efforts are made to achieve a list of central committee members that
will be selected by unanimous consensus by the convention. The Likud
central committee in 2003 became the battleground for control of the
selection of the party list and the setting of party policy.

The 2004 Labor Party had a 4,739-member convention, which elected
a central committee of 2,363 members, which in turn selected a leadership bureau of 170 members plus elected mayors, which in turn elected
a smaller executive. Because so many competing groups struggled for
representation in the central committee, the Labor Party convention had
been enlarged from 2,847 members in 1996 and 1,240 members in 1981,
while the central committee grew to 1,150 from 880. This allowed many
groups to feel politically satisfied, made many activists proud to be central committee members, and maintained the proportionate power relations within the party.

Mapam's convention in 1996, before it merged into Meretz, had more
than 1,100 members; its central committee, some 600; and its executive,
50. In addition, it had a 25-member committee and a select committee
made up of the general secretary, the political secretary, and the central
committee secretary. Mapam used a method of rotating members of its
governing council in order to afford greater participation. The membership of the convention was constructed so that 45 percent were from
Kibbutz Haarzi, 45 percent from urban branches, and 10 percent from
moshavim and Arab sectors.

Meretz elections, held in 2000, chose a central committee of 3,001 elected members plus officeholders. The council of 901 (20 percent appointed and 80 percent elected by the branches) also included 25 officeholders, and the directorate was made up of 57, including 25 officeholders. These were the institutions that led the metamorphosis to the Yahad Party in 2004.

The 1,000 delegates to the NRP convention were last selected by its 125,000 members in 1993. The NRP central committee in 2004 had 1,045 members and selected a 72-person secretariat. In 1979 the Mizrachi and Hapoel Hamizrachi held a joint convention, and each was represented in the formal decision-making bodies, with an executive committee of 264. This last organization was the joint meeting of two separate executive committees of the NRP and Hapoel Hamizrachi, each committee having 76 members. When the two groups sat in joint meeting, 110 additional members were added. Democrats might say that this inclusiveness increases representation; political analysts would point out that it also increases honorific appointments while lowering the probability that key decisions will be made.

Party conventions are the supreme governing bodies of parties, but they provide imperfect examples of democratic practice. The most important point is that most party conventions do not result from secret elections by party members, for in many parties the election for the convention turns into an act confirming the existing leadership of the branch. In all the Israeli parties, the vote for a convention delegate is for an individual, with the exception of the NRP, where the election is by list. While it may be possible for an opposition group to organize successfully in a district or two or in a few branches, it is almost inconceivable that an opposition group could pose a serious challenge to the party leadership at the convention because of the enormity of the organizational task facing it. If one must canvass hundreds of branch members in order to be elected, let alone elect enough convention delegates around the country with similar views, the advantage obviously lies with established party leaders and local activists. This is why successful opposition to the established leadership is rarely fielded from the grassroots. What is more likely is for dissension among leaders to galvanize the grassroots into action.

Often, local elections are dispensed with altogether. For Herut's party convention in 1975, only 11 out of 100 party branches held elections, the others being appointed according to agreements worked out by local activists. This arrangement has characterized the Independent Liberals as well.[9]

Yet another limitation of the democratic nature of the party convention lies in the fact that additional convention members are often appointed by the convention without undergoing election anew. For example, it is customary to elect en bloc, as delegates to the new convention, such notables of the party as ministers, Knesset members, and members of the outgoing central committee. This serves the dual function of adding more establishment votes and avoiding the embarrassment of having a national leader lose his election to the party's convention. Usually there is an upward limit to the number of additional members permitted in this fashion, and often they serve in an advisory capacity to the convention without the right to vote.

Thus, Shinui's governing council in 2004 numbered 150 members, plus three young people and the party's fifteen Knesset members, for a total of 168. The secretariat included fifteen members selected by the council, the council's president, and the Knesset delegation, for a total of thirty-one.

The more supreme a political body, the less authoritative it is—this cynical point of view sums up the general assessment of party conventions in Israeli politics. Party conventions are large, unwieldy affairs requiring careful control, which is almost always provided by the party leadership. Usually conventions are staged for public relations purposes, attempting to portray a party characterized by harmony, cooperation, and common cause. There have been notable exceptions to this pattern: the 1942 and 1965 Mapai conventions predated the splits in the party, and the 1981 convention was the site of Peres's victory over Rabin for head of the party; it was at the Herut convention that Geula Cohen attacked Begin for the Camp David agreement, left the party, and set up Tehiya. But, on the whole, party conventions are orchestrated demonstrations of organizational control and political compromise.

Party leaders generally promote a "central list." In the case of Mapai, and later Labor, this list usually included leaders of the local labor councils who were members of the party, leading party figures in the municipality or local council, and key members of the secretariat of the local party council. When contests have developed, they have tended to be over personalities and not over national or party issues. In the 1964 election for Mapai delegates, only six out of eighty-four branches had hard-fought contests—and even these were related to personality clashes—at a time when the nation was agonizing over the Lavon Affair and Ben-Gurion's call for a judicial investigation.

The convention delegates, elected and appointed, are usually individuals dependent on the party and the leadership. Sometimes this dependency is material, as when large numbers of delegates are employed in party or party-related jobs.[10] Sometimes the debt is political, as when a delegate's continued political success is dependent on a good relationship with the party hierarchy and leaders. Often the dependency is psychological, because individuals can develop feelings of organizational loyalty and solidarity with the party. Regardless of the source of the dependency, its existence makes convention delegates instruments in the hands of party leaders and not active representatives of the rank-and-file.

Party leaders feel they have the power to commit their membership regardless of the loose linkage they have with members. This is clearly seen by the fact that no founding convention of newly merged parties in Israel has ever been preceded by an internal election among the membership for convention delegates called upon to ratify the merger—not in the case of Mapam in 1948, of the NRP in 1956, of the Liberals in 1961, of the Labor Party in 1968, or of the Likud in 1988. Instead, the composition of the merged party's conventions were arrived at by negotiation among the leaders of the merging parties, and the delegates were appointed by agreement. Should we be surprised that the conventions meekly ratified the mergers?

The key body in determining the smooth operation of the party convention is the standing committee. This committee has had total control over the convention in the Mapai and Labor parties, controlling the agenda and the preparation of the convention, and generally presenting proposals to the convention that have been adopted unanimously. The control of the standing committee has been the crucial element in controlling the convention and those bodies that determined its composition. Once the control of the committee has been gained, the rest is only a matter of detail, best understood in terms of ritual and ceremony.[11]

The frequency of the convention is also a sore point of Israeli party democratic practice. The NRP's constitution, for example, calls for a convention once every fourth year (although it does allow for postponement). In reality, conditions are much worse: NRP conventions were held in 1956, 1963, 1969, and 1973, and all except that of 1973 were "agreed" conventions, with the leaders' factions determining the delegates to the convention among themselves without holding elections in the party.[12]

The convention, the supreme body of most Israeli parties, provides an imperfect link with the membership because of the shortcuts used in its elections. The committee then becomes the agent that embodies the principles of indirect representation by selecting the party's central committee. The central committee, a smaller group than the convention, meets more often and plays a more central role in the ongoing life of the party. In the past, the central committee approved the party's platform and list of candidates, and debated important policy issues. As we have seen, much effort is made to select for a convention those who will conform to the leadership's wishes, and the efforts extended toward the selection of the central committee are no less great. The selection of the central committee is the focus of considerable political activity on the part of political activists and party hacks because the best way to determine the outcome of a vote is to control the composition of the electing body. On the surface the procedure is smooth enough, with a nominating committee presenting a suggested list to the convention—a list that is almost always approved. The real action is behind the scenes in the nominating committee, where intense political and personal pressure is often applied to increase the membership in the central committee of this or that group. It is the job of the nominating group (whether that be a special committee, the standing committee, or a small group of party leaders) to accommodate competing demands and end the process of selection of the central committee with a show of party unity. The factional parties, the NRP and the Liberals, saw to it that the factional division in the convention was simply perpetuated in the central committee.

The central committee tends to number a few hundred members and meets no more than a dozen times a year, if that. Generally it has the last word in electing the secretary-general and approving the party platform. In most parties in the past it was this group that rubber-stamped its approval of the list of candidates for the Knesset.[13]

The central committee is a microcosm of the convention, whose importance is as symbolic as it is practical. What the central committee does is to choose the body next up in the hierarchy, whatever its name. This is a smaller group, and hence a more powerful one. This rule is partially suspended when the party is in power, however, for then the leaders who made the small-party institution powerful by their presence and personal authority are concentrating their efforts in other matters. When most of the leaders are government ministers, their consultations become crucial not only for national policy but for party policy as well.

Another modifier of the rule of the inverse relationship between size and power of party committees is that the top party leaders must be involved. During the years that Herut was in opposition, its practice was for the parliamentary party to decide the party's stand on issues and report to other party institutions; the dominance of the parliamentary party assured that its path would be followed by the party. When in power, however, the parliamentary party was overshadowed by the government and its Herut/Likud leaders—Netanyahu's original period as prime minister displayed a total disregard for the Likud and its institutions. The direct election of the prime minister thus gave power to the leader and diminished the importance of the party institutions.

Ben-Gurion's interest in party affairs shifted when he became secretary-general of the Histadrut and then leader of the Jewish Agency. As prime minister he had even less time for party affairs, and much of the real decision making regarding party policy shifted to the Mapai ministers in the government. This process became even more acute in 1954 when the party executive was increased to nineteen members in order to accommodate pressures from ministers, parliamentarians, Histadrut officials, party branches, women, young members, ethnic groups, kibbutzim, moshavim, and workers in *moshavot* (smaller agricultural towns). Moshe Sharett, then prime minister, instituted meetings that consisted of Mapai ministers together with the secretary-general of the Histadrut and in effect bypassed the executive. Sharett was anxious to have the support of his colleagues and needed this form of collective leadership, especially after having followed the charismatic Ben-Gurion in office. When Ben-Gurion returned to office, he continued the meetings of this informal, extra-constitutional device.[14]

Once decisions were made in this fashion, the participants were expected to follow the line in public and see to it that it was adhered to in decisions made by the party and governmental bodies. Such an informal network is infinitely stronger than formal constitutional provisions, but it relies on a very high degree of group solidarity and common purpose. A leader who finds himself at the head of such a network is blessed, for he can utilize the formal arrangements in a much more successful manner.

Developments in Mapai continued in the same direction; after Secretary-General Lavon of the Histadrut stopped participating in the meetings in 1959, Sharett's committee became a committee of cabinet ministers. The executive had grown to thirty members, and since no real power was at stake, more groups could be given representation. And so, as we should have come to expect by now, another more compact group was selected—the leadership bureau—and in establishing it (without any constitutional sanction), the executive abdicated much of its own authority.

This is not the place to document the ins and outs of intraparty politics, but the general picture is clear. Groups jockey for power, and the organizational structure is made to accommodate the tides of battle. Control over the party is at stake, and resources are not spared in the effort. The mass of members is generally not brought into the fight— probably most of them do not know of it. Temporary truces are reached, usually giving time to marshal forces for the next battle. When a leader emerges whom the party can rally around, his authority can be brought to bear if he is willing to alienate one side in order to find favor in the eyes of the other, but this infighting consumes enormous amounts of time and energy. While the politicians' ambitions and future careers are at stake, it is also important because the winners will be the ones to determine policy.

A larger number of tiers generally means that effective control is that much farther from the rank-and-file. Additional tiers are usually introduced to solve organizational problems, as in the case of Sharett, and not deliberately to introduce antidemocratic tendencies into the organization. The proliferation of tiers usually has its origins in a desire to settle problems or distribute representation among the groups, sections, leaders, officeholders, pretenders to power, and bureaucracies that make up the party.

The impression should not be given that the internal life of a party is static, held in control by the ruling oligarchy. Often the contrary is the case, with the oligarchy striving mightily to keep diverse elements of the party satisfied. Turbulence occurs especially when a group thinks that it should be stronger in the party hierarchy than it actually is in terms of positions, representation, or prestige. Sometimes it can be bought off easily by being provided with more jobs for its people or by having its leader appointed to an honorary position. Sometimes it can be co-opted, a process by which dissidents are included as a minority in decision-making bodies, making them privy to deliberations and responsible for decisions without there being a real possibility that their points of view or program will carry the day. Sometimes there is no other choice but to accommodate them by granting them real power; because replacing members of existing bodies would likely upset other fine-tuned relationships, one strategy for doing so would be to bypass existing groups by setting up yet another body within the decision-making structure of the party.

Efficient structure or neat textbook-like organizational charts are not goals of political parties; control and political success are. Even if the organizational structures are messy, the questions we should ask ourselves as political scientists must center on political effectiveness, control, collegial relations, and the generation of an image of unified leadership. The latter will likely count for far more in the end than conforming to the abstract, and unproved, rules of rational administrative science. Party structures become more, rather than less, complex because changes tend to be made to existing bodies; it is unusual to start from scratch. Solving a problem by patching an already barely understandable structure tends not to clarify that structure but to make it even harder to understand.

Once the process is entered into, the momentum toward oligarchy increases quickly. Defenders of the form insist that it provides a satisfactory solution to the conflicting demands of democracy and organizational efficiency, allowing the membership to vote and yet concentrating power in the hands of the party leadership. Critics of the system identify this structure as one of the prime resources in the hands of the party leadership, which allows it to perpetuate its control over the organization. For if enough members of the broad-based convention can coalesce around a candidate or point of view, they can see to it that their view prevails in the smaller tier above the convention. In that body, the majority point of view of the convention can also be perpetuated when selecting members for the next higher tier, and so on. Power is not only perpetuated but is likely to be distilled and made stronger. As the body becomes smaller, the proportion of those with divergent views is likely to shrink. This, critics say, is the ultimate result of the system and its principal fault.

Widespread participation is a cherished value of a democracy but one seldom realized. The tension between democratic values and organizational control and efficiency are clearly evident in the case of the party primary. Primaries are not common in democratic politics—that they are widely held only in the United States and in Iceland gives an indication of the way other countries view them.[15] Primaries raise the crucial issue of the relationship between party members and broad-based representative bodies in the party. What is the appropriate role for these bodies? Should they be ignored or converted into rubber stamps? Sometimes decisions or nominations are brought before broad-based party groups and are approved by near-unanimous votes; the authority of the leadership is often brought into play, and the convention is not about to upset the precarious compromises worked out in late-night sessions. The convention feels a sense of responsibility to the party and its leadership, and typically abdicates its authority. This is a very understandable, very human, reaction and yet it causes critics of the system to question whether the party must remain as centralized and hierarchical as it sometimes appears.

It should be pointed out very clearly that this is not a dilemma invented by the Zionist movement or even by Israeli politicians. This is a fundamental problem in the life of organizations in all times and in all places, and is faced by kibbutzim, labor unions, university councils, voluntary organizations—by any organization that considers it a positive value to order its internal life in a democratic manner.

Candidate Selection

The way to get on a party's list in the past was to be appointed to it by the party's top leadership. The proposed list was generally presented to the party central committee for approval, and that approval was almost always automatically given since the list had been prepared by a nominating committee often peopled by the leaders or their cronies.

A major break in that pattern occurred with the first primary elections in Israel in 1977, held by the DMC. Reacting to the criticism of the role of machine politicians in other parties in choosing their lists, the DMC decided to hold a primary election among its 30,000 members to determine its list for the Knesset. Paradoxically, but not surprisingly, the most well-known candidates received the most votes; if democracy implies free access to decision-making positions, it was not attained by the DMCs primaries. The DMC list, chosen democratically, was most heavily peopled by luminaries, whereas the list of the Labor Party, selected in 1977 in a smoke-filled room by party stalwarts, was much more representative.

Herut had been another pioneer in a more participatory form of list formation. Herut's central committee had an active role from the 1980s in determining its Knesset list, selecting the candidates for the Knesset list in a ranking procedure within clusters of seven. Herut has traditionally exempted its leader (first Begin, then Shamir) from the rigors of competition, reaffirming the leader's selection by acclamation. In 1988, however, the Herut central committee was identical to the Herut convention, because the latter was bitterly divided among the followers of Yitzhak Shamir, Ariel Sharon, and David Levy, and was unable to select a smaller central committee. Thus, in 1988, with some 3,000 participating, the election of the clusters of seven proceeded.

In 1988, the Citizens Rights Movement selected its candidates by using a secret ballot in its council. Many competed, including five who were then members of the Knesset. Not surprisingly, the first five on the CRM list were the five Knesset members, and they then were installed as the CRM Knesset delegation after the list won five seats.

The 1988 Labor Party decentralized the system somewhat, providing for two ways of getting on the Labor list: through the party's districts and through election by the central committee. Competition took place for fifty places—twenty-three positions on the list reserved for the party's districts, and twenty-seven to be selected by the central committee by secret ballot. The district elections were held in the various districts (Tel Aviv, Jerusalem, kibbutzim, moshavim, etc.) by the district councils of the party. Meanwhile, eighty-six candidates competed for nomination to the twenty-seven slots to be filled by the party central committee. To assure representation, provision was made that at least one Druze, one Arab, one young person, three women, and one candidate from development towns be selected. After these first rounds of selection, the 1,340 members of the central committee met. (The central committee itself had been selected by the 3,201-member Labor convention. The constitutional size of the convention was 3,001 members, but another 200 members had been co-opted for organizational and political reasons.) The central committee's task was to determine the positions on the Knesset election list of the fifty candidates selected by the two methods, using a system of voting for clusters of ten.

The results indicated the difficulties inherent in democratization: the big losers were the districts, whose candidates were ranked in low positions in the runoffs that determined how high on the list a candidate would be. Of the twenty-three district candidates, only nine were finally elected to the Knesset—and seven of them were in the last ten places on the list of those elected. Although the districts may be closer to "the people," they controlled fewer votes in the central committee; those who were known by many central committee members and enjoyed national visibility were more likely to be elected. Still, an unusually large percentage of new and young candidates emerged. Its initial attempt at decentralization at least a partial success, Labor followed Herut into an era of greater—if not perfect—democracy in the selection process. In

1992 Labor switched to a primary election in which all dues-paying members could participate, while the Likud (dominated by Herut) retained its cluster system in the party central committee.

The task of the primaries was to select a fixed list to be presented to the voters on election day. A variety of considerations came into play, since the job is different from simply selecting one of a number of candidates to represent the party. Two competing goals, both desirable to those who wrote the rules, were broad participation and representation. The dilemma was that popular elections often select well-known people; how does a list generate a balance between well-known and lesser-known figures, between representatives of majority and minority groups, between representatives from various geographical regions, and so forth?

By 1996, both Likud and Labor employed primary elections to select their candidates for the Knesset. Both parties adopted a mixed national-district system, in which members had multiple votes, but the party institutions had almost no role to play in them, other than approving the rules and supervising the election. Both parties held membership censuses that ended close to the day for primary elections. Mass enrollments were alleged by vote-brokers or by labor organizers; there were charges that workers had been coerced by their employers in public or Histadrut-owned enterprises to register as Labor members and pay the dues. An internal Labor inquiry regarding the 1992 primary had confirmed many of these charges. Complaints had come especially from the Israel Electric Corporation and the Egged bus cooperative: in the IEC's Jerusalem district, over 90 percent of the employees registered as Labor members; Egged employees also reported pressure from their superiors, who threatened that failure to sign up would result either in firing or loss of tenure, perks, or advancement.

The mixed national-district selection system used by both Labor and Likud solved the problem by assigning positions on the list to various categories of winners in advance. Thus, Likud rules gave the first place to Binyamin Netanyahu, since he had been selected as party leader in a separate election, the next sixteen slots to those who had been named on the national list, place 18 to the Jerusalem district, place 19 to Tel Aviv, place 20 to Haifa, place 21 to the Negev, place 22 to the Galilee, place 23 to the next national list winner, and so forth. In addition, place 31 was reserved for a new immigrant, place 32 for a non-Jew, places 33 and 36 for women, and place 37 for a young person. David Levy had withdrawn from Likud and formed Gesher because he felt that the ratio of national to district seats in the composition of the list would weaken his chances to secure slots for his activists. Fifty percent of Likud's registered members actually voted in the primaries.

Labor used the same principle with different details. Peres was unopposed in 1996 for first place and so no ballot was required. For the rest of the list, Labor allotted twenty-one of the first forty-four slots to its national list, the remaining twenty-three to district candidates. A voter had to select no fewer than eleven and no more than fifteen of the fifty-six candidates. Labor had one-, two-, and three-member districts; a voter could vote for no more than two in the multimember districts. Candidates had to reside in the district they sought to represent. Two-thirds of Labor's 285,000 members actually voted in the primaries.

The 1996 primaries were flawed, however, because the leaders of the two biggest parties, Likud and Labor, could not avoid the temptation of tampering with the results of the primaries vote. The Likud's tampering was the more blatant of the two, as its politicians altered the primary results significantly by agreeing to form a joint Likud-Gesher-Tzomet list after the primaries were held, thereby relegating Likud primary winners to lower positions on the new three-party list. One Likud candidate, a Druze Knesset incumbent, applied to the courts—and was denied—when his place 32 was changed to place 46 because of the three-party merger. Since the polls showed that the Likud was likely to win about forty seats, the change would have meant the difference between victory and defeat (had the polls been correct).

The Labor leadership engineered a change in the results of its party primaries as well. Its rules reserved the 29th place on the list for a new immigrant—with more than half a million new immigrants from the former Soviet Union, this was a crucial group, representing some 15 percent of the electorate. But the new immigrant elected in the primary was an Ethiopian Jew, Adiso Massalla, whose compatriots represented about 1 percent of the electorate. His election followed the revelation a few weeks earlier that the government's medical authorities had systematically destroyed blood donations from Ethiopian Jews because of a higher incidence of HIV-positive blood in this donor population; furious Ethiopians attacked police at a rally, and the public observed them abandoning their generally passive demeanor in calling for an end to discrimination against them. This evidently struck a chord as Labor Party members went to vote in their primaries, and Massalla won the place on the list reserved for the new immigrant.

Labor leaders, however, still had the problem of attracting the votes of the immigrants from the former Soviet Union. And so they called for a special election to fill the place vacated by Ora Namir, the minister of social welfare. Namir, the only Labor woman minister in the government, had won the twenty-sixth place in the primaries, while Dalia Itzik, a young firebrand, had won the ninth place. This raised the delicate problem of which woman would serve in the cabinet if Shimon Peres were elected. The problem was solved by convincing Namir to resign her cabinet position and accept an appointment as ambassador to China, and by then calling a special primary to fill her slot on the list— except this time, only Labor Party members who were new immigrants from the former Soviet Union were entitled to run for the spot. As designed, Sofia Landver, a "new" immigrant from the Soviet Union (in the country since the 1970s and, not coincidentally, Peres's Russian language teacher), won the race against weak opposition and filled the slot Namir had originally won. Either because of this manipulation or in spite of it, many of the new immigrants voted for Sharansky's Israel b'Aliyah list.

The selection of leaders and the construction of the lists of candidates for the Knesset provide fascinating material for understanding the role of organization in a democratic setting. Before 1977, the oligarchs ruled the parties and controlled the selection of candidates. In that year, however, the Likud began selecting its Knesset list in the party's central committee; candidates competed in several rounds, adding seven names in each round. Labor changed in 1988 to a similar system, using ten-candidate rounds. Labor adopted a radical reform in 1992, introducing mass party primaries to choose both party leader and the Knesset list. Moreover, Labor promised new members the immediate right to participate in upcoming primaries, a practice that opens up a party to unexpected outside influences. Whether any of these factors played a role or not, Labor's Rabin won the 1992 elections, and so other parties felt the need to follow Labor's lead or face accusations of being oligarchic and undemocratic.[16] Within a year, five of the six largest parties announced plans to introduce some form of primaries in electing their candidates to local and national office, and most parties used a form of primaries for the selection of their 1996 list.[17]

After the democratic interlude of 1996, only Labor retained internal party primaries. With the direct election of the prime minister and serious campaign irregularities in the internal party primaries, other parties preferred less costly selection methods that could be more easily controlled by the party leadership. Likud and Meretz returned to having the central committees in each party select their Knesset lists.

In 2002 Amram Mitzna, then mayor of Haifa, was elected in the Labor primaries to head its list for the 2003 elections, and Sharon beat Netanyahu in the Likud primaries. Labor used the primaries system to compile its list, but public interest focused instead on the Likud central committee and the list of candidates that it selected. The abolition of the Likud primaries led to other excesses; expenditures were not reduced and control was not returned to the leadership. Activists attempted to ensure support among members of the party's central committee and to maintain the loyalty of those supporters. In 2003, for example, Likud vote-brokers turned their attention from mobilizing large numbers of primary voters for Knesset candidates to arranging the election of members of the party's central committee. Ironically, by abolishing the primaries, the vote-brokers' influence with potential Knesset candidates was enhanced. These brokers fashioned deals turning the Likud's central committee (as well as that of several other parties) into a job-placement operation in which committee members and their relatives were appointed to executive boards and granted lucrative civil service positions in return for mobilizing and maintaining support. Charges of bribes, votes for sale, and involvement of activists with criminal records in the Likud Party list selection process surfaced, and Prime Minister Sharon hastened to fire Deputy Minister Naomi Blumental, who refused to cooperate with a police investigation of the charges. Corruption scandals continued to plague the public agenda during the election campaign, as Labor Party candidates were accused of wrongdoing as well, and Sharon himself was personally implicated.

Public Financing

Israel adopted public financing of electoral campaigns for the general elections of 1969, granting parties government funding according to their proportional Knesset representation while permitting the solicitation of private donations as well.[18] Parties were obliged to disclose income and expenditures, expenditures were limited, and contributions from corporations were prohibited. Originally, parties were able to receive unlimited donations from private persons, including non-Israeli citizens, but large contributions by private donors were limited before the 1992 elections to NIS 55,000 ($22,000 at the time). Additional restrictions and stricter conditions of transparency and accountability were passed in 1994 as part of a deal that helped the parties cover their accumulated deficits but also slashed the ceiling of legal campaign contributions by 98 percent, from

NIS 55,000 to NIS 1,000 ($380). Contributions were also confined to Israeli citizens only, both as donors and as recipients. For internal elections, the expenditure ceilings in December 2002 were $115,000 per candidate for Knesset primaries, and $383,000 in primaries for party leader. The maximum individual contributions were set at $2,000 for Knesset primaries and $8,000 in primaries for party leader. Parties were allowed, however, to set lower ceilings for different internal elections, and most of them have done so.

Today parties rely almost entirely on public funding, with private contributions accounting for only one or two percent of reported campaign expenses. This has led parties to all but cease their fund-raising activities, leaving contributors open to the appeals of individual candidates competing in internal party races for parliamentary representation and party leadership. Menachem Hofnung estimated that in 2003 campaign costs reached almost half a million dollars to win a safe seat in primaries within the two major parties.[19] Candidates can accept individual contributions up to $2,000 or spend their own money, but there is no state subsidy and contributions from corporations are not allowed. Because of the involvement of the central government in many economic activities, personal contacts in government offices can pave the way for grants, licenses, and building authorizations; accordingly, businesspeople are willing to "invest" in politicians, to contribute to their campaigns, and to offer campaign services.

The lack of serious competition in the 2003 elections was associated with reduced campaign expenditures by the parties. All parties' spending was 40 percent lower than in 1999, even though state subsidies to cover the parties' election expenses were cut by only 6 percent. However, despite generous state funding for the Knesset elections, politicians still tended to disregard campaign finance regulations, using every available source in pursuit of electoral victory. Netanyahu, Barak, and Sharon were all suspected of breaching campaign finance laws and were subject to police investigation soon after winning their respective prime-ministerial campaigns.

The public financing of parties and their election campaigns was obviously favored by party leaders since, unlike other contributions from other sources, there was no uncertainty about receiving government funds. Also, the decisions regarding the use of this funding were completely in their control, for this money is not provided to individual members but given to the Knesset delegation.[20] The regulations mandate payments to the parties in proportion to their representation in the

Knesset: a party receives one "unit" for each Knesset member. In 2003 the "unit" was about $28,000 per Knesset member per month—for a total of more than $40 million per year. There is an additional mechanism to fund election activities from the public treasury, and this funding in 2003 came to an additional $350,000 per Knesset member, or another $40 million. The total $80 million of public money for the 3.2 million votes cast in 2003 comes to $25 per vote, making Israel the most expensive democracy per voter in the world. The rationale is democratic because parties are central to a functioning democracy; the outcome is that the biggest winners are also the biggest earners for their organizations' ongoing expenses.

In 1992 the "unit" was set at $300,000 per Knesset member per year, with an additional unit in an election year to defray campaign expenses doubling the total. That was an increase of a third over the amount in effect in May 1991. However, litigation prevented the increase from taking effect—the High Court of Justice ruled that it would have to be approved by an absolute majority of the entire Knesset since the Finance Committee's decision to link the quarterly increase in the unit to the cost-of-living index had not been included in the original legislation— and it remained at "only" $200,100 per year. Had the "reform" taken effect, the total of public funds going to the parties in an election year would have been $72 million, or about $29 per vote! This was about the level of 1988. Since the increase was thwarted, the election-year bill for the parties in 1992 was $48 million, coming to "only" $19 per vote. Politicians from different parties, who are often split by deep ideological divisions, usually manage to agree on raising the funding unit for the parties. In 1992, they were stymied by the High Court, but not before going to unusual lengths, the most flagrant of which occurred when members of the Finance Committee who opposed the increase were replaced by their party leaderships with members who supported it.

The public treasury's generous payments to the political parties have been accompanied by the introduction of more public oversight and scrutiny of the affairs of the parties. Most notably, legislation passed in 1994 took the task of setting the amount of the "unit" out of the hands of the Knesset Finance Committee and delegated it to a public commission headed by a retired Supreme Court justice. However, the "unit" is linked to the cost-of-living index and increases regularly. In addition, Knesset members have legislated additional moneys for the parties for purposes outside the scope of existing laws, such as the strengthening contacts with the voters.

Special funding is provided for election periods, and lists are granted a proportion of the funds based on the size of the delegation in the outgoing Knesset. Parties that do better in the new elections are reimbursed; if they lose strength, they may owe the treasury. One outrageous feature of the 1996 legislation, which applied only to that election year, was to base the allocation on 126 members of the outgoing Knesset, and not on the actual 120 number. This allowed financing of 6 members who had broken with their parties and were running on separate lists, while simultaneously allowing the original parties to enjoy the public funding that they had expected, as if the renegade Knesset members still belonged to their parties. The large parties in 1996 were big losers of Knesset seats and of public financing as well.

The Iron Law of Oligarchy

Robert Michels's "iron law of oligarchy" is an insightful concept that is especially relevant to the reality of Israeli politics. Although he wrote about German parties and not Israeli ones, and died twelve years before Israel was declared a state, Michels foretold almost prophetically that "the social revolution would not effect any real modification of the internal structure of the mass. The socialists might conquer, but not socialism, which would perish in the moment of its adherents' triumph."[21]

The iron law of oligarchy posits that true democracy in any organization is impossible. Autocratic tendencies in an organization are neither accidental nor temporary—they are inherent in the nature of organization. "He who says organization, says oligarchy," sums it up well. Michels details the reasons that the masses are unable to control their destinies. There are technical reasons, such as the difficulty of assembling in one place and the need to make quick decisions on complex issues that demand great expertise. There are psychological reasons, including the fact that most people are apathetic about public issues, neither knowledgeable enough nor engaged enough to participate in decision making. More important, argues Michels, most people want to be led. The many financial, political, diplomatic, and informational tasks that must be performed cannot be performed by all. Organization implies a division of labor and a hierarchy of command. Whenever something must get done, someone has to do it; someone must see to it that this thing is done. Leadership necessarily arises in an organization and will act independently of the will of the masses. The leaders will likely speak in the name of the masses and of a democratic ideology, but Michels would counsel that we pay very little attention to what the leaders say and instead look at what they do.

One indicator of the psychological dependence that develops between the leadership and the mass is a phenomenon that might be called the customary right to office. Although formally a leader can be replaced when new elections are held, the fact that he has held office is thought to give him a moral claim on that office or some other leadership post in the organization. Playing to these sentiments may lead a politician to threaten resignation, which is generally very threatening to the masses because it causes uncertainty and denies security—and to other leaders because it may lead to unpleasant confrontations and disclosures—and tends to be avoided, with the necessary concessions generally made to the threatening leader. Of course, there is always the chance that the resignation will be accepted, and the prudent politician assesses these probabilities before he undertakes the gamble. On both grounds—the customary right to office and the use of resignation as a bargaining chip—Michels would be quite comfortable in Israeli politics. Ben-Gurion, Golda Meir, Yitzhak Ben-Aharon, among many others, successfully used the threat of resignation as a powerful tool to force their will on the group.

As Machiavelli pointed out, when the mass is deprived of its leadership in time of action, its members abandon the field in disordered flight, and this happens in politics and organizations as well. This need for leadership on the part of the passive masses makes them dependent on leaders and grateful for their efforts; concomitantly, it makes leaders of mass parties or the state extremely busy people. Soon the leaders as a group are perceived by the masses, and perceive themselves, as indispensable to the organization. The leadership develops power independent of the mass membership and is constituted as an informal subgroup. This effect is clearly evident in the salaries, expense accounts, and fringe benefits they vote for themselves from organizational funds—amounts that are larger than the wages of the workers they represent. This they justify by reference to their enormous efforts and indispensability to the organization; the members, after rightly protesting such autocratic maneuvers, approve the increases.

The leaders develop a sense of group superiority with regard to the masses, and soon the leaders themselves change. This drive for power is not only self-seeking but is also based on the belief that what most benefits the organization is their own continuance in power, because of their superiority, sacrifice, and indispensability. The extreme form of this development is the stage at which the leader "identifies himself completely with the organization, confounding his own interests with its interest. All objective criticism of the party or nation is taken by him as a personal affront. . . . If, on the other hand, the leader is attacked personally, his first care is to make it appear that the attack is directed against the party or nation as a whole."[22]

Peter Medding's book on the role of Mapai during the first twenty years of statehood details many of the situations and manipulations discussed by Michels. For example, Medding notes that Mapai "stood at the apex of a whole interconnected network of organizations and institutions which it controlled and directed from within" and that "the party was thus left as final referee, arbitrator or decision maker."[23] Medding writes that the party displayed a wide latitude in conducting the affairs of institutions it ran on behalf of the party—it was rarely upset by "lack of concern with constitutional formality [which] led to centralization of control in the hands of narrower executive bodies, and the inevitable lessening of the influence of the wider representative bodies." Strangely, after all this and more, Medding concludes that "the internal decision making process as we have analyzed it provides impressive evidence against Michels's theory of political party organization." Since many decisions were made in Mapai in many committees and institutions, and not all were made by the handful of major leaders, Medding concludes that Mapai was an example of "consensual power relations: the views of many groups were put forward or taken into consideration, and bargaining and mutual compromise characterized the discussions." Medding's analysis confronts the iron law of oligarchy with essentially trivial exceptions to the thrust of Michels's argument. Mapai was an excellent example of Michels's iron law of oligarchy, and Medding's thorough research chronicles an oligarchical party at the height of its power.

To those who despair of democracy in view of the inevitability of oligarchy, Michels's words are important. He expresses that famous dictum about democracy compared with all other forms: "If we wish to estimate the value of democracy, we must do so in comparison with its converse, pure aristocracy. The defects inherent in democracy are obvious. It is none the less true that as a form of social life we must choose democracy as the least of evils." His view of the role of scientific observation is an important one. Democracy is to be desired, but oligarchy will always remain. The goal must be to put some limit on the absoluteness of oligarchy, for which detachment and objective analysis are needed. "Nothing but a serene and frank examination of the oligarchical dangers of a democracy will enable us to minimize these dangers, even though they can never be entirely avoided."[24]

Israeli political life, as exemplified by its parties, its organizations, the Knesset, and the government, is oligarchical and hierarchical. Politics, especially in its democratic form, means hard work, frustrations, and setbacks. Those who cherish democracy must ponder the appropriate balance among competing values. Those who work within the existing parties must learn the rules of representation and the secrets of organization. Those who despair of the existing parties and attempt to set up new structures must take into account that past history and the laws of social science indicate that their new organization will not be immune from the rules of oligarchy described here.

7   THE ELECTORAL SYSTEM

THE VOTING ACT is conditioned by influences and pressures brought to bear on the citizen and by political arrangements that characterize the system within which the vote takes place. Electoral laws have political consequences, hence many constitutional issues in the realm of elections—reapportionment, extension of suffrage, financing elections, type of ballot, use of voting machines, single-member district as opposed to proportional representation, rules of party and candidate eligibility, and formulas for distributing the leftover vote—are matters that provoke the politician's serious concern and attention. The multiplicity of electoral arrangements is clearly a monument to the ingenuity of political man and a manifestation of his striving for power. Far from being objective rules to regulate the game, electoral laws are never neutral; they favor one political rival at the expense of another.

Legal arrangements are not the only constraints on the system of political competition. Social and historical factors can be just as powerful in limiting the range of potential outcomes the development of a system may produce. These factors may not be causal in determining who shall rule and for how long, but they set parameters on the political struggle and its possible outcome.

Knesset Elections

The voter chooses the entire list as submitted and cannot alter the order of names on the list or delete candidates, as is possible in some other electoral systems. If a party wins a third of the vote, entitling it to forty seats, the first forty names on the list become members of the Knesset. If during the Knesset's tenure a seat is vacated, the next person on the list automatically fills it. Neither special elections (as for the British House of Commons or for the U.S. House of Representatives) nor appointments (used to fill vacancies for the U.S. Senate) are permitted.

Voting for the Knesset is actually done by choosing the letter symbols of the competing lists. Each party chooses a Hebrew letter or group of letters, which must be approved by the Central Elections Committee, and campaigning and voting are conducted using these letter symbols. An interesting sidelight of the campaign is the symbolism involved in the parties' choices.

The letter combination the Labor-Mapam Alignment requested and was assigned was AMT—*aleph, mem, taf.* A good argument could be made for this combination, since the aleph (revealingly, the first letter of the alphabet) was traditionally the letter of Mapai, the *mem* the symbol of Mapam, and the *taf* that of Ahdut Haavoda, all of which were in the Alignment until 1984. But this special combination of letters was more than a throwback to the days when these parties ran as separate entities. For AMT (pronounced *emet*) means "truth" in Hebrew. And who can be against truth? The letter B used by the NRP and the D used by Poalei Agudat Israel, both religious parties, have both been used in campaign rhetoric in highly symbolic and suggestive ways.[1] So was the Z (besides the name of the letter, a signifier for the male sexual organ) used in the 1970s by the Black Panthers, a group of Sephardi Jews who felt they were discriminated against by the authorities, and by the Male Rights in the Family Party in 1996, indicating succinctly that each group felt that it was being "screwed."

If the list submitted by the party (or a group of parties) receives 1.5 percent (2 percent since 2004) or more of the vote, it wins representation in the 120-seat Knesset. The citizen, on entering the voting booth, chooses from the letter or group of letters assigned to the party and places the slip of paper with the letter(s) of his choice into an envelope. Votes are counted on a nationwide basis, and Knesset seats are allocated in direct proportion to the strength of the lists at the polls.

Israel's Knesset is elected by a proportional representation list system in which very few procedural or technical obstacles face a group choosing to compete. The minimum age for a candidate is twenty-one. The list must be submitted some thirty-five days before the election date. The Central Elections Committee, made up of representatives of the various parties in proportion to their strength in the outgoing Knesset and headed by a Supreme Court justice, is responsible for conducting the election, including the approval of lists.

Until 1964 there was no legal restriction on the right to run for public office. In anticipation of elections for the Sixth Knesset, the Court upheld the disqualification by the defense minister of an Arab list, many of whose members were from the outlawed El-Ard organization, thus limiting for the first time the right to run for office and accepting the principle that the state had a right to defend itself from those who opposed its existence. Legislation followed in 1985, with the addition of Section 7a to the Basic Law: The Knesset, which states that a list may not take part in Knesset elections if its goals or actions include one of the following:

1. Negation of the right of the State of Israel to exist as the state of the Jewish people.

2. Negation of the State's democratic nature.

3. Incitement to racism.

This legislation was a reaction to the polarization and extremism that characterized the 1980s, when the issues of the future of the territories became agitated. Before the 1984 elections, the Central Elections Committee disqualified two lists: Kach, a Jewish extremist list, and the Progressive List for Peace, an Arab list at the opposite end of the political spectrum. The Supreme Court overturned the Committee's decision and enabled both parties to participate in the elections; Kach won one seat, the PLP two seats. After the elections, the Section 7a legislation was passed, establishing the three causes for disqualification, which themselves were the result of a political tradeoff balancing those who sought to negate the state's democratic nature, including inciters to racism (the intention was to disqualify Kach's candidacy) with limits on lists negating Israel's right to exist as a Jewish state (the Progressive List for Peace).[2] This same formula was used in the 1992 Parties Law, thus limiting the right to organize. In that case, an additional cause for disqualification was specified—that of the existence of conclusive evidence that the party in question would serve as a front for illegal activities.

In 2002 two additional limits on the right to run for election were passed in reaction to the ongoing conflict with the Palestinians, the fight against terrorism and the dilemmas posed by Arab Knesset members. First, a new cause for disqualifying Knesset candidacy or for nonregistration of a party was added: support for the armed struggle of an enemy country or a terrorist organization fighting against the State of Israel. This cause is compatible with the concept of the "self-defending democracy," but its formulation indicates that it was directed toward the Arab minority, since it does not address individuals and organizations such as Jewish terrorist groups. The second new limitation introduced the possibility of disqualifying an individual candidate as opposed to a list. This revision stemmed in part from the sense of unease at disqualifying an entire list based on the behavior of a single candidate.

In 2003 the politically constituted Central Elections Committee disqualified one Arab list, Balad (National Democratic Alliance), and two Arab candidates, Balad's leader, MK Azmi Bishara, and MK Ahmad Tibi of Hadash (Democratic Front for Peace and Equality). At the same time, the committee sanctioned the participation of Baruch Marzel, former leader of the extreme right-wing, debarred Kach Party. All these decisions were later reversed by the Supreme Court.

Constitutional Provisions

Section 4 of The Basic Law: Knesset states that "the Knesset shall be elected in general, national, direct, equal, secret and proportional elections." These are the six features of the relatively pure form of proportional representation by which Israel's Knesset is elected:

1. *General:* allowing no discrimination among qualified voters. Every Israeli citizen eighteen years of age and older is entitled to vote. The issue of suffrage was a major scene of political battle in Western democracies, but Israel was spared these battles, always opting for universal suffrage. In the Yishuv period, religious groups demanded the exclusion of women from the list of voters because, the argument ran, women have no role to play in public affairs. So furious was the debate that some groups boycotted the elections of Yishuv institutions because of the rules on women suffrage in the election. Other institutions permitted only males to vote and then had the weight of the male vote doubled in order to compensate for the lack of women votes.[3]

2. *National:* that votes will be counted on a national basis, although administrative provisions are made for conducting elections and reporting results on regional, city, district, subdistrict, and precinct levels.

3. *Direct:* that each voter must complete the voting act by himself or herself. No delegation of authority, except for the blind or infirm, is permitted. Nor is absentee balloting permitted, although special arrangements are made for some people to vote even though they do not present themselves at their polling station, including persons serving with the Israel Defense Forces on election day, those in official positions abroad and their families (a few thousand eligible voters), eligible sailors working on Israeli flagships with at least ten voters (none met these requirements in 2003), those hospitalized, and prisoners.

4. *Equal:* that each voter has the same amount of influence as every other voter. This ideal is probably unattainable in the real world because in all electoral systems some votes are "wasted," and those who cast "wasted" votes have less influence on the election results than do other voters. The percentage of nonvalid or "wasted" votes in the 2003 Knesset vote was 1.6 percent, and an additional 4.1 percent cast ballots for parties that received less than the 1.5 percent minimum required. On the whole, the Israeli electoral system receives high grades for equality in its election of the Knesset (with two reservations to this generalization, discussed later).

5. *Secret:* that it not be possible to identify the vote of a particular voter.

6. *Proportional:* that each list be represented according to its strength in the electorate, providing that it achieves at least 1.5 percent of the vote (2 percent since 2004).

The two reservations regarding the equality principle stem from the fact that, ultimately, the result of the electoral process is to select the 120-member Knesset, which is apportioned by determining the "quota" for each seat. If there are 1,200,000 valid votes, a list will win a seat in the Knesset for each 10,000 votes that it gets. But reality is not that neat: parties do not win votes in increments of 10,000; instead, one party wins 9,994 and the other 14,968. What is to be done?

The first reservation regarding the general equality of the system is that the minimum needed for winning a Knesset seat is 1.5 percent of the valid voters.[4] That is, for the first seat in our hypothetical example, 10,000 votes would not be enough. Since 1.5 percent of 1,200,000 is 18,000, that is the number of votes it would take to win the party's first seat—a higher price must be paid for this first seat than for those following it. The second seat is cheapest by far, since $2 \div 120 = 1.67$ percent, only 0.17 percent more the 1.5 percent already paid for the first seat.

This minimum rate for winning the first Knesset seat was raised before the 1992 elections with the express purpose of limiting the number of single-member parties. And it worked very well: single-member parties have been eliminated since 1992, and the overall number of parties that won representation decreased from fifteen in 1988 to ten in 1992. In 1996 eleven parties won representation and most received at least four seats, with only one winning two seats. In 2003 there were thirteen winning lists, with two lists receiving two seats each in the Knesset. There is constant discussion of raising the minimum even higher; in 2004 legislation raised it to 2 percent.

The second reservation about the equality of the system concerns the distribution of the "surplus vote"—the below-quota portion remaining in the columns of parties that achieved the minimum percentage needed after the initial allocation of seats. Between 1961 and 1969, the party with the largest remainder won the vacant seat or seats. In 1949 and since 1973, however, the Hagenbach-Bischoff formula for the allocation of remainder seats has been used. Widely used in Europe, in Israel the method is popularly known as the Bader-Ofer Amendment, after the Likud and Alignment politicians who sponsored the bill and saw it through the legislative process.

The Hagenbach-Bischoff system provides for a floating quota after the original allocation of seats has taken place. Each list has its quota recalculated in order to allocate the surplus votes; the new quota is the number of votes won by a party divided by the number of seats already allocated to that party plus one. Inflating the denominator in this manner obviously works in favor of larger parties to the detriment of smaller ones (see table 7.1).

The method works as its proponents desired. Of the seven additional seats allocated in the 2003 elections, the Likud won two and Labor one under the Bader-Ofer calculation, while five small parties missed out on extra representation that they would have received according to the largest remainder formula. In 1977 the three largest parties (Likud, Alignment, and DMC) won a total of five seats more than they would have received under the largest remainder formula, and the middle-sized NRP did not win or lose, but five small parties lost five Knesset seats among them compared to what they would have had under the largest remainder system. In 1996, three of the six additional seats went to the

Table 7.1 Largest Remainder and Hagenbach-Bischoff Methods of Allocating Surplus Votes

Party	Votes	Seats	Surplus votes	Largest remainder	Hagenbach-Bischoff calculation	Hagenbach-Bischoff index	Hagenbach-Bischoff allocation
A	667,000	66	7,000	+1	667,000/67	9955	+1
B	415,000	41	5,000	0	415,000/42	9880	+1
C	118,000	11	8,000	+1	118,000/12	9833	0
Total	1,200,000	118		2			2

Note: Voters = 1,200,000 ; seats = 120 ; quota = 10,000.

two largest parties (two to Likud and one to Labor), while the others went to smaller parties.

Proponents of this deviation from the principle of equality argue that the relative size of the electorate that supports a list must also be taken into consideration in determining the allocation of seats. A party supported by a million voters must be treated differently from a party supported by 20,000 voters. The Hagenbach-Bischoff formula expresses this preferential treatment. Opponents argue that this is a case of the majority legislating against the minority; indeed, all the small parties in 1973 banded together, regardless of ideology, to oppose the passage of the Bader-Ofer Amendment. In a system in which the multiplicity of opinion and political organization is legitimate and even encouraged, it is unfortunate that the two large parties "ganged up" on the smaller ones, even if the overall damage to the principle of equal representation is relatively slight. In order to safeguard the principle of majority rule, the law states that a party will not win a majority of the seats in the Knesset if it fails to win a majority of the valid votes in the electorate, and this contingency clause contained, slightly, the hue and cry that the amendment generated.

An offsetting feature of the distribution system comes from *apparentement,* the French term for the formal linking of party lists at the stage at which parliamentary seats are allocated. The term roughly translates into English as "cartel" or "association,"[5] and is referred to as a "surplus vote agreement" in Hebrew. Party lists appear separately on the ballot, and the initial allocation is for each party. If there are still seats to be distributed after the count is completed, parties that have entered an *apparentement* participate in the next stage, with the surpluses of the associated parties merged. In 2003 six surplus vote agreements were made: between Labor-Meimad and Meretz, Shinui and the Greens, Shas and Yahadut Hatorah, the National Union and Israel B'Aliya, the NRP and Am Ehad, and Hadash and Balad. The law states that both parties of the *apparentement* agreement must win more than the minimum 1.5 percent of the vote; since the Greens failed to do so, only five party-couples participated in the calculations.

Table 7.2 reflects the 2003 Knesset election results, in which the quota was established at 25,138—3,016,624 votes for the thirteen parties that achieved the 1.5 percent minimum, divided by 120 seats. Division of the votes of each party by 25,138 allocated 113 seats disregarding remainders, leaving 7 seats to be allocated to reach the full 120-member Knesset. The next step was to add together the votes and seats of those

Table 7.2 Israel's 2003 Election Results: Largest Remainder and Bader-Ofer Methods of Allocating Surplus Votes

Party	Votes[a]	Seats based on quota[b]	Numerical remainder[c]	Largest remainder	Bader-Ofer calculation	Difference	Total
Likud	925,279	36	**20,311**	+1	+2	+1	38
Labor-Meimad	455,183	18	2,699	0	+1	+1	19
Shinui	386,535	15	9,465	0	0	0	15
Shas	258,879	10	7,499	0	+1	+1	11
National Unity (Ha-Ihud Haleumi)	173,973	6	**23,151**	+1	+1	0	7
Meretz	164,122	6	**13,294**	+1	0	−1	6
National Religious (Mafdal)	132,370	5	6,680	0	+1	+1	6
Torah Judaism	135,087	5	9,297	0	0	0	5
Democratic Front for Peace & Equality (Hadash)	93,819	3	**18,405**	+1	0	−1	3
One Nation (Am Ehad)	86,808	3	11,394	0	0	0	3
National Democratic Assembly (Balad)	71,299	2	**21,023**	+1	+1	0	3
Israel B'Aliya	67,719	2	**17,443**	+1	0	−1	2
United Arab List	65,551	2	**15,275**	+1	0	−1	2
Total	3,016,624	113		7	7		120

a. There were 4,720,079 eligible voters; 3,200,773 participated in the elections. Of those who voted, the ballots of 52,409 (1.6%) were disqualified, and 131,740 (4.1% of those who voted) cast ballots for parties that received less than the 1.5% minimum required.

b. Qualifying threshold for representation (1.5% of valid votes) = 47,226 votes. Quota per Knesset seat = 25,138 votes.

c. Boldface numbers indicate the seven highest numerical remainders.

parties that had entered into surplus vote agreements. For example, Labor-Meimad's total of 455,183 votes, when divided by the quota, yielded 18 seats and left 2,699 surplus votes in the party's column. Its associated party, Meretz, which received 164,122 votes, won 6 seats on the first allotment, leaving it 13,294 votes in surplus beyond the seats it had won.

Apparentement calls for the calculation of the new quota by dividing the two associated parties' *total* votes by their *total* seats plus one (619,305 ÷ 25); the new quota was 24,772. Even though the two parties only had 15,993 surplus votes between them, that new quota was high enough to win one additional seat for the two parties together. The next step was to determine whether Labor or Meretz would get this seat—which required referring back to the numbers won by the individual parties to the agreement. Labor's new quota was 23,957 (455,183 ÷ 19), and the new quota for Meretz was 23,303 (163,122 ÷ 7). Accordingly, Labor won this seat because its quota was higher.

Shinui suffered because its surplus agreement partner, the Green Party, failed to pass the minimum 1.5 percent threshold, and thus, its 12,833 votes were lost. Likud signed no agreement in 2003; its leaders were slow in getting around to it and by the time they did, their preferred partners had already signed with others.

The Bader-Ofer system worked as intended by favoring large vote-getters over smaller ones. Most of the parties that benefited were larger ones, and most of those smaller vote-getters that would have won additional seats under the largest remainder system did not do so under the Bader-Ofer system.

Setting the Date of the Elections

Elections in Israel are held every four years unless earlier elections are called. Determining the date for the elections can, like most topics in Israel, become intensely political. Early elections can be decided on by the Knesset; the prime minister with the concurrence of the country's president can disperse the Knesset and bring about early elections; early elections are mandated if the Knesset fails to pass the budget three months after the beginning of the fiscal year or if the designated process fails to result in the formation of a government approved by the Knesset.

The Knesset's term is four years unless earlier elections are called. Elections are to be held on the third Tuesday of the Hebrew month of Heshvan (which usually occurs around November) of the year in which the Knesset ends its term, unless the previous year is a leap year according to the Hebrew calendar, in which case the elections are held on the first Tuesday of Heshvan. According to the Basic Law: Knesset, if a parliament disperses before the end of its legal term in office, the next parliament will hold office until the month of Heshvan after it has completed four full years in office; if a parliament lasts its regular term in office, the next parliament will hold office until the month of Heshvan before the end of its fourth year.

The matter of setting the date for the parliamentary elections to follow those of 2003 became embroiled in controversy: should the next elections be held in November 2006 or October 2007, assuming that the Knesset would complete its full term? In the past, when the Fifteenth Knesset (elected in 1999) had been dispersed before the end of its four-year term, it was assumed, in accordance with the law, that the next Knesset should last longer than four years. According to the original Basic Law: Government, if the prime minister disperses parliament, it is to be regarded as though the Knesset has dispersed itself, and, therefore, the next Knesset is to last more than four full years.

But prior to the 2003 elections, the Knesset made a mistake in passing a relatively minor amendment to the Basic Law: Government having nothing to do directly with the question of the date of new elections. In seeking to extend the time between the dispersal of parliament and the next election from sixty days to ninety days, the writers of the amendment failed to include the words that had appeared in the original Basic Law: Government to the effect that if the prime minister disperses parliament, it is to be regarded as though the Knesset has dispersed itself.

In 2002 Sharon dispersed parliament. According to the original law, his act should have been regarded as if parliament had dispersed itself. But the 2003 amendment to the law did not contain that provision. Everyone agreed that the words had been deleted by mistake, but the Supreme Court ruled that it could not assume the Knesset's intentions when the provision was not specifically included. Accordingly, the Court ruled, the elections must be held no later than 2006.

The tenure of the Knesset has been substantially shortened a number of times and postponed once. The elections that followed those held in 1949, 1959, and 1981 were in 1951, 1961, and 1984 respectively. In 1973, when elections were scheduled for the end of October and the Yom Kippur War broke out at the beginning of that month, elections were postponed for two months until the end of December.

The 1996–2003 period of the direct election of the prime minister was characterized by early elections. Both Netanyahu in 1999 and Barak in

2001 lost the support of their own governments, and when early elections were called, both were dismissed by the public. The 2001 election was a special election for the prime minister only, with the Knesset continuing its tenure.

The ruling party would probably attempt to manipulate the election date for political advantage, if it thought it could do so. But because the campaign period is so long and political developments are so unpredictable, Israeli politicians seem to understand that trying to turn a swing in public opinion into electoral advantage is a risky bet. A shortened Knesset term in the past has generally resulted from political crises. After the Six Days' War of 1967, at certain stages of the peace negotiations with Egypt in 1978, and after the Rabin assassination in 1995, the Alignment, Likud, and Labor, respectively, probably could have benefited from early elections, but they were not called.

One explanation is that elections must be called well in advance. A Knesset law mandates a 100-day cooling-off period for a civil servant who wishes to run in the elections (although in 1996 it was shortened to 60 days because an early election date was decided on). Since many parties infuse their political ranks with fresh blood from the military, diplomatic, or administrative services, it is customary to set the date for elections well past the 100-day period. A politician knows that in three-and-a-half months his rosy prognostication may well change, and he might regret the move.

The history of the 1996 election provides a case in point. The Labor Party and Shimon Peres, its leader, enjoyed a cascade of popular support in the months following Rabin's assassination in November 1995. However, since the government was in the midst of negotiations with Syria over the future of the Golan Heights and Lebanon, it remained committed to the mandated election date of late October 1996. Peres preferred an election campaign based on a draft peace treaty with Syria and thought that face-to-face negotiations with President Assad of Syria were necessary to reach an agreement in time. When Assad finally agreed to negotiate but would provide no firm date for the meeting, Peres decided that Syria would not be forthcoming. Labor therefore opted for elections at the end of May 1996, and the party leaders reached out to the leaders of other parties regarding the election date.

However, the crowded Hebrew and Israeli calendars of the spring (Passover, Holocaust Day, Memorial Day, Independence Day, Lag BaOmer, Jerusalem Day, the feast of Shavuot, and memorial commemorations for those killed in the 1967 Six Days' War and the 1982 Lebanese war) combined with very practical political considerations to complicate the task of setting a date. Influenced by the wording of the new law regarding the runoff elections for the direct prime minister vote, and by Israelis' patterns of behavior in leisure time, Labor favored elections in May. The Likud and the religious parties preferred June. At this point— before two of the other announced candidates for prime minister, Raful Eitan of Tzomet and David Levy of Gesher, swung their support to Netanyahu as part of the deal they had worked out to form a joint list with Likud—it seemed likely that a runoff election would take place for the prime ministry. If a runoff were to be held, it would take place on the Tuesday "two weeks after the announcement of the original vote results." And if the first round of elections were held in the beginning of June, the official results announced a few days later, and the runoff two weeks after that, many Peres voters might be out of the country on summer vacation on the day of the runoff.

There were constraints on calling the elections too early as well as too late. The Interior Ministry official in charge of overseeing the elections warned that holding elections on May 20 would not give his office enough time to update the lists and include in the official roster all those who were eighteen years of age on election day. Labor wanted the voting done by June 20, the last day of classes in Israel's high schools—after that date (and certainly by June 30, when the elementary school students finish), many families make travel plans, and the national attention is difficult to focus. Besides, the European Cup soccer finals were to be held in the last weeks of June, and the politicians wanted no distractions from their show. Summer elections in the past had dealt unkind blows to Labor; it reasoned that its relatively affluent voters were more likely to be away than were those of the Likud and the religious parties. Moreover, the groundswell of grief over the Rabin assassination seemed to be spearheaded by young, first-time voters. It seemed unwise to risk their being shut out for administrative reasons if the elections were held too early, or their being out of the country if the elections were extended to late June or to July.

One practical thing could be done to reduce risk: to control some of the uncertainty by having a firm date for the second round of voting. Even though this matter of setting election dates was part of a Basic Law (supposedly one of the building blocks of Israel's constitution), the politicians had no qualms about altering it to fit their immediate needs. The revised wording timed the runoff two weeks after the original elections, rather than two weeks after the announcement of the results.

Although it preferred June, the Likud also favored May 21, a few days after Jerusalem Day, on the supposition that the call for keeping Jerusalem united as Israel's capital, and the media attention to Jerusalem on that day, played in its favor and against Peres's more conciliatory positions. However, May 21 was only days before Shavuot, the holy day commemorating the receiving of the Torah at Mount Sinai; for haredim and other religious Jews, the days preceding that holy day are for prayer and withdrawal in symbolic preparation for receiving God's word. The thought that some 300,000 haredim might be too withdrawn to turn out and vote made the Likud and Netanyahu reconsider the May date.

In the end, the elections were scheduled for Wednesday, May 29, 1996. In the past, elections had always taken place on Tuesdays—but political expediency led to calendar flexibility. While Israeli politicians are ever cognizant of political advantage (even in such matters as setting the date of elections), it is doubtful that their willingness to manipulate the situation is matched by their success in effecting the desired results. At the end of February 1996, when these weighty decisions were being taken, no one could have predicted either the series of suicide bombings awaiting Israel or the inconclusive result of the Grapes of Wrath campaign in Lebanon, nor the impact these events would have on the voters.

Alternative Electoral Systems

Electoral laws are as much a result as they are a cause of the political culture of a country. They project the political values and interests of the times and the ruling groups. Like other laws, they benefit certain interests and groups at the expense of other interests and groups. Electoral laws have political consequences. They provide no magic formula for curing the ills of the nation. The laws are incapable of making politicians honest, officeholders responsible, or voters wise. In a simplistic sense, when officeholders perceive that it is in their or their party's interest to be more responsive to the demands of the electorate, they are likely to be so. A change in the electoral laws may also coincide with this perception, but the change in behavior (responsive officeholders) cannot be attributed solely to a change in the rules. The system is much too complex and the interrelations too many to use a simple mechanistic model to expect change in the political system as a result of legislation.

Israel is an example of a representative parliamentary democracy with authoritative decisions being made by the duly elected legislature.[6]

In truth, the Knesset is eclipsed by the prime minister and other government ministries, but in a formal, legal, and moral sense, authority rests with the Knesset.

Techniques of direct democracy, such as the referendum, are often considered.[7] The principle of republican government exemplified in the Israeli system rests on the belief that an elected parliament weighing alternative proposals will best serve the national interest, while forms of direct democracy run the risk of having key decisions made by shifting majorities of varying degrees of intensity. Israel experimented with an expression of direct democracy with the adoption of the direct election of the prime minister, but the policy was aborted after five years.

No referendum has ever been held in Israel, although the method has been suggested a number of times. Ben-Gurion suggested it in 1955 as a means to reform the electoral system. In 1958 Begin proposed legislation that would allow 100,000 citizens to demand a referendum. In a Knesset debate in 1994, Deputy Defense Minister Mordechai ("Mota") Gur, obviously representing Prime Minister Rabin, promised a referendum regarding a possible withdrawal from the Golan Heights as part of a peace treaty with Syria. This effectively defused the political opposition to the continuing negotiations, and since those negotiations did not end in an agreement, no referendum was held. Similarly, in the 1996 election campaign Prime Minister Peres promised a referendum before signing the permanent status agreement with the Palestinian Authority, but since he was not reelected, that promise was never put to the test.

A 1999 law states that any government decision to withdraw from territories in which Israeli law applies must be approved by an absolute majority of the Knesset. (Israeli law has applied to East Jerusalem since 1967 and to the Golan Heights since 1981; the other territories are considered "liberated" or "occupied" or "disputed," but they have not been annexed to Israel.) Furthermore, if the Basic Law: Referendum is in effect at the time—it has yet to be passed—such a withdrawal must also be approved in a referendum with the support of a majority of the participants. This requirement would apply only *if* the Basic Law: Referendum were promulgated—that is, the rules for holding a referendum would have constitutional status.

One crucial question regarding the holding of a referendum is defining the majority required for passage: A majority of those voting or a majority of voters? Half or some other fraction? Many Israelis champion the proposal that only Jews (and not Arab citizens) be allowed to participate in decisions regarding the country's borders, making these issues political dynamite. Stipulating a majority of voters and not a majority of those voting would allow abstainers to influence the outcome of the referendum. Using anything other than a simple majority formula would mean that Jews would have to disproportionately support the proposal to pass it, assuming the near unanimous support of Arab voters (about 15 percent of the electorate).

Two major democratic systems of elections—the single-member district system (SMDS) and proportional representation (PR)——reflect the distinction between systems of representation that are based on more direct expressions of the public will or on parliamentary democracy.[8] The single-member district system, which is widely used in Anglo-Saxon countries, is thought to foster government stability, while proportional representation, more prevalent in continental Europe, promotes democratic representation. In SMDS, the candidate who wins a majority of the vote is elected; variations include electing the candidate who receives the most votes even if he fails to receive a majority, or electing the candidate who receives the most votes provided that it is more than a certain amount (say, 40 percent, as in the election of mayors in Israel).

Proportional representation, in contrast, provides for the election of representatives in proportion to the strength of the competing groups in the electorate. Usually individuals do not compete in this system, although in some variations the voter may rearrange or delete names on a party list or even choose candidates from different lists. Other details also vary from one example to another. For instance, a country may consist of one electoral unit (as in Israel) or it may be divided into districts, with competition taking place in each district according to the rules of proportional representation (as was the case in Italy). Another variation may specify a minimum percentage needed to win representation—such as a single arithmetic function of the size of the group to be elected and the number of voters (1.5 percent or 2 percent of the 120-member Knesset, as in Israel)—or the number of votes needed for winning a seat may be fixed. Regardless of variations, the principle of representation according to electoral strength is the key. Usually, proportional representation generates many competing parties (there were twenty-seven in Israel in 2003). Small parties generally oppose reform since they would be disadvantaged by a change to a constituency system.

The size of electoral districts is the critical factor in approximating the ideal of proportional representation: the larger the electoral district in terms of seats, the more proportional the representation will be.[9] This is why the NRP, a party that has traditionally opposed electoral reform to a constituency system, argued in 1977 for dividing the country into five large districts; and why the DMC, whose platform heavily stressed electoral reform, opted for sixteen. The DMC reform would have increased local visibility of the constituency's representative at the expense of proportionality.

Reform is proposed in many systems, but it is implemented only occasionally. Discussions for revamping the American electoral college or the British constituency system have continued for decades. The French are much more active than most, having changed their system for electing the National Assembly from a constituency method to a proportional system and back again since the 1980s. The 1990s have seen a rash of electoral reform, including the Italian shift from a proportional system to a mixed proportional-constituency system, the New Zealand move from a constituency method to a proportional one, and the Japanese, from a multi-member, single-alternative vote to a more proportional method. The Israeli shift from a pure parliamentary system to a mixed parliamentary direct election of prime minister system, also occurred at that time.[10]

Since there is no perfect system, and since electoral reform is not a magic formula to cure the ills of political or social systems, what is electoral reform meant to achieve? In other words, in order to make up your mind regarding electoral change, it is important to know what goals you are trying to reach. What are the important criteria for judging electoral systems? What is the experience of other democratic countries? Which system tends to be associated with which results? Four important criteria are *system stability, democratic representation, the link between the elected and the electorate,* and *the role of the party.*

Stability

In a parliamentary system in which the executive is elected by the legislature and the parliament is fragmented into many parties, the probability of instability rises. Often no clear majority is achieved by any party, coalitions are necessary for organizing the parliament and for passing legislation, and no easy agreement can be reached as to who should serve as prime minister. This condition has prevailed in many countries in Europe—in France before the Second World War and in Italy after it. The British system, by contrast, is more stable because only two or three large parties are represented in Parliament and the leader is more clearly discernible; coalitions are rarely needed. After some fifty years and fifty-five governments, Italy abandoned its proportional system in 1995–1996 and adopted a mixed proportional and single-member district system.

In presidential systems such as in the United States, France, Russia, and Mexico, the identity of the head of government is determined by popular vote and is not decided by parliamentary coalitions. In the United States, of course, this distinction is not technically achieved, since the electoral college actually selects the president. And the system of the French Fifth Republic has been termed semi-presidential,[11] since it features both a president elected by the voters and an elected parliament that selects a prime minister in the tradition of parliamentary systems.

In a parliamentary system, the stability of the executive is predicated on control of the legislature because the parliament chooses the prime minister. The presidential system, on the other hand, provides for stability of the executive and the government but does not ensure that the executive's relations with the legislative branch will be trouble-free, especially if the legislature is in the hands of another party. The Israeli direct election of the prime minister did not separate the prime minister from dependency on the government coalition.

Paradoxically, Israel did not suffer from excessive governmental instability before it switched to the direct election of the prime minister. There was, however, a perception of instability because the fact that the two large political blocs were almost evenly matched seriously complicated the task of the prime minister in keeping the governing coalition together. The reform was designed to allow the elected prime minister the stability needed to govern. When Netanyahu led the government as its first directly elected prime minister, forty-eight years after the establishment of the state, the Knesset had held its fourteenth election and he headed the twenty-seventh government. Over the next five years, Israel had three elections and three different prime ministers.

Stability is not only a matter of numbers but also a matter of political control. The parties of Israel's prime ministers have been, for the most part, in firm control of the political situation. There has rarely been a feeling of instability, despite the fact that Yitzhak Rabin headed minority governments both in 1974 and in 1994, when religious parties were not part of the government coalition.

But if politics is about ruling, and ruling demands a majority, then coalition politics are at the center of a polity like Israel's. The largest party has never won a majority in the elections, and hence coalitions are a constant feature of Israeli politics. Winning parties can choose to coalesce with some or all of the religious parties, as they have done most of the time, or they can coalesce with the second biggest winner (and others), as they have in 1967, 1984, and 1988, calling this exercise the formation of National Unity Governments.

The reformers hoped that, by being directly elected, the prime minister would be relieved of the stressful pressures of intense and costly bargaining with medium-sized and smaller parties to form a coalition. Potential partners would have to cooperate with the directly-elected prime minister, the thinking went, because there was no way of changing the candidate for prime minister short of new elections. In addition, some who supported the reform hoped that the number of parties would decrease because winning the prime ministry would require winning an electoral majority, and thus splintering of the vote would no longer be rational in terms of electoral and political success.

These expectations were cruelly dashed, as the new electoral procedure generated the most fractionalized political party system that Israel had known. Never in Israeli political history had there been winning parties (once Likud, then Labor) with such small Knesset delegations. Moreover, the total number of seats won by the two largest parties was also unusually small. One must look to the 1949 elections and those in the early 1950s to find the two major parties commanding so few of the votes of the electorate as they did in 1996; in 1999, together they were the smallest ever. The results led to the emergence of sectarian interests, such as the new immigrants, the religious, and the Arabs, and a weakening of the concentration on national issues. This effect was obviously facilitated by split-ticket voting, in which a voter felt that he could send differentiated messages because he voted twice—once for the prime minister and once for the Knesset. This sophisticated use of the ballot box by the Israeli voter left in its wake a party system in shambles, and a Knesset fractionalized and weakened compared to the prime minister and the executive branch.

The extent of bargaining with small and medium-sized sectarian parties to form the coalition was as great as it had been in the past, if not greater. The prime minister had to satisfy many different demands and that put pressure on the public treasury. What emerged was a very costly agreement that was likely to be renegotiated often during the lifetime of the government as new issues posed threats to the stability of the coalition. The prime minister would also have to expend more of his own time to calm his coalition partners and more of the national budget in order to keep the coalition together.

Democratic Representation

The premise of proportional representation is that opinions expressed in the legislature accurately reflect opinions held in the population. This is unlikely, if only because many people do not have firm opinions on many issues of public importance, and even those who do are unlikely to follow the "party line" on each of them. Furthermore, many voters are influenced by matters peripheral to the central issues, such as the candidate's television appeal, the persuasiveness of the campaign, or some emotional attachment with one party or another.

The modern political party should not be understood as the mechanism for reflecting distribution of opinion in the population; it is more accurate to think of the party as the mechanism that translates votes into public policy and political power. What the voter "really" meant is always a matter of interpretation. Thus, proportional representation must be understood in terms of proportional representation of political parties and not in terms of proportional representation of public opinion or policy alternatives.

On the whole, proportional representation may not produce an identical image of the electorate in the legislature, but the distortion is not nearly as great as it usually is in the constituency system. Choosing someone to represent a district may pinpoint responsibility, but it denies representation to all those voters who did not support the person elected. The ideal of proportional representation, in contrast, is the faithful representation of all shades of opinion. This is a profoundly democratic notion and is in fact relatively modern. The idea of a single-member constituency originated in predemocratic days when legislators were expected to represent corporate bodies such as localities, universities, and economic corporations rather than individuals. The British idea of constituency representation grew out of its feudal heritage and has remained the dominant political expression of the British system.

The anomalies of the constituency system are well known. For example, in the 1988 Canadian elections, those who opposed the free trade treaty with the United States were in the majority, but, because of the constituency system used in Canada, a majority of the parliament members favored the bill. While public opinion was not accurately reflected in the vote, what was more important was that Canadians saw the results of the elections as a legitimate expression of the nation's will, and the free trade treaty was ratified.

The Electorate and the Elected

A third criterion for the assessment of electoral systems is the proper relationship between the electorate and the elected. Two classic models are the *free agent* and the *delegate*. A free agent will vote his conscience regardless of the interests of party or constituency; the delegate will, to the best of his ability, do as he has been instructed. Modern representative government involved the search for the proper relationship between the representative and his constituency. The free agent model assumes that the representative is only remotely attached to his constituents and that his understanding of the national interest will guide him.

In the Israeli system, an oft-heard criticism of the electoral system is that voters do not know who represents them. The party, especially the large party, is too anonymous for many voters; technically there is no representative who can protect interests, hear pleas, or present proposals. Israeli parties have been seeking to strengthen the connection with their members. Five of the largest parties—Likud, Labor, Meretz, Tzomet, and the NRP—introduced some type of primary among registered party members to select their lists before the 1996 elections, and many continue to use the system. Israel went through an intense period of primaries, but efforts to limit headline-grabbing sensationalism and to regulate expenditures were largely unsuccessful.

The fundamental question is on what basis groups are represented. Many Knesset members were selected by their party leaders in the past because they were part of an important ethnic, occupational, geographical, or ideological group. Both the Likud and Labor based their primaries partly on district representation and partly on assured representation for special groups such as women, ethnic groups, or Arabs. Also, many seated Knesset members are later approached by interested parties to promote legislation or to solve a personal problem.

Whereas the single-member district system promotes geographical representation, proportional representation promotes functional representation. In England or the United States, a representative is identified by his association with a given district or state. In Israel he is identified by the fact that he is Moroccan (or Polish), lives in a city (or development town), is for an aggressive settlement policy (or against it), and so on, regardless of where the representative lives. Obviously, in a single-member district system, it is simpler to identify your representative.

Even in constituency systems, however, many do not know who their representative is, let alone come in contact with that person for political purposes. We should not be misled into thinking that if we know who our representatives are, we suddenly become better citizens by participating more in debate over public issues. In Great Britain about half of the population knows the party of their district's representative in Parliament; a lower percentage knows the representative's name. In the United States the parallel figures are even lower. The proper relation between the electorate and its elected representatives is an extremely important issue, but it will not be determined simply by legislating a constituency system.

Once the lists are presented, the Israeli voter chooses among them as they are, without the possibility of adding, subtracting, or changing the order of the names that appear on any list. Contact with the candidate is minimal, both before and after the election. While the argument can be made that exposing the candidate to the judgment of the electorate should make him or her more responsive, the other side of the coin is that perhaps responsiveness to the momentary whim of the public is not in the national interest—in short, is not a responsible act. We return to the dilemma of the free agent and the delegate—which, in turn, leads us to the next major topic.

The Role of the Party

The fourth criterion is the proper role of the party, especially that of the party machine. Israeli parties in the past tended to be hierarchical, with small elite groups appointing the candidates for the party's list. This system began to crumble in 1977, to the point that in 1996—with the introduction of the primaries and the direct election of the prime minister—the role of the political party itself was called into question. In 2003 Labor was all but moribund, and the Likud appeared to have been taken over by vote-brokers and even criminal elements, leaving it out of touch with both the Likud leaders and the Likud voters.

The direct election of the prime minister put enormous power in the hands of the prime minister but did not provide for accountability to a political party. In the past, party leaders not elected by the public had acted as kingmakers, but under the direct election system, the public itself was to select the king, and so the leader had little obvious reason to consult with his party. While the law required that the prime minister be the head of a Knesset list, it did not require that he consult with his party. The Likud's constitution did not require approval of the prime minister's appointments or policies by the any party body, although Labor's constitution did.

A very difficult question for Israeli democracy in the past was whether it was appropriate to have unelected leaders select candidates for high office, which, in effect, limited the choice of the public come election day. The answer to that question was that Israel was a free country, and anyone who disliked the way a certain party selected its list could either vote for another party or set up another list. As long as competition was open and unhindered, proponents of this view argued, no damage was done to the democratic ideal. Alternatively, they argued, individuals who felt this way could involve themselves in the party's affairs and work to change the rules. The general argument was that a party was the keeper of an ideology, and as such it was in the best position to determine who was qualified to serve that particular ideology in the Knesset.

As the institution that has traditionally mediated between the people and the government, the political party needs discipline in order to govern. Party discipline demands Knesset members who are willing to be "delegates." On the other hand, it is important to attract to the Knesset individuals with skill, ambition, and talent. Is a talented person likely to want to play the role of party faithful and be disciplined when matters of importance are at stake? Will party interests always, or even often, meet the criteria of personal or national responsibility? Will a dynamic, thinking individual be appealing enough to meet the test of popular success in parties with primaries, or acceptable in parties that use nominating committees? An independent thinker who is not looked upon kindly by primary voters or by nominating committees may be left off the list or placed in a low spot the next time around. And yet these are the very people needed by a dynamic, creative party. The dilemma is that discipline enhances stability but also stagnation and a lackluster effect. Recruiting first-rate people to the Knesset means allowing them more creativity; this demands a high degree of visibility to win a primary and an ability to overcome the power of the party bosses. This problem is not unique to Israel. Some countries try to solve it by allowing voters to alter the lists presented by the parties, others by allowing the constituency to select its candidate pending approval of the central office (as in Britain).

With these four criteria in mind—stability, representation, the elector-elected relationship, and role of party—we face the question of electoral reform. Different priorities will generate different systems. If democratic representation is considered more important than a direct link between voter and representative, proportional representation may be preferred. If government stability is considered more important than the under-representation of minority viewpoints, then a form of constituency system may be preferred. All criteria cannot be fulfilled equally; some ranking of priorities will inevitably occur.

Electoral Reform

Discussion of electoral reform is a constant feature of Israeli politics. The interest shown by the press and the involved public stems from the belief, strongly rooted in the Israeli political culture, that changes in the law can change behavior, that the formal rules of the game are central in determining the nature of the game and the way it is played. In a sense, this is correct because the electoral laws ultimately determine who is elected and how much support they will have. But the debate regarding electoral reform is usually cast in much more general terms. Reform is championed as the way of changing the nature of the political system, making the members of the Knesset responsible and responsive to voters, and altering the very moral climate of the country.

In the early 1950s, Prime Minister David Ben-Gurion's problems with religious party partners in his government coalition led him to suggest that a referendum be held to adopt the British electoral system of single-member constituencies. The central committee of Mapai adopted this position in 1954, and since then electoral reform has been a constant issue of Israeli politics. Rafi in 1965 and the DMC in 1977 both made it the central issue of their election platforms. Tinkering with details of the system has been rather frequent, including the shift to the Bader-Ofer system of allocating surplus votes before the 1973 elections, and the raising of the minimum needed for representation from 1 percent to 1.5 percent before the 1992 elections.

Many reform proposals have been made over the years, and many of them contain provisions similar to those the Knesset approved by a wide margin in a first reading just before the 1988 elections, although they never became the law of the land. The common feature of the legislation's two proposals was that part of the Knesset would be elected by districts and part on a proportional list basis. It is likely that this sort of proposal will reemerge in the future.

Gad Yaacobi of Labor had spearheaded such proposals for years.[12] An early version of his plan called for eighteen five-member districts accounting for ninety members, with thirty others to be elected proportionally. This change would have added districts to the electoral system but not direct elections of representatives in the British or American sense, because all Knesset members would be elected on a proportional basis, only instead of having one national constituency, there would be eighteen smaller constituencies and one national one. Each party would submit up to nineteen lists: eighteen five-person lists and a single thirty-person list. The winner of each seat would be determined by the number of votes won by the party in the district, not by the candidate himself. The voter would not be able to identify his or her representative directly nor be able to influence the party's choice of candidates. Under this system, the minimal price paid for each seat, in terms of vote percentage needed, would increase dramatically. Under the present system the minimum is 1.5 percent; under the reform proposal it would in effect be 20 percent in the districts (one in five) and 3.3 percent for the national list.

An important question with this type of system concerns the acts that would be required of the voter. Would the voter have two ballots or one? That is, would he (or she) be able to split the ballot between an attractive district list of the Likud, say, and still vote his national preference by casting his ballot for Labor? Or would he be forced to choose only one party? Would the voter be allowed to alter the order of the names submitted by the party? Would he be obliged to vote for five candidates, or could he decide how many candidates (up to five in a five-person constituency) he wanted to vote for?

Another problem is that of gerrymandering, or drawing arbitrary districts, in order to benefit the party that controls the apportionment process. An example would be putting predominantly religious neighborhoods in with four or five religious kibbutzim in order to make more likely the election of religious candidates. In fact, while gerrymandering comes to politicians easily, it is not too difficult to prevent. A nonparty body headed by a Supreme Court justice in charge of apportionment would likely be above reproach. In the Yaacobi proposal, the districts envisaged would be relatively equal in size and contiguous in land area in order to avoid gerrymandering.[13] Alternatively, administrative districts could be made into electoral districts and the number of the representatives could be adjusted depending on population shifts.

There have been tremendous groundswells in favor of electoral reform. Rafi stressed electoral reform as one of its chief planks in 1965. Yigael Yadin was active in the electoral reform movement long before he entered national politics in 1977. Amnon Rubinstein's Shinui and the Yadin's DMC spoke enthusiastically of electoral reform, although most politicians preferred to speak in generalities and avoid details. The evidence of public support for electoral reform was striking. In 1972, 30 percent of a sample reported support for a mixed proportional-district system; by 1977 that figure had almost doubled, to 59 percent. After the 1988 elections, as the religious parties made enormous demands in order to join in a governing coalition, appeals for electoral reform surged again. Many who called for electoral reform really wanted to change the political outcome of the election, but instead, they concentrated on changing the electoral system.

Faced with public pressure for change, politicians were forced to react, and almost all parties indicated some degree of support for electoral reform in the 1977 elections. But in reality, party politicians were very uneasy about electoral reform because it would add yet another element of uncertainty to their already precarious occupation. The foot-dragging could be clearly seen in negotiations among the Likud, the NRP, and the DMC to expand the coalition government set up after the 1977 elections to include the DMC. The DMC had an ideological belief in and had made a public commitment to electoral reform, but the NRP, as a middle-sized party with most of its voters in a few concentrated geographic areas, had every reason to oppose reform. The Likud, and especially Herut and Prime Minister Begin, were never enthusiastic supporters of reform, but had committed themselves to it in the election campaign.

The lines of argument reflected the interests of the parties. The NRP wanted five districts of sixteen members each—recall that large districts increase the chances of approximating proportional representation—while the DMC argued for many districts with few delegates, since their concern was district representation. The problem was solved in a typical Israeli way: a decision was made not to decide. The parties agreed to set up a committee that would bring a proposal within a certain time, but that period passed and no recommendation was made. The lack of enthusiasm on the part of most politicians was hard to hide.

The coalition agreement setting up the 1984 and 1988 National Unity Governments called for a special committee to examine changing the electoral system. With Labor and Likud controlling the government coalition and the Knesset, it would have been an ideal time for the two large parties to legislate reform that would favor their political interests. But the perceived need of having a good working relationship with the religious parties—potential future coalition partners—proved overpowering. An implicit part of the bargain with the smaller parties that also joined the National Unity Government in 1984 was an understanding that reform would be deferred; after all, the coalition agreement only called for setting up a committee. In 1988 the pressure was even greater, but the countervailing forces were also substantial. Electoral reform had not yet come about.

The proposal to have part of the Knesset elected by districts and part on an national list was approved by the Knesset on a first reading before the elections held in 1988. Knowing full well that they would be threatened by such reform, and forcefully reminding Prime Minister Shamir that he was likely to need their support in forming a coalition after the upcoming elections, leaders of the religious parties appealed to Shamir to prevent further action in the last moments of the legislative session. Shamir acceded to their pleas, and further legislative action was stymied. Although Shamir could have formed a coalition with the religious parties after the elections, he ultimately constructed the 1988 National Unity Government with the Labor Party and other parties.

After the inconclusive elections of 1988, it seemed that the only way to set up a governing coalition was to give in to the demands of the religious parties (who had collectively won 15 percent of the vote) for amending the "Who is a Jew?" definition in the Law of Return and to provide substantial additional funding for their schools. It appeared that the religious parties controlled the future of Israeli politics because they could determine which of the large parties would form a governing coalition in the Knesset. Accordingly, strong appeals rose to prevent in future the exaggerated power of the minority over the majority.

It was in this period of sharp political division over the future of the territories and a perceived stalemate between the major parties that the one major reform of Israeli constitutional transformation—the direct election of the prime minister—began to gain momentum. The ills of the parliamentary system became more obvious than ever because of the "dirty trick" of 1990, the name given by Yitzhak Rabin to the failed attempt by Shimon Peres to replace the Likud-led National Unity Government with a Labor-led coalition.

The background of the story of the "dirty trick" was a peace initiative put forth by Israel. It gained support in Washington and Cairo, but when U.S. Secretary of State James Baker pressed the Israeli government to be more flexible regarding details, Prime Minister Yitzhak Shamir recoiled. The Knesset expressed "no confidence" in its government for the first time in Israeli history, and the National Unity Government fell.

Yitzhak Modai, minister of finance, and his group of four other Knesset members (former members of the Liberal faction of the Likud), with a total of five votes, demanded recognition as an independent Knesset faction in return for their support of Shamir's position. The approval of their demand was granted just before the vote of no confidence. On March 15, 1990, the government fell by a 60–55 vote, defeated by the combined opposition of Labor, the Arabs, the left, and ultra-Orthodox Agudat Israel. The key to the "victory" of Peres and Labor was the fact that five of the six Knesset members of the ultra-Orthodox Shas Party absented themselves from the vote.

With the fall of the government, President Chaim Herzog appointed Shimon Peres to form a government. Peres had to placate his own party, made up of hawks and doves, and to fashion a government of religious parties and the extreme left. He needed the votes of Arab parties too, but he could not plan on negotiating away territory if their support was seen as pivotal. To succeed, Peres had to find Knesset members of the other camp who were willing to desert to the Labor side (Israeli constitutional practice at that time did not prohibit the Knesset member from switching allegiance). The three most likely turncoat candidates had all been placed on the Likud list in deals cut to solve previous coalition crises. One was Yigael Horowitz, leader of Ometz (two seats), who had left the Labor Party years before; another was Aharon Abu-Hatzeira, former head of the Tami list; finally, there was the Modai group, with five seats, recently liberated from the Likud and now recognized as an independent Knesset faction.

Things went poorly for Peres. Agudat Israel, the ultra-Orthodox haredi party, agreed not to participate in a Likud government and to support a Labor government without formally joining it, but, on the other hand, the deciding rabbinical council of the Sephardi, ultra-Orthodox, haredi, non-Zionist Shas, decided to back a government headed by Shamir. Charlie Biton, of the Communist list (Rakah), was wooed to Labor's ranks. Avraham Sharir, one of Modai's group who felt that Prime Minister Shamir had slighted him in the past, seemed to be leaning to Labor, and Modai was also reportedly wavering. It was a seller's market. Peres and Labor agreed to appoint Shamir minister of transportation and to give him a sure place on the Labor list for the next two elections.

Meanwhile, the Likud was busy trying to block Peres's attempt, and pre-negotiating their own government. Shamir met with Modai; the Likud promised him an important ministry (foreign, defense, or treasury), another for one of his colleagues, five certain places in the next Likud election list, and a $10 million security deposit to guarantee these pledges. After petitions to the judicial system, and a massive demonstration calling for constitutional reform, Modai backed down from his demand for a cash deposit and agreed to make do with the signatures of all of the Likud ministers backing the agreement with him. When four of them refused to go along, Modai reopened negotiations with Labor.

Peres planned to present his government to the Knesset on the last day of his twenty-one-day mandate to form a government. By adding Sharir to the sixty votes that had brought down the National Unity Government, Peres thought he had enough votes. But his plans unraveled when two of the Aguda supporters bolted, despite the discipline that Aguda Knesset members had always demonstrated to the dictates of their party's Council of Torah Sages—Verdiger and Mizrahi chose to disobey party dictates rather than to allow the creation of a government headed by Peres. President Herzog gave Peres a fifteen-day extension to form the government. The Aguda lined up Verdiger, one of its two wayward Knesset members, after extracting a promise from Peres that new elections would be held before any territory was returned. Mizrahi was to be tried before a rabbinical tribunal for breaking his promise to follow the dictates of the Council of Torah Sages. Ultimately, he resigned from the Aguda and set up his own one-member faction in the Knesset (to run unsuccessfully in 1992).

The uncertainty grew. After a meeting with David Levy, Shamir seemed ready to shift his support back to the Likud. The deal with Modai's group drew sharp criticism; many Herut members were incensed that much of the next Likud list was being given away. Once Peres failed, it was Shamir's turn, and he faced troubles of his own. But at last, he won the support of Mizrahi of the Aguda list and turned a Labor Knesset member, Ephraim Gur; both were rewarded with appointments as deputy ministers, and Gur was given a promise of a secure place on the Likud list for the next Knesset. With them, the Likud could count on sixty-two Knesset members.

Reform followed. In February 1991 the Knesset reacted to this unseemly chain of events by passing legislation that was intended to change basic parliamentary norms. The legislation established penalties for any Knesset member who resigned from the party on whose list he or she had been elected, or who voted no confidence against the decision of the party on whose list he or she had been elected: the offending Knesset member would not be recognized as being a member of any other party-grouping within the Knesset; would not be allowed to run in the next elections on a list represented in the current Knesset; would not be allowed to serve as a minister or a deputy minister during the term of the Knesset in which the prohibited act occurred; and would not be entitled to party financing from the public treasury.

The other reform to emerge from this messy political period was the direct election of the prime minister. Originally conceived of as one of a series of constitutional reforms by a group of law professors,[14] the proposal took on a life of its own and led to a well-funded public campaign sparked by petition drives and demonstrations.[15]

The reform was presented as governmental reform—more to protect the incumbent parliamentarians (the cynics said) than to increase governmental efficiency. The opposition Labor Party supported the direct election of the prime minister proposal, mainly out of short-term electoral considerations; Likud wavered, with Prime Minister Shamir explicitly and publicly opposing the plan. The vote of a young Likud politician, Binyamin

Netanyahu, would prove crucial, ultimately ensuring Knesset approval of the direct-election bill, against the Likud leadership.[16]

The legislation, though passed in the Twelfth Knesset, prior to the 1992 election of the Thirteenth Knesset, would be applied only from the Fourteenth Knesset in 1996. But the politicians were alert to the potential of the new electoral system. Labor conducted its 1992 election campaign as though these were direct elections for the prime ministry, placing Rabin firmly at the center of its campaign and exploiting the themes of change and Likud's opposition to reform. In anticipation, the Labor Party went so far as to officially call itself "The Labor Party Headed by Rabin." Netanyahu, meanwhile, was preparing for the election of a new head of Likud should that party lose in 1992.

The direct election of the prime minister was Israel's first major electoral reform. While it weakened the Knesset in comparison to the prime minister, the law did not tamper with the method of electing the Knesset. The politicians could declare that they had passed reform, without changing the manner by which they themselves had learned to be elected. Thus the "dirty trick" of 1990 set the stage for major changes in Israeli political life: the direct election of the prime minister; the major parties' primaries; the ascendancy of Rabin over Peres; Labor's election victory in 1992; the primaries victory of Netanyahu in the Likud after Shamir stepped down as party head; and then Netanyahu's ascendancy as the first directly elected prime minister.

Before the direct election of the prime minister was actually carried out in 1996, a head count of Knesset members revealed that 77 of the 120 would support repealing or delaying the implementation of the plan, if party discipline were lifted so that they could vote freely. Shimon Peres, who had consistently opposed the plan, felt an obligation to the assassinated Rabin, who had consistently supported it. And so Peres blocked delay or repeal, and paid for it with his job. Had the old system been in place, he would have been given the first opportunity to form a government, since his party was the biggest winner in the 1996 election.

After the 1996 elections, there were calls to return to the parliamentary pattern of having the Knesset select the prime minister, or having the prime minister be the head of the largest party in the Knesset, but the Netanyahu camp and the middle-sized parties that had done well in 1996 were not anxious to undo the system that had brought them power.

Three elections were held under these rules, in 1996, 1999, and 2001.

The elections of 2001 would turn out to be the final scene in the political saga of the direct election of the prime minister. The new constitutional order provided the setting for the downfall of the

Netanyahu government in 1999 and the calling of early elections: because he feared losing a vote of confidence in the Knesset, Netanyahu opted instead to support moving up elections by two years, and he lost in a landslide to Ehud Barak. When Barak, in turn, faced the same dilemma two years later, he resigned rather than acceding to new elections for prime minister and Knesset, thus bringing on special elections only for the prime minister, in which he was beaten badly by Sharon and drummed out of office. Neither Netanyahu nor Barak had invested sufficient energy in cultivating relations with key power-brokers within their respective political parties, or in the elections of the party Knesset lists. Eventually their efforts to lead without looking back at their followers caught up with both of them. Both Netanyahu and Barak resigned from the Knesset and from political life (at least temporarily) upon their electoral defeats.

A month after the 2001 election and just before Sharon's National Unity Government took office, the provisions for direct election of the prime minister were repealed and Israel returned to the previous method of selecting its prime minister. Also, the constructive vote of confidence was introduced, whereby the Knesset would have to select a replacement for the prime minister if it wanted to vote no confidence in the current prime minister and remove him from office.

Public support for repealing the law had grown over the years as it became clear that the reform had not brought about more acceptable behavior on the part of those negotiating for coalition benefits. On the contrary, coalition negotiations became more prevalent and political blackmail was suspected frequently, including one infamous case that allegedly tied support for a political agreement with the Palestinians regarding Hebron with the proposal to appoint the country's attorney general.

Whether electoral reform should take place is a matter of belief, preference, and evaluation; whether it does take place is a matter of politics. Public support has generally been stronger for electoral reform than has been the resolve of the political leadership to bring it about, as those who have done well under the old system find little reason to explore a new one. Reforming the electoral system generally happens only when politicians back into the project with their eyes closed—and that is precisely what happened with the adoption of the direct election of the prime minister.

8 ELECTORAL BEHAVIOR

THE DISTRIBUTION OF political power in a democracy is determined by the electoral rules employed, by the party system and the actions of parties, by political events, and by the behavior of the voters (see tables 8.1 and 8.2 for election results for the Knesset and for the direct election of the prime minister).[1]

Voting Participation

Voting turnout in Israel was high until the elections at the beginning of the twenty-first century. About 80 percent of the eligible voters voluntarily cast ballots on voting day between 1949 and 1999; the highest rate of participation was in the first Knesset elections in 1949, in which 86.8 percent of the eligible population voted. In 2001, however, the rate fell to 62.3 percent (in an election only for prime minister), and in 2003 it was only 67.8 percent—the lowest ever for Knesset elections. Before that, 75.1 percent in 1951 had been the lowest rate, and the drop-off in that year was probably a result of dislocation created by the large-scale immigration that had increased the number of eligible voters by 70 percent since the 1949 elections. By 1955, the rate was back up to 82.8 percent.

There has been a slight decline in participation over time: elections through the 1960s averaged above 80 percent, and those since the 1970s have fallen slightly below that level. With the exception of 1951, all elections through 1969 had turnout rates greater than 80 percent, while no election since has reached the 80-percent mark.

Table 8.1 Knesset Election Results (120 seats)

Election Year	1949	1951	1955	1959	1961	1965	1969	1973	1977	1981	1984	1988	1992	1996	1999	2003
Participation rate (%)	86.9	75.1	82.8	81.6	81.6	83.0	81.7	78.6	79.2	78.5	79.8	79.7	77.4	79.3	78.7	67.8
Labor and Left																
Mapai[a]	46	45	40	47	42	45	56	51	32	47	44	39	44	34	26	19
Ahdut Haavoda[b]			10	7	8											
Rafi[c]						10										
Mapam[d]	19	15	9	9	9	8						3				
DMC/Shinui[e]									15	2	3	2			6	15
CRM/Meretz[f]								3	1	1	3	5	12	9	10	6
Arab lists	2	1	4	5	4	4	4	3	1		2	2	2	4	7	5
Communist	4	5	6	3	5	4	4	5	5	4	4	4	3	5	3	3
Likud and Right																
Independent Liberals[g]	5	4	5	6		5	4	4	1							
Liberals[h]	7	20	13	8	17											
Herut[i]	14	8	15	17	17	26	26	39	43	48	41	40	32	32	19	38
Tehiya/Tzomet[j]										3	5	5	8			
Moledet/Kach/ National Union[k]											1	2	3	2	8	7
Religious																
NRP	16	10	11	12	12	11	12	10	12	6	4	5	6	9	5	6
Aguda parties[l]		5	6	6	6	6	6	5	5	4	8	7	4	4	5	5
Shas											4	6	6	10	17	11
Others	7	7	1			1	8[m]	3	5[n]	5[o]	5[p]			11[q]	14[r]	5[s]

a. Aligned with Ahdut Haavoda in 1965; Labor formed from Rafi, Ahdut Haavoda and Mapai in 1968; Labor-Mapam Alignment through 1984; in 1999 One Israel with Gesher and Meimad; in 2003 One Israel-Meimad.

b. See note a.

c. Ben-Gurion's party; joined the Labor Alignment in 1969 minus the State List.

d. Ahdut Haavoda included in Mapam in 1949 and 1951; Mapam included in Labor-Mapam Alignment between 1969 and 1984; Mapam included in Meretz after 1992.

e. DMC in 1977; Shinui between 1981 and 1988 and then most of party joined with Meretz. Fraction continued as Shinui.

f. Meretz from 1992 made up of CRM, Mapam, and Shinui.

g. Included in Liberal party in 1961 and independent again since 1965; in 1984, part of Labor-Mapam Alignment.

h. Until 1959 known as General Zionists, joined Herut to form Gahal in 1965, and part of the Likud from 1973.

i. Jointly with the Liberals since 1965 and part of the Likud from 1973.

j. Tehiya in 1981 and 1984; in 1988, 3 seats for Tehiya, 2 for Tzomet; Tzomet in 1992; from 1996 Tzomet part of the Likud.

k. Kach in 1984, since 1988 Moledet. In 1999 Israel Beiteinu 4 members and National Union 4 members.

l. Poalei Agudat Israel, Agudat Israel, and Degel Hatorah.

m. Includes the State List (4 members), the Free Center (2 members), and Haolam Haze (2 members). The first two joined Herut and the Liberals in 1973.

n. Includes Shlomzion (2 members), which joined the Likud after the elections, Shelli (2 members), and Flatto-Sharon (1 member).

o. Includes Tami (3 members), and Telem (2 members).

p. Includes Yahad (3 members), Tami (1 member), and Ometz (1 member).

q. Includes Israel b'Aliya (7 members) and the Third Way (4 members).

r. Includes Center party (6 members), Israel b'Aliya (6 members), and Am Ehad (2 members)

s. Includes Am Ehad (3 members) and Israel b'Aliya (2 members).

Table 8.2 Results of Prime Minister Elections, 1996–2001

				Votes	
Year	Number of eligible voters	Voter turnout (%)	Candidate (party)	N	%
1996	3,933,250	79.3	Netanyahu (Likud)	1,501,023	50.5
			Peres (Labor)	1,471,566	49.5
1999	4,285,428	78.7	Barak (Labor)	1,791,020	56.1
			Netanyahu (Likud)	1,402,474	43.9
2001	4,504,769	62.3	Sharon (Likud)	1,698,077	62.4
			Barak (Labor)	1,023,944	37.6

The steep declines in 2001 and 2003 reflected lower rates of participation among both Jewish and Arab voters. In 2001 (the special direct election of the prime minister), 68 percent of Jews voted, compared with only 19 percent of Arabs, bringing the overall turnout rate to 62.3 percent. The 2001 election was held shortly after the eruption of the Al-Aqsa Intifada and the October 2000 disturbances within Israel, in which thirteen Palestinians, twelve of them Israeli citizens, were killed by the police. Arab voters blamed the government, and the disaffection of many Arab citizens was greater than ever. Deeply alienated and affronted, Arab political parties as well as civic organizations campaigned vigorously for a boycott of the 2001 elections.[2] In 2003 the Jewish turnout level was about the same as in 2001, at 69 percent, but the Arab turnout rate rebounded to 62 percent, raising the overall rate to 67.8 percent.

In the past, voting participation was not associated with levels of modernization, with the possible exception of the Bedouin tribes. In 1977 the Bedouin voting rate was only 64.3 percent, much lower than other groups at that time, but high by the standards of other countries— and even of Israel twenty-five years later.

Non-Jews have had high rates of participation in elections. Even in Arab cities where protest was strongly felt and the antiestablishment Rakah won 70.8 percent of the vote, the voting rate in 1977 was 77.4 percent. By 1981, however, the participation rate in non-Jewish settlements had fallen to 69.7 percent, and the rate for Bedouin tribes to 53.3 percent. In 1988 voting participation in Arab communities was 73.8 percent. By 2003, lower turnout patterns familiar in other industrialized democracies were evident in Israel as well, among both non-Jews and Jews.

Nonvoting among the Arab minority in Israel has usually been construed as political, while the common factors in abstention among Jews before 2001 were technical ones such as illness, improper registration, or lack of identification. The dominant reason for nonvoting among non-Jews was thought to be a preference not to vote. In 1973, 54.6 percent of non-Jews gave purposeful abstention as the reason for not voting, compared to 12.8 percent of the sample of Jewish nonvoters.[3] In 1981, following a very divisive campaign, many Arabs refrained from voting; in 1988, in the midst of the first intifada, Arab citizens again voted at high rates, hoping to influence the political process.

The option of abstaining for political reasons was on the public agenda and a matter of lively debate among both Jews and Arabs during the 2001 election campaign (but not in 2003). This period was dominated by the breakdown of the Oslo process following the failed Camp David summit in July 2000 and the eruption of the Al-Aqsa Intifada in September of that year. Both elections were noncompetitive, as almost everyone assumed that Ariel Sharon would win. The gloomy political context was characterized by disillusionment with the peace process and with the Palestinians as partners; anguish with regard to the future; and disappointment in the situation, in government performance, and in the alternatives presented by the major parties. Prospective rather than retrospective evaluations seemed to matter: in both election campaigns, the abstainers were the more disillusioned—they did not see a way out of the situation. And as in other countries, in both elections abstainers were the less involved politically and the less integrated socially: they were younger, of lower socioeconomic background, less religious, less sophisticated politically, and of lower political efficacy.

The act of voting is not only a rational calculation of cost and benefit but a social act carried out within a certain normative climate of opinion. The widespread disaffection and despair in 2001 and 2003 encouraged abstention among all those who felt hopeless, but in particular among those voters who were less "connected" socially and politically. Abstention appeared to be election-specific—related to dissatisfaction with the particular political actors and the current situation—rather than an indicator of disaffection from more general political objects such as regime institutions or principles.

Explaining the Vote

In addition to asking whether people vote, political scientists are concerned with why people vote as they do.[4] As a rule, people learn political symbols and values in much the same way they learn other values—through the family, the school, and peer groups. In the case of an individual whose political learning is reinforced by all the socializing agents with which he or she comes in contact, the result is likely to be high levels of belief and behavior consistent with the expectations of the environment. A good example is the voting behavior of kibbutz members, who generally show very strong support for the party with which their kibbutz federation is associated; the pressures for voting for the party are rarely opposed by significant others. Just as most Israeli Jews accept their Judaism as a matter of course, so most kibbutz members accept their socialism and identification with a political party as a matter of course.

The situation is more complex when cross-pressures come to bear. Among residents of a city, for example, where levels of political organization are much lower, socialization into political life or into voting for a specific party is likely to be less intense. Voters who have been affiliated with party-sponsored youth groups, internalizing the values and identity of the party, and have been reinforced by the home environment in this learning, are obviously more likely to continue voting for that party in later years.

It is almost impossible to know why people really vote the way they do. One way of trying to assess the vote is to ask voters what factor was most important in determining their vote. Another way is to ascertain what factors are associated with voting for one party and not another. In both cases we must take into account that factors we have not tapped are also at work.

The Israeli political system is, and is perceived to be, ideological in nature. Israeli voters report that ideological considerations are important in motivating their vote, and they tend to make this claim even when strong, popular leaders—such as Golda Meir in 1969, Menachem Begin in 1981, Yitzhak Rabin in 1992, Ariel Sharon in 2003—are running for reelection. Based on the discrepancy between the frequent assertion that it is ideology that drives the vote and the obvious popularity of such leaders, one is tempted to say that the ideology of the system is to declare the importance of ideology. In none of the nine surveys regarding the Knesset vote reflected in figure 8.1 does the candidate carry as much weight with the voters as the platform (ideology) of the party. Always in the 20-percent to low 30-percent range, the reported importance of party identification peaked in the 1980s and waned in the 1990s; in 1999 party identification, at 21 percent, was as low as it had been in 1969. The year 1999 saw the introduction of primaries in the parties and an increase in party membership. Although the role of the candidate is growing in the television-dominated election campaign, and party differences are made to seem larger during the campaign than they really are, Israelis still report that their voting decision is dominated by ideological considerations. The Israeli voter has internalized the expectation of democratic theorists that voters make their decision by virtue of rational, cognitive processes.

Figure 8.1   Determining Factor for Knesset Vote, 1969–2003 (in percentages)

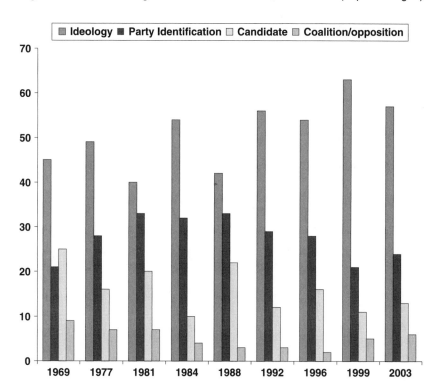

Source: Israel National Elections Studies.

Obviously other factors are also at work, but this is the way Israelis see themselves and present themselves to others.[5]

The data show that party identification grew in importance with the stiff competition between the two blocs during the 1980s, then declined in the 1990s and especially in the elections of 1999 and 2003. The response of "candidate" as the major factor in the voter's decision was in third place in all the surveys except that of 1969, a striking finding when one considers the adoption of the direct election of prime minister system in the mid-1990s as well as the general trend—in Israel as in other Western democracies—toward "candidate-centered politics."[6] According to the respondents, the candidate's appeal had a limited role, while the ideology factor increased in importance during the decade of the 1990s and in 2003. The "candidate" response fluctuated most over time, but it never exceeded 25 percent of responses, and a slight downward trend was in evidence.

In the years in which the electoral system requiring direct election of the prime minister was in place, the question about the major factor determining the vote for prime minister was asked a second time in the surveys, and the ranking order of the elements was the same: ideology was most important, followed by party/bloc identification, and then candidate. The consistency of these self-reports suggest that voters may have focused on the candidate as ideology bearer—and not only because he was leader of a party or bloc or because of his telegenic image.

These data seem to be challenged by the fact that the candidates for office in Israel are very important in attracting voters or, on the contrary, in repelling voters, but this effect has often been offset by the fierce debate on the future of the territories, which reinforces the centrality of the party platform or ideology. On many other issues ideological differences among parties are not great, although their style, emphases, and images might be. In an ironic twist in 1996, when the system changed to direct election of the prime minister, Netanyahu tried to present himself as less militant than his image and his party platform, while Peres tried to present himself as more militant. Both were appealing for the votes of the center, and both feared that they had positioned themselves incorrectly for that task.

Amid growing criticism of government and erosion of the public's trust in government in postindustrial democracies, political parties are held in especially low esteem by voters. Surveys on the trust in institutions conducted in Israel consistently place political parties in last place; an April 2003 survey found that only 32 percent of respondents had trust in political parties, which was significantly lower than the level of trust in other institutions.[7] When long-term factors such as party identification decline in the vote calculus, there is a rise in short-term forces related to issues and candidates. Assessments of candidates' performance in office become more important, and issue voting increases.[8]

Vote Choice

Patterns of support for the major political parties have been quite constant; political change came about because the strength of support of various parties has shifted from time to time. The dominant Mapai, now Labor, found support among all groups of voters, but especially among those who identified with the epoch in which the party rose to its peak and with the dominant values of that epoch. The greatest of Mapai's (Labor's) achievements was the gaining of independence, which highlighted all the projects undertaken by the Jews in Eretz Israel—immigration, building the land, security. After the founding of the state, these undertakings were continued, sometimes within different organizational settings and institutional arrangements, but with much of the same symbolism and ideological justification. Those who lived through the independence epoch in Israel were more likely to identify with the dominant party. As the party and movement values permeated the society, the distinction between party and state was often blurred; achievements of state accrued to the benefit of the party. Jews who immigrated to Israel before independence and immediately thereafter continued to support Labor heavily, although the rate of support fell off among those who immigrated after 1955 and among Israeli-born voters.

Much of the program and appeal of the dominant Labor Party at the time of independence must be seen in light of the social and political realities that the Labor leadership had known in Eastern Europe in the first decades of the twentieth century. The precarious position of the Jews, the restrictions on economic and political activity, the unbalanced nature of their occupations, the spread of rationalist feeling, the undermining of traditional religious belief and behavior—all these pressures led to the creation of the socialist-Zionist experiment. The Labor leadership, almost exclusively of East European origin, developed a party and an ideology that answered the needs of the nation as they saw and experienced them.

The Likud saw the problems of the country from a different ideological perspective and consequently found its support among different groups. Whereas Labor was notably successful among earlier immigrants and among those born in Europe and America, Likud appealed more to the native-born than to any immigrant group, and more to the Asian- or African-born than to the European- or American-born. The symbols Labor used to evoke the epoch of independence and nation-building were more effective among the old than with the young, more effective among those who came before independence than among those who came after independence or were born in Israel, and more effective among those born in Europe than those born in Asia or Africa.

The Likud, in opposition until 1977, gave the appearance of being broadly based in its electoral support (as was the Labor-Mapam Alignment) because it blended the preferences of its two major components: the right-wing, nationalistic Herut movement and the bourgeois Liberal Party. But much of this wide spread was a reflection of the difference between the groups that supported Herut and the Liberals. Herut was a party that appealed disproportionately to the lower class and to lower-middle-class workers, and to Israelis born in Asia or Africa, although obviously many Ashkenazim also supported it. The Liberals, on the other hand, were a bourgeois party that drew most of its support from middle-class and upper-middle-class merchants and businessmen. Since the followers of the Liberal Party had higher levels of education than did supporters of Herut, the apparent broad base for the Likud was a balancing of two countertendencies; thus it is misleading to read into the data a suggestion that the Likud before 1977 was beginning to generate the appeal characteristic of a dominant party.

The support for the Likud came heavily from the young, from native Israelis, from Israelis of Asian or African background, and from those with lower education and income levels. Undeniably, many of these cleavages overlapped with strong differences in political opinion and religious observance. The voters who supported the Likud tended to have hawkish opinions on foreign and defense policy. Those who were older, had more education, came from a European background, and supported Labor, tended to hold more conciliatory views.

The religious parties generally received about 15 percent of the vote—although in 1996 their total shot up to 20 percent—and they were regular coalition partners in the majority of governments, whether headed by Labor or Likud. Their support came from the following groups: traditional Jews from Asian or African backgrounds, with low income and low education levels; highly educated intellectuals of European origin; and Israeli-born youth imbued with religious ideals through formal schooling in the state-supported religious schools. The NRP lost votes in 1988 to the Likud for ideological reasons and to Shas for ethnic ones. Its rebound in 1996 was the result of moderating its ideological appeal, retaining its nationalist base, and undertaking successful organizational efforts.

On the whole, the religious parties were relatively more successful among those with lower levels of education, but the picture grew more complex when place of origin was considered in conjunction with education. Among the European- or American-born, support for religious parties tended to decrease with educational attainment, while the Israeli-born exhibited the opposite tendency of religious party support increasing with higher levels of education. In the 1980s and 1990s, Shas emerged as the major religious party. A Sephardi ultra-Orthodox party, it won its major support from traditionalists with lower incomes, lower levels of education, and Asian or African backgrounds.

Issue Voting and Demography

Issue voting grew dramatically in Israel in the 1980s and 1990s, especially regarding the divisive issue of the future of the territories, while the grasp of social allegiance on voting patterns remained constant. Social and economic differences have traditionally been considered good predictors of voting behavior, although there has been a general decline in the importance of such cleavages throughout the Western world, and a simultaneous increase in issue voting.[9] As the electoral importance of the territories issue grew, the role of demographic factors tended to remain stable.[10]

Consider table 8.3, in which the voting intentions of Jewish respondents for the 2003 Knesset election are broken down by demographic background categories. Age was a good predictor of the vote, with the

Table 8.3 Demographic Profile of Jewish Voters, 2003 (in percentages)

Sample	Size	Left	Labor	Shinui	Likud	Religious	Right
Total	100	10	18	14	38	13	7
	(N = 831)						
Age							
18–21	9	6	5	16	36	25	12
22–29	16	12	10	21	28	21	8
30–59	56	10	17	14	42	11	6
above 60	19	9	35	8	36	6	6
Gender							
Male	50	8	18	16	41	10	7
Female	50	12	18	12	36	15	7
Education							
up to 8 years	3	—	30	—	52	18	—
9–12 years	46	6	17	11	47	14	5
above 12 years	51	14	19	17	29	12	9
Continent of Birth							
Asia-Africa	8	3	17	5	62	10	3
Europe-America	32	9	16	19	38	6	12
Israel (father, Israel)	24	12	17	14	33	19	5
Israel (father, Europe-America)	18	18	32	17	19	11	3
Israel (father, Asia-Africa)	19	5	10	7	56	17	5
Religious Observance							
All	11	—	1	1	28	65	5
Most	17	1	6	4	51	25	13
Some	40	8	24	15	45	2	6
None	32	20	25	23	27	—	5

Source: Israel National Elections Studies.

old more likely to support Labor, while the young supported Shinui, the right, and the religious parties; Likud was able to attract substantial numbers of voters in each age category. As usual, gender was not a good predictor of the vote in 2003, although men tended to support the Likud and Shinui at higher rates, while women favored by small percentages the left and the religious parties. Men and women supported Labor at the same rate. The Likud did very well among those with lower levels of education, and Shinui was successful among those with higher levels.

Continent of birth was strongly related to vote choice. Those born in Asia or Africa, or whose fathers were born there, were much more likely to choose Likud, while those with a European-American background were prone to select Labor. Shinui did well among the Israeli-born, and especially among those born in Europe or America.

The strongest predictor of the vote reported in table 8.3 was the extent of religious observance. As observance decreased, the probability of voting for the left and Labor increased; as observance increased, the chances were greatest of choosing a religious party. The Likud was especially successful among those at moderate levels of religious observance. Among the very observant, the Likud attracted only partial support, evidently because religious parties were available to be voted for; on the whole, however, the Likud did much better among observers than among nonobservers, and certainly much better than Labor did with this group.

The correlations in table 8.4—between the Labor-Likud vote and various demographic and issue variables for the 1969–2003 period, and the prime minister vote between 1996 and 2001—provide important clues as to the nature of partisanship in Israel. Age has had a consistent relationship with vote, with the young somewhat more likely to vote Likud, and the old, Labor. This relationship has been generally regarded as indicating generational rather than life-cycle effects.[11] This correlation peaked in 1973 and 1977, reached its nadir in 1992, and was again high in 2003, although the number of respondents in 2003 who chose either Labor or Likud was the lowest ever. The 1977 reversal was lead by the young, who abandoned Labor for the promises of the Likud or the Democratic Movement for Change (DMC). The Likud, always strongest among this group compared to other age cohorts, won 36 percent support in 1969, compared to 44 percent in 1973 and 51 percent in 1977 and 1981. The Labor-Mapam Alignment lost half its support in this youngest age group between 1973 and 1977, the same amount of support that the DMC attracted. The Alignment more clearly than ever became the party of the older, more conservative voter; the Likud was

Table 8.4 Correlations between Likud and Labor, Demographics and Issues, 1969–2003

			Demography							Issues	
Survey[a]	(N)	Age	Gender	Density	Education	Income	Religion	Ethnicity	No territories for peace[b]	Capitalism/ socialism[c]	State/ religion[d]
Oct 1969	1,017	.17	(.05)	.07	(.00)	(−.04)	.08	.13	.15	.23	.12
May 1973	1,062	.27	(.01)	.15	(−.02)	(−.01)	(.04)	.13	.23	.17	e
Mar 1977	620	.29	(−.03)	.18	(.01)	(−.06)	.18	.32	.28	.22	.17
Mar 1981	798	.13	(.06)	.07	.09	(.00)	.19	.23	.27	.16	.20
July 1984	807	.20	(−.03)	.25	.22	.08	.37	.53	.57	.32	e
Oct 1988	532	.16	(.04)	.09	.15	(.01)	.27	.27	.61	.30	.24
June 1992	657	.10	(.07)	.13	.24	(−.02)	.40	.35	.57	(.05)	.29
May 1996	798	.13	(.04)	.18	.21	.12	.36	.30	.65	(.07)	.35
May 1999	599	.11	(.07)	.19	.14	(.05)	.33	.35	.67	.17	.40
Jan 2003	470	.23	(−.03)	.18	.15	(.05)	.29	.25	.53	.13	.20
PM 1996	1,113	.09	(.06)	.20	.18	.12	.44	.28	.63	(.08)	.41
PM 1999	898	.07	(.04)	.21	.11	.08	.37	.24	.67	.21	.40
PM 2001	972	.16	(.02)	.24	.12	(−.06)	.35	.25	e	.08	.35

Note: All are Pearson correlations, significant above the .05 level, except those in parentheses. The coding for these correlations was Likud = 1, Labor = 2, Netanyahu/Sharon = 1, Peres/Barak = 1, Peres/Barak = 2. Low scores for the other variables indicate young age, female, high density, low education, low income, high religiosity, Sephardi, unwillingness to concede territories for peace, favoring capitalism over socialism, and favoring public life in accordance with Jewish religious law, respectively.

a. Preelection surveys of Jewish population used. In a year for which multiple surveys were available, the one that contained the most variables used in the table was chosen.

b. Before 1984, a question concerning the maximum amount of territory Israel should give up in order to achieve a peace settlement. In 1984 and after, constructed from two questions, the first asking preference between return of territories for peace, annexation, or status quo, and a follow-up question forcing a choice of those who chose the "status quo" option. In 1996 through 2003 a 7-point answer was used.

c. The question asked about preference for the socialist or capitalist approach. The 1973 question asked if the Histadrut labor union should both own industries and represent workers.

d. The question asked whether the government should see to it that public life in Israel be conducted according to the Jewish religious tradition.

e. Not asked.

the choice of the young, even though the DMC was a party of young adults. In 1992 both the young and the old forsook the Likud; young voters were more attracted by the parties further to the right, while Labor was more successful than in the past in attracting voters across generations. The high correlation of 2003 reflects the fact that many of the young and middle-aged chose Shinui.

It was in the youngest voting group that the significant change came about. A tantalizing change emerged in the 1988 data, with Labor and Likud getting almost the same percentage of support among first-time voters. This hinted at a changing pattern from that of the last two decades, in which the young chose the Likud, but Labor's optimism was only partially fulfilled, because young voters in 1988 and 1992 tended to support parties of the extreme left and the extreme right as well as Labor and Likud. Nonetheless, Labor and Rabin won in 1992 by managing to attract a substantial part of the youth vote, while the Likud lost a sizable portion of it.

In 1996 first-time voters split in favor of Netanyahu at about a 3-to-2 rate despite the general assumption that the Rabin assassination had galvanized the young generation on Labor's behalf. The assassination did mobilize emotional support for Labor among the young, but its effect was especially felt among those first-time voters who would have supported Labor anyway. Although much was made of the "candles generation" of young people supporting Peres while grieving for the slain Rabin in 1996, there was no evidence that this promise materialized in the elections.

Voters under thirty split evenly between Netanyahu and Barak in 1999, but those older than sixty preferred Barak. In the Sharon landslide of 2001, these patterns were almost reversed: almost three in four voters under thirty supported Sharon, while Sharon and Barak split the vote of those over sixty about equally.

Gender has never been related to vote choice to a statistically significant extent in Israeli surveys.

Class differences have mattered to a degree, although correlations have been neither consistent nor strong.[12] There has usually been no relationship between the Likud-Labor vote and income, but the income variable is not the best measure of class in Israel, as it is the kind of topic an Israeli is unlikely to discuss in an open manner with an interviewer-stranger. Two other measures of class, living density (the number of persons per room) and education, tell a different story.

Class differences appeared with the reversal of 1977, as lower-class voters abandoned Labor in favor of the Likud. Education gained in importance after 1981, with the return to Labor of more highly educated voters, who had deserted for the DMC in 1977. This process of class stratification continued in the 1980s and was still in evidence in 1992, although over time the education variable was stronger than the living-density indicator. But based on the inconsistent and rather weak correlations of the vote with class indicators, combined with the pattern of correlations between the vote and socialist versus capitalistic views, the class cleavage does not seem to be a driving force behind electoral choice and change in Israel. Note that in 1996 and 1992 there was virtually no relationship between voters' preferences as to the structure of the economy and their vote, and in 1977 the correlation was of the same magnitude as throughout the 1970s. Moreover, the responses to this question are to be seen more as an indicator of whether or not a voter belongs to the camp of socialism-Zionism socially, politically, and culturally, rather than of ideological commitment. Again, class is not the most potent correlate of the vote in Israel.

Religion and ethnicity were strongly correlated with the vote decision. For both of these variables, the critical election year was 1977. Before that year, both dimensions barely distinguished Labor voters from Likud voters. Religion (measured by extent of religious observance) gained in importance over time, reaching all-time highs in the 1992 election and in the vote for prime minister in 1996. The relationship between ethnicity and the vote reached its highest point in the 1984 election, but it has receded since.

The ethnic theme has changed over time as the proportions of the groups in the electorate have changed. In 1977 the majority of the electorate (53 percent) was Ashkenazim, 43 percent were Sephardim, and 4 percent were Israeli-born with fathers also born in Israel. In the 1988 election, the Jews of Sephardi background outnumbered the Jews of Ashkenazi background in the electorate for the first time. In 1992, following the mostly Ashkenazi mass immigration from the former Soviet Union, the proportions were 48 percent Ashkenazim, 44 percent Sephardim, and 8 percent Israeli-born with fathers also born in Israel. By 1996, the Ashkenazim had grown to 50 percent, the Sephardim had gone down to 39 percent, and the Israeli-born with fathers born in Israel had grown to 11 percent. The electoral impact of the immigrants from the former Soviet Union has been enormous: they were important forces in the three turnovers in the 1990s and in the election of Sharon in 2001, casting a protest vote against the incumbent in each election and bringing about the victories of Rabin, Netanyahu, Barak, and Sharon.

The relationship between voting and origin is not a new one in Israeli politics. In the 1948–1977 period of Labor dominance, the party regularly won support from most groups in the society. This was especially true of new immigrants, who were often in awe of the "miracle" that had returned them to the land of their fathers and dependent on the bureaucracies of the establishment for the whole gamut of economic, educational, health, social, and cultural needs. An increasingly large share of the electorate was of Sephardi origin, and Mapai maintained its dominant role as the largest plurality party and the leader of every government coalition. More than that, attempts to appeal to the Sephardi population at election time by lists set up by Sephardim largely failed. It was only before the mass immigration of the early 1950s that any lists manifestly linking themselves with Sephardim and Yemenites achieved representation in the Knesset.

The Sephardi shift away from Labor was gradual, becoming more pronounced in the 1970s and going beyond the general trend of Likud growth and Labor decline. Ethnic voting among the Israeli public continues: ethnicity predicts the vote for both the Likud and the Alignment. In 1984 the preference ratio for the two parties among each ethnic group was about 3 to 1, with the Sephardim preferring the Likud, and the Ashkenazim the Alignment. In 1988 and 1992 the preference ratio declined, as smaller parties of the extreme left and right won more of the Ashkenazi and Sephardi votes, respectively. In 1996 both parties performed poorly, but the respective preference of the ethnic groups persisted.

The ethnic cleavage manifested itself in voting behavior dramatically in the 1977 election when many voters abandoned their long-standing practice of supporting Labor, shifting largely along ethnic lines. Sephardim gravitated to the Likud, and Ashkenazim to the DMC. These two defections so weakened Labor that the Likud could take over the reins of power, resulting in the beginning of the Likud era of Israeli politics. In 1981 and 1984 many of the Ashkenazim were back with Labor; the campaigns were especially bitter and focused on the sense of exploitation by Labor felt by many Sephardim. The ethnic vote was most pronounced in the 1984 elections, although the 1981 election campaign was most taken up with the ethnic cleavage.

The fortunes of the Likud and Labor were transferred to the second generation as well: the Likud generally retained the loyalties of the Sephardim born in Israel, while Labor did better among Ashkenazim who immigrated and among their Israel-born children. The Likud gained most among the youngest and fastest-growing groups in the 1980s; the

Alignment, losing support within all groups over time, did best in the group that was oldest and shrinking rapidly.

In the elections of the 1980s, the term *ethnic voting* was used often, supposedly in reference to the support of Jews from Asia and Africa and their children for the Likud. The fact was, however, that the Alignment was closer to being an "ethnic party" in this sense than the Likud was, for about two-thirds of Labor's voters were Ashkenazim, while a similar percentage of Likud voters were Sephardim. This had not always been the case: in the past the bulk of both the Likud's and Labor's support had come from Ashkenazim, who, after all, constituted a majority of the electorate. Polls going back to the late 1960s indicate that then, too, about two-thirds of the Alignment vote was from Ashkenazim, even though Sephardim also often voted for the Alignment. In the late 1960s both parties were predominantly Ashkenazi; by 1981 the Alignment had stayed that way, but the Likud had become predominantly Sephardi. The turnabout seems to have occurred in the election of 1977, when a majority of the Likud vote was Sephardi for the first time in history.

In 1992 Likud was more heavily Sephardi than in 1977; two-thirds of its votes came from that group in 1992, compared with about half in 1977. Labor was much more balanced, with half its voters Ashkenazim, a third Sephardim, and the rest second-generation Israelis. The Likud came close to being left with its hard-core supporters only, while Labor in 1992 was able to enlarge the circle of its voters. However, Labor and Peres were unable to accelerate this trend in 1996, leading to a very close race and ultimately to defeat. Between 1996 and 2001, the period of the direct election of the prime minister, the large parties lost support from all groups. Many Sephardim found the ultra-Orthodox Shas attractive, and many Ashkenazim turned to parties of the left, such as Meretz and Shinui.

The question of the relationship of ethnicity to vote choice may also be turned around by asking how members of the two ethnic groups divided their votes between the two large parties. Again, a mirror image is provided: In general about 60 percent of the Ashkenazim voted Labor, about a third Likud, while approximately 60 percent of the Sephardim voted Likud, about a third Labor. By 1984, the Ashkenazi vote was more concentrated in the Alignment (about 70 percent) than the Sephardi vote was in the Likud (about 60 percent). In 1988, with the relative success of Mapam and Meretz among Ashkenazim, Labor's support among that ethnic group fell to about half; Likud's support among Sephardim came close to 60 percent.

As the proportion of Sephardim grew in the electorate, it was clear that Labor would have an uphill battle in trying to regain power until it could increase its share of the Sephardi vote. That shift occurred in 1992. The trend was not overwhelming, but the movement of Sephardim to Labor was substantial enough to provide the bounce that Labor needed to regain power. This transformation worked only because it occurred in conjunction with two other developments: the movement of other former supporters away from the Likud to parties of the right, and the impetus given Labor by the new Soviet immigrants who supported it. In 1996 Netanyahu won two-thirds of the Sephardi vote, a third of the Ashkenazi vote, and 40 percent of the Israel-born whose fathers were Israel-born. Peres's support within the two ethnic groups was reversed.

Meretz did more than three times better in 1992 among Ashkenazim and second-generation Israelis than among Sephardim, and the parties of the right were twice as popular among Sephardim as they were among Ashkenazim. Most of Meretz's support came from Ashkenazim, similar to the 3-out-of-4 rate of the DMC in 1977.

Two-thirds of the voters for the parties of the right in 1992 were Sephardim. The most notable shift was toward the religious parties, who had successfully adapted to the demographic shifts in Israel after 1977. From a situation in which three-quarters of their vote had come from Ashkenazim, in 1992 their supporters were half Sephardi, one-third Ashkenazi, and one in seven was a second-generation Israeli. The religious parties drew equally from all ethnic groups in 1992, a very different pattern from their 1977 showing, which reflected strong support among Ashkenazim.

In 1996 Netanyahu's vote came primarily from Sephardim, Peres's from Ashkenazim. The surge of religious parties in 1996 was based on broad ethnic support, with different ethnic groups supporting the three religious parties. Yahadut Hatorah was largely Ashkenazi, Shas mostly Sephardi, and the NRP drew from both ethnic groups.

In 1999, 60 percent of the Sephardim voted for Netanyahu and 60 percent of the Ashkenazim voted for Barak. In 2001, even though there was a general hemorrhaging of support for Barak, he still won 60 percent of the Ashkenazi vote. By contrast, Sharon received 80 percent of the Sephardi vote.

If indeed the two major parties in the 1990s could be defined as ethnic parties, it was only in terms of their electorate, for one has to keep in mind that about one-third of each ethnic group voted for the "wrong" camp. Neither party organized to promote specific ethnic ends or along ethnic lines. Both Labor and the Likud were run by Ashkenazim, as has been the case with most parties in Israel. Sephardim were high on the lists, but representation was not the issue. The Likud and Labor were ethnic parties only in the sense that the vote for each of them was closely associated with ethnicity.

The important Jewish ethnic lists were Shas and the two parties of immigrants from the former Soviet Union, Israel b'Aliya and Israel Beiteinu. Shas had seen its strength grow phenomenally, from four seats in 1984, to six seats in each of the 1988 and 1992 elections, ten seats in 1996, and seventeen seats in 1999. Israel b'Aliya won seven seats in 1996 and six in 1999; Israel Beiteinu won four in 1999. In the 2003 Likud victory and with the repeal of the system of directly electing the prime minister, Shas and the Russian parties suffered; Shas went from seventeen to eleven seats, Israel b'Aliya from six to two; Israel Beiteinu was part of the National Union.

Despite the fact that it had held power since 1977 only in the periods 1984–1986, 1992–1996, and 1999–2001, the Alignment remained identified by many as the party of the establishment. Sephardim, and especially their Israeli-born children, tended to reject Labor because of the persistent inequalities these voters perceived, while Ashkenazi voters tended to reject the populism of Likud governments and longed to return to a more familiar and pragmatic past. The hawkish image of the Likud also correlated with attitudes prevalent among Sephardim, who tend to be more traditional about religion than Ashkenazim. Begin (although not the Likud Party generally) was very successful in utilizing the symbols and language of religion. Many thought of Labor as antireligious, especially because of its support for Meretz positions during the 1992–1996 period and because of its attacks on the religious parties for what Labor termed disproportionate gains through coalition bargaining. During the races for prime minister, Labor candidates Peres and Barak pleaded with the rabbis for the support of the religious vote, but to no avail.

The twin issues of God (religion) and nationalism (the territories) were powerful predictors of the vote. On the state-religion issue, the trend of increasing correlations persists over time: the identification of Labor as an anticlerical party has strengthened, while the Likud has played to the traditional sympathies of much of its voting base, even though the origins and ideology of the Likud are very secular.

Since 1984, the elections in which Shamir replaced Begin as the head of the Likud, the correlations of the territories issue with the vote have been high. Over time, Labor has more unambiguously identified itself as the territories-for-peace party, making its platform less vague on this issue. Barak's offers to the Palestinians in the period leading up to the elections of 2001 went beyond what most Israelis were willing to contemplate at that time.

Since 1996 many voters have said that the territories would be an important consideration in their voting decision. In the 2003 sample, 67 percent reported that the issue of the territories would very greatly influence their vote, compared with 65 percent in 1999 and 71 percent in 1996. In 1992, 52 percent reported that it would be a very great influence, while less than a third had said so in previous elections. Adding the next category of response, 90 percent in 2003, 92 percent in 1999, 90 percent in 1996 and 81 percent in 1992 said that it would influence them greatly or very greatly, compared with 63 percent in previous elections.

Although the territories issue may drive the vote, it does not necessarily dominate the campaign. One way of assessing the mood of the times is to consider the recurring question asking respondents to identify the major issue that the government should deal with. Breaking the answers down into foreign and security issues (security, terrorism, peace, and so on) on the one hand and domestic issues (housing, health, education, immigrant absorption, and the like) on the other shows how much the public agenda has varied over the years (see figure 8.2.). In 2003 foreign and security issues were mentioned by

Figure 8.2 Security and/or Peace as Major Vote Issue, 1969–2003 (in percentages)

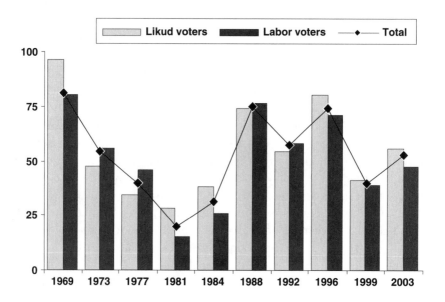

50 percent of respondents, compared with 70 percent in 1969, 1988, and 1996. In 1981 and 1984 less than 30 percent mentioned those issues and concentrated instead on domestic matters. In terms of support for Labor and the Likud, voters shift their attention in the same direction, with very small differences. It is easy enough to "predict the past" and to provide "explanations" for these differences, but it is much more difficult to forecast them. But it is important to note that the years in which the security response was high came on the heels of important security developments: the Six Days' War of 1967, the beginning of the intifada in 1987, and the Oslo Accords with the PLO in 1993 and 1995.

Shifting Voters

Despite social and economic change, the Israeli political system seemed on the surface to be remarkably stable until 1977, with one party (Mapai, later Labor) consistently receiving a plurality of the votes. But the system was hardly static; appearances notwithstanding, it would be misleading to depict the election results as robotlike behavior on the part of the public, election after election. To sustain this kind of analysis, we would have to make herculean assumptions about the unimportance of population change due to the exit of some from the voting public (death, emigration) and the entrance of others (coming of age, immigration). The anomaly of the Israeli case stemmed from the coincidence of very large changes in the voting public (primarily due to immigration) from election to election and the apparent stability of the voting results. Part of this effect was illusory: votes changed, but the government did not.

In reality, voting shifts have been a dominant feature of Israeli elections: between a third and a half of the voters have been known to select a different party from the one selected in the previous election. The proportional representation system and the emergence of a dominant party system in Israel prevented the translation of voting change into government change until 1977. Changes in the vote, however, were accurately reflected in the size of the delegations that represented parties in the Knesset. In 1965 and 1969, 25 percent of the respondents reported that they had voted for different parties in the two elections. A stability rate of 74 percent is very similar to the results obtained in Britain in a study that concluded that "electoral change is due not to a limited group of 'floating' voters but to a very broad segment of British electors."[13]

Prior to 1973, a good deal of the vote shifting in Israel was among factional groupings. For example, the parties of the left lost voters to one another, so although one party might exhibit a substantial swing in its vote totals from election to election, a much more stable picture would emerge in terms of its factional grouping. Parties of the left (including the communists) never won fewer than 64 nor more than 69 seats in the 120-seat Knesset in the seven elections through 1969; in 1973 they won 59 seats. The center parties ranged between 27 and 34 seats (43 in 1973), and the religious parties between 15 and 18 (15 in 1973). When an analyst divided the parties into six such groupings and calculated the average deviation for each grouping between 1949 and 1969, that for the parties in the Labor grouping (excluding the communists) was only 1.0 percent.[14] The average deviation for the center and religious groupings was even lower: 0.8 and 0.6 percent, respectively. The overall strength of factional groupings remained relatively stable; changes were occasioned by mergers and splits, alignments and divisions that characterized the relationships among the parties within factional groupings. But these swings should not obfuscate the basic fact that the parties of the Labor grouping, especially Mapai, dominated the voting results and politics of the entire period.

The Likud was in power for most of the period following its 1977 victory despite the high degree of competitiveness that characterized the end of Labor's dominance of Israeli politics. The Likud prime ministers were Menachem Begin (1977–1982), Yitzhak Shamir (1982–1984, 1986–1992), Benjamin Netanyahu (1996–1999), and Ariel Sharon (2001–). By contrast, the Labor prime ministers seemed to provide only a counterpoint to the Likud theme (Shimon Peres 1984–1986 and 1995–1996, Yitzhak Rabin 1992–1995, and Ehud Barak 1999–2001). In the ten elections between 1969 and 2003, the right bloc consolidated its domination, while the left lost support. Although the left bloc managed three times to achieve an absolute majority of the Knesset in that period—which the right never did—the right and the religious blocs in tandem have won sixty or more seats in every election since 1977, except 1992.

The period following the Yom Kippur War of 1973 is best thought of in terms of a realigning electoral era. In a realigning election (or a "critical election, " in V. O. Key's phrase), a new party balance is created. Key characterized an election as critical when "more or less profound readjustments occur in the relations of power within the community, and in which new and durable election groupings are formed."[15] Many thought that the 1973 war could be seen as a turning point in Israeli politics because it shattered so many myths and previously held conceptions. The publication of the 1973 election results soon after the war provided a rare opportunity to compare the voting behavior of large segments of the population. Since much of the population was serving in the army on election day, the results were especially informative, for the army is rather homogeneous in its composition—predominantly young and male (although women and the not-so-young are also represented).

If the experience of the 1973 war was to have far-reaching effects in the future, it would have been best to search for signs of these realigning effects in groups directly involved in the war and among those whose political beliefs and partisan attachments were still relatively flexible. If the army went for the Likud by a large majority, the war might be interpreted as a shared experience of the generation then reaching maturity that would have an impact on the politics of the future. The new tendency would be different from the dominant one in the previous generation; the younger generation, which made up a larger share of the electorate and was raising its children in a new climate of opinion, would eventually prevail.

The 1973 election results, however, did not indicate that the voters had behaved very differently on election day from the way they had behaved before. The army results gave the Likud 41.3 percent of the vote, as opposed to 39.5 percent for the Alignment. In the general population, the division was 30.2 percent to 39.6 percent, respectively. (In 1977 the results were even more dramatic in the army: 46 percent Likud, 22 percent Alignment, 16 percent DMC.) It is true that the Likud outpaced the Alignment in the army returns, but even before the war it had been well known that the Likud was strong among younger voters. Nonetheless, the Alignment won from army voters the same share as it received from the general population. This indicator, therefore, showed that it was inappropriate to regard the 1973 elections as critical; at most, tendencies already in process were accelerated as a result of the war. There was no clear, large-scale shift of group allegiances from one party to another. Previous patterns were accelerated, but no new patterns were obvious.

In a dominant-party system it may be more useful to discuss a "realigning electoral era"[16] rather than a critical election. During such an era the dominant party's electoral support slips from its grasp. As time passes, as "dominant doctrines" shift, the power base of the dominant party may well be eroded, although no one act or failure is enough to explain this decline. The Labor Party, the pivot of all government coalitions until 1977, became entrenched in office, and, socialist values notwithstanding, it grew conservative—anxious to preserve the gains it had won for the state, for the citizenry, and for its functionaries as well.

Many of the revolutionary socialist ideals that were part of Labor's legacy became only verbal goals. The fact that Labor had difficulty in attracting the votes of the young—the generation that had grown up since independence—indicated a partial shortcircuiting of the party's claim to dominance. This decline was evident in the voting results.

The 1977 elections ended the realigning era by deposing the dominant party. As we would expect in a dominant-party system, the opposition itself did little to depose the ruling party. The Likud's strength increased steadily, for demographic and ideological forces were harnessed behind it. The Alignment's greatest loss was to the Democratic Movement for Change (DMC); Alignment votes that went to the DMC determined the fall of the Alignment and the rise of the Likud. Later victories by Labor in 1984, 1992, and 1999 could not restore its dominant position. Dominance, which is both a set of power relations and a state of mind, is difficult to deny to the party that has it and extremely hard to win back by the party that has lost it.

The results of the 1981 elections strengthened the impression that a basic change in Israeli politics had come about as a result of the realigning electoral era. Despite its relative success compared with the 1977 election, the Alignment was unable to stymie the continued growth of the Likud. In 1984, although the Alignment won more votes than any other party, it was far from a position of dominance and had to share power with the Likud in a National Unity Government. In 1988 Labor lost additional votes and found itself smaller than the Likud. Labor finally agreed to continue the National Unity Government with the Likud, but it could not demand that the prime ministry rotate out of the hands of the Likud's Prime Minister Shamir. The 1992 elections brought Labor back to power, but that advantage was lost again in 1996.

In 1973, after the postponement of elections as a result of the Yom Kippur War, the rate of vote stability remained remarkably high. To be sure, the Alignment was weakened and the Likud strengthened: the Likud won 8 percent of the Alignment's 1969 vote while losing only 1 percent of its own 1969 vote to the Alignment. But when the overall rate of stability is calculated by dividing the number of stable votes in the two elections by the number of voters who reported a 1969 vote, the stability rate was 68 percent. The religious parties voters were most loyal, with 79 percent reporting identical votes in 1969 and 1973. Only two-thirds of the 1969 Alignment voters reported that they had voted for the Alignment in 1973, with 17 percent reporting a vote for the Likud and 4 percent for the Citizen Rights Movement list.

If the rates of stability and floating or shifting vote were not all that different in 1973 from what had occurred earlier, what was different was the unbalanced nature of the tradeoff. Usually the floating vote is a multisided affair, with the losses of one party made up by its gains from another. Many of the losses sustained by the Alignment this time, however, were net gains for the Likud. Perhaps this was the uniqueness of the 1973 results—not in the scope of the shift but in the relatively uniform movement of its direction.

Respondents have regularly been asked in preelection surveys how they were about to vote and how they had voted in the previous elections. In the late 1960s, the stable vote was around 75 percent, contracted to two-thirds in 1973. The stable vote in 1977 represented a historical low, with only 54 percent voting as they had in 1973. The rate increased to 60 percent in 1981 and returned to the 75-percent level in the 1980s. In 1992 it stood at about two-thirds, decreasing to almost 60 percent in 1996, and exceeding 60 percent of the electorate in 1999. In 2003 the stability rate was again very low at 57 percent—its lowest level since 1977 (see table 8.5).

Most of the change in 1977 was among those who had supported the Alignment in 1973. Of those (44.5 percent of the sample), less than half voted for the Alignment again in 1977, with 20 percent going to the Likud and 18 percent to the DMC. The 1973 Likud voters remained loyal on the whole, with some 8 percent supporting the DMC in 1977. Those who had not voted in 1973 gave the Likud 40 percent of their vote in 1977, the DMC 16 percent, and the Alignment a scant 4 percent. The DMC gained two-thirds of its voters who had participated in the 1973 elections from the Alignment, and the Likud almost 30 percent of its 1977 vote from the same source.

In 1981 a very tense and polarized campaign led to low levels of trade-off among the Likud and Alignment voters of 1977. Most of them stayed with their previous choice, with the Alignment picking up 3 percent of the sample from those who had voted Likud in 1977, compared with 2 percent of the sample who had voted Alignment in 1977 but shifted to the Likud in 1981. The major movement was among the 1977 DMC voters, who went overwhelmingly for the Alignment, at a ratio of 4 to 1 compared with those who chose the Likud. Some 1977 Likud voters voted for other parties, especially Tehiya. But the most crucial datum regarding the future was the attraction to the Likud of those who had not voted in 1977 (mostly young voters): the Likud outdrew the Alignment among this group by a ratio of 2 to 1.

Table 8.5   Stable and Floating Voters (in percentages)

A. 1973–1977

1973 vote	1977 vote						
	Alignment	DMC	Likud	Religious	Other	No answer	Total
Alignment	**20.0**	8.0	9.0	0.5	1.0	6.0	44.5
Likud	0.5	2.0	**19.0**	—	0.5	2.0	24.0
Religious	—	—	2.0	**5.0**	—	—	7.0
Other	—	2.0	1.0	–	1.0	2.0	6.0
No vote	0.5	2.0	5.0	0.5	0.5	4.0	12.5
No answer	–	—	—	—	—	6.0	6.0
Total	21.0	14.0	36.0	6.0	3.0	20.0	100.0
							(*N* = 465)

Note: Based on June 1977 survey; stable vote in boldface type.

Total stable vote = 54% (stable votes/1973 party voters; 44/81.5)

B. 1999–2003

1999 vote	2003 vote								
	Left	Labor	Shinui	Likud	Religious	No Right	Other	answer	Total
Left	**5.0**	1.5	1.0	—	—	—	—	1.0	8.5
One Israel	2.0	**11.5**	3.0	3.0	—	—	0.5	4.0	24.0
Center	0.5	—	**3.0**	0.5	—	—	—	0.5	4.5
Likud	—	0.5	1.5	**19.5**	1.0	2.5	0.5	4.0	29.5
Religious	—	—	—	2.5	**5.0**	0.5	—	1.0	9.0
Right	—	—	—	1.0	—	**1.5**	—	1.0	3.5
Other	—	—	0.5	—	—	—	—	0.5	1.0
No vote	0.5	0.5	1.0	2.0	1.5	1.0	—	1.0	7.5
No answer	0.5	1.0	1.5	2.5	2.0	—	1.0	4.0	12.5
Total	8.5	15.0	11.5	31.0	9.5	5.5	2.0	17.0	100.0
									(*N* = 1,034)

Note: Based on January 2003 survey; stable vote in boldface type.

Total stable vote = 57% (stable votes/1999 party voters; 45.5/80)

In 1984, 23 percent of the total sample repeated their 1981 votes for the Alignment or the Likud. Four percent of the I984 sample who had voted Likud in 1981 switched to the Alignment; 5.5 percent switched to other parties. The Alignment lost 0.5 percent to the Likud, 2 percent to others. Among the army voters, the Likud and Tehiya won about 50 percent, the Alignment, Shinui, and the Citizen Rights Movement about 40 percent.

In the 1988 elections, the two big parties retained their 1984 voters at about the same rate. Some Alignment voters drifted to the left, but others moved to the Likud and the right. A similar pattern for the Likud voters was evident, but in the opposite direction. The pattern among new voters (no vote in 1984) indicated just how fractured the political system had become, with 5 percent of the total sample selecting the right and the Likud and 5 percent selecting Labor and the left.

Rates of retention were very different for Labor and Likud between 1988 and 1992. Labor retained most of its 1988 vote, while the Likud lost more than a third of its 1988 vote; those defecting Likud voters went to Labor and to parties of the right. The result was a much-weakened Likud, allowing Labor and Rabin to take office in 1992. New voters split evenly among the right and the Likud on the one hand, and the left and Labor on the other, with a substantial number of them choosing religious parties.

The 1996 and 1999 elections were different because of the addition of the direct election of the prime minister to the vote for the Knesset lists. That era saw very high rates of mobility because the large parties emphasized the importance of the prime ministerial vote and were willing to give up much of the voting support for their party lists. Meanwhile, sectarian parties such as Shas and the Russian immigrant parties flourished, since the pressure on voters by the big parties was not focused on the party vote. In 2003 the appeal of Shinui heightened, and that party won votes from former Labor voters and from those who had voted for the Center Party in the past.

The factors associated with consistent voting are the same factors associated with a "conservative" vote. Age, for example, has always been a very powerful factor: the older one is, the more likely one is to retain previous patterns of behavior, including vote preferences. Education is also related to voting stability: the lower the level of education, the higher the stability of the vote. Voters with higher education levels change their voting choice more often, and they vote less often for the larger parties and more often for smaller ones.

Party Images

There are many reasons for the change in fortunes of the two parties; the passing of leadership, the weakening of dependency relations, and demographic changes have already been discussed. All of these developments are connected with the images the electorate holds of the parties.

Just as a social myth is a convenient way of ordering reality, the party's or leader's image is no less important than the actual opinion or personality. While reality is usually complex, myths and images have a simplifying quality that makes them easily grasped and widely accepted. If Peres is thought of as soft and Sharon as tough, conflicting evidence can easily be put aside in favor of the widely held image, which allows one to grasp the essence of the person more easily. And when conflicting images are widely held by polarized groups, beliefs tend to be held and expressed all the more strongly.

A key aspect of voting behavior involves prospective evaluations of the competing parties—the answer to the question "Who can deliver?"[17] Such evaluations have been found to be very important in explaining Israeli elections.[18] In 1988 short-term issues such as dealing with the Arab uprising were less important than considerations of the long-term future of the territories. An analysis of the 1992 elections showed the security aspect to be crucial in the voting decision, rather than the economic one. In the 1996 elections, the risks involved in peace-making were contrasted with the threats evident in everyday life. Taking all these analyses together, it is clear that the images of the parties in terms of their ability to achieve goals that are generally favored by the electorate are significant factors in voting behavior.

Regarding security matters, the desirable party would be one able to put an end to uprisings and terror on the one hand and to achieve peace on the other. Respondents have been asked over the years to evaluate which political party (Labor or Likud) would best be able to achieve different goals. Labor presented itself as the party of peace and the better one to lead the country in negotiations with the Arabs, while the Likud tried to project a firm image regarding security. In 1992 Labor evidently achieved that image with Rabin at the head of the list; in both 1988 and in 1996, with Peres, Labor gambled and lost. In 1999 Labor and Barak were seen as better able to bring both peace and security than Netanyahu. In 2003 Sharon was faced with terror that did not end and with peace that did not come, yet he and the Likud were preferred over Mitzna and Labor. In the 2003 survey leading up to the elections, the Likud led Labor in almost every category: more likely to bring true peace, to preserve democracy in the country, to know how to fight terror, and to separate Israel from the Palestinians (Mitzna's platform). Labor was seen as slightly more likely to close the social gaps, and the Likud was seen as more corrupt than Labor, although a large majority thought both parties corrupt (see figure 8.3).

Figure 8.3   Party Images, 2003 (in percentages)

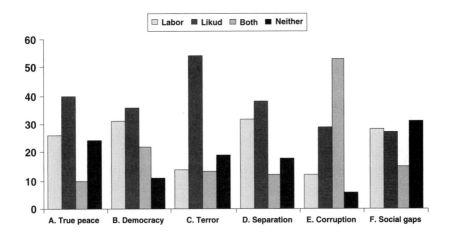

Source: Israel National Election Study, 2003.

"Which party . . . ?"

A. will secure true peace with the Arabs.
B. will preserve democracy in Israel.
C. will contain terror.
D. will achieve separation from the Palestinians.
E. is corrupt.
F. will decrease social gaps.

The images of being tough and desirous of peace can be parlayed into a winning program, as Ben-Gurion, Begin, Rabin, and Sharon have demonstrated. This type of appeal has overarching success in Israel and reaches across social groups. However, the chances for the continued success of a democratic regime rest in part on having social groups overlap. In Israel today we witness a lack of overlapping social cleavages, so much so as to point to a possible danger to Israeli democracy. When the political system is polarized so that one group concentrates within it the religious, the Sephardim, and the less educated and lower-status workers voting for the Likud and religious parties, while the other group has a disproportionate share of secular, upper-class Ashkenazim voting for Labor and Meretz, the likelihood of intolerance, lack of communication, misunderstanding, and violence grow. In many countries the amount of vote variance explained by social structure and attitudinal variables has been reduced over the years from the 1960s through the 1990s. This has not been the case in Israel; the difference lies in the nature of the issues that have captured the agenda. In most Western countries, issues involving postbourgeois versus materialist values, gender issues, public versus private consumption, and state employment have gained ascendancy. In Israel, however, these issues have energized only limited publics and have not become as central, critical, and engulfing as the major issue dimension: the territories and the Israeli-Arab conflict. Voting in Israel has become more structured, and security issues have become a more important determinant of it over time.

9 THE GOVERNMENT, THE KNESSET, AND THE JUDICIARY

THE ISRAELI SYSTEM, like most democratic regimes, has legislative, executive, and judicial branches and espouses separation of powers and checks and balances. The Knesset, which is the supreme legislative body of the state, has tremendous symbolic importance as the seat of the people's sovereignty and the most important deliberative assembly of the nation. Its Speaker stands in for the president of the country should the latter be out of the country or indisposed, and he receives the reports of the state comptroller. But symbolism should not be confused with power, which rests in the executive branch, headed by the government cabinet. The court system represents the third branch of government, led by the highly respected Supreme Court of Israel.

The branches are hardly equal or separate. Inevitably there is mixing, as when judges fill administrative functions regarding implementation of judicial decisions, the division of land, and bequests; when the administration deals with secondary legislation to an extent that surpasses the output of the Knesset in primary legislation; and when administrative justice becomes more important as the degree of intervention of the central government grows, or when the Knesset takes on judiciary powers in deciding to revoke the immunity of a Knesset member.[1]

Formally, the legislature generates and controls the government, but the legislature is not the equal of the executive in terms of political power. The hierarchical party system makes it a political inevitability that the dependent Knesset members will tend to support their party leaders who are also government ministers. While the other branches can be important and in some situations even crucial, in a political sense the Knesset is generally a staging ground for the government and the executive branch.

The Executive Branch

Parliamentary Government

The one true expression of mass democracy—elections—determines the composition of the Knesset, Israel's parliament. *Knesset* means assembly, while *parliament* denotes discourse and deliberation. Perhaps that dual designation hints at the primary function of the Knesset: to assemble and select the government coalition.

The elementary fact of Israeli political life is that the government, and not the Knesset, is the focus of political power in the country. In that sense, Israel is a good example of the parliamentary system; the Knesset is elected by the people, and it in turn approves the prime minister and his or her government. The president of the state appoints a Knesset member who undertakes to form a government, and that person has twenty-eight days to perform this task, although the president may grant up to fourteen additional days. The appointee is usually the leader of the largest party in the Knesset, but it need not be so. In 1983 the president gave the job of forming the government to Yitzhak Shamir following Prime Minister Begin's resignation, even though the Likud's Knesset delegation was smaller than the Alignment's. It is more likely that the head of the largest party will be successful in winning majority support in the Knesset, but if this is not possible, another Knesset member will be chosen to attempt to form a government.

The prime minister's success can be measured by his or her effectiveness in achieving the government's policies and maintaining majority support in the Knesset. Since no party has ever won a majority of the votes in the elections, pursuing policy and stability has always entailed coalition government. The strength of the government is achieved by a process of condensation in which, at each successive stage, the potency of the remaining actors is increased. Within a voting population of 3 million, the power of an individual voter is not great. Among the 120 members of the Knesset, the relative influence of each one is obviously greater. If members of the government coalition parties number, say, 65, and members of the government 18, power is concentrated even more. Now, if you were one of the seven ministers who were members of the major party, and if, among those seven, you also happened to be in the dominant faction, of which there were only three members, your power would grow greatly.

Formal and informal power rests with the government and its ministers. The government cabinet declares war and ratifies treaties. While there are gradations of power, the prime minister and those close to him are near the top of the scale. The Israeli system has always emphasized the role of the prime minister. Ben-Gurion could conceive of and plan the Sinai operation without prior knowledge by his cabinet. Golda Meir's decisions regarding Egyptian overtures in the early 1970s, Begin's decision regarding the feasibility of a peace treaty with Egypt at the end of that decade, and Sharon's suggestion of unilateral withdrawal from the Gaza Strip in 2004 demonstrate that the predispositions and conclusions of the prime minister can have far-reaching influence in the system. Although surrounded by colleagues with differing opinions, each of these leaders knew that his or her opinion would likely be the one to prevail.

The prime minister occupies a superior position, in both law and politics, and is the undisputed focus of power. The individual leader's political acumen, personality, or coalition imperatives might lead to the sharing of power and even to responsiveness to party or public opinion, but the prime minister's near-monopoly on power resources must never be underestimated. The incumbent in any political situation has an advantage, which, used judiciously, is almost irrepressible.

The prime minister is in a privileged position compared with the ministers of his cabinet. He commands the public spotlight, is likely the head of the Knesset's largest party, and is the head of the many aspects of his administration. Even in the face of criminal allegations, the prime minister's position is special. While the High Court of Justice held in the cases of Ministers Rafael Pinhasi and Arye Deri that a minister indicted for a crime could no longer serve in office, the Basic Law: Government specifically treats the prime minister differently. The law states that the prime minister must resign only after a final verdict in the case, meaning that it is likely that his or her term will end before the decision is finally made. This article was carried over in the law of the direct election of the prime minister even though the logic of that legislation was entirely different because the prime minister was no longer invested through a vote of confidence in the Knesset. The ethical ramifications of a prime minister's continuing to make decisions of state while his case proceeds through the legal system is problematic in both cases, but especially so in a parliamentary system in which legitimacy is granted to the ruling coalition and not only to the prime minister. When Ariel Sharon faced possible indictment in 2004 on charges of bribery, these matters weighed heavily on the political system.[2]

Generally, cabinet ministers are leaders of the political parties in the coalition. As ministers, they not only have political power and prestige but with the ministerial office they gain patronage and budget to enhance their political positions and that of their parties. As members of political parties that tend to operate in an oligarchic manner, the other Knesset members of their party realize that it is in the interest of the party—and often in their personal interests—to toe the line. Ministers are not department secretaries in the American sense of being advisers or experts serving at the pleasure of the president, nor are they advisers of the prime minister, for they have not been appointed for their expertise in the fields controlled by their ministries. Instead, they have become cabinet members generally because of their political role as politicians whose parties have decided to join the ruling coalition. There have rarely been more than one or two ministers at a time who were not Knesset members. During the 1996–2003 period of the direct election law, which allowed up to half of the cabinet ministers be non–Knesset members, Netanyahu's 1996 government had two ministers who were not Knesset members.

The government has often had two dozen or more Knesset members engaged as ministers and deputy ministers. This means that almost a quarter of the Knesset is involved in the work of the government ministries and that the work of legislation falls on the remaining members. During National Unity Governments (which existed during a third of the period between 1967 and 1988), there have been fewer Knesset members in the opposition than there were in the government cabinet. The 2001–2002 government had thirty ministers, seven of whom had no assignment to a specific ministry but served as ministers without portfolio. In these cases, coalition parties in the Knesset were led by second-level leaders because the first-rank leaders were busy in the cabinet. And this, of course, weakened the Knesset politically.

This situation has driven support for the so-called Norwegian law, which would have ministers automatically resign from the Knesset upon being appointed to the government in order to make room in the Knesset for the next person on the party list; also, not surprisingly, the law would allow a minister who resigns from the cabinet to resume his place in the Knesset automatically at the expense of the newcomer. Adoption of this plan would strengthen the ranks of the government coalition supporters in the Knesset and reward more of the party activists. The reform would be expensive because so many new officeholders would be involved, but the real reason that the plan will be accepted or rejected, however, will be political and not economic.

Each cabinet minister is appointed by his party and is responsible for the voting behavior of his delegation in the Knesset. Generally prime ministers do not interfere with the selection of ministers by their coalescing parties, notwithstanding Golda Meir's exceptional refusal to appoint Yitzhak Rafael to her cabinet. Until 1981 the prime minister did not have the formal power to dismiss a minister, although, in practice, incumbent ministers could be pressured by the prime minister to resign, as Moshe Sharett was in June 1956. Upon resuming the role of prime minister in 1955, Ben-Gurion appointed the reluctant Sharett foreign minister, but disagreements over defense policy soon emerged, with Sharett advocating a more moderate position than Ben-Gurion. When the position of secretary-general of Mapai opened, Sharett jokingly offered to be a candidate, whereupon Ben-Gurion insisted that he take the position, thus bringing Sharett to resign from the cabinet.[3] In 1976 Prime Minister Rabin used as a pretext for early elections the support on a no-confidence vote by three ministers from the National Religious Party, in effect firing them from his cabinet.

In 1981 new legislation authorized the prime minister to dismiss a minister by stating his intention to do so to the Knesset. A minister's appointment was to terminate forty-eight hours later, giving both the prime minister and the minister time to reconsider. The reform made cabinet ministers more directly accountable to prime ministers, thus strengthening prime ministerial power. The coalition agreement of the National Unity Government in 1984 suspended this provision, authorizing the prime minister to dismiss only ministers from his or her own party. Nonetheless, the relations between Prime Minister Peres and Minister Yitzhak Modai of the Likud were so strained that the agreement was stretched to its limits.

Only twice did such a dismissal actually occur in the years before the direct election of the prime minister, and both incidents involved Prime Minister Yitzhak Shamir. The prime minister dismissed Ezer Weizman in December 1989, following a Weizman meeting with a PLO representative despite the cabinet's decision banning such meetings. In March 1990 Shamir dismantled the National Unity Government and fired Foreign Minister Shimon Peres when he learned that Peres, head of Labor, was attempting to bring down the governing coalition in a no-confidence vote and to form a new coalition. In 1999 Prime Minister Benjamin

Netanyahu discharged Defense Minister Yitzhak Mordechai, knowing that Mordechai intended to quit the Likud Party and oppose Netanyahu as head of the newly formed Center Party.

The Israeli governing system is based on the principle of collective responsibility to the coalition in the Knesset. This norm, while vocally praised, is applied with great flexibility, and there have been many instances of ministers voting against the government in which they serve, especially on controversial issues such as the Camp David agreements and the Oslo Accords. The essence of collective responsibility is that cabinet members may object or vote against a cabinet decision, but once taken, they must support it unless specifically released from their obligation. Ministers are also held responsible for the voting behavior of Knesset members from their party, and they can be removed by the prime minister upon his notification to the Knesset.

The government sets up its own rules of procedure, and most of its official decisions have to do with legislation that the government approves before forwarding it to the Knesset. What really happens in cabinet meetings is a function of the personality of the prime minister and of the issues on the public agenda. Unfortunately, little is known in a systematic way about the dynamics and interactions within the cabinet. We know the procedures for asking the various ministries involved for their comments on pending legislation. We are sometimes aware of acrimonious debate that takes place in a cabinet meeting, especially if there is a leak or if the disagreement continues on the evening's television news or in the newspapers. We also know the quantity of legislation and decisions taken, and we may debate about their quality. But the cabinet and its meeting must be thought of as a rather formalized setting for the continuation of the political game.

The supremacy of the prime minister, as well as matters of coalition politics, electoral politics, and bureaucratic politics can never be far from the minds and actions of the ministers and the government. Because they are first and foremost politicians, however, it is clear that their motivations are complex and do not always flow directly from dedication to the greater good. When there is a conflict within the cabinet, the dynamics become more focused and this makes it easier to determine the lineup of the players and to assess why they act as they do and what they hope to achieve. The personalities of the major actors, and especially that of the prime minister, determine much of the governing style of the cabinet.

The government sometimes delegates matters to one of its committees of ministers, which can make decisions in place of the cabinet. A 1991 law required that a ministerial defense committee be established, headed by the prime minister, deputy prime minister, and the ministers of defense, foreign affairs, and finance, and others up to half the members of the cabinet.[4]

The prime minister may participate in any meeting of a government committee, and if he so desires, he may serve as chairman of that meeting. Deliberations of the government and the ministerial committees are secret. The ministers are responsible for the actions of their ministries, and the minister is also responsible for the decisions of the government as a whole. This means that once a decision is taken in the government, all the ministers must support it, in the Knesset and publicly, even if they opposed it in the cabinet meeting. Ministers must also see to it that Knesset members of their delegation vote for the government's position unless given permission to do otherwise.

Throughout Israeli political history, the resignation of most ministers from the government can be explained in political terms. While there may have been matters of principle or policy at the heart of the issue, the resignation itself must be thought of in terms of its effect on the political structure of the coalition. Parties (and hence ministers) have resigned from the government over religious issues and matters of foreign policy. The examples offered earlier in this chapter can be cited as cases of leaving the government on political grounds connected with party principle. Another example would be the exit in 1970 of Gahal from the National Unity Government because it could not agree to the government's position on the plan presented by U.S. Secretary of State William Rogers, with its acceptance of UN Resolution 242.

Rarely does an individual minister resign on an issue of principle, as Yitzhak Berman did in 1982 after the government refused (only to reverse itself a week later) to set up an official commission of inquiry regarding the events in the Palestinian refugee camps of Sabra and Shatilla in Beirut. Government ministers almost never resign out of ministerial responsibility. For example, Prime Minister Meir and Defense Minister Dayan did not resign as a result of the Yom Kippur War, in part because of the support given their view by the Agranat Commission that decisions regarding the war involved the collective responsibility of the entire government.

Coalition Politics

The two words *coalition* and *politics* are almost synonymous. In order to construct winning majorities in committees or legislatures, coalitions must often be formed. Forming coalitions comes naturally to politicians— in the parliamentary systems of Europe it has become accepted as a basic characteristic of politics. A recent feature of Israeli constitutional law is that coalition agreements (in local government too) must be made public.

As a general rule, we would expect coalitions to be formed with the smallest surplus over the resources necessary to maintain a majority in the Knesset.[5] There are costs involved in having another party support your party's platform, so, obviously, one would try to keep costs down by entering coalitions with as few other parties as possible. The "minimum size" principle applied to the Knesset would lead us to expect a coalition of 61 in the 120-member Knesset. In fact, the Israeli experience has rarely adhered to the minimum-size principle.

Most governments formed in Israel between 1949 and 2003 rested on oversized coalitions, solid majorities in the Knesset that were well above the minimum size needed to rule. These comfortable majorities gave the governments more leeway in action and discouraged smaller parties from causing coalition crises—because by simple arithmetic it is clear to smaller parties that they are dispensable. Of the thirty governments between 1949 and 2003, only two had support from fewer than sixty-five members at the outset. The cabinet formed by Prime Minister Sharett in 1955 was made up of a coalition of only sixty-four votes, but it lasted only two months. The 1995 government formed by Peres after the Rabin assassination began with the formal support of only fifty-six Knesset members, but it also had the informal support of five Arab Knesset members and was in consultation with the six-member Shas delegation about the possibility of its joining the coalition. The special conditions that existed after the assassination allowed the government to continue through the elections a half-year later. The government formed by Barak in 1999 was supported by seventy-five Knesset members, but by the time of his decision to call for elections in 2001, his government could rely on only thirty-two Knesset members.

Governing coalitions were quite stable during Labor's dominance between 1949 and 1977, when it headed every government and pursued policies with little interference from coalition partners or from the opposition. Knesset fragmentation did not really matter much as long as junior coalition partners could be compensated with secondary ministerial portfolios and relatively limited budget allocations. Once Labor lost its dominant position, however, fragmentation became more problematic as smaller parties increased their demands for payoffs, making consensual policies much more difficult to form. At the same time, smaller parties became increasingly aware of their crucial leverage in making or breaking coalitions.

After 1977, the bargaining over portfolio allocations and budget shares became more demanding and complex. The junior coalition partners demanded a larger share of ministerial and budget payoffs in return for their support, as well as control over high-spending ministries. Consequently, the coalition-forming parties increased the total number of ministries and allocated more senior ministerial portfolios and larger shares of the budget to the smaller parties. The number of portfolios increased in proportion to the decrease in the size of the prime minister's party. In response to mounting public criticism regarding these additions and the escalating cost of government ministries, their number was fixed at eighteen in the same reform that legislated the direct election of the prime minister. However, this limit was removed in 1999 when Prime Minister Barak capitalized on his landslide victory to expand his governing coalition and solidify his power in office.

In the 1996–2003 period of the direct election of the prime minister, a fragmented party system weakened the institutional power of the Knesset and accelerated the concentration of prime ministerial power, but at the same time it impaired the ability of governments to rule effectively and accountably. A major flaw with the direct-election system was that it encouraged small parties to pressure the bigger parties to accommodate their policy preferences at multiple points in the process: before the first round of elections, before the second round, during the bargaining process for the formation of the coalition government, and then whenever a crucial policy decision was about to be made. Under the system in use before and after the direct election of the prime minister phase, the small parties could pressure the big ones only during the coalition-formation phase, and then only if they were genuinely pivotal—that is, if their support was needed by the party forming the coalition.

In many parliamentary regimes, governments are formed with more than the minimum necessary support in the legislature because parties have multiple actors and policy goals that are expressed in various ways in coalition-formation negotiations.[6] A party desires both to maximize the number of portfolios it controls and to achieve its policy goals. But the strategy of party leaders who form coalitions is also influenced by their determination to secure their leadership within their respective parties. They may thus support allocating important portfolios to coalition partners and broadening the government, thereby weakening political rivals within their own parties and simultaneously strengthening their own positions.

The loss of Knesset seats by the two bloc leaders to smaller parties reduces the share of portfolios held by the party that has formed the coalition. The coalition-forming party must obtain the support of a minimum of sixty-one Knesset members in order to present the coalition for the vote of investiture, a central institution in multiparty parliamentary systems, by which the coalition becomes the formal government. The reduced number of Knesset seats won by the parties that have formed a coalition means an increase in the number of coalition partners needed to form a coalition and win the approval of the Knesset.[7]

A strong core party can reduce considerably the side-payments to smaller parties in the coalition-formation process—an advantage that empowers it to pursue relatively consistent, long-term policies and to reward coalition partners with only secondary portfolios in order to obtain their support of the government and its policies. In this way, government capabilities increase. Small parties gained a significantly higher share of the government portfolios when the Knesset had an empty core between 1977 and 1992, compared to the situation that prevailed when a party core could be identified, as in the years between 1951 and 1977, between 1992 and 1996, and after 2003 (see table 9.1).[8]

During the term of office of a coalition, its size may be reduced to the point that it is in danger of losing its parliamentary majority. Thus the Ben-Gurion government of 1951 had the support of only sixty Knesset members after Agudat Israel and Poalei Agudat Israel left the cabinet over the issue of compulsory army service for women. As a result of defections from the Likud and the splitting up of the DMC, Begin's Knesset support fell drastically in 1979. After the 1981 elections, Begin set up a government based on the support of only sixty-one members of the Knesset.

Until 1977, the consistent leader of the coalition was the Mapai-Labor Alignment. As the pivotal figure in all arithmetical calculations regarding the coalitions, the dominant party consolidated its position by controlling the key ministries of defense, foreign affairs, finance, education, and the prime ministry. Budget allocations, key appointments, and important matters of policy were all in the hands of the Labor Party. With the ascension of the Likud in 1977, the government coalition was constructed for the first time by another party, but its political behavior in terms of forming the coalition was not much different from that displayed by the Alignment over the years.

The basic partner in the Likud coalition of 1977 was the same as that linked with the various Labor governments earlier: the National Religious Party. With twelve Knesset votes, the NRP was attractive to the Likud without being threatening. Moreover, the NRP was experienced

Table 9.1 Parties and Coalitions, 1949–2003

Prime minister	Term	Initial size of coalition	Size of largest party	Number of ministers	Number from PM's party	% of ministers from PM's party
Ben-Gurion	Mar 49–Oct 50	73	46	12	7	58.3
Ben-Gurion	Oct 50–Feb 51	73	46	13	8	61.5
Ben-Gurion	Oct 51–Dec 52	65	45	13	9	69.2
Ben-Gurion	Dec 52–Dec 53	87	45	16	9	56.3
Sharett	Jan 54–June 55	87	45	16	9	56.3
Sharett	June 55–July 55	64	40	16	11	68.8
Ben-Gurion	Nov 55–Dec 57	80	40	16	9	56.3
Ben-Gurion	Jan 58–July 59	64	40	16	11	68.8
Ben-Gurion	Dec 59–Jan 61	86	47	16	9	56.3
Ben-Gurion	Nov 61–June 63	68	42	16	11	68.8
Eshkol	June 63–Dec 64	68	42	15	10	66.7
Eshkol	Dec 64–Nov 65	68	42	16	11	68.8
Eshkol	Jan 66–Feb 69	75	45	18	12	66.7
Meir	Mar 69–Oct 69	107	56	22	14	63.6
Meir	Dec 69–Dec 73	102	56	24	14	58.3
Meir	Mar 74–Apr 74	68	51	22	17	77.3
Rabin	June 74–Dec 76	61	51	19	16	84.2
Begin	June 77–June 81	62	45	17	9	69.2
Begin	Aug 81–Sep 83	61	46	18	15	83.3
Shamir	Oct 83–July 84	64	46	18	15	83.3
Peres	Sep 84–Oct 86	97	40	25	9	36.0
Shamir	Oct 86–Nov 88	96	40	25	10	40.0
Shamir	Dec 88–Mar 90	95	40	26	11	42.3

Table 9.1 Continued

Prime minister	Term	Initial size of coalition	Size of largest party	Number of ministers	Number from PM's party	% of ministers from PM's party
Shamir	June 90–June 92	62	40	19	9	47.4
Rabin	July 92–Nov 95	62	44	17	13	76.4
Peres	Nov 95–May 96	58	44	20	15	75.0
Netanyahu	June 96–May 99	66	32	18	9	50.0
Barak	July 99–Aug 99	75	26	18	8	44.0
Barak	Aug 99–Feb 01	75	26	23	10	43.5
Sharon [a]	Feb 01–Jan 03	82	26	26	9	34.6
Sharon	Feb 03	68	38	23	13[b]	56.5

a. Since this government resulted from a "special election for the prime minister," the largest party was Labor, elected in 1999, and not Sharon's Likud.

b. This includes Natan Sharansky, whose Israel b'Aliyah Party, with two seats, joined the Likud immediately after the elections.

in the politics of compromise, which is the essence of coalition politics. The alternative partner was the DMC, with fifteen seats, but it had a reformist bent and, in the coalition negotiations, insisted on items such as electoral reform, to which the Likud preferred to pay only lip service. Once the government was set up, it was harder for the DMC to stand by its principles; ultimately it acquiesced in entering the government coalition without receiving the assurances it had sought.

A good working relationship developed between Mapai and the religious parties, although the major crises in the history of coalitions in Israel are often associated with problems of religion. In a country so hard-pressed by security and economic problems, it is enlightening to note that cabinet crises usually center on matters peripheral to immediate concerns of government and pertaining more to matters of philosophy and theology. Perhaps this indicates special cultural attainments of Jews and the Jewish state, but it also means that the ruling coalitions are relatively successful in governing; government policy is generally assured of support before it reaches the Knesset, and only in matters on which cleavage cannot be overcome do partners sometimes quarrel in public.

Three examples will suffice. The first crisis in Israeli cabinet history occurred in early 1950, over the religious education of children in immigrant camps. A compromise solution was worked out whereby religious schools would be set up in predominantly religious camps and two systems, secular and religious, would operate in others. By the end of 1950, the issue emerged again; the cabinet recommendations were rejected by a Knesset vote of 49–42, with many opposition parties using the opportunity to strike a blow against Mapai as much as to support the claims of the religious parties. Ben-Gurion immediately announced the resignation of the government, and new elections were called for July 1951. This crisis gave impetus to Ben-Gurion's assessment that a national system of education must be established, thereby abandoning party-related tracks that had characterized education in the pre-state period. At the government level, he was convinced that effective ways must be found to assure collective responsibility in order to prevent cabinets failing as a result of the defection of coalition members. This experience also convinced him that electoral reform was needed in order to free the political system from the stranglehold that strong parties had over it.

A second crisis occurred in July 1958, when the two NRP ministers resigned from the cabinet over a directive issued by Minister of the Interior Israel Bar-Yehuda of Ahdut Haavoda. Bar-Yehuda's instructions to registration officials stated that "any person declaring in good faith that he is a Jew shall be registered as a Jew and no additional proof shall be required." This infuriated the religious authorities, for the question of "Who is a Jew?" has historically and traditionally been their province. Indeed, it can be argued that the issue is of prime concern to them because matters of group exclusivity are meaningful only in terms of some preconceived notion of the history and destiny of the group. Ultimately, the NRP resigned from the cabinet and experienced the taste of opposition for the first time. The real issue was not "Who is a Jew?" but *who decides* who is a Jew? The most significant political outcome of the crisis was that between 1959 and the late 1980s, the minister of the interior, who is responsible for registration of citizens, was from the National Religious Party. This pro-NRP conclusion was reached while the party was not a member of the coalition, indicating that even in opposition it had considerable leverage.

The story of the third example of a coalition quarrel began in January 1970, when the Supreme Court ruled that a person's statement that he was a Jew was sufficient to define him as a Jew. The government headed by Golda Meir subsequently amended the Law of Return by defining a Jew as "one who is born to a Jewess or is converted." This is in accord with rabbinical practice and was considered by many a major victory for the religious forces. But the further issue soon arose—converted by whom? Conversions undertaken by non-Orthodox rabbis were not regarded as valid by the establishment of Israeli religious leaders. The demand was made that the Law of Return be further amended to have conversion valid only if performed in accord with Jewish rabbinical law, *halacha*.

Golda Meir's efforts to form a new government after the 1973 elections were held up until March 1974 by this issue. After much effort a formula was developed: the prime minister issued a statement that since the amendment of the Law of Return, "no non-Jew had been registered as a Jew, and the government intended to continue in like fashion." The NRP gave in for all intents and purposes, joining the Meir government in the light of "compelling security considerations" occasioned by reports of the deteriorating situation on the Syrian border. When Meir resigned as prime minister soon after having established the government, however, the process had to begin again. In this second round, the opponents of the coalition, especially the NRP Youth Faction led by Zevulun Hammer and Yehuda Ben-Meir, hardened their line and successfully prevented the NRP from participating in the new Rabin government.

The NRP was concerned, however, about losing its powerful base in the Ministry of Religious Affairs, which allowed it to control religious councils and chief and local rabbinates. This had happened in the 1958–1959 crisis, and the leadership was afraid that it would happen again. By November 1974, the NRP replaced the Citizen Rights Movement members in supporting the government without achieving any change in the "Who is a Jew?" issue.

Coalition involves a large number of issues, such as ideology, government ministries, programs, and money. Many of them are tied together, and sometimes behavior explained at the public level in one way is really motivated by something altogether different. It is possible to explore the nature of the payoffs in coalition politics by examining the ministries assigned to the various parties, but this is harder than it appears, because not all ministries are of equal importance and even the size of the budget is not always an indicator of a ministry's importance. When using government ministries as an index of the payoffs of coalition behavior, we must therefore focus on the quality rather than the quantity of the positions awarded: the important ministries have historically been placed in the hands of the major party of the coalition. During parts of their terms of office as prime minister, David Ben-Gurion, Levi Eshkol, Menachem Begin, Shimon Peres, and Yitzhak Rabin were also their own defense ministers. The appointment of Moshe Dayan to the post of defense minister on the eve of the Six Days' War of 1967 was important not only because Prime Minister Eshkol was relinquishing the post but also because it was being given to a member of Rafi, a party that had been outside the government coalition before the establishment of the National Unity Government. Moshe Dayan figured in another important exception when, after the 1977 Likud victory, Menachem Begin offered him the post of foreign affairs minister, even though Dayan had been elected on the opposition Alignment list.

The second National Unity Government was set up in 1984, after the election had produced a stalemate. In an unprecedented manner, the Alignment and the Likud agreed that Peres would be prime minister for the first twenty-five months, and then he would relinquish the post to Yitzhak Shamir for the next twenty-five months. Also, most of the other elected lists supported the government, making its promised strength in the Knesset 97 of 120 members. A careful balance was struck between the two large parties over ministries, timetables, and commitments to the smaller parties associated with each of the bigger ones.

The National Unity Government that followed the 1988 elections highlighted many of these considerations. Likud (with forty members) and Labor (with thirty-nine members) were almost equal in size; the religious parties, with eighteen members, seemed to be likely candidates for coalition. But these parties demanded, among other things, iron-clad guarantees that the Law of Return would be amended so that only those converted according to *halacha* would be considered Jews. *Halacha* is strictly observed by Orthodox Jews, but in lesser degrees by others; accordingly, Jewish communities around the world (overwhelmingly non-Orthodox) and many Israelis opposed this demand vehemently. A Likud-Labor unity government emerged, but without the features of rotation in power that had existed after 1984. Most of the religious parties joined the ruling coalition in the end, but as junior partners. The beginning of Sharon's term in 2001–2002 was also characterized by a Likud coalition with Labor in a National Unity government.

In addition to ministries, many other things are bargained over in coalition negotiations. Policy is a crucial one. The government sets up guidelines that are, in effect, the government's platform, and these are presented to the Knesset when the cabinet is approved. But the guidelines do not have binding status; they reflect promises made by partners of the coalition to each other. Usually, no timetable is set on promises for enacting policy, and often such promises can be overlooked. If the coalition is fragile, however, or if the other party must acquiesce in supporting a policy, the payoff may be that the coalition leadership fulfills its promise by enacting legislation or pursuing certain policy goals. The coalition has the resources to do this because its Knesset members can be pressured to follow the party line.

Other chips in the bargaining process include deputy ministers, chairmanships of Knesset committees, and budgets. A deputy minister must be a Knesset member; members enjoy the status of minister and many fringe benefits. Responsibilities and powers depend on their relations with the minister of their offices, or on their importance to the coalition. Another chip is budgets, which may be promised to kibbutzim or yeshivas or any other favored organization of the party being wooed to join the coalition. The public treasury often pays a high price for the continued existence of the government coalition.

A Brief Experiment

Israel has employed a parliamentary system since independence except in the period between 1996 and 2001, when it experimented with prime ministerial government by adopting the direct election of the prime minister.[9] After the return to the parliamentary system in 2001, the one major constitutional reform that was retained was the constructive vote of no-confidence, which stipulates that the prime minister can be replaced by the Knesset only if a majority of Knesset members have already agreed to invest the task of forming an alternative government in a specific Knesset member. In a parliamentary system, confidence in the government is assured as long as the coalition remains intact.

In the system used between 1996 to 2001, the prime minister was elected directly by the voters (a feature of a presidential system) and could be replaced by new elections if he found it difficult to win the legislative majority needed to govern, though not by the emergence of an alternative coalition in the Knesset (a feature of a parliamentary system). Before the constructive-vote reform, lack of confidence was often moved: there were 99 votes of no-confidence in the 1992–1996 period, and 150 in the 1988–1992 period, although none of the motions was successful. Indeed, only one government has failed a vote of confidence in Israel's political history: in 1990, when Shimon Peres orchestrated the fall of the National Unity Government headed by Yitzhak Shamir with his "dirty trick" maneuver. In the end Peres was unable to win a majority of the Knesset, and Shamir formed another government without Labor (see chapter 7).

The system of the direct election of the prime minister created a "balance of terror" between the Knesset and the prime minister, since each could dismiss the other. The prime minister could dissolve the Knesset by resigning, an act that mandated elections for both prime minister and the Knesset. The Knesset was empowered to dismiss the prime minister by a no-confidence vote of at least sixty-one of its members or by not approving the annual budget within three months of its submission—although that would bring about new elections for both the Knesset and the prime minister (see table 9.2). The Knesset could dismiss the prime minister but remain in power if a vote of no-confidence was sustained by at least 80 (two-thirds of 120) of its members, in which case "special elections" for the prime minister alone would be held.

The system of simultaneously electing both the Knesset and the prime minister was a unique and problematic parliamentary regime with presidential attributes. The prime minister was elected twice on election day, both as prime minister and as head of the party in the parliamentary elections. Elected directly by the voters for four years, a prime minister who had served for seven consecutive years could not run for reelection; there was no term limit on Knesset membership.

Table 9.2 Constitutional Framework before, during, and after the Era of Direct Election of the Prime Minister

	Before direct election (1949–1996)	Under direct election (1996–2003)	After direct election (2003–)
Position of prime minister	First among equals	First	First among equals
Selection of prime minister	Knesset member (usually the leader of the largest party) appointed by the president to form a government	Elected directly by the voters	As before direct election
Ministerial appointments	Prime minister appoints ministers; since 1981, prime minister authorized to dismiss ministers	Prime minister appoints between 7 and 17 ministers subject to Knesset's approval; prime minister and/or Knesset can remove ministers; limits on size of cabinet removed in 1999	As before direct election
Consequences of prime minister resignation	Knesset must approve new prime minister	New elections held for prime minister	As before direct election
Government dissolution power	New elections can be called by Knesset	Prime minister can dissolve Knesset In consultation with the president	Prime minister can dissolve Knesset in consultation with the president
Parliamentary confidence	Government is subject to parliamentary confidence by simple majority vote	Prime minister and cabinet require parliamentary confidence	Constructive vote of no-confidence: alternative candidate must be designated before vote of no-confidence
		Failure to pass budget within 3 months leads to elections of Knesset and prime minister	Failure to pass budget leads to elections of Knesset
Term limit	Unlimited	Prime minister cannot be reelected after seven consecutive years in office	Unlimited

The prime minister had considerable resources under his control, but the direct-election system created new ambiguities because of the dependence of the prime minister and the cabinet on a legislative majority. While provisions of this electoral reform empowered the Knesset in such matters as subsidiary legislation and the declaration of a state of emergency, it also eroded the Knesset's power over governance and policymaking more generally and concentrated even more formal and informal power in the hands of the executive. Prime ministerial powers were strengthened, but prime ministers were ultimately dependent on Knesset coalition, and because neither Netanyahu in 1999 nor Barak in 2001 could sustain this support, their governments fell. Both prime ministers found themselves running in early elections rather than risking the loss of a confidence vote in the Knesset, and both of them lost.

Israel is a good example of a parliamentary system in both the period before the direct election of the prime minister, and again since its repeal in 2001. The Knesset selects the prime minister and approves his cabinet; these appointees can be removed from office if a majority of the legislature loses confidence in them. The ruling coalition is expected to muster the votes needed to support the ruling government; while a coalition holds, it is highly unlikely that a government would fail to pass its legislative program in the Knesset.

In the post-2003 regime, the government ceases its term if the Knesset agrees on an alternative candidate for prime minister, if the Knesset decides to resign, if the prime minister no longer can or no longer wishes to serve in that capacity, or if a new Knesset is elected. In all four situations, the outgoing government continues as a caretaker government until a new one is appointed. A caretaker government has all the powers of a regular government and none of the political liabilities; it is hermetically closed (Joshua 6:1)—ministers cannot be appointed or replaced, nor can a no-confidence vote be taken against a caretaker government.

None of these situations, however, necessarily entails new elections. Before the direct-election reform, the only way in which new elections could be called in Israel was through a law of the Knesset; the Knesset could not be dissolved. This was changed dramatically during the period of the direct election of the prime minister; since the repeal, the prime minister can dismiss the Knesset with the concurrence of the president of the state. There are few other checks and balances in place to regulate the interactions between the executive and legislative branches: the prime minister cannot veto legislation, nor can the Knesset overturn prime ministerial actions. The Knesset can summon the prime minister no more than once a month upon the request of forty Knesset members. The true recourse to political crisis is renewed negotiations or new elections, and increasingly, appeal to the courts.

The Knesset

The Knesset is organized along party lines: committee appointments are made by party, and even seating arrangements are determined by party. Some aspects of the Knesset can be traced back to the British Parliament, others to continental usage and procedure. The Jewish state, deprived of autonomous independence and institutional development for some 2,000 years, took up parliamentary forms of the late nineteenth century, bypassing the long evolutionary process of the emergence of a supreme parliament—a protracted struggle that was crowned with success in England only in the eighteenth century. The acceptance of the Knesset as the omnipotent legislative body was natural, but the lack of this historical perspective makes it more difficult, and more necessary, to evaluate the functions, strengths, and weaknesses of the Knesset.

The nineteenth century can rightly be considered the golden age of legislative supremacy—it was the prevailing tendency in America and Europe, and representative institutions could successfully cope with the relatively simple conflicts of democratic societies. Governmental expenditures were small, and the state tended not to interfere with the economy, so that the legislature could delve into the details of budget-making.[10] At this point of legislative evolution, the Zionist revolution adopted parliamentary procedures. The Zionist Congresses reflected parliamentary practice in turn-of-the-century Europe, and this is the legacy of the Knesset. The link between the Congresses and the Knesset was the Electors' Council (Asefat Nivharim) of the Yishuv, which served as the assembly for the Jewish community under the Mandate.

Two structural features of the Knesset indicate the Israeli parliament's affinity to the continental style rather than the English. First, speakers in the Knesset, as in continental parliaments, speak from the rostrum; this encourages prepared speeches and lengthy oratory and decreases the likelihood of sharp interchanges between the speaker and his listeners. In the English Parliament one speaks from one's seat. At one time Israeli practice introduced microphones at the seating place of each member to assure that interlocutions be heard, but this was discontinued. As a rule, the speaker who has the floor now comes to the rostrum and addresses the Knesset from there.

The second feature is the matter of permanent seating and the capacity of the house to hold all the members. The British case is unique in this sense; members do not have fixed seats, and the hall is too small to accommodate all the members comfortably. In contrast, Knesset proceedings take place in a spacious hall, wherein each member is assigned a seat. Members of the government sit at an oblong table in the center of the chamber, with members of the Knesset around them in a semicircle. They all face the chairman of the meeting and the rostrum.[11] The party that controls the ruling coalition sits to the left of the speaker, not for ideological reasons, but because that provides the most advantageous angles for the television cameras that broadcast the proceedings.

Knesset Members in Action

Knesset members play a more complex role than simply that of legislators. Concerned with their own careers, and especially with the upcoming primaries in the party (if they exist), as well as with the fortunes of their party and its adherence to their ideals, they must maintain ties with those groups within the party or in the public at large that supported them, and with the interests that they represent. As legislators, they also are concerned with the public welfare. Their hardest task is synthesizing these sometimes competing roles.

The need to grant special legal status to legislators is recognized by all democratic countries. Representatives must be free to go about their business without harassment by the authorities, the exceptions being treason and apprehension in the act of committing a crime. There are good reasons to protect the independence of the legislator, but it must be done in a sensible manner.

By law, Knesset members are granted immunity, which, by comparative standards, is extensive. The basic concept is to allow legislators freedom of speech and freedom of action while pursuing their duties. Parliamentary immunity, which pertains to their actions in the legislature, is irrevocable. A second form of immunity extends to matters not directly connected to legislative work: Knesset members are protected from criminal proceedings against them for the entire period of their membership in the Knesset, even for acts committed before their election, although this immunity can be removed by the Knesset on recommendation of the House Committee. Immunity once extended to traffic violations, but this exemption has been reformed (although crass affronts to civic sensibilities still surface).

The removal of immunity is now decided by a public vote in the Knesset. In the past, a secret ballot was used, allowing the impression that at times extraneous considerations were at play. In the case of Rafael Pinhasi of Shas, an accusation of misuse of funds given to his party from the public treasury under the party financing laws was based on an inquiry conducted by the state controller. In 1993, upon the request of the attorney general and after the recommendation of the House committee, the Knesset approved the removal of Pinhasi's immunity, but he was granted a second vote by the High Court of Justice on technical grounds; the final vote was 50 in favor, 54 against, and 8 abstaining. In the 1996 coalition negotiations, Pinhasi was given the chair of the Knesset House committee, the very committee that makes recommendations to the Knesset on such matters. When the attorney general renewed his petition to remove Pinhasi's immunity so that he could stand trial, he had to make that case before the committee that Pinhasi headed.

During the Ninth Knesset (1977–1981), there were three sensational cases of immunity removal: NRP minister Aharon Abu-Hatzeira was accused of improperly using public funds and found not guilty; Shmuel Rechtman of the Likud was sentenced to prison on bribery charges; and Shmuel Flatto-Sharon was accused of illegal campaign practices and later found guilty. More than twenty members have had their immunity removed so as to face criminal charges while serving in the Knesset. The Knesset elected in 2003 continued in the same direction, with eighteen members (15 percent!) either indicted or under investigation within a year of election.[12]

One notorious case in 2003 was that of Deputy Minister Naomi Blumenthal, who was accused of buying votes in the Likud central committee to ensure her reelection; when interrogated by the police, she refused to testify. Prime Minister Sharon thereupon removed her from her position as deputy minister—an act that was criticized because his own son (not a Knesset member) Gilead had used that same tactic in the police investigation of his father and his brother, Knesset member Omri Sharon. The Knesset declined to remove Blumenthal's immunity despite the request by the attorney general to do so.

Other cases included Knesset members who voted twice on important legislation and members accused of incitement to riot. After a series of contentious cases with various conclusions, it was little wonder that some thought of the Knesset—and even the government of Israel—as a house of refuge protecting members from the shortened arm of the law.

Public opinion reflected a very negative opinion of the Knesset and its members.[13]

In 2004 preliminary legislation passed the Knesset that would establish a public committee not composed of Knesset members to determine the removal of immunity. It was felt that this move would improve the legitimacy of the Knesset and its members after many cases of questionable ethical practices regarding the immunity issue. After hearings were held in the Knesset's Law, Constitution, and Justice Committee, however, the proposal was quashed and immunity remained the task of the Knesset.

The Knesset may remove a member from its ranks by a vote of two-thirds of the members if he or she is convicted of a criminal act and sentenced to at least one year in jail. In the case of a sentence that is not yet final, a Knesset member may be suspended until the legal proceedings are completed.

The Knesset member is entitled to serve out his term regardless of his political behavior, and this is an important exception to the central rule of Israeli politics that the political party dominates the Knesset. Even if the Knesset member leaves the party on whose list he was elected and joins another party, he remains a member of the Knesset. Such a resignation by a Knesset member from his list is always an agonizing affair. The list claims that he must resign from the Knesset, because the voters voted for the party and its ideology, not for the individual. The Knesset member invariably answers that if he had not been on the list, his former party would not have done nearly as well.

As discussed in chapter 7, a Knesset member who resigns from the party on whose list he was elected, or who votes no-confidence against the decision of the party on whose list he was elected, can be penalized by not being recognized as a member of any other party-grouping within the Knesset; can be prohibited from running in the next elections on a list represented in the current Knesset; can be barred from serving as a minister or a deputy minister during the term of the Knesset in which the prohibited act occurrs; and can be denied party financing from the public treasury.

The Knesset is a fairly reliable prism through which the Israeli political system can be viewed, but it is not to be confused with the heart of the system. The composition of the Knesset is determined by elections, and the relative strength of the parties determines the government coalition and national policy. Even the organization of the legislature is influenced by the party composition of the Knesset. The delegation of a party

or list to the Knesset is the major building block of the house's organization: political calculations in forming the government are based on the
size of the delegation; the assignment of committee membership and
chairs is done by the delegation, and for important debates, speaking
time is allocated to delegations, which in turn divide it among their
members; motions of no-confidence must be made by a delegation; and
even office space in the Knesset building is provided to the delegation
rather than to an individual Knesset member.

The parliamentary delegation is obviously an important political
force within its own party. Generally, there is overlap between the leadership of the party and the leadership of the parliamentary delegation.
Party policies are guides for the parliamentary delegation, but if the
party is represented in a government coalition, government policy in
effect dictates the stand of the parliamentary delegation. Often, then,
the parliamentary delegation of the party must accept this state of
affairs or be open to the accusation that its party platform has been
flouted by the government. The overlapping membership of an individual in government, parliamentary delegation, and party can be used to
pressure the government in a direction more amenable to the party
platform. This may happen when, behind the scenes, a minister encourages a stand against a proposed government policy and even has the
party issue an ultimatum that its continued support in the government
will be conditioned on the altering of government policy. Small and
medium-size coalition partners, such as the NRP, Mapam, and the Liberal Party, used this ploy often. In major coalition parties, the party
leadership is also leading the government, and thus the usual pattern is
for the parliamentary delegation and the party institutions to pass
declaratory resolutions supporting the government policy and wishing
it continued success.

In ideological parties (Hadash, Agudat Israel, Shas) the primacy of
the party institutions over the Knesset delegation appears in the
party constitution and in its operative procedures. This situation can be
manipulated by the political leader when some outside group superior
to him, such as the Council of Torah Sages in the case of Agudat Israel
and Shas, "demands" that he conform to the group's dictates. The party
establishes the identity of the ideological authority, and the Knesset
member, as powerful as he may seem, is only a messenger of the ideological party. He, too, may compromise in the end, as all politicians do,
but in the interim he can cite the superior authority of the party's decision to explain his seeming intransigence.

An example of a Knesset delegation being given voting instructions by the party council on a specific issue occurred in 1975, when the Knesset voted on the interim agreement with Egypt worked out by U.S. Secretary of State Henry Kissinger. The Yaad Party's four Knesset members thought it would be best to abstain or reject the agreement because it did not go far enough. But the party council, after strenuous debate, requested that the Knesset delegation support the agreement, and all four members, against their better judgment, did so.

This example of party control of the Knesset delegation is rare in Israeli politics because usually the party councils and the parliamentary delegations are dominated by the same people. The triangle of relationships—party/Knesset delegation/Knesset member—is the source of many conflicts.[14] Party rules state specifically that the Knesset member is subject to the decisions of the party, generally leaving it that vague, but it is clear that in the logic of the Israeli political system hierarchical relations exist among the three, with the party usually taking precedence, followed by the desires of the Knesset delegation, and lastly the Knesset member. The member is elected on the party list representing a program or ideology, and he must decide—especially in a party with primaries—whether his personal career will be better off in the long run if he is a loyal party member. Most Knesset members do not have the financial, organizational, or personal qualities necessary for risking a political career on a given issue. For most members, the Knesset is the culmination of a political career, not the beginning of one.

The purpose of party discipline is to allow the Knesset to legislate and the government to rule in a stable manner; clearly, this is a political matter, and not necessarily an ideological one. Its advocates argue that party discipline is the only way for many coalition programs to be passed, while dissenters charge that party discipline promotes mediocrity among Knesset members, who no longer think for themselves, as well as cynicism in the public at large when parties change long-held views for political advantage and then force their Knesset delegation members to toe the line. Party discipline is even reflected in the Knesset law that makes a minister responsible for the behavior of his Knesset delegation members; if the delegation's members fail to vote in conformity with the government's decisions on certain issues, the minister may forfeit his office.

The government coalition has at times permitted abstention on crucial issues by members of coalition parties and has even allowed verbal opposition to its proposals along with abstention on the vote. As a rule, however, members of delegations that participate in the coalition are expected to support government proposals. The major exception applies to issues that the coalition decides are matters of conscience, such as certain religious matters. Party discipline may also be rescinded when the government is willing to gamble on its success, as when the Begin government brought the peace treaty with Egypt before the Knesset. Some Likud members opposed or abstained in the vote, but the prime minister correctly calculated that the votes of remaining Likud members and the votes of many more moderate opposition parties would assure the passage of the treaty and support the evacuation of the Sinai. In 2002 Sharon solidified his leadership when he fired five Shas ministers and four deputy ministers because the party had failed to support his economic plan. Rarely is such a sanction applied to a wayward party, but the potential is there.

Two areas in which Knesset members can supposedly influence the Knesset and the government are question time and motions for the agenda. Unlike the British system, in which question time is an opportunity for a sharp exchange between government minister and parliament member, in Israel question time is fairly dull. Attention focuses on the question submitted and not on the answer, which can take six weeks or longer in coming. Although the eventual answer can be followed up by a short oral question to the minister by the Knesset member who asked the original question (if he happens to be present), the whole procedure is usually lackluster.

Motions for the agenda allow matters of public importance to be aired even if no specific legislation is to be debated and even if the government has not requested the debate. At the end of a ten-minute introductory speech, the minister concerned replies. The issue may then be deferred for a general Knesset debate on the matter, rejected, or referred to a committee for examination and report to the Knesset. A quota system has been instituted based on a party ratio (with a slight advantage to the opposition parties) so as not to clog the Knesset with motions for the agenda and private members' bills. Urgent motions fall outside these quotas, if the urgency has been recognized by the chairman of the Knesset.

The organization of the Knesset follows party lines. The chairman is almost always from a major faction of the largest party, and his deputies are generally chosen from the large parties in the house. Aside from his symbolic and ceremonial importance, the chairman has considerable authority over the routine affairs of the Knesset because he largely determines the agenda and is responsible for the day-to-day operation of the legislature.

No quorum is necessary for Knesset deliberations and action, and this laxity is sometimes criticized by those who believe that a legislator should sit in the house when business is being conducted. Attendance is very low at most times. The contention made by some Knesset members that they do not attend the plenum because they are busy with the Knesset's really important work in its committees is on the whole unfounded, for many Knesset members absent themselves from committee meetings as well, and the importance of the Knesset committees has often been overstated. A more plausible explanation is that as politicians they must juggle varied and time-consuming activities; it makes little sense for them to listen to speeches on matters that they, or their parties, have already settled. Because of the centrality of the party, the dominance of government ministries on legislation, and the nature of the profession of politicians, it is difficult to argue that the absence of Knesset members from debates in the plenum is a major problem of Israeli democracy. It is a symptom, but not the disease.

Knesset membership imparts important advantages and additional resources to the individual seeking election. Especially in the age of primaries and television, a shrewd Knesset member can develop clout and visibility. The franking privilege is another major resource, although it is no longer unlimited following the public outrage when one Knesset member sent out 450,000 letters concerning pending legislation regarding the rights of veterans (this was prior to the 1992 elections, in which 2.66 million voted). Knesset members are entitled to a considerable amount of free telephone time, a parliamentary assistant, and a car, along with many other fringe benefits.

In addition to their political and administrative clout, Knesset members are well off by Israeli standards. It is important to note that Knesset members are often established (if not wealthy) before entering parliament. Many are lawyers, professors, rabbis, kibbutz or moshav members, retired generals, or apparatchiki in the labor unions or other organizations related to party life. They earn a handsome salary in Israeli terms from the Knesset, but many of them would do even better if they were not Knesset members.

Current rules prohibit the earning of additional income or the holding of another public position. This restriction is especially important for mayors and union leaders, and for professionals such as lawyers and accountants, since some in the past used their position in the

Knesset to advance their careers. Also prohibited is receiving expenses or other material goods such as a car, a driver, or office space from any source other than the Knesset member's political party. A member may also retain ownership of property or stocks and may receive royalties from literary or artistic efforts. A yearly financial report must be filed.

During the first forty years of statehood, Knesset membership was not an exclusive undertaking; Knesset members could continue their private concerns while serving in the legislature. A political party would have a political reason for wanting a public officeholder to be a Knesset member: it afforded control over centers of power. For the individual, Knesset membership established a power base for additional exposure and influence, and at the same time allowed the legislator to espouse the interests of his constituency. An interesting exception to this principle is a rule passed by the Labor Party that prohibits representatives from holding more than one elected post. The actual reason for this ruling was that in opposition, the party has to provide positions for its activists and therefore needs to limit the number of positions held by each individual; the official reason given was the principle of rotation. However, from the perspective of the Knesset, the new rule strengthens the body as a legislative institution since more time can be devoted to matters of the Knesset.

Knesset members once enjoyed extraordinary health benefits and pension rights, but these have been reduced or abolished. Other benefits and rights still exist, however, and they are hard to dislodge. Sensitive to the charge that they regularly raise their own salaries, Knesset members set up a committee to make recommendations regarding their remuneration; its proposals must then be reviewed by the Knesset's Finance Committee. Two revealing incidents occurred in 1996: in partial compensation for the new antimoonlighting law, the commission recommended an increase of members' salaries by a third (to a hefty amount about five times the national average in that year), while lowering their pension rate to 2 percent per year, which was the general pension rate among salaried workers in Israel (Knesset members had enjoyed a 4-percent rate). The Finance Committee approved the first recommendation and turned down the second.

The regulations for cabinet ministers have been more stringent for some time. A minister is expected to devote all of his time to his job. Rules against professional and commercial conflicts of interest have been established, and although these expressed expectations have proven largely unenforceable, they make clear the norms of behavior expected of ministers.

Within the Knesset, especially among those more active in the day-to-day operations of the house, a clublike atmosphere develops, for common interests and shared experience bring people closer together regardless of party background. As in other social situations and in legislatures around the world, this esprit de corps is an important social feature of the informal life of the Knesset. It undoubtedly gives many Knesset members an enhanced feeling of purposive behavior in legislating for the nation and its needs, and the collegial atmosphere cushions the uncertainties surrounding the decisions to be made and the unpredictable nature of the life of the politician. However, such general acceptance by colleagues is sometimes erroneously translated by Knesset members into a sense of success and satisfaction that promises invincibility at the polls the next time around. Needless to say, while the clublike atmosphere is functional for legislation and for reducing tensions between ideological opponents, some Knesset members are rudely shocked when they find themselves removed from the club by party leaders or the voters.

Committees

The committees of the Knesset are formed along party lines. Soon after the elections, an arranging committee headed by a member of the largest party is established to determine the composition of the committees. The work of the arranging committee is quintessentially political, since it must balance the size of the delegations with the attractiveness of the committees. Opposition members regularly chair some of the less important committees.

There are twelve standing committees of the Knesset: the House Committee; the Law, Constitution, and Justice Committee; the Finance Committee; the Foreign Affairs and Security Committee; the Immigration and Absorption Committee; the Economics Committee; the Education and Culture Committee; the Interior Affairs and Environment Committee; the Labor and Welfare Committee; the State Control Committee; the War on Drugs Committee; and the Committee for the Advancement of the Status of Women. Committee size varies; in 2004 the House Committee had twenty members, while the Law, Constitution, and Justice Committee and the Finance Committee had sixteen each. Joint, special, and ad hoc committees are also established from time to time.

Assignment to committees is made by the arranging committee, and representatives of the various delegations determine for their own parties where they want their stronger delegates placed. Most members sit on one or two committees, but some have served on three or more. These assignments can enhance a Knesset member's career by placing him on an important committee or weaken him by not doing so. Small delegations are faced with a difficult dilemma because they do not have members on all the committees; they must convince their Knesset colleagues to grant them representation on the committees they deem most important. Committee appointments are for the duration of the Knesset's tenure. If a member resigns from his party, the place on the committee reverts to the party, even though the member remains a member of the Knesset.

The temporary replacement of committee members who disagree with the government's position is an excellent example of a mechanism of control by the ruling coalition and the passivity of the individual Knesset member. Two important instances of this practice were the vote on an appeal of the government decision regarding the settlement of Jews in Hebron in 1980 before the Foreign Affairs and Security Committee, and the Finance Committee's approval of a decision to close El Al on the Sabbath and Jewish holidays in 1982. In the first case, the Likud had agreed to permit the DMC the right of appeal on settlement issues; in the second case, the courts had ruled that a decision by the government to change the charter of a government corporation was not sufficient unless approved by the Finance Committee of the Knesset. Since defeat of the appeal on the first issue and passage of the necessary approval on the second were important to the Likud, and since party discipline did not hold in Knesset committees, the leadership "temporarily" replaced unreliable coalition members on the committee until after the votes were taken. Subsequently, the rules were changed so that the members of the Foreign Affairs and Security Committee could not be replaced during the three-month period of the Knesset's term.[15]

Committee chairmen are formally elected at the first meeting of the committee, upon nomination by the House Committee. The chairmanship of committees has been used as a bargaining chip in coalition negotiations for setting up the government after an election: rather than another ministry or deputy minister, an important Knesset committee chairmanship may suffice as an incentive for a bargaining party. Coalition parties always have a majority in the committees of the Knesset, although sometimes a chair may be from an opposition party, depending on the size of the opposition and the importance of the committee.

As a rule, the chairmanships of important committees—such as the House Committee, the Foreign Affairs and Security Committee, and the Finance Committee—are reserved for members of the ruling coalition. The House Committee is important because it has virtual control over the day-to-day operations of the Knesset; its chair in 2004 was Roni Bar-On. Since the Knesset is often in the public eye and is the formal decision-making organ of the state, the ruling majority must be able to control procedural decisions. In this situation, where majorities are automatic, rules of order can determine how effectively the coalition or the opposition will be able to use parliamentary procedure to its advantage.

A second committee usually headed by a member of the ruling party is the Foreign Affairs and Security Committee; in 2004 it was headed by Yuval Steinetz of the Likud. Although its membership is select and the matters brought before it are often very grave, this committee's impact on policy is relatively small. Instead, it has been used as a sounding board or as a mechanism for consulting with members of the opposition on important international matters or sensitive security issues without involving the entire house. Various chairs have made valiant efforts to increase the committee's role in policymaking, especially since the membership of the committee has often included former prime ministers, defense ministers, and chiefs of staff, but these efforts have largely been in vain. In addition, sensitive matters regarding topics such as intelligence and the security budget are discussed in subcommittees, thus weakening the committee even more.

The Finance Committee, which plays an active role in policymaking, has usually been headed by a member of a coalition party. In both the Ninth and Tenth Knessets, between 1977 and 1984, the committee was headed by Knesset members from Agudat Israel, which was willing to forego government ministries and agreed to support the coalition on the conditions that a string of legislation (including tighter controls on abortion, tighter observance of the Sabbath and holidays, and more financial support for yeshivas) be adopted and that the party be assigned the chairmanship of the Finance Committee. Not being in the government itself gave the Aguda a certain amount of distance from ongoing government policy; the party could support the ruling coalition without being responsible for its policies. At the same time, it could bargain for budget, legislation, and power—commodities that were more easily available to coalition members than were ministries. In 1988 Labor demanded and received the chairmanship of the Finance Committee; Shimon Peres agreed to be finance minister in the National

Unity Government but knew very well that his economic policies would have a better chance of success if a member of his own party were chairman of this vital committee. The chair of the Finance Committee after the 2003 elections was Yair Hirschzon of the Likud.

The annual budget is discussed at length in the Finance Committee, and its recommendations to the Knesset on the subject generally are passed. The Finance Committee is also given statutory authority to approve changes in the budget during the fiscal year. The Knesset has allocated decisions regarding the salaries of judges, Knesset members, and ministers to its Finance Committee, as well as the responsibility for setting the amount of money to be allocated for financing political parties. In turn, public commissions have been set up to deal with these two topics and to bring recommendations to the Finance Committee.

The committees meet on a regular basis, and there are Knesset members who claim that the major task of a Knesset member is work in committee. This statement must be seen in perspective, however. The power of Knesset committees does not come close to approximating the power of committees of the U.S. Congress, which play a key role in the legislative process. In fairness, it must be pointed out that the American case is unusual; in Europe as a whole, and even in Great Britain, committees of the parliament do not reach this level of importance. There are two important reasons for this state of affairs. First, the American Congress is conceived of as the legislative branch of government, independent of the executive. The parliamentary notion is different. The parliament cooperates with the government it chose, while the Congress may compete with the president. The Knesset has historically not perceived itself as operating independently or at cross-purposes to the government of the day, although that situation may develop over time.

This cooperative stance explains the relative weakness of Knesset committees. Under certain circumstances, committees can subpoena witnesses and documents, but this privilege is rarely sought or used. They can invite, persuade, and cajole, but, for the most part, there has been no sanctioning of those who refuse to cooperate. For example, the Government Control Committee can establish a state investigating committee with the agreement of the state comptroller, and it can also demand the testimony of any officeholder discussed in the state comptroller's report—except the president of the state, the Speaker of the Knesset, and judicial authorities.

The second reason for the relatively minor role played by Knesset committees in the legislative process is budgetary: in order to function properly as an independent agency in legislation or to provide oversight for the activities of the administration—a Knesset committee would need to have a large staff of professionals who could gather information, assess it, and put it at the disposal of members of the committee. An example is the field of education: almost a third of Israel's population is in school, which makes overseeing the ministry and collecting, processing, and analyzing data just too much even for a conscientious and hardworking member of the Education Committee, who is likely also to serve on a second Knesset committee as well as being a member of a party and having a constituency to attend to—in short, a politician whose tasks are numerous and whose time is limited. Providing the Knesset Education Committee with the kind of staff needed to fill this function would be very expensive. Besides, there is an easy alternative: the information requested can be provided by the minister and his ministry's staff, who have already gathered the information and supposedly have made their policy proposals based on these data. But this is exactly where the independence of the legislature breaks down, for the members of the Knesset committees become dependent on the data, experts, and points of view of the ministry and so cannot exercise their governmental function of overseeing and legislating independently.

Knesset committees do have staff, but not nearly enough. A committee may be granted legal assistance, since the conception is that drafting legislation is the job of a lawyer—although, as a moment's reflection will indicate, this is only partially the case. On occasion the Finance Committee has had economists in a consulting capacity, as have other committees, but a part-time consultant or testimony before the committee by a university professor simply cannot replace staff work done over a long time in a consistent manner. The reason given for the failure to set up independent staffs for the Knesset committees has been the cost of such a proposal. At the same time, however, Knesset members will agree that being dependent on experts from the ministries weakens the effectiveness of the committees. What these Knesset members gloss over is that the matter is fundamentally in their hands, for the practice in Israeli government has always been that the government does not discuss or approve the budget of the Knesset. (This is one of the only areas of real independence on the part of the legislature in Israel.) Since this is the case, if many Knesset members feel that the committees should be strengthened, they could simply appropriate moneys for this purpose and establish a staff system for the Knesset committees.

It may be that this is only a utopian suggestion, for significant participation by Knesset committees in the legislative process would mean
that the responsibility for legislation would also shift (at least partially)
from the government ministries to the Knesset. As members of hierarchical political parties, however, Knesset members in actuality may
decline to take this more active role in the legislative process because
they are content in knowing (and keeping) their place in a system that
does not encourage confrontation between the executive and legislative
branches.

Legislation

The formal stages of the legislative process will be familiar to students
of European parliaments. There are three readings of a bill, which most
often is initiated as a proposal introduced by the government. It must be
placed on the table of the Knesset forty-eight hours before the Knesset
takes it up for a first reading. The minister responsible for the legislation
generally presents the explanation of the bill at the first reading, and a
member of the opposition opens debate on it, after which the bill is voted
on. Returning a bill to the government is in effect a defeat for the government, because the Knesset has chosen not to consider legislation it has
proposed. Almost always, however, the first reading ends with a decision
to send the bill to committee, which is tantamount to approval.

The committee by which the bill is considered is generally suggested
by the minister, whose suggestion is almost always accepted. Important
matters are certain to end up on the table of a "friendly" committee. If
there is dissent, the matter is decided by the Knesset's House Committee. No time limit is set on the committee's deliberations, and no mechanism can be used to force a committee to report on a bill, short of the
efforts of committee members themselves to have the bill read out of
committee.

In the committee, the bill is discussed in detail and amendments are
suggested. Changes may be introduced by the committee, which then
reports back to the Knesset with its version of the bill. The second reading of the bill is concerned with any amendments proposed by the committee. If no changes have been made in the committee's version, the
second and third readings of the bill can proceed immediately, but if
additional changes were introduced at the second reading, the third
reading is postponed in order to study the ramifications of the changes
and to give the government the opportunity to withdraw the proposed
law in view of the changes made.

A bill becomes law after being signed by the prime minister, the president, the Speaker of the Knesset, and the minister responsible for the bill; it is then published in the official gazette. The right of veto does not exist—the signatures on the bill are mandatory, not discretionary.

The work of the Knesset has suffered from a lack of coordination with the executive branch. In the Fifteenth Knesset (1999–2003), 4,458 pieces of proposed legislation were submitted, 95 percent of them by private members. Of the 401 laws passed, 60 percent had originated as private members' proposals, made without consideration of how they would be funded. By contrast, during the Third Knesset (1955–1959), 326 bills were proposed, 7 percent of them by private members; in that same period, 285 laws were adopted and 7 percent of them were private members' bills.[16] A bill proposed by a private member follows the usual procedure except that there is a preliminary reading before the bill goes to committee to be reported back for the "first" reading.

The increase in private members' bills becoming law in the late 1990s was an example of the government and the political parties being weakened without the Knesset being strengthened. The visibility afforded by the private members' bills in an age of television coverage and a party system dominated by primaries explained why members proposed legislation. These private members' bills (such as a bill, which passed, providing for cash payments to veterans) were sometimes very expensive to implement but too popular to oppose. The tremendous volume of private members' bills, much higher than in other Western democracies, eventually led to reform: in 2003 the Knesset changed its rules so that legislation initiated in a private member's bill must not exceed $1 million in expenditures and must be passed by at least fifty members.

In the past, most private members' bills had been submitted by members of the opposition. One that passed in 1960 was known as the Kanovitz law, intended to regulate the pollution caused by motor vehicles (Shimon Kanovitz was a member of the Progressive Party). While the intentions of the Knesset were good, it took two and a half years for the ministries responsible (Health, Transportation, and Interior) to publish the necessary regulations, and even after that the Kanovitz law remained a classic example of a law not enforced. The fact that enforcement of a law is no less important than its ratification reinforces the tendency to rely heavily on government ministries for bill initiation. Government-proposed legislation is initiated only after it has been cleared with the various ministries involved, especially the ministries of Finance and

Justice. Since most legislation either involves financial costs for additional manpower to enforce it or impinges on other legislation, government ministries are naturally active in determining the content and form of legislation that reaches the Knesset floor. This was obviously a great source of frustration to many individual Knesset members.

The Judiciary

The judicial system provides one of the greatest paradoxes in Israeli civil life. In a culture that is very highly politicized, the judicial system is professional and impartial despite charges that it too is being politicized. Although there is no written constitution, the political system as a whole and particularly the judicial system respect the principle of limited government and have exercised self-restraint in many areas. The country has been declared to be under emergency conditions since independence, yet in many areas of civil liberties (at least within its pre-1967 boundaries) Israel's record is good. The rule of law is much respected as an ideal, although in fact access to justice is stratified by one's wealth, determination, and patience for dealing with the judicial system. In a system where most appointees in public life must meet some political requirement, the appointment of judges is widely perceived as based on professional attainment and potential. Increasingly, as the Supreme Court has become more activist in matters of civil rights, it is perceived by some as part of the political battle. On the whole, however, the Israeli judicial system is professional and unpolitical and, in that sense, very un-Israeli. This is what makes it such an important bastion of Israeli democracy in a sea of forces that would hasten the erosion of its foundations.

The tension between the limited government implied by a constitutional system and the security problems of Israel is best evidenced by the constant state of emergency that has existed since May 19, 1948—five days after the achievement of independence. The legal arrangement is an announcement by the Knesset, or by the government if the Knesset cannot be convened, or by the prime minister if the government cannot be convened, of the existence of a state of emergency. The existence of a state of emergency allows the government to change or suspend any law (except the right of access to the courts, post facto punishment, or infringing upon human dignity), to increase taxes, and to issue other emergency regulations intended to provide for "the defense of the state, the security of the public and upholding necessary distribution and service."[17] These regulations are generally for a three-month period and can be extended only by Knesset legislation. In effect, emergency regulations, often used in defense matters and in economic matters involving labor disputes or taxation, have afforded the government an alternative method of legislation with which to sidestep deliberations that might be time-consuming and controversial.

Like most other activities of Israeli government, however, the judicial system is controlled by the executive branch. For example, the budget of the judicial system is not determined by the Knesset but by the executive branch, meaning the Finance Ministry. This is an unhealthy arrangement, especially for an activist court that adjudicates government actions and regulations on a regular basis.

Elements of the Law

Israeli law is influenced by four major traditions: (1) Ottoman law, (2) British common law, (3) religious law, and (4) Israeli law. Each element represents a different historical period or cultural influence in the developing Israeli laws.[18]

Ottoman law reflects the impact of the rule of the Turks in Palestine before World War I. A composite of Koranic precepts and Islamic customs, along with a heavy influence, especially since the beginning of the twentieth century, from French legal models and sources, Ottoman law was not influential in regard to personal laws for the Jews, for at that time non-Muslim groups were under the jurisdiction of their own community. But Ottoman law was very influential regarding property law, especially land. The French influence was introduced by the Turks in the nineteenth and early twentieth centuries in regard to civil and criminal procedures and commercial and maritime law. During the Mandate period, the British enforced Ottoman law and practice unless specific British mandatory regulations had been issued in their stead. The scope of influence of Ottoman law is constantly decreasing as Israeli legislation replaces aspects of the Ottoman law.

The British Mandate lasted from 1922 to 1948. In this period legislative power was vested in the high commissioner, who was bound by provisions of the Mandate but had full power and authority to pass ordinances needed to maintain peace, order, and good government, while according complete freedom of conscience and exercise of religion. He was prohibited from discriminating in any way between inhabitants on the ground of race, religion, or language.

By the time of the establishment of the state, the substance of British common law and the doctrines of equity and stare decisis—the binding force of judicial precedent—had been firmly established in the judicial system. These principles in particular and the British influence on the Israeli judicial system in general are probably the most significant heritage of the British Mandate.

Personal law is largely under the jurisdiction of the courts of the recognized religious communities—Jewish, Muslim, and Christian. In the Jewish communities, this means the Orthodox rabbis (see chapter 10), for neither Conservative nor Reform rabbis are recognized in Israel for performing religious ceremonies. This issue has the potential for creating ill will among the various organizations of Jewry because outside Israel the two latter groups are powerful and growing.

The jurisdiction of Jewish religious courts extends to all Jews in Israel, whether Israeli citizens or not. The religious courts' decision is subject to appeal both within the appellate system of the religious courts and through the High Court of Justice. With few exceptions, such as bigamy and abortion, the Knesset has not undertaken to legislate in the field of personal law. In other matters, Jewish law is often taken into account, but wide-ranging precedents from the Western world are usually dominant in legislative and judicial matters.

Israeli law has developed from the special nature of the country's problems. There are still laws from the Mandate period on the books, and occasionally one hears a call to update them. But, as would be expected, the proportion of Knesset-made law is growing over time.

Basic Laws and a Constitution

A basic notion of a liberal democracy is the limiting of the powers of government through the existence of a constitution, which sets the outer limits of the permissible and also implies a form of redress through the courts if that limit is breached. Democracy consists of both the formal procedures of electing governments and the freedoms from government interference that protect minorities and individuals from having their liberties infringed upon by government action. The Israeli experience has always taken a formalistic approach in its understanding of democracy. This is nowhere better seen than in the fact that the issue of electoral reform is studied in schools and debated at length in the press, while the lack of a basic law that covers human and civil rights is taken for granted as a political necessity. The beginnings of a bill of rights have emerged with the passage of the basic laws regarding the freedom of occupation and human dignity and liberty, but much work is still to be done before the bill of rights is completed.

Great Britain has no written constitution, but it has a tradition of hundreds of years of guarding civil liberties and developing their meaning. Israel's experience is too fragile to leave the guarding of civil rights to the goodwill of the authorities; the glaring shortfall in the Israeli system is the absence of a written constitution.[19] After the 2003 elections, a flurry of activity in drafting a possible constitution was undertaken by the Knesset's Law, Constitution, and Justice Committee, as well as by independent organizations such as the Israel Democracy Institute.[20]

The Israeli solution to the lack of a constitution has been the stage-by-stage approach.[21] In 1950, when debates over the writing of a constitution were at their peak, it was clear that the two major bodies of opinion had created a standoff. Secularists insisted that Israel must have a constitution like other modern, Western, liberal states, while religious spokesmen claimed that the Torah and its rabbinical commentaries made up the written constitution of Israel and that this was superior to any secular legislation since it was of divine origin. As consensus is usually an important goal in Israeli politics, especially regarding matters of principle and public concern, it was then decided not to attempt to write a complete document but rather to put together, stage-by-stage and as conditions permitted, legislation that would, at a later date, form Israel's constitution.[22] This solution has been known as the "Harari decision," named after the Knesset member who introduced it. It is also likely that the leaders of the fledgling state did not want the provisions of a constitution to limit their freedom of action and therefore delayed completing the work of writing the constitution. The Harari decision called for the Law, Constitution, and Justice Committee of the Knesset to prepare the appropriate legislation. The First Knesset, which passed the resolution, was perceived to be a constitutional convention and was in fact called a constituent assembly.

The basic laws are (1) The Knesset; (2) Israel Lands; (3) the State President; (4) the State Economy; (5) the Israel Defense Forces; (6) Jerusalem, Capital of Israel; (7) the Judiciary; (8) State Comptroller; (9) Freedom of Occupation; (10) Human Dignity and Liberty;[23] and (11) the Government. Before the three basic laws passed in 1992 (Government, Freedom of Occupation, and Human Dignity and Liberty), all the basic laws except for those regarding the Knesset and Jerusalem were prepared and approved by the government and not by the Knesset Law, Constitution, and Justice Committee. Many of the basic laws do not have limiting clauses, a condition necessary if the legislation is to serve as a constitutional provision.[24]

Fine-tuning the legislation required that some of these laws be modified; the Freedom of Occupation and the Human Dignity and Liberty basic laws were substantially rewritten and legislated again to pass judicial scrutiny. For example, the Basic Law: Freedom of Occupation was redone in 1994 after the Supreme Court ruled that the law prevented the government from limiting the economic activities of a business that wanted to import pork (the eating of which is prohibited by both Jewish and Islamic religious law).

The status of the basic laws was intended to be higher than that of regular legislation, among other reasons, because in passing a basic law the Knesset is continuing the work of the First Knesset, the constituent assembly. This higher status is made even clearer when entrenched provisions in the basic law require that changes be made only by special majorities. In general, legislation in the Knesset is passed by a simple majority of those present (abstentions not counting); some constitutional provisions have been adopted by very small numbers of Knesset members. For example, in 1992 the Basic Law: Freedom of Occupation was passed by the votes of twenty-three Knesset members, with no objections or abstentions, and the Basic Law: Human Dignity and Liberty was passed 32–21, with one abstention.

The Basic Law: Knesset has several entrenched provisions that can be modified only by unusual majorities: Article 4, which deals with the electoral system, can be changed only by an absolute majority during each stage of legislation; Articles 44 and 45 exempt the law from being changed by emergency regulations unless two-thirds of the members (at least eighty) concur; and clause 9a states that a law to expand the term of office of the Knesset must be passed by eighty members at least. The Basic Law: Freedom of Occupation and the Basic Law: Government can be amended only by a majority of sixty-one members. Article 41 of the Basic Law: Government makes that law immune to emergency regulations.

The Courts

If the judicial system is based on a complicated legal order influenced by many sources, the court system is much more straightforward. The courts have a hierarchical structure, with little overlap among the various levels. The two major systems are the civil and the religious courts; in addition there are special courts for military, labor, traffic, municipal, family matters, and juvenile matters, to name but a few.

The civil court system has three levels: magistrates' courts, district courts, and the Supreme Court. Magistrates' courts deal with offenses that carry relatively light sentences (a maximum of three years' imprisonment except in the case of drug offenses) and relatively small monetary claims. District courts may accept appeals from magistrates' courts; jurisdiction of the former covers civil and criminal matters exceeding the limits of the lower courts. There are five district courts in Israel—in Jerusalem, Tel Aviv, Haifa, Beer Sheva, and Nazareth. Trials in district courts generally have a single judge. No jury trials are held in Israel.

The Supreme Court, composed of fourteen permanent justices and one temporary justice as of 2004, is the country's highest appellate court. In addition, it has original jurisdiction over petitions seeking relief against administrative decisions that are not within the jurisdiction of any court. In this role the Supreme Court sits as the High Court of Justice and may restrain or direct government agencies or other public institutions by such writs as habeas corpus and mandamus, as is customary under English common law.

The Supreme Court generally hears cases before a panel of at least three justices, although larger odd numbers are sometimes used. In the appeal of John ("Ivan the Terrible") Demyaniuk, a former Nazi prison camp guard, five justices were impaneled; in the 1968 case regarding the registration as Jews of the children of Binyamin Shalit (see chapter 10), a panel of nine justices decided the case. In a case involving the future of frozen sperm of a dissolved marriage, a court of eleven justices was impaneled.[25] Still pending in 2004 were decisions regarding citizenship and the minimum standard of living, both cases being considered by panels of thirteen judges.

The court system in general and the Supreme Court in particular are held in high esteem in the country.[26] An important reason for the independence and stature of Israel's judiciary is the method of selecting judges. This is done on the recommendation of a nine-member appointments committee, which consists of the president of the Supreme Court and two other justices of that court, the minister of justice and one other cabinet minister chosen by the cabinet, two members of the Knesset elected by secret ballot by majority vote, and two practicing lawyers who are members of the Israel Bar Association and approved by the minister of justice. The justice minister serves as chairman of the appointments committee; the nominees of the committee are formally appointed judges by the president of the state.

This appointment system has produced good results because five of the nine members come from professional legal groups (the courts, the bar association) and four from political life (representatives of the government and the Knesset). Increasingly, however, there has been pressure to represent groups and value systems outside the main-stream legal profession, with some calling for changing the system. Orthodox religious groups are especially critical of many of the liberal decisions made by the court; they demand that Jewish religious law become more central in informing the court's decisions. A moderate change was attempted in 2004, when the committee interviewed many more candidates than vacant places on the court before voting on appointments; in the past, candidates brought to it by the majority members were approved. It remains to be seen if such moderate reforms will quell the waves of discontent with the court expressed in recent years.

Judges serve until mandatory retirement at the age of seventy (seventy-five for judges of religious courts). Salaries are fixed by the Finance Committee of the Knesset and are graduated according to the level of the court and tenure on the bench. The salary of the president of the Supreme Court is usually equivalent to that of the prime minister, and the salary of Supreme Court justices is equivalent to that of ministers. The court system is technically under the jurisdiction of the Ministry of Justice—too close to the government administration to ensure a large measure of independence by the judiciary.

While the Israeli experience has shown that justices can be chosen in a manner that neutralizes the highly political nature of the national cul-ture, other considerations are still active. For example, it is customary to have at least one religious justice on the high court, with representation also considered important for Sephardim and women. In 2004 there were three religious justices and five women on the high court. The first Arab judge had recently been appointed.

Previous judicial experience is not required in the appointment of judges. Two-thirds of the thirty-six Supreme Court justices who served between 1948 and 1978 had prior judicial experience: of the first five appointed, only one did; of the next twenty, fourteen did; of the next eleven, nine did. Of the judges promoted from the district court to the Supreme Court, none had obvious political affiliations. Others were more visible in the public spotlight; their previous posts included general consul in a diplomatic mission, legal adviser to the government, legal counsel of the Histadrut, and university professor.

The judicial elite of Israel is similar to the political elite discussed in chapter 4 in terms of its demographic characteristics. Of the thirty-six judges who served on the court during the country's first forty-five years, all were Jews and thirty were Ashkenazim. Ten had been born in Poland, nine in Germany, eight in Israel, six in Russia and Lithuania, and one each in Iraq, England, and the United States.[27]

Since there is no written constitution and no bill of rights, the judicial system is the foremost guardian of civil liberties in Israel.[28] Most legislation is designed to permit the authorities to limit freedoms by, for example, giving the Interior Ministry the task of licensing printing houses or giving the police the task of granting permits for demonstrations. The record of the Interior Ministry and the police has been generally good in protecting the rights of the individual to freedom of the press, speech, and assembly, but these rights are granted to the individual by the authorities rather than assured by a written constitution. It is true that in moments of crisis laws cannot thwart a determined antidemocratic force, yet the existence of a constitutionally endowed right sets up norms that may be difficult to overcome. In contrast, limiting rights is a matter of interpretation as to whether the public safety is jeopardized; the burden of proof is placed on those whose rights are being limited. If rights were constitutionally protected, they could of course still be abused, but then the burden of proof would fall on the government that had attempted to limit individual freedom.

The court system is crowded and slow.[29] While the quality of judging is generally considered to be high, and the system is adding staff and acquiring equipment, access to justice is painful, costly, and not speedy. Reforms are often discussed and many are instituted, but problems remain.[30] A public defender system has been operating to provide legal representation for all. Lawyers proliferate; the system seems so built that only they can manage to navigate in the murky waters of bureaucrats and special regulations. The Israel Bar Association is a statutory body whose tasks include licensing and controlling practitioners.

In general, Israel is a nonpunitive society. Penalties prescribed by law for many crimes are low compared with those imposed in other countries. The death penalty appears on the books, but it is never applied, with a sole exception in the case of the Nazi Adolf Eichmann. The increasing crime rate is a topic of public concern, but it rarely becomes a political issue as it has in other Western countries.

Civil Liberties and the High Court of Justice

When it sits as the High Court of Justice, the Supreme Court is empowered to act before an action is taken by the authorities. The common-law principle is that damages can be recovered after the act has been perpetrated. Imagine that a wall is shared by you and your neighbor, who decides to tear down the wall without any concern for your rights or your house. After your house has fallen in because your wall was destroyed, you can collect damages. Equity, however, demands the ability to pursue justice even before the act is committed—that you be entitled to petition the court to prevent the neighbor from tearing down your joint wall without your permission. The same principle applies to actions of the authorities in Israel. The High Court of Justice can prevent government actions that have been instituted illegally and that will be harmful to your rights or property. A private citizen may petition to challenge the actions of a government agency, a ministry, the army, a minister, and even the prime minister.

Israel's Supreme Court has acquired, by tradition and by the abdication of other institutions, the task of major guardian of justice and civil rights in Israel. The court was initially reticent about interfering in political issues, and its first foray into the field of judicial review—in the *Bergman* case (discussed later in this chapter) was tentative and unsustained. Since the mid-1980s, however, the Court has developed into a very dynamic actor in the governmental system: it has not shied away from questions brought to it, but has extended itself in broadening the meaning of justice throughout the system and in ensuring for itself the role of fearless guardian of inherent rights.[31]

Israel's courts are highly aware of civil rights and respect the tradition of the Enlightenment that places individual rights at the heart of the society. The role of the Supreme Court is to protect rights and to limit the authorities in their unwarranted use of power. However, with no constitution and few laws on which to base such protection, it fell to the Court to set the tone of self-control for the authorities in respecting rights. The Court has moral weight, as well as the power to hold in contempt those who do not obey its rulings, but it has no police or army with which to enforce its decisions, and so it must be aware of the prevailing norms in the society.

Considering that civil liberties are not firmly entrenched in law and that the system rests on the discretion of the authorities, Israel's record in this field is quite good. The few blemishes on the system include some religious requirements that, when applied, restrict certain liberties that are taken for granted in other liberal systems, and the emergency regulations that transfer to the executive functions that would otherwise demand the public deliberation of the legislature.

Beginning in the early 1980s, the judicial activism of the Court intensified. In the political sphere, the Court overturned the ban by the Central Elections Committee of two parties before the 1984 elections (see chapter 5), and it did the same thing in 2003. Citing the public's right to know, the Court required political parties to make public the details of coalition agreements, which became a provision in the revised Basic Law: Government. Apprehension about the Court's possible decision caused Labor and Shas to remove a clause in a draft coalition agreement stipulating that the government would introduce legislation circumventing any Supreme Court decision that impinged on the religious status quo.

In censorship cases, the Court virtually eliminated the practice in regard to theater productions, reduced it for the movies, and decided that the army censor could not block publication of an article that included criticism of the head of the Mossad unless there was a "near certainty" that the content of the article posed a danger to national security. It also backed the right of newspaper reporters not to reveal their sources.[32]

In the religious sphere (see chapter 10), the Court ordered the registration as a Jew and the granting of new immigrant status to an American woman who had undergone a Reform conversion; forced a political leader who also served as a judge in the High Rabbinical Court to relinquish his judicial position; ordered the inclusion of women in religious councils and in the electoral groups that selected candidates for religious councils; and ordered El Al, the national airline, to provide a homosexual employee's partner the same benefits it provided other married workers.

Defending the civil rights of Israel's minority groups presents difficult challenges.[33] Israeli Arabs are full-fledged citizens, granted all formal rights; they vote and are represented in the Knesset and in municipalities. But since they do not serve in the army (and probably do not want to), they are deprived of access to the whole of the system, including welfare benefits provided for veterans, political access to the highest levels of decision making, and the psychological satisfaction that goes along with the identification of country, religion, and nation. Psychological satisfaction may not be a civil right, but it would be shortsighted to assess the position of Israeli Arabs in terms of only formal legalisms; indeed, reforms in the 1992–1996 period were intended to remove some of the existing bureaucratic inequalities. There may be no easy solution for this dilemma, but denying its existence, as many Israelis do, is no solution either.

West Bank and Gaza Arabs have presented even more difficult problems.[34] Before the establishment of the Palestinian Authority, they could petition the High Court of Justice, although they were not citizens of Israel. If their situation were conceived of as living in a battle zone, then the Israeli record of dealing with them would seem reasonable in the history of warfare. But if the judgment were based on the norms of a regular country, the Israeli record would appear much weaker. Military occupation is difficult under any circumstances, and the chances that it will be perceived as humane over time are very low.

The Barak Court

One dominant personality driving all this increased activism has been Aharon Barak, a justice since 1978, and president of the Supreme Court since 1995. Barak was appointed attorney general in 1975, and Prime Minister Begin drafted him to head the legal team at the Camp David peace talks with Egypt. Soon after, at forty-two, he went to the Supreme Court.

As attorney general, Barak decided to press charges against Asher Yadlin, who was about to become governor of the Bank of Israel but was accused of financial misconduct while heading Kupat Holim; Yadlin was eventually imprisoned. Barak was also involved in probing the case of Avraham Ofer, a Labor housing minister who was charged with financial malfeasance; as the probe dragged on, Ofer shot and killed himself. Barak also decided to press criminal charges against Leah Rabin in 1977, rather than allowing her to quietly pay an administrative fine, because she had a U.S. bank account—a violation of Finance Ministry regulations that barred Israelis from holding bank accounts abroad. As a result, her husband, Prime Minister Yitzhak Rabin, decided not to run at the head of the Labor-Mapam Alignment list in the 1977 elections, thereby opening the decades-long competition between him and Shimon Peres.

Barak has been directly involved in the constitutional revolution taking place in the country.[35] In addition to his role in judicial review, he was instrumental in expanding the right of citizens to petition the Supreme Court. In the past, a citizen could petition the Court only if he had been directly affected, but now the Court will hear any petition it deems to be in the public interest.

Barak has led in applying the test of "reasonableness," under which the Court can annul a cabinet or Knesset decision if it is deemed unreasonable in the extreme.[36] This doctrine signifies the Court's changed perception of its role in the political system, going beyond adjudication to the application of substantive criteria in its review of laws and policies.[37] The use of the doctrine of reasonableness to invalidate legislation or administrative action, known as substantive due process in the United States, was accelerated in the 1980s. In one important case, the Court overturned the government's appointment of former Shin Bet agent Yossi Ginossar as Housing Ministry director general, determining that he was not fit for public office because he had perjured himself in two security service scandals. Although Ginossar had never been convicted, the High Court struck down the nomination on the ground that such an appointment was so unreasonable that it could be regarded as illegal, and therefore null and void. In other cases, the Court forced the resignations of Shas Minister of the Interior Deri and Shas Deputy Minister Pinhasi, who were being investigated on criminal charges, although Deri had promised in writing to resign if charges were pressed in court. The High Court also forced the attorney general to reconsider decisions not to file charges against bank managers involved in the 1983 bank shares debacle.

Activist courts raise active opposition, and the Barak court is no exception. Political opponents, especially in religious circles, accuse the High Court of pursuing its own liberal political agenda. Calls have been made to have the Knesset alter the Basic Law: The Judiciary to limit the scope of the Court's jurisdiction. The Court's reputation for liberal decisions is complemented, however, by its restraint regarding matters of security.[38] Thus, the Court upheld the expulsion of 418 Hamas activists without a prior hearing, it approved demolishing the homes of terrorists, and it did not overturn the practice of using "moderate physical force" in interrogations of Islamic fundamentalists. Similarly, after declaring null and void the Interior Ministry's criteria for recognizing conversion to Judaism (and thus being eligible for citizenship under the Law of Return), the Court referred the matter to the legislature rather than ordering the ministry to register the petitioner as a Jew.

Judicial Review

The entrenchment clause in the Basic Law: Knesset was the background for the first case that hinted at judicial review in the Israeli system. Judicial review is the power of a court to invalidate on constitutional grounds a governmental action, whether it be committed by the executive (administrative) or legislative branch. In this regard, it is important to distinguish between cases in which judicial review is applied using a test of reasonableness of government action, and those in which it weighs the constitutionality of the legislation challenged. The former has been regularly applied by the Israeli Supreme Court and has not been much criticized; the latter is much more controversial.

The *Bergman* case presented a situation in which the Israeli Supreme Court declared an act of the Knesset void for violating a basic law. Aharon A. Bergman had brought an action before the Supreme Court, sitting as the High Court of Justice, to block the implementation of the (Campaign) Financing Law of 1969; Bergman's complaint was that the law unfairly discriminated against new political parties because it provided government funds only for those parties already represented in the outgoing Knesset. He argued that the financing law violated the equality required by section 4 of the Basic Law: Knesset, which had been entrenched and could be changed only by a majority of Knesset members. The financing law had passed its first reading in the Knesset by a vote of 24 to 2.

Writing for all five justices who participated in the case, Justice Moshe Landau agreed that the financing law was in conflict with the equality required by section 4 of the Basic Law: Knesset. The absolute refusal of funds to a new list constituted a major denial of equal opportunity in the democratic electoral process. Justice Landau acknowledged the absence of any provision in Israel's written law that expressly authorized the Court to construe statutes in terms of the natural justice principle of equality of all before the law. "Nevertheless, this principle that is nowhere inscribed breathes the breath of life into our whole constitutional system." It was therefore right and just, Justice Landau argued, for the Court to use it in interpreting the law. This story of judicial innovation has a political ending. The Knesset enacted the financing law again—this time by an absolute majority—but incorporating changes in light of the court's remarks. The issue of judicial review was skirted, and the supremacy of the Knesset was upheld.[39]

The power of judicial review of legislation was expanded significantly with the passing of three basic laws in 1992.[40] The Basic Law: Human Dignity and Liberty and the Basic Law: Freedom of Occupation were intended as the first pieces of a bill of rights. While the laws appeared limited in scope, they were interpreted to grant the Supreme Court powers to overturn legislation that violates the rights they list.

The Basic Law: Human Dignity and Liberty contained in clause 8 the constitutional basis for reviewing, and possibly declaring unconstitutional, future legislation that did not conform with the law:

> The rights according to the Basic Law shall not be infringed upon except by a statute that befits the values of the State of Israel and is directed towards a worthy purpose, and then only to an extent that does not exceed what is necessary, or by regulation enacted by virtue of express authorization in such law.

The Court quickly made it clear that it would declare unconstitutional ordinary laws that did not comply with the new basic laws. This had a noticeable impact on legislators and administrators who had to consider whether their laws or their actions would survive the scrutiny of the Court. The Court also made it clear that it was prepared to give new liberal interpretation to previous legislation that restricted basic human rights. Thus, for example, the Supreme Court compelled the air force to allow a woman to enter a combat pilot course on the grounds that previous administrative regulations violated the principles of the Basic Law: Human Dignity and Liberty.[41]

The basic laws have yet to yield a constitution, nor have they been used by the legislature as a means of training itself and the public to think in terms of a body of law that limits later legislation and governmental action. Despite the need to complete the work of drafting a constitution and despite the fact that the Knesset has the constitution-writing function in addition to that of the regular legislative function, the basic laws have yet to develop a constitutional aura. They can and have been changed and amended with ease, thus losing their strength as limitations on the governing authorities. In 1997, when the coalition parties wanted to appoint a second deputy prime minister in order to solve problems of prestige and coalition formation, and in 1996, when the issue of the election date was being debated (see chapter 7), the Basic Law: Government was amended with ease.

A severe impasse developed over the Basic Law: Freedom of Occupation in 1993 when a Court panel overruled a government ban on importing nonkosher meat as a violation of the importers' right to earn a living.[42] The government had decided to relinquish its monopoly over the import of meat as part of its privatization policy; but the Ministry of Commerce denied a company permission to import nonkosher meat. After the High Court of Justice declared the ministry's refusal unconstitutional, a revised basic law was worked out, under the pressure of the religious parties, that would allow an ordinary law to be modified by an absolute Knesset majority so as to be considered an exception to the provisions of the basic law. Such a law, forbidding the import of nonkosher meat, was enacted. However, in amending the Basic Law: Freedom of Occupation in 1994, a reference to Israel's Declaration of Independence was added. This may come back to haunt the Orthodox proponents of the amendment, since the Declaration refers to the principle of equality among religious groups, which in the future may be the basis for judicial review of special preferential treatment to Jewish Orthodox institutions.

10   INTEREST GROUPS AND PUBLIC POLICY

IT IS APPROPRIATE for political scientists to concentrate on groups that try to influence public policy. We do well to remind ourselves that policy decisions benefit some groups at the expense of others, that political decisions are made by a small portion of the population, and that groups try to influence decisions.

The right to assemble and organize has long been regarded as a fundamental political right, and that is precisely why it is one of the first rights denied by authorities in periods of tension or upheaval. That like-minded citizens can organize to have their interests expressed in policy is a keystone of the democratic process. Unlike a political party, whose primary function is to aggregate various interests in order to compete in elections with a view to gaining control of the government, the interest group articulates the demands and attitudes (the "interests") of group members in order to bring about policies in line with their views. Whereas the party is primarily concerned with elections and ruling, the interest group is geared to the policy outputs of the system. Political theorists have often taken the existence of a large number of active interest groups as evidence of the vitality of democratic institutions in the country.

The theory of political pluralism posits the struggle among myriad interest groups as a highlight of the democratic process. For a writer like David Truman, the extensive organization of competing groups is evidence that power is widely shared and that no group ever loses completely, although none always wins either. While the pluralist school points to some groups as stronger than others, they also recognize that new groups ("potential groups" in their parlance) can organize and take part in the political process to their advantage.[1]

The terms interest and interest group, although pervasive in political science, are also very difficult to employ as analytical tools. What is an interest? The empirical referents of the term are many at best and ambivalent at worst. In the final analysis it appears that most commentators have employed the term interest as synonymous with group activity to achieve desired results. But are we not all characterized by the interests we support? And if we only support interests but do nothing to achieve them, can we be thought of as participating in the political process?

We all have interests. At the most basic level there are the interests of survival and sustenance, but even these "interests" involve policy issues. Are subsidies to be enlarged, reduced, or maintained? Do security demands take precedence over other issues? May a soldier refuse to serve in the territories or to remove settlers from their homes?

Quickly it becomes clear that interest is often synonymous with politics. What we want is, almost by definition, opposed by others and hence part of the political game. And if there were no groups or individuals fighting over it, if there were no interests, we would not be concerned with it. Years ago, before there was widespread awareness of the limits of our planet's natural resources, clean air was not a political issue. And precisely because there was widespread belief that there were sufficient amounts of clean air for all of us, no interests were seen as jeopardized and no groups felt vulnerable. But with the development of greater awareness of the finiteness of the earth's resources and of the role that these matters play in maintaining our quality of life, the issue entered politics. Interests were perceived in maintaining low levels of ozone in the atmosphere or low degrees of chemical concentration in lakes and rivers. Economic "interests" brought on an era of concern with nuclear plants for the production of electricity and the safety of automobiles on the roads, with material fire-resistant enough for the making of children's pajamas, with where to locate electricity generating plants, and with the carcinogenic character of the foods we eat.

"Interest" is so pervasive a phenomenon, and so closely related to the group organization designed to further it, that it must be used very carefully. It is important to keep in mind that in order to understand the phenomenon better we must characterize two things: the interest and the group. Interests may relate to personal interests or social or general ones. Increasing the minimum wage may stem from personal motivation for a low-paid unskilled worker, or it *may* be an altruistic goal for greater social equality on the part of a group or political party. One's orientation is likely to be affected according to whether a personal interest is involved. Another helpful distinction may be between sectoral interests, such as business or labor, and promotional groups that have more altruistic goals in mind.

The organization of the group is also a key to understanding the role of interest groups. A loosely coordinated group with part-time leadership and a low budget behaves very differently and most likely has a different impact on the system than a well-organized, bureaucratic group with a large budget. The outcome is not a foregone conclusion. The former group and its membership may be sufficiently motivated for a large effort on a relatively short-term basis—stop the war, or lower taxes— while the latter organization is better able to handle long-range protracted contacts with government authorities. A bureaucratized interest group inevitably faces organizational problems from the growing conservative nature of its bureaucracy and a tendency to oligarchy; the other kind of organization may remain more dynamic, at least in the early phases.

A popular notion of interest group activity is that it must be public and loud. This notion must be reconsidered; the most effective pressure groups are those we hear of least. Confrontational politics and long petitions are not necessarily a sign of strength in a system such as Israel's. The popular notion of interest group behavior in pluralistic political cultures features the lobbyist waging a brave fight in the name of the interests of the masses. But the truly effective lobbyist is the one known only by those he needs to maintain the policies desired by patrons. The basic fact is that most policy matters are indeed decided behind closed doors on issues most of us would not understand or become agitated about. It is the rare issue that excites public passion; on such an issue unusual tactics might be employed. But for most policy matters, interests are expressed, promoted, and transformed into policy in much more subtle and mundane ways.

Some groups have won reputations as effective lobbyists for positions they favor. Politicians are likely to fear the clout of such groups long before they have organized petitions, mass mailings, or demonstrations. In the United States, the National Rifle Association (which opposes limiting the right of Americans to bear arms) and the so-called Israel lobby are two examples of groups whose potential is enhanced by their previous behavior and successes. Israeli counterparts to such groups are difficult to find because Israeli interest groups are more likely to be ide-ologically, if not organizationally, linked to a political party or point of view. The appeal of Gush Emunim, Peace Now, or the Histadrut would tend to reinforce existing political divisions rather than to add a new dimension to the forces at work on a given policy area.

Other groups, such as the Council for the Prevention of Traffic Acci-dents or various ecological groups, are largely financed by public mon-eys and promote causes that are rarely embroiled in partisan politics. One clear success was achieved by a group called "The Four Mothers," formed after the tragic crash of two army helicopters ferrying soldiers to Lebanon in February 1997. Each of the women founders had sons who had fought in Lebanon, and in May 2000 the army withdrew from the security zone there largely because of their activity.

Rather than think of competing interest groups, it is best to think of political parties attempting to colonize bureaucracies or public policy issues or both. The ruling party, either Likud or Labor, has dominated defense, Labor has run the Histadrut and has colonized the agriculture bureaucracies, and the NRP and haredi parties have nationalized the religious issue and made it their own. Pluralism is not in evidence; competing political parties are.[2]

The Israeli Case

An analysis of interest group activity must begin with a careful consid-eration of the system to be influenced. The trait that makes the pluralis-tic model described above not completely relevant to Israel is the relative lack of points of access in the Israeli political system. In a large, decen-tralized system such as the American one, points of access are many, and the role of the media in launching nationwide campaigns is crucial. With a Congress composed of 435 congressmen and 100 senators and a pres-ident whose political antennae are always up, the potential for interest group activity is great. But in a centralized, bureaucratized system such as Israel's, the same rules do not apply. In Israel, the major focus of pol-icy-oriented pressure must be the few senior civil servants responsible for the area under discussion or the leaders of the two or three impor-tant parties in the government coalition. This handful of people is likely to have the political and administrative power needed to satisfy the demands of the group making application.

Israel, a small country whose politics and politicians are thoroughly familiar to those active in the field, is a case of a democratic system whose interest groups work in a very compacted environment. Groups organize and jockey for power and influence, but because the space is so small and the system so intense and so dense, the interplay that might exist in other countries is not evident.[3] This is so for at least three reasons.

First, Israel's system is so centralized and party-dominated that there are only two or three effective access points into the system. The Knesset, as we have seen, is run by a coalition of parties that also controls the government. Most legislation is initiated by the government and is generally assured of passage by coalition parties in the Knesset. Why, then, lobby individual Knesset members? The effective interest group would concentrate on the two or three major parties that make up the government coalition. Within each party there is likely to be a handful of individuals whose support would be critical in bringing the issue onto the agenda and having it passed. But since the Israeli system is so centralized, so party-dominated and bureaucratic, lobbying can be much more concentrated and even secret. How different from the 535 members of Congress and the president who can be lobbied in the American system! The American lobbyist's techniques of sophisticated communication networks and computerized mailing lists become less relevant in Israel, where having access to the party leadership or the hierarchy of the government ministry dealing with the issue is infinitely more important.

Second, there is a lack of free-floating issues in the system. It is very hard to find an issue that might raise public attention that is not already being discussed, debated, studied, or researched by a government, public, or semipublic agency. The absence of free-floating issues decreases the potency of interest groups and gives a tremendous advantage to the ruling party, if it can regulate the introduction of issues being processed by the system. The timing of the infusion of issues into the system, as much as anything else, allows power-holders to forestall movements that might otherwise gain public momentum and to divert attention to the areas they favor.

The success or failure of the ruling party in managing demands has depended very little on ideological differences between the parties. Issues of labor relations, wages, and economic policy have been troublesome for any finance minister who has tried to deny the workers what they wanted. Labor governments might have had a slightly easier time when the Histadrut was also under their party's control, but the differences have been more of style than of substance. Likud governments have had no control over the Histadrut and hence could be sniped at by this Labor-dominated institution. Religious issues have generally been called up by the religious parties according to a political clock that they have controlled, although the success of the anticlericalist Shinui has tempered that monopoly. At times, religious issues have been raised at moments in which the coalition they participated in have appeared to be in danger, and when their votes have been needed to avert its fall. Sometimes the religious issue has been propelled into the public sphere by intrareligious competition among various religious parties and factions.

Insertions of issues by groups outside the party system have traditionally been more easily contained. The number of demonstrations and petitions in Israeli politics is high,[4] but this does not mean that they are effective on the whole. What it seems to mean is that an extraparty level is sought for asserting pressure because party channels are either clogged or overloaded. The Wadi Salib riots in 1954 and the Black Panthers in the early 1970s, both examples of the introduction of the ethnic issue into Israeli politics, were handled by setting up committees, by coopting a number of the leaders, and/or by initiating some policy changes. These groups tended to be small, their efforts episodic, and their achievements in concrete terms marginal.

It is instructive that in the Israeli system the largest returns for the least effort are always won by groups affiliated with one of the major parties. Numbers can certainly make a difference, but numbers in themselves are not enough. The fact that hundreds of thousands had signed a petition supporting the annexation of the Golan certainly was noted when the annexation was finally legislated, but in and of itself it was insufficient. After all, the petition had been circulating for years; poll after poll and election after election had indicated that popular support for the idea existed. Numerical strength, coupled with the appropriate political and diplomatic conditions and the political will of the leadership, preceded the legislation.

The third reason that Israeli interest groups must be understood as existing in a compressed environment is that interest group leaders are often situated in a hierarchical relation with the party politicians they are trying to influence. They are likely to be not anonymous callers lobbying for some obscure issue but members of the party's institutions whose votes were or will be needed on one issue or another, or for some candidate. More crucially, it is likely that the party leadership approved, or at least did not veto, the appointment of these individuals. We are talking of a process of severe selection in which those who come to make the case of the kibbutzim are not anonymous farmers from the back country but leaders of the kibbutz or moshav movements whose interests often define the actions and policies of the Labor parties. What is more, these movement leaders themselves may one day become important party influentials.

This process occurs even in the army. At the highest levels of the army, meetings may be held between politicians serving as government ministers and officers who are potential and even aspiring politicians. The military has always been an important recruiting ground for party politicians, and it is likely that the politicians at the meeting will on some occasion be consulted about the promotion or appointment of these senior military leaders to their next military or political positions. As in other social situations, people tend to like those who agree with them and agree with those they like; a community of interest builds up based on a commonality of positions and lifestyles. Interest group activists are often the product of the process of selection that will determine the cast for years to come. The point is that the cast is limited in number, in background, and in social class. Once, the member of the cast was born in Europe and was an immigrant of the second or third *aliyot;* today he is likely to be Israeli-born and university-educated. Efforts are increasingly being made to raise the number of Sephardim in this group, but overwhelmingly it is still Ashkenazi. Women and Arabs are almost totally absent from this group.

It is useful to think of Israeli politics as being of the closet and not of the caucus. Then it will be easier to understand that surface motion is not motion, that basic policies are set far from the displays in the Knesset or the headlines in the papers. Important policies are set and important groups operate without fanfare, without headlines, without the public knowing about it. For most groups with economic interests, publication of their victories would be counterproductive. If the pilots win concessions that are likely to upset the delicate balance of wage differentials in the country, neither the pilots nor the government want to broadcast this fact—the pilots because they want to retain their relative advantage, the government because it wants to prevent others from seeking similar concessions. If the kibbutzim win favorable water allocations, they are not likely to gloat in public over their achievement; we are much more likely to hear about their water allocations when they lose favorable water allocations. Most interest group activity is covert; an interest group's being often in the news is likely to be an indicator of setbacks (perhaps temporary) to its interests and not a sign of strength.

Notice how different this description is from the pluralistic theory of interest group representation alluded to earlier. Absent is the assumption that these groups provide a key linkage between the people and their government, or that groups compete with one another. There is no safeguard against one group's interest becoming dominant, and it is not at all clear that resources are substitutable, with, for example, numbers taking the place of budget in the case of a budget-meager group with a popular cause. Most important, the definition of the "public interest" that emerges from pluralistic interest group theory must be changed in a basic sense: if the competition among groups competing fairly for policy goals is the best assurance that the public interest will be served, in the Israeli system the game is clearly stacked in favor of the ruling parties, allowing them to define the public interest if they have the will to do so. Add to this the corporatist arrangements wherein the government, the Histadrut, labor unions, and manufacturers meet to work out wage guidelines, and the understanding of the limitations of spontaneous groups is more complete.[5]

Based on this analysis of the role of interest groups in setting public policy in Israel, it is clear that questions that might be important to scholars in other settings are less important here. For example, whether Israelis join voluntary groups to a great or a limited extent becomes a moot point. Voluntary organizations, when not party-affiliated, tend not to be crucial in setting public policy. The numbers themselves do not provide an indication of political power. An estimated 600 public organizations exist in Israel, and 30 percent of Israeli adults belong to a voluntary organization other than the Histadrut. There are almost 40,000 registered nonprofit organizations, and 60 percent of Israeli adults perceive themselves as connected to one of those groups of the civil society.[6]

In Israel, as in any other country, nonformal, nongovernmental processes play a role in decision making, and in this field the role of the interest group looms large. The major function filled by interest articulation is formulating and expressing political demands. A useful typology of interest groups includes the institutional interest group, the associational interest group, the nonassociational group, and the anomic interest group.[7]

The *institutional interest group* is a formal organization or a long-lasting informal group within a social institution whose manifest function is something other than interest articulation. A group of military or bureaucratic leaders who are formally authorized to undertake some task but who include in their activities influencing policy outputs would be an example of this. The *associational interest group* is constituted in order to express the interests of the group it represents. To do this it usually develops a staff and orderly procedures for achieving the goal for which the group was established. The *nonassociational group* would include kinships and ethnic, regional, or status groups that lack formal organization and through which interests are articulated on an intermittent basis by individuals, family heads, and other spokesmen. The *anomic interest group* is of shortest duration and is not characterized by formal organization or long-range planning; examples would be riots, demonstrations, assassinations, and other more or less spontaneous penetrations into the political system from the society.

Various means of access, styles of operation, and environmental factors affect articulation patterns, and these differences have been used to characterize the level of political modernization based on interest articulation. The emergence of differentiated infrastructures, such as associational interest groups, indicates higher degrees of political development. As the polity becomes complex and issues increase in number and severity, articulation of interest becomes more institutionalized.

It is instructive to think of Israeli politics in terms of these four types of interest groups. While we can certainly think of instances of all four types, most interest articulation—and certainly most influence—is institutional and associational. For example, the Israel Electric Company derives its authority from its monopoly status granted by law, rather than by recruitment of public opinion and support. Its employees form what is among the most successful organizations because of the threat that they will disrupt the flow of electricity to the country. No ruling party has been willing to confront them or to fundamentally change either the monopoly status of the company or the fringe benefit of free electricity enjoyed by the company's workers.

Associational interest groups such as the Histadrut are also very important. It seems reasonable to speculate, although no empirical work on the subject has been done, that these two kinds of groups (institutional and associational) are the most active and the most successful in the Israeli decision-making process. Nonassociational and anomic interest groups are observed only rarely, although their occurrence is more likely to be noted in the newspapers than is the mundane, day-to-day operation of the first two types. A demand for ethnic representation or a sit-in in apartments by young couples or a demonstration in support of some foreign policy is more unusual—and therefore more likely to appear in the news—than is a report by a committee of experts or a secret political twist of the arm by a Histadrut official to a senior civil servant. But the latter are likely to have the political weight necessary to influence policy; the former probably do not.

There is a close link between political parties and interest groups in all political systems. The Israeli case presents a fascinating laboratory to consider the contention that a weak party system facilitates a strong pressure group system.[8] The primacy of party in Israel was once evident but is now in question. Will the relative weakness of the autonomous system of interest groups change as well? The answer to this question will be offset by the generalization that a fragmented decisional system tends to encourage associational groups, while a centralized hierarchical one tends to discourage them. Israeli political parties are in decline, but the decision-making structure is still very centralized. Add to this the preference of the system for a rhetoric of absolute-value orientations. Pragmatic bargaining was always permitted and even desirable behind closed doors; at the public level, however, the pragmatic style that thrives on bargaining was downplayed.

In the compact conditions of the Israeli political and bureaucratic cultures, those groups do best in terms of policy outcome that are closest to decision-making bodies or decision makers themselves. Lobbying—the effort to secure specific policy decisions or the appointment of favorably disposed government personnel—is undertaken in discreet, covert ways as opposed to the more overt methods that characterize a more open system. One example of "painless lobbying" was the existence in Israel of multiple office-holding, which made it acceptable for a legislator simultaneously to hold an executive position in a major decision-making organization such as the Histadrut or the Jewish Agency. Although it is now forbidden, in the past mayors were sometimes elected to the Knesset, thus affording the municipal interests an ideal carrier and object for lobbying efforts. Levi Eshkol, while serving as prime minister and defense minister, retained for a time the post of chairman of the settlement division of the Jewish Agency—a politically sensitive post, but hardly one demanding the attention of the prime minister. But it is reasonable to assume that the head of the division had a good deal of access to the very highest decision makers in the land.

Elite interaction is usually a little less intense than in this example, but it exists nonetheless. Keeping in mind the pyramidal structure of Israeli political life and the relatively small numbers of people at the apex of the pyramid reminds us that the probability of elite members meeting often—formally and informally, in official capacities and socially—is very high. And if these individuals also belong to the same party, the interaction is likely to be frequent and cooperative. The informality and ambiguity attendant on an "off the cuff" conversation between a mayor and a minister introduce severe analytic difficulties for the student of interest groups, but they are likely to be more frequent and significant in terms of policy outcomes than many more overt kinds of pressure.

Activities such as formal lobbying and mobilization of the public are not infrequent occurrences, but it is reasonable to conclude that their impact is slight. Lobbying as a recognized institution does not exist in Israel; there are no requirements to register, nor are there legal limitations on activities such as there are in the United States. The Knesset recently instituted a set of rudimentary rules regarding lobbyists, but these are unlikely to affect the workings of the lobbyist. Demonstrations, hunger strikes, and petitions are regular occurrences in Israeli politics, but they are generally conducted by groups at the fringes of the power network and not by significant ones. If a group such as the Histadrut or Gush Emunim calls for a mass rally or march, it is likely to be for purposes of group arousal as much as for direct influence on a specific policy area. The demonstrations that these broad, politically well-connected groups organize have more of a symbolic role to play than a policy role.

In the British House of Commons, a substantial proportion of the members have explicit and acknowledged ties to organized groups, and the groups perceive the election of their members as advantageous to their general policy interests.[9] This condition sometimes exists in Israel as well; the election of an "interested member" is yet another indication of the group's connection with the party involved. A kibbutz member, a leader of the Histadrut or some cooperative, a rabbi, or a leader of a trade organization indeed represents the interests of his constituency, but the connections between his organization and his party are pervasive and continuous. Groups are often active at the party level, campaigning for the election of their leader to the party list. The efforts of the group for the leader and the efforts of the leader for the group are often two sides of the same coin because sometimes the leader speaks for the group on his own behalf in seeking election.

Perhaps the most important mechanism used by groups in attaining access is influencing the appointment of officials on bureaucratic and statutory boards, including key civil service or political appointments. Groups utilize their proximity to party leaders to try to influence these appointments. During the three decades of Labor dominance, it was well understood in Israeli politics that the way ahead led in some fashion through the parties of the Labor Alignment or the parties in coalition with them. Such membership was an important, necessary, although not sufficient, condition for appointment and power. Individuals could be sponsored by groups close to the parties; if an endorsement could not be had, the absence of a veto was also occasionally sufficient. In the first period of Likud rule, a good deal of carryover of Labor appointments was in evidence, and it was attributed either to a desire on the part of the Likud to adopt a merit-based civil service philosophy or, less kindly, to a paucity of candidates who could pass the Likud loyalty test after its long period in opposition. With their later victories since the 1980s, it became evident that Likud appointments were influenced by endorsements of groups close to the Likud and its allied parties.

Independent groups that organize to influence policy are generally short-lived and unsuccessful unless co-opted by some party-affiliated group. More important, in the Israeli system the number of groups proves nothing because of their extreme inequality in terms of power. Power in the system is in the hands of leaders of the party or parties in the government coalition. This power is fortified by an extensive system of interlocking directorates with these leaders or their chosen proxies, in this way concentrating power in the key organizations.

We next consider some major topics of public policy and of interest group activity. Four areas are discussed with an eye to gaining a clearer picture of the issues that excite the political system and the ways these issues are handled and influenced by interest groups operating in each area. The four areas to be discussed are defense, the Histadrut, agriculture, and religion.

Defense

Defense policy provides the best example of an institutional interest in the Israeli political system, for it is the policy area that commands the most attention, the largest concentration of budget, and years of active service of most Israelis. This policy area has overshadowed all others in Israel's existence, often recruiting top-level individuals to serve its demands and rewarding many who have reached the top of its hierarchies with prominent second careers in politics, business, and administration.[10] Placing a priority on defense has become part of the Israeli way of life; an overwhelming proportion of the population sees it as the central issue facing Israel. The defense issue penetrates the value system of the country: symbols of military strength, self-sacrifice, and heroism are given positive recognition in the culture. Complex political issues of international relations are often simplified, and military aspects of problems are often stressed at the expense of the political. Borders and settlements are often the focus of the debate regarding Israel's future, with issues such as the interest of other nations given lesser roles. In recent years, however, public criticism of the military and questioning of security symbols has been fomented by the crisis of military effectiveness in dealing with the intifada, the war in Lebanon, and geopolitical shifts resulting from the decline of the Cold War and the Gulf Wars.

In the first fifty-six years of independence (1948–2004), 20,196 persons died in the line of duty, in addition to 2,978 civilian casualties; in the same period, 23,000 died in traffic accidents. Yet, the centrality of the defense issue in Israel is maintained by leaders of the major government parties, whose dominance is only rarely penetrated by outside groups. Peace Now and Gush Emunim have clearly articulated points of view regarding security matters on opposite sides of the spectrum. Propelled by the Lebanon War and the first intifada, new protest movements entered the political scene, among them, "Yesh Gvul" ("There's a Limit"), which advocated conscientious objection in the face of the IDF's attacks on the civilian population, and "Four Mothers," a group that demanded the IDF's withdrawal from Lebanon. In fact, the Barak government's decision to withdraw unilaterally from Lebanon in 2000 was ascribed to the impact of this latter group. Another manifestation of the growing influence of interest groups is the heightened involvement of parents within the military on issues that previously were protected from civilian interference, such as reactions to training accidents and operational mishaps. A notable feature of these activities has been the central role played by women in these groups.

The defense challenges facing Israel are enormous, and Israel's success in this field has become legendary. The prolonged state of conflict and the risks taken on the road to peace shaped its perception of reality and influenced its societal and economic arrangements. It is precisely because the topic is so salient and the issue boundaries so impermeable that it remains central to understanding the Israeli political system.

The impact of the defense issue is clearly seen in the arrangements that have been worked out regarding national service, which provides for many a major form of identification with the country, while for others, it signifies their being apart from the mainstream of Israeli life. The defense issue segregates the Jewish from the Arab population by requiring army-service from the former while denying it (except for the Druze and

Bedouin) to the latter. Military service is still an important requisite for many positions of power and importance in Israeli life, as well as for certain welfare benefits, and non-Jews are effectively shut out from them. Arabs are excluded for security reasons; given their choice, it is likely that many would not be willing to risk their lives for the Jewish state.

Of the 88,000 Jews liable for service in 2002, only 77 percent actually served; another 12 percent were discharged within a year. In other words, one-third of Jewish Israeli men were not inducted or did not complete their compulsory army service. Only half the women served, but they are always exempted from their two years of service in higher numbers.

Two Jewish groups are exempted from army service for political reasons. The conscription of some yeshiva students is formally deferred—in effect they are exempted—while they are studying. This arrangement began in the early days of statehood, when Ben-Gurion agreed to the demands of the ultra-Orthodox that some 400 of the 7,000 yeshiva students be exempted from army service; technically, they were granted extensions of their call-up date. The number of those receiving exemptions ballooned, and their number has increased more than a hundred-fold, to 50,000.[11] Religiously observant women may also avoid active service. Both groups are regularly attacked for shirking their duty. While alternative forms of national service are often suggested for religious women and Arabs, none have never been implemented. Pressured by the courts, secular parties, and disgruntled reserve soldiers, the government took steps in the early 2000s to limit the exemption of yeshiva students.

Service in the reserves, estimated at 425,000, or more than 70 percent of Israel's potential military manpower, is also not a universal phenomenon. Only one in five performed more than ten days' reserve service in 2002. Some arrange to be excused; most are not called.

Military service has become less inclusive, and, as the army becomes more professional, it is likely that in the future the society will be divided among those who served and those who did not. An example of this divide is provided by the army records of those elected to the Knesset in 2003: about a quarter of the 120 Knesset members (mostly Arabs and ultra-Orthodox Jews) had not served in the Israel Defense Forces. If peace should develop and the army demand less manpower in the future, this process will be accelerated. This decreasing need has special relevance for the large immigrant group from the former Soviet Union. The army historically played an important role in the integration of successive waves of immigrants; it was widely known as a people's army.[12] But since the military now has more recruits from which to choose, it can be more selective, thus denying many immigrants the rite of passage that once offered such an important way to get ahead in Israeli social life. In fact, even today less than half the relevant age group now completes military service.

Many Jews do serve in the military, however, and for many years. Men often serve in reserve units into their forties; women are exempted after having borne a child. Interestingly, political positions are often not altered by service in the territories or exposure to combat training, although after these experiences there is a tendency to be more critical of the army as an institution and less optimistic about its future than people who have not served or who have served under less demanding conditions.[13] In the past, the pervasive structure of the military enterprise assured that most families had a connection—some more direct than others—with the army. The universality assured a high level of salience for military matters and tended to lend implicit public support to the policies followed. The military, certainly until the Yom Kippur War, enjoyed a very high level of prestige in the society, partially because of the sacrifice inherent in the job and partially because of the successes of the military since independence, especially in 1967. This combination of high participation, high prestige, and the admitted importance of the issue made the defense establishment one of the most important areas of interest group activity in the country.

No area of Israeli public life is immune from its impact. Major economic decisions in such varied fields as industrial infrastructure, natural resource development, privatization, and urban planning take defense considerations into account. The number of buses available in the country, the future of an airport close to the heart of a city, the routing of roads and their capacity, and the kinds of industries to be developed are specific examples of this range of concern. The defense issue also has an impact on cultural matters ranging from religious law to the development of an army slang that makes the army one of the most fertile areas for development of the Hebrew language. The structure of the education system is influenced by the demands of defense in ways ranging from the curricula of vocational high schools to the fact that Israeli university students tend to begin their studies after a number of years of army service and remain likely to be called up for reserve service, along with many of their teachers, during their years of study. The impact of this reality on Israel's youth is a topic of justified concern among parents, educators, psychologists, and philosophers. Can moral, humanistic values be glorified in an environment of training to kill and destroy? Can the value of life be upheld in a structure calculated to bring death? The answers are not simple, and no single type has emerged as the Israeli soldier, but the dilemma provides the backdrop for the attempt to merge the rich morality of Judaism with the historical developments of Zionism.

The successes of the Israeli army must also be seen against the backdrop of the Holocaust and the image of the defenseless Jew being led meekly to death. The trauma of that image undoubtedly goes a long way to explain the primacy of the military in Israeli thought and life. The objective challenges the country faced from a hostile environment before the peace treaties and accords reinforced this trauma. One of the difficulties in the pursuit of peace has been the difficulty in conceiving the neighborhood and former enemies in a new way. The process of differentiating between good Arabs and bad Arabs is far from complete for many Israelis. It is difficult to shift from being a nation in arms, a nation besieged, especially when suicide bombers explode on urban buses. During the decades of strife, Israel has been called upon to do what few nations have done successfully: to maintain democratic and liberal traditions under conditions continuously working against those traditions.

Considering the enormous economic, psychological, and cultural burden of defense, Israel's record in maintaining democratic forms and civil rights (at least within the pre-1967 borders) is admirable. Although part of the explanation for this success is the small size of the country, Israel's army depends on a vast reserve of manpower that is continually called up and trained. The aphorism that Israelis are soldiers on eleven months' leave catches the spirit of the situation.[14] The dominant values of the country are reflected in the army, and vice versa. No isolated class has developed, no feeling of being aloof or different from the rest of the population. While the image of the army as more efficient or successful than those of other countries is weaker than it once was, feelings of pride in its strength are not concentrated in a narrow class of officers but dissipated throughout the society.

The dilemma posed by the military forces of any nation is clear. Because the state is supposed to monopolize the use of violence and because military might rests with the army, it is essential that the army be under the control of the civilian authorities of the state. Both democratic and communist regimes desire the subjugation of the military to the civilian forces, for fear of being replaced by those officers to whom the means of violence have been entrusted. Imbuing a "professional" commitment in the army to obey the duly elected leadership is not a matter of empty ideological posturing but of neutralizing a dangerous potential threat to the continuation of the regime.

In Israel, the army was seen as a partner with the political forces in bringing about the national revolution of independent statehood and not as a competing power. A pattern of dual control developed during the Yishuv period, in which the Haganah was responsible to the dominant party, Mapai, and to the voluntary national institutions that were the functional equivalent of civilian authorities of the state. Upon the achievement of statehood, this dual pattern of loyalty to party and state persisted and prevented the emergence of an instrumentalist army solely controlled by the civilian branch of the state—the ideal model of liberal democracies.[15]

The existence of separate armies with competing political loyalties presented a major problem that was resolved by Ben-Gurion in 1948, when separate commands of the Haganah, Palmach, Irgun, and Lehi were abolished and the Israel Defense Force (IDF) established. But because Ben-Gurion feared that the new army would be open to the same kind of coalition pressures as were other aspects of Israel's public life, the army was never domesticated in the sense of being controlled by the civilian Ministry of Defense. Ben-Gurion wanted to keep control in his own hands, and while he served as both prime minister and defense minister (1948–1953 and 1955–1963) this arrangement was possible. But when Ben-Gurion's personal stature was removed from the equation, it became clear that the subordination of the military to the civilian government had not been properly institutionalized.

It was fashionable to talk of the depoliticization of the army, and there was much evidence of this new instrumental pattern emerging. But the basic flaw in the process was the attempt to devise a nonparty solution to a political problem in Israel's governmental culture, which rests squarely on political parties. Who can keep the army under civilian control and yet away from the politicians and their party interests? Ben-Gurion's answer was to extol the virtues of civilian control while keeping personal control over the major decisions of the IDF. All three times that Ben-Gurion retired from the dual roles of prime minister and defense minister (1953, 1954, and 1963), he suggested that the roles be filled by two separate individuals. During his tenure he tried to make the defense sphere independent of the civilian sphere and in so doing ultimately made their interpenetration inevitable. "The end result was, therefore, that the dual control failed to achieve either of Ben-Gurion's aims. Though deprivatized, the IDF did not

develop into an apolitical, instrumentalist army under the absolute supervision of the state institutions. Instead it ultimately became an army working as a partner in the political process, integrated with the civil power
even beyond the national-security field." [16]

The nominal civilian control instigated by Ben-Gurion largely succeeded in keeping other parties' influence out of the IDF but made the
interpenetration of the highest echelons of Mapai and the highest echelons of the army very intimate. No strong autonomous civilian ministry
was set up to oversee the functioning of the military. Since Ben-Gurion
the civilian was in charge of the IDF, his oversight was deemed sufficient.
The Defense Ministry became a civilian aide for the army, with all major
functions of budgeting, procurement, and military strategy situated in
the army itself or duplicated in the Defense Ministry. At certain levels,
internal party developments influenced the army. Senior ministers
would court army leaders for support in conflicts with other ministers
regarding policy. The support of the officers was important not just in the
sense of professional advisers but as the opinion of the major interest
group involved in the area. In periods of generally accepted leaders such
as Ben-Gurion and Begin, the role of the military was similar to that of
the professional adviser, but when the role of leader was less secure, as
with Eshkol and Rabin (both in the 1970s and in the 1990s) and
Netanyahu, the position of the military leadership became an important
part of the political calculus.

After Ben-Gurion, the fact that civilian control had not been institutionalized became obvious. One writer categorized relations between the
defense minister and the political system as follows: Ben-Gurion had
almost complete authority over the IDF and the Defense Ministry.
Lavon, his successor as defense minister, had almost none, and not surprisingly from this perspective, the Lavon Affair (discussed in chapter 5)
occurred during this period. Levi Eshkol is called a "representative"
defense minister: between 1963 and 1967 he held both positions of
prime minister and defense minister, representing the demands and programs of the military to the political leadership, but this was hardly control. In the period 1969–1974, when Golda Meir was prime minister,
Moshe Dayan was defense minister, and Pinhas Sapir was finance minister, Dayan and Sapir differed over economic and defense matters; also,
Dayan had split from Mapai with Rafi while Sapir was leader of the
Mapai political machine. This left Golda Meir in the role of arbiter,
balancing between the two prominent ministers in her government. The
period between 1974 and 1977, in which Yitzhak Rabin was prime

minister and Shimon Peres defense minister, was characterized by cabinet rivalry between the two and by professional control of the military by Peres.[17]

Begin's experiences were more varied. His support for a harder foreign policy line, especially regarding Egypt, than that espoused by his defense minister, Ezer Weizman led to a tacit coalition between Begin and Chief of Staff Raful Eitan and ultimately brought about Weizman's resignation in 1980. Until Ariel Sharon was appointed to the post in 1981, Begin also served as his own defense minister, becoming somewhat more actively involved in defense matters than when he had a defense minister, with Eitan playing a dominant role. Sharon's appointment after the 1981 elections removed the political conflict within the triad, because Begin, Sharon, and Eitan were all hard-liners. Sharon tended to dominate army as well as government policy until 1983, when he was forced to resign from the Defense Ministry as a result of the Kahan Commission report concerning his role in the events in the Palestinian refugee camps of Sabra and Shatilla.

As defense minister during 1984–1990, the years of the National Unity Government, Rabin had to work closely with the Security Cabinet, a group that was made up equally of Likud and Labor politicians. He resumed the dual role of defense minister and prime minister after being elected in 1992 and held it until his assassination. Moshe Arens was appointed defense minister by Likud prime ministers in 1983, 1990, and 1999. Arens exemplified the "civilian" type of defense minister and was successful in inducing structural reforms in the IDF, the most important of which was the introduction of the Ground Forces Command. But when retired generals again took the reins, such as Yitzhak Mordechai (1996–1999), Ehud Barak (1999–2001), Benjamin Ben-Eliezer (2001–2003), and Shaul Mofaz (2003–), the old pattern repeated itself: defense ministers functioned as a kind of "supreme chief of staff" while weakening civilian aspects of control.

The pattern that has emerged is that top government leaders (who are, by definition, politicians) are very active in army policy, especially relating to procurement and personnel appointments. The boundaries between the civilian and military in Israel are not clear; outside of the active political group there is no institutionalized civilian counterpart to the military bureaucracy in the Israeli defense establishment. Top military leaders have been called upon to be very active in matters of policy that, according to a purist model, should be the exclusive area of the politicians. The army's influence reached unsettling heights during the Al-Aqsa Intifada that began in 2000, when the IDF actively partici-pated in defining political goals—an approach that led to the extensive (some called it excessive) use of deadly force against the Palestinians. In an effort to counter the preponderance of influence by the defense establishment, a National Security Council was set up in the prime minister's office in 1999 (during Netanyahu's tenure).

Retired army officers have been deeply involved in the political debate, especially since the beginning of the intifada in 1987. Before elections are held, groups of senior reserve officers organize to express authoritative opinions about the strategic value of the territories in defense of the country. On the one hand, the Peace and Security Coun-cil announces that the nation's security would be furthered by exchang-ing territories for peace. On the other hand, the Security and Peace Council, also made up of senior reserve officers, reacts promptly by declaring that holding the territories is necessary for the security of the country.

The problematic nature of civil-military relations is seen more clearly in periods of crisis and war. During the War of Independence, Ben-Gurion had to contend with a revolt among his generals, who were opposed to his proposed appointments, which were intended to purge the high command of officers who were not Mapai members. Ultimately, Ben-Gurion won the battle by compromising with the generals while demanding total political support from his cabinet in such matters. In the Sinai Campaign of 1956, the war was well under way before Ben-Gurion apprised his government of the battle plan. Civilian control, yes, but not governmental control. In the days before the 1967 Six-Day War, intense political negotiations ultimately led to Dayan's appointment as defense minister after Eshkol removed himself from the position. Not only were other political parties active in this negotiation, but the lead-ership of the army also took part in it, pressing its desire to go to war.

In the 1973 crisis of the Yom Kippur War, the porous relations between the civilian government and the military were most obvious. Ministers were given military appointments, and generals publicly criti-cized political decisions. The Agranat Commission ultimately focused blame on the military, largely ignoring the acts of omission and commis-sion by the political leadership. In the 1982 Lebanon war, the military was divided on the goals and the tactics of the war, as was the civilian community; the lack of a national consensus split the army, creating crises of morale and resignations, demonstrations, and petitions. This pattern repeated itself again and again during the periods of Israel's presence in the territories, the occupation of south Lebanon, and the two intifadas. The lines of demarcation between the civil and military are not clear partially because the army is such an integral part of Israeli society and partially because basic institutions of civilian control have never been established.[18] Given that the army is so esteemed, so prominent, and so important, it is not surprising that it is also so powerful.

Even in a constitutional sense, civilian control over the military is blurred. We know who the chief of staff is, but it is more difficult to determine who the commander in chief is. Collective responsibility lies with the government, and many ministers often speak out on military matters to the discomfort of the minister of defense and the prime minister. The Basic Law: Israel Defense Force, passed in 1976 in response to the evidence of a lack of clear lines of authority in the 1973 Yom Kippur War, formalized the constitutional responsibility. The army is under the authority of the cabinet, and the minister of defense acts through cabinet authority in defense matters. The commander is the chief of staff, who is appointed by the cabinet on the recommendation of the minister of defense. While this better defines the hierarchical relations, the roles of the prime minister and the other ministers are still left vague. The defense minister's role is defined neither as delegate of the cabinet nor as leader of the army—it could be both or neither depending on the circumstances.

The appointment of the chief of staff must incorporate both professional and political considerations. At that highest of levels, not even the strongest proponent of civilian-military separation would pretend that a complete divorce of the two is possible. But which quality should be more prominent: professional competence or political loyalty? Leaders such as Ezer Weizman, Ariel Sharon, and Yitzhak Mordechai have been candid in expressing their opinions that they were best qualified, but they were passed over because Labor leaders did not trust them politically: each became defense minister without being chief of staff. Chiefs of staff have done very well politically. The list includes Yigael Yadin, Moshe Dayan, Yitzhak Rabin, Chaim Bar-Lev, Mota Gur, Ehud Barak, and Shaul Mofaz. Rabin and Barak also became prime minister. The fact that the chief of staff is so important in the political system both during and after his tenure indicates how close the apexes of the political and military pyramids are.

The civilian Ministry of Defense—which Rabin called a ministry of supply for the army—exists in the heavy shadow of the IDF, and even in those spheres in which its formal authority is recognized, it does not succeed in exerting it. It was Ben-Gurion who made the double decision that the Ministry of Defense would be separate from the army but that it would not supervise the army. Later defense ministers have followed Ben-Gurion's practice of utilizing the uniformed officers of the general staff extensively in the decision-making process and in his practice of choosing not only the chief of staff but other senior officers. Ben-Gurion's practice of keeping research, manufacturing, procurement, finance, and conscription under civilian management was maintained until 1996, but in many of these spheres the dictates of the IDF carried the day, and the civilian Defense Ministry was swept along.

The defense minister is an extremely important actor in Israeli politics because of the centrality of the defense issue, but the Defense Ministry as an implement of civilian control is relatively unimportant. The topic was so sensitive that the statement of a senior civil servant to the effect that "the army dominates the defense establishment" was banned by the censor.[19] The rationale of the concentration of power in the hands of the military is that the army, as the body responsible for implementation, must also be responsible for planning, procurement, and deployment of arms and forces. This may be based on a naive belief that Israel is immune from social forces that have led to military takeover in other countries, or it may be an expression of the high esteem that many Israelis have for their army. While there exists the formality of separation, and while the minister of defense and the cabinet have dominated military planning and moves, Israel lacks the patterns of civilian control in a more institutionalized sense that exist in other countries.

A good example of this is the defense budget. As we saw in chapter 3, the defense budget in effect defines Israel's budget both in terms of domestic spending and in its reliance on funds from foreign sources to offset the purchase of weapon systems abroad. The military, in turn, defines Israel's defense needs. The head of the budget division of the Ministry of Defense (who also holds the title of financial adviser to the chief of staff) prepares a proposal after extensive consultation. In the case of major change—redeployment of forces as a result of political negotiations or military readjustments—a new plan might be needed. The cancellation of plans for the advanced jet fighter Lavi because the United States refused to continue to underwrite its development and production, the unanticipated expenses of combating the extended Arab uprising, and the redeployment of IDF forces from the territories are examples of how budget plans may change in midstream, even in the absence of war. But the budget process takes last year's budget as a given and tends to grow from that point; no zero-based budgeting methods are used to attempt to determine what is really needed to achieve the desired results.

If a single budget proposal emerges from the whole process, it is forwarded through the defense minister to the Finance Ministry and the cabinet. If there are disagreements among general staff members or between the army and the Defense Ministry, the matter is brought to the minister. In such a case, however, his role is that of judge rather than leader. When such disagreements are brought to other civilian leaders, the tendency has been to give as much as possible. Eshkol tended to press the officers to ascertain that their budget was sufficient, and Sapir perceived his role as cashier for the defense establishment. Rabin and his chief of staff, Ehud Barak, redesigned the budget in the 1990s in terms of a leaner and smarter army, thus allowing the defense budget to take a smaller part of the country's economic resources, a commodity always in short supply. The cabinet has been actively involved in the process usually only when the defense and finance ministers have disagreed. While budget decisions need cabinet approval, that step tends to be a formal ratification of decisions made elsewhere. In the mid-1990s, civilian oversight was increased. The economic recession of the early 2000s again pushed the IDF to adjust its structure in light of the shrinking available national resources; military considerations began to be subordinated to economic values.

The Knesset has developed a special procedure for working on the defense budget. Because it is a subject that requires much secrecy, the entire Knesset is not involved. Instead, a special subcommittee composed of members of the Finance Committee and the Committee for Foreign Affairs and Security scrutinizes the budget in closed session and approves it item-by-item, and then the whole Knesset approves the total as part of the national budget. The structure of its preparation and the political process it undergoes assure that the defense budget approved will be quite close to the proposals approved by the general staff and the defense minister, for only those groups at the heart of the preparation stage have a realistic chance of affecting it. Matters as important and far-reaching as the production of a new tank or a new jet aircraft are, for all intents and purposes, decided by the defense establishment. The Finance Ministry, the cabinet, and the Knesset, in order of decreasing effectiveness, may slow the decision-making process, but it is unlikely that they can turn it around. Arguments can be made about the tremendous expense involved and about alternatives that might be economically more sound, but they usually do not, at so late a date, abort the decision. If indeed the Israeli system is a partnership between civilian and military spheres, there is at least some evidence that the military is the senior partner.

The pattern of civil-military relations in Israel is complex. In a formal sense, the civil branch dominates, but in a deeper sense, the military is not confined to its barracks but is active in the political life of the country at its highest reaches. What is more, some military leaders enter active political life after retiring from the army. The boundaries between the two spheres are porous and shifting, and this very feature may allow Israel to retain formal civilian control over the military.

The Histadrut

If politics played an important role in an institutional interest group in the defense field, party politics was even more prevalent in an associational interest group such as the Histadrut. The Histadrut was conceived as the organization of the workers movement run by the labor parties, which would compete among themselves in elections. The Labor Party was clearly dominant in the Histadrut until 1994, so the organization became an important staging ground for political fights within the Labor Party, an important aid to power when Labor ran the government, and an important source of opposition when it did not. Power within the Histadrut was a possible resource to be used in national politics by ambitious groups and individuals within the Labor Party because the budget controlled by the Histadrut was considerable and the jobs that could be allocated were numerous.

The Histadrut is a voluntary organization of workers that functions as a trade union, but it was also much more than that in the pre-state period, playing a key role in building the infrastructure of the country's economy, in absorbing immigrants, and in preparing for the political and military challenges that Israel would face (see chapter 3). It claimed more than 1.8 million members before its 1994 reorganization, after which it plunged to some 700,000 members in the early 2000s, although still representing a major fraction of the Israeli workforce. Obviously, such an organization must be taken into account when policies important to it are being considered.

Since its inception in 1920, and until 1994, the Labor Party controlled the Histadrut. The ideology of the organization was that it represented the interests of the workers, but in reality, the Histadrut represented the interests of the Labor Party, which controlled the Histadrut. Even the 1994 elections may ultimately be viewed as a fight within Labor for control of the Histadrut: Chaim Ramon, minister of health in the Labor Party government of the day, headed a list that ran against his own party (Labor) and won 46 percent of the vote to Labor's 32 percent.[20]

Since 1994, the economic activity of the Histadrut and its role in social service delivery have changed dramatically. Kupat Holim, the sick fund, is still a Histadrut activity, but the National Health Insurance Law provides that most of its operations will be funded and regulated by the government. The Histadrut redesigned itself so that trade union activity was its major function.

Socialist parties are often associated with labor unions. The support may be more direct, as in Germany and Great Britain, where the unions actively support a labor party, or less direct, as in the United States, where organized labor generally supports the Democratic Party. Often in continental countries each political party has its own trade union and recruits labor's support in that way. Israel's pattern is unique; the Histadrut fits none of these descriptions, for it is made up of workers who elect their governing officers from competing parties. Until the 1960s, the parties that competed were workers' parties or parties that accepted socialist ideals. But since the 1965 Histadrut elections and the participation of a Herut-Liberal list (Gahal), the full spectrum of parties that competes in the Knesset elections also competes in the Histadrut elections, making them an important stage in Knesset elections.

The New Histadrut (the post-1994 regime changed the name) downsized the organizational structure, disbanding the Histadrut Assembly, a middle-level body of no great organizational importance. The member still has many opportunities to vote, for the Histadrut convention, consisting of 2,001 delegates, elects the 171 members of the Histadrut House of Representatives, in which each gender must comprise at least 30 percent of the membership. The seventy workers' councils are also elected, although they were reorganized into thirty regional units, costing many activists their jobs. Members also vote for the trade union council in their craft or profession, and for the workers' committee at the individual workplace. Women also vote for Naamat, a women's workers council.

The elections for the convention and workers' councils use a proportional representation, fixed-list system similar to that used in Knesset elections. The minimum percentage needed to win representation in the Knesset is 1.5 percent, but for the Histadrut national convention, the minimum has been 2 percent since the 1981 elections. In 1977 it was 1 percent, and before that time, no minimum percentage was required. Some of the national trade union leaders and most of the workers' committee members are elected on a plurality basis, which promotes the election of visible and popular leaders; the fixed-list system retains the processes of selection and promotion in the hands of the labor establishment.

In addition to streamlining the decision-making structure, organizational reform has cut the number of workers in the Histadrut administration (executive committee, workers' councils, and tax collection agency) from 3,924 workers in 1994 to 1,040 in 2002. The Histadrut had a $350 million deficit in 2002.[21]

Losing control of the Histadrut was a serious blow to the Labor Party. No longer could it count on cooperation with the leadership of the Ministry of Finance (as it could when party loyalists headed both institutions) in the process of wage negotiations when Labor was in power. Without this cooperation, the negotiations could be long and stormy. Historically, much depended on the relations between the government and the Histadrut. After the establishment of the state, the Histadrut lost much of its power and leading personnel to the newly formed government. By and large, the Histadrut was relegated to second-rank status in terms of setting social and economic policy, although its ideas and leaders were often heard and sometimes promoted to more prominent positions. In the Likud era, the Histadrut became a major focus of opposition to the government. There were two major reasons for this: First, the long years in government had weakened the Labor Party as an effective organization, and the Histadrut was more able to fill the gap. Second, the important base of power and patronage for Labor after 1977 was the Histadrut and its related enterprises. Paradoxically, the Histadrut and its leadership were strengthened as a result of the 1977, 1996, and 2003 Likud victories over Labor.

The appropriate way to conceptualize labor relations in Israel in general is by seeing the Histadrut as trying to further the interests of the workers and its own interests as well. In the pre-1994 period, it was most likely that the Histadrut and the government would resolve labor friction through compromise. When arguments developed, they were due to differences over implementation, not policy. Or—as happened not infrequently—a group of worker leaders would strive for concessions above and beyond what the Histadrut had agreed to; then, without the support of the Histadrut, wildcat strikes or work actions would wreak havoc on an economic sector. What was fascinating to observe in these situations was how much more effective Histadrut leaders were in communicating with the government and/or the employers than they were in dealing with the workers.

Under the Likud, the government and the Histadrut seemed to perpetuate the kind of relations that had existed under Labor in the field of labor relations, but on more general topics—such as social-economic policy or proposals for legislation regarding compulsory arbitration, national health insurance, or state pensions—the differences between Histadrut and Likud government leaders were great.[22] In the post-1994 period, the Histadrut tried to generate an image of militant trade-unionism, free from having to juggle the organization's economic interests with its role as labor leader.

Within the Labor Party, the Histadrut was an important resource in another sense. The local leadership often used the office of secretary of the local council as political patronage. If it wanted to reward an active member, the party might provide him with that job. If, on the other hand, a member achieved prominence within the council and became its secretary, she or he almost automatically acquired an important position in the local party branch and possibly beyond it as well. It was the nature of the extended scope of the Histadrut in Israeli labor relations that the secretary of the workers' council had the potential for helping to solve individual as well as collective grievances and for dispensing patronage jobs within the Histadrut network. The economic and service institutions of the Histadrut, weighted down by enormous deficits, became a tremendous economic burden rather than an ideological imperative or a political boon, and they crumbled in the end.

With the decline of its electoral fortunes in 1988, Labor was faced with a two-fold problem: (1) to secure government funds, credits, and guarantees for Hevrat Ovdim (the holding company for the Histadrut's industrial and economic activities), with its overextended industries, cooperatives, and service providers; and (2) then to use the Histadrut as a vehicle to regain political power. The wheel had turned: for forty years, Labor had wielded political power by controlling the economy. When Shimon Peres became finance minister in 1988, he hoped to be able to restructure the economy in a way that would save both the economic future of the Histadrut and the political future of the Labor Party. Grabbing the reins of the weakened Histadrut in 1994, Chaim Ramon was able to gain status and power for himself while depriving the Labor Party of its past bastion of strength. He also changed its structure beyond recognition by downsizing its economic activity and by bringing about the nationalization of the health services.

Paradoxically, as the Histadrut became more important for Labor's future, the role of Histadrut leaders diminished. This pattern was a reversal of what had occurred with independence. In the pre-state era, the Histadrut was the focus of action, but, as the Jewish Agency and later the state became centers of activity, the major party leaders reduced their activity in the Histadrut. As we saw in chapter 4, that was the pattern followed by Ben-Gurion himself. In the 1996 elections, Labor suffered from the lack of the organizational effort that the Histadrut had provided in previous elections. Determined to be single-minded trade unionists, Histadrut leaders were very careful not to involve their organization in Labor's election campaign; the huge reservoir of personnel and vehicles that the Histadrut institutions controlled was not employed during the campaign. Peres's loss by only 30,000 out of 3 million votes indicates how crucial added organizational effort might have been. Peres, the man whom Yitzhak Rabin finally replaced as the head of the party in 1992, appointed Ramon, the man who had run Rabin's successful campaign in 1992, to be his campaign organizer in 1996. Perhaps this was the greatest irony of all.

Agriculture

Agriculture is an excellent example of an important policy area in which interest-group activity is more covert than overt, relying on party, parliamentary, and government contacts that are available because of the strategic location of proagriculture persons in the system. Agriculture was a penultimate value in the period before the establishment of the state, ranking high along with absorption of immigrants and defense. Through agriculture the Zionist movement could realize two of its major goals: returning to the land of Israel in the most literal sense, and making the Jewish people productive rather than centering their economic activities on trade, craftsmanship, and scholarship. Over time, especially after the 1930s, agriculture was also identified with defense imperatives because it allowed for spreading the population and establishing a physical presence and a kind of military early-warning system.

The earliest traces of modern Jewish agriculture go back to the first *aliyah* and the plantations set up by Baron de Rothschild at the end of the nineteenth century. These efforts permitted Arab labor and discouraged Jewish labor because the former was cheaper and more experienced. The

second and third *aliyot*, however, pioneered new forms of agricultural settlement, including the kibbutz and the moshav, and based their program
on using Jewish labor while avoiding the exploitation of others by
employing only members in their enterprises. These pioneering ventures
became the ideological and organizational strongholds of the labor movement, and even though most of the Jews of Eretz Israel were always
urban dwellers, agriculture became associated with the highest ideals in
the system of values that existed before independence. Agriculture was
perceived as a mission of the movement and the nation; the leadership,
ideology, and organization of the entire labor movement presented themselves as stemming from the agricultural sector.

The bourgeois farmers and plantation owners associated with nonsocialist ideas were extraordinarily negative in opposing the socialist
organization of agriculture. They were divided among themselves and,
after the 1930s, became more and more marginal in the politics of the
country. One of their leaders, Yosef Sapir, even argued that only with
decentralized organization could they be true to the ideals of the "free"
farmer.[23] The right accepted the socialist ideology, seeing in agriculture
a way of life that would lead to national rejuvenation. For the parties
associated with Labor, these settlements and their leadership became
heads of the entire movement and ultimately of the nation, while the
agriculturists of the Likud parties were soon eclipsed and could do little
more than make feeble attempts at interest group activity.

Independence and the establishment of the Agriculture Ministry
decreased the autonomy of the Histadrut and the Agriculture Center, the
cooperative organization of kibbutzim and moshavim, in agricultural
matters and ultimately led to substantive changes. But at least in the first
decade of independence, the dominance of the Agriculture Center
remained intact. Most of the ministers came from agricultural backgrounds in the settlement movements and usually from the kibbutz
movement affiliated with Mapai. The organizational and ideological
strength of the settlement movement prevented Mapai from actively
interfering in agricultural policy; in fact, the opposite was true—leaders
of the agricultural movements achieved prominent roles in the party and
dominated in party affairs out of all proportion to their numerical size.
After the 1949 and 1951 elections, by contrast, some thirty Knesset
members were kibbutzim and moshavim. In 1965, six of Ahdut
Haavoda's eight-member delegation were from kibbutzim, six of nine in
Mapam, and eight of forty-two in Mapai. One can sense the political
decline of the kibbutz movement and of the agriculture "lobby" by

comparing those numbers with later figures: in 2003 there were only nine members from kibbutzim and moshavim, including one kibbutz member from Labor and two from Meretz. By contrast, settlers from the territories accounted for eleven Knesset members in 2003.[24]

The supremacy of Labor and Mapam was obvious when the matter of land allotment was considered. Israel did not have a history of large landowners, and so there was no need for agrarian reform. Land was purchased by the World Zionist Organization through the Keren Kayemet (the Jewish National Fund) and distributed or leased by it primarily to settlements organized in the Agriculture Center. The Agriculture Center incorporated settlements (kibbutzim and moshavim) affiliated with the Histadrut. This arrangement gave the Histadrut enormous power, and in the early years it was the kibbutzim that won the battle, receiving preferential treatment at the hands of the Agriculture Center from the resources provided to it by the Keren Kayemet.[25] The kibbutzim were preferred over the moshavim (the private farmers of the right were almost totally ignored) because the kibbutzim were more closely associated with the dominant party, while the moshavim had their closest contacts with a rival party. The kibbutzim were dominant in the Agriculture Center, and that made all the difference.

The interpenetration was so complete that various kibbutz movements, affiliated with different socialist parties, competed with one another within the Agriculture Center. The settlement division of the Jewish Agency handled training, research, and budget but left the allocation of land to the settlement movements, which set up a committee comprised of leading activists. When Mapai won control over the WZO and the Jewish Agency, it quickly took advantage of the resources placed at its disposal to further national, party, and sectoral goals. Since decision-making positions had been "colonized" by the kibbutz, there was no need to exert great pressure to secure favorable policies.

After independence, the dominance of agriculture continued. Huge sums were poured into settlement movements, resulting in impressive achievements in agriculture; in addition, the settlement movements provided organizational strength and a supply of party activists and leaders to Mapai and other parties. This was especially sensible for the kibbutz movement, whose lifestyle provided for the member's and his family's needs and could allow him to absent himself from work on the kibbutz to further the interests of the nation, the party, and the kibbutz. National federations could recruit members—from 5 to 7 percent—from the federated kibbutzim for work within the movement or in national capacities.[26]

In 1959 Moshe Dayan was appointed minister of agriculture. This shocked the political establishment because Dayan was young and many faithful politicians were itching to be appointed, because Dayan had only recently completed his turn as IDF chief of staff, but mostly because Dayan was seen to represent the moshavim and not the kibbutzim. Dayan changed the sectoral outlook of Israel's agriculture ministers and adopted a statist approach (see chapter 11). This was upsetting to the old order whose interests had been secured by having their people appointed to key positions. Dayan rejected the practice of having the Agriculture Ministry deal with the old-time settlements established before the state was founded and the Jewish Agency deal with new ones founded after statehood. The new settlements were predominantly populated by new immigrants from Asia and Africa who were untrained in agricultural methods and largely without the accompanying ideology with which the early European settlers had begun their settlements. The new settlements were generally set up on poorer land and were very dependent on the bureaucracies, which issued credit, training, and marketing—and which tended to be run by veteran Europeans. When Dayan took over the Agriculture Ministry, he found that the average kibbutz landholding unit was 105 dunams (1 dunam = 1,000 square meters, or 0.222 acres), compared with the average 36.7 dunams for moshavim, and that the average water quota for the kibbutz unit was 24,300 cubic meters, compared with 10,600 for the moshavim. Dayan undertook major changes in this balance, allocating 100,000 dunams to the new kibbutzim, lowering the kibbutz water quota to 17,100 cubic meters, and raising that of the moshavim to 13,500 cubic meters.[27]

Moshe Dayan was the first minister of agriculture who did not perceive himself as a representative of the settlement movements, although he had been born in the first established kibbutz and raised in one of the pioneer moshavim. During his term, the bulk of the country's land was formally nationalized with the passing of the Basic Law: Lands of Israel (1960). The law regulated the allocation of land and made the Lands of Israel Administration (and not Keren Kayemet) responsible for the national lands, which comprised more than 90 percent of the country's land. The minister of agriculture became chairman of the Lands Administration.

Under the Labor-Mapam Alignment, the settlement movements could greatly influence government policy because they could count on majority representation on the commissions that interested them. (The commissions for tobacco and olives had a majority of Arabs, since much of the production of these items was in Arab hands.) Most of the settlement representatives came through the Agriculture Center, and the government representatives were also favorable to the sectoral demands of agriculturists. Even in the Likud years, the federations affiliated with the Labor-Mapam Alignment were well-represented on the commissions because they have organized most of the agriculture of the country. Although the government representatives have tended to be less cooperative in following the sector's demands, the influence of the settlements on agricultural policy has been substantial; agriculture as an issue area, however, has lost its centrality.

Competition in agriculture between the kibbutzim and the moshavim has a long history. Historically, the kibbutzim dominated Mapai and hence policy. The other source of conflict, festering over the years and becoming more and more evident as the ethnic polarization of the country grew, was the divide between the kibbutzim and veteran moshavim, which were mainly Ashkenazi, and the moshavim peopled by Sephardi immigrants. Whereas the older settlements had pioneered in statesmanship, diplomacy, agriculture, and security, they absented themselves—either because of fatigue, overload, or dismissal—from the effort of absorbing the new immigrants who came soon after the state was founded. Abandoning the task of absorbing new waves of immigrants to the bureaucracies they had helped set up, and thus depersonalizing the process, the labor settlement movements accelerated feelings of alienation on the part of the new immigrants toward the more established farmers. The veteran kibbutzim and moshavim, perceived as a landed gentry in affluent Israel, were characterized by others as arrogant, as assuming that leadership of the country was their natural and indispensable role. These people were easily singled out in the antiestablishment, anti-Labor campaigns of the 1980s, as their previous image of folk heroes became tarnished and their political power dissipated.

In the past, settlement and agriculture had been associated with the shared value of building the homeland; by the 1990s, building the homeland raised contentious issues of territories and relations with the Palestinian Authority. With the exception of the Golan Heights and the Jordan Valley, the established kibbutz movement refrained from settling in disputed areas; the symbol of agriculture could no longer sustain a national ideology.

Even the appointment of a kibbutz member as minister of agriculture in 1988 could not help much, because by then the agricultural sector was in deep economic and political trouble. As the country industrialized, and as the service sector became more important, agriculture found itself unable to play the central role it had once held in the politics of the nation. The government arranged to take over some of the kibbutz debt in the mid-1990s (see chapter 3), but even those improved conditions could not restore the movement's previous wealth, power, and status.

In the dominant party, Mapai, agricultural interests were assured because of the ideological tone of the pre-state era and the early years of statehood and the leadership positions that members of the settlement movement attained—which also ensured that the party refrained from interfering in the affairs of the agricultural movements. Party interference was greatest in the agricultural organizations of the smaller parties, set up to try to compete with the successful organizations of the labor movement. These parties included the minuscule movements of Herut, the Liberals, and the Independent Liberals, and the slightly larger movements of the NRP and Poalei Agudat Israel. Their agricultural movements often achieved representation within party institutions but never achieved the importance of labor movement organizations.

Four of those who served as agriculture ministers—Pinhas Lavon, Levi Eshkol, Moshe Dayan, and Ariel Sharon—eventually became ministers of defense, and two of them—Eshkol and Sharon—became prime ministers. Especially in the case of Sharon, agricultural policy was defined by his activities and concern for settlement of the territories taken in the 1967 war, thus continuing the tradition of the pre-state era, which equated agriculture with settlement and defense needs. The ministry was dominated in its early years by ministers favorable to the kibbutz, a dominance that could be seen in both policy and appointments.

The control of water allocations is so important an economic and political resource that it caused a furor when Netanyahu attempted to set up a Ministry for National Infrastructure in 1996, to be headed by Ariel Sharon. Water was a key to building a powerful base for Sharon, but water was the province of Raful Eitan, the minister of agriculture and another important power broker in Netanyahu's climb to the prime minister's office. Eitan was not willing to have control over the water commission taken from him, so a compromise was reached, stipulating that Eitan would continue to have control over water for agriculture, including the amounts used and the rates charged, and that Sharon would control other aspects of water allocation.

Water also has international implications. In 2000 the Barak government decided in principle to purchase water from Turkey as part of a strategic effort to ensure good relations between the two countries. As the water crisis in Israel deepened, the Sharon government endorsed that decision in 2002, and an agreement to buy 50 million cubic meters of water over a twenty-year period was signed in 2004.

A production commission for the control and marketing of citrus fruit was formed in the 1940s and continued in existence until 1991, when its marketing was privatized. Later, commissions were introduced for all branches of agriculture; they were empowered to oversee production, to assure a regular supply of each product, to facilitate its marketing, and to deal with surpluses. Today, the commissions are statutory authorities that can enter into contracts and enterprises (six other commissions relating to agriculture have been incorporated). The composition of these commissions involve those active in the branch; the government has no more than 25 percent of the membership (with representatives of the Agriculture, Finance, Industry, and Commerce Ministries and sometimes the Ministry of Health); the producers (represented by settlement groups) have 50 percent, and the marketers 15 percent; and the rest are retailers and consumers. The commissions have a great deal of authority and can set quotas, minimum prices, surplus policy, subsidies and incentive bonuses, and funds to encourage export and industrial usages; they even deal with packaging and categorization. Recent legislation envisages the consolidation of these commissions into a single body; proponents see this as an efficiency move, while opponents regard it as greater centralization and control by the minister of agriculture.

Voting patterns in 2003 reflect the weakened links between the political party and the organizational affiliation of both kibbutzim and moshavim (see table 10.1). Kibbutz members supported Labor at a 45-percent rate, moshav members at a 22-percent rate. In the kibbutzim, the Likud won almost no support, while in the moshavim it received the votes of more than a third of the voters.

Members tended to vote for the party with which their kibbutz movement had been affiliated. In 2000, members of the United Kibbutz Movement (Takam), which was affiliated with Labor, merged with the Kibbutz Haarzi, led by Mapam, to form the "New Kibbutz Movement." In the past, movement affiliation had been an excellent predictor of the vote in kibbutzim, but this association seemed to have been muted after the merger. Table 10.2 displays the voting behavior in Yagur and Negba, two kibbutzim affiliated with the Takam and the Kibbutz Haarzi, respectively. Kibbutz Yagur voters supported Labor at a rate exceeding 70 percent in both the 2003 and 1999 elections; Meretz, the social democratic party farther to the left of Labor, won a much smaller fraction of their

Table 10.1 Voting in 2003 (and 1999) Knesset Elections in Selected Settlements (in percentages)

	Likud	Labor-Meimad	Shinui	Meretz	NRP	Shas
National Total	29.1 (14.0)	14.5 (20.1)	11.9 (4.9)	5.1 (7.4)	4.1 (4.2)	8.3 (13.1)
Jewish settlements	31.9 (15.5)	15.2 (21.6)	13.2 (5.4)	5.2 (7.6)	4.6 (4.5)	8.9 (14.1)
Non-Jewish settlements	3.5 (1.3)	7.7 (7.7)	—	4.2 (5.2)	—	3.1 (4.2)
Jewish agricultural settlements	24.1 (10.9)	27.9 (36.3)	12.7 (4.4)	12.8 (15.7)	5.4 (5.1)	5.2 (8.4)
Kibbutzim	6.9 (1.8)	45.5 (50.5)	7.8 (2.4)	27.0 (31.9)	3.7 (2.7)	—
Moshavim	32.5 (16.3)	22.1 (30.8)	12.1 (4.4)	6.8 (7.6)	6.5 (6.4)	8.6 (14.6)
Jews in						
West Bank	29.2 (20.9)	3.1 (6.6)	6.0 (4.1)	1.0 (2.0)	11.2 (11.2)	9.0 (11.6)
Gaza Strip	21.5 (11.8)	—	1.7 (1.0)	—	29.7 (15.4)	9.3 (14.5)
Golan Heights	25.1 (9.2)	15.2 (23.3)	15.2 (4.6)	5.7 (6.8)	14.4 (8.6)	2.6 (4.5)
Bnei Brak	9.1 (6.5)	2.3 (4.4)	2.4 (1.2)	0.4 (1.1)	5.4 (6.7)	20.7 (22.6)
Jerusalem	27.8 (15.2)	9.0 (14.0)	6.9 (4.3)	4.8 (7.1)	6.5 (5.9)	12.6 (17.4)
Tel Aviv	28.4 (15.4)	22.6 (27.4)	15.5 (6.3)	11.1 (13.1)	2.5 (3.1)	7.2 (10.8)

Source: Official election results of the Central Elections Committee, as reported in *24 Hours* supplement of *Yediot Aharonot*, January 30, 2003, 2.

Table 10.2 Voting for Labor and Meretz in Two Kibbutzim, in 2003 and 1999 (in parentheses)

2003 (1999) vote	Labor	Meretz
Yagur (Takam)	70.5 (75.8)	9.3 (12.7)
Negba (Haartzi)	32.5 (20.5)	51.2 (74.1)

Source: Same as table 10.1.

vote. On the other hand, the rate of support for Labor increased from Negba kibbutz voters. Meretz continued to win more votes at Negba, but at a lower rate than before.

Members of moshavim founded after independence were largely Sephardim, and they have been less successful on the whole than the veteran moshavim. The farmers of the younger moshavim are the least loyal to Labor; they have shifted to other parties, especially Likud, just as their urban cousins have. Kibbutzim did not absorb many post-independence immigrants, and so they have been immune from this pattern, maintaining a record of support for their party. But that record is weaker than it was in the past. As recently as 1981, the kibbutz federations associated with the Labor-Mapam Alignment supported their party at rates above 90 percent regardless of when the kibbutz was established.

The NRP's kibbutz federation was loyal to its mother party in 2003. In one religious kibbutz, Kvutzat Yavne, the NRP won 46.6 percent of the vote (compared to 38.8 percent in 1999), and the Likud won 23.6 percent (compared to 8.7 percent in 1999). In the past, some of the leadership of the religious kibbutz federation had been active in a religious party with a more conciliatory stance on defense issues, Meimad. Meimad, however, did not compete in 1996 and since 1999 has fielded a joint list with Labor.

Religion

The clearest case of political parties reflecting and promoting a set of interests is the religious parties' advocacy of the role of religion in the state. For the NRP, Shas, and Agudat Israel, the first a Zionist and the other two non-Zionist parties, the major plank of political ideology is to have the State of Israel organize its public life in accordance with Jewish religious law, *halacha*. This is the overriding concern of all three parties; after that, issues of economic policy, the future of the territories, and all other matters with which a political party concerns itself are addressed.

In these parties, the religious lobby and the party are synonymous. They have been at least partially successful in creating in Israel a Jewish state that adheres to Orthodox rabbinical law, and this effect has been achieved not by impressing legislators with this vision through an articulate lobby but by succeeding in the games of electoral and coalition politics.

Religion is a central issue in Israeli political life. It is crucial because the broad consensus within the Jewish population is that Israel should be a Jewish state. Conflict arises over the degree to which legislation and civil life in Israel should reflect the norms and decisions of established (Orthodox) religious authorities.[28] The Knesset has passed legislation regarding some of these matters, including, for example: (1) the 1950 Law of Return, assuring the right of every Jew to immigrate to Israel; (2) the 1952 Law of Citizenship, granting citizenship to every Jew, his or her spouse, children and grandchildren; (3) the 1953 law establishing sole jurisdiction to the Orthodox rabbinical courts regarding marriage and divorce among Jews; (4) a 1951 law making the Jewish Sabbath an official day of rest for Jews and requiring a permit to employ a Jew on the rest-day; (5) the 1962 law prohibiting the raising of pigs in Israel except in areas in which there is a concentrated Christian population; (6) the 1986 law prohibiting Jews from displaying leavened food for sale during the days of Passover; and (7) the 1990 law allowing local authorities to regulate whether enterprises involved in entertainment (movies and theaters) will be allowed to operate on the Sabbath and holy days.

The issue is made more complex because of the various meanings of Jewishness. Judaism may be thought of as a religion, a nationality, a culture, or all of these, and more. For Orthodox Jews, religion and nationality are one and the same. Religious observance and belief, while desirable, are not essential criteria for membership in the community.[29]

Israelis are split over these matters, as is demonstrated in figure 10.1. It is fascinating to note the different patterns over time in the distribution of answers to questions regarding personal religious behavior on the one hand and the role of religion in public life on the other. Despite enormous change along most dimensions of Israel's existence, the rate of those responding that they observe "all" or "most" of Jewish religious law is amazingly stable at 25 to 30 percent; the other responses provided were "some" and "none." These numbers are consistent with the estimate that about a quarter of Israeli Jews are observant in an Orthodox sense or even beyond that, including 6 to 10 percent haredi, or ultra-Orthodox; that about 40 percent are determinedly secular; and that the rest are somewhere between those poles.

Figure 10.1 Religious Observance and Role of Religion in Public Life

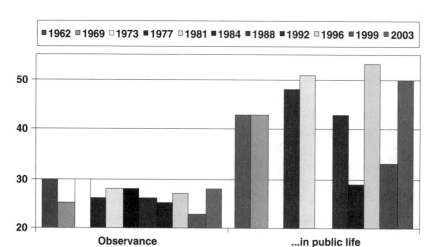

Regarding desired public behavior, the responses vary widely from one period to another. About half of respondents agree to having public life conducted in accordance with religious tradition; about half disagree. The question seems to act as a barometer for government policy: when religious parties are in the coalition and the pendulum seems to have gone in their direction, as in the 1960s and 1980s, less than half the respondents answer that they want public life to be conducted according to *halacha*. The 1992 response seems to indicate a sense that the power of the religious has increased too much and should be curtailed. The 1996 rate indicates that the majority feels that the secular point of view has become too dominant in public policy, while the 2003 even split may suggest a momentary sense of equilibrium.[30]

The cause of Jewish religious law in public life is promoted by all the religious parties, and most other parties are secular or noncommittal. The first appearance of an antireligious party occurred in 2003, with the campaign of Shinui, which argued strenuously against the special privileges that had been granted over the years to religious individuals and institutions in terms of army service and government budgets. The new party opposed what it saw as the pilfering of the public treasury in order to benefit one group in the name of religion. Having declared that it would refuse to join a coalition in which Shas also participated, Shinui, as the big winner of the 2003 elections, got its way. Shas did not participate in the governing coalition, and programs that favored religious institutions were cut back.

Many Israelis would support a pluralistic approach that would allow both freedom of religion and freedom from religion. The problems begin when one group perceives that the behavior of the other is impinging on its rights. The norm of the Israeli political system has been to legitimize both the role of Orthodox religion and the ethic of a single Jewish people; these are important political issues because it is so difficult to achieve these goals.

The call for the separation of religion and the state has never had wide appeal, although it has been discussed. Before the 1992 elections, Avraham Burg became very popular by sponsoring and winning approval in the Labor Party center of a resolution calling for the separation of synagogue and state, but party leaders were so concerned that the resolution would hinder future coalition-building plans with the religious parties that they called a special session to overturn the decision at the next meeting. This episode underscores the political reason that separation of religion and state in the near future is unlikely. Religious parties have been active in the ruling Zionist and Israeli coalitions since the 1930s. This cooperation gave rise, when the state was founded, to the concept of maintaining the status quo, which meant that arrangements in effect during the pre-state period regarding religion and religious practice would be extended into the state period. And so it has been.

There is also a symbolic-ideological obstacle to the separation of synagogue and state. With minor exceptions, most Israelis support the notion of Israel as a Jewish state, and while there are furious debates about what this could possibly mean in an age of liberal democracy, most identify with this value (see chapter 12). To be sure, there are other than religious options to the question of how to express the Jewishness of Israel, but once the basic premise is accepted, the status quo version becomes at least appropriate, if not exciting. Even when the socialists ruled and preferred a different form of expression of the Jewishness of Israel, their coalition calculations and obligations led them to accept the status quo arrangements.

The arrangements in effect appear natural to many Israelis because they are the only ones they have known. But there is evidence that the current arrangements are grating and may present serious burdens or inconveniences. While most people do not drive on the Sabbath in areas that the ultra-Orthodox want blocked from traffic, and although most rituals can be ignored if one so chooses, there are cases, such as marriage, that increasingly pose problems. The Orthodox rabbinate will not sanction a marriage between a Jew and a non-Jew, for example, so if one partner's Jewishness is in question by the rabbinate, no religious ceremony can be held. Since no other branch (such as Conservative or Reform) of Judaism is recognized, and civil marriage does not exist, many couples find that there is no state-sanctioned institution through which they can marry. Many Jews who might qualify nevertheless choose not to be married by the Orthodox rabbinate; as many as half the marriages registered by the Ministry of the Interior are not performed by Orthodox rabbis. The number of marriages recorded by the rabbinate actually went down between 1998 and 2002, despite the large growth in population of the marrying-age cohort.[31] This drop is explained by the large number of couples marrying outside the country, in Cyprus, for example. A marriage performed elsewhere is recorded by the appropriate clerk in the Ministry of the Interior, but the Jewish nature of the bonding is not certified by the rabbinate, and this may emerge as a problem later, as in the case of divorce. While only a small minority is directly affected negatively by rabbinical rulings, a large segment of the public is very much dissatisfied with the situation.

In a broader sense, the call for the separation of religion and the state is foreign to much of the experience of Jewish history and the people of the Middle East. The focus of religion on the individual is a modern, Western notion, especially evident in Christian contexts, whereas religion in the traditional sense was a community undertaking, wherein the individual was identified by his membership in the community. The Yom Kippur service recites that "we have sinned"—not that "I have sinned." Jews were dealt with as members of a community throughout their history of dispersion, sometimes achieving large measures of communal autonomy. The Ottoman Empire recognized communities, and this millet system became the basis of practice during the British Mandate and ultimately within the State of Israel.

From this heritage, it is a natural development to have marriage and divorce and other matters of personal law regulated by the religious community to which one belongs. Religion, then, connotes social belonging and jurisdiction, not only theological belief. Accordingly, notions of individual choice have never taken hold in Israel. While one might not believe in God, one's personal status would still have to be settled by the religious court. Political authorities and religious authorities have worked hand-in-hand to strengthen the power of each other. Questions of inclusion and exclusion in the community—that is, Who is a Jew?—were given religious answers with the authoritative backing of the secular state.

Israel is not a theocracy; it is a modern parliamentary regime that has opted to allocate decisions on certain aspects of public and private life to religious authorities. For the Jewish population, it is the Orthodox rabbinate whose interpretations are binding; for members of other religions—Muslim, Druze, and almost a dozen Christian sects—it is the rules of the recognized religious authority of those other recognized communities that are binding.

In regulating religious affairs in Israel, the Knesset did not give the Jewish religious courts superior status to the courts of other religions, but it did give the Orthodox religious courts a monopoly within the Jewish community regarding marriage and divorce.[32] The 1953 law gives the rabbinical courts complete jurisdiction over marriage and divorce of the Jews in the country, whether citizens of Israel or not. Until then, membership in Knesset Israel ("the community of Israel") was voluntary, but from that point on, jurisdiction over all Jews was in the hands of the rabbinical courts. The various solutions adopted by Jews denied the right to marriage by the religious courts—marrying in Cyprus or marrying through the mail in Mexico or other places—are permitted not by *halacha* but by the secular state and its rules of registering the marriage of citizens.

The registration of one's personal status is in the hands of the Ministry of the Interior. Control over this ministry has therefore become extremely important for religious circles, and, indeed, two NRP leaders, Chaim Moshe Shapira and Yosef Burg, held the post in most of the governments and for most of the years of the country's first decades. The ministry used to register both "religion" and "nationality." According to *halacha*, the two categories are interchangeable, "Jew" connoting both religion and nationality.

Many versions of the relation between religion and nationality are possible—for example, atheists may claim that they are Israeli nationals with no religion, or extreme antinationalists may claim that they are Jews with no special connection to the secular state of Israel. The debate led to a modification of the registration procedure in 2002: "nationality" no longer appears on the identity card, thus easing a visible irritant to many. When hard cases are introduced, the authorities can grapple with these difficult questions.

Such a case was that of Brother Daniel, a Catholic Carmelite monk who had been born, reared, and educated as a Jew in pre–World War II Poland; he had even spent a number of years in training to immigrate to Eretz Israel. Although he had since converted to Catholicism and become a monk, Brother Daniel claimed the right, under the Law of

Return, to come to Israel. The Law of Return, passed in 1950, grants Israeli citizenship to any Jew coming to Israel. Rufheisen (Brother Daniel's name before his conversion) claimed that as a Jew who had converted to Catholicism, he was entitled to the same status and privileges granted other Jewish immigrants. In 1962 the Supreme Court ultimately backed the position of the religious parties, that Brother Daniel was no longer a Jew because he had converted.[33] But the court distinguished between *halacha*, which regards him still as a Jew by virtue of the fact that he was born of a Jewish mother, and the secular usage, which recognized a convert to another religion as no longer a Jew. The court's support of the religious parties' position denying Brother Daniel's request was based on secular grounds.

Another hard decision was made in the two cases brought by Binyamin Shalit in 1968 and 1972.[34] Shalit, an Israeli-born Jew and naval officer, had married a non-Jewish woman abroad. When they tried to register their two children as Jews under the nationality category, the request was denied. The NRP-run Interior Ministry wanted them to leave both the religion and nationality categories blank; Shalit, an atheist, was willing to leave the religion category blank but wanted his children registered as being of the Jewish nation. The Supreme Court, by a 5–4 majority, agreed to his request. This important decision differed from the Brother Daniel case in that the status of the plaintiff in the Daniel case was cloudy according to *halacha*, whereas in the Shalit case, the children were not Jews according to *halacha* yet the court ruled that they must be registered as of Jewish nationality. The Knesset, under NRP pressure, then amended the law to read that a Jew is one born of a Jewish mother or converted. When the second Shalit case arose, regarding the couple's third child, the court denied the request, and the child was not registered as a Jew.

The "Who is a Jew?" issue continues to plague Israeli politics. In 1983, for example, the High Court of Justice instructed the Interior Ministry to register as a Jew a woman named Suzie Miller, an American immigrant to Israel whose conversion in the United States by a Reform rabbi had been declared "suspicious" by the Orthodox rabbinical authorities in Israel. The Shas Party's Minister of the Interior, Yitzhak Peretz, resigned from the cabinet over this decision and resisted attempts to return him to the government unless the Law of Return was changed. It was impossible to placate him and he remained outside the government until after the 1988 elections.

The Miller decision, along with others related to the legal status of individuals converted in other places and with varying degrees of observance of *halacha*, led to a firm demand by the religious parties that the law be changed. Because of the fact that many conversions to Judaism (especially in the United States) are performed by Conservative or Reform rabbis, the religious parties in Israel have labored to have the law changed to recognize only conversion according to *halacha*, which would mean limiting legal conversion to Orthodox rabbis. Although most secular politicians oppose these changes, whether they will be accepted depends on coalition calculations and not on philosophical or theological considerations. After the 1988 elections, with the religious parties in a strong bargaining position regarding the future coalition, both Likud and Labor toyed with the idea of agreeing to amend the "Who is a Jew?" definition of the Law of Return so that only conversion according to *halacha* would be acceptable. Vociferous appeals by Jewish communities abroad, demonstrations within Israel, and the intercession by the president of the country finally led to a National Unity Government, obviating the need to agree to this demand by the religious parties.

Had the law been amended at that time, it would have pertained to only a handful of individuals each year. But the symbolic importance of the proposed amendment was enormous. Many Jews abroad have family members who are not Jews according to *halacha*—either through intermarriage or after conversion by non-Orthodox rabbis. To have their children (or grandchildren) labeled as anything but Jewish was considered an affront by many of these Jews. Besides, the argument went, why should this theological issue be decided by the Knesset, a political body whose members include non-Jews? The 1988 skirmish ended without changing the amendment, but it was clear that the war was not over. It will be fought another day because it is important to both sides.

The 1988 fight over amending the definition of conversion led many to the conclusion that religious parties held power disproportionate to their electoral strength. Many were convinced that changing the electoral system to the direct election of the prime minister, thus insulating him from coalition pressures, would solve the problem. The argument employed to raise money from Reform and Conservative Jews abroad by those promoting the direct election of the prime minister was that it would lessen the hold of Orthodoxy. It was especially ironic, then, that in the first election held under the new system, the Orthodox religious parties were strengthened more than ever in the past: the guidelines agreed to by the parties that set up the Netanyahu government in 1996 called for legislation recognizing only conversions approved by the Israeli Chief Rabbinate.

For the Orthodox parties, the Reform and Conservative movements of Judaism are much more threatening than is secularism, or even atheism. The more liberal movements are seen as usurpers, perverting the titles, prayers, and ceremonies of the religion. The common roots are not overlooked; the Orthodox see the other groups as manipulating holy symbols in a subversive manner. As the role of Orthodoxy in Israel grows, and the proportion of Diaspora Jews who are not Orthodox expands, nothing less than the unity of the Jewish people may be called into question in the future.

A different but related problem stems from the mass immigration from the former Soviet Union, which has introduced hundreds of thousands of people who are directly affected by the issue of Who is a Jew? Under *halacha*, Jews are either children of a Jewish mother or converts, but under the Law of Return, which regulates immigration, one Jewish grandparent is deemed sufficient. Estimates are that almost a third of the immigrants who have come to Israel from the former Soviet Union since 1989 would not be considered Jewish under *halacha*. When their children apply to the Orthodox rabbinate to marry someone recognized as a Jew, they will be turned away and the public pressure for change will grow.

Most of these people are not Jews because their mothers were not Jews and they have not undergone the lengthy conversion process. Thousands of people in this category insist that their mothers were Jewish but have been unable to prove it to the satisfaction of the Orthodox rabbinate. These people—full Israeli citizens under the Law of Return—are sometimes the subject of heart-breaking inequities, as in the cases of a soldier killed in action, or a two-year old killed in a traffic accident, both of whom were denied burial rights in the local cemetery because their mothers were not Jewish. In addition, a growing number of cases involve individuals whose social existence is rooted in the Jewish community of Israel, yet they are not allowed to marry the partner of their choice because one of them is not Jewish according to *halacha*. Furthermore, in death, they may not be buried in cemeteries near their Jewish loved ones.

By 2004 there were about 350,000 non-Jewish immigrants in Israel, but in 2003 only 923 conversions were performed, about the same number as in each of the previous seven years.[35] The number of conversions is limited both by decisions of the rabbinical establishment and by the high cost involved. When elected in 1993, Sephardi Chief Rabbi Eliyahu Bakshi-Doron ordered a limit to the number of converts, reflecting the ultra-Orthodox view that conversion should be granted only to those committed to living a fully Orthodox lifestyle. This demand is often treated as a legal fiction, but the stipulation can be applied if the presiding rabbis so decide. Very few immigrants from the former Soviet Union are willing to accept this provision, and they therefore see the application of this ruling as discriminatory. Those who come to Israel married to a Jew find it difficult to obtain a divorce in Israel because the rabbinical courts have sole jurisdiction over Jews and there is no alternative recourse for divorce. These strict rules have led to the emergence of a permanent underclass of people who cannot get married in the generally accepted manner and who are also isolated from the mainstream in other matters of the life cycle and of personal status. Regarding the high cost of conversion, the Ministry of Religious Affairs at the end of the 1990s refused to cover the $1,000 expense of circumcision for converts, as it did for uncircumcised immigrant males who were able to prove their Jewishness to the rabbis' satisfaction.

The actors who determine developments in this issue area are the religious political parties, the factions within them, and the rabbis affiliated with them. Secular political parties are drawn into these dilemmas because of their desire to have the support of the religious parties in a coalition or to prevent religious parties from supporting the rival secular political party. The religious groups compete with one another, often attempting to win public support within the religious community by being more exacting than others in their interpretations of current events in terms of *halacha*. This is especially effective with the more dogmatic: calling into question groups that are more lenient is exactly the tactic used by the opposition factions within each party, by the more ultra-Orthodox parties against the Orthodox (usually the Aguda and Shas against the NRP), and by rabbis affiliated with one party against rabbis of another party.

When the election of the president of Israel can be determined by religious party votes in the Knesset, political deals are rumored. When religious legislation might be defeated because antireligious members of the coalition threaten to either vote against the bill or abstain, the leaders of the secular party heading the coalition have been known to put tremendous pressure on the upstarts, including threatening the downfall of the government if the bill fails. When in a pivotal position, religious parties may treat the government budget as a political football, pressing for added funds for their projects. In all these instances, the point is that much of the activity in this issue area is motivated by purely political considerations. Israel is divided on the religious issue, but it would be inappropriate to measure that division by the legislation passed on the subject since the impact of coalition politics must also be factored in.

The clear political success that the religious parties have had rests on their pivotal role in coalition formation. The results of this success are obvious: a series of laws and administrative rulings that have, on the whole, gone in the direction desired by the religious parties on questions relating to such issues as abortion, marriage and divorce, public transportation on Sabbath and holy days, enforcement of the Jewish dietary laws, and the definition of Who is a Jew? From the point of view of the religious parties, many matters are yet to be settled as they would wish, but no one can deny the achievements they have scored.

As we have seen, the background to their success is cultural, based on the symbol system and the basic premises on which the society rests. But would things change drastically if the religious parties were no longer needed in the government coalition? To what extent is the Jewish character of Israel one of political expediency, and to what extent is it part of the civic culture? There is no certain answer to this hypothetical question, but it seems likely that the forms regarding religion and religious usage that have evolved in Israel are more permanent than many secularists would like to think.

There have been thoughtful and creative attempts to bridge the gaps between the various positions without forcing either side to surrender cherished principles. One such example is the Gavison-Medan Covenant, which purports to provide a basis for a new social covenant between observant and secular Jews in Israel.[36] The project addresses many of the basic issues confronting the two groups, including the Law of Return, the right to marry and establish a family, and the observance of the Sabbath and holy days. Such efforts reflect an awareness of the deep divide between the two sides and the importance of seeking consensual solutions.

The arrangements in place as a result of the status quo are more flexible than is commonly thought. Local authorities have leeway in how strenuously they apply laws concerning commerce or entertainment on the Sabbath and holy days, and the strength of the religious parties in the local jurisdiction plays an important role in the matter. On national issues, uniformity is maintained. All institutions that receive moneys from the government—including the army, schools, hospitals, and government missions abroad—must observe Jewish dietary laws. The issue of whether El Al, the national airline, would operate on the Sabbath and holidays occupied the country's attention in 1982 until the government decided, in accordance with the demands of the religious parties, to stop these operations. The list of laws and public policy decisions based on religious precepts is a long one, not long enough for some, too long for others, and always changing.

One fascinating dilemma concerned television on the Sabbath. The secularists saw television as an extension of radio, which existed before the establishment of the state and hence was continued into the state period as part of the status quo. (Indeed, early Israeli television was not much more than radio with pictures.) The religionists saw television as especially insidious on the Sabbath—interfering with family solidarity, to say nothing of enticing weaker souls from endeavors of prayer and study. In 1969, when the Broadcast Authority Executive Committee approved television broadcasting seven days a week (except for Yom Kippur), the minority appealed the decision to the prime minister, who decided to bring it before the government. In the meantime, however, the Supreme Court ruled that there was no reason to suspend the decision until the government met, and Sabbath television began on November 7. Other legal arguments regarding the legality of work permits issued to those who were to transmit the broadcast also failed in court. In this case it was the court that spared the politicians from facing the decision of how to interpret the status quo.

The religious parties, especially the NRP, have been constant partners in the ongoing story of Israeli politics. While these parties straddle the fence that divides principle and pragmatism, depending on whether they are in the government coalition or not, the NRP in particular has had to guard its flank from the political sniping of the Agudat Israel and Shas— the NRP is a firmly Zionist party; the Aguda and Shas are non-Zionist. For both ideological and practical reasons, the NRP became the champion of the movement that encapsulates developments since the founding of the state—the nationalization of religion.[37] The goal of the NRP was to have religious institutions, which might have been temporary or voluntary in the past, become permanent fixtures of the religious community by having them established, and funded, by law. The NRP has invested great efforts to promote this legislation and to dominate these institutions, which include the Ministry of Religious Affairs, the chief rabbinate, the rabbinical courts, and the religious councils. Through these efforts, the NRP hoped to establish itself as the major representative of the Jewish religious community.

The institutional instincts of the NRP were excellent. The web of relations between the party and these religious institutions provided budget and patronage for the party's leaders for years. However, in 2004, the Ministry of Religious Affairs was abolished. Shinui claimed that it had delivered on its 2003 election platform; the NRP, a partner in the Sharon government that abolished the ministry, claimed that its participation in the coalition had assured the continuation of budget and services to the observant community even if the ministry was closed.[38]

When its electoral fortunes came on hard times, as its Knesset representation decreased from twelve to four seats between 1977 and 1984, the NRP had a hard time retaining control of these institutions. The haredi parties, and especially Shas, penetrated the systems that the NRP had built, and transformed them in the process. One of the most spirited fights regarding the 1996 coalition was over the Ministry of Religious Affairs. Both Shas and the NRP wanted it, but after they agreed on rotating the minister's position, they found it impossible to agree on who would begin the rotation. As that fight was going on, the Aguda demanded its share of the ministry as well.

The Ministry for Religious Affairs had important administrative, legal, and political functions. It provided and administered technical services for all the various religious sects in Israel. Along with the chief rabbinate, the ministry was very active in the Jewish community—enforcing Jewish dietary laws for public institutions not under the supervision of a local rabbinate and overseeing the ritual purity of imported food, especially meat; providing grants for the building of synagogues and ritual baths; supervising the activities of burial societies; administering holy sites such as the Western Wall; subsidizing needy yeshiva students; and encouraging the development of yeshivas. On the legal level, the ministry initiated legislation on religious affairs and implemented legislation after it was passed. In 1994, when Shas left the Rabin government, the ministry was given to Shimon Sheetrit of Labor, whose activities in matters such as burial rights and lists of those ineligible for marriage heartened many secularists and infuriated many of the Orthodox leaders. Being out of power was so upsetting to them, both in terms of office and of policy, that the leaders of the religious parties all but declared that they would participate in the coalition after the 1996 elections no matter who headed it.

The Ministry of Religious Affairs was also important because of the patronage it controlled, including the selection of personnel of almost every religious institution in the state, Jewish and non-Jewish. This included the chief rabbinate and the local rabbinates, the rabbinical courts and the religious councils, as well as the state religious school system.

There are two chief rabbis in Israel, an Ashkenazi and a Sephardi. Both the fact that there is a Chief Rabbinate at all and the fact that there are two chief rabbis stem from historical considerations; neither is mandated by Jewish tradition. Judaism does not require a rabbinical hierarchy; the Chief Rabbinate emerged primarily for purposes of managing contacts with the authorities outside the Jewish community. Because of the separation clause in the U.S. Constitution, no chief rabbi was needed in the United States and none emerged. But in 1921, under the British Mandate and following the practices of the Ottoman Empire's millet system, a rabbinical council was convened in 1921 to manage the affairs of the Jews in Palestine. This council was ultimately recognized by the mandatory power, and the Chief Rabbinate was institutionalized. Only in 1972, however, were its existence and the rules for its election mandated in law by the Knesset. The Chief Rabbinate was recognized as the supreme authority regarding *halacha*, although after the establishment of a hierarchy of religious courts, it ceased to double as the Supreme Rabbinical Court of Appeals.

An electoral college to select the chief rabbis was to be composed of eighty rabbis and seventy laymen, equally divided between Ashkenazim and Sephardim, with the mayors of the country and the heads of local religious councils playing a role in the election. The makeup of the electoral college was meant to ensure the joint influence of the NRP (through the rabbis appointed) and Labor by virtue of their influence in local government when the law was passed. This joint influence has persisted despite the emergence of Shas as a major religious party and the Likud as a major political force at both the national and local levels. The election of the chief rabbis is always accompanied by intense bargaining among political parties; although the balloting is secret, the results show that the parties have high levels of influence on the rabbis. The Aguda, which rejects the religious authority of the chief rabbis, occasionally calls for the abandonment of the institution and at other times backs candidates of its own. Despite such appeals to abandon the practice of having chief rabbis, the practice persists, more for political and personal reasons than for philosophical or theological ones.

The local religious councils were established to provide services funded by the public treasury. After much party bickering, a Religious Council Law was passed in 1967, calling for the religious councils to be recomposed every four years. The law provides that 45 percent of the members be appointed by the minister of religious affairs, another 45 percent by the local authority, and 10 percent by the local rabbi. The members are to be personally religious, but the appointment system is meant to reflect the ethnic and political composition of the community. When the political fortunes of the Likud, Shas, and Aguda improve, they naturally strive to reap for themselves the benefits that flow from the arrangements instituted under Labor and the NRP.

In 1987 a new type of crisis emerged in the ever-engaging sphere of religion and the state. A woman—Lea Shakdiel—an observant Jew and a member of the town council of Yeruham, was selected as a member of the town's religious council. The minister of religious affairs, Zevulun Hammer of the NRP, refused to confirm the election of Shakdiel because she was a woman. In 1988 the High Court of Justice ruled, in a decision written by a justice who himself was an observant Jew, that the selection of Shakdiel was perfectly legal and binding, and that denying her this position violated the requirement of equality of the sexes as required by law. Moreover, he argued, *halacha* did not deny women the possibility of having a role in the selection of public office-holders. Needless to say, the furor was intense: three years passed before she was seated.

In other cases in Tel Aviv, Haifa, and Netanya, the municipal councils also appointed persons who were unacceptable either to the electoral college for the religious councils or to the religious councils, and again passions soared. In some of these cases, women had been appointed; in others, men who were observant, but only according to Conservative or Reform ritual, were chosen. The Orthodox would have none of it. The inauguration of the Ashkenazi chief rabbi for Tel Aviv was postponed for a year and a half, until the legal and political battles subsided. The battles do not end, but the issue may dwindle away because of delay, failure to convene relevant committees, or sometimes the withdrawal of the offending nomination.

The rabbinical court is another institution that the NRP successfully brought under the jurisdiction of the law of the state, thus perpetuating it. In principle, the rabbinical courts have exclusive jurisdiction over all Jewish citizens in the area of personal-status law. While formally separate from the Chief Rabbinate, the chief rabbis serve as presidents of the Supreme Rabbinical Court of Appeals. The chief rabbis must approve all religious judges before their appointment. The Religious Judges Law of 1955 is similar to the Judges Law of 1953, with the exception that the latter sets out the qualifications for secular judges, whereas qualifications for religious judges are set by the Chief Rabbinate. A further difference is that secular judges swear allegiance to the state and its laws, whereas religious judges must swear allegiance to the state only. There are twenty district courts and the Supreme Rabbinical Court of Appeals in Jerusalem. The Israeli Supreme Court, in its capacity as the High Court of Justice, retains the right to determine whether the religious courts have jurisdiction in a given matter, and by precedent it has also intervened when it finds that principles of "natural law" have been violated by the rabbinical courts. For example, the court held in a 1994 case that in divorce, religious court rulings had to be based on the principle of equal rights to joint property, thus requiring them to follow civil law rather than religious law on this matter.

Religion is a potent issue area in Israeli politics. However, the density of action within the area makes it unlikely that groups from outside will successfully penetrate and win influence within it. The political parties have large stakes invested in the system and are committed to compromises developed over the years. Many of these compromises have been enacted into law by the Knesset, which makes it even more difficult to alter past practice. The NRP has had to pay a political price for its nationalizing legislation by sharing power with other religious parties and with secular parties. But this "price" has worked both ways: the secular parties also committed themselves to structures that enhanced the worldview of the religious groups, not to mention their political power and patronage.

11 PUBLIC POLICY, ADMINISTRATION, AND LOCAL GOVERNMENT

IN A HIGHLY CENTRALIZED state, issues of public policy and administration are closely entwined. Both are seen as political resources as well as political opportunity. The balance between group and personal benefit on the one hand, and the public good on the other, is never firmly settled. The gradual but steady transfer of the delivery of social services from political parties, with their particularistic approach, to the universal criteria of a national service conflicted with the desire by some of the parties to enlarge their budgets by adding more members. The civil service was also embroiled in tensions between principles of good government and the tendency of many politicians to see the bureaucracy as an extension of their own political will. The roles of the state comptroller and national commissions of inquiry have improved the image of impartiality of some state authorities. Local government is the public body most closely in touch with citizens and provides many services to them.

Statism

Many of the services in the pre-state era were provided by voluntary organizations; the largest and most resourceful of these groups was the Histadrut. This activity proved important in establishing the Histadrut and its ruling party in a dominant position throughout the pre-state period and the first generation of the independent state. With independence, however, came a wave of nationalization of these services—the ideology was called *statism*, and Ben-Gurion was its major champion. Labor and other parties historically important in delivering these services paid for the transfer of control of these services with decreased patronage and power. In later years, when it became clear that the state would not or could not deliver these services (especially education and welfare), other parties (especially Shas) built a constituency by tapping the public treasury to provide these services again. The irony is that the founding parties refrained from doing so, and their power base weakened accordingly.

The call for statism was taken up by sections of Ben-Gurion's Mapai Party before he left it in 1965, and it was a major plank in the platform of Rafi, the party he founded after leaving Mapai. When most of the members of that party returned to the Labor fold in 1968, Ben-Gurion persisted in rejecting the Labor Party and in maintaining his call for statism. In 1969, after the Rafi list disintegrated, he formed the State List, which even included the idea in its name. When the State List later dissolved and became part of the Likud, the move brought Ben-Gurion's call more forcefully to the right side of the political spectrum. There were two elements to the idea: that "services required by all citizens must be provided by the state,"[1] and that the Labor Party was unable to separate party interests from national interests, which must prevail.

The process of nationalization of services in Israel is a long, unfinished story. Since the transfer has been in stages and is still incomplete, the administration of public services has had to face unique challenges. But as the transfer includes more areas, as when health services or pensions are nationalized, the power of the central government increases. Power is transferred from the service-providers controlled in the past by the political parties to the civil servants who run the ministries, and to the ministers who head them.

This unfinished transfer of service provision was the product of a political system characterized by coalition politics, and it was not hurried along by those whose political power was enhanced because they knew how to manipulate the structural complexities of the system. This closed circle was not easily penetrated; interests, symbols, and careers were all involved. The tension between those who attempted to achieve a more complete transfer and those who supported a partial transfer (or no transfer at all) was a major theme in the country's story. Examination of four areas will indicate the complexities: defense, education, employment, and health services.

Defense

After independence in 1948, there was no question about Israel's need for a single national defense force. Immediately after the state was established, the Haganah (the largest military organization in the Yishuv, controlled by Mapai) became Israel's army; the future of the other military organizations—Irgun, Lehi, and the Palmach—was in doubt.

The Irgun (also known as Etzel) and Lehi were underground organizations that sprang from the Revisionist movement, the right-wing organization that had opposed Ben-Gurion and the Mapai establishment in the pre-state period. The Irgun, headed by Menachem Begin, was the larger and had the support of most Revisionists; when the state was established, the Irgun was dominated by the Herut movement. Lehi was smaller but more extremist in its methods of activity against the British; Yitzhak Shamir was active in its ranks. It had split off from the Irgun in 1940 and was less strongly identified with the Revisionists. The Palmach was identified with the Kibbutz Hameuhad (the kibbutz branch of Ahdut Haavoda) and, to a lesser extent, with Hashomer Hatzair.

Disbanding the Irgun and Lehi can be seen as part of the struggle to ensure the legitimacy of the regime. Neither organization was represented in the provisional government, and thus Mapai had no need to compromise with them. Disbanding the Palmach was more problematic because Mapam, to which the Palmach owed its allegiance, was an integral part of the labor movement and was Mapai's partner in the government when the Palmach command was disbanded. At that time, however, the composition of the coalition was such that Mapam did not have the power of veto, because it could not leave the government and abandon Mapai in a minority position. Nevertheless, disbanding the Palmach formations was postponed until Mapam was in opposition. Disbanding the Palmach did not threaten the organizational infrastructure of either the labor movement or the Histadrut; Mapai thus had the support of the party machinery on this issue. The Histadrut, firmly in Mapai's control, also supported the dissolution of the Palmach, which it had funded, because dissolution brought the economic benefit of moneys released for other activities. Disbanding the Palmach is best considered as the means by which the dominant party prevented other political bodies from retaining their own militias within the newly formed sovereign state.

Education

The nationalization of the education system in 1953 did not create a unified school network. A number of divisions are relevant: (1) the demarcation between predominantly Jewish and Arab schools; (2) the partition between state and independent schools, and (3) the distinction between nonreligious and religious schools.

Schools are not segregated, but because of dwelling patterns and with communal preferences, most Jews go to predominantly Jewish schools and most Arabs go to schools with other Arabs. Arab schools are conducted in Arabic, with a substantial part of the curriculum devoted to learning Hebrew and topics related to Israel and Judaism, but Jewish schools generally have no noticeable Arabic component.

The state system, the largest segment, involves a decreasing percentage of the country's students. An "independent" track was established for haredi students, and the number of these students is growing. The schools in the independent track are connected with Agudat Israel, Degel Hatorah, or Shas. The haredi tracks are truly independent, enjoying both state money and freedom from state supervision. Some have the status of "recognized but not official," others are granted an exemption from supervision. In 2003, 23.6 percent of Jewish elementary schoolchildren were in independent schools compared with 5.7 percent in 1979. In the past, kibbutz movements each retained autonomy over the educational systems of kibbutz schools, but as the pressure grew for their members' children to enter universities, they tended to accept standards used in the general educational system.

When the Arab students are added to the haredi students, we find that half the first-graders of the country in 2004 were entering schools in which Zionist values were either tolerated but not celebrated (the Arab schools) or were rejected (the haredi schools). And over time, the number of these schoolchildren is likely to grow, because these groups have very high birthrates compared to other groups in Israel.

The third division within the school system regards religious education, which may be sponsored by either the state-religious track or one of the independent haredi tracks. Religious schools serve more than a third of the students in the country; more than half the teachers in training colleges in 2004 were in religious-track education, up from a third in 1994.[2] Both tracks receive funds from the state, and the state-religious track is under state supervision. The nonreligious state school share fell from 74.7 percent in 1979 to 57.6 percent in 2003, while that of the religious state schools declined from 20.1 percent to 18.8 percent. In sum, while most Jewish children in Israel attend schools whose curriculum is controlled by the government, a growing number do not.

When Labor controlled the Ministry of Education from 1948 to 1977, it generally had an NRP deputy minister to deal with matters of religious education. When the National Religious Party won control of the Education Ministry in 1977, the institutions of religious education received a serious boost, as they did again when the NRP's Zevulun Orlev headed the ministry in the 1996–1999 period. When Meretz leaders (Shulamit Aloni, Amnon Rubenstein, and Yossi Sarid) served as education ministers sporadically after 1992, they attempted to add secular, universalistic content to the schools' curriculum. In 2001 the Likud's Limor Livnat became education minister, and she attempted to reassert nationalist values in the curriculum.

The labor movement entered the field of education at a relatively late stage in the development of the school system of the pre-state period. It developed a socialist track that existed in competition with the "general" one (identified with the General Zionists) and the religious track. Following the establishment of the state and the advent of massive waves of immigrants from Europe, Asia, and Africa, education became a prime political issue; the socialist track experienced pronounced growth compared with the general track. In 1948–1949 only 29.3 percent of pupils were registered in socialist schools, while 43.8 percent were enrolled in general schools. Three years later, the general schools accounted for only 27.4 percent of all pupils, while the share of the socialist schools had increased to 42.6 percent.[3] The labor schools movement achieved outstanding success in the settlements of the new immigrants, but this was the cause of a bitter struggle with the religious parties, which at one stage even boycotted government meetings because of the dispute.

The transfer of the education system to the hands of the government in 1953 did not generate a coalition crisis because Mapam was then in the opposition, and thus effectively isolated and prevented from allying with possible sympathizers in Mapai. The leaders of Mapai knew that Mapam would be satisfied with a guarantee of educational autonomy for its kibbutzim, and when the support of the religious parties was obtained in return for strengthening the influence of the religious faction (Hapoel Hamizrachi) in the religious state schools, no real opposition remained. Thus, in 1953 the socialist and general tracks were, in effect, merged into the nonreligious state schools controlled by the Ministry of Education, which in turn was controlled by the labor movement. The NRP retained effective control over the national religious schools, and after 1977 the NRP often controlled the Ministry of Education. Of the parties that had been active in education during the pre-state period, only the General Zionists did poorly in the 1953 nationalization of the system. This is especially ironic, since they had strongly supported the idea of statism and the State Education Law.

Employment

Labor exchanges were an employment service or job-placement bureau run by the Labor Ministry. They were set up by law in 1959 after a long history of party competition over the provision of employment.[4] These employment services were politically important in the pre-state period and the first years of nationhood, during which unemployment was widespread; their importance decreased once the assistance ceased to be required by the majority of the population. In the post-independence era, the Labor Exchange Centers are more important in times of mass immigration and economic slowdown.[5]

Cooperation of sorts developed among the parties in the pre-state era. Due to a scarcity of jobs at the time, Ben-Gurion reached an agreement with Jabotinsky and the Revisionists with regard to job allocations in 1935, but Ben-Gurion's premature statism was defeated in a referendum of Histadrut members. Still, other joint ventures were pursued in the labor field, and by the time of statehood, cooperation was widespread. A Labor Exchange Center was established and gradually concentrated on employment, despite frequent squabbling among the groups involved. Because it was already dominant in the Labor Exchange Center and felt that other parties had achieved overrepresentation there, Mapai gave silent consent to the nationalization of the employment service.

Health Services

The total expenditure on health in Israel is large and growing; in 2002 it accounted for 8.8 percent of the GNP, compared with 6.1 percent in 1975.[6] The parallel U.S. figure was 13.9 percent in 2003.[7] Life expectancy in Israel is among the highest in the world, while infant mortality is among the lowest. The ratio of physicians to population, the number of specialists, and the level and quality of resources invested in health services all compare favorably with those prevalent in the Western world.

The National Health Insurance Law, in effect since 1995, set forth the state's responsibility to provide health services for all residents of the country.[8] The law stipulated that a standardized basket of medical services (including hospitalization) would be supplied by one of the four comprehensive health care organizations that had insured most of the population. Every resident would register as a member with one of these organizations, each having equal status. These "sick funds" or health care organizations could not bar applicants on any ground, including age or state of health, and after a year, a person could transfer to a different sick fund. The sick funds were required to supply the services enumerated in the standardized basket, within reasonable time and distance from the insured person's home.

The funding sources would include health insurance premiums paid by each resident, parallel-tax payments by employers and self-employed persons, National Insurance Institute funds, funds from the Ministry of Health budget, and consumer participation payments. Payment of health insurance premiums is compulsory; the National Insurance Institute (parallel to the U.S. Social Security Administration) collects them in the same way it collects national insurance premiums. Employees have the premium deducted by their employer; self-employed persons remit them directly to the Institute.

The rates of health insurance premiums are progressive, with low-income earners paying less and high-income earners paying more. When both spouses are employed, they pay separate health insurance premiums. Employers and self-employed persons pay 3.1 percent of the portion of the salary that is equal to half of the average wage, and 4.8 percent of the rest of the salary, up to a maximum of four times the average wage. Workers who receive retirement pensions or benefits from the National Insurance Institute, or from the Ministries of Defense or Finance, pay health insurance premiums only on their income from work; the pensions and benefits are exempt. Persons receiving old-age pensions pay a minimum of $20 per month.

In 2002 the Histadrut's Kupat Holim sick fund (one of the four sick funds in the country) provided services for 55.6 percent of the citizenry, while the Maccabi fund accounted for 23.5 percent. Before the new law took effect in 1995, the Histadrut's fund had covered about 75 percent of the insured. In 2002 some 31 percent of the country's hospital beds were in government hospitals, 29 percent in private hospitals, and 15 percent in Histadrut hospitals.[9]

The National Health Insurance Law was passed over the initial opposition of the Labor Party. Its convention passed a resolution in January 1994 that would have made Kupat Holim membership conditional on union membership, would have had the Histadrut continue to collect the dues and turn part of them over to the National Insurance Institute to fund health insurance, and would have allowed the Histadrut to keep 0.8 percent of members' salaries for Histadrut activities.[10] But Labor lost on each of these issues.

Before the law was passed, the Histadrut's Kupat Holim played a primary role in the delivery of services, but increasingly it had had to rely on state funds to meet its deficits.[11] Half of the Ministry of Health budget in the past was earmarked for transfer to the sick funds, and other moneys were added indirectly. During Labor governments, ministers of finance were known to provide direct support to the Histadrut's sick fund above the 10 percent of budget received from the Ministry of Health. The Health Ministry opposed these added funds provided by the Finance Ministry because it wished to maintain control over the health field despite its a small budget. In the 1983 and 1987 doctors strikes, similar interdepartmental tensions were evident.[12]

Kupat Holim also competed with other Histadrut functions for budget. By the late 1960s, the proportion of Histadrut dues allocated to the sick fund had increased to almost 60 percent. Another source of income was an employers' contribution paid to the sick fund for their workers. After 1973, this employers' contribution was paid to the National Insurance Institute, which apportioned it among the different sick funds. Since the payment to the Histadrut fund incorporated a contribution to the Histadrut, this arrangement in effect obliged employers to contribute to a trade union.

In the mid-1980s, support from the government treasury to Kupat Holim decreased substantially. Commissions, committees, and experts made suggestions intended to make more rational a system that had both an important social mission and a very heavy political and bureaucratic overlay. The non-Histadrut planners, including experts from the Finance Ministry, attempted to reduce the subsidy by having the Histadrut and its members pay more nearly the real cost of medical care; the politicians and the bureaucrats tried to avoid that. The public was not anxious to pay more, but it was also restive about the delivery of health care.

Before the National Health Insurance Law of 1994, Kupat Holim insured 75 percent of the population and had some 30,000 employees. The prime motivation of many members in remaining in the Histadrut was to benefit from the health services it provided; the Histadrut itself benefited because a fraction of members' dues was used for political and cultural purposes. Proposals to transfer the delivery of health care to the state were opposed, because leaders of the Histadrut did not want to lose control over the many jobs that a complex bureaucracy such as Kupat Holim controlled for the supplying of medicines, linen, food, forms, and other goods needed to run such an operation; most of these services could be provided by firms owned by the Histadrut and by workers who were members of the Histadrut. Not least, it was assumed that the requirement of belonging to the Histadrut's Kupat Holim would ultimately accrue to the ideological and organizational advantage of the Labor Party; so long as membership was to be attained through Histadrut membership, a large bureaucracy could be employed to collect dues and service the clinics, and these workers could be turned into party activists during election periods. The transfer of health services was a major blow to the Histadrut and to the Labor Party; both lost their most important source of funds and patronage.[13]

In the past, the Kupat Holim fund had provided services not only for its members but also for members of the religious parties. In 1979 those affiliated with the NRP accounted for 6.7 percent of the insured and those of Agudat Israel for 1.2 percent. These religious party members received services by virtue of their membership in organizations affiliated with the sick fund, although they themselves are not individual members of the Histadrut. These special relations, which came with an understanding that these religious parties would not compete in Histadrut elections, formed one of the bases of the long-term political cooperation between the religious parties and the labor movement. One of the important reasons for the religious parties' longstanding opposition to the nationalization of the health services was the historic connection these parties had with Kupat Holim. This connection was continued even after the advent of the National Health Insurance Law and the reorganization of the Histadrut following its 1994 elections, adding some 37,000 affiliated workers and their families from the NRP and Agudat Israel workers' organizations to the Histadrut, and assuring that the organization tax of 0.9 percent of their salaries would be paid to the labor federation. The agreement was that the Histadrut would refund to the religious parties more than half of this organization tax.

The Histadrut's Kupat Holim was by far the most important actor in laying the foundation of the health system during the pre-state period. Before the British Mandate at the end of World War I, diseases such as dysentery, malaria, typhus, and trachoma were rampant and health facilities practically nonexistent in the land, then a backward and neglected part of the Ottoman Empire. By 1948, however, when the State of Israel was established, the country's medical infrastructure was already well-developed, immunization was standard procedure, and frameworks for improving environmental conditions were operative. In the early years of the state, the health services had to readdress some of the problems previously overcome in order to cope with the needs of hundreds of thousands of refugees from postwar Europe and various Arab countries.

The Labor Party and the Histadrut had always opposed national health insurance; in the past they had supported proposals for making health insurance compulsory but leaving the provision of services to the existing sick funds. Kupat Holim, Histadrut, and Labor Party leaders appreciated the enormous financial power and patronage opportunities they would lose if sick fund activities were nationalized. Of course, ideological invocations of the virtues of mutual aid, self-help, and worker solidarity were voiced, but it was clear that the sick fund was the labor movement's main source of strength and that its transfer to the state would mean the collapse of the movement's organizational and financial bases. In the past, only parties that did not have their own health schemes—the General Zionists, the Progressives, and Agudat Israel— had supported the introduction of a national health insurance law, a movement that started in the 1950s and culminated in success in 1994.

Attempts at complete nationalization were thwarted regularly. The terms of reference for a governmental commission set up in 1957 called for general health insurance, preserving the multiplicity of sick funds and the autonomous management of the insurees' organizations. The majority report complied; a minority report claimed that the terms of reference were inconsistent with principles of good management and financial efficiency and proposed a unitary structure. As the debate heated up, suggestions were even made by party leaders keen on statism (including Ben-Gurion) that the sick fund and the Histadrut should be separated and the sick fund left on its own.

Much of this debate coincided with the split in Mapai in 1965. After the elections, in which Rafi took 8 percent of the vote (disappointing for it, but heartening for Mapai, headed by Eshkol), another committee was set up to plan for general health insurance "provided by the insurees' sick funds," in the words of the letter of appointment. The committee again split between those who were loyal to the needs of the government and those who felt that the goals of supervision, avoidance of duplication, planning, and compulsory insurance were not attainable by the proposed method. It was a standoff between the professionals and the politicians.

Within the Labor Party the argument centered on the way in which the sick fund's organizational and budgetary independence could be ensured after the enactment of such a law. All factions of the labor movement demanded that funds not operating in the more remote settlements would have to subsidize the provision of health services in those areas; since the Histadrut sick fund was the only organization to do so, this would mean a significant weakening of the smaller sick funds. If such a national health scheme were introduced, the labor movement intended to exploit it for its own ends, namely, to ensure its fund's dominance in the field of health care while ensuring a substantial budget from the national treasury that would both reduce the pressure on the

Histadrut and ensure the sick fund's organizational independence. In the ministerial committee that discussed the issue in 1969, the labor ministers were united in their opposition to the demand made by the NRP and the Independent Liberals to channel the collection of sick fund dues through the National Insurance Institute.

Minister of Labor Yosef Almogi suggested this compromise, by which members' contributions would be paid directly to the sick funds, while employers contributions would be collected by the National Insurance Institute, which would make the allocation to the different funds. The labor movement wanted to be sure that Histadrut members knew their contribution was going to the Histadrut and that it could continue to use the collection offices for patronage; with regard to the employers' contribution, the fund's only concern was to guarantee its income. The sick funds and the Histadrut were prepared to accept a certain degree of state supervision in return for an expansion in the scope of their activities and an increase in their power. In this case, the banner of statism was used as camouflage for trade union and party interests.

In 1973 the government proposed to the Knesset a Medical Insurance Law, which it had developed during the previous two years largely to meet the needs of the Histadrut sick fund and without excessive consultation with the other funds or the Ministry of Health. The proposal was presented a few months before the elections in the hope of impressing the electorate with the legislative activity of the Alignment, although it was uncertain that there was enough time to enact the proposal into law. Items on which the Histadrut sick fund was not prepared to compromise included service provision by the many sick funds, collective membership, and dues collection. No single fund was to be established, although principles for supervision and standardization were proposed. Membership was compulsory, but the Histadrut refused to agree to freedom of choice of sick fund by employees who belonged to organizations (mainly the Histadrut) that had collective affiliation contracts with a sick fund. The proposal to have fees collected by the National Insurance Institute was resoundingly rejected by the Histadrut and its sick fund for fear of losing control of the funds and the patronage of the jobs involved.

The proposed bill included a division of responsibility between the ministries of Health and Labor in providing different elements of the health service. This was crucial, for while the Labor Party never deemed it important enough to control the Health Ministry, it almost always controlled the Labor Ministry, for both practical and ideological reasons. At subsequent stages, the bill was stalled by opposition from those who feared reduction of their influence following the passage of the bill in its proposed form—the smaller sick funds, the Ministry of Health (which basically objected to the role proposed for the Ministry of Labor), and the Histadrut, which feared that the proposed law would lead to an increase in the sick fund's membership and increase its autonomy within the Histadrut.

The ascension to power of a non-Labor government in 1977 raised expectations that legislation would be quickly forthcoming in the health field. But the Begin government soon became deeply involved in negotiating a peace treaty with Egypt and controlling runaway inflation. The Health Ministry went ahead with preparations for national health insurance legislation based on two concepts: organizational unification and administrative regionalization.[14] The plan was to divide the country into regions and "provide health services based on the facilities available in the region—sick funds, public hospitals, institutes, laboratories, etc." No nationalization of health facilities was foreseen; agreements would be arrived at between the Health Ministry and the providers of health services. But most significant, "there [would] be no more membership and no more membership fees, rather residents [would] be eligible to receive all health services by virtue of their being insured by National Insurance." It was not at all surprising that even without seeing the detailed proposal, the Histadrut, its sick fund, and the Labor Party immediately and emphatically rejected the proposal; the legislation was abandoned.

There were many in Labor who were certain that nationalizing the health services would injure the Histadrut in the long run, just as other transfers of services had done in the past. To this day one can hear heated debates in Israel about the disbanding of the Palmach or the nationalization of the education system. Ideologues as well as pragmatists argue that the movement toward statism was one factor that brought about the downfall of the Labor Party in the 1977 elections, and there are indications that a lack of organizational vigor in 1996, after the downsizing of the Histadrut, was instrumental in Netanyahu's victory over Peres. Bases of spiritual and political dominance had been relinquished over the years to anonymous forces opposed to the continued rule of the left.

Another social service of considerable importance has been the Histadrut's pension plans. In addition to providing for pensioners, the funds amassed great sums of money that could be used to finance other Histadrut projects. This ability was severely limited in the mid-1990s when the government agreed to ensure the solvency of these pension funds on condition that the financial activities of these funds be controlled and monitored by the Finance Ministry, thus further limiting the clout of the Histadrut. In sum, the Histadrut, once in many ways a world unto itself in which were concentrated economic, social, and political powers, has been in steady decline. Its many functions, considerable patronage and economic prowess has been severely curtailed by overextension and nationalization of services.

Public Administration

Israel's public administration reflects many elements of the country's political culture. There is a plethora of rules, bureaucrats, and committees; but the political element is never far from the surface, especially if the issue is considered an important one. Lip service is paid to professionalism and nonpartisanship, but these values are likely to weaken the higher up the civil service ladder one climbs. There is a pretense of modern rational structure, and increasingly computerized techniques have been introduced; still, a solid core remains of a more personal and traditional form of dealing with the citizenry by the administration. Outright corruption is relatively rare or is small in scale, but *protektzia*—the use of pull or personal acquaintance to speed up processes or obtain favorable treatment—is rampant.[15]

Israel's administrative culture is composed of four strands. The first is the Middle Eastern style, which is characterized by "deference to authority and status, bargaining skills and displays of bureaucratic officiousness." At the same time, there is the British legacy, which "is a no-nonsense, orderly, condescending, bureaucratic approach, with little room for bargaining, local initiative or disruption." Third is the strand of traditions brought by Jewish immigrants: "Paranoic ghetto attitudes mingle with dynamic, cosmopolitan, liberal entrepreneurship." The fourth strand—the Israeli—reflects the differing experiences of a generational culture. The older ones, "skilled in political infighting and insurgency tactics, affirm their inherent visionary powers, their pragmatic 'feel' of things, and their confidential, in-group decision-making." Their children, more middle-class and likely to be native-born, turn more to models experienced in military service or learned in the university, although improvisation is always a possibility.[16]

Israeli public administration is a direct extension of the pervasiveness of bureaucracy. Bureaucracy is a feature of the modern state everywhere, but in Israel it seems even more prevalent. Part of this impression stems from the fact that such a large portion of the population is employed in jobs related to one bureaucracy or another, and part from the extremely large role of government and its related agencies in the economy and society. This employment pattern fortified the inclinations of the Jews who came to Israel to continue living in urban areas and to find work in commercial or service sectors.

Bureaucracy is important in a modern society because it provides for a division of labor and is immune from reliance on a single individual. As transactions are based on written rules and records, it allows for neutrality and constraint. These positive features also provide the background for bureaucracy's limitations and perversions: too much paperwork, too many authorizations needed, too many organizations involved, too little coordination. The proper functioning of the bureaucracy is as much an art form as any human endeavor; ultimately it depends on the people involved, their motivations, and their attitudes. Faults are often to be found not in the instrument but in the way the instrument is employed.

Bureaucracy is seen as a neutral form that facilitates executing policies. In this theoretical world, politicians *set* policy; the public administration and its civil servants merely *execute* policies. In the real world, however, relations are not nearly that simple. Politicians usually lack expertise in highly complex and technical areas such as welfare delivery, water distribution, or defense allocations, so they turn to senior civil servants for advice and opinion. Civil servants often present to the decision maker a choice between various alternatives, but the structuring of the problem and the implications of the policy are in their hands. Politicians have been known to prefer one policy over another for political reasons; bureaucrats have been known to promote one policy over another because they think that the policy better meets the political goals of the politician. Not least important in this list of circumstances that blur the line between administration and politics is the fact that administrators tend to remain, but politicians rotate out of office when their party loses or they move on to other positions.

These considerations point to two major questions regarding the civil service. The first has to do with the degree to which it is motivated by professional as opposed to political considerations. In other words, to what extent do appointments and promotions result from merit considerations, as opposed to a spoils system in which the victors divide jobs and privileges among their camp followers? The second question has to do with the degree to which the civil service is responsive to public demands and responsible in its actions to the executive, legislature, and ultimately, the voters.

The answers to these questions in Israel are not straightforward.[17] Certainly much lip service is paid to creating a professional, nonpolitical, responsive, and responsible service. And there is evidence that progress has been made, but the evidence is mixed. For example, merit consider-ations are often spoken of, especially at the lower ranks of hierarchies. But as we move up the ladder of power and prestige, the prevalence of extraprofessional considerations grows.

Israel is a small country, and among the few candidates for a senior position, the front-runners are likely to be known. Past performance and the groups with which a candidate is affiliated cannot easily be separated in the minds of an appointments committee. Charges of politicization have frequently been heard from various sides of the political fence.

The dilemma is not an easy one to solve. It is important that years of service in the public administration be rewarded with promotion; on the other hand, politicians in decision-making positions must be able to work with and trust the judgment of senior civil servants. Obviously, this trust will be facilitated by appointing people known to the politicians and who have demonstrated their loyalty. For most of the bureaucrats, pro-fessionals, and clerks in public administration (some 60,000 in 2002, not counting the army, police, and teachers), these considerations are not relevant, but they may be very relevant in determining who will lead their ministry, department, or regional office. The specter of politiciza-tion has grown more acute as each political party accuses the others of indulging in political appointments. For our purposes, there is no better indicator of the problems of public administration than its failure to develop as a neutral, professional arm of government.

It is a rule of thumb that when a civil service is strong, it is a meritocracy; when it is weak, it is not. In Israel, the civil service is not very strong, nor is the system exclusively meritocratic because the political element is never far from the surface in matters of policy, appointment, and execution. So much of foreign and defense policies is traceable to the prime minister and defense minister, and so much of economic and social policy to the finance minister, that seeking an independent and autonomous civil service is futile. The power of the Finance Ministry is evident from the structure of the arrangements: the Civil Service Commission is a department of the Finance Ministry and thus control tends to be centered in the ministry and not at the cabinet level.[18] In 1977 many career bureaucrats made the tran-sition from Labor to Likud without difficulty, but since this was Israel's first transition, it was more of a personal feat than a characteristic of the system. Since then, other transitions have occurred, and it is clear that the rules of a smooth and responsible transition are yet to be written.[19]

The relative weakness of the Israeli civil service is obvious from the compartmentalization that characterizes the system. There is very little real career mobility, although almost everyone is rewarded with occasional promotions within the department, division, or ministry. In the United Kingdom, it is relatively easy to move horizontally within a department; in the United States, it is easy to move vertically from department to department. Both systems provide training for senior civil servants in a variety of tasks and fields. In Israel, neither kind of movement is widespread. Everyone in the system crawls forward together, receiving gradual promotions but rarely breaking the pattern of employment in which he or she began work. The lack of lateral transfer promotes inbreeding, which ultimately works to the detriment of the organizations.

Those individuals in direct contact with the minister—the director-general of the ministry, the minister's secretary, driver, and various aides—are expected to be loyal to the minister, and rules of professional distance are relaxed. These are sanctioned political appointments.[20] The future of these people depends on their ability and perseverance, and on the political fortunes of their minister. Young aides have been known to use such protégé relations to enhance their career mobility. Successful directors-general have been known to use their experience and connections to good political advantage in promoting their careers; two examples are Levi Eshkol and Shimon Peres, both of whom served as director-general of the Defense Ministry before becoming prime minister.

It would be too narrow an understanding to think of the public administration as obediently administering policies made elsewhere. The ministries are the major repositories of knowledge and the major collectors of data regarding the topics under their control. As we have seen, most legislation originates in the ministries. Recommendations may or may not be adopted, but whether they are adopted or not is likely to be a political or budget issue as much as an administrative one.

The role of the minister in the political system is the key to determining how strong the ministry will be. It works the other way as well: top political leaders head the important ministries. A small ministry such as Welfare may become important if the minister holds the balance of power in coalition calculations in the government and Knesset. The major point here is that the public administration is an extension of the political system. The organization of the government is primarily affected by political considerations and not by abstract models of rational public administration.

The fact that the minister's political clout is often a key to the ministry's success gives her or him the potential for prestige within the ministry. On the other hand, since the minister is often an outsider to the subject matter of the ministry and dependent on professionals in the ministry for aid, and since success as minister is partially connected with the cooperation received from his ministry, the minister may instead become a captive of the administration. Then the minister represents not only the ministry's policies but also its interests. He becomes committed to retaining or even enlarging the ministry's budget and areas of activity. Universal rules are the goal, but they can be reached only if they are given political backing. There have been cases of a strong minister, mayor, or director who achieves benefits for employees that are a function of the actor's political strength even while they are counter to stated policy. The center then appears weak because it cannot, or has chosen not to, confront the issue of irregular salaries and benefits.

Decision making in Israel tends to take one of two forms. One is the crisp, often unexpected, decision made by a handful of people that effectively bypasses the public administration. Such decisions reflect the centralized nature of the system and the enormous political power in the hands of a few. The second form is one of organized randomness, with myriad sections and departments within ministries often expressing conflicting points of view, and fights between ministers and ministries regarding policies. In these latter situations, the system is the opposite of hierarchical; it is chaotic. Either no clear policy is articulated because of the conflicting demands, or a series of contradictory rules emerge that tend to defeat the policy purpose of any one group.

If leaders think the matter is acute, the first form of decision making is used; if not, the second. The difference is between issuing clear-cut edicts or allowing a situation to develop haphazardly. Michael Brecher has studied foreign policy decisions in times of crisis, and his figures illustrate the situation in Israel. Of the crucial decisions regarding the Six-Day War in 1967 and the Yom Kippur War in 1973, Brecher documents the concentration of decision-making power in the hands of the prime minister and a small number of handpicked politicians and senior officials. By way of illustration, we may consider the following figures: In the 1967 crisis, Brecher identifies 97 consultative meetings. Of these, 31 involved two participants, 23 had three or four, and 24 had five to ten participants. Of these meetings, 65 were of an ad hoc nature, while only 13 were institutional. Brecher counts 111 meetings in 1973, 42 of them attended by two participants, 8 by three or four, and 25 by five to ten. Of these, 25 were of an ad hoc nature, and 50 were institutional.[21]

There tends to be an inverse relationship between the importance, in terms of national security, of the issue being discussed and the number of people involved in the decision-making process. The Sinai Campaign of 1956, the destruction of Yamit before withdrawing from Sinai in 1982, the decision to withdraw from Lebanon in 2000, and the decision of unilateral separation from the Gaza Strip in 2004 are examples of decisions taken by Ben-Gurion, Begin, Barak, and Sharon, respectively, with minimal if any advance consultation. In each case, the administrators became very active after the decisions had been made. In many other areas, however, the effort that would have to be made to coordinate policy or the political capital that would have to be expended to sort out conflicting interests and goals would be greater than it seems to be worth. Israeli public administration has learned to live with this dual reality of sometimes being ignored in influencing policy and sometimes being frustrated in achieving clear-cut policy.

Planning exists in the system, but it is often irrelevant to the political exigencies in force when projects are actually implemented. Planning demands an assumption of stability regarding the future environment, and that is precisely the characteristic that is lacking in Israel. Parties in power shift, influence within the coalition changes, a new administrator is more important than his predecessor, new interests must be placated—all of these circumstances and others are insidious to the planner. In addition to political surprises, there are other uncertainties that interfere with planning: large-scale immigration, a war, a peace treaty, or an economic crisis can all have devastating effects on plans.

Another problem is bureaucratic conservatism. In-place structures generate interests and jobs and a built-in inertia. Conditions often change more quickly than structures do. For example, national bureaucratic structures planned and implemented the creation of water supplies. When that challenge was successfully met, with the establishment of a national water carrier, distribution of water became the pressing bureaucratic problem, and the old structures persisted even though they were clearly unequipped to handle the new challenge.[22]

Powersharing with Nonelected Authorities

Governance involves powersharing between elected institutions and nonelected authorities.[23] As government has expanded in size and in the scope of its activities, policy decisions have become increasingly more complex, highly specialized, strongly interdependent, and to a large extent, technical in orientation. Correspondingly, the significance of professional, nonelected public officials in the policymaking processes and the extent of their legitimacy have dramatically evolved along with their discretionary power. The rationalization of executive governance—characterized by greater specialization, organizational differentiation, professionalism, and political neutrality as means for enhancing government effectiveness and accountability—has led to the proliferation of nonelected authorities.

Nonelected institutions are increasingly independent within government, but obviously they are not independent of it. Consequently, an inherent tension, occasionally erupting into downright conflict, characterizes the relations between nonelected and elected officials. The very performance of elected political executives, and often their political fortunes, depend to a large extent on decisions made by nonelected authorities.

In most democracies, including Israel, the attorney general and the governor of the Central Bank are key wielders of power. The attorney general has the discretionary authority to define the public interest, to ask for the removal of parliamentary immunity, and to initiate criminal proceedings against elected officials. Central bankers can make or break a presidency or a prime ministership. The role of the state comptroller and the attempt to oversee and occasionally contain executive power are also relevant here.

The Attorney General

The attorney general, who is appointed by the government based on the support of the prime minister and the formal recommendation of the minister of justice, is one of the most senior nonelected officials. Attorneys general play a number of important roles in the government. First, they are public prosecutors, in which capacity they are designated by the state to enforce criminal law, including making appearances in courts in relevant cases. Although in the past the attorney general would personally appear in court, in recent years, due to increasingly heavy workloads, court appearances mostly have been made by their representatives. Second, attorneys general represent the State of Israel in legal suits in all proceedings that are not criminal in nature. In their third significant role, attorneys general provide the government and government agencies with legal counsel and regularly attend government meetings. Next, the attorney general provides professional assistance to the government, particularly to the minister of justice, in preparing legislation to be submitted to the Knesset; in this context, the attorney general assesses how proposed bills cohere with other public laws. Finally, the attorney general is responsible for representing the public interest on a variety of additional subjects arising from the provisions of special legislation.[24]

As the domains of legal counsel have expanded considerably over the years, the attorney general's authority is to a large extent a corollary of evolving legal norms and ethical standards as well as reactions to social and political developments. The range of issues on which attorneys general have provided legal-professional counsel has dramatically expanded, and their role in advising the government has made them even more powerful. In fact, since 1977 attorneys general have been regularly invited to participate in cabinet meetings.

The attorney general is involved with government policy against terrorism and subversive groups; the personal and political status of elected and appointed officials in general, and Knesset members, ministers, and the prime minister in particular, which may determine the survival of government coalitions; and the formation and implementation of public policies on substantive issues such as the privatization of government companies and services, with its inevitable consequences on the redistribution of wealth. The attorney general's decisions have a strong potential for influencing public opinion on all these matters.

The substantial power of the attorney general stems from four principal sources. First, the law explicitly grants him a large degree of authority regarding issues that are deeply entrenched in the essence of the democratic state. Attorneys general play a central role in the democratic process and in fostering a culture of obedience to the law through their responsibility for filing criminal suits.[25] The second source are the legal norms and political practices that secure the attorney general's institutional autonomy and independence from those who appoint him, although in the Bar-On Affair (discussed in greater detail later in this chapter), this principle was violated. These norms and practices include granting the attorney general a lengthened term in office and not replacing him following changes in the governing coalition. Furthermore, to date no attorney general has been dismissed, although Attorney General Gideon Hausner resigned because of profound disagreements with Justice Minister Dov Yosef. Attorney General Yitzhak Zamir was replaced after announcing his intention to retire although he had yet to complete the intricate "Bus Line # 300 Affair," a case that involved the 1984 killing of captured terrorists by the Shin Bet, Israel's Secret Service.

The third source of the attorney general's authority has evolved over the years, deriving from societal values and legalized norms. In Israel as in other Western democracies, the prevalent myth sees the law as completely neutral, a strictly professional apparatus that upholds and promotes objective justice, thus contributing to societal welfare and progress. Indeed, the law is a fundamental component of the rational-legal persuasion that is characteristic of the modern democratic state. This orientation has been strengthened by recommendations from public committees on the status of the attorney general that were adopted by the government, such as the Agranat Commission report in 1962, and on the rulings of the Supreme Court, which are as binding as ordinary laws, as long as the Knesset does not pass contrary legislation.

The fourth major source of the authority and influence of the attorneys general derives from their professional prestige as jurists. Their status is similar to that of Supreme Court justices; indeed, since the early 1960s, the government has embraced the principle that the qualifications of attorneys general should be similar to those required of Supreme Court justices. The position has been regarded as professional and nonpartisan, to be filled by jurists who are presumably devoid of political aspirations. Their authority is boosted by the public expectation that as representatives of the rule of law, attorneys general will oversee the judicious, fair, and accountable work of government. Even former Attorney General Zamir, a proponent of the rule of law in its strict sense, accentuated the obligation of the attorney general to promote the rule of law in its broadest sense. Certainly Zamir was well aware of the difficulties inherent in this approach, for it entails legalism as well as moral judgments.[26]

The transfer of authority from elected officials to the attorney general is broad and relates to three major factors. The first factor is associated with sociocultural developments in Israeli society; the second is specific to the Israeli institutional arrangements concerning the attorney general's roles. The third factor is in many ways related to the first two, but it also stands on its own, embodying the very basic philosophical ambiguities inherent in the concepts "rule of law," "legal interpretation," and "public interest."

With respect to the first factor, the Israeli Supreme Court has been taking an increasingly active role in a variety of highly controversial public concerns. The most obvious reasons for the Court's activism are the consolidation of big government and its regulatory activities, increased professionalization throughout the economy and society, and the disintegration of the political hegemony established by the founding generation, as evidenced in the Likud Party's rise to power in 1977. Other reasons include the erosion of the collectivist ethos, the intensification of social and economic cleavages, and the increase of social rifts due to questions of national identity.[27]

Since elected officials have failed to deal with such politically volatile issues through appropriate public policies and legislation, the Court has increasingly been filling the void, in the process becoming the most experienced and credible branch of government in resolving disputes. Moreover, new justices appointed to the Court have shared a more activist approach to the judicial role in Israeli society. Changes in legal practices and regulations, particularly in the principles governing the right to appear in court, have significantly increased the number of parties eligible to appeal to the Supreme Court and the variety of appeals on which the Court is willing to render judgment. Thus a subsidiary process, rapid and multifaceted in nature, has given the Court a new, central role in a wide range of governance-related issues that it had avoided in the past. Supreme Court justices also have become more extensively involved in public policy and administrative issues, setting criteria that require public authorities to act reasonably, and not, for example, just in good faith. Court justices have also become involved in the appointment procedures of senior civil servants and in social-political policies.[28] Furthermore, Supreme Court justices have begun to exercise judicial oversight in national security issues, ignoring the self-imposed restrictions that the Court willingly adhered to in earlier years. For example, the Court did not hesitate to get involved in questions of military censorship, overruling the censor's exercise of discretion and permitting the publication of criticisms of the Mossad, or to intervene in the case of admitting women to air force training courses, or to decide where the fence separating Israel from the Palestinians should be built, even balancing moral and political issues such as security and excessive encroachment on the rights of Palestinians.

The 1992 Basic Laws on Human Dignity and Liberty and Freedom of Occupation have reinforced these trends, strengthening the authority of the Supreme Court and bringing judicial review to a new stature by authorizing the Supreme Court to exercise judicial oversight over Knesset legislation—a radical departure from previous practice.

As governing authorities have become more exposed to judicial scrutiny, the need for legal advice and representation has increased. Thus the attorney general, the most senior adviser on matters of law and legislation, is asked to advise and provide representation on an ever-increasing variety of topics, while, concurrently, the span of his discretionary authority has expanded. Furthermore, the Supreme Court itself bolstered the attorney general's formal status by conferring unprecedented authority on a nonelected official in two rulings: Supreme Court justices determined that the attorney general was the official interpreter of the law with respect to the government and stipulated that his decision obligates the government as well as other government authorities. Moreover, when attorneys general represent a government authority, they must be faithful to their understanding of the law, even if the government authority has a different interpretation.[29]

The second factor related to the attorney general's increasing authority is that the institutionalization of diverse roles into a single position contributes to role ambiguity and to tensions within the office, impairing its accountability and transparency. For example, when Knesset Member Arye Deri, the leader of Shas at the time, was indicted (see fuller discussion later in this chapter), Attorney General Ben-Yair performed three roles: as the official responsible for handling the prosecution, he filed an indictment against Deri and requested the Knesset to remove Deri's immunity; in his role as the senior legal adviser to the government, he advised Prime Minister Rabin to dismiss Deri because the indictment was about to be filed; and, when Rabin did not heed this legal advice, Ben-Yair refused to represent the prime minister in the Supreme Court, thus putting Rabin in an unfavorable position during the Court's deliberations in September 1993.

The inherent tension among the roles of the attorney general, coupled with the inevitable conceptual vagueness of the concepts "law" and "justice" strongly reinforce the power of this nonelected authority. This is the third factor related to the transfer of power to the attorney general: law and justice are ambiguous concepts with broad implications that change over time and between societies. In its broadest sense, the law guides the attorney general, but the law is amenable to different interpretations influenced by the interpreter's worldview and values, by his or her professional and socioeconomic background and political inclination. As a result, the person who presents his rendering of the law to the authorities, and then guides and represents them in applying it, wields a great deal of discretion that may also be open to various interpretations. Although the attorney general's interpretation is subject to judicial scrutiny by the Supreme Court, in fact the Court rarely intervenes. Similarly, in his capacity as public prosecutor, the attorney general acts to the best of his understanding and interpretation in a system in which interpretation itself is a central and significant component. Moreover, while a private party in need of legal consultation and assistance can turn to any legal advisory body, government authorities and the government itself are limited. Formally, they can obtain legal counsel only from the attorney general, and they must be represented by him. Furthermore, attorneys general are personally obligated to advance the cause of justice in its broadest sense, which involves them in a legal relationship that is distinctly different from the relationship between a private party and a private attorney. Even if attorneys general are committed to advancing the government's interests, their commitment to promoting the rule of law is more encompassing than that of an attorney representing a private client.

This threefold background of the attorney general's authority—as senior legal adviser and representative of the government in an increasingly activist judicial arena, as the holder of multifaceted roles within the system, and as guardian of the very concepts of law and justice—provides the officeholder with an unusual degree of power and a great deal of influence over executive governance in Israel. Indeed, attorneys general have been involved in many significant political events, some of which have shaken the political system, as the following cases exemplify.

The Kastner Affair in the 1950s evolved as a citizen named Malkhiel Gruenvald published a scathing critique of the behavior of Yisrael Kastner, who at the time was spokesman for the Ministry of Supplies and Rationing. Attorney General Chaim Cohen decided to file an indictment against Gruenvald, despite Kastner's objection. Cohen stipulated that if Kastner did not file an indictment to clear his name, Kastner would have to draw personal conclusions and resign. Pursuant to instructions from the attorney general, a criminal investigation was instigated that led to a public scandal over Kastner's role in the Holocaust, as well as that of the Mapai Party's leaders in that era. In the early stages of the trial, Attorney General Cohen conducted the prosecution himself, reasoning that the public prosecutor was incompetent. On June 22, 1955, the judge ruled that Kastner had "sold his soul to the devil" and cleared Gruenvald of most charges.

Despite sharp criticism from influential politicians, including Prime Minister Sharett, regarding the rigid position he had taken as attorney general, Cohen decided to appeal to the Supreme Court. This decision inflamed the public controversy on an issue that the government had no interest in pursuing, and it was reviewed in the government's weekly meeting on June 26, 1955. Two days later, the Knesset debated the affair, sharply criticizing the Ministry of Justice and the attorney general; Cohen's decision to indict Kastner was criticized because it would humiliate the State of Israel. Chaim Ariav of the General Zionist Party, a member of the Knesset and the governing coalition, publicly announced that in light of the attorney general's error, his party would abstain in the Knesset's vote, and, as a result of this abstention, Prime Minister Sharett resigned.[30] Cohen's controversial decision had an extraordinary impact, for it brought back extremely painful memories of the destruction of European Jewry to the public agenda, and it raised critical questions concerning the roles of the Zionist leadership in saving Jews.

Attorney General Cohen interpreted the law quite literally, which not only caused trouble for the political leadership and the government but also influenced the public discourse on one of the pivotal issues of the Jewish Israeli experience. In other cases, an attorney general's decision to let the political process unfold without his intervention had no less of an impact. One of the most tragic and complex examples of this approach was Attorney General Michael Ben-Yair's hands-off prosecution policy regarding political expression by extreme right-wing groups engaged in political protest, leading up to the assassination of Prime Minister Yitzhak Rabin.

Ben-Yair granted extremist groups a great deal of latitude, and his decision, in turn, influenced the temper of the public debate in Israel over the Oslo Accords and the government's policies on political protests. Had indictments been filed against the extremists, the political controversy might have been better managed, although it is also possible that indictments might have exacerbated it. In any case, the attorney general's decision not to file any indictments restricted the ways in which government authorities could react to incitement by extreme groups, leaving the government and its leaders exposed to scathing, at times incendiary, public criticism. Following the assassination of Prime Minister Rabin, the attorney general instituted a much stricter prosecution policy.

The conceptual ambiguity over the interpretation of the "rule of law" is clearly evident in the attorney general's policy of filing indictments against elected officials, including the prime minister. In these cases, the attorney general's decisions have sweeping implications on the political future of elected officials, political parties, and governments. Such was the case when Ben-Yair decided to file an indictment against cabinet minister Arye Deri. Having approved Prime Minster Rabin's decision to include Deri in his government pending Deri's resignation upon formal indictment, the attorney general later changed his decision and demanded that Deri resign earlier. Immediately following his request to the Knesset to revoke Deri's immunity, Ben-Yair asked Rabin to fire Deri so that an indictment could be filed. It was agreed that Deri would not have to resign until the indictment was actually filed. Rabin agreed with the attorney general's interpretation, a decision that led to the collapse of his governing coalition.

Another stirring political case of the attorney general's immense political influence was Elyakim Rubinstein's 1997 decision not to indict Prime Minister Netanyahu in the Bar-On affair. The attorney general is the only official authorized to file an indictment against a prime minister, a decision that is likely to determine the prime minister's political future and possibly affect the entire political system. The Bar-On affair is particularly instructive because the senior staff in the prosecution office was not in complete agreement with the attorney general's decision not to indict Netanyahu,[31] underscoring the fact that legal interpretations tolerate opposing positions.

At the end of 1996, a few months after Netanyahu's election, Attorney General Michael Ben-Yair announced his intention to retire from public life. Prime Minister Netanyahu and Minister of Justice Tzachi Hanegbi were not disappointed by this development, for they were anxious to appoint their "own" attorney general with views closer to their right-wing ideology. From this familiar beginning in governmental transition, the story developed in an ugly fashion, leading to a recommendation by the police that the investigation of the prime minister continue and that others, including the minister of justice, be indicted for suborning justice and for disregarding their oaths of office. In the end, a new attorney general concluded that there was insufficient evidence for the continuation of the investigation or for the indictments, save one. Attorney General Rubinstein wrote in his report:

> Nothing in the history of the State of Israel is similar to this affair in terms of its sensitivity, the ranks of those involved, or the heavy shadow of suspicion that there was a premeditated attempt to threaten the rule of law in a manner well-known in certain countries by appointing an attorney general, the chief of the prosecution system, someone who might be beholden to certain individuals who do not hold the public interest or the rule of law as matters of prime concern. . . . The interweaving of politics and law is a slippery and dangerous area. The use of political power to further personal interests is a slope with disastrous potential.[32]

The story, as determined by the police investigation and other sources, began on December 2, 1996, when Ben-Yair resigned as attorney general after some three years in office. The prime minister and the minister of justice accepted the resignation, which was to go into effect on January 1, 1997. On December 10, 1996, Minister of Justice Hanegbi listed in a speech to the Knesset three criteria for the next attorney general: (1) a strong backbone, integrity, and an upright character; (2) extraordinary legal expertise; and (3) a basic affinity to the ideology of the party that appointed him or her. In the meantime, the search for a successor to Ben-Yair had begun in earnest.

The appointment of Roni Bar-On as attorney general occurred at the weekly cabinet meeting on January 10, 1997. Soon after the meeting began, the prime minister added a "Miscellaneous" item to the agenda—the appointment of the attorney general. Netanyahu announced that he had decided to appoint Roni Bar-On to the office and asked the cabinet's approval. This caused much consternation, since some of the ministers had never heard of the candidate, others had their reservations about him for this position, and none of them had been given a chance to consider the appointment before the surprise announcement at the cabinet meeting. They asked that the matter be deferred until another meeting, but under pressure from Netanyahu and Hanegbi, the cabinet approved the appointment, with one minister voting against it and five others abstaining.

One of the most upsetting aspects of the case was that Minister of Justice Hanegbi misrepresented the reaction of the president of the Supreme Court to the proposal. During the cabinet meeting Hanegbi reported that he had informed Chief Justice Aharon Barak and the outgoing Attorney General Ben-Yair of his intention to recommend Bar-On and that they had supported the appointment.

The appointment caused an uproar: Bar-On was not considered a major figure in the relatively small and tight-knit world of Israeli jurisprudence; what is more, he was an active Likud supporter and a member of the party's Center, one of its decision-making bodies. Petitions were made to the High Court of Justice to have the prime minister and the justice minister explain why they had proposed Bar-On and to have the appointment suspended until the hearing. After intense negotiations between the Court and the prosecution, it was decided that Bar-On would not take on his new job immediately. Bar-On then resigned without ever having actually served as the attorney general, although the cabinet had approved his appointment—he offered the politicians his resignation if they wanted it, and they accepted.

On the evening news program of Channel One on January 22, 1997, Ayala Hason reported the following scoop: the people behind the appointment of Bar-On were David Apple, a wealthy contractor and Likud supporter, and Knesset member Arye Deri of Shas, the ultra-Orthodox party. Deri was on trial for misuse of public funds, but the ten Shas votes were crucial to Prime Minister Netanyahu and his coalition, so Deri had both the motivation and the ability to influence who would be the next attorney general. Deri went so far as to threaten that he and his party would not support the government's agreement with the Palestinians to withdraw from Hebron if Bar-On were not appointed attorney general (hence the nickname the "Hebron-Bar-On affair"). Netanyahu and Hanegbi had been considering Avi-Yitzhak, Deri's chief legal counsel, for the position, but that would not do for Deri because he would thereby lose an attorney familiar with his case, and in the event of a plea-bargain or a later request for pardon, his former lawyer would have to recuse himself from deliberations. According to newspaper reports, Deri made the threat in a meeting with Netanyahu and Yvette Liberman, the general director of the Office of the Prime Minister; evidently, Hanegbi was not aware of the pressure at this stage. Likud Party sources later confirmed that it was Deri, not Hanegbi, who first suggested Bar-On's name.

Claiming to be shocked by the allegations that criminal deeds had been committed, the prime minister called for a speedy and comprehensive police investigation of the matter. Minister of Commerce and Industry Natan Sharansky was quoted as saying that the government would have no moral basis to continue in office if even 10 percent of the allegations against it were substantiated. The police investigation lasted eleven weeks, and fifty witnesses were interrogated. Among them was Prime Minister Netanyahu; it was the first time in Israeli history that a serving prime minister had been interrogated by the police "under warning," meaning that he was suspected of performing criminal acts and that his testimony might be used against him at a later time. According to newspaper reports, Netanyahu told the police about a series of candidates for the job of attorney general. He admitted that he had not known Bar-On personally and that he had relied on the recommendations of others; moreover, he conceded that he knew there were better lawyers than Bar-On but that he was very interested in appointing someone close to his own political point of view. Netanyahu had had his eye on Avi-Yitzhak, but was notified that he was about to be investigated by the State Prosecutor's Office and hence would not be able to serve; it was then that he returned to the idea of appointing Bar-On.

The police report to Attorney General Rubinstein recommended indicting Knesset member Deri of blackmail while using threats, and of indicting Minister of Justice Hanegbi and General Director of the Office of the Prime Minister Liberman on charges of deceit and of disregarding their oaths of office. The police further recommended continuing the investigation of Prime Minister Netanyahu, based on the charges of deceit and disregard of the oath of office, but closing the investigations against Roni Bar-On and David Appel. The State Prosecutor's report concluded that the appointment of Bar-On was the result of a sordid forbidden association between Deri, Appel, and Bar-On. Deri and Appel were under criminal indictment, and Deri had used his considerable political power—as head of a ten-member Knesset delegation that was key to the survival of the coalition—in order to further Bar-On's candidacy to head the office that would play an important role in determining Deri's personal future.

In September 2000, former Prime Minister Netanyahu won a chance for a political comeback when the attorney general decided against prosecuting him on corruption charges. The police had investigated Netanyahu and his wife for conspiring with a contractor in a kickback scheme, illegally keeping gifts given them while in office, and obstructing justice. The police recommended prosecution, as did the state's attorney. However, Attorney General Rubinstein decided not to prosecute due to "difficulties with the evidence."[33]

Appel's name emerged again in the Greek Island affair, which threatened to lead to the indictment of Prime Minister Ariel Sharon in 2004. Appel had attempted to win the Greek government's approval for plans to develop a gambling resort on a Greek island, and to get lands in the vicinity of Lod annexed to the city. Although both efforts failed, Appel was suspected of bribing Sharon by paying Sharon's inexperienced son Gilead more than $3 million as a "marketing adviser" to research the tourism habits of European retirees. Attorney General Menahem Mazoz finally decided against filing an indictment because of insufficient evidence, thereby removing a serious threat to Sharon's continued functioning as prime minister.

Beyond such momentous prosecutorial decisions, the attorney general's extensive involvement in governance is also manifested in the counsel given to elected officials in cases not necessarily related to the law. An obvious example is the recommendation to ministers during government transitions. By law, the outgoing prime minister continues to serve after the elections as long as the newly elected prime minister has not formed a government that has won the confidence of the Knesset. Legally, the outgoing government is considered the government for all intents and purposes, and it possesses the full range of political authority, yet the attorney general advises the outgoing ministers not to make any political appointments or unnecessary policy decisions that might restrict the new government. This practice is not based on law, but it is a generally accepted norm during government transitions.

The attorney general is also involved in civil service appointments. Thus, during the transition period between the Netanyahu and Barak administrations in 1999, Attorney General Rubinstein instructed the legal advisers in government ministries to examine the appointments made or authorized by the government but not yet examined by appointment committees. There are three such committees: the appointment assessment committee, as defined in Chapter 18b of the Government Companies Act; the appointment committee headed by the civil service commissioner; and the advisory committee for senior public officials appointments. The assessments by these various bodies are intended to advise ministers whether candidates are professionally and ethically suitable for their designated positions.

The attorney general's formal authority and influence stem from the general conceptual perspective that in certain types of cases it is best if elected officials do not intervene. When necessary to preserve the rule of law, democratic government must constrain elected officials by the authority of nonelected authorities committed primarily to professional values. As the scope of the attorney general's influence has increased, demands and concrete proposals for larger institutional measures of accountability and transparency have also increased.[34]

The Governor of the Bank of Israel

The dilemma of institutional powersharing with the executive in a democracy is also evident in economic policymaking. Since the establishment of the Israeli state, the pattern of state-led growth and economic policymaking has followed a dynamic driven as much by political expediency as by professional economic considerations. Institutionally, the powerful Ministry of Finance, usually headed by an experienced politician close to the prime minister, has been in charge of fiscal policy, while the authority over monetary policy has been delegated to the Bank of Israel, headed by an appointed, professional economist. Historically, the Ministry of Finance—and its dominant budget office in particular—has had an exceedingly strong influence over the making of economic and social policy.[35] More recently, as monetarism has received much greater emphasis in macroeconomic policymaking, primarily due to its success in controlling inflationary pressures, central banks worldwide have gained considerably more influence, along with the upgrading of their institutional independence.[36] In practice, the Bank of Israel has followed this development, although the 1954 law that established the Bank remains intact.

Consequently, the governor of the Bank of Israel has become one of the most powerful nonelected officials in government. The governor's decisions directly influence the Israeli economy in terms of the rate of growth, the level of unemployment, the level of imports and exports, currency exchange rates, and, above all, the stability of market prices and the level of inflation, which are strongly influenced by decisions on interest rates.

Under institutional arrangements similar to those in most Western democracies, the governor can use his discretion in the many areas of the Bank's jurisdiction. The governor's formal authority is specified in the Bank of Israel Law of 1954, passed by the Knesset during the Moshe Sharett government. Clause 3 defines the Bank's role as "The management, organization and supervision of the currency system, as well as supervision of the credit and banking system in Israel, in accordance with the economic policy of the government of Israel and the instructions of the Bank of Israel Act. This in order to promote the value of the Israeli currency, using monetary measures, and to reach a high level of production, employment, national income and capital investments in Israel." Clause 9 states that the president, upon the recommendation of the government, is to appoint the governor. To ensure the governor's independence from the elected politicians, a term of five years was decided upon; the appointment can be renewed only once. Clause 15 provides for the removal of the governor in rare cases, such as major differences on policy between the governor and the government, or if the governor engages in behavior unbefitting the position or is incapable of fulfilling his responsibilities.

The formal authority granted the governor by law is supplemented by informal sources of authority. First, the governor is expected to be an eminent professional economist. Second, since the governor is not a political actor, his exercise of discretion is to be matter-of-fact, professional, and neutral, with no political or populist short-term motivation. Third, as Israel's representative in international economic organizations such as the International Monetary Fund and the World Bank, the governor is a member of an international economic elite. Fourth, as a member of the Israeli and international communities of academic economists, his decisions are likely to be congruent with mainstream paradigms.

The institutional independence of the Bank of Israel is essential to achieve its missions, for it enables the governor to ascertain and project the monetary stability of the economy and to reach long-range objectives that are likely to conflict with elected officials' short-term interests. The inevitable problem of dynamic inconsistency reinforces the emphasis in macroeconomic policy on passing laws and regulations to constrain the short-term goals of elected officials from interference with optimal long-term plans.[37] In other words, were it not for the institutional independence of the central bank and discretionary power of the governor, monetary policy would be likely to favor short-term political rather than long-term economic considerations.

Historically, despite the institutional independence of the Bank of Israel, its governors have been unsuccessful in influencing—and at times they have even cooperated with—populist elected officials.[38] One striking example was the full cooperation of Governor Moshe Mandelbaum with Finance Minister Yoram Aridor's populist policies, which led to hyperinflation in 1982–1983. Since the mid-1980s, and to a large extent in response to that economic crisis, governors have become considerably more assertive. Their power stems from four major sources: ideological, professional, the blurring of the roles of the governor, and political.

Economic policy is based on ethical assumptions and socioeconomic viewpoints. As in all social sciences, schools of thought in economics are contradictory and promote different socioeconomic objectives.[39] Therefore, governors may espouse a particular socioeconomic philosophy while elected officials support a different one. There are many examples of this discrepancy, none more striking than the one that emerged during the 1992–1995 Rabin administration, in the open friction between Finance Minister Avraham Shochat and Governor Yaakov Frenkel of the Bank of Israel. (Shochat was reappointed finance minister in 1999 by Prime Minister Barak, shortly before Frenkel's decision to retire from his second-term appointment.) As a practitioner of the liberal classic monetarist persuasion, Governor Frenkel advocated a very restrained monetary policy despite the short-term risks of recession and higher unemployment. By contrast, Finance Minister Shochat, in consultation with his economic advisers, espoused the neo-Keynesian approach: immediate expansion of economic activity to be triggered by lowering interest rates, with the emphasis placed on increasing employment even at the risk of a higher budget deficit. Both strategies were legitimate, but the two leaders' philosophical differences led to a ceaseless confrontation between the Ministry of Finance and its minister and the Bank of Israel and its governor, limiting the government's capacity to carry out an integrated economic policy.

The existence of different macroeconomic approaches enables the governor to maintain an interest rate policy that may contradict the economic policy preferred by the government. Furthermore, opinions also differ on what methods should be used to meet specific economic objectives and on the interpretation of relevant economic information, especially in the realm of forecasts and their implications for policy. A striking example of such divergence occurred during the economic stabilization program of 1985, when the governor intervened in setting the exchange rate, while the government decided to freeze the rate. Apparently, the governor was motivated by personal umbrage because he had not been involved in the formation of the stabilization program. Officially, his position was presented as based on professional grounds; however, he had no faith in the merits of the stabilization program.[40] Eventually, Prime Minister Peres stepped in and persuaded the governor to alter the bank's management of foreign currency to better suit the government's goals.

The governor's influence on economic policymaking is also manifested in other, more subtle ways related to his official roles. He is the government's economic adviser and also the sole authority in determining interest rates and regulating foreign currency. In many other democracies, by contrast, it is regarded as inappropriate to have these roles performed by the governor; instead, a board or a monetary council makes decisions collectively on monetary policy, thus enhancing both institutional and personal accountability. In Israel, the most problematic situations occur when the governor supports setting a particular inflationary target or exchange rate that differs from those preferred by the government. In these situations, he may use his formal advisory role, as well as media and political connections, to influence government decisions. In the bargaining process thus created, the governor can use his authority as economic adviser to make particular proposals to the government; in exchange for acceptance of these proposals, he may use his authority at the Bank to accommodate a request by the government.

This was the case in June 1997, when Bank Governor Frenkel proposed a change in the range of the "diagonal band" (the formula for adjusting the exchange rate), which would cause an increase in the range of the Israeli shekel's appreciation. Although exchange rate policy was not within the jurisdiction of the Bank, the government decided to accept the governor's proposal, and the interest rate was reduced that same day by 1.2 percent. Although the governor publicly claimed that he had not lobbied ministers on behalf of his proposal, the fact that he agreed to change the interest rate made his influence felt. Significantly, the governor's proposal contradicted the policy advocated by Finance Minister Dan Meridor. Prime Minister Netanyahu supported the governor's proposal and not the policy of his finance minister, and seized upon the change of policy as an opportunity to bring about the resignation of the finance minister who had been forced on him by the Likud's party leadership.[41] The governor's power is capable of influencing government decisions and, due to the multiplicity of his roles, may become either intentionally or inadvertently involved in partisan and personal conflicts.

The governor of the Bank of Israel is also a political actor intent on promoting certain economic objectives. Some governors have refrained from becoming actively involved in the political process, while others have clearly had political ambitions; most wish to gain professional prestige among their international peers. Governors have been influenced by various reference groups, including the governors of central banks in other industrialized countries, senior economists involved in international finance and banking, and top officials in the International Monetary Fund and the World Bank. Oftentimes, these top officials endorse the Israeli governors' policies, which in turn strengthens their professional standing and legitimizes their policies.

The quality of the personal relationships among the governor, the prime minister, and the finance minister is a significant factor in policy-making. In some governments, the governor is closer to the finance minister; in others he has a closer relationship to the prime minister. Arnon Gafni, who was especially close to Finance Minister Yehoshua Rabinowitz, served as director-general of the ministry until, with Rabinowitz's strong endorsement, Gafni was appointed governor. Governor Michael Bruno, on the other hand, had enjoyed a close personal relationship with Prime Minister Shimon Peres before Bruno was appointed to the position. Sometimes the governor develops a relationship with government ministers or with the prime minister based on similar philosophies or political ideas. Such a relationship evolved between Prime Minister Netanyahu and Governor Yaakov Frenkel: the governor earned the prime minister's trust, and Netanyahu even considered appointing Frenkel to be his finance minister, an unprecedented move that would have been detrimental to the credibility of the central bank. As monetary policy has become most consequential in macroeconomic policymaking, the governor has become one of the most powerful nonelected officials in government.

The State Comptroller

The formal and informal status of the state comptroller differs from that of the attorney general or the governor of the Bank of Israel. In contrast to the governor or the attorney general, the state comptroller is directly accountable to the Knesset and is regarded as serving a watchdog function for it. The institutional and political importance of this nonelected authority has increased over the years, primarily in reaction to the great expansion of executive governance. The state comptroller is neither a policy expert nor an executive authority, but he has a great deal of institutional power and public support that can be used to affect governance and politics. Eliezer Goldberg, a retired Supreme Court justice, was selected by the Knesset to be state comptroller in 1998 for a seven-year term.

At first glance, the state comptroller could be regarded as an institution of the legislative branch. The restraints and sanctions that the comptroller's office can place on government activities might be seen as part of a system of checks and balances. Such a system of accountability exists in other parliamentary democracies, in which executive authority functions by virtue of having the confidence of the legislature and is subject to its confidence. In Israel, however, the Knesset usually does not initiate or formulate public policies. Therefore, the role of the state comptroller cannot be understood as an independent authority in a system of separate institutions. Instead, the state comptroller evolved as a hybrid institution: by law, the institution is subject to the Knesset's authority, but in practice it operates within the boundaries of executive authority.

The power of the state comptroller derives from a Basic Law that establishes the institution's status and discretionary authority for overseeing and evaluating all government activities. He prepares annual and special reports that are transmitted to the reviewed offices, to the Knesset, to the official responsible for implementing the recommendations on behalf of the government, and often to the media. Section 2 of the Basic Law places the obligation of scrutiny on each government authority and on each party the Knesset deems subject to oversight; the section also stipulates that the state comptroller may investigate questions regarding "legality, integrity, proper management, efficiency and economy" of the parties under review. Section 10 adds even more extensive powers to the state comptroller, who is authorized to investigate "any matter that he deems necessary." The law specifies that the comptroller has the authority to "demand any document needed for the investigation from any party under review at any time." If a criminal deed is suspected, the state comptroller is to submit the report to the attorney general, who is to inform the comptroller within six months of the measures taken in light of the findings. The state comptroller is also authorized to petition the Knesset State Oversight Committee to appoint a commission of inquiry, and he is obligated to submit an opinion on any matter if a government institution or the Knesset requests it. For example, the state comptroller played an important role in establishing the Bejski Commission of Inquiry regarding the commercial banks shares crisis in the 1980s.

Since 1971, the state comptroller performs also as ombudsman, reviewing complaints regarding the deeds and misdeeds of public authorities that have been sent directly to the public complaints commission by the public at large. The law grants the state comptroller extensive discretionary authority, but the power of the office derives from other sources as well.

First, the state comptroller's authority stems from the same developments in Israeli society that have brought extensive power to the attorney general: the strengthening and expansion of the power of the courts in arbitrating public policy conflicts that do not find resolution in the government or in the Knesset. Moreover, the state comptroller is actively involved in personal conflicts between central players in the political system, which are due to the upsurge in social polarization, as well as to changes in the rules of the political game. The comptroller is increasingly asked to examine and give his opinion on matters related to the political futures of senior government officials. An example of this role was State Comptroller Miriam Ben-Porat's involvement in the exchange of accusations between Police Commissioner Yaakov Turner and Interior Security Minister Moshe Shahal in 1993. When Shahal claimed that Turner had become involved in political negotiations before his discharge from the position, Turner petitioned for the state comptroller's professional opinion of what had transpired between him and Shahal, thus demonstrating the considerable influence of such reports and their impact on the reputations of elected and nonelected public officials. Turner, who felt adversely affected by the report, then petitioned the Supreme Court, claiming that the state comptroller had deleteriously affected his right to plea and that his reputation was severely damaged. The Supreme Court unanimously accepted this petition (4914/94).

State Comptroller Eliezer Goldberg released a report that examined the conduct of Ehud Barak during a military accident in November 1992 at the Ze'elim Training Camp when Barak was chief of staff. Investigated while Barak was campaigning for prime minister in 1999, this case involved allegations that Barak had left the scene of the accident without attending to wounded soldiers, a charge that was seen as a major obstacle to his election bid. Barak himself asked that the investigation be expedited so that suspicions against him could be cleared up; the report was released weeks before the elections of 1999.[42]

The state comptroller, unlike the attorney general and the governor of the Bank of Israel, enjoys the "power of the weak," benefiting from extensive public support in comparison to other government institutions. He also enjoys broad freedom regarding topics to be investigated and the methods to be used. Although not subject to laws of evidence or legal practice, the state comptroller has adopted the legal rhetoric and semilegal methods that give him the professional validation and prestige needed when involved in legal matters.[43]

Another source of power is the publication of the reports of the state comptroller in the mass media, which have shown great interest in them for three main reasons. First, the media consider the reports an important source for criticizing the government, which is one of the media's principal roles. Second, the comptroller's reports enable the media to report information on topics that are of considerable public interest. Last, the reports are perceived as credible due to the institutional and professional prestige that the comptroller projects.

The media coverage provides the comptroller with a great source of power, especially at election time. An instructive example is the report on the Ze'elim Bet Affair released in 1999. Had the state comptroller determined that Barak had not functioned properly as chief of staff, this judgment might have been detrimental to his election campaign. In another case, about a month and a half before the 1992 elections, the state comptroller publicized a particularly critical report on wrongdoing by government ministers, including reckless spending and improper management of their ministries, especially the Ministry of Housing. As a result, government corruption became a central theme in Labor's campaign against the Likud. Labor used this report in planning its strategic campaign,[44] although there is conflicting evidence about whether government corruption was a significant factor in voters' decisions in the 1992 elections.[45]

The institutional framework provides the state comptroller with extensive discretionary authority regarding the subjects of investigation, enabling him to play an important role in shaping the public agenda. Thus in August 1999, a special report was published regarding preparations of government ministries for the "Y2K bug." The comptroller determined that ministries were not properly prepared for the problems anticipated, and the report's findings were given particular attention in the media. Still, the report's reverberations could also be attributed to the fact that the public was already preoccupied with this topic.

Like the attorney general and the governor, the official who holds this office draws an additional source of power from the lack of conceptual-theoretical clarity as to the quality of the state comptroller's work, its standards and methods. A clear example is the term *integrity.*

The comptroller must assess, methodically and professionally, whether "integrity" inheres in the decisions and activities of various government authorities. But there is no precise definition of integrity in either a cultural or professional sense. In many cases, the comptroller's subjective ethical outlook influences a particular interpretation, and at times a new interpretation is created. In these cases, the comptroller shapes new norms, subject to his discretion and professional experience, and relying on the support of the media and the public. A striking political example is Ben-Porat's decision to publicize the names of campaign contributors who made contributions exceeding a certain amount, even though the contributions were permitted by law. In this way, the state comptroller brought the issue of campaign funding to the public agenda and helped in shaping a new norm of conduct.[46] Similarly, the state comptroller played an active role in addressing the issue of political appointments to senior positions in the public service and in government-owned companies; following the 1987 report, the issue was placed on the public agenda. As a consequence, three government committees were established to examine the credentials of designated appointees, and the attorney general took an active role in overseeing the appointment processes.

In sum, the state comptroller has considerable authority to oversee a broad range of subjects and a variety of public organizations. He enjoys strong public support, and his reports receive extensive media coverage. At the same time, the centralized decision-making processes in the state comptroller's office, the lack of clear conceptual and methodological guidelines for oversight activities, and the secretive deliberations within the office have been causes of increasing concern.

Oversight of the Public Service

Nonelected institutions have become an integral component of executive governance in Israel. Their strong influence on public policy and democratic performance is an indication of a transition to the greater professionalization, specialization, and centralization characteristic of the rational-bureaucratic paradigm. Furthermore, the more frequent breakdowns of governing coalitions, as discussed in the next chapter, have created even more opportunities for nonelected officials to influence public policies. At the same time, the concentration of power within nonelected institutions, coupled with the lack of institutionalized norms requiring greater measures of transparency and accountability to the public and the Knesset strongly reinforce the centralization of executive governance and contribute to the public's feelings of ambivalence toward executive power.

Oversight of the activities of the public service is highly developed. The state comptroller regularly probes into the practices and policies of ministries and other organizations that receive state funds. Reports tend to be professional and unbiased. Serious failings are uncovered in each report, and some shortcomings are found to recur year after year. There must be a formal, ministerial response to the report, but that does not mean that the problems are fixed. The very act of revealing is important, but it is a giant step from controlling.

Another institution that has achieved public acceptance is the commission for citizens' complaints, or the ombudsman. In 2002 almost 6,129 complaints were received, and in 35.7 percent of the cases completed, the ombudsman found that the complaint was justified.[47] This was about the same rate as in 1980. In the mid-1970s, the percentage of complaints justified had been almost 50 percent of those decided.[48]

Israel's public administration, like many of the country's other institutions, has many rules that reflect the lawmakers' intention that it be run in a modern, apolitical, and detached fashion. Unfortunately, rules are not enough to determine the outcome. The human element—the kinds of people attracted to the civil service, their motivations and professional competence, the satisfaction they have in their jobs—influences the way in which the administration operates. Add to this the political dimension, which always must be taken into account in Israel, and the resulting picture is one of an administration that does not always live up to the lawmakers' original intention.

Commissions of Inquiry

In Israel's charged political atmosphere, a detached appraisal of a situation is hard to achieve. In 1968 the Knesset passed the Commissions of Inquiry bill, which allows the government to decide to establish such commissions on vital public matters. The law also empowers the president of the Supreme Court to appoint the members of the commission—usually there are two members and the commission's chair, who must be either a Supreme Court or district court judge.[49]

The commission decides on its agenda, its procedure, the list of witnesses to appear and the material to subpoena, and it has the power to ensure that these witnesses and evidence be brought before it. If a person might be damaged by the commission's findings, that person must be notified by the commission of that possibility, and then he has the right to be represented by counsel, to interrogate witnesses, and to bring additional evidence. In principle, the proceedings are public, but sensitive security, foreign policy, or economic matters may be discussed behind closed doors.

The end result of the commission's deliberation is a report to the government, reviewing its findings and making recommendations. Unless sensitive security matters are involved, the report is to be public, although the government may also decide not to publish part or all of it. The government is not obliged to accept the recommendations of the commission, but it has always done so in regard to disciplining public servants either by removing them from office or by limiting the responsibilities they can bear in the future.

Between 1969 and 2003 fifteen national commissions of inquiry have been established. Their topics have included such varied topics as the investigation of the fire in the al-Aksa Mosque in Jerusalem (1969); corrupt practices in the national football (soccer) league (1971); the management of the oil fields in Sinai (1971); conditions in the prison system (1979); the 1933 murder of Chaim Arlozoroff (1982); the health system (1991); the massacre of dozens of Arabs at the Cave of Mahpelah in Hebron (1994); the disappearance of Yemenite babies in the period following independence (1995); the assassination of Yitzhak Rabin (1995); and the safety of building construction following the collapse of a wedding hall in Jerusalem (2001).

Five other commissions have been especially important to the country's political history:

1. The Agranat Commission, established in 1973, was charged with examining the preparedness of the army and the country prior to the surprise attack of Yom Kippur. This commission, chaired by the president of the Supreme Court, had four other members, including two former chiefs of staff, and it held only secret sessions. Its report recommended relieving Chief of Staff David "Dado" Elazar, the head of the southern command, and the chief of intelligence, of their commands. It did not place personal responsibility on Prime Minister Golda Meir or Defense Minister Moshe Dayan.

2. The Kahan Commission of 1982 investigated the carnage at the Palestinian refugee camps of Sabra and Shatilla during the Lebanese war of that year. The slaughter was carried out by elements of the Christian Falangists, but the commission determined that Minister

of Defense Ariel Sharon, Chief of Staff Raful Eitan, and two other generals were indirectly responsible for the mass murder and that they should be relieved of their command positions.

3. The Bejsky Commission of 1985 was established after the publication of the report of the state comptroller regarding the bank-shares collapse of 1983. The report concluded that Finance Ministers Yigael Horowitz and Yoram Aridor, the governor of the Bank of Israel, and the directors of the four largest banks bore personal responsibility for the collapse of the shares. The governor of the Bank was removed from office; the bank managers were ultimately tried and found guilty. The politicians were untouched.

4. The Landau Commission of 1987 dealt with the methods of investigation used against terrorists by the Shin Bet, Israel's internal security service. The hearings were held behind closed doors, and the most often cited of its public findings was that it was permissible for the Shin Bet to use "mild physical force" on suspects, and especially nonviolent psychological pressure. The commission recommended that the Shin Bet and its activities be more carefully supervised by authorities outside of the service because of the instances of perjury in court by service members when interrogated about the methods used.

5. The Or Commission report dealt with the deadly confrontation between Israeli Arabs and the police in October 2000, in which thirteen Arabs were gunned down. The commission concluded that the government and the police had failed in their handling of the crisis. Prime Minister Barak was criticized, and it was recommended that Police Minister Shlomo Ben-Ami not be permitted to hold that position in the future, that some police officers be removed from the force, and that others be prevented from serving in leadership positions in the police in the future. It also determined that Arab leaders, including Knesset members, had incited violence, but since they had no operational responsibility, no sanctions were recommended.

Commissions of inquiry enjoy a high degree of prestige in the system, and their findings are generally viewed as impartial. What is striking in these cases is how frequently the political leaders are left unscathed while harsh punishment is meted out to persons acting at the operational level. Yet the commissions' recommendations are taken seriously:

when Netanyahu was putting together his government in 1996, it was clear that both Sharon and Eitan would be in it but that neither would be defense minister because of the Kahan Commission report. In the end, Sharon became minister of national resources and Eitan was made minister of agriculture and the environment. When Sharon was elected prime minister in 2001, he refrained from taking for himself the defense minister's portfolio even though many other prime ministers had simultaneously served in that capacity.

In addition to the national commissions of inquiry, the government and the Knesset both have rules for setting up committees of inquiry made up of ministers and Knesset members, respectively. These committees have lesser powers for forcing witnesses to appear and to present documents and other material upon demand. They are generally less widely respected because they are peopled by sitting politicians, whereas the national commissions of inquiry are appointed by the Supreme Court president and so are presumed to have no political stake in their findings.

Local Government

Local government and the quality of the services it provides affect every citizen directly. In Israel, local government is highly dependent on the national government ministries, but it must be considered as a component of public administration. Local government is important because it pioneered the direct-election method of selecting the mayor and because it has become a major source of recruitment of young and promising leaders. Although the national government is dominant, local government provides services, and the local government budget is a vehicle for redistribution among communities.[50]

The municipal elections of November 1978 were the first to be held using two separate systems: direct election of the mayor and proportional election of the council. Until then, the proportional system had been used exclusively, and the mayor was elected by the council. Under that system, the selection of the mayor had become political, influenced by coalition maneuvering within the council. More than that, it was not unknown for national parties to take an interest in the selection of mayors; parties sometimes used coalition negotiations, especially in the larger cities, to achieve added leverage in the national negotiations for the composition of the coalition.

In addition to being a pawn in national negotiations, local policy sometimes involves acts that may be interpreted as promoting a politician's status. The exploitation of a political situation to further personal goals is not unknown in politics; in Israel it has a special name, Kalanterism, which is derived from a municipal crisis that occurred when a majority of the Jerusalem city council decided to remove Mapai Mayor Gershon Agron from the mayor's seat in August 1956. At that time mayors were elected by the city council in much the same way that prime ministers were elected by the Knesset. The religious parties were displeased by Mayor Agron's support for establishing an Institute of Archeology and attached chapel affiliated with the Reform movement in Jerusalem. The opposition General Zionists denounced the economic policies of Agron's administration, but Rahamim Kalanter, a member of Hapoel Hamizrachi, defected from the anti-Agron group, voted for Agron, and was subsequently appointed deputy mayor in charge of religious affairs and responsible for the sanitation department. Thus, Kalanter's defection, which was attacked by his political opponents (and former allies) as treason and defended by his new allies as civic-minded behavior, enabled him to improve his immediate political fortunes and to become immortalized in Israel's political vocabulary.

Political clashes between the council and the mayor occurred in about 10 percent of the cases. In the period between 1950 and 1973, the mayor was switched in midterm fifty-three times during the five election cycles in the 98 Jewish municipalities.[51] Usually these crises ended with the formation of a new coalition with a different allocation of responsibility, patronage, and offices.

A new law regulating municipal elections was passed in 1976 and is still in effect. The mayor is now elected by direct vote, the winner being the candidate who receives the most votes, providing that he wins at least 40 percent. If no candidate receives 40 percent of the vote, a second round is held two weeks later, in which the two biggest vote-getters of the first round compete with each other.[52] In the 2003 municipal elections, about a quarter of the 156 mayoral contests were decided by a second round. The council is still elected using proportional representation and a fixed list; the minimum required for representation is 0.75 percent.

This law reflected the growing popular support for electoral reform before the elections to the Knesset of 1977, and it would ultimately serve as a precursor to the direct election of the prime minister twenty years later. Unfortunately, the structure invites political clashes between the popularly elected mayor and the municipal party activists on the council. Even though the mayor is directly elected and cannot be replaced, council members have many opportunities to hinder the efficient administration of local affairs if the mayor does not have majority support in the council. This effect at the local level was another precursor, this time of the failure of the national system of direct election of the prime minister: it is no easier to form a ruling coalition, nor can it be shown that coalition deals made are more benign.[53] Since the Interior Ministry is ultimately responsible for the smooth functioning of local administration, appeals are made to authorities in the central government to disband the council in extreme cases.

Until its ascent to national power in 1977, the major political base of the parties of the Likud was in local government. The General Zionists (later the Liberal Party) controlled major cities such as Tel Aviv, Ramat Gan, and Netanya, while Haifa, Holon, and Bat Yam were long considered safely in the Alignment camp. In 1959, however, the Mapai candidate became the Tel Aviv mayor, and the party held the post until 1973. Competitiveness has become characteristic of local elections, especially since the advent of local lists, which have often shifted the distribution of the vote between the major parties within a locality.[54] The 1989 and 1993 municipal elections witnessed a weakening of the power of the Labor Party in an arena that it had long dominated. In 1989, in cities such as Holon, Beersheva, and Petach Tikva, Labor mayors were defeated, and even in Haifa, long a bastion of the Labor Party, the Likud candidate came very close to unseating his Labor Party opponent. The relative success of religious parties among Jewish voters (and of fundamentalist Islamic parties among the Arabs) prevented the conclusion that these municipal elections represented a clear Likud victory, but it was clear that they had presented Labor with a resounding political defeat.

The change in the local electoral system captured the spirit of a process that was developing and helped perpetuate it. At the same time, young and ambitious politicians, especially from the development towns, were emerging in local politics and using this exposure as a base to enter national politics. The young generation of Sephardi Knesset members, especially in the Likud, is the best example: David Levy of Beit Shean, Maxim Levy of Lod, Meir Sheetrit of Yavne, Moshe Katzav of Kiryat Malachi, and David Magen of Kiryat Gat. These politicians have counterparts in Labor, but those in Labor have not reached the levels of visibility and power enjoyed by those in the Likud. Part of the explanation is that Labor has a larger reservoir from which to draw, but there is also a feeling that the emerging Likud leaders are more "authentic" because they have been active and successful in electoral politics at the local level for years, whereas many of their opposite numbers in Labor were drafted as pseudorepresentatives without the same roots in local politics. Two Sephardi Labor leaders who were former mayors did succeed: Amir Peretz of Shderot became a Knesset member and head of the Histadrut, having followed Chaim Ramon in the breakaway group in 1994 and then rejoining Labor in 2004; another was Eli Dayan of Ashkelon, whose political career did not develop on the national scene as did those of some of his Likud colleagues. There was no clear evidence, however, that their place on the list improved Labor's success among Sephardim.[55]

The pioneering aspect of electoral reform and the generating of political leadership notwithstanding, the proper perspective for understanding Israeli local government is its extreme dependence on the center. The legacy of Ottoman rule, the British Mandate, and Yishuv politics created a heavy bias toward politics from the capital. The politics of independent Israel reinforced this tradition, and the center retains a vital role in the budgeting, planning, and development of local affairs.

It is not that local authorities are unimportant, but that government ministries are so dominant in determining what goes on at the local level. Past practices of overt favoritism and withholding of funding have largely disappeared as the system has become more rationalized and bureaucratized. But the political element has not been eradicated: local governments succeed when they are adept at the political tasks of bargaining and applying political leverage. For it is the Ministry of the Interior (which is in charge of local authorities) and the Ministry of Finance (which releases the money) that must be penetrated if a municipality or local council is to enjoy a budget for developing beyond the minimum required by law and regulation.

The most important actor in determining local government affairs, and the clearest indication of the retention of the forms of the British Mandate, is the district field officer. Appointed by the Interior Ministry, he has wide-ranging discretionary power regarding local governments, up to and including dismissal of the elected councilors and the appointment of administrators to run the affairs of the local authority. This position is in the tradition of direct rule as practiced in British colonies; that the Israeli system carried over this tradition seemed natural given the pressing problems of the independence period, but it has become an important instrument of central control over local affairs and a symbol of the dominant status of the central government and its Interior Ministry.

The bargaining that can be entered into between the local and central governments concerns the size of budget, the programs to be supported, and the timing of program execution. The services provided by the local government are varied, and the forms of payment are complex. What determines the success of the local authority—especially the mayor—is access to and influence with bureaucrats, ministers, and party politicians active in the decision-making process regarding local affairs. When it was permitted for mayors also to be Knesset members, special leverage was possible; perhaps these Knesset members were also mayors because of their political traits. Now that Knesset members are not allowed to have another job, however, this advantage has disappeared. Going beyond the authorized plans demands special approval, which cannot be divorced from the political process.

The functions of local government, including education and health services, are closely monitored and influenced by national rules. The budget and the number of approved job slots are determined by the size of the community and its past activities. Education is a good example of the relation between central and local governments: it is the biggest item for most local authorities, yet most of the important decisions regarding education come from Jerusalem. Teachers are hired, trained, and licensed by national supervisors, and although they are paid by the municipal authority, the budget funding to pay them comes from the center. Teachers throughout the country are paid according to the same contract. Up to a quarter of the curriculum is left to local discretion on the part of parents, but since most communities do not take advantage of this opportunity, curriculum is mostly dictated by the Ministry of Education. The local government is left with the superintendence of buildings (which must meet nationally dictated standards), the administration of the payroll, and staffing tasks such as hiring guards and nurses for the schools. A frequent complaint of local government officials is that the rules are upgraded while the budgets are not increased.

Between one-half and two-thirds of the budget of a local authority comes from the central government; the amount varies by community and type of service. For example, in Kiryat Shmona, a town close to the Lebanese border and made up of many Sephardi families, as much as 90 percent of the welfare budget comes from central authorities. In Givatayim, a middle-class suburb of Tel Aviv, the figure may be a third that of Kiryat Shmona. Not only are there more welfare cases in Kiryat Shmona, but the authorities there are anxious to bolster the social fabric and morale of the border town, which became the symbol of vulnerability to terrorist shelling before the Lebanese wars of 1982 and 1996. Money channeled to the local authorities plays a redistributive role, because block grants are used to encourage poorer local authorities to provide better services, though uniformity of service is not sought.[56]

Local governments finance the rest of their activities by collecting taxes, especially property taxes. But only a dozen or so of the more than two hundred local authorities have the wealth and economic activity needed to generate support for the activities of local government. Accordingly, most localities, representing a majority of the country's population, have to rely on support from the center for their budgets. Central authorities attempt to use this dependence to promote universal rules of property tax collection and zoning practices, activities that can be very difficult in poor, small, economically depressed communities. This structure leads politicians of the central government authority down the enticing path of using rules, patronage, and budgets to further goals of the party and of fellow party members. Influential land developers and other economic interests have been known to place strong temptations in the path of local government officials, leading to charges of corruption and cronyism. Many local governments in Israel are too poor, their politicians too ambitious, and the political center too removed to resist these temptations.

Two other methods developed over the years to fund local activities are special municipal endowment funds, especially for cultural purposes, and Project Renewal. The endowment funds, usually collected from wealthy contributors outside Israel, allow mayors to be more flexible and more creative in handling the affairs of the city. This method was most successfully used by Teddy Kolleck, former mayor of Jerusalem, whose initiatives were widely acclaimed. The mayors of Tel Aviv and Haifa have also been successful, but beyond Israel's three largest and most important cities, the record of success in using this method dwindles as we continue down the list. Most local authorities cannot compete with the historical and emotional attraction of Jerusalem or the appeal of large cultural, business, and industrial centers like Tel Aviv and Haifa. Thus the amount of funds at their disposal is relatively smaller.

Project Renewal was set up as another attempt to help local authorities by raising funds from Jewish communities abroad. The funds are earmarked to renew deteriorating neighborhoods; the money is to be spent on housing, ecology, and cultural and educational projects. Despite a slow start—occasioned by a complex method of coordinating the desires of citizens with the plans of the local authority, the various government ministries involved, and the Jewish Agency—Project Renewal has begun to help communities and to give a psychological lift to many of their residents.[57]

The role of local government is relatively weak, as is obvious when one considers the structure of the planning and zoning process in Israel: local, regional, and national commissions must approve plans. The local level plays an important role because its city council, which is popularly elected, must first approve plans. But the approval of local government is not sufficient; plans are then forwarded to the regional commission and in some cases to the national commission. These last two are composed of members who represent government ministries and major local governments. This composition obviously reflects the strength of the political parties in the government, in ministries involved, and in the local councils.

Planning is hindered because of the lag between approval and performance. In the past, well-connected politician-mayors could ignore plans and "create facts." Large projects have at times been approved by various commissions well after the projects were complete. Illegal construction is widespread; even making minor changes in a building often demands a license, and licenses are often not obtained. Enforcement of these laws is sporadic—rather than forcing compliance with the plans, the authorities usually assess fines, and the infraction is not corrected.

Local government plays an important role in setting the cultural atmosphere of the city or town. The uneven enforcement of laws prohibiting entertainment on the Sabbath provides a good example. In Tel Aviv, movies and theaters operate on the Sabbath, but buses do not run. In Haifa some buses run (supposedly because of the Arab population and in accord with the rule of maintaining the status quo), and movies are open. In Jerusalem, there are no buses on the Sabbath, and entertainment was once prohibited. Then, in 1987, the situation changed when a judge dismissed the indictment brought by the Jerusalem municipality against a private club that was showing movies on Friday evening. The decision caused an uproar and led to moves by the religious parties in the coalition to overcome the court decision. The issue heated up again in view of the results of the municipal elections in 1989, in which the religious parties did well and were positioned to play pivotal roles in local coalitions. There was no doubt that the religious parties would press for a change in public policy and legislation.

In 1990 a law was passed giving the municipality the authority to regulate activities within its jurisdiction. The competing values in this case are the individual's freedom of religion, on the one hand, and the right of freedom from religion, on the other. Can the majority in a locality regulate behavior that infringes on the rights of individuals? Of course, this dilemma cuts both ways: religious persons want a quiet neighborhood on their days of rest, while seculars want direct paths of travel. Should streets be closed along main traffic arteries? The issue becomes acute because the police in Israel are a national force and might be expected to apply uniform rules in law enforcement. What is obvious is that the political climate of the city (especially the size and concentration of the religious population and its political power) influences law enforcement. In the powersharing balance between national and local government, the former is clearly dominant, but the latter is also an actor.

12 ASPECTS OF POLITICAL CULTURE

Because I know that you are obstinate, and your neck is an iron sinew and your forehead brass . . .

Isaiah 48:4

EVERY OBSERVER, MOST journalists, and many tourists are alert to differences among countries. The prophet Isaiah had a clear idea of the qualities of the people with whom he was dealing, and some observers still subscribe to this description of Israelis.

Whether the description is accurate or not, those who research political culture attempt to explore differences among populations by focusing on the distribution of such factors as norms, attitudes, and behaviors as they relate to government and politics. The left-right continuum in political ideology, dominant values, political communications and socialization, and democratic norms and political tolerance are a few of the many aspects included in the study of political culture.[1]

Left-Right Political Ideology

An ideology is a system of ideas that is normative in nature in that it depicts and justifies an ideal, is based on assumptions concerning the nature of man and social reality, and is action-oriented. Politics, being a normative activity, must be accompanied by guidelines against which the actors gauge their behavior. Political ideology is a set of attitudes employed in answering questions of political priority.

Ideology, much like politics, is a concern of the elite, whose members not only produce ideology but are also its largest distributors and

413

consumers. They distribute it to their constituents in programs and statements; they consume ideological output because, trained in the language of ideological discourse, they tend to communicate with their peers in that idiom and to remain alert and sensitive to messages that have an ideological cast.

In ideological intercourse the elite tends to be active, the people passive. Since ideology is less than salient to the population at large, deviations from ideological purity by the elite are accepted by the electorate. Ideologues in power invariably find that they must modify and adjust ideological pronouncements to fit policy imperatives. Both phenomena can exist simultaneously: ideology may be modified, yet ideological discourse continues at a high level of intensity.

Two principles to be kept in mind, therefore, are that ideology is largely an elite affair and that it is not necessarily a good predictor of policy. Political communication in Israel tends to be highly ideological, public policy much more pragmatic. Israel has developed an economy in which there is a very high level of government activity and in which principles of market forces and profitability are ascendant. The pre-state and early state periods featured socialist ideologies but also fostered policies that were centralized while encouraging private investment. This dualistic form has been developed by ministers of the Labor left and augmented by officeholders of the Likud right. While the rhetoric of their parties still identifies them as socialist or capitalist, respectively, the policy practices of these ministers do not lend themselves to neat categorization.

Political discourse, and the ideologies and parties associated with it, is generally based on the assumption that political groupings can be ordered on a continuum from left to right. The concepts *left* and *right* (or *liberal* and *conservative* in the American version) are common terms in politics. Nevertheless, their meaning is multifaceted at best, elusive at worst, and divergent over time and across polities.

Most often in political discourse, the left-right continuum has been given economic meaning, referring to equality as opposed to inequality, government intervention as opposed to free enterprise, tolerance of change as opposed to adherence to the status quo. Other issues, such as abortion, foreign aid, and integration, have all been subsumed under these headings in their time. On closer examination, however, it becomes clear that notions of left and right are too simplistic to capture the complexity of reality. It is important to consider the problems related to a left-right continuum.[2]

First, the assumption of unidimensionality is explicitly made in discussing a left-right continuum, yet it is questionable whether so simple a concept is adequate. The test is whether the continuum provides an ordering of parties such that if we know, for example, that a party is on the right of the continuum, we then know its views on the issues of the day. Clearly this is not the case. The positions of Israeli parties on issues raised by the role of religion in the state are not related to their locations on the continuum when arranged by social welfare policy or foreign policy. The left would be expected to be least amenable to the religious position, the right more so, yet many Likud leaders and supporters are fervent secularists on these questions, and some Labor people accept religious policy not only because they feel they must do so to maintain coalitions when in power but because they are so inclined personally. Different issues are salient for various parties. In Israel at least two, and possibly more, dimensions are needed for making sense of the orderings of political parties.

A second problem relating to the left-right continuum has to do with the meanings of the terms *left* and *right*. Broadly, the left represents the socialist values of equality, social justice, and international cooperation and brotherhood; the right has historically been associated with capitalist values such as freedom of opportunity, competition, restricted government activity, and nationalism. In certain senses this description fits Israel, but in other important senses it is incomplete. For many years, and certainly since the Six-Day War, the major Zionist parties have competed in their nationalism, placing the highest value on security and on the survival of Israel as a Jewish state. The Likud has argued that these goals can be achieved using a firm, nonconciliatory policy, while Labor favors more flexibility and concession. Nevertheless, it was the Alignment that began the policy of settling the territories, the Likud that ceded the Sinai to the Egyptians, and Ariel Sharon who accepted the principle of the unilateral withdrawal from Gaza—none of these government actions could have been anticipated with only the left-right continuum for a guide. Being a party of the "left" did not prevent Ahdut Haavoda from taking a very strong militant line against neighboring Arab states in the 1950s; it was on this very issue that the party split from Mapam in 1954.

Parties near the center of the continuum tend to differ in ideology but to be more similar in policy. Parties at the extreme edges, rarely tested by the exigencies of power, are generally more consistent in their ideology. Regarding the future of the territories, it was relatively easy to differentiate between the extreme parties of the left and the right but harder to do so regarding the parties at the center. The two large parties were in the middle, tending toward the right—meaning that the left-right continuum failed to distinguish easily between them on this most critical issue. The major parties were close on this issue, with the extremes much more divergent.

This pattern would hold as well for social and economic issues such as compulsory arbitration in public-sector labor disputes or welfare benefits for the underprivileged. Again, the large parties would cluster toward the center, but much variation would be evident among extreme, and weaker, political groups. On religious matters, however, the problem is more complex: almost all secular parties stress the importance of religious freedom and civil rights, and the religious parties promote the importance of behavior in accordance with Jewish religious law. Secular parties tend to release their Knesset members from the obligation of party discipline on Knesset votes on these issues by referring to such issues as matters of personal conscience. Often, however, the coalition needs of the party in power offset the principle of freedom of conscience, and the Knesset member faces the dilemma of choosing between personal views, the party's ideological stand, and the party's political needs.

A third difficulty has to do with the lack of a fixed structure in the continuum. The meaning of "left" and "right" may well change over time, making the ranking provided by today's continuum somewhat different from that of earlier years. Party positions change. The NRP was much less militant in its foreign policy before the 1967 war than after it; since then, it has become a prominent spokesman for the positions of Israeli settlement in all of Eretz Israel. This stunning change must be understood in terms of the changes in the mood of the times, the ascension of a young generation of leaders in the NRP, and the increased salience of these issues in the public mind.

Labor and Likud also moved in this sense. Labor abandoned its long-standing opposition to negotiations with the PLO *after* the 1992 elections and removed the plank opposing the establishment of a Palestinian state—without explicitly stating that it supported the establishment of such a state—*before* the 1996 elections. The Likud had little choice but to reluctantly follow Labor on the first change and then hope it would not be tested regarding the second.

The difficulty of a fixed structure in the continuum is clearest in the lack of necessary connection between party platform and policy when a given party is in power. Power tends to modify extreme positions, because responsibility is more keenly felt as problems are confronted. Opposition affords a politician the luxury of being judged by his words and not by his deeds. The economic policies followed by Pinhas Sapir when he was finance minister in the 1960s would not have been anticipated by a student of socialist economic theory. But as a dynamic leader faced with difficult problems, Sapir conceived his program as an answer to national needs; only then was the question of ideological purity addressed. His socialist Labor party could encourage private investment and even subsidize it to achieve goals thought important. Leaders such as Sapir have no problem with ideology because ideology is never rigid; only some ideologues are.

The surprises that followed Prime Minister Begin's turnabout on the question of peace negotiations with Egypt, which culminated in the Camp David agreements in 1978, the change in policy by Prime Minister Rabin regarding recognition of the PLO in 1993, and Sharon's changed positions when in power are good examples of the inadequacy of the continuum to provide precise indication of the behavior of the politician in a given situation. Begin had been associated with tough, nationalist stands throughout his twenty-nine years of parliamentary opposition. After his accession to power, and following Sadat's visit in November 1977, Begin altered many of his views. Rabin had been a leader of the tough Labor Party opposition to negotiating with the PLO because it was a terrorist organization; feelings were so intense that at one point it was made illegal for an Israeli to have contact with the PLO or any of its members, and yet Rabin went on to agree to mutual recognition with the PLO and to sign the Oslo Accords. In 2002 Sharon tried to avoid the vote by the Likud's central committee rejecting the establishment of a Palestinian state, but the vote took place and passed. Then, in 2004 he adopted a policy of unilateral separation from the Gaza Strip even after the plan had been rejected in a referendum among Likud members. Sharon continued to pursue his policies of choice against the votes of his party, suggesting that party ideology had been replaced by the pragmatic political needs of a leader seeking to win American and international favor as well as continued support from Israeli voters at the center of the continuum.

A fourth problem of the left-right continuum is the difficulty in determining what a party's position is on a given issue. In the 1970s and for much of the 1980s, the larger parties refrained from clearly stating ideological positions in order to retain the support of diverse elements. The two biggest groupings, the Likud and the Labor-Mapam Alignment, were composed of separate and autonomous political parties. Often the platforms of the Herut and Liberal Parties (or the Labor Party and Mapam) were not identical, so there was great pressure to generalize ideological positions, to make them lose specific meanings that might divide these constituencies.

A good example of this generalizing strategy could be found in the party platform planks on security policy prior to the 1969 elections, which took place after the Six-Day War:

> *Alignment (Labor):* Until peace comes, our forces will remain on all the cease-fire lines. . . . Israel will never return to the armistice lines used before the Six-Day War. . . . Additional settlements will be established in the border areas.
>
> *Gahal (later Likud):* Our security requirements in peace treaties with Arab states, stemming from our experience, demand our ruling in areas that served as the basis of our enemies' aggression. . . . Large-scale Jewish settlement . . . must be given priority in the development plans of the state.
>
> *NRP:* . . . will work for continued large-scale, speedy urban and rural settlements in the liberated areas.

The most striking feature of these excerpts from the platforms of the country's three strongest parties was their similarity; both the Alignment and Gahal platforms were straining toward the middle. Within the Labor Party, in fact, there was considerable difference of opinion regarding security policy, Abba Eban and Pinhas Sapir supposedly being much more dovelike than Moshe Dayan, Yigal Allon, or Golda Meir. As if these differences were not enough, the platform committee had to attend to the demands of Mapam, the group farthest to the left in the Alignment. That the final document turned out as tough as it did caused much ill-feeling among Mapam members. The possibility of returning territory— the word *retreat* is never used—is mentioned only in a positive form: "Until peace comes, our forces will remain on all the cease-fire lines." But the next sentence—"Israel will never return to the armistice lines used before the Six-Day War"—quickly recovers the momentarily lost initiative of the more hawkish.

It used to be that you could tell a party's position by whether it talked about the "conquered territories" or the "liberated territories." Both Gahal and the NRP used the phrase "liberated territories." The Alignment talked only of the "territories," and when speaking of settlements, it could not bring itself even to use the word *territories;* instead, it stated that "additional settlements will be established in the border areas." Gahal too strained a bit toward the center, though not nearly as hard: anyone looking for the statement "Not one inch of land will be returned" would look in vain. The choice not to include this Herut principle was made in deference to its coalition partner, the more centrist Liberal Party, many of whose leaders became uncomfortable when categoric language was used.

By the 1980s, some movement was evident on this issue. The Likud government spoke only of Judea and Samaria instead of the West Bank territories, thereby annexing them semantically. The Alignment approved a platform calling for territorial concessions for a true peace, placing itself in firm opposition to the Likud government. The NRP, after losing half its electoral strength in 1981, attempted to moderate some of its more extreme statements on the territories. This move toward moderation became more difficult as the mood of the times shifted further, from the more militant 1980s to the more conciliatory 1990s.

All these changes indicate that the election platform is a compromise among the factions of a party and the constituent parts of a list. On very difficult issues, the surest formula is not to mention them. According to an old saying, party platforms are like train platforms—something to get in on, not to stand on. In addition, a party platform does not commit the party in any legal sense; if a party wishes, it may ignore part of its platform entirely. A good example of this is the recurring commitment of the platform of the U.S. Democratic Party to move its country's embassy to Jerusalem from Tel Aviv. Just as consistently as the platform has promised it, Democratic presidents have ignored it, or even opposed it, as in the case of President Clinton's reaction to a Republican-sponsored resolution in the U.S. Senate.

A fifth problem relates to how the continuum is perceived and understood by the electorate. In Israel, as in other countries, only people with high levels of sophistication in conceptualizing politics concern themselves with the left-right continuum. For most people, politics is a matter of leaders and parties, whose images are no less important than ideological issues of left and right. Alternately, some think of politics in terms of specific questions facing the polity or in terms of the ability of a party to satisfy group demands. The left-right continuum in Israel often fills a political function more than an ideological one.

The left-right continuum is a useful shorthand for the initiated to understand and order the political scene.[3] But it is misleading to expect the parties on our man-made continuum to conform their behavior to our expectations. For most people, left and right are political labels used to make sense of the party system. The left-right label is part of one's political vocabulary, of one's political education, and it is learned in the same way one learns about other labels—being Jewish or being Israeli. Behavior reinforces this labeling. The process seems to work this way: having voted Likud and learned that it corresponds with "right," one identifies with that label. Most people do not start by being for a certain policy, identifying that policy with left or right and then searching for the appropriate party. The left-right label seems to be related to, and probably stems from, one's party identification.

The best evidence of this learning process is the distribution of left and right in the Israeli population over the past forty years. Israel is often characterized as being evenly split between left and right, but a more accurate description would identify an overall drift to the right (see table 12.1). In surveys conducted by various research groups, support for the right increased from 8 percent in 1962 to 16 percent in 1969 to 52 percent in 2003. Not only has the answer become more legitimate in the system—so too has the word. When the Israel Institute of Applied Social Research ran a pretest before its 1962 study, the "right" political identification was found to be so discredited that it was decided to substitute the political party of the right—Herut—in the questionnaire; the final version of the question had as its extremes "Marxist left" and "Herut," with "moderate left" and "center" as the other two categories. By 1969 this problem had disappeared, and the terms *left* and *right* were used for the extreme responses. By 1981 some studies began splitting the "right" response into "right" and "moderate right," because the distribution had so shifted over time.

The support for the left eroded in parallel with the erosion of the dominant party system that spawned it. In 1973 the two camps were about equal in size, but by 1977, with the turnabout in government, the right had superseded the left. The right continued to grow until 1988, when it comprised almost half the Jewish population, but during the peace process years of the 1990s, its upsurge halted and its strength decreased. The fortunes of the left presented a mirror image, with low points in 1977 and 1981, after which it increased in size. Left identification reached its high points in the 1990s, with the peace process unfolding, declining threat, and increased hope for a peaceful resolution of the Israeli-Arab conflict. By 1999, the size of the two groups was again almost equal. In 2003, over two years into the al-Aqsa Intifada, the left had dwindled by almost 30 percent, and a majority of respondents identified with the right—a feat never before observed in these surveys.

Table 12.1 Left-Right Self-Identification, 1969–2003 (in percentages)

Q: "With which political tendency do you identify?"

	1962[a]	1969	1973	1977	1981	1984	1988	1992	1996	1999	2003
Left/moderate left	31	25	22	18	17	23	26	30	36	39	27
Center	23	26	33	29	39	21	11	18	16	11	17
Right/moderate right	8	16	23	28	33	38	49	42	39	40	52
Religious	5	6	7	6	6	2	4	3	3	2	2
No interest in politics/no answer	33	27	15	19	6	15	10	7	6	9	2
Center plus no interest/no answer	56	53	48	48	45	36	21	25	22	20	19
Percentage of right among all left+right identifiers:	21	39	51	61	66	62	65	58	52	51	66

Sources: From 1962 through 1977 the surveys were conducted by the Israel Institute of Applied Social Research; from 1981 through 1992 by the Dahaf Research Institute; in 1996 by Modi'in Ezrachi; and in 1999 and 2003 by Mahshov.

Note: The "left"/"center"/"right" responses were suggested to the respondent; the "religious" and "no interest in politics/no answer" responses were not.

a. In 1962 "left" and "right" were not used; "Marxist left" and "Herut" were offered in their place.

Another trend seen in table 12.1 is the growing relevance of the left and right labels since the end of Labor dominance. These labels organize the multiparty system, combining politics and ideological stance. Politicians use them, as do political commentators and the general public. As the two-bloc party system established itself beginning in the 1980s, the terms *left* and *right* became more meaningful, useful, and prevalent, and there was an increase in the number of respondents defining themselves as "right" or "left" over time. By 1988, 75 percent did so, compared to 50 percent in 1981, and 45 percent in 1969. In the 1999 and 2003 surveys, 79 percent placed themselves in one of the two blocs. The depletion of the center and no-identification categories is the other half of the same process. Adding together those who defined themselves in the center and those who did not identify themselves along this continuum presents a convincing trend. From about half of the sample up to and including the 1981 elections, this group declined to about a third in 1984, and to between a quarter and a fifth in the next five elections.

Another reflection of changes in the party system can be seen in the responses of those who identified themselves as "religious" using this measure. Through the 1981 elections, about 6 percent were not willing to identify themselves in left-right terms but voluntarily offered self-identification with the religious camp. From 1984 on, this number shrank by about half, as the religious dimension became more and more associated with the hawkish, right-wing position on the Israeli-Arab conflict dimension—the major dimension of the left-right continuum. This dimension evidently overrode other calculations for many religious voters.

The electorate had become more and more identifiable using the left and right labels, and it had also become more polarized, with fewer center and nonidentified respondents, and more left and right identifiers. If we take only those respondents who defined themselves as either left or right, in every election since 1973 there were more Jewish voters identifying with the right than with the left (last row in table 12.1). In 2003, as in 1981 and 1988, two thirds of the total left or right identifiers chose "right."

According to these data, the most polarized years were 1996 and 1999 (during the Oslo period), when the number of left and right sympathizers was nearly equal. In 1973 the number of left and right sympathizers was also almost equal, but their combined number was much lower than it would be in the 1990s, and thus the overall polarization of the system was much lower.

If the left-right continuum were a representation of ideological differences in Israel, we would expect that as the right grows, so too should the distribution in attitudes identified with a "right" ideology. But even as the "right" response has become more prevalent and the parties of the right more prominent, there is a gradual growth of conciliatory attitudes over time in the society. What has happened in Israel over the past few decades is a process of political change followed by ideological change. The growth of the Likud and the growth of the right must be understood as a reaction to the years of dominance of the Labor-Mapam Alignment and the left. Likud means not only "right" but also non-Alignment, hence non-"left." The left-right continuum thus has a greater importance in its labeling function than in its ability to predict the answers to ideological questions.

Most people do not impute issue meaning to *left* and *right*. When asked at the beginning of the 1980s about the meaning of these terms, 70 percent mentioned nothing. Of the 30 percent who did respond, the farther to the right one was, the more likely it was that there would be a response. This pattern seemed to indicate that the formerly dominant left was in retreat ideologically as well as politically and that its adherents were less equipped to confront the issues than the more assertive voters of the right. As the political pendulum in Israel then was swinging in their favor, the respondents of the right were more prone to talk about it. These data are similar to findings in the United States, Britain, and other countries regarding the prevalence and function of ideology and the left-right continuum.[4]

That political labels should fill a veto function by pointing out whom we want to avoid is not surprising to observers who know the nature of political communication in Israel. This function was filled by the left in the period of dominance in the pre-state and early state eras, when the left was widely considered to be the appropriate legitimate authority in the system. As that basic understanding was being reconsidered, the term *right* filled the role of identifying the bad guys (the left) as much as it did that of identifying the group with which one might wish to identify (the right). The prime motivation was the identification with one of the political parties; from that flowed identification with one of the political labels.

In a basic sense, all politics in Israel is ideological. Messages are packaged in ideological containers, and code words are frequently attached. "Isms" and expressions such as "fascism," "socialism," "Revisionism," and "the basic values of the labor movement" abounded in the campaigns of the 1980s; yet for many of the voters, they were empty sounds. The style of Israeli political communication has become as important as the substance.

Ideological differences among the large parties in Israel have been proclaimed regularly, and while the rhetoric remains distinct, in reality these differences seem to have diminished over time. Elections have turned on party image and leader popularity, with ideological themes underscoring these more individualistic features. The rhetoric is important because attitudes on the future of the territories still predict voting behavior well, and they also predict left-right labeling. Political differences matter to public opinion, with class lines being less powerful as a predictor.[5] The appeal of a party or a leadership group could possibly bring about change in the public stand regarding policy; indeed, this prospect seems more likely than the possibility of class or group interests emerging to redefine public policy, and it gives the political leaders enormous leverage. They can change policy, if they so decide, secure in the knowledge that they will be able to swing public opinion to their position if they present it properly—in short, if they lead. No less important, they can retain the status quo by making a case for that position as well.

At the end of the 1980s, Israeli politicians and public opinion were rather hard-line regarding return of the territories and opposition to the establishment of a Palestinian state. Following the Rabin-Peres decision to enter negotiations with the Palestine Liberation Organization (PLO), a clear difference became apparent between the parties. But when in power after the 1996 and 2003 elections, the Likud found itself constrained by the policy initiatives that had been undertaken by Labor; there seemed to be no political necessity or ideological will to do otherwise.

Elites decide as they see fit, with little or no accountability or threat of reprisal from an incensed public. Even with an informed, interested, and articulate citizenry, as in Israel, politicians are free to do as they choose when the distribution of opinion is relatively balanced. Under these conditions, "elections are virtual lotteries because the two sides cancel each other out."[6] Precisely because of the balanced division of public opinion, the elite can do as it sees fit.

Elections can thus foster experiments in public policy, with no direct relationship to the party platform or the campaign. This effect has resulted from Israeli elections, and it is the root explanation of why the fit between public opinion and policy is less than good. The vote is the important ingredient in determining who will decide, but not in determining the direction policy will take. Begin, Rabin, and Sharon are all examples of this principle. Elections are sometimes portrayed as referendums regarding important issues, but that portrayal is almost always inappropriate.

Values

Politics is conflict over what to decide (and who should make the decision) about desirable things that are in short supply, such as power, money, or status. Often we think of politics in terms of competing ideologies, but it is often more accurately portrayed as competition among cherished values.[7] That is the real stuff of politics.

The concept of right and left is a conflictive way of thinking about politics. Concentrating on various values instead of one overall ideology represents a way of thinking about politics that does not expect or require people to develop an integrated system of beliefs. Instead, the focus is on discrete values that, like ideology, may provide the vehicle to explain reality and to posit standards of desirability. These values serve as shortcuts to guide people's interpretation of a complex and changing world, but they may or may not be connected, integrated, or coherent.

This approach recommends itself because values in political situations often conflict, and trade-offs are required. Many societal values are consensual—that is, they are supported by almost all members of a society or at least by a large majority. People vary on the rank they assign to a value when it is in conflict with another cherished value rather than on how much they support that idea in isolation. The order of priorities becomes the bone of contention.

The basic values in conflict in Israeli political culture are: (1) Israel as a Jewish state; (2) Greater Israel, the idea of retaining control of all of Eretz (the land of) Israel; (3) democracy; and (4) peace. Each of these may be an end in itself, or it may be a means to achieve other ends. In principle, for example, most Israeli Jews might support any one of these values if it were cost-free, but in reality trade-offs must be made. Thus, for many on the right and among religious Jews (but not only them), Greater Israel is an end in itself; for others, it is a means for achieving peace and security, or for absorbing more immigrants. Each of the values considered may be instrumental for some, serving as a means for achieving another value, or it may be an ultimate value, an end in itself, for others.

These four values are enunciated in Israel's Declaration of Independence, which includes the basic values of Israeli society. While not legally binding, the declaration has great symbolic importance, for the right of the Jewish people to its homeland embodies the Zionist justification for the establishment of the State of Israel. This value of Israel as a Jewish state is the most pervasive one in the culture. In a 1988 survey, 97 percent said that it was important or very important that the Jewish character of the state be preserved—that there be a Jewish majority.[8] Eretz Israel is referred to in the opening section of the declaration, thus binding the notion of the national home closely to the land, and is a value deeply ingrained in the Zionist ethos of national revival.

Democracy in the broadest sense of equality of political rights is also generally supported, at least in the abstract, with the courts bolstering these rights in principle and in practice over the years. In the same survey, 82 percent said it was important or very important that the democratic character of the state be maintained—that every resident have equal rights. Peace is a common aspiration, reiterated by politicians, sung about in popular songs. Being accepted among the nations of the world, and in particular by states of the region, was always one of the major goals of Zionism and of Israeli policy, and an important dimension of Israel's national interest.[9] After almost half a century of independence, peace has seemed progressively more feasible.

The issue of the territories is the basic dividing line in Israeli politics because of the trade-offs it involves. If it were not for the indigenous Palestinian population (the "demographic problem") and international pressure, and if holding on to the territories were not perceived as an obstacle to peace, most Israeli Jews would prefer a Greater Israel (the post-1967 war boundaries) to the smaller Israel that was militarily more vulnerable. If Israel could keep these territories with no price attached, just about every Israeli Jew would support that situation.

But to opt for Greater Israel means either restricting the political rights of the Arabs in the territories or facing the possibility of a country without a Jewish majority—or perhaps raising the probability of war. Preferring a democratic state with a Jewish majority makes keeping the territories less attractive. Wanting a Greater Israel with a Jewish majority means that the demographic imbalance between the Jewish and Arab populations must be redressed, in which case some support the notion of transferring Arabs from Israel to other Arab lands, others think denying civil and political rights to the Arabs in the territories makes the issue unthinkable, while others believe that large Jewish immigration would solve the problem.

Peace would be made possible, many on the left have argued, only by returning the territories and avoiding the need to deal with the Arabs under Israel's military rule. Activists on the right have argued that the strategic depth provided by the territories, coupled with massive Jewish immigration, would strengthen the state, offsetting the demographic advantage of the Arabs in the territories, and would be the best recipe for a low probability of hostilities. The permutations are many; the substance of these trade-offs is the stuff of contemporary Israeli politics.

The tensions and dilemmas revolving around these values are not new; they have accompanied Zionism from the outset.[10] Consider the following value priorities as expressed by Israeli Jews in a 2004 survey. Most Israeli Jews would be happy to achieve every one of them, if they did not conflict with achieving other goals. Were they to be observed in a political vacuum, one would learn little; much more can be understood by considering them in terms of competing values in specific contexts.

Respondents were asked the following question: "In thinking about the various paths along which Israel can develop, there seem to be four important values which clash to some extent, and which are important to different degrees to various people: Israel with a Jewish majority, Greater Israel, a democratic state (with equal political rights for all), and peace (that is, a low probability of war). Among these four values, which is the most important to you?" The phrase "Jewish majority" was invoked because it seemed closest to the original Zionist idea, as well as to common usage in Israel, although competing specifications of a Jewish state, such as a state where Jewish culture and tradition are dominant, or a theocratic state where the Torah is the law of the land, are also possible. The Hebrew term for Greater Israel is commonly recognized and widely used in political discourse. Democracy was conceived of as equal political rights for all, including the franchise to Arabs under Israel's jurisdiction. Peace was explained as a situation in which there was a low probability of war, so as to set it clearly apart from more formal aspects of peace agreements. The respondents were asked to rank all four values, and they had no apparent problem with the task.

Two values—Jewish majority and peace—were ranked high by a vast majority of the population, and the two other values—Greater Israel and democracy—ranked generally low (see figure 12.1).[11] Peace was mentioned first by 41 percent of the sample, with a Jewish majority close behind at 37 percent. The other two values, democracy and Greater Israel, which were mentioned as the first priority by 14 percent and 8 percent, respectively, were directly related to the political disposition of the territories—Greater Israel reflected concern for the land, democracy for the citizen's rights of the people in the land. Forced to choose among the four goals, most respondents placed neither Greater Israel nor democracy high on their priority lists.

Figure 12.1 Ranking of Basic Values, 2004 (in percentages)

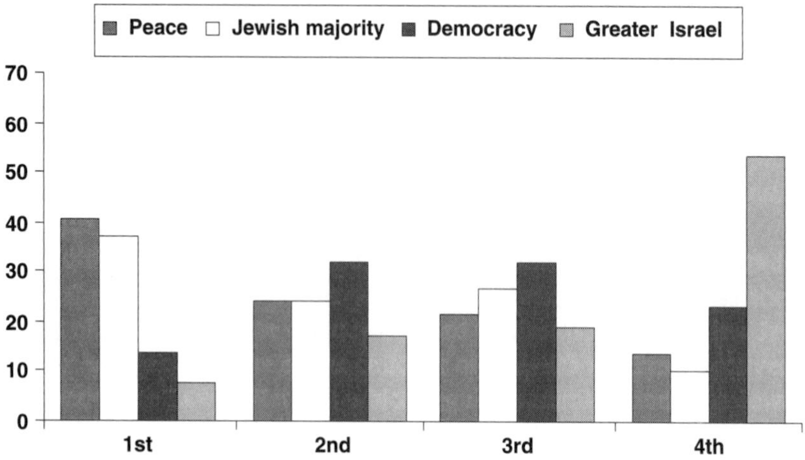

Source: Asher Arian, Shlomit Barnea, Pazit Ben-Nun, *The 2004 Israeli Democracy Index: Auditing Israeli Democracy* (Jerusalem: The Guttman Center at The Israel Democracy Institute, 2004). Jewish respondents only: http://www.idi.org.il/.

These results accentuate how superficial it is to portray politics in Israel as a struggle between a camp that wants to keep the territories and a camp that is willing to give them up if it would lead to a secure Jewish state. The more meaningful picture that emerges is of a population firmly supporting a Jewish majority in their state, with a very strong desire for peace. Keeping Israel Jewish by maintaining in it a Jewish majority is a major value of political consensus; peace is also, though to a lesser extent. The values of land and democracy are less important. While there is consensus regarding democracy as an abstract principle, and Greater Israel could also be an agreed-upon goal, their collective lower priority amid contemporary political circumstances makes them the substance of debate and conflict. Indeed, they have been transposed into divisive position issues in Israeli politics.

This picture is made even clearer in figure 12.2, where these value rankings are examined through self-placement on the left-right ideological scale, the same scale used and explained in chapter 1. Those who identified with the right ranked Jewish majority very high, placing peace and Greater Israel at lower levels. For left identifiers, peace was the highest priority, followed by Jewish majority and democracy. The sum of these preferences means that both ends of the continuum could share a commitment to both a Jewish majority and peace, while democracy and

Figure 12.2   Ranking of Basic Values by Left-Right Self-Placement, 2004 (in percentages)

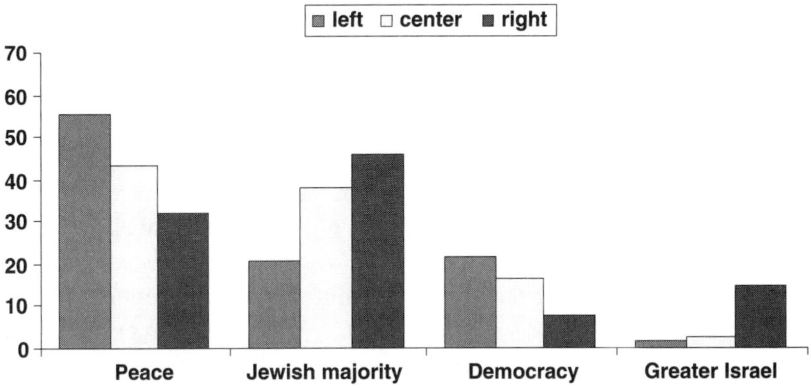

Source: Asher Arian, Shlomit Barnea, Pazit Ben-Nun, *The 2004 Israeli Democracy Index: Auditing Israeli Democracy* (Jerusalem: The Guttman Center at The Israel Democracy Institute, 2004). Jewish respondents only: http://www.idi.org.il/.

Greater Israel raised the possibility of contention. Politicians could raise the consensus issues of Jewish majority and peace in every campaign speech throughout the society, while stressing the more contentious ones made sense when addressing like-minded people: Greater Israel for the right, and democracy for the left.

Political Communication

A free press is a major prerequisite of a democratic system, and Israel's record on this score is a good one. The dilemmas posed by the difficult security problems Israel faces make its tradition of having a lively press even more impressive. Two conflicting sets of priorities underlie these dilemmas: on the one hand, there are the values of free speech, freedom of the press, and the right of the people to know—all of them basic democratic rights; on the other hand, there is the legitimate demand to prevent publication of information that will be of use to the enemy. Some cases are clear-cut: divulging information about troop strength and location may legitimately be suspended, but quoting an opposition politician who thinks the government's policy is wrong must be allowed. The difficulties are at the borderline: should stories about low morale or rising emigration or a minister's declaration that he has no faith in the senior army command be permitted or not?

The answer to the question of the necessary limits of a free press in Israel is difficult; its implementation is even more so, since freedom of the press is not safeguarded by constitutional or legal provisions. On the contrary, almost all the legislation enacted enables the prevention of publishing or broadcasting news. In fact, the Israeli press operates freely because the authorities allow it to do so through voluntary arrangements worked out by them and the editors of the largest daily newspapers.[12]

The State Security Ordinance (Emergency Regulations) of 1945 is the legal basis for the military censorship of news published in Israel or abroad that could "endanger the defense of Israel, or the well-being of the public, or public order." Appeals may be heard by a special committee of three, representing the press, the military, and the general public. While unanimous decisions are final, majority decisions can be appealed to the chief of staff. The Press Ordinance of 1933, issued during the Mandate and still in effect, requires licensing of all newspapers and printing houses by the Interior Ministry. The license may be revoked for incitement "endangering public order."[13] Interior Minister Avraham Poraz agreed in 2004 to transfer the authority to revoke licenses to the courts but that change has not been effected.[14]

The voluntary agreement between the defense minister and the Committee of Newspaper Editors broke down in 1992 when the editor of *Haaretz* withdrew from the agreement because of the military censor's decisions regarding the paper's coverage of an accident. In 1995 the editors of *Yediot Aharonot* also withdrew from the voluntary agreement, in opposition to a proposed law regulating newspapers. In 1996 a new voluntary agreement was reached, under which the rules would apply to all newspapers, including Arab ones, and editors would be allowed to appeal decisions of the censor to the High Court of Justice.

Israelis consume news at very high rates. In 2004 more than three-fourths of the Jewish population claimed that they kept up with the news every day or several times a week.[15] Half over the age of fourteen read a newspaper at least one day a week, and about two-thirds read a weekend newspaper.

The Hebrew press is active and competitive. The two largest newspapers are the mass-circulation afternoon tabloids *Yediot Aharonot* and *Maariv*. In 2003 *Yediot* had more than half the weekend market, *Maariv* about a third; on weekdays, *Yediot* had 45 percent, *Maariv* about a quarter.[16] Both papers are independently owned and present a wide range of opinions in their signed columns; the editorial tone of both papers tends to be right of center. The important Hebrew morning paper is *Haaretz*, with 8 to 9 percent of the market. It is probably the most prestigious of Israel's papers, blending liberal values and pragmatic Zionism in its editorial columns.

Newspapers affiliated with political parties were much more important during the Yishuv and in the early state years.[17] They provided the political line to activists and served as important channels of communication among segments of the party. With statehood, however, their partisan function was eclipsed by the more general mass-circulation papers, which appealed to the growing market and downplayed political and ideological matters. The most prominent party paper was *Davar*, the Histadrut newspaper, renamed *Davar Rishon*, in its last period. *Davar* steadily lost readership, even in Histadrut strongholds such as the kibbutz movement. In the mid-1970s its circulation was 45,000 newspapers, but that fell to 25,000 in the mid-1980s, and to 10,000 in the mid-90s, less than 1 percent of the public. In recent years, its editorial staff has been increasingly free from political interference, but the newspaper was always heavily subsidized by the Histadrut and was identified with the Labor Party. With Labor's loss of hegemony in the Histadrut, and the emergence of a leadership dedicated more to labor unionism and the bottom-line, *Davar* published its last issue in 1996, some seventy years after its founding.

Newspapers depend on good reporting, and reporters are only as good as their sources. Even reporters for independent newspapers must enter tacit agreements with politicians if they are to receive information. The politician's interest is to have his name in print, preferably with his point of view as well; the reporter wants to know what is really going on. Symbiotic relations are bound to develop. And in Israel, a small country where everyone who counts knows everyone else, and a country with a competitive press and a news-attentive population, these symbiotic relations are useful to both reporter and politician. Information or opinions that would be inappropriate for a minister to reveal can be released through the friendly reporter. Such a release may be intended for public consumption, or for international targets, or it may be part of an intragovernmental or intraparty battle taking place at the moment.

Leaks are generated the same way. Rather than being created by reporters from government meetings or secret deliberations, leaks are fed to reporters by the ministers who take part in these consultations and who have an interest in having information that may be helpful to them or harmful to their opponents brought to public attention. Periodically, there is a public uproar regarding the secrecy of deliberations and the lack of professional discipline on the part of the newspapers, but the real culprit is, of course, the minister who provides the information. In the debate over the role of the press in the 1982 Lebanese war, for instance, it was maintained that the antigovernment position expressed by the Alignment opposition was detrimental to the morale of the troops and the civilian population. Reports of dissent within the government itself were even more harmful to public morale—and the source of these reports was not the opposition but members of the government.

Preventing leaks is a matter of concern to all governments. In the 1950s Ben-Gurion resigned the premiership over leaks from within his government and then returned to the job only after extracting support for legislation making all cabinet proceedings secret. That was not as successful a solution as the arrangement worked out in 1966, in which deliberations of the Cabinet Security Committee were defined as "state secrets," meaning that unauthorized publication could be punished as severe espionage.[18] In the 1970s, a practice developed of declaring cabinet meetings special sessions of the Security Committee, thus achieving total secrecy. This practice can easily be abused: the Begin government attempted, unsuccessfully, to consider settlement policy under these total blackout rules. The line that protects the government's right to keep its secrets safe is also the line that may infringe on the public's right to know. The balance is a difficult one, but one that it is crucial to maintain in a democracy.

Competition and diversity are now a fact in television and radio, and Israel has undergone a revolution in the past decades in this regard. Where there was one public broadcasting authority, one television channel, and two radio stations (including one run by the IDF), there is now a proliferation of channels and stations.[19] In addition to the public authority's Channel 1, there are commercial Channels 2 and 10, an educational channel, cable, and regional outlets; the same is true of radio. In the early 1980s, 95 percent of all television viewers watched the evening news on the government authority's channel; in 1994 the parallel figure was 30 percent, and in 2004 it was 10 percent.[20] It is not that Israelis are less interested or less well-informed, but that they now have a choice about what and how to consume their news.

Radio and television operate under the Israel Broadcasting Authority, set up in 1965, which was patterned on the British Broadcasting Corporation. Before the law establishing that authority was passed, radio had been located in the prime minister's office (television did not yet exist), and political interference in broadcasting was not unknown. The Broadcasting Authority has brought much more autonomy to the world of the airwaves but does not divorce programming and news broadcasting from the political sphere. The plenum of the authority, which meets three times a year, has thirty-one members; the board, which meets weekly, has seven. Members are appointed by the government according to a party key that assures coalition control of the authority, at least at the moment of appointment. The British model calls for nonpolitical appointments based on ability, professional expertise, and independence, but the Israeli system clearly deviates from that norm. The authority's director general, who is appointed by the board in Britain, is chosen by the government in Israel; again, political rather than professional considerations predominate.

The composition of the authority and its exposure to the political process mean that the staff has to keep political considerations in mind, even if it is not given clear-cut political dictates. Deliberations within the authority often reflect the political debate in the country. Members from parties participating in the government coalition are likely to argue that the authority emphasizes negative aspects of life in Israel, while its mandate should call for encouraging the public by emphasizing the positive. Opposition party members are likely to be critical of reporting they perceive as propaganda for the party in power. Who should be interviewed, how much weight should be given to a story, and what is news are not only professional questions of radio or television journalism; in Israel they are very important political questions.

Channel 2, the first commercial channel, began broadcasting in 1993 after intense political maneuvering, and Channel 10, the second commercial channel, in 2002. The law approving the structure of Channel 2 called for the division of broadcast time among three equal franchise groups, each broadcasting for two days, with joint broadcasts on Saturday and a shared news department. The three groups that won the franchises were controlled by three families prominent in newspaper publishing, raising serious issues of overlapping ownership and control. The Moses family of *Yediot*, the Nimrodi family of *Maariv*, and the Schocken family of *Haaretz*, as well as banking interests and other investors, were leaders in the organizations that received the franchises. Channel 10 was financed by Yossi Meimon and Ron Lauder, each with 40 percent, and Shlomo Ben Zvi with 20 percent. In addition to commercial and economic interests, political interests were close to the surface: the prime minister, education minister, and minister of communications had formal responsibility for the various public broadcasters, including educational television and the army radio station, the second channel and the cable channels.

The Broadcast Authority is funded by a user's fee; Channels 2 and 10 are funded commercially; cable users pay the companies directly. The Broadcast Authority allows sponsorship of productions—not quite commercials, but close. Cable stations have no commercials—yet. Netanyahu, once prime minister, then finance minister, has called for the privatization of public broadcasting partially because this is in tune with his economic view, and partially because of the feeling on the part of leaders of the right that the media is a stronghold of the left. The opponents of privatization fear that having only commercial broadcasting will deprive the minority of higher-quality art and entertainment, to say nothing of more in-depth coverage of worthy topics.[21]

Channel 2 has been very successful both commercially and in drawing a larger share of the viewing population than does the Broadcasting Authority's Channel 1. Politicians are very anxious to appear on the popular shows of these channels, some of which develop into raucous debating opportunities. The boisterousness and energy of these shows are an accurate reflection of the political debate in Israel—loud, rude, energetic, and unlikely to convince anyone to change a position previously held.

In internal politics, Israeli journalists can be as inquisitive and courageous—although few are—as any in the world. In most security areas, however, they are more restrained than foreign journalists. This restraint stems from national loyalty, a desire to maintain good relations with sources, and a self-imposed mechanism of self-censorship. Because foreign correspondents usually work without these restraints, sometimes the impression is created that Israeli journalists are lackeys of the government. In the government's attempt to win the battle of public opinion, it must walk the hazardous line between controlling the news and those who report it and respecting the right of the people—and the world—to know. The more controversial the policy that lies at the heart of the story, the harder this dilemma is.

Public opinion is a phantom that is often worshipped by politicians and the press. More than simply a computation of the attitudes of members of the population, public opinion must be understood in terms of the distribution of opinions within the population, the intensity with which they are held, their stability, and the organizational means used to translate the opinions into actions that will have an impact on policy.[22] Demonstrators outside Mapai party headquarters in 1967 are said to have had an impact on the decision to appoint Moshe Dayan minister of defense before the Six-Day War. A mass rally of hundreds of thousands in the summer of 1982 preceded the government's decision to reverse itself and set up a commission of inquiry into the alleged massacre that occurred in the Palestinian refugee camps of Sabra and Shatilla in Beirut. These were expressions of "public opinion," but they were also carefully organized demonstrations in support of ideas frequently expressed in the press.

In the era of individualism, television has become a major focus of the electoral campaign. In the past, the mass rally and the visit of politicians to the neighborhood or place of work were the usual ways in which the public was exposed to competing politicians. In order to prevent giving unfair advantage to one party, the rule was that no candidate's picture could be shown on television during the month preceding the election, but that rule was abandoned as of the 1999 elections.

Broadcast time for the parties on television and radio is provided free of charge during the campaign and is allocated in proportion to the party's strength in the outgoing Knesset. Each competing list is provided with a base of ten minutes on television, with six additional minutes for each member of the outgoing Knesset. Thus the Likud and Labor have enjoyed a good deal of free television time, while small and new parties have had very little.

The impact of these broadcasts on the electorate is not great. The Israel Rating Committee found during the 2003 election campaign that viewing ranged from 20 percent of viewers during the first week of the free political broadcasts to 12 percent during the third week. In 1996 about a quarter of the population said they viewed most of the party political broadcasts, compared to about half in 1977. The variety of other programming choices available evidently makes the repetitive political broadcasts not very appealing, but the state continues to provide the parties with free prime-time slots for their political commercials. Only 2 percent said that the broadcasts would help them very much in deciding how to vote, a quarter said somewhat, and 76 percent said not at all. Comparable numbers in 1981 had television helping 7 percent very much, a third somewhat, and 60 percent said that it did not help at all.

Opinion polls have proliferated in the past few decades, and they now dominate much of the campaign. In the 1969 elections, three dailies reported polls, and the total number of reports on polls was 16; in 1992, fifteen dailies reported on polls, and there were 421 such reports.[23] More than half of survey respondents follow the polls, and 42 percent believe them. More than a third believe that people are influenced by the polls in determining how to vote. When asked about the proposal to ban the publication of the polls in the preelection period, only 29 percent agreed.

Political Socialization

Political socialization is the process by which values important to the political system are internalized. The way a person responds to authority, the way he (or she) perceives his responsibility toward the collectivity, whether he sees himself as active or passive in the political system— all these topics are affected by one's political socialization. More party-specific and issue-specific dimensions are also involved: For whom should I vote? What is my attitude regarding the territories?

Any individual is influenced both by early experiences (the primacy hypothesis) and by current political developments and issues (the recency hypothesis). Political socialization studies place great emphasis on the formative years of childhood, adolescence, and early adulthood in determining one's political outlook and later behavior. There is no doubt that one's primary reference groups in the formative years influence one's political ideas. Most Israelis report that they vote as their families do, and this is true in other countries as well. The exact rate of congruence between the voter and his or her family is difficult to ascertain because "one's family" may be understood to include only spouse or parents or a much more extended group. In 1981, when asked whether "your family" votes as you do, 55 percent said yes, 25 percent said no, and 18 percent reported that they did not know how their family voted. An interesting reversal on this matter reflects the independent temperament of Israelis. In 1988, when the question was phrased, "Do you think you are influenced by the way members of your family vote?" a much lower agreement rate was recorded: only 14 percent gave a definite yes, and 55 percent answered with a definite no. The respondent is the leader, and the family acts as he does, not vice versa.

In a multiparty system such as that in Israel, intergenerational transmission is clearest in respect to the left-right division, less so regarding the party group, and least of all in terms of the actual party voted for. In a study in the mid-1990s, Raphael Ventura found that 81 percent of respondents voted for the same left or right side as did their father, while 76 percent voted for the same party group (left, center, religious, right), and only 52 percent voted for the same party. This finding held for mothers, too, and for the voting patterns of married respondents and their spouses.[24]

Schools and the youth culture are important sources of influence in political socialization. The inherited wisdom regarding the Israeli polity is that in the pre-state period and in the first years of statehood, schools and youth movements were influential agents in the hands of political parties. Therefore, it is not surprising that much of the curriculum dealt with material that could strengthen identification with Zionism and with the political struggle that the Yishuv had undertaken. After independence and the changes in the school population as the result of mass immigration, the school curriculum began more fully to represent the complexity of Israeli society. Schools, especially high schools, were no longer regarded as sources of elitist education but of public and mass education, and they achieved almost universal attendance through the age of sixteen. The change is clear in high school civics instruction: whereas early texts barely mentioned political parties, although the role of the political party was dominant in almost every sphere of life, over time, issues salient in public life began to be discussed in the schools, and representatives of various points of view were invited to speak.

The decline of the youth movements in the secular neighborhoods paralleled the general decline of party-related activity after the founding of the state. In the religious areas, however, the investment in education and youth groups expanded just as it was contracting among the seculars. Alternative frameworks within the school system competed with the particularistic youth movements. Nonetheless, peer-group pressure remains strong among Israeli youth in general, and one discerns high levels of conformity in dress, entertainment, leisure-time activity, and lifestyle. These are direct carryovers of the more organized pressures of youth movements, even though fewer youths are organized in these political and ideological movements.[25]

The army service of young Israelis coincides with their entrance into active participation in politics by virtue of their right to vote, and with the period in which historical events can have their strongest lasting impact on the future political behavior of an individual. A good case in point is the vote of the army in 1973. Some two months after the Yom Kippur War, army voters supported the Likud at a higher rate than did the general population. For some time, the young had tended to support the Likud at higher rates, but evidently the war accelerated this phenomenon.[26] Army service is important not only in terms of specific acts of voting. Perhaps more crucially, it is in the army that the young citizen receives his first independent taste of the systems of hierarchy and bureaucracy that are such important features of Israel's political culture. As this service becomes more selective (see chapter 10), the structure of the society will likely change.

The agents of socialization—family, friends, schools, army—are usually crucial for relatively set periods of time. The system also acts to reinforce attitudes and predispositions. The most obvious examples are the national pageants associated with events such as Holocaust Day and Independence Day, which tug at the collective memory and attempt to rekindle feelings of collectivity, shared destiny, and patriotism. More subtle are the presentation of Jewish holidays in ways that reinforce national and patriotic feelings. In these efforts the governing system—ministries, television and radio—play a central role.[27]

Political socialization leads to the internalization of values and attitudes, but it does not occur in a vacuum. It is clear that the family and its social environment are important conditioners of the results of political socialization. In Israel's varied society, different patterns are obviously at work on different parts of the population. Extreme examples are provided by groups that are relatively isolated from general society, such as kibbutz members and the ultra-Orthodox, who live in relatively hermetic communities. Both groups seem relatively successful in socializing their later generations politically if we use community perpetuation and voting patterns as indicators. There are many cases of people leaving these groups and out-voting, but compared to the general society, rates of conformity there are high.

As a country built on immigration, Israel has had experience with the resocialization of immigrants, usually adults who arrive after the early phases of their political socialization are over. Their experiences before arriving in Israel may be thought of as important in determining their political predispositions in Israel. For many, especially Europeans, the various Zionist parties were active in their countries of origin and exposed the potential immigrants to the ideological differences among them well before their arrival in the country. For many others, Israel was a place of refuge after the displacements experienced before the move, so ideological issues were not really at stake. For many Sephardim who arrived in Israel, religious motivation and messianic vision were more central than earthly divisions among competing political groups.

Almost all these immigrant groups came from political systems that lacked democratic traditions. Being introduced to a democratic regime was as novel for Russian immigrants in 1991 as it was for Poles or Moroccans in the 1950s. After carefully studying the political resocialization of Soviet and American immigrants in Israel in the early 1970s, Zvi Gitelman concluded that the process "affects attitudes toward specific issues most, abstract political ideas less, and fundamental orientations to politics least."[28] The children of Israel who wandered in the desert for forty years before entering the promised land were a transitional generation, not capable, we are told, of independence. As Israel approached its fiftieth anniversary of independence, however, the system was dominated by citizens born in Israel. Those born and raised in Israel have known no other—predemocratic or nondemocratic—experience. Unlike their forefathers, they were born to democracy. They have witnessed the institutionalization of democratic processes in the country and the periodic rotation of power in a peaceful manner from one party to another, even as the system still faces severe challenges.

Democratic Norms

Political Tolerance

Israelis support abstract democratic norms at high rates: belief in majority rule, in freedom of expression, in the right of the citizen to criticize the government, and in equality before the law is supported by sizable majorities.[29] But when the question becomes less abstract and more salient in the political context, the rate of democratic support falters. In a 2004 survey, 75 percent agreed that minority-opinion groups should be allowed to operate freely to gain majority support for their positions.

The support for abstract notions of democracy does not automatically extend to concrete policy issues, however. This finding is replicated worldwide and certainly holds for many Jews in Israel. A sizable portion of Jewish citizens sampled assessed Israeli Arabs negatively and displayed negative policy attitudes toward Israel's Arab citizens (see figure 12.3). Most Israelis oppose including Arab parties in coalition governments, they believe that Israeli Arabs are disloyal to Israel, and they oppose having Israeli Arabs participate in crucial national decisions, such as the future borders of the country. Moreover, a majority favors having the government pursue policies of encouraging Arabs to emigrate from Israel, and about a third favors a policy of transfer, or removal, of Israeli Arabs from Israel.[30]

The disparity between abstract norms and practical tolerance is seen even more clearly when the problem is concretized by referring to the group least liked by the respondent. In Israel in the 1980s, the "least liked" groups most often mentioned were on the political left, especially Arab groups, and outside the Zionist consensus—in 1980, 73 percent of the sample mentioned these groups. In 1984, after Meir Kahane's election to the Knesset and the growing salience of his presence on the public scene, many more—22 percent, compared to 3 percent in 1980—named his

Figure 12.3   Jewish Opinion about Israeli Arabs, 2000–2004 (in percentages)

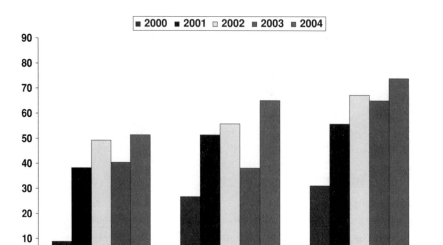

A. Oppose including Arab parties in coalition government.
B. Believe Israeli Arabs are disloyal to Israel.
C. Oppose having Israeli Arabs participate in crucial national decisions, such as the future borders of the country.

Source: Periodical Surveys, The Guttman Center at The Israel Democracy Institute. Jewish respondents only: http://www.idi.org.il/.

group as least liked. But still most respondents (52 percent) mentioned groups on the left, in particular Arab groups (43 percent). About one-sixth of the respondents identified as least liked the ultra-Orthodox anti-Zionist Neturai Karta. When the abstract norm of free speech was applied to the least-liked group, support for this democratic principle shrank by more than half.

Overall levels of political tolerance in Israel, while not high, are similar to levels found in the United States in the 1980s.[31] Moreover, in Israel, crucial variables such as ethnicity, religiosity, and social status relate to the selection of the least-liked group but not to the level of tolerance. More closely related to political tolerance are such factors as psychological security, political ideology, and the threat that the least-liked group is perceived to pose to the individual and the political system.

Political Efficacy

The feeling that one has influence in the political system, or can have if one chooses to, is generally considered an important feature of a democratic system. Israelis are interested in politics, discuss the subject quite a bit, vote in great numbers, change their government from time to time, and believe in the potency of elections to change policy; but they do not have much faith in their own ability to influence policy (see table 12.2). What is more, the sense of little or no influence has consistently grown. In 1969, 51 percent reported that they had little or no power to influence

Table 12.2   Political Efficacy, by Place of Birth

Q: "To what extent can you and people like you influence policy?"

	N	Very much[a]	Somewhat	Little	Not at all
1969					
Asia or Africa	296	19%	26%	23%	32%
Israel (father Asia or Africa)	89	15	23	26	37
Israel (father Israel)	68	5	39	29	26
Israel (father Europe or America)	213	14	43	29	14
Europe or America	629	15	34	27	24
Total	1,295	15	33	26	25
1981					
Asia or Africa	316	22	18	28	33
Israel (father Asia or Africa)	190	18	22	22	38
Israel (father Israel)	127	10	20	28	43
Israel (father Europe or America)	196	12	26	28	35
Europe or America	321	10	24	29	38
Total	1,150	15	24	24	37
1996					
Asia or Africa	170	9	17	37	37
Israel (father Asia or Africa)	324	11	24	39	26
Israel (father Israel)	186	12	27	39	22
Israel (father Europe or America)	208	8	24	39	28
Europe or America	267	6	23	38	28
Total	1,155	9	23	39	29
2003					
Asia or Africa	78	10	20	39	31
Israel (father Asia or Africa)	201	7	28	35	30
Israel (father Israel)	240	10	28	32	30
Israel (father Europe or America)	191	6	19	39	36
Europe or America	346	4	15	30	51
Total	1,056	7	22	33	38

a. "To a very great extent" and "To a great extent" in 1969 and 1981.

policy; the comparable numbers were 61 percent in 1981, 68 percent in 1996, and 71 percent in 2003.

Based on the 1969 results, it seemed that the *lower* on the social scale the Israeli citizen was, the more likely he or she was to feel efficacious. The Asian- or African-born felt most efficacious based on the "very much" column in table 12.2, the European- or American-born least efficacious. Among those who claimed no efficacy, the pattern was even more striking. Those born in Asia or Africa and their Israeli-born children stood out as feeling least influential, with the Europeans and Americans, and especially their children, having the lowest nonefficacious rate. The inverse relationship between efficacy and social status (as measured by place of birth and education) was explained by greater sophistication in understanding the essentially closed nature of the Israeli political system. As the Israeli moved up the social ladder, he became more realistic and realized that his chances of penetrating the political system were slight.

By 1981, changes had taken place. Efficacy on the whole declined, falling most dramatically among those European- or American-born groups that evidently perceived most clearly their loss of power with the ascent of the Likud in 1977. This analysis is strengthened by the relatively high levels of efficacy reported by the Asian- or African-born and their children. The data are especially fascinating since no real change of political power in ethnic terms was evident in Israel between the two time periods. But the high rates of low efficacy, especially among the Israeli-born whose fathers were also Israeli-born, are striking.

In 1996 and 2003, the overall rate of efficacy had fallen even lower, with the least efficacious still the European- or American-born and those born in Israel of a father born there. Low levels of efficacy are reported by the Asian- or African-born and their children. The most change was shown by those born in Israel of an Israeli-born father; they were the most efficacious, or more accurately, the least nonefficacious. These data provide a mixed message. There has been a decrease in feelings of efficacy, and in the 2000s there is evidence of alienation from the system, as demonstrated by the lower rates of voter turnout.

Participation

There are obvious tensions between the high rates of support for abstract democratic norms and the evidence of recoiling from democratic policies, lowering rates of voter turnout, and low levels of political efficacy. Despite these tensions, Israelis have been shown to have high levels of political information, with 87 percent knowing the correct answers to a series of politics-related questions in a recent survey—compared with 53 percent in a comparable American sample. Almost two-thirds of respondents knew the number of terrorists involved in an exchange of prisoners deal and the size of defense as a percentage of the government budget. Respondents were also asked about the rights of Arabs in the territories; since most Israeli Jews have no meaningful social contact with Arabs, these questions identify those who had made an effort to gain and retain information on subjects of importance. The two questions asked were "Do the Arabs of Judea, Samaria, and the Gaza Strip have the right to apply to the High Court of Justice?" and "Do the Arabs of Judea, Samaria and the Gaza Strip have the right to vote in Knesset elections?" More than 55 percent answered the first question correctly (yes) and more than three of four answered the second one correctly (no).[32]

Compare these levels to the 46 percent of Americans in the 1990s who could name their representative in Congress, and to the 30 percent who knew that the term of a U.S. House member is two years. Only 38 percent knew in 1964 that the Soviet Union was not a member of NATO, and only 23 percent in 1979 knew that the United States and the Soviet Union were the two nations involved in the SALT talks. In 1987, at the height of the Iran/*contra* scandal, only half knew that the United States was supporting the rebels rather than the government in Nicaragua.[33]

Israelis live politics, with 57 percent (compared with 33 percent in the United States) reporting that they talk about politics at least once a week. They have high rates of news-media consumption, which peaks before elections. Participation is high, though less party-based and now often centered in extraparty protest. More than 20 percent of the Israeli public have participated in demonstrations—a high figure by international standards.[34] The major parties are no longer the vehicle of articulating interests, but the political system remains vibrant and dynamic. Protest groups and movements arise, and activists find ways of making their demands felt. The responsiveness of the system is another matter.

Rule of Law

In times of security threat, all democracies reveal a tension between upholding the rule of law and pursuing national security interests. Liberal principles demand respect for the rights of individual liberties and of property, but these values may seem like a luxurious excess to those who feel that the freedom of the country, if not its very existence, is at stake. These issues emerge strongly in cases in which the government has seemed to be ignoring the principle that all government actions must be in accord with the law. Implementing the rule of law is often frustrating, since what seems right and necessary at the moment often must be deferred because of abstract principle and legal maneuvering. Whether fighting crime or fighting wars, government always feels the temptation to suspend the rule of law.

The choice between the two polar extremes—security on the one hand, and the rule of law on the other—is a stark one, but most situations allow for obfuscation and interpretation so that a clear choice between two extremes is unnecessary. Still, this basic dilemma has characterized the public debate in Israel. In the face of the Lebanon campaign in 1982, and then with the onset of the intifadas in 1987 and 2000, both the relations between the political and military spheres and the manner in which the military operated within the framework of the rule of law were closely scrutinized by the public.[35]

The issues were especially complex regarding the intifadas, because the defense forces were not designed or trained for the type of police action that resulted from the low level of hostilities, almost always involving stone-throwing demonstrators, that characterized the early stages of the uprisings. The tactics used to repress and deter the Arab population called into question the army's commitment to the rights of the demonstrators and focused attention on the zeal of certain officers and soldiers in interpreting the orders of commanders and political leaders.

The cover-up of Shin Bet activities in the 1984 "Bus 300 incident" by the authorities was an example of the tension between security concerns and democratic principles of upholding the rule of law, although government officials at the highest levels denied any wrongdoing. The Israeli public comes down on the side of security interests even if the rule of law must be abridged: two-thirds regularly choose security interests in a hypothetical choice between the two; about a quarter choose the rule of law; the remaining respondents choose the middle category between these two poles.

This ability to give a tough-minded evaluation of the security situation is an important characteristic of Israeli public opinion. And turnabout is fair play, as was exemplified in the responses to a set of questions asked in 1987 about spies and spying. In the period before the survey was conducted, Jonathan Pollard, an American Jew working for the U.S. Navy, had been convicted of spying for Israel. When asked whether it was "justifiable for Israel to spy on the United States in order to procure information vital for Israel's security," 40 percent of the sample thought that this was acceptable. That percentage is almost identical to the proportion of those who thought it "justifiable for the United States to spy on Israel in order to procure information vital for America's security."

Trust in Institutions and Strong Leadership

Trust in institutions is seen as an indication of the public's assessment of democracy. The Israeli pattern has been quite stable, and the 2004 distribution reflects the prevailing preferences (see figure 12.4). The Israel Defense Forces and the Supreme Court are widely trusted, indicating their success in avoiding excessive partisan identification. At the other extreme, political institutions such as parties, the Histadrut (labor unions), government ministers including the prime minister, and the Knesset fail to engender widespread trust.

A different question that has been asked over the years is whether politicians pay attention to the opinions of the ordinary citizen. Since 1969, only a quarter to a third of the respondents thought they did. Overall, the data portray a citizen who is very attentive and interested in politics, who is lacking political efficacy, and whose participation is decreasing. One trait is probably influenced by the other: the more you

Figure 12.4   Trust in Institutions, 2004 (in percentages)

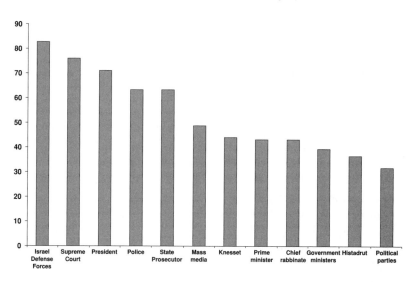

Source: Asher Arian, Shlomit Barnea, Pazit Ben-Nun, *The 2004 Israeli Democracy Index: Auditing Israeli Democracy* (Jerusalem: The Guttman Center at The Israel Democracy Institute, 2004). Jewish respondents only: http://www.idi.org.il/.

know, the more frustrated you are; the more frustrated you are, the less likely you are to participate.

The consistent pattern in this skein of conflicting threads is the desire for assertive political leadership. This pattern was noted in the 1960s, and it persists. The rate of preferring strong leadership to "all the debates and laws," has always been above half, and it reached a high point of 72 percent in 1981. In 2004, 58 percent agreed to the statement. Despite the surface support for democratic norms, there is a stubborn respect for the strong personality in Israeli politics. This explains at least in part the overwhelming popularity of leaders like Ben-Gurion, Begin, and Sharon.

Impressive achievements in military and other areas have fashioned a nation that seems to be impressed with doing, creating, acting. The élan of a leader compares very favorably to the humdrum of the cumbersome parliamentary process, with its weak personalities and compromising atmosphere. As opposed to magnetic leadership, the political system seems inefficient; politicians appear to lack imagination and resourcefulness. We must seek an explanation for these findings by noting that Israel is a nervous, energetic nation. The doers—pilot, manager, builder, settler—are rewarded heavily, both materially and symbolically. Much of this nervous energy is evident in army activities and in more anonymous moments in civilian life, such as on the highways and in buses, where it merges with Mediterranean friendliness to produce a fundamental Israeli characteristic, a jaunty assertiveness. Hemmed in on many sides by bureaucratic regulation and anxious about terror and possible international isolation, this unruly condition expresses itself in less formal, less structured situations. Yet the need for guidance, for structuring, and for leadership remains strong.

The resulting syndrome appears paradoxical, but its elements actually mesh nicely. On the surface there is a cockiness and self-assurance about running the country—and many less important issues, for that matter. At a more fundamental level, there is also a desire for order, for security, and for leadership. The former provides the semblance of the latter: in place of the desired authority comes an assertive dogmatism. Whether this fundamental insecurity has its roots in the individual psyche or in the educational system—or in one of any number of other sources—is unclear. At the public level, however, it provides a very fertile soil for cultivating widespread support for positions associated with leaders invested with legitimacy. Public opinion in Israel is volatile and can be brought to support the dominant position of the appropriate leaders when the proper symbols and appeals are applied.

***

The chances for the continued success of a democratic regime rest in part in having social groups overlap. In Israel today, we witness so profound a lack of overlapping social cleavages as to point to a possible danger to Israeli democracy. When the political system is polarized so that one group concentrates within it the religious, the Sephardim, and the less-educated and lower-status workers voting for the Likud and religious parties, while the other group includes a disproportionate share of secular, upper-class Ashkenazim voting for Labor and Yahad (Meretz), the chances for intolerance, lack of communication and understanding, and violence grow. And then there is the Arab-Jewish division among Israelis about which it is impossible to prophesy, but which generates very disturbing signals.

Some patterns are not immutable, and some will be more conducive to change; it may be that with changes in the parties, the system will become fluid, allowing new affiliations to emerge within the polity and new policies to be explored. It is not easy to decide which are greater, Israel's achievements or Israel's problems. Both contribute to make the Israeli political system at once fascinating and unpredictable.

NOTES

Chapter 1. Introduction

All voting statistics are from official publications of the Central Bureau of Statistics. *Haaretz, Maariv,* and *Yediot Aharonot* are Hebrew daily newspapers.

1. Giovanni Sartori, *Parties and Party Systems* (Cambridge: Cambridge University Press, 1976); Arend Lijphart, *Democracy in Plural Societies* (New Haven: Yale University Press, 1977); Amos Perlmutter, *Military and Politics in Israel* (London: Cass, 1969); Gabriel Ben-Dor, "Politics and the Military in Israel," in *The Elections in Israel—1973,* ed. A. Arian (Jerusalem: Jerusalem Academic Press, 1975), 119–144; and S.N. Eisenstadt, *Israeli Society* (London: Weidenfeld and Nicolson, 1967).

2. Arend Lijphart, "Israel Democracy and Democratic Reform in Comparative Perspective," in *Israeli Democracy under Stress,* ed. Ehud Sprinzak and Larry Diamond (Boulder, Colo.: Lynne Rienner, 1993), 107–123; and Michael N. Barnett, ed., *Israel in Comparative Perspective* (Albany: SUNY Press, 1996).

3. See "A Jewish and Democratic State," a special edition of *Iyunei Mishpat* 19, no. 3 (1995) [in Hebrew]; Baruch Kimmerling, "State-Society Relations in Israel," in *Israeli Society: Critical Perspectives,* ed. Uri Ram [in Hebrew] (Tel Aviv: Breirot, 1993), 328–350; and Rebecca Kook, "Between Uniqueness and Exclusion: The Politics of Identity in Israel," in Barnett, *Israel in Comparative Perspective,* 199–225.

4. Yair Auron, *Jewish-Israeli Identity* (Tel Aviv: Sifriat Poalim, 1993); and Simon N. Herman, *Jewish Identity in the Jewish State* (Beverly Hills, Calif.: Sage, 1977), 175, 184.

5. Yaron Ezrahi, "Democratic Politics and Culture in Modern Israel: Recent Trends," in Sprinzak and Diamond, *Israeli Democracy under Stress,* 255–272.

6. Yitzhak Samuel and Ephraim Yuchtman-Yaar, "The Status and Situs Dimensions as Determinants of Occupational Attractiveness," *Quality and Quantity* 13 (1979): 485–501.

7. *Haaretz,* March 9, 1983.

8. On the importance of history in political culture, see Robert D. Putnam, *Making Democracy Work: Civic Traditions in Modern Italy* (Princeton: Princeton University Press, 1993).

Chapter 2. People of Israel

1. Data on Israeli and Jewish population are plentiful. An authoritative source, from which most of the data in this chapter are taken, is Dov Friedlander and Calvin Goldscheider, *The Population of Israel* (New York: Columbia University

Press, 1979). See also Calvin Goldscheider, *Israel's Changing Society: Population, Ethnicity, and Development* (Boulder, Colo.: Westview, 1996); Gershon Shafir and Yoav Peled, *Being Israeli: The Dynamics of Multiple Citizenship* (New York: Cambridge University Press, 2002). For material on world Jewish statistics, see Roberto Bachi, *Population Trends of World Jewry* (Jerusalem: Institute of Contemporary Jewry, Hebrew University, 1976); and for material on Israeli population statistics, see Roberto Bachi, *The Population of Israel* (Jerusalem: Institute of Contemporary Jewry, Hebrew University, 1977), and from the annual *Statistical Abstract*.

2. *Statistical Abstract, 2003*, 2–10.

3. See, for example, Joseph Gorni, "Changes in the Social and Political Structure of the Second *Aliya*, 1904–1914" [in Hebrew], *Zionism* 1 (1970): 204–246. Cf. Drora Kass and Seymour Martin Lipset, "America's New Wave of Jewish Immigrants," *New York Times Magazine*, December 7, 1980.

4. Discussions of the Zionist idea are found in Ben Halpern, *The Idea of the Jewish State* (Cambridge, Mass.: Harvard University Press, 1961); Arthur Herzberg, *The Zionist Idea* (New York: Meridian, 1960); and Shlomo Avineri, *The Making of Modern Zionism: The Intellectual Origins of the Jewish State* (London: Weidenfeld and Nicolson, 1981).

5. Important treatments of the pre-state period include S.N. Eisenstadt, *Israeli Society* (London: Weidenfeld and Nicolson, 1967); and Dan Horowitz and Moshe Lissak, *The Origins of the Israeli Polity: Palestine under the Mandate* (Chicago: University of Chicago Press, 1978). For good overall historical treatments, see Walter Laqueur, *A History of Zionism* (London: Weidenfeld and Nicolson, 1972); and Noah Lucas, *The Modern History of Israel* (New York: Praeger, 1974).

6. Anita Shapiro, *The Frustrated Struggle: Jewish Labor* [in Hebrew] (Tel Aviv: Hakibbutz Hameuhad, 1977).

7. Friedlander and Goldscheider, *Population of Israel*, 16.

8. See Shabtai Tevet's discussion in his *David's Jealousy: The Life of Ben-Gurion*, vol. 1 [in Hebrew] (Jerusalem: Schocken, 1977).

9. See Dan Giladi, *The Yishuv at the Time of the Fourth Aliya (1924–29): Economic and Political Aspects* [in Hebrew] (Tel Aviv: Am Oved, 1977).

10. Cited in Friedlander and Goldscheider, *Population of Israel*, 97.

11. For a thorough discussion, see Zvi Gitelman, *Becoming Israelis: Political Resocialization of Soviet and American Immigrants* (New York: Praeger, 1982).

12. Ruth Westheimer and Steven Kaplan, *Surviving Salvation: The Ethiopian Jewish Family in Transition* (New York: New York University Press, 1992).

13. Tamar Horowitz, "The Absorption of Immigrants from the Former Soviet Union in Israel: Integration or Separatism?" *EuroSocial Report* 54 (1995): 75–96.

14. Ministry of Immigrant Absorption, "The Absorption of Immigrants," March 1996. See also Zvi Gitelman, "The 'Russian Revolution' in Israel," in *Critical Issues in Israeli Society*, ed. Alan Dowty (Westport, Conn.: Praeger, 2004), 95–108.

15. The Israel Association for Ethiopian Jews Web site, hppt://www.iaej.co.il/pages/community_news_facts.htm (accessed January 20, 2004).

16. Abe Kay, *Americans "On the Map"* [in Hebrew] (Jerusalem: American Jewish Committee, 1996); and Nadav Zeevi, "Uncle Sam's Other Contribution," *Haaretz Weekend Supplement,* January 12, 1996, 21.

17. Ministry of Immigrant Absorption Web site, http://www.moia.gov.il/neutnim/hoshi/olim.10.htm (accessed January 20, 2004).

18. Gideon Alon, "270,000 Israelis Left Country Over 10-Year Period," *Haaretz,* January 22, 2004; and Gallya Lahav and Asher Arian, "Israelis in a Jewish Diaspora: The Multiple Dilemmas of a Globalized Group," in *International Migration and the Globalization of Domestic Politics,* ed. R. Koslowski (New Brunswick, N.J.: Routledge, forthcoming).

19. Asher Friedberg and Aharon Kfir, "Jewish Emigration from Israel," *Jewish Journal of Sociology* (June 1988): 5–15.

20. Yinon Cohen, "From Haven to Heaven: Changing Patterns of Immigration to Israel," in *Challenging Ethnic Citizenship: German and Israeli Perspectives on Immigration,* ed. D. Levy and Y. Weiss (New York: Berghahn Books, 2002); and S. Gold, "Israeli Americans," in *Multiculturalism in the United States: Current Issues, Contemporary Voices,* ed. Peter Kivisto and Georganne Runblad (Thousand Oaks, Calif.: Pine Forge Press, 2000), 409–420.

21. Asher Arian, David Nachmias, Doron Navot, and Danielle Shani, *Auditing Israeli Democracy* [in Hebrew] (Jerusalem: Israel Democracy Institute, 2003), 203–205.

22. "Absorption of Immigrants," 57.

23. Arian et al., *Auditing Israeli Democracy,* 205.

24. Salo Wittmayer Baron, *The Social and Religious History of the Jews,* 2nd ed., vol. 2 (New York: Columbia University Press, 1952).

25. For a thorough discussion, see Raphael Patai, *Tents of Jacob* (New York: Prentice-Hall, 1971).

26. *Encyclopedia Judaica,* s.v. "demography." For a broader analysis, see Sammy Smooha, *Israel: Pluralism and Conflict* (Berkeley: University of California Press, 1978).

27. *Statistical Abstract, 2003,* 3–34.

28. Ibid., 2–10.

29. Central Bureau of Statistics, press release, February 1, 2004.

30. David Kretzmer, *The Legal Status of the Arabs in Israel* (Boulder, Colo.: Westview, 2002); Majid Al-Haj, "The Status of the Palestinians in Israel: A Double Periphery in an Ethno-National State," in Dowty, *Critical Issues in Israeli Society,* 109–126. See also the Web site of the Arab Association for Human Rights, http://www.arabhra/org.

31. Nadim Rouhana and As'ad Ghanem, "The Democratization of a Traditional Minority in an Ethnic Democracy: The Palestinians in Israel," in *Democracy, Peace, and the Israeli-Palestinian Conflict,* ed. E. Kaufman, S. Abed, and R. Rothestein (Boulder, Colo.: Lynne Rienner, 1993), 163–184.

32. As'ad Ghanem, "The Palestinians in Israel as Part of the Problem and Not the Solution," *State, Government, and International Relations* [in Hebrew]

(forthcoming); Baruch Kimmerling and Joel S. Migdal, *Palestinians: The Making of a People* (New York: Free Press, 1993). See also William M. Brinner, "The Arabs of Israel: The Past Twenty Years," *Middle East Review* 20, no. 1 (Fall 1987): 13–21; and Nadim Rouhana, "The Collective Identity of Arabs in Israel," *New Outlook,* July/August 1987, 22–23.

33. Oren Yiftachel, "The Shrinking Space of Citizenship, Ethnocratic Politics in Israel," *Middle East Report 2002,* 223. See www.merip.org.

34. See Martin Gilbert, *The Arab-Israeli Conflict: Its History in Maps* (London: Weidenfeld and Nicolson, 1974); and Baruch Kimmerling, *Zionism and Territory: The Socio-Territorial Dimensions of Zionist Politics* (Berkeley: University of California Press, 1983).

35. See Benny Morris, *The Birth of the Palestinian Refugee Problem, 1947–1949* (New York: Cambridge University Press, 1988) and *The Birth of the Palestinian Refugee Problem Revisited* (New York: Cambridge University Press, 2004).

36. Uzi Benziman and Atallah Mansour, *Subtenants* [in Hebrew] (Jerusalem: Keter, 1992).

37. Yehoshafat Harkabi, *Fateful Decisions* [in Hebrew] (Tel Aviv: Am Oved, 1986); and Aryeh Shalev, "Unilateral Autonomy in Judea and Samaria: Israel's Option," *Jerusalem Quarterly* 43 (1987): 71–86.

38. Herbert C. Kelman, "The Palestiniazation of the Arab-Israeli Conflict," *Jerusalem Quarterly* 46 (1988): 3–15.

39. See Meron Benvenisti (with Ziad Abu-Zayed and Danny Rubinstein), *The West Bank Handbook: A Political Lexicon* (Jerusalem: Jerusalem Post, 1986), 49–50; and the annual reports of Benvenisti's West Bank Data Base Project, published by the American Enterprise Institute and the *Jerusalem Post.*

40. Asher Arian, *Security Threatened: Surveying Israeli Opinion on Peace and War* (New York: Cambridge University Press, 1995).

41. Peter Jones, "The Middle East in 1995: The Peace Process Continues," *SIPRI Yearbook 1995* (Oxford: Oxford University Press, 1995), chap. 4.

42. Khalil Shikaki, "The Peace Process, National Reconstruction, and the Transition to Democracy in Palestine," *Journal of Palestine Studies* 25 (1996): 5–20.

43. Benny Morris, "Camp David and After: An Exchange: An Interview with Ehud Barak," *New York Review of Books* 48, no. 13 (August 9, 2001); Hussein Agha and Robert Malley, "Camp David: The Tragedy of Errors," *New York Review of Books* 49, no. 10 (June 13, 2002); and Jeremy Pressman, "Visions in Collision: What Happened at Camp David and Taba?" *International Security* 28, no. 2 (Fall 2003): 5–43.

44. Asher Arian, "Israeli Security Opinion 2004," Jaffee Center for Strategic Studies, Tel Aviv, at www.tau.ac.il/jcss/ (forthcoming).

Chapter 3: Political Economy

1. Avi Ben-Bassat, ed., *The Israeli Economy, 1985–1998: From Government Intervention to Market Economics* (Cambridge, Mass.: MIT Press, 2002).

2. Reviews of Israel's economy can be found in Assaf Razin and Efraim Sadka, *The Economy of Modern Israel: Malaise and Promise* (Chicago: University of Chicago Press, 1993); Yair Aharoni, *The Economy of Israel* (New York: Routledge, 1991); and Yakir Plessner, *The Political Economy of Israel: From Ideology to Stagnation* (Albany: SUNY Press, 1994).

3. *Ka'adan and Ka'adan v Israel Lands Authority et al.*, High Court of Justice 6698/95; *High Court of Justice Decisions*, vol. 54 (1) 258.

4. Background material on the Histadrut can be found in Rachel Tokatli, "Political Patterns in Labor Relations in Israel," Ph.D. dissertation [in Hebrew], Tel Aviv University, 1979; and Dan Horowitz and Moshe Lissak, *The Origins of the Israeli Polity: Palestine under the Mandate* (Chicago: University of Chicago Press, 1978).

5. Amnon Barzilai, *Ramon* (Tel Aviv: Schocken, 1996).

6. Arie Shirom, "Changing the Histadrut, 1994" [in Hebrew], *Economic Quarterly* 42 (April 1995): 51–52.

7. D. G. Blanchflower and R. B. Freeman, "Unionism in the United States and in Other Advanced OECD Countries, *Industrial Relations* 31 (1993): 56–80.

8. Chaim Ramon, "Report of the Chairman of the Histadrut—July 1994 to November 1995," New Histadrut (n.p., n.d.).

9. Michal Shalev, *Labor and the Political Economy of Israel* (New York: Oxford University Press, 1992); and Asher Arian and Ilan Talmud, "Electoral Politics and Economic Control in Israel," in *Labor Parties in Postindustrial Societies*, ed. Frances Fox Piven (London: Polity Press, 1991).

10. Ira Sharkansky, *Wither the State? Politics and Public Enterprise in Three Countries* (Chatham, N.J.: Chatham House, 1979), 75.

11. Lev Grinberg, *Split Corporatism in Israel* (Albany: SUNY Press, 1991).

12. "The Histadrut—Whither?—A Symposium" [in Hebrew], *Economic Quarterly* 42 (April 1995): 7–81.

13. Emanuel Sharon and G. Rosenthal, "The Pensions System: Policy Alternatives," in *Resource Allocation in Social Services: 1993–1994*, ed. Y. Kopf [in Hebrew] (Jerusalem: Israel Center for Policy and Social Research, 1995), 53–87.

14. Elkana Margalit, *The Trade Union in Israel—Past and Present* [in Hebrew] (Tel Aviv: Ramot, 1994).

15. Yair Aharoni, *Structure and Performance in Israeli Economy* [in Hebrew] (Tel Aviv: Gomeh, 1976), 222–263.

16. Israel Ministry of Finance, *Report on Government Companies, 2001*, 111.

17. E. S. Savas, *Privatization—The Key to Better Government* (Chatham, N.J.: Chatham House, 1987); and Yitzhak Katz, "Privatization in Israel—1962–1987" [in Hebrew], *State, Government, and International Relations* 35 (1991): 133–145.

18. *Yediot Aharonot*, May 2, 2001.

19. *Maariv*, January 14, 2004.

20. General Auditor's Office, Unit Managing the Government Debt, *Annual Report 2002*, 50.

21. Bank of Israel, *Economic Development in the Past Months*, No. 104, 2.

22. Avi Ben-Bassat, "The Obstacle Course to a Market Economy in Israel," in Ben-Bassat, *Israeli Economy, 1985–1998*, 1–58.

23. See Haim Barkai, "Israel's Attempt at Economic Stabilization," *Jerusalem Quarterly,* Summer 1987, 3–20.

24. Ben-Bassat, "Obstacle Course."

25. Haim Barkai, "The Public Sector, the Histadrut Sector and the Private Sector in the Israeli Economy," *Sixth Report 1961–63* (Jerusalem: Falk Project for Economic Research in Israel, 1964), 28–30.

26. *Statistical Abstract, 1979,* 292.

27. Assaf Razin and Efraim Sadka, *The Economy of Modern Israel: Malaise and Promise* (Chicago: University of Chicago Press, 1993), 190.

28. *Statistical Abstract, 1985,* 176.

29. *United Nations Human Development Report* (New York: Oxford University Press, 2002), 295. See SIPRI Military Expenditure Database, http://first/sipri.org/non_first/result.

30. David Dery and Emanuel Sharon, *Bureaucracy and Democracy in Budgetary Reform* (Tel Aviv: Israel Democracy Institute and Hakibbutz Hameuhad, 1994).

31. *Statistical Abstract, 2003,* table 15–5.

32. *Statistical Abstract, 1981,* 190; *Statistical Abstract, 1995,* 252; *Statistical Abstract, 2003,* table 15–2.

33. Gabriel Sheffer and Yohanan Manor, "Fundraising: Money Is Not Enough," in *Can Planning Replace Politics? The Israeli Experience,* ed. Raphaella Bilski et al. (The Hague: Martinus Nijhoff, 1980), 283–319; and United Jewish Appeal, *Annual Report.*

34. "Israel in the World Economy: Israel as an East Asian State?" in *Israel in Comparative Perspective,* ed. Michael N. Barnett (Albany: SUNY Press, 1996), 107–140.

35. Hanan Sher, "Riding High-Tech," *Jerusalem Report,* July 11, 1996, 36–39.

36. *Statistical Abstract, 2003,* table 11–10.

37. Arie Shirom, "Changing the Histadrut, 1994" [in Hebrew], *Economic Quarterly,* 42 (April 1995): 58.

38. Yonatan Reshef, "Political Exchange in Israel: Histadrut-State Relations," *Industrial Relations* 25, no. 3 (1986): 303–319.

39. Yoram Ben-Porath, "The Years of Plenty and the Years of Famine—A Political Business Cycle?" *Kyklos* 28 (1975): 401.

40. Gideon Doron and Boaz Tamir, "The Electoral Cycle: A Political Economic Perspective," *Crossroads,* Spring 1983, 27, table 4.

41. Eli Arom, "Economic Motivation for DMC Support," graduate paper [in Hebrew], Political Science Department, Tel Aviv University, 1978.

42. *United Nations Human Development Report* (New York: Oxford University Press, 2003), 282, 248.

43. Chanoch Bartov, "Not to Feel Too Good," *Maariv Sabbath Supplement,* January 6, 1989, 10.

44. Shlomo Swirski and Eti Konor-Atias, "A Picture of the Social Situation 2003," Adva Center, 2003.

45. M. Semyonov and N. Levin-Epstein, *Hewers of Wood and the Drawers of Water: Noncitizen Arabs in the Israeli Labor Market* (Ithaca, N.Y.: Institute for Labor Relations Press, 1987); and E. Yaar-Yuchtman, "Economic Entrepreneurship as

a Socioeconomic Mobility Route: Another Aspect of Ethnic Stratification in Israel" [in Hebrew], *Megamot* 29 (1986): 393–412.

Chapter 4: The Political Elite

1. Gaetano Mosca, *The Ruling Class* (New York: McGraw-Hill, 1939), 50.

2. See Robert D. Putnam, *The Comparative Study of Political Elites* (Englewood Cliffs, N.J.: Prentice Hall, 1976).

3. Yonathan Shapiro, "Generational Units and Inter-Generational Relations in Israeli Politics," in *Israel—A Developing Society*, ed. A. Arian (Assen: Van Gorcum, 1980), 161–179.

4. See Pippa Norris, ed., *Passages to Power: Legislative Recruitment in Advanced Democracies* (Cambridge: Cambridge University Press, 1997).

5. Mosca, *Ruling Class,* 144–145.

6. Asher Arian, "Incumbency in Israel's Knesset," in *The Victorious Incumbent: A Threat to Democracy?* ed. Albert Somit, Rudolf Wildenmann, Bernhard Boll, and Andrea Rommele (Aldershot: Dartmouth, 1994), 71–102; and Gideon Doron and Moshe Maor, *Barriers to Entry into Israeli Politics* [in Hebrew] (Tel Aviv: Papyrus, 1989).

7. Yael Yishai, *Between the Flag and the Banner: Women in Israeli Politics* (Albany: SUNY Press, 1996).

8. For the judiciary, see Elyakim Rubinstein, *The Judges of the Land* [in Hebrew] (Jerusalem: Schocken, 1980), chap. 6; and Martin Edelman, *Courts, Politics, and Culture in Israel* (Charlottesville: University Press of Virginia, 1994). For the army, see Yoram Peri, *Between Battles and Ballots* (Cambridge: Cambridge University Press, 1983), chap. 5. For the mass media, see Yitzhak Galnoor, *Steering the Polity: Communication and Politics in Israel* (Beverly Hills, Calif.: Sage, 1982), 250–253; and Dan Caspi and Yehiel Limor, *The Mass Media in Israel 1948–1990* [in Hebrew] (Tel Aviv: Am Oved, 1995).

9. Walter Laqueur, *A History of Zionism* (New York: Schocken, 1976), 308–309.

10. Emanuel Gutmann and Jacob Landau, "The Political Elite and National Leadership in Israel," in *Political Elites in the Middle East*, ed. George Lenczowski (Washington, D.C.: American Enterprise Institute, 1975), 166–167.

11. Avraham Brichta, "The Social and Political Characteristics of Members of the Seventh Knesset," in *The Elections in Israel—1969*, ed. A. Arian (Jerusalem: Jerusalem Academic Press, 1972), 109–131.

12. Max Weber, "Politics as a Vocation," in *From Max Weber: Essays in Sociology*, ed. H. H. Gerth and C. Wright Mills (New York: Oxford University Press, 1946), 84.

13. Zbigniew Brzezinski and Samuel Huntington, *Political Power: USA/USSR* (New York: Viking Press, 1963), 150–173.

14. "The Cincinnatus and the Apparatchik: The Israeli Case," *Jerusalem Quarterly*, Winter 1984, 105–112.

15. Dan Horowitz and Moshe Lissak, *The Origins of the Israeli Polity: Palestine under the Mandate* (Chicago: University of Chicago Press, 1978), 159.

16. Emanuel Gutmann and Jacob Landau, "The Israeli Political Elite: Characteristics and Composition," in *The Israeli Political System,* ed. Moshe Lissak and Emanuel Gutmann [in Hebrew] (Tel Aviv: Am Oved, 1977), 192–228.

17. Peter Medding, *Mapai in Israel* (Cambridge: Cambridge University Press, 1972), 158–160.

18. Shevah Weiss, *Israeli Politicians* [in Hebrew] (Tel Aviv: Ahiasaf, 1973), 51.

19. Aharon Lapidot, "Informal Election: Predicting the Results of the Election of the Fifth President" [in Hebrew], *State, Government and International Relations* 13 (1979): 111–113.

Chapter 5: Political Parties

1. Larry Diamond and Richard Gunther, eds., *Political Parties and Democracy* (Baltimore: Johns Hopkins University Press, 2001).

2. Maurice Duverger, *Political Parties* (New York: Wiley, 1963), 308.

3. T. J. Pempel, *Uncommon Democracies* (Ithaca, N.Y.: Cornell University Press, 1990).

4. Amitai Etzioni, "Alternative Ways to Democracy: The Example of Israel," *Political Science Quarterly* 74 (1959): 196–214.

5. Ibid., 312.

6. See the sources listed in chapter 2, note 5, especially Lucas, *Modern History of Israel.*

7. See Zvi Even-Shushan, *The History of the Workers' Movement in Eretz-Israel* [in Hebrew] (Tel Aviv: Am Oved, 1963).

8. Michael Bar-Zohar, *Ben-Gurion: A Biography* (London: Weidenfeld and Nicolson, 1979); and Peter Medding, *Mapai in Israel* (Cambridge: Cambridge University Press, 1972).

9. Natan Yanai, *Split at the Top* [in Hebrew] (Tel Aviv: Lewin-Epstein, 1969).

10. Uri Bar-Josef, *Intelligence Intervention and the Politics of Democratic States: The United States, Israel, and Britain* (University Park: Pennsylvania State University Press, 1995), chap. 7.

11. See Yonathan Shapiro, "The End of a Dominant Party System," in *The Elections in Israel—1977,* ed. A. Arian (Jerusalem: Jerusalem Academic Press, 1980), 23–38; and Ariel Levite and Sidney Tarrow, "The Legitimation of Excluded Parties in Dominant Party Systems: A Comparison of Israel and Italy," *Comparative Politics* 15 (1983): 295–327.

12. Dan Korn, *Time in Gray* [in Hebrew] (Tel Aviv: Zmora Bitan, 1994).

13. See the sources listed in chapter 2, note 43.

14. Asher Arian, "Israeli Security Opinion 2001," Jaffee Center for Strategic Studies, Tel Aviv, 2001, at www.tau.ac.il/jcss/.

15. See Joseph B. Schechtman, *Rebel and Statesman, Vladimir Jabotinsky: The Early Years* (New York: Thomas Yoseloff, 1956); Menachem Begin, *The Revolt*

(London: W.H. Allen, 1951); and Rael Jean Isaac, *Israel Divided: Ideological Politics in the Jewish State* (Baltimore: Johns Hopkins University Press, 1976).

16. Nakdimon Rogel, *Tel-Hai* [in Hebrew] (Tel Aviv: Yariv, 1979).

17. Miriam Geter, *Chaim Arlozoroff, A Political Biography* [in Hebrew] (Tel Aviv: Kibbutz Hameuhad, 1978); and Shabtai Tevet, *The Murder of Arlozoroff* [in Hebrew] (Jerusalem: Schocken, 1982).

18. Yaacov Shavit, *The Season of the Hunt: The "Season": The Confrontation between the "Organized Yishuv" and the Underground Organizations, 1937–1947* [in Hebrew] (Tel Aviv: Hadar, 1976).

19. Shlomo Nakdimon, *Altelena* [in Hebrew] (Jerusalem: Idanim, 1978).

20. Efraim Torgovnik, "Likud 1977–81: The Consolidation of Power," in *Israel in the Begin Era,* ed. Robert Freedman (New York: Praeger, 1982), 7–27.

21. For background, see Gerson Shafir and Yoav Peled, "'Thorns in Your Eyes': The Socioeconomic Basis of the Kahane Vote," in *The Elections in Israel—1984,* ed. Asher Arian and Michal Shamir (New Brunswick, N.J.: Transaction, 1986), 189–206.

22. Gary Schiff, *Tradition and Politics: Religious Parties of Israel* (Detroit: Wayne State University Press, 1977); and Menachem Friedman, *Society and Religion: Non-Zionist Orthodoxy in Eretz Israel, 1918–1936* [in Hebrew] (Jerusalem: Ben-Zvi Institute, 1978).

23. Ehud Sprinzak, "Three Models of Religious Violence: The Case of Jewish Fundamentalism in Israel," in *Fundamentalisms and the State,* ed. Martin E. Marty and R. Scott Appleby (Chicago: Chicago University Press, 1993), 462–490; and Samuel C. Heilman and Menachem Friedman, "Religious Fundamentalism and Religious Jews: The Case of the Haredim," in *Fundamentalisms Observed,* ed. Martin E. Marty and R. Scott Appleby (Chicago: Chicago University Press, 1994), 197–264.

24. Yoram Bilu and Eyal Ben-Ari, "The Making of Modern Saints: Manufactured Charisma and the Abu-Hatseiras of Israel," *American Ethnologist* 19, no. 4 (1992): 672–687.

25. See Ehud Sprinzak, "Gush Emunim: The Tip of the Iceberg," *Jerusalem Quarterly,* Fall 1981, 28–47; Danny Rubinstein, *Gush Emunim* [in Hebrew] (Tel Aviv: Kibbutz Hameuhad, 1982); and Gideon Aran, "Jewish Zionist Fundamentalism: The Bloc of the Faithful in Israel (Gush Emunim)," in Marty and Appleby, *Fundamentalisms Observed,* 265–344.

26. Aviezer Ravitzky, "The Contemporary Lubavitch Hasidic Movement," in *Accounting for Fundamentalism,* ed. Martin E. Marty and R. Scott Appleby (Chicago and London: University of Chicago Press, 1994), 303–328.

27. For a geographical insight into the competition, see Yosseph Shilhav, "Spatial Strategies of the Haredi Population in Jerusalem," *Socio-Economic Planning Science* 18, no. 6 (1986): 411–418.

28. For information on Rafi, see Yanai, *Split at the Top.* For information on the DMC, see Amnon Rubinstein, *A Certain Political Experience* [in Hebrew] (Jerusalem: Idanim, 1982); Nachman Orieli and Amnon Barzilai, *The Rise and*

Fall of the DMC [in Hebrew] (Tel Aviv: Reshafim, 1982); and Miri Bitton, "Third Reformist Parties," Ph.D. dissertation, City University of New York, 1995.

29. Jacob Landau, *The Arabs in Israel* (London: Oxford University Press, 1990).

Chapter 6: Party Organization

1. Russell J. Dalton and Martin P. Wattenberg, "Unthinkable Democracy: Political Change in Advanced Industrial Democracies," in *Parties Without Partisans: Political Change in Advanced Industrial Democracies,* ed. Dalton and Wattenberg (Oxford: Oxford University Press, 2000), 3–16; Richard Gunther and Larry Diamond, "Types and Functions of Parties," in *Political Parties and Democracy,* ed. Diamond and Gunther (Baltimore: Johns Hopkins University Press, 2001), 3–39.

2. Peter Medding, *Mapai in Israel* (Cambridge: Cambridge University Press, 1972), 88.

3. Yaacov Shavit, *From Majority to State—The Revisionist Movement: The Settlement Program and the Social Idea, 1925–35* [in Hebrew] (Tel Aviv: Yariv, 1978), 101–103.

4. Otto Kirchheimer, "The Transformation of West European Party Systems," in *Political Parties and Political Development,* ed. Joseph LaPalombara and Myron Weiner (Princeton: Princeton University Press, 1996), 177–200.

5. Morris Fiorina, *Retrospective Voting in American National Elections* (New Haven: Yale University Press, 1981).

6. Richard S. Katz and Peter Mair, "Changing Models of Party Organization and Party Democracy," *Political Parties* 1 (1995): 5–27.

7. Dan Avnon, ed., *The Parties Law in Israel* [in Hebrew] (Tel Aviv: Israel Democracy Institute and Kibbutz Hameuhad, 1993).

8. Maurice Duverger, *Political Parties* (New York: Wiley, 1963), quotations from 140–141.

9. Most of the examples are from Natan Yanai, *Party Leadership in Israel* (Ramat Gan: Turtledove, 1981).

10. Shevah Weiss, *Politicians in Israel* [in Hebrew] (Tel Aviv: Ahiasaf, 1973).

11. Myron J. Aronoff, *Power and Ritual in the Israeli Labor Party* (Assen: Van Gorcum, 1977), chaps. 2 and 6.

12. Gary Schiff, *Tradition and Politics: Religious Parties of Israel* (Detroit: Wayne State University Press, 1977), 81.

13. Giora Goldberg and Steven Hoffmann, "Nominations in Israel: Politics of Institutionalization," *The Elections in Israel—1981,* ed. A. Arian (Tel Aviv: Ramot, 1983).

14. Medding, *Mapai in Israel,* quotations from 122–124.

15. Aliza Bar, *Primaries and Other Methods of Candidate Selection* [in Hebrew] (Jerusalem: Israel Democracy Institute and Kibbutz Hameuhad, 1996).

16. Gideon Doron and Barry Kay, "Reforming Israel's Voting Schemes," in *The Elections in Israel—1992,* ed. Asher Arian and Michal Shamir (Albany: SUNY Press, 1995), 313.

17. Gideon Rahat and Neta Sher-Hadar, *Interparty Selection of Candidates for the Knesset List and for Prime-Ministerial Candidacy 1995–1997* [in Hebrew] (Jerusalem: Israel Democracy Institute, 1999).

18. Menachem Hofnung, "Fat Parties—Lean Candidates: Funding Israeli Internal Party Contests," in *The Elections in Israel—2003*, ed. Asher Arian and Michal Shamir (Jerusalem and New Brunswick: Israel Democracy Institute and Transaction, forthcoming); and Menachem Hofnung, "Corruption, Political Finance and the Rule of Law," in *Critical Issues in Israeli Society*, ed. Alan Dowty (Westport, Conn.: Praeger, 2004).

19. Hofnung, "Fat Parties—Lean Candidates."

20. Menahem Hofnung, *Party Funding and Campaign Funding in Israel* [in Hebrew] (Tel Aviv: Israel Democracy Institute and Kibbutz Hameuhad, 1993).

21. Robert Michels, *Political Parties* (New York: Hearst, 1915), 391.

22. Ibid., 228.

23. Medding, *Mapai in Israel*, quotations from 301–305.

24. Michels, *Political Parties*, 407–408.

Chapter 7: The Electoral System

1. Shlomo Deshen, *Immigrant Voters in Israel* (Manchester, England: Manchester University Press, 1970).

2. Ami Pedahzur, "Who's Defending the Democracy? The Battle among the Elites over the Elections to the 16th Knesset," in *The Elections in Israel—2003*, ed. Asher Arian and Michal Shamir (Jerusalem and New Brunswick: Israel Democracy Institute and Transaction, forthcoming); and Michal Shamir and Keren Weinshall-Margel, "Disqualification of Political Party Lists and Candidates for the Knesset—Were the 2003 Elections Unique?" in Arian and Shamir, *Elections in Israel—2003*.

3. Moshe Atias, *Knesset Israel in Eretz Israel* [in Hebrew] (Jerusalem: The National Committee, 1944), 20–21.

4. The minimum percentage was raised to 2 percent after the 2003 elections.

5. Arend Lijphart, *Electoral Systems and Party Systems* (Oxford: Oxford University Press, 1994), 134–135.

6. Dana Arieli-Horowitz, *The Labyrinth of Legitimacy: Referendum in Israel* [in Hebrew] (Jerusalem: Israel Democracy Institute and Kibbutz Hameuhad, 1993).

7. Dana Blander and Gideon Rahat, *The Referendum: Myth and Reality* (Jerusalem: Israel Democracy Institute, 2002).

8. Harry Eckstein, "The Impact of Electoral Systems on Representative Government," in *Comparative Politics—A Reader*, ed. Harry Eckstein and David E. Apter (Glencoe, Ill.: Free Press, 1963), 247–254.

9. Douglas Rae, *The Political Consequences of Electoral Laws* (New Haven, Conn.: Yale University Press, 1967); and Rein Taagepera and Matthew Søberg Shugart, *Seats and Votes* (New Haven, Conn.: Yale University Press, 1989).

10. Ofer Kenig, Gideon Rahat, and Reuven Y. Hazan, "The Political Consequences of the Introduction and the Repeal of Direct Elections for the Prime Minister," in Arian and Shamir, *Elections in Israel—2003.*

11. Maurice Duverger, "A New Political System Model: Semi-Presidential Government," *European Journal of Political Research* 8 (1980).

12. Gideon Doron and Barry Kay, "Reforming Israel's Voting Schemes," in *The Elections in Israel—1992,* ed. Asher Arian and Michal Shamir (Albany: SUNY Press, 1995), 299–320.

13. Stanley Waterman and Eliahu Zefadia, "Israeli Electoral Reforms in Action," *Political Geography* 11, no. 6 (November 1992): 563–578.

14. U. Reichman, B. Bracha, A. Rosen-Zvi, A. Shapira, D. Friedman, B. Susser, K. Mann, A. Maoz, and A. Klagsveld, *A Proposal for a Constitution for the State of Israel* (Tel Aviv: A Constitution for Israel, 1987).

15. Guy Bechor, *A Constitution for Israel* [in Hebrew] (Or Yehuda: Maariv, 1996); and Tamar Hermann, "The Rise of Instrumental Voting: The Campaign for Political Reform," in Arian and Shamir, *Elections in Israel—1992,* 275–297.

16. Gideon Alon, *Direct Election* (Tel Aviv: Meidan, 1995).

Chapter 8: Electoral Behavior

1. All voting statistics are from official publications of the Central Bureau of Statistics.

2. Amal Jamal, "Abstention as Participation: The Labyrinth of Arab Politics in Israel," in *The Elections in Israel—2001,* ed. Asher Arian and Michal Shamir (Jerusalem: The Israel Democracy Institute, 2002), 105–133; Nadim Rouhana, Nabil Saleh, and Nimer Sultany, "Voting without Voice: About the Vote of the Palestinian Minority in the 16th Knesset Elections," in *The Elections in Israel—2003,* ed. Asher Arian and Michal Shamir (Jerusalem and New Brunswick, N.J.: Israel Democracy Institute and Transaction Press, forthcoming).

3. Uri Avner, "Non-Voting in the Elections for the Tenth Knesset (1981) and Its Causes" [in Hebrew], *Statistical Monthly of Israel* (1982): appendix 5, pp. 79–101; Michal Shamir and Asher Arian, "Introduction," in Arian and Shamir, *Elections in Israel—2001,* 7–27.

4. A. Arian, *The Choosing People: Voting Behavior in Israel* (Cleveland: Press of Case Western Reserve University, 1973), chap. 6.

5. The literature on voting is extensive. Among the important contributions are Bernard Berelson, Paul E. Lazarsfeld, and William N. McPhee, *Voting* (Chicago: University of Chicago Press, 1954); David Butler and Donald E. Stokes, *Political Change in Britain* (London: Macmillan, 1969); Angus Campbell, Gerald Gurin, and Warren E. Miller, *The Voter Decides* (Evanston, Ill.: Row Peterson, 1954); Angus Campbell, Philip E. Converse, Warren E. Miller, and Donald E. Stokes, *The American Voter* (New York: Wiley, 1964); Morris P. Fiorina, *Retrospective Voting in American National Elections* (New Haven: Yale University Press, 1981);

Norman G. H. Nie, Sidney Verba, and John R. Petrocik, *The Changing American Voter* (Cambridge, Mass.: Harvard University Press, 1976); and Russell J. Dalton and Martin P. Wattenberg, eds., *Parties without Partisans: Political Change in Advanced Industrial Democracies* (Oxford: Oxford University Press, 2000).

6. Martin P. Wattenberg, *The Rise of Candidate-Centered Politics* (Cambridge, Mass.: Harvard University Press, 1991), and *The Decline of American Political Parties 1952–1996* (Cambridge, Mass.: Harvard University Press, 1998).

7. Susan J. Pharr and Robert D. Putnam, eds., *Disaffected Democracies—What's Troubling the Trilateral Countries?* (Princeton: Princeton University Press, 2000); and Asher Arian, David Nachmias, Doron Navot, and Danielle Shani, *The Israeli Democracy Index—2003* [in Hebrew] (Jerusalem: The Israel Democracy Institute, 2003).

8. Michal Shamir and Asher Arian, "Collective Identity and Electoral Competition in Israel," *American Political Science Review* 93 (1999): 265–277.

9. Russell J. Dalton, *Citizen Politics: Public Opinion and Political Parties in Advanced Industrial Democracies,* 3rd ed. (Chatham, N.J.: Chatham House, 2002); Stefano Bartolini and Peter Mair, *Identity, Competition and Electoral Availability: The Stabilisation of European Electorates 1885–1985* (Cambridge: Cambridge University Press, 1990); and Mark N. Franklin, Thomas T. Mackie, and Henry Valen, *Electoral Change: Responses to Evolving Social and Attitudinal Structures in Western Countries* (Cambridge: Cambridge University Press, 1992).

10. Michal Shamir, "Realignment in the Israeli Party System," in *The Elections in Israel—1984,* ed. Asher Arian and Michal Shamir (New Brunswick, N.J.: Transaction, 1986), 272–275.

11. Paul R. Abramson, "Generational Replacement, Ethnic Change, and Partisan Support in Israel," *Journal of Politics* 51 (1989).

12. Michael Shalev, with Sigal Kis, "Social Cleavages Among Non-Arab Voters: A New Analysis," in *The Elections in Israel—1999,* ed. Asher Arian and Michal Shamir (Albany: SUNY Press, 2002), 67–96.

13. Butler and Stokes, *Political Change in Britain,* 293.

14. See H. Smith, "Analysis of Voting," in *The Elections in Israel—1969,* ed. A. Arian (Jerusalem: Jerusalem Academic Press, 1972), 63–80.

15. V. O. Key Jr., "A Theory of Critical Elections," *Journal of Politics* 17 (1955): 4. See also V. O. Key Jr., *The Responsible Electorate* (Cambridge, Mass.: Harvard University Press, 1966); and Angus Campbell, "A Classification of Presidential Elections," in *Elections and the Political Order,* ed. Angus Campbell, Philip Converse, Warren Miller, and Donald Stokes (New York: Wiley, 1966), 63–77.

16. Duverger, *Political Parties,* 307.

17. Morris Fiorina, *Retrospective Voting in American National Elections* (New Haven: Yale University Press, 1981); Arthur H. Miller and Martin P. Wattenberg, "Throwing the Rascals Out: Policy and Performance Evaluations of Presidential Candidates, 1952–1980," *American Political Science Review* 79 (1985): 359–372.

18. Michal Shamir and Asher Arian, "The Intifada and Israeli Voters: Policy Preferences and Performance Evaluations," in *The Elections in Israel—1988,* ed.

Asher Arian and Michal Shamir (Boulder, Colo.: Westview, 1990), 77–92; Roni Shachar and Michal Shamir, "Modelling Victory : The 1992 Elections in Israel," in *The Elections in Israel—1992,* ed. Asher Arian and Michal Shamir (Albany: SUNY Press, 1995).

Chapter 9: The Government, the Knesset, and the Judiciary

1. Amnon Rubinstein, *The Constitutional Law of Israel,* 4th ed., 2 vols. [in Hebrew] (Tel Aviv: Schocken, 1991), 343.

2. Gideon Alon, "Could the Prime Minister Continue in Office as a Convicted Felon? Definitely a Possibility," *Haaretz,* February 16, 2004.

3. Daniel Korn and Boaz Shapiro, *Coalitions* [in Hebrew] (Tel-Aviv: Zmura Bitan, 1997).

4. Yehuda Ben Meir, *Civil-Military Relations in Israel* (New York: Columbia University Press, 1995), 31–32.

5. William H. Riker, *The Theory of Political Coalitions* (New Haven: Yale University Press, 1962); David Nachmias, "Coalition Politics in Israel," *Comparative Political Studies* 7 (1974): 316–333; and Norman Schofield, "Coalition Politics: A Formal Model and Empirical Analysis," *Journal of Theoretical Politics* 7, no. 3 (1995): 245–281.

6. Michael Laver and Kenneth A. Shepsle, *Making and Breaking Governments: Cabinets and Legislatures in Parliamentary Democracies* (Cambridge: Cambridge University Press, 1996).

7. Schofield, "Coalition Politics," 245–248.

8. Asher Arian, David Nachmias, and Ruth Amir, *Executive Governance in Israel* (London: Palgrave, 2002), chap. 5; David Nachmias and Itai Sened, "The Basis of Pluralism: The Redistributional Effects of the New Electoral Law in Israel," in *The Elections in Israel—1996,* ed. Asher Arian and Michal Shamir (Albany: SUNY Press, 1999).

9. Gideon Alon, *Direct Election* [in Hebrew] (Tel Aviv: Bitan, 1995); and Yossi Beilin, *An Accident Called the Direct Election* [in Hebrew] (Tel Aviv: Kibbutz Hameuhad, 1996).

10. Walter Bagehot, *The English Constitution* (London: Watts, 1964); and Ivor Jennings, *The British Constitution* (Cambridge: Cambridge University Press, 1966).

11. Material for this section is from Basic Law: Knesset. Other sources are Shevah Weiss, *The House of the Elected* [in Hebrew] (Tel Aviv: Ahiasaf, 1977); Asher Zidon, *Knesset* (New York: Herzl Press, 1967); and Rubinstein, *Constitutional Law.*

12. Baruch Krah, "A Suspect Knesset, Knesset Members Investigated," *Haaretz,* April 26, 2004, B8.

13. Shachar Ilan, "Organized Crime Penetrates the Knesset," *Haaretz,* April 26, 2004, B3.

14. R. T. McKenzie, *British Political Parties* (New York: Praeger, 1963).

15. Rubinstein, *Constitutional Law,* 437, n. 56.

16. Dana Blander and Eran Klein, *Private Members' Bills: Comparative Analysis and Recommendations* (Jerusalem: Israel Democracy Institute, 2002), 42–44; and Knesset Web site: www.knesset.gov.il. Not including bills originating in committee.

17. Clauses 49 and 50 of the Basic Law: Government. See Rubinstein, *Constitutional Law,* 616–618. See also Baruch Bracha, "Restriction of Personal Freedom without Due Process of Law According to the Defence (Emergency) Regulations, 1945," in *Israel Yearbook of Human Rights, 1978,* 296–323.

18. See J. E. Baker, *The Legal System of Israel* (Jerusalem: Israel Universities Press, 1968).

19. Ruth Gavison, *Constitutions and Political Reconstruction? Israel's Quest for a Constitution,* (Beverly Hills, Calif.: Sage, 2003).

20. For the Israel Democracy Institute publications on its Constitution by Consensus project, see http://www.idi.org.il/.

21. Philippa Strum, "The Road Not Taken: Constitutional Non-Decision Making in 1948–1950 and Its Impact on Civil Liberties in the Israeli Political Culture," in *Israel: The First Decade of Independence,* ed. S. Ilan Troen and Noah Lucas (Albany: SUNY Press, 1995), 83–104.

22. Knesset Proceedings 5 [in Hebrew], 1721–22.

23. Menachem Elon, "The Way of Law in the Constitution: The Values of a Jewish and Democratic State in Light of the Basic Law: Human Dignity and Freedom" [in Hebrew], *Tel Aviv University Law Review* 17, no. 3 (1993).

24. Rubinstein, *Constitutional Law,* 449.

25. The *Nahmani* Case 2401/95, decision 50(4), 661.

26. Asher Arian, David Nachmias, Doron Navot, and Danielle Shani, *The Israeli Democracy Index—2003* (Jerusalem: Israel Democracy Institute, 2003).

27. Martin Edelman, *Courts, Politics, and Culture in Israel* (Charlottesville: University Press of Virginia, 1994), 36–37; and Rubinstein, *Judges of the Land,* chap. 5.

28. Pnina Lahav, "Foundations of Rights Jurisprudence in Israel: Chief Agranat's Legacy," *Israel Law Review* 24 (1990): 211–269.

29. Shalev Ginossar, "Access to Justice in Israel," in *Access to Justice,* ed. Mauro Cappelletti and Brian Garth (Milan: Giuffre, 1978), 1: 627–648.

30. Shachar Goldman, ed., *The Proposed Reform of the Court System* (Jerusalem: Israel Democracy Institute, 2000).

31. Pnina Lahav, "Rights and Democracy: The Court's Performance," in *Israeli Democracy under Stress,* ed. Ehud Sprinzak and Larry Diamond (Boulder, Colo.: Lynne Rienner, 1993), 125–152.

32. Rubinstein, *Constitutional Law,* chaps. 28, 29.

33. David Kretzmer, *The Legal Status of Arabs in Israel* (Boulder, Colo.: Westview, 1990).

34. Ian Lustick, *Unsettled States, Disputed Lands: Britain and Ireland, France and Algeria, Israel and the West Bank-Gaza* (Ithaca, N.Y., and London: Cornell University Press, 1993).

35. Aharon Barak, *Judicial Interpretation* [in Hebrew] (Jerusalem: Nevo, 1992), and "The Constitutional Revolution: Human Rights Protected" [in Hebrew], *Law and Government in Israel* 1, no. 1 (August 1992): 9–35.

36. Aharon Barak, *Judicial Discretion* (New Haven: Yale University Press, 1989), and *Interpretation of Law* [in Hebrew] (Jerusalem: Nevo, 1993).

37. Menachem Mautner, *The Decline of Formalism and the Rise of Values in Israel Law* (Tel Aviv: Ma'agalay Da'at, 1993): 34–35.

38. Moshe Negbi, *Above the Law* [in Hebrew] (Tel Aviv: Am Oved, 1987); and Menachem Hofnung, *Israel—Security Needs vs. The Rule of Law* [in Hebrew] (Jerusalem: Nevo, 1991).

39. *Bergman v. Minister of Treasury,* Israeli Supreme Court 23 (1) 693.

40. Menachem Hofnung, "The Unintended Consequences of Unplanned Legislative Reform: Constitutional Politics in Israel," *American Journal of Comparative Law,* forthcoming.

41. *Alice Miller v. Minister of Defense,* High Court of Justice 4541/94, decision 49 (4) 94.

42. See *The United Mizrahi Bank* case regarding judicial review, High Court of Justice 6821/93, decision 49 (4) 221; 512–3.

Chapter 10: Interest Groups and Public Policy

1. David Truman, *The Governmental Process* (New York: Knopf, 1951).

2. The term is developed in Brian Chapman, *The Profession of Government* (London: Allen and Unwin, 1959); and by H. Gordon Skilling, "Groups in Soviet Politics: Some Hypotheses," in *Interest Groups in Soviet Politics,* ed. H. Gordon Skilling and Franklin Griffiths (Princeton: Princeton University Press, 1971), 19–45.

3. Clive Thomas, ed., *First World Interest Groups: A Comparative Perspective* (Westport, Conn.: Greenwood Press, 1993).

4. Gadi Wolfsfeld, *The Politics of Provocation: Participation and Protest in Israel* (Albany: SUNY Press, 1988); and Sam N. Lehman-Wilzig, *Wildfire: Grassroots Revolts in Israel in the Post-Socialist Era* (Albany: SUNY Press, 1992).

5. See Suzanne D. Berger, *Organizing Interests in Western Europe: Pluralism, Corporatism, and the Transformation of Politics* (Cambridge: Cambridge University Press, 1981); and Alan Cawson, *Corporatism and Political Theory* (Oxford: Basil Blackwell, 1986).

6. Yael Yishai, *Civil Society in Israel* [in Hebrew] (Jerusalem: Carmel, 2003); and Benjamin Gidron, Michal Bar, Hagai Katz, *The Third Sector in Israel: Between Welfare State and Civil Society* [in Hebrew] (Tel Aviv: Hakibbutz Hameuchad, 2003).

7. Gabriel Almond and James Coleman, eds., *The Politics of Developing Areas* (Princeton: Princeton University Press, 1960).

8. Marcia Drezon-Tepler, *Interest Groups and Political Changes in Israel* (Albany: SUNY Press, 1990).

9. Samuel Finer, *Anonymous Empire: A Study of the Lobby in Great Britain* (London: Pall Mall Press, 1966).

10. Yoram Peri, *Between Battles and Ballots* (Cambridge: Cambridge University Press, 1983), chap. 5.

11. The Tal Report on Recruiting Haredim, 2002, Part 4.

12. Yagil Levy, *Trial and Error: Israel's Route from War to De-Escalation* (Albany: SUNY Press, 1997), chap. 2.

13. Asher Arian, Ilan Talmud, and Tamar Hermann, *National Security and Public Opinion in Israel* (Boulder, Colo.: Westview, 1988), chap. 5; and Asher Arian, *Security Threatened: Surveying Israeli Opinion on Peace and War* (New York: Cambridge University Press, 1995), chap. 3.

14. Baruch Kimmerling, *The Interrupted System: Israeli Citizens in War and Routine Times* (New Brunswick, N.J.: Transaction, 1985); and Uri Ben-Eliezer, *Through the Target-Sights, Derech Hakavenet* [in Hebrew] (Tel Aviv: Dvir, 1995).

15. Peri, *Between Battles and Ballots,* chap. 2; and Yehuda Ben Meir, *Civil-Military Relations in Israel* (New York: Columbia University Press, 1995).

16. Peri, *Between Battles and Ballots,* 50–51.

17. Daniel Shimshoni, *Israeli Democracy* (New York: Free Press, 1982); and Ben Meir, *Civil-Military Relations,* chap. 6.

18. Avner Yaniv, *Dilemmas of Security: Politics, Strategy and the Israeli Experience in Lebanon* (New York: Oxford University Press, 1987).

19. Dina Goren, *Secrecy, Defense and Freedom of the Press* [in Hebrew] (Jerusalem: Magnes Press, 1976), 203–206, cited in Peri, *Between Battles and Ballots,* 200.

20. Amnon Barzilai, *Ramon* (Tel Aviv: Schocken, 1996).

21. *Yediot Aharonot,* April 10, 2003.

22. See Yonatan Reshef, "Political Exchange in Israel: Histadrut-State Relations," *Industrial Relations* 25 (1986): 303–319.

23. Yosef Sapir Institute, *Yosef Sapir* [in Hebrew] (Tel Aviv: Yosef Sapir Institute, 1977), 125.

24. Nadav Shragai, "The Settlers Replace the Knesset Members in the Knesset as Well," *Haaretz,* April 26, 2004, B5.

25. Dan Horowitz and Moshe Lissak, *The Origins of the Israeli Polity: Palestine under the Mandate* (Chicago: University of Chicago Press, 1978). For later developments, see Jay Abarbenel, *The Cooperative Farmer and the Welfare State: Economic Change in an Israeli Moshav* (Manchester, England: Manchester University Press, 1974); and Alex Weingrod, *Reluctant Pioneers* (Ithaca, N.Y.: Cornell University Press, 1966).

26. Neal Sherman, "The Agricultural Sector and the 1977 Knesset Elections," in *The Elections in Israel—1977,* ed. A. Arian (Jerusalem: Jerusalem Academic Press, 1980), 149–170.

27. Moshe Dayan, *Pathmakers* [in Hebrew] (Tel Aviv: Idanim, 1976), 379.

28. Differing viewpoints may be found Gershon Weiler, *Jewish Theocracy* [in Hebrew] (Tel Aviv: Ofakim, 1975); Yeshayahu Leibowitz, *Judaism, the Jewish People and the State of Israel* [in Hebrew] (Jerusalem: Schocken, 1976); Amnon Rubinstein, "State and Religion in Israel," *Journal of Contemporary History,*

October 1967, 107–121; and Charles Liebman, "Religion and Democracy in Israel," in *Israeli Democracy Under Stress,* ed. Ehud Sprinzak and Larry Diamond (Boulder, Colo.: Lynne Rienner, 1993), 255–272.

29. Menachem Friedman, "The Structural Foundation for Religio-Political Accommodation in Israel: Fallacy and Reality," in *Israel: The First Decade of Independence,* ed. S. Ilan Troen and Noah Lucas (Albany: SUNY Press, 1995), 51–81.

30. On the history of religious-secular relations, see Asher Cohen, *From Reconciliation to Intensification* [in Hebrew] (Jerusalem: Schocken, 2003). On the distribution of other attitudes regarding religion, see Shlomit Levy, Hanna Levinsohn, and Elihu Katz, *Beliefs, Observances and Social Integration among Israeli Jews* (Jerusalem: Louis Guttman Institute of Applied Social Research, 1993).

31. Central Bureau of Statistics, Monthly Report, March 2004, vol. 55, table 3G.

32. Martin Edelman, *Courts, Politics, and Culture in Israel* (Charlottesville: University Press of Virginia, 1994).

33. *Rufheisen v. Minister of Interior,* High Court of Justice 62/72, decision xv 2428.

34. *Shalit v. Minister of Interior,* High Court of Justice 68/58, decision xxiii (2) 477; and *Shalit v. Minister of Interior* 72/18, decision xxvi (1) 334.

35. *Haaretz,* May 27, 2004, 13A.

36. Yoav Artsieli, *The Gavison-Medan Covenant: Main Points and Principles* (Jerusalem: Israel Democracy Institute and AVI CHAI Foundation, 2004).

37. Gary Schiff, *Tradition and Politics: Religious Parties of Israel* (Detroit: Wayne State University Press, 1977).

38. Anshel Pepper, "The Budget and Authorities of the Ministry of Religious Affairs Were Dispersed, but Not the Workers," *Haaretz,* March 8, 2004.

Chapter 11: Public Policy, Administration, and Local Government

1. David Ben-Gurion, *Eighth Histadrut Convention* [in Hebrew] (Tel Aviv: Histadrut Executive, 1956).

2. *Statistical Abstract, 2003,* table 8.35.

3. A. Shmaltz, ed., *Educational and Cultural Statistics* [in Hebrew] (Tel Aviv: Histadrut Executive, 1956).

4. On the establishment of the Labor Fund for Israel and the political debate that followed, see Giora Goldberg, "The Labor Exchanges as a Political Instrument in a Developing Society" [in Hebrew], M.A. thesis, Tel Aviv University, 114–117.

5. Louis Avraham, "The Government Employment Services—Changing Roles," M.A. Thesis in Public Policy, Tel Aviv University, 1993.

6. *Statistical Abstract, 1995,* 709; Yael Yishai, *Doctors and the State: Creating Hospital Trusts in Israel* (Jerusalem: Jerusalem Institute for Israel Studies, 1994); and Yaacov Kopf, *Resource Allocation to Social Services 2003* [in Hebrew] (Jerusalem: Israel Center for Policy and Social Research, 2004), 141.

7. World Health Organization Report 2003 Web site. http://www.who.int/pub/en/

8. David Chinitz, "Hiding in the Market Place: Technocracy and Politics in Israeli Health Policy," in James Bjorkman and Christa Altenstetter, *Comparative Health Policy* (London: Macmillan, 1996).

9. Kopf, *Resource Allocation,* 148.

10. Amnon Barzilai, *Ramon* (Tel Aviv: Schocken, 1996), 304–306.

11. See Yair Zalmanovitch, *Policy Making from the Margins of Government: The Case of the Israeli Health System* (Albany: SUNY Press, 2001).

12. Yael Yishai, *The Power of Expertise: The Israel Medical Association* [in Hebrew] (Jerusalem: Jerusalem Institute for Israel Studies, 1990).

13. Asher Arian, "Health Care in Israel: Political and Administrative Aspects," *International Political Science Review* 2 (1981): 43–56.

14. Ministry of Health, "Principles for a National Health Insurance Law" [in Hebrew], 1978.

15. Brenda Danet, *Pulling Strings: Biculturalism in Israeli Bureaucracy* (Albany: SUNY Press, 1988).

16. Gerald E. Caiden, *Israel's Administrative Culture* (Berkeley, Calif.: Institute of Governmental Studies, 1970), 18–19.

17. Jacob Reuveny, *The Israel Civil Service* (Ramat Gan: Massada, 1974); and David Nachmias and David H. Rosenbloom, *Bureaucratic Culture: Citizens and Administrators in Israel* (New York: St. Martin's, 1978).

18. Yitzhak Galnoor, *No, Mister Commissioner!* (Tel Aviv: Yediot Aharonot Hemed Books, 2003).

19. Asher Arian, David Nachmias, and Ruth Amir, *Executive Governance in Israel* (London: Palgrave, 2002), chap. 7.

20. David Dery, *Political Appointments in Israel* (Jerusalem: Israel Democracy Institute and Kibbutz Hameuhad, 1993).

21. Michael Brecher, *Decisions in Crisis: Israel, 1967 and 1973* (Berkeley: University of California Press, 1980), 239.

22. Yitzhak Galnoor, "Water Planning: Who Gets the Last Drop?" in *Can Planning Replace Politics? The Israeli Experience,* ed. Raphaella Bilski et al. (The Hague: Martinus Nijhoff, 1980), 137–215.

23. Ibid.

24. Avraham Weinrot, "Difference in the Roles of the Attorney General" [in Hebrew], *Hamishpat* 6 (1995): 54–55; and Ruth Gavison, "The Attorney General—A Critical Review of the New Trends" [in Hebrew], *Plilim,* 5, no. 2 (1996): 34.

25. Mordechai Kremnitzer, "The Role of the Prosecutor in a Criminal Action" [in Hebrew], *Plilim* 5, no. 2 (1996): 173–187.

26. Yitzhak Zamir, "The Attorney General and the Battle for the Rule of Law" [in Hebrew], *Iyunei Mishpat* 11 (1986): 411–421.

27. Baruch Kimmerling, "Elections as a Battle Field for National Identity," in *Elections in Israel—1996,* ed. Asher Arian and Michal Shamir (Albany: SUNY Press, 1999).

28. Menachem Mautner, "The Probability of Politics" [in Hebrew], *Theory and Criticism* 5 (1994): 25–53.

29. Ruth Gavison, *The Judicial Revolution* [in Hebrew] (Jerusalem: Israel Institute for Democracy, 1998).

30. Yechiel Gutman, *A Storm in the Shin Bet* [in Hebrew] (Tel Aviv: Yediot Aharonot, 1995).

31. *Haaretz,* April 23, 1997.

32. Elyakim Rubenstein, "Decision of the Attorney General in the Matter of the Appointment of Roni Bar-On as Attorney General," April 20, 1997.

33. *Haaretz,* September 27, 2000.

34. Gad Barzilai and David Nachmias, "Governmental Lawyering in the Political Sphere: Advocating the Leviathan," *Israel Studies* 3, no. 2 (1998): 30–46.

35. David Dery and Emanuel Sharon, *Bureaucracy and Democracy in Budgetary Reform* [in Hebrew] (Jerusalem: Israel Democracy Institute, 1994).

36. Alex Cukierman, *Central Bank Strategy, Credibility and Independence: Theory and Evidence* (Cambridge, Mass.: MIT Press, 1992).

37. Finn E. Kydland and Edward C. Prescott, "Rules Rather than Discretion: The Inconsistency of Optimal Policy Plans," *Journal of Political Economy* 85, no. 3 (1977): 473–492.

38. Yair Aharoni, *The Political Economy of Israel* [in Hebrew] (Tel Aviv: Am Oved, 1991).

39. Edmund S. Phelps, *Seven Schools of Macroeconomic Thought* (Oxford: Clarendon Press, 1990).

40. Michael Bruno, *Crisis, Stabilization and Economic Reform* (Oxford: Clarendon Press, 1993).

41. *Haaretz,* June 19, 1997, A1.

42. Hanan Kristal and Ilan Kafir, *The Sixth Medal of Honor—Elections '99* [in Hebrew] (Tel Aviv: Keter, Alfa Communications, 1999), 155–159.

43. Ronen Shamir, "The Politics of Probability" [in Hebrew], *Theory and Criticism* 5 (1994): 7–24.

44. Gideon Doron, *Election Strategy* [in Hebrew] (Rehovot: Kivunim, 1996).

45. Roni Shachar and Michal Shamir, "Modeling Victory in the 1992 Election," in *The Election in Israel—1992,* ed. Asher Arian and Michal Shamir (Albany: SUNY Press, 1995).

46. Amnon Rubinstein, *Constitutional Law in the State of Israel* [in Hebrew] (Tel Aviv: Schocken, 1996), 594–607, 680.

47. *Haaretz,* July 10, 1996, A6.

48. *Statistical Abstract, 1981,* 599.

49. Rachel Gruman and Moshe Peleg, *Democracy in Israel* [in Hebrew] (Jerusalem: Carmel, 1995).

50. See David Dery and Binat Schwarz-Milner, *Who Governs Local Government?* [in Hebrew] (Jerusalem: Israel Democracy Institute and Hakibbutz Hameuhad, 1994); Efraim Ben-Zadok, ed., *Local Communities and the Israeli Polity* (Albany:

SUNY Press, 1993); and Daniel Elazar and Chaim Kalchheim, eds., *Local Government in Israel* (Lanham, Md.: University Press of America, 1988).

51. Arye Hecht, "Municipal Councils Opposed to the Mayors in Israel's Local Government," Jerusalem Center for Public and National Issues, August 1993, 4.

52. Mordecai Ben-Porat, "The Election System for the Local Authorities" [in Hebrew] (Jerusalem: Ministry of the Interior, 1978). Mimeographed.

53. Hecht, "Municipal Councils," 9.

54. Shevah Weiss, *Local Government in Israel* [in Hebrew] (Tel Aviv: Am Oved, 1972).

55. Hanna Herzog, *Realistic Women: Women in Local Politics* [in Hebrew] (Jerusalem: Jerusalem Institute for Israel Studies, 1994).

56. Efraim Torgovnik and Yeshayahu Barzel, "Block Grant Allocation: Relationship between Self-Government and Redistribution," *Public Administration* 57 (1979): 87–102.

57. Fred Lazin, *Politics and Policy Implementation: Project Renewal in Israel* (Albany: SUNY Press, 1994).

Chapter 12: Aspects of Political Culture

1. Gabriel Almond and Sidney Verba, *The Civic Culture* (Princeton: Princeton University Press, 1966); Mary Douglas and Aaron Wildavsky, *Risk and Culture: An Essay on the Selection of Technological and Environmental Dangers* (Berkeley: University of California Press, 1982); and Robert D. Putnam, *Making Democracy Work: Civic Traditions in Modern Italy* (Princeton: Princeton University Press, 1993).

2. Donald E. Stokes, "Spatial Models of Party Competition," *American Political Science Review* 57 (June 1963): 368–377.

3. This section is based largely on Asher Arian and Michal Shamir, "The Primarily Political Functions of the Left-Right Continuum," *Comparative Politics,* January 1983, 139–158.

4. Philip E. Converse, "The Nature of Belief Systems in Mass Publics," in *Ideology and Discontent,* ed. David E. Apter (New York: Free Press, 1964), 206–261; David Butler and Donald E. Stokes, *Political Change in Britain* (London: Macmillan, 1969); Ronald Inglehart and Hans D. Klingemann, "Party Identification, Ideological Preference and the Left-Right Dimension among Western Mass Publics," in *Party Identification and Beyond,* ed. Ian Budge, Ivor Crewe, and Dennis Farlie (London: Wiley, 1976), 243–273.

5. This discussion is based largely on Michal Shamir and Asher Arian, "Collective Identity and Electoral Competition in Israel," *American Political Science Review* 93 (June 1999): 265–277.

6. George Rabinowitz and Stuart E. MacDonald, "A Directional Theory of Issue Voting," *American Political Science Review* 83 (1989): 115.

7. This section is based largely on Michal Shamir and Asher Arian, "Competing Values and Policy Choices: Israeli Public Opinion on Foreign and Security Affairs," *British Journal of Political Science* 24 (1994): 111–133.

8. Elihu Katz, "Forty-nine Percent Lean towards 'Transfer' of Arabs," *Jerusalem Post International Edition*, August 20, 1988; and Charles Liebman and Eliezer Don-Yehiya, *Civil Religion in Israel: Traditional Judaism and Political Culture in the Jewish State* (Berkeley: University of California Press, 1983).

9. Yehoshafat Harkabi, *Israel's Fateful Decisions* (London: I.B. Tauris, 1988).

10. Dan Horowitz and Moshe Lissak, *Origins of the Israeli Polity: Palestine under the Mandate* (Chicago: University of Chicago Press, 1978); Baruch Kimmerling, *Zionism and Territory* (Berkeley: University of California Press, 1983); and Dan Horowitz and Moshe Lissak, *Trouble in Utopia: The Overburdened Polity of Israel* (Albany: SUNY Press, 1989).

11. Asher Arian, Shlomit Barnea, Pazit Ben-Nun, *The 2004 Israeli Democracy Index: Auditing Israeli Democracy* (Jerusalem: The Guttman Center at the Israel Democracy Institute, 2004). See http://www.idi.org.il/ for Jewish respondents only. See also Asher Arian, *Security Threatened: Surveying Israeli Opinion on Peace and War* (New York: Cambridge University Press, 1995), chap. 8.

12. For an assessment of freedom of the press in conjunction with Israeli democracy, see Asher Arian, Shlomit Barnea, and Pazit Ben-Nun, *Auditing Israeli Democracy 2004: Attitudes of Youth* (Jerusalem: Israel Democracy Institute, 2004).

13. Daniel Shimshoni, *Israeli Democracy* (New York: Free Press, 1982), 83–84.

14. Meirav Yudelevitch, "Poraz: The Mandate's Newspaper Law Should be Abolished," ynet [a *Yediot* news service on-line], Culture, April 29, 2003.

15. Arian, Barnea, and Ben-Nun, *Auditing Israeli Democracy 2004*; and Yael Yishai, *Civil Society in Israel* [in Hebrew] (Jerusalem: Carmel, 2003), 62.

16. The TGI /Teleseker ongoing survey of "readership" of newspapers, including the Jewish population 18 and older (3.541 million people), January–December 2003. See also *Statistical Abstract of Israel 2003*, table 7.9.

17. Dan Caspi and Yehiel Limor, *The Mass Media in Israel 1948–1990* [in Hebrew] (Tel Aviv: Am Oved,1995).

18. William Frankel, *Israel Observed* (London: Thames and Hudson, 1980), 138.

19. Rachel Lael, ed., *Channel 2—The First Year* [in Hebrew] (Jerusalem: Israeli Democracy Institute, 1994).

20. The Israeli Rating Committee, "Data on Viewing" [in Hebrew], at http://www.midrug-mt.org.il/index.asp.

21. Caspi and Limor, *Mass Media*, 122–133.

22. V. O. Key Jr., *Public Opinion and American Democracy* (New York: Knopf, 1961); Benjamin I. Page and Robert Y. Shapiro, *The Rational Public: Fifty Years of Trends in Americans' Policy Preferences* (Chicago: Chicago University Press, 1992); James A. Stimson, *Public Opinion in America: Moods, Cycles, & Swings* (Boulder, Colo.: Westview, 1991); and John R. Zaller, *The Nature and Origins of Mass Opinion* (Cambridge: Cambridge University Press, 1992).

23. Gabriel Weimann, "Caveat Populi Quaestor: The 1992 Pre-Elections Polls in the Israeli Press," in *The Elections in Israel—1992*, ed. Asher Arian and Michal Shamir (Albany: SUNY Press, 1995), 258.

24. Raphael Ventura, "The Influence of the Close Family Circle on the Voting Patterns of the Individual in Israel," Ph.D. dissertation, Tel Aviv University, 1996.

25. Arian, Barnea, and Ben-Nun, *Auditing Israeli Democracy 2004*.

26. A. Arian, "Were the 1973 Elections in Israel Critical?" *Comparative Politics,* October 1975, 152–165.

27. On this and related topics of culture, see Nurith Gertz, *Captive of a Dream: National Myths in Israeli Culture* [in Hebrew] (Tel Aviv: Am Oved, 1995); Tamar Katriel, *Communal Webs: Community and Culture in Contemporary Israel* (Albany: SUNY Press, 1991); and Tamar Katriel, *Talking Straight: 'Dugri' Speech in Israeli Sabra Culture* (Cambridge: Cambridge University Press, 1986).

28. Zvi Gitelman, *Becoming Israelis: Political Resocialization of Soviet and American Immigrants* (New York: Praeger, 1982).

29. Arian, Barnea, and Ben-Nun, *Auditing Israeli Democracy 2004*.

30. Asher Arian, *Israeli Security Opinion 2004,* Jaffee Center for Strategic Studies, Tel Aviv University, 2004.

31. Michal Shamir and John Sullivan, "The Political Context of Tolerance: A Cross-National Perspective from Israel and the United States," *American Political Science Review* 77 (1983): 911–928. See also Carol Gordon and Asher Arian, "Threat and Decision Making," *Journal of Conflict Resolution,* April 2001, 196–215.

32. Arian, *Security Threatened,* chap. 9.

33. Page and Shapiro, *Rational Public,* 9–11.

34. Gadi Wolfsfeld, "The Politics of Provocation Revisited: Participation and Protest in Israel," in *Israeli Democracy Under Stress,* ed. Ehud Sprinzak and Larry Diamond (Boulder, Colo.: Lynne Rienner, 1993), 199–220.

35. Ehud Sprinzak, *Political Violence in Israel* (Jerusalem: Jerusalem Institute for Israel Studies, 1995); Ehud Sprinzak, *The Ascendance of Israel's Radical Right* (New York: Oxford University Press, 1991); and Moshe Negbi, *Above the Law* [in Hebrew] (Tel Aviv: Am Oved, 1987).

GLOSSARY

AGUDAT ISRAEL (also AGUDA). Ultra-orthodox religious political party with a non-Zionist ideology.

AHDUT HAAVODA. *(a)* Political organization founded in 1919 and dominant in the politics of the Yishuv; *(b)* left-wing party that joined Mapai and Rafi in 1968 to form the Israel Labor Party.

AL-AQSA INTIFADA. Arab uprising that began in September 2000 with the visit of Ariel Sharon, then the leader of the opposition, to the Temple Mount in Jerusalem.

ALIGNMENT. *(a)* Name of election list in 1965 composed of Mapai and Ahdut Haavoda; *(b)* name of election list between 1969 and 1984 composed of Labor and Mapam.

ALIYAH (plural ALIYOT). Waves of mass immigration to Israel. Literally, going up.

ASHKENAZIM. Jews whose background is generally the countries of Europe.

BADER-OFER AMENDMENT. Law that sets the method of distributing the last seats to be allocated in Knesset elections. Based on Hagenbach-Bischoff method.

BALAD. Arab party with a vigorous nationalist platform. Won three seats in 2003.

BALFOUR DECLARATION. Statement by British secretary of state for foreign affairs in 1917 supporting the establishment of a Jewish national home in Palestine.

BASIC LAW. Legislation of constitutional stature. Collection of Basic Laws to form the Israeli constitution.

BEITAR. Youth group of the Revisionist movement and later of the Herut movement.

BLACK PANTHERS. Jewish protest movement to better social and economic status of Sephardim. Affiliated in electoral list with Rakah.

CAMP DAVID ACCORDS. Israeli-Egyptian peace agreements worked out in 1979 between Prime Minister Menachem Begin and President Anwar Sadat, mediated by U.S. President Jimmy Carter at Camp David, Maryland.

CITIZENS RIGHTS MOVEMENT (CRM). Small party of the left led by Shulamit Aloni.

COUNCIL OF TORAH SAGES. Committee of rabbis that provides political and religious instruction to Agudat Israel.

DEGEL HATORAH. Ultra-Orthodox non-Zionist political party.

DEMOCRATIC MOVEMENT FOR CHANGE (DMC). Party headed by Yigael Yadin; ran only in 1977 and won 15 seats.

DOMINANT PARTY. A political party in power for some time with spiritual and wideranging dominance.

DUNAM. 1 dunam = 1,000 square meters, or 0.222 acres, or 9,700 sq. ft.

EDA HAHARIDIT. Ultra-orthodox group that rejects Zionism.

EL AL. National airline of Israel.

ELECTORS COUNCIL (ASEFAT NIVHARIM). Elected assembly of the Yishuv.

ERETZ ISRAEL. Land of Israel, denoting the biblical Promised Land.

FREE CENTER. Splinter group from Herut in 1967, a part of the Likud between 1973 and 1977, and a component of the DMC in 1977. Headed by Shmuel Tamir.

GAHAL (acronym for the Herut-Liberal bloc). Established as a joint list in 1965; expanded in 1973 and called the Likud.

GENERAL ZIONISTS. Right-of-center bourgeois party that joined with the Progressives between 1961 and 1965 and was known as the Liberal Party.

GESHER. Party led by David Levy, stressing social and economic equality and a militant security policy. Levy emerged from within the Likud, then became Ehud Barak's foreign minister, later returning to the Likud.

GREATER ISRAEL. Notion of completeness and indivisibility of Eretz Israel.

GUSH EMUNIM. Settlement movement, largely religious, active in the territories acquired after the 1967 war and staunchly opposed to any territorial compromise.

HADASH (Hebrew acronym for the Democratic Front for Peace and Equality). Left-of-center party (including Israeli communists) with a strong base among Israeli Arabs.

HAGANAH. Defense force of the Yishuv.

HAGENBACH-BISCHOFF METHOD. Allocation of seats in parliament based on consideration of the relative strength of the competing lists.

HALACHA. Jewish religious law.

HAPOEL HAMIZRACHI. Religious workers' movement and a major component of the National Religious Party.

HAPOEL HATZAIR. Political party in the Yishuv period representing labor.

HAREDI (plural HAREDIM). Ultra-Orthodox, non-Zionist parties. (The word *haredi* connotes awe-inspired, fearful of God's majesty).

HASHOMER HATZAIR. Settlement movement and youth group of Mapam.

HERUT. Political party with nationalist ideology and a major component of the Likud.

HEVRAT OVDIM. Holding company of the Histadrut.

HISTADRUT. General Federation of Labor; formerly a key economic and political force in Israel.

HOVEVEI ZION. First organized national Jewish groups that encouraged immigration to Eretz Israel at the end of the nineteenth century.

IDF (ISRAEL DEFENSE FORCES). Israel's army.

INDEPENDENT LIBERALS. Formerly the Progressive Party. Part of the Liberal Party between 1961 and 1965. Since 1984, part of the Alignment.

INTIFADA. Arab uprising, connoting both the 1987–1990 period and the Al-Aqsa Intifada, which began in 2000.

IRGUN (also known as Etzel, Irgun Zva Leumi, National Military Organization). Pre-independence military organization associated with the Revisionist movement.

ISRAEL B'ALIYAH. Party of immigrants from the former Soviet Union. Especially successful in 1996 and 1999.

ISRAEL BONDS. Interest-bearing securities issued by the State of Israel whose proceeds are designated by the Finance Ministry for general use. A traditional source of support for Israel by Jews around the world and especially in the United States.

ISRAEL LABOR PARTY. *See* Labor-Mapam Alignment.

JEWISH AGENCY. Executive body of the World Zionist Organization.

KACH. List of the Jewish Defense League headed by Rabbi Meir Kahane.

KALANTERISM. Exploitation of a political situation to further personal goals, in particular switching support from one party to another, thereby determining the party that will be able to form the governing coalition.

KEREN HAYESOD/MAGBIT. Institution of the World Zionist Organization charged with raising funds for the movement.

KEREN KAYEMET. Institution of the World Zionist Organization charged with purchasing and reclaiming land in Eretz Israel.

KIBBUTZ (plural KIBBUTZIM). Communal settlement sharing production and consumption.

KNESSET. Israel's parliament, with 120 members.

KNESSET ISRAEL. Communal organization of Jews in the Yishuv in which membership was voluntary.

KUPAT HOLIM. A health clinic plan, the largest of which is associated with the Histadrut.

LA'AM. Political party that developed from the Rafi faction of Mapai; in 1968 it refused to support the Labor Party, then joined the Likud.

LABOR-MAPAM ALIGNMENT. List that included the Labor Party and Mapam; 1969–1984.

LADINO. Language combining Spanish and Hebrew; spoken by many Sephardim.

LAVON AFFAIR. Political conflict in Mapai with far-reaching implications within the party. Conflict began as a question regarding the role Defense Minister Lavon played in a security mishap in 1954.

LAW OF RETURN. Law passed in 1950 by the Knesset granting to every Jew in the world the right to immigrate to Israel.

LEHI. Extreme rightist pre-state underground organization opposed to cooperation with the British.

LIBERAL PARTY. Middle-class party; a member of Gahal and Likud. Formerly the General Zionists.

LIKUD. Joint list of Herut, Liberal Party, La'am, and others founded in 1973; often in power after 1977.

MAKI. Israel Communist Party, especially active in the first decades of statehood.

MANDATE. The British administration of Palestine by a decision of the League of Nations after the First World War until 1948.

MAPAI (acronym for Israel Workers' Party). Created in 1930, it was the dominant party in Israel until its merger in 1968 with Ahdut Haavoda and Rafi to form the Israel Labor Party.

MAPAM (acronym for the United Workers Party). A left-wing socialist-Zionist party, Mapam was part of the Alignment between 1969 and 1984.

MEIMAD. Orthodox Jewish party with moderate foreign policy positions. Ran with Labor in 1999 and 2003.

MERETZ. Left-of-center party formed by the merger of the Citizens Rights Movement, most of Shinui, and Mapam before the 1992 elections.

MIZRACHI. A major component of the National Religious Party.

MOLEDET. 1988 list led by Rehavam "Gandhi" Zeevi, calling for the voluntary transfer of Arabs from Israel.

MORASHA. Religious party established before 1984 elections.

MOSHAV (plural MOSHAVIM). Cooperative settlement in which production (but usually not consumption) is collective.

MOSHAVA (plural MOSHAVOT). Small agricultural town.

MOSSAD (Hebrew for "institute"). The Institute for Intelligence and Special Tasks, with responsibility for human intelligence collection, covert action, and counterterrorism in Israel.

NAAMAT. Women's branch of Histadrut labor federation. Formerly Pioneer Women.

NATIONAL COMMITTEE (VAAD LEUMI). Executive committee of the Yishuv.

NATIONAL RELIGIOUS PARTY (NRP). A Zionist religious party; historical partner of Likud and Labor in government.

NATIONAL UNITY GOVERNMENT. Government formed in times of national emergency, representing most major parties in the Knesset.

NATURAI KARTA. Anti-Zionist ultra-Orthodox Jewish religious group.

NEW ZIONIST ORGANIZATION. Established in 1935 by Revisionist movement led by Jabotinsky after splitting with the World Zionist Organization.

OSLO ACCORDS. 1993 agreements between Prime Minister Yitzhak Rabin and Foreign Minister Shimon Peres for Israel and the Palestine Liberation Organization's head, Yasser Arafat, calling for mutual recognition and negotiations to end the Israeli-Arab conflict.

PALMACH. Elite striking force of the Yishuv's military arm, the Haganah.

PARTY KEY. Distribution of resources based on the proportional strength of the parties.

PEACE NOW. Movement formed after the 1973 Yom Kippur War, urging policies of conciliation and moderation toward Arabs and Arab states. Opposes most settlement in the territories that resulted from the 1967 Six Days' War.

POALEI AGUDAT ISRAEL (also POALEI AGUDA). Ultra-Orthodox religious party with a workers' orientation. In 1984, a component of Morasha.

POALEI ZION. Major socialist political party in the Yishuv period.

POGROM. Organized massacre, especially of Jews.

PROGRESSIVE LIST FOR PEACE (PLP). Established in 1984 as a joint Arab-Jewish list supporting the creation of a Palestinian state alongside Israel.

PROGRESSIVES. Political party originally supported and dominated by German immigrants. In 1961, merged with General Zionists to form the Liberal party. This party split in 1965 and the Progressives took the name Independent Liberals. In 1984, part of the Alignment.

PROTEKTZIA. Political pull; favoritism shown or access achieved because of informal connections with an official or clerk.

RAFI. Party founded by David Ben-Gurion and others who split from Mapai. Ran once in 1965 and won 10 seats. In 1968, most of the activists (excluding Ben-Gurion) returned and formed the Labor Party along with Mapai and Ahdut Haavoda.

SEPHARDIM. Jews whose background is generally from the countries of Asia and Africa.

SHAS. Ultra-Orthodox religious party established in 1984 with special appeal to Sephardim. Split from Agudat Israel. Surged in 1999.

SHELLI. Leftist group that split before the 1984 elections. Part of the group ran in elections with the Citizens Rights Movement and part with the Progressive List for Peace.

SHINUI. Centrist political party whose name means "change." Established as a protest movement after the 1973 Yom Kippur War; part of the DMC in 1977. Succeeded in 1999 and surged in the 2003 elections.

SIAH B. Leftist opposition faction in Mapai.

SICK FUNDS. Health clinics, funded by government subsidy and user fees, that provide services and preventive care to all.

SIX-DAY WAR. 1967 war between Israel and Arab states resulting in Israeli capture of East Jerusalem, West Bank of Jordan, Gaza Strip, Sinai Peninsula, and Golan Heights.

SHIN BET (Hebrew acronym for the General Security Services). Israel's internal security organization.

SMDS. The single-member district system of electoral representation.

STATE OF ISRAEL. Founded in 1948.

STATE LIST. A political party made up originally of Rafi members who refused to reunite with Mapai in 1968.

STATISM. The policies championed by David Ben-Gurion, placing the state above political parties and sectarian movements.

STATUS QUO. Regarding the role of the Jewish religious law in Israel, perpetuating the arrangements that existed in the Yishuv period.

TAMI. Political party set up in 1981 after its leader, Aharon Abu-Hatzeira, split from the NRP. Its appeal was ethnic, especially to Israelis of North African descent.

TEHIYA. Party of the extreme right whose platform rejected the Camp David accords, the Israel-Egypt peace treaty, and the return of the Sinai to Egypt.

TORA VEAVODA. Hebrew for "religious law and toil."

TORAH RELIGIOUS FRONT. Joint list of Agudat Israel and Poalei Agudat Israel.

TRANSFER. The proposal to remove Arabs from Israel, voluntarily or involuntarily, by relocating them in Arab lands.

TZOMET. Right-wing party established for the 1988 elections led by "Raful" Eitan; split from Tehiya. Ran with Likud in 1999.

WESTERN WALL (sometimes known as the Wailing Wall). Remnant of outer wall of the Second Temple in Jerusalem. Considered the most holy site in Judaism.

WHITE PAPER. Policy statement of the British government. Used during the Mandate period to announce restrictions on Jewish immigration.

WORLD ZIONIST ORGANIZATION (WZO). Established by Theodor Herzl in 1897 to promote plans of Jewish nationalism.

YAHAD. (*a*) List established in 1984 and headed by Ezer Weizman; (*b*) separate organization with same name established in 2004 headed by Yossi Beilin with former Labor members and Meretz.

YERIDA. Out-migration from Israel. Literally, going down.

YESHIVA (plural YESHIVOT). Seminaries of higher learning of Jewish religious law and ritual.

YIDDISH. Language combining German and Hebrew; spoken by many Ashkenazim.

YISHUV. Jewish settlement and communal organizations in the pre-state period.

YOM KIPPUR WAR. Fought from October 6 (the day of Yom Kippur) to October 22/24, 1973, between Israel and a coalition of Egypt and Syria. After initial military victories by the Arab states, their advances were repulsed by Israel.

YOUTH FACTION. Group within the NRP.

ZIONIST CONGRESS. Governing body of the World Zionist Organization.

INDEX

ABOUT THE AUTHOR

Asher Arian was born in Cleveland, Ohio, in 1938. He studied in Cleveland and received an A.B. degree from Western Reserve University. His graduate work was completed at Michigan State University where he received his doctorate in political science in 1965.

In 1966 he was appointed to Tel Aviv University where he was the Romulo Betancourt Professor of Political Science. He served as chairman of the Political Science Department and as dean of the Faculty of Social Sciences there. In 1986 he was appointed executive officer of the M.A./Ph.D Program in Political Science at the Graduate School of the City University of New York and holds the rank of Distinguished Professor there. He is a senior fellow of the Israel Democracy Institute in Jerusalem and professor of political science at the University of Haifa. Arian has had visiting appointments at the University of California at Berkeley, Columbia University, Brandeis University, University of Michigan, University of Minnesota, and Hebrew University.

Arian's professional writing has concentrated on Israeli politics, especially elections, public opinion, and political parties. He is the author of many books, including *Ideological Change in Israel, The Choosing People: Voting Behavior in Israel,* and *Security Threatened: Surveying Israeli Opinion on Peace and War.* Since the 1969 elections Arian has edited the series titled *The Elections in Israel.* His articles have appeared in journals such as the *American Political Science Review, Journal of Conflict Resolution, Electoral Studies, Comparative Politics, Journal of Politics, Western Political Science Quarterly,* and the *British Journal of Political Science.*

Arian has served as president of the Israel Political Science Association, and as a member of the Executive Committee of the International Political Science Association.